1st International Workshop on Computational Approaches to Historical Language Change 2019

Florence, Italy
2 August 2019

ISBN: 978-1-5108-9105-0

Printed from e-media with permission by:

Curran Associates, Inc.
57 Morehouse Lane
Red Hook, NY 12571

Some format issues inherent in the e-media version may also appear in this print version.

Copyright© (2019) by the Association for Computational Linguistics
All rights reserved.

Printed by Curran Associates, Inc. (2019)

For permission requests, please contact the Association for Computational Linguistics
at the address below.

Association for Computational Linguistics
209 N. Eighth Street
Stroudsburg, Pennsylvania 18360

Phone: 1-570-476-8006
Fax: 1-570-476-0860

acl@aclweb.org

Additional copies of this publication are available from:

Curran Associates, Inc.
57 Morehouse Lane
Red Hook, NY 12571 USA
Phone: 845-758-0400
Fax: 845-758-2633
Email: curran@proceedings.com
Web: www.proceedings.com

ACL 2019

The 1st International Workshop on Computational Approaches to Historical Language Change

Proceedings of the Workshop

August 2, 2019
Florence, Italy

©2019 The Association for Computational Linguistics

Introduction

Welcome to the 1st International Workshop on Computational Approaches to Historical Language Change (LChange'19) that was co-located with ACL 2019 in Florence, on August 2, 2019.

Human language changes over time, driven by the dual needs of adapting to ongoing sociocultural and technological development in the world and facilitating efficient communication. In particular, novel words are coined or borrowed from other languages, while obsolete words slide into obscurity. Similarly, words may acquire novel meanings or lose existing meanings. This workshop explores these phenomena by bringing to bear state-of-the-art computational methodologies, theories and digital text resources on exploring the time-varying nature of human language.

Although there exists rich empirical work on language change from historical linguistics, sociolinguistics and cognitive linguistics, computational approaches to the problem of language change – particularly how word forms and meanings evolve – have only begun to take shape over the past decade or so, with exemplary work on semantic change and lexical replacement. The motivation has long been related to search, and understanding in diachronic archives. The emergence of long-term and large-scale digital corpora was the prerequisite and has resulted in a slightly different set of problems for this strand of study than have traditionally been studied in historical linguistics. As an example, studies of lexical replacement have largely focused on named entity change (names of e.g., countries and people that change over time) because of the large effect these name changes have for temporal information retrieval.

The aim of this workshop is three-fold. First, we want to provide pioneering researchers who work on computational methods, evaluation, and large-scale modelling of language change an outlet for disseminating cutting-edge research on topics concerning language change. Currently, researchers in this area have published in a wide range of different venues, from computational linguistics, to cognitive science and digital archiving venues. We intended this workshop as a platform for sharing state-of-the-art research progress in this fundamental domain of natural language research.

Second, in doing so we want to bring together domain experts across disciplines. We want to connect those that have long worked on language change within historical linguistics and bring with them a large understanding for general linguistic theories of language change; those that have studied change across languages and language families; those that develop and test computational methods for detecting semantic change and laws of semantic change; and those that need knowledge (of the occurrence and shape) of language change, for example, in digital humanities and computational social sciences where text mining is applied to diachronic corpora subject to lexical semantic change.

Third, the detection and modelling of language change using diachronic text and text mining raise fundamental theoretical and methodological challenges for future research in this area. The representativeness of text is a first critical issue; works using large diachronic corpora and computational methods for detecting change often claim to find changes that are universally true for a language as a whole. But the jury is out on how results derived from digital literature or newspapers accurately represent changes in language as a whole. We hope to engage corpus linguists, big-data scientists, and computational linguists to address these open issues. Besides these goals, this workshop can also support discussion on the evaluation of computational methodologies for uncovering language change. Verifying change only using positive examples of change often confirms a corpus bias rather than reflecting genuine language change. Larger quantities and higher qualities of text over time result in the detection of more semantic change. In fact, multiple semantic laws have been linked to frequency rather than underlying semantic change. The methodological issue of evaluation, together with good evaluation testsets and standards are of high importance to the research community. We aim to shed some light on these issues and encourage the community to collaborate to find solutions.

The work in semantic change detection has, to a large extent, moved to (neural) embedding techniques in recent years. These methods have several drawbacks: the need for very large datasets to produce stable embeddings, and the fact that all semantic information of a word is encoded in a single vector thus limiting the possibility to study word senses separately. A move towards multi-sense embeddings will most likely require even more texts per time unit, which will limit the applicability of these methods to other languages than English and a few others. We want to bring about a discussion on the need for methods that can discriminate and disambiguate among a word's senses (meanings) and that can be used for resource-poor languages with little hope of acquiring the order of magnitude of words needed for creating stable embeddings, possibly using dynamic embeddings that seem to require less text. Finally, knowledge of language change is useful not only on its own, but as a basis for other diachronic textual investigations and in search.

A digital humanities investigation into the living conditions of young women through history cannot rely on the word *girl* in English, as in the past the reference of *girl* also included young men. Automatic detecting of language change is useful for many researchers outside of the communities that study the changes themselves and develop methods for their detection. By reaching out to these other communities, we can better understand how to utilize the results for further research and for presenting them to the interested public. In addition, we need good user interfaces and systems for exploring language changes in corpora, for example, to allow for serendipitous discovery of interesting phenomena. In addition to facilitate research on texts, information about language changes is used for measuring document across-time similarity, information retrieval from long-term document archives, the design of OCR algorithms and so on.

In response to the call we received 53 submissions, each of which were carefully evaluated by at least two members of the Program Committee. Based on the reviewer's feedback we accepted 34 full and short papers, which were then presented orally or as poster papers. We were also delighted to have two keynote presentations by Claire Bowern (Yale University) and Haim Dubossarsky (University of Cambridge). We hope that you will find the included papers as insightful and inspiring as we have.

We would like to thank the keynote speakers for their stimulating talks, the authors of papers for their interesting contributions and the members of the Program Committee for their insightful reviews. We also express our gratitude to the ACL 2019 workshop chairs for their kind assistance.

Nina Tahmasebi (University of Gothenburg)
Lars Borin (University of Gothenburg)
Adam Jatowt (Kyoto University)
Yang Xu (University of Toronto)
LChange'19 Workshop Chairs

Organizers:

Nina Tahmasebi, University of Gothenburg (Sweden)
Lars Borin, University of Gothenburg (Sweden)
Adam Jatowt, Kyoto University (Japan)
Yang Xu, University of Toronto (Canada)

Program Committee:

Yvonne Adesam, University of Gothenburg (Sweden)
Rami Aly, Universität Hamburg (Germany)
Avishek Anand, L3S Research Center (Germany)
Timothy Baldwin, University of Melbourne (Australia)
Pierpaolo Basile, University of Bari (Italy)
Barend Beekhuizen, University of Toronto Mississauga (Canada)
Meriem Beloucif, Universität Hamburg (Germany)
Klaus Berberich, MPI-INF (Germany)
Aleksandrs Berdicevskis, University of Gothenburg (Sweden)
Chris Biemann, Universität Hamburg (Germany)
Damian Blasi, University of Zürich (Switzerland)
Ricardo Campos, Polytechnic Institute of Tomar / INESC TEC, (Portugal)
Annalina Caputo, Trinity College Dublin (Ireland)
Brady Clark, Northwestern University (USA)
Paul Cook, University of New Brunswick (Canada)
Dana Dannells, University of Gothenburg (Sweden)
Pavel Denisov, University of Stuttgart (Germany)
Yijun Duan, Kyoto University (Japan)
Haim Dubossarsky, University of Cambridge (UK)
Stian Rødven Eide, University of Gothenburg (Sweden)
Michael Färber, KIT (Germany)
Antske Fokkens, Free University of Amsterdam (The Netherlands)
Mats Fridlund, University of Gothenburg (Sweden)
Mika Hämäläinen, University of Helsinki (Finland)
Johannes Hellrich, Friedrich Schiller University Jena (Germany)
Simon Hengchen, University of Helsinki (Finland)
Louise Holmer, University of Gothenburg (Sweden)
Abhik Jana, IIT Kharagpur (India)
Péter Jeszenszky, Ritsumeikan University (Japan)
Dirk Johannßen, Universität Hamburg (Germany)
Richard Johansson, University of Gothenburg (Sweden)
Antti Kanner, University of Helsinki (Finland)
Tom Kenter, Google (UK)
Jey Han Lau, University of Melbourne (Australia)
Nicholas A. Lester, University of Zürich (Switzerland)
Liina Lindström, University of Tartu (Estonia)
Behrooz Mansouri, Rochester Institute of Technology (USA)
Animesh Mukherjee, IIT Kharagpur (India)
Luis Nieto Piña, University of Gothenburg (Sweden)

Bill Noble, University of Gothenburg (Sweden)
Kjetil Norvag, NTNU (Norway)
Ella Rabinovich, University of Toronto (Canada)
Taraka Rama, University of Oslo (Norway)
Jacobo Rouces, University of Gothenburg (Sweden)
Sylvie Saget, University of Gothenburg (Sweden)
Eyal Sagi, Northwestern University (USA)
Asad Sayeed, University of Gothenburg (Sweden)
Dominik Schlechtweg, University of Stuttgart (Germany)
Vidya Somashekarappa, University of Gothenburg (Sweden)
Andreas Spitz, EPFL (Switzerland)
Ian Stewart, Georgia Institute of Technology (USA)
Suzanne Stevenson, University of Toronto (Canada)
Susanne Vejdemo, Stockholm University (Sweden)
Mikael Vejdemo Johansson, CUNY CSI (USA)
Barbro Wallgren Hemlin, University of Gothenburg (Sweden)
Melvin Wevers, KNAW Humanities Cluster (The Netherlands)
Guanghao You, University of Zürich (Switzerland)
Yihong Zhang, Osaka University (Japan)

Invited Speakers:

Claire Bowern, Yale University (USA)
Haim Dubossarsky, University of Cambridge (UK)

Table of Contents

Conference Program

August 2, 2019

9:00–9:15   *Introduction*

9:15–10:30   **Session 1**

9:15–10:00   *Semantic Change in the Time of Machine Learning, Doing It Right!*
Haim Dubossarsky

10:00–10:30   *From Insanely Jealous to Insanely Delicious: Computational Models for the Semantic Bleaching of English Intensifiers*
Yiwei Luo, Dan Jurafsky and Beth Levin

10:30–10:45   *Coffee Break*

10:45–12:30   **Session 2**

10:45–11:15   *Computational Analysis of the Historical Changes in Poetry and Prose*
Amitha Gopidi and Aniket Alam

11:15–11:35   *Studying Semantic Chain Shifts with Word2Vec: FOOD>MEAT>FLESH*
Richard Zimmermann

11:35–11:55   *Evaluation of Semantic Change of Harm-Related Concepts in Psychology*
Ekaterina Vylomova, Sean Murphy and Nicholas Haslam

11:55–12:25   *Contextualized Diachronic Word Representations*
Ganesh Jawahar and Djamé Seddah

12:30–13:30   *Lunch Break*

Semantic Change and Emerging Tropes In a Large Corpus of New High German Poetry
Thomas Haider and Steffen Eger

Conceptual Change and Distributional Semantic Models: an Exploratory Study on Pitfalls and Possibilities
Pia Sommerauer and Antske Fokkens

Measuring the Compositionality of Noun-Noun Compounds over Time
Prajit Dhar, Janis Pagel and Lonneke van der Plas

Towards Automatic Variant Analysis of Ancient Devotional Texts
Amir Hazem, Béatrice Daille, Dominique Stutzmann, Jacob Currie and Christine Jacquin

Understanding the Evolution of Circular Economy through Language Change
Sampriti Mahanty, Frank Boons, Julia Handl and Riza Theresa Batista-Navarro

Gaussian Process Models of Sound Change in Indo-Aryan Dialectology
Chundra Cathcart

16:00–16:40 Session 5

16:00–16:20 *Modeling a Historical Variety of a Low-Resource Language: Language Contact Effects in the Verbal Cluster of Early-Modern Frisian*
Jelke Bloem, Arjen Versloot and Fred Weerman

16:20–16:40 *Visualizing Linguistic Change as Dimension Interactions*
Christin Schätzle, Frederik L. Dennig, Michael Blumenschein, Daniel A. Keim and Miriam Butt

16:40–17:15 *Discussion and Closing*

From *insanely jealous* to *insanely delicious*: Computational models for the semantic bleaching of English intensifiers

Yiwei Luo[1] **Dan Jurafsky**[1,2] **Beth Levin**[1]
[1]Stanford Linguistics   [2]Stanford Computer Science
{yiweil, jurafsky, bclevin}@stanford.edu

Abstract

We introduce novel computational models for modeling semantic bleaching, a widespread category of change in which words become more abstract or lose elements of meaning, like the development of *arrive* from its earlier meaning 'become at shore.' We validate our methods on a widespread case of bleaching in English: de-adjectival adverbs that originate as manner adverbs (as in *awfully behaved*) and later become intensifying adverbs (as in *awfully nice*). Our methods formally quantify three reflexes of bleaching: decreasing similarity to the source meaning (e.g., *awful*), increasing similarity to a fully bleached prototype (e.g., *very*), and increasing productivity (e.g., the breadth of adjectives that an adverb modifies). We also test a new causal model and find evidence that bleaching is initially triggered in contexts such as *conspicuously evident* and *insanely jealous*, where an adverb premodifies a semantically similar adjective. These contexts provide a form of "bridging context" (Evans and Wilkins, 2000) that allow a manner adverb to be reinterpreted as an intensifying adverb similar to *very*.

1 Introduction

Developments in computational semantics and availability of large diachronic corpora have renewed interest in studying historical semantic change. Recent work has moved away from documenting and qualitatively categorizing types of changes (Bréal, 1964; Stern, 1931) to focus on detecting semantic shifts (Gulordava and Baroni, 2011; Rosenfeld and Erk, 2018; Frermann and Lapata, 2016; Mitra et al., 2014; Kulkarni et al., 2015), distinguishing gradual linguistic drifts from cultural ones (Hamilton et al., 2016a) and assessing laws of change (Hamilton et al., 2016b; Dubossarsky et al., 2017; Xu and Kemp, 2015; Ramiro et al., 2018; Luo and Xu, 2018).

Building off prior work, we propose the first computational study of semantic bleaching, one of the most widespread changes in word meaning. Work in historical linguistics characterizes bleaching as an abstraction or loss of some initial elements of meaning, such as in the example *arrive*, which has broadened from 'become at shore', or *amazing*, which has undergone a change from 'stupefying' to 'great'. However, we know very little about how this change happens as a quantifiable and continuous process. For example, can we measure to what extent a bleached word continues to bear its root meaning? How much of the meaning of "awefulness" does *awfully* have, and to what extent does *awfully* now mean *very*? Finally, the fundamental question of what drives bleaching remains open.

Answering these questions requires a way to model the nuances of semantic bleaching separately from general semantic shifts. Thus, our work asks the following:

Q1: Can we build computational models of the bleaching process that match known semantic reflexes of bleaching?

To answer this question, we develop methods for quantifying three known reflexes of bleaching from the theoretical literature on semantic change: loss of original lexical meaning, gain of bleached target meaning, and increasing productivity. We focus on the case of English de-adjectival adverbs (***awfully nice, insanely delicious***), which originally have a manner meaning derived from the semantics of their root adjective and later bleach into intensifying adverbs (or *intensifiers*) (Tab. 1). We choose this case of bleaching as it represents an open class of semantically diverse adverbs that experience exceptionally rapid change and speaker innovation (Bolinger, 1972; Peters, 1994).[1]

---

[1]Though he focuses on synchronic properties of degree words, Bolinger (1972, 18) observes: "[Intensifiers] afford

1

Proceedings of the 1st International Workshop on Computational Approaches to Historical Language Change, pages 1–13
Florence, Italy, August 2, 2019. ©2019 Association for Computational Linguistics

Original usage	Bleached usage
awfully behaved	**awfully** nice
wildly flailing	**wildly** easy
insanely muttering	**insanely** delicious
abundantly endow	**abundantly** at ease
singing **terribly**	**terribly** sorry
aggressively demanded	**aggressively** sunny

Table 1. Examples of the bleaching phenomenon: de-adjectival **adverbs** in their original, manner usage and in their bleached, intensifier usage.

Next, we apply our methodology for modeling bleaching to answer open questions concerning *how* bleaching happens over time:

Q2: Can bleaching be explained in terms of reanalysis, by which certain contextual factors lead to one interpretation being favored over another?

Q3: If bleaching is a form of reanalysis, what are the contexts that trigger this re-interpretation?

We use the same semantically diverse set of bleaching de-adjectival adverbs to formulate and test hypotheses pertaining to these questions (Study 2, Sec. 4), building on previous diachronic work on intensifiers that have focused on a single word (Lorenz (2002), Macaulay (2006), Beltrama and Bochnak (2015), Tagliamonte (2008)). In particular, we hypothesize that a high semantic similarity between an adverb and the adjectives that it initially modifies is a crucial contextual factor that triggers the reanalysis of manner adverbs into intensifiers. This criterion (exemplified by collocations such as *conspicuously evident, terribly gruesome*) is what allows a manner adverb to be interpreted as an intensifier in the first place.

2   Methods for modeling bleaching

We translate three known reflexes of semantic bleaching from the literature—loss of lexical meaning; gain of intensifier meaning; increased productivity—into relationships between word embeddings and n-gram parse context. For our n-gram data, we use the English fiction portion of the Google Books English n-grams corpus (Lin et al., 2012) and for the historical word embeddings, we use the HistWords dataset trained on the same portion of the n-gram dataset (Hamilton et al., 2016b). The full corpus spans the years

a picture of fevered invention and competition it would be hard to come by elsewhere [...] They are the chief means of emphasis for speakers for whom all means of emphasis quickly become stale and need to be replaced."

1800 to 1999 but we restrict our temporal range to 1850 to 1999, inclusive, due to data sparsity. We test two different sets of HistWords embeddings: Word2Vec (W2V) representations and SVD representations. All data are aggregated to the granularity of decades, yielding 15 decades total.

2.1   Similarity of adverbs to *very* (SIMVERY)

As a manner adverb bleaches into an intensifying adverb, we expect the meaning of the adverb to grow more similar to the meaning of *very*, the prototypical example of a completely bleached intensifier (Peters, 1994). We measure this similarity via the cosine similarity between the HistWords embedding for an adverb and the embedding for *very*, both retrieved for a given decade. The bleached status of *very* is empirically verified in the embedding space: the self-similarity between consecutive decades is comparable to words expected to change extremely little over time, such as determiners, numerals, and pronouns (*the, two, three, four, them, they, us*, etc.) (Pagel et al., 2007).

2.2   Similarity of adverb to original lexical meaning (SIMLEX)

As a manner adverb like *awfully* bleaches into an intensifier, its meaning diverges from its root adjective's lexical meaning of "awfulness." We formalize this intuition of a bleaching adverb's divergence from its lexical meaning as the average cosine similarity of an adverb to a set of lemmas (L) related to its lexical meaning (eq. 1). We constructed these lemma sets by retrieving WordNet (Miller, 1998) synonyms for the root adjective and supplementing these with additional synonyms according to the *Oxford English Dictionary (OED)* (Simpson et al.) (Tab. 2).

Adverb	Lexical source lemmas
disgustingly	filthy, filth, repulsive, aversion
beautifully	elegance, elegant, style, gorgeous, beauteous
wildly	savage, rage, fierce, barbarian, uncivilized
remarkably	impact, stun, awe, wonder, amazement, terror

Table 2. Examples of adverbs and lemmas related to the lexical source meaning for computing SimLex.

$$\text{SIMLEX}(adv) = \frac{1}{|L|} \sum_{l_k \in L} \texttt{sim}_t(adv, l_k), \quad (1)$$

where L is a lemma set of lexical meanings and $\texttt{sim}_t(adv, l_k)$ is the cosine similarity at time t between an adverb and a lemma l_k in L.[2]

2.3 Productivity of adverb (BREADTH)

As an adverb bleaches, we expect to see greater productivity, i.e., an increase in the variety of the adjectives that it modifies. For example, we expect to see *terribly* modifying a greater range of sentiment adjectives over time. We suggest two distinct ways to quantify this semantic breadth. The first is *type diversity* (TYPEDIV)—the number of types modified—which is shown in Bybee (1995) to be important in determining productivity. The second is BREADTH, which we measure as negative cosine similarity of the adjectives, to capture how semantically similar the set of modified adjectives is. The more similar the adjectives modified by an adverb are to each other, the less semantically broad they are. This more general approach is useful since an adverb might modify a larger number of distinct adjectives while becoming more restricted in the meanings of adjectives that it modifies.

We extract all adjectives modified by an adverb for a given decade from the Google Syntactic n-grams corpus (Goldberg and Orwant, 2013). To calculate a single value for similarity among many adjectives, we subset the top 50 adjectives ranked by log odds, then take the grand average of all the pairwise similarities between each distinct adjective type (eq. 2). We also weight each pairwise similarity by each adjective's odds of being modified. The BREADTH B of an intensifier I at time t can be expressed as:

$$B(I,t) = - \sum_{a_i \in A_{I,t}} \sum_{\substack{a_j \in A_{I,t} \\ i \neq j}} \texttt{sim}(a_i, a_j) o(a_i) o(a_j)$$

$$(2)$$

where $A_{I,t}$ is the set of all adjectives modified by an intensifier I at time t, $\texttt{sim}(\cdot, \cdot)$ is the cosine similarity between two words, and $o(\cdot)$ is the odds of an adjective being modified by an adverb.

---

[2]To increase the robustness of this metric, we restricted lemmas in L to those whose embeddings remained relatively stable over time by verifying that their self-similarities over successive decades did not differ significantly from a highly stable word set composed of determiners, numerals, and pronouns ($t = 8.2$e-01, p = 0.85).

3 Study 1: Do our methods capture bleaching?

We hypothesize that our methods can be used to distinguish adverbs undergoing bleaching into intensifying adverbs from non-bleaching control adverbs. In particular, we expect to see significant correlations among the set of intensifiers between each metric and time in the following directions (Tab. 3) after fitting linear regressions on $\{y_t, t\}_{t=1850}^{2000}$, where y_t represents a bleaching metric evaluated at decade t.:

metric	sign of slope over time
SIMVERY	+
SIMLEX	—
BREADTH	+

Table 3. Predicted correlations between each bleaching metric over time (as the dependent variable) and time (as the independent variable) for bleaching adverbs.

To test these predictions, we introduce a set of bleaching intensifiers and a frequency-matched control set of non-bleaching adverbs. We expect to see significantly increasing similarity to *very* (SIMVERY), decreasing similarity to original meaning (SIMLEX), and increasing productivity (BREADTH) over time for intensifiers, and we expect that the slopes over time of these metrics are significantly greater for intensifiers than for the control adverbs.

3.1 Datasets

For both the intensifier and control sets, we restrict to de-adjectival adverbs (also known as *ly* type adverbs).[3] We sample these de-adjectival adverbs from lexical classes of adjective roots identified by Bolinger (1972) and supplement these with synonyms from WordNet (Miller, 1998). The result is a set of 250 intensifiers, shown partially in Table 4. (See Appendix A for the full set.)

Our control set consists of 178 frequency-matched adverbs sampled from the British National Corpus (BNC) (shown partially in Tab. 5, see Appendix B for the full set).[4] We obtained

---

[3]We also discard adverbs for specific years due to OOV-ness at random from either the W2V or SVD embeddings.

[4]Examples of usage taken from the British National Corpus (BNC) were obtained under the terms of the BNC End User Licence. Copyright in the individual texts cited resides with the original intellectual property right holders. For information and licensing conditions relating to the BNC, please see the web site at http://www.natcorp.ox.ac.uk/.

Root adjective type	Examples
magnitude	enormously, vastly, immensely, greatly, abundantly, massively
strength	overpoweringly, strongly, vigorously, exuberantly
singularity	distinctly, unusually, abnormally, mysteriously
evaluation	marvellously, brutally, dramatically, luxuriously, terribly, monstrously
irremediability	desperately, abominably, pathetically, disastrously
purity and veracity	undoubtedly, thoroughly, absolutely, fully, sincerely

Table 4. Examples of intensifiers, categorized by root adjective type according to Bolinger (1972).

average (relative) frequency estimates from the Google Books corpus over the period 1850-1990 and we selected the control adverbs from semantic categories such as time adverbs (*firstly, formerly, finally, temporarily, eventually*) and speed adverbs (*rapidly, quickly, slowly, promptly*), avoiding semantic categories of intensifiers that have been identified in the literature (Bolinger, 1972; Morzycki, 2008; Nouwen, 2011; Paradis, 1997).

abruptly	accordingly	frankly
ironically	locally	loudly
nationally	newly	officially
privately	quietly	simultaneously
happily	neatly	originally

Table 5. Examples of control adverbs.

3.2 Comparison of BREADTH to TYPEDIV

To determine whether or not BREADTH is independent from TYPEDIV (the number of adjective types modified by an adverb), we compute Spearman correlation coefficients between the metrics for individual adverbs as well as a single correlation between BREADTH and TYPEDIV averaged across all adverbs. We find that there are no significant correlations between average TYPEDIV and average BREADTH, nor do we find significant correlations between the two metrics within individual adverbs, indicating that our weighted BREADTH measure captures differences in productivity independent from the number of types that an adverb modifies. In fact, 200 of the 250 intensifiers in our dataset show a decrease in the number of types they modify within the last 5 decades of our data, but an increase in BREADTH.

3.3 Study 1 Results

We computed the 4 metrics (SIMVERY, SIMLEX, BREADTH, and TYPEDIV) on the intensifier and control adverbs described in Section 3.1 over the

14 decades from 1850 to 1990. As a reminder, SIMVERY measures an adverb's average semantic similarity to *very* and SIMLEX measures an adverb's average semantic similarity to its root adjective meaning (e.g., *completely* to {*full, entire, whole, ...*}). Both BREADTH and TYPEDIV measure the collocational freedom of an adverb, with the latter taking into account only the type diversity of adjectives that the adverb modifies and the former also incorporating the semantic similarity of those modified adjectives to each other. We then fit linear regressions with each bleaching metric as the dependent variable and time as the independent variable.[5] We take the natural log of BREADTH so that values are linear after weighting by adjective frequencies. We also compute each bleaching metric separately with Word2Vec (W2V) and SVD embeddings, expecting the strength and direction of the correlations to be unaffected by the choice of embedding.

The 10 most and least bleached intensifiers by each metric using W2V embeddings for 1990 are shown in Tab. 7; examples showing increasing BREADTH over the period 1850-1990 are shown in Tab. 6. A visual of increasing BREADTH is shown in Fig. 1.

The results of our regressions somewhat support our predicted temporal correlations (Fig. 2). As a caveat, we note that the increasing size of the syntactic n-grams corpus over time likely biases BREADTH, since a larger corpus has more contexts for each word, thus potentially inflating the strength of the correlation with time. While weighting BREADTH by each adjective's likelihood of being modified may mitigate this bias to an extent (since each likelihood is expected to decrease as corpus size increases), we recognize that future work should seek more robust forms of nor-

---

[5]We performed all regressions using ordinary least squares models in the StatsModels Python module (Seabold and Perktold, 2010).

	1850	1990
terribly	deficient, deformed, diseased, beaten, broken, fatal, unorthodox, guilty...	relieved, smitten, small, important, valid, goodlooking, generous, tired, pregnant...
abundantly	fat, large, flowing, fertile, rejoicing, grateful...	available, fraught, intelligible, loud, eager, familiar...
enormously	rich, large, high, long, great, fat, wealthy, thick...	popular, successful, important, complex, influential, difficult, helpful...

Table 6. Three bleaching adverbs and examples of adjectives they modify in the Google Books corpus at 1850 vs. 1990, showing an increase in productivity of the bleaching adverb.

	most bleached	least bleached
SIMVERY	**extremely**, terribly, truly, awfully, *definitely*, remarkably, **absolutely**, precisely, honestly, seriously	amply, vigorously, richly, *heavily*, violently, mysteriously, profusely, severely, furiously, miraculously
SIMLEX	entirely, decidedly, *heavily*, supremely, **particularly**, sorely, literally, deeply, especially, sharply	pleasantly, abundantly, enthusiastically, intensely, delightfully, *definitely*, furiously, curiously, *evidently*, **profusely**
BREADTH	wholly, completely, **particularly**, deeply, *evidently*, distinctly, **absolutely**, **extremely**, perfectly, clearly	grievously, gorgeously, stupendously, surpassingly, outrageously, miraculously, deliciously, extravagantly, **profusely**, ludicrously

Table 7. The 10 most and least bleached intensifiers in 1990 according to each metric computed using W2V embeddings. Intensifiers **in bold** are most or least bleached according to more than one metric. Intensifiers *in italics* are categorized as most bleached by one metric but least bleached by another.

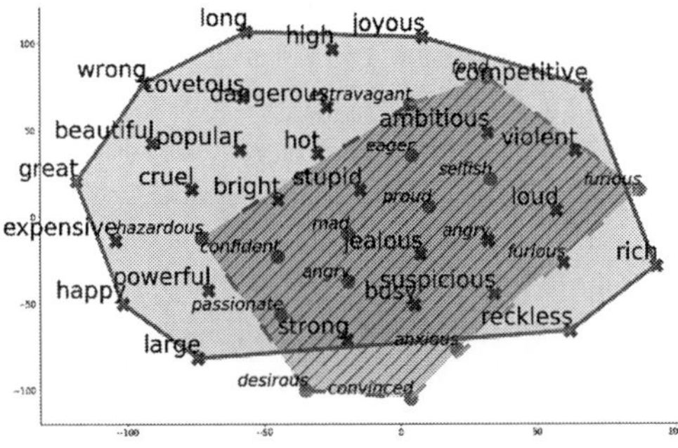

Figure 1. t-SNE visualization of adjectives modified by *insanely* in 1850 (plotted as circles; italicized) vs. in 1990 (plotted as x's), with convex hulls of each decade's adjectives shown in hatched purple and solid green, respectively, showing that the category of adjectives that are modified by *insanely* has expanded over 140 years.

malization.

The signs of the slopes match our predictions for all metrics and across embedding types for the intensifier set. Moreover, the strength of the correlation is significant for SIMVERY (p<1e-01) as well as for BREADTH (p<1e-4) when computed using both W2V and SVD embeddings. For SIMLEX, the strength of this correlation is also signif-

icant (p<1e-05), but only when computed using W2V embeddings.

For the control set, we find that there are no significant correlations for SIMLEX computed using either embedding type (p>0.50), which matches our predictions. Nor do we find significant correlations for SIMVERY when computed using SVD embeddings. However, we do find a significant positive slope (p<1e-06) for SIMVERY+W2V, indicating that the control adverbs in our dataset are also becoming more similar to *very* over time. Nevertheless, the slope over time is still significantly greater for intensifiers than control adverbs (t = 3.1, p<1e-02).

Finally, the correlation for BREADTH is significant for both intensifiers and control when computed using W2V embeddings as well as using SVD embeddings (p<1e-63, p<1e-05), suggesting that our current metric for change in productivity might be heavily dependent on corpus size. While we did not find any correlations between BREADTH and TYPEDIV, we find that the latter measure of productivity also shows significant trends of increase for both intensifiers and control (again, likely due to increasing corpus size). However, we find that the size of the slope for

TYPEDIV is significantly greater for intensifiers than control (t = 4.28, p<1e-04), indicating that this metric can identify a bleaching adverb given a control set of non-bleaching adverbs.

3.4 Discussion

We find that the combinations SIMVERY+SVD and SIMLEX+W2V successfully distinguish between bleaching and non-bleaching adverbs, yielding significant slopes over time for the former and no significant slopes for the latter. Surprisingly, SIMVERY+W2V shows a significant increase over time for both intensifiers and control, despite the fact that the principal meaning difference between the two sets is the new meaning of intensification that only the bleaching adverbs acquire. However, we note that this metric is still useful for identifying bleaching adverbs when a control set of non-bleaching adverbs is defined, since the size of the slope is significantly larger for the former. We find that BREADTH does not work in distinguishing bleaching from non-bleaching adverbs, most likely due to its dependence on corpus size, though possibly also because it captures changes that are not due strictly to bleaching (such as metaphorical extension, though we do not investigate this suspicion here). However, we find that TYPEDIV (just as SIMVERY+W2V) does work in the setting of a control set being available, as the size of the slope is significantly greater for intensifiers compared to control adverbs.

It is also possible that SIMLEX may show some bias toward adverbs that are less morphologically transparent with respect to their root—for example, we see that *sorely, especially,* and *decidedly* are among the 10 most bleached intensifiers identified by SIMLEX in Tab. 7. We hope to explore refinements to SIMVERY[6] and our two productivity measures (BREADTH and TYPEDIV) in future work that may better distinguish between bleaching and non-bleaching adverbs even without a control set readily available.

4   Study 2: Testing a causal theory

Ultimately, we are interested in modeling bleaching in order to test hypotheses concerning *how* a change like **awfully** *behaved* to **awfully** *nice* took

---

[6]We perform the same analyses with a modified version of SIMVERY that measures the average cosine similarity of an adverb to {*very, really*} but find that the results are slightly poorer in distinguishing bleaching from non-bleaching.

place. In particular, we hypothesize a reanalysis-driven account of this change:

H1: When an adverb begins to modify adjectives that are semantically similar to itself, the adverb begins to be re-interpreted as an intensifier.

We now turn to the logic behind our hypothesis and the predictions made by our theory.

4.1   A theory of reanalysis-driven bleaching

For our causal theory, we adopt the framework of reanalysis as in work by Bybee et al. (1994), Hopper and Traugott (2003), and Evans and Wilkins (2000). In these works, interpretations that initially arise out of pragmatic enrichment become conventionalized over time due to regularly occurring contexts that provide support for the enriched interpretation. Following Evans and Wilkins (2000), we refer to these supporting contexts as "bridging contexts."

In the case of the reanalysis of a manner adverb into an intensifier, we hypothesize that the bridging context crucially involves the premodification of an adjective, *A*, that denotes a semantically similar property. To develop an intuition for how this criterion can give rise to the contextual ambiguity *very A*, we refer to examples (1-3) below from The Corpus of Historical American English (*COHA*) (Davies, 2010-). In (1-3)(b), the adverb and modified adjective denote independent properties: abnormalness is independent from being developed, awfulness is independent from being behaved, etc. However, in (1-3)(a), both adverb and adjective are associated with a shared semantic property such that the adverb reiterates the modified adjective in a way that is analogous to intensification.

(1) a.   There   is   an   **abnormally** disproportionate lack of demand.

   b.   The most **abnormally** developed organs [...]

(2) a.   [...] but it has left these rooms **awfully** dirty.

   b.   [...] most **awfully** behaved girl she had ever met.

(3) a.   The scenery on the river was **beautifully** picturesque [...]

   b.   The country is **beautifully** broken, highly fertile, and cultivated like a garden.

Our theory hypothesizes that only for the (a) contexts involving an adverb and adjective pair both

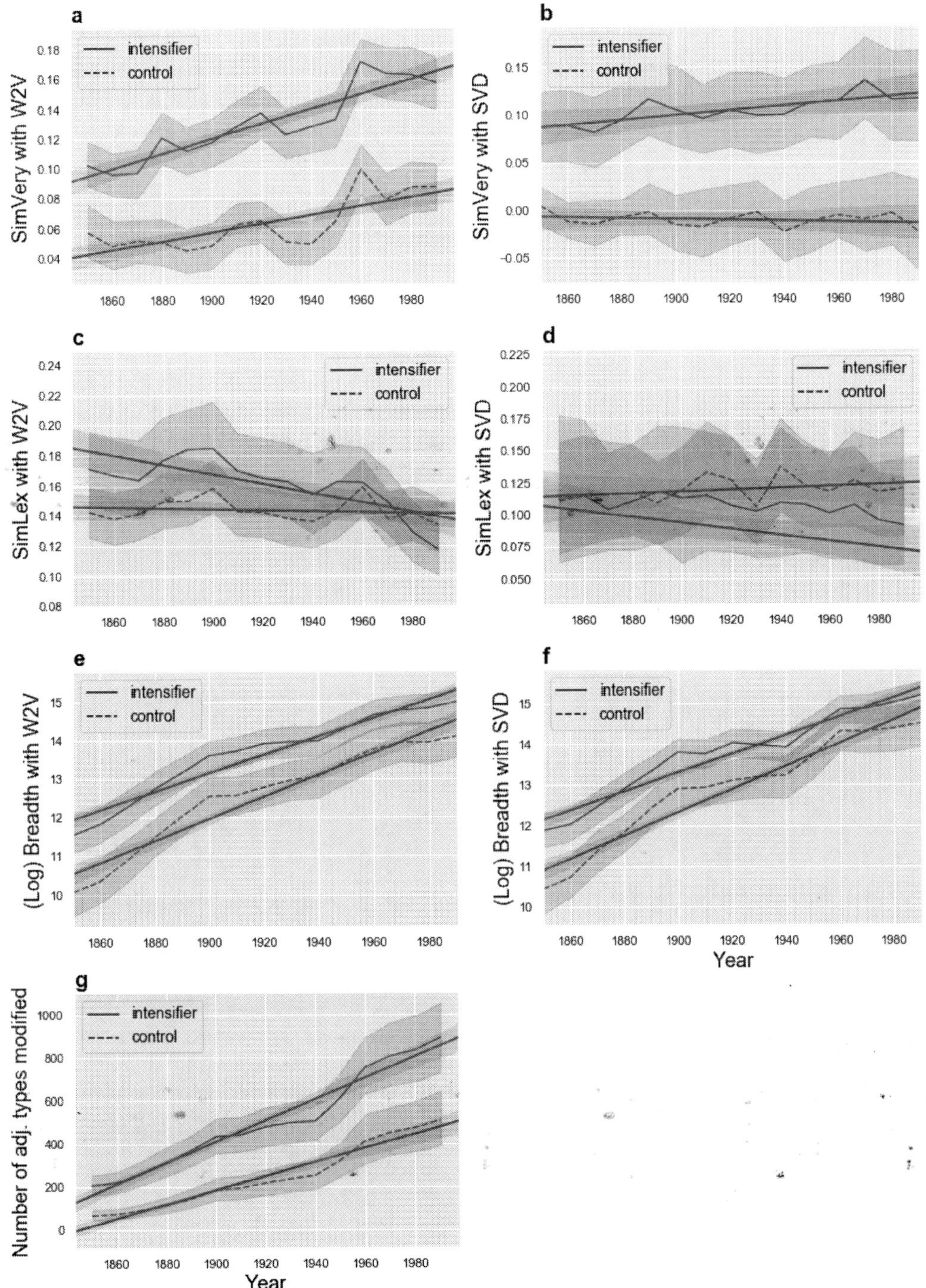

Figure 2. Raw extents of bleaching over time and lines of best fit from OLS linear regressions, showing partial confirmation of predicted trends. Intensifiers show significantly greater increases in W2V similarity to *very* (SIMVERY) over time compared to control adverbs (**a**), intensifiers show increasing SVD similarity to *very* over time while control adverbs show no trend (**b**). Intensifiers show decreasing W2V similarity to their original lexical meanings (SIMLEX) over time whereas control adverbs show no trend (**c**). Neither intensifiers nor control show a significant trend with SIMLEX using SVD embeddings (**d**). Intensifiers and control adverbs both show increasing productivity over time measured as BREADTH (**e-f**) and as raw type diversity, but intensifiers show significantly greater increases over time compared to control for TYPEDIV (**g**). Error bars on raw values show 95% bootstrap confidence intervals.

related to a single property p does their combination yield a synergy such that language users can infer the meaning 'very p.' As these bridging contexts increase in number, there is eventually enough evidence for users to infer the adverbial meaning 'very' even in the absence of the initial bridging context. In this way, the adverb becomes increasingly free to modify new adjectives without injecting its literal meaning as in (1-3b), effectively becoming bleached. Thus, the prediction we will test in order to evaluate our theory is as follows:

- **P1.** Rate of bleaching (for an adverb, over a given decade) is positively correlated with the similarity between an adverb and the adjectives modified by the adverb (henceforth SIMADJMOD).

4.2 Setup

We calculate rates of bleaching by taking the first derivative of extent of bleaching with respect to time, according to eq. 3:

$$\frac{d}{dt}(B(K,t)) = \frac{\Delta B}{\Delta t} = \frac{B(K, t+10) - B(K, t)}{10}$$

(3)

where $B(K, t)$ is rate of bleaching for an adverb K at time t according to one of the three bleaching metrics (SIMVERY, SIMLEX, BREADTH), giving us three different time series for rates of bleaching per adverb.

Since we are interested in examining how rate of bleaching over a given decade correlates with SIMADJMOD, the semantic relatedness between an adverb and the adjectives it modifies, we compute this variable (for a given adverb and decade) according to eq. 4:

$$\text{SIMADJMOD}(K,t) = \frac{\sum\limits_{a_i \in A_{K,t}} \text{sim}(K, a_i) o(a_i)}{|A_{K,t}|}$$

(4)

where $A_{K,t}$ is the set of all adjectives modified by an adverb K at time t. Essentially, we take the average cosine similarity between an adverb and the adjectives it modifies, weighted by the odds of each adjective being modified (for a given decade).

4.3 Results

We present results using rates of bleaching computed from SVD embeddings (see Appendix C for results based on W2V embeddings). We find that our prediction is borne out: across all adverbs (both intensifiers and control), rate of bleaching over a given decade $D = [t_0, t_1)$ is positively correlated with SIMADJMOD at t_0 (the semantic relatedness between an adverb and adjectives modified at t_0), implying that at a given time, adverbs that modify semantically similar adjectives will bleach faster into intensifiers over the following decade. Lines of best fit from ordinary least squares regressions are shown in Fig. 3.

Moreover, what distinguishes intensifiers from non-bleaching control adverbs in our data is the variable SIMADJMOD: averaged across 1850-1990, SIMADJMOD is higher among the set of intensifiers compared to the set of control adverbs (Fig. 4). We further performed paired t-tests and found that SIMADJMOD is significantly higher for intensifiers than for the control adverbs ($t = 7.3\text{e}{+}1$, p$<$1e-20).[7]

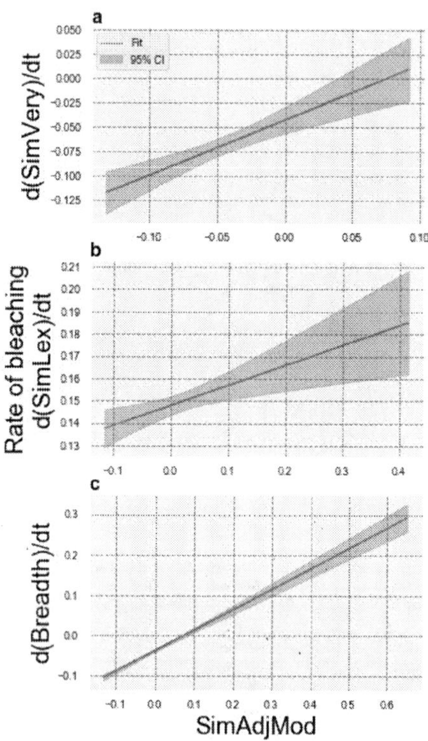

Figure 3. The more semantically similar an adverb is to the adjectives that it premodifies (the greater SIMADJMOD), the greater its rate of bleaching according to SIMVERY (**a**), SIMLEX (**b**) and BREADTH (**c**). Rates are computed using SVD embeddings and data are for all adverbs (intensifiers and control) at all years. Shaded areas show 95% confidence intervals.

---

[7]We also found the proportion of adjectives modified by an adverb relative to verbs to be significantly higher among intensifiers vs. control ($t = 4.4$, p$<$1e-04).

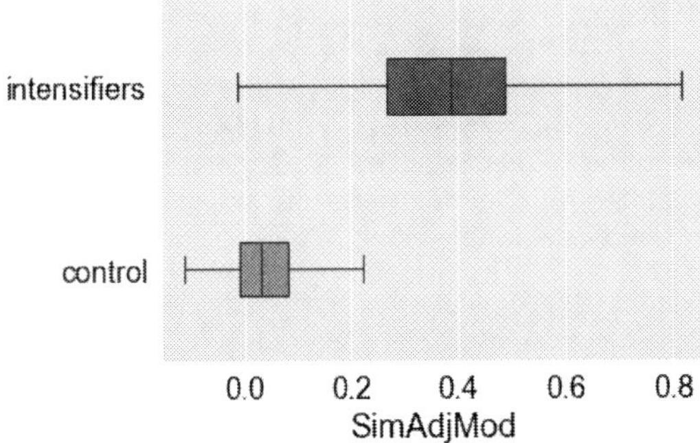

Figure 4. Intensifiers on average modify semantically more similar adjectives compared to control adverbs.

5 Discussion

In this work, we show how word embeddings and n-gram parse context can be used to model the semantic bleaching of manner adverbs into intensifiers. In particular, we empirically show that the bleaching of adverbs is associated with intuitive changes that have not previously been evaluated on large scale data: loss of root meaning, gain of target meaning, and increasing productivity. While our diachronic metrics may be biased by increasing corpus size over the years in our study, we find that the metrics SIMVERY, SIMLEX, and TYPEDIV still show significantly larger increases for the intensifiers compared to the control set. Thus, even though increasing corpus size presumably affects both wordsets equally, we have evidence to suggest that there are significant additional increases for intensifiers that may capture the fact that they are bleaching. We recommend that future researchers apply these metrics in conjunction with a control set (matched in frequency) when using other corpora subject to changes in size over time so that they may test for these significant relative differences between the bleaching and control words.

We also find that these two classes of adverbs can be distinguished in the absence of a control set when modeled using SIMLEX, an adverb's similarity to its root adjectival meaning. This metric also has the benefit over BREADTH of operationalizing a fundamental feature of bleaching that is not shared by other kinds of semantic change (e.g., metaphorical extension), as well as being generalizable (unlike SIMVERY) to cases of bleaching beyond manner adverbs becoming intensifiers. Thus, we recommend this metric to researchers interested in modeling bleaching more generally.

We also show the utility of our methodology in evaluating explanatory hypotheses regarding how bleaching into intensifiers happens. We found that there is empirical evidence to support a reanalysis story: an adverb's tendency to modify adjectives that are semantically similar to itself is positively correlated with its subsequent rate of bleaching. This pathway of change is intuitive, as it is collocations such as *awfully disgusting* and *clearly obvious* that invite the re-interpretation of an adverb as a marker of emphasis, similar in function to an intensifier.

In future work, we are interested in refining BREADTH by normalizing for increasing corpus size as well as trying different weightings to capture the landscape of adjectives that an adverb modifies. It also remains an open question how generalizable our findings concerning bleaching of manner adverbs into intensifiers are. It would be interesting to see if other examples of adverb bleaching, such as the development of "moderators" (*slightly*, *hardly*, etc.) can be modeled as reanalysis. Another under-explored example of adverb bleaching concerns the development of maximizing adverbs into reinforcing adverbs. Beltrama and Staum Casasanto (2017) study the change undergone by *totally*, but the larger tendency remains unexplored.

Furthermore, among English adverbs, there are many other semantic factors that have potential effects on bleaching. For example, Sweetser (1989) suggests that words which explicitly highlight semantic facets of the source domain that cannot be mapped onto the target domain are unlikely candidates for grammaticalization as they require "active suppression" of the foregrounded meanings.[8] It would be interesting to study the bleaching of intensifiers with this question in mind—for example, the adverb *vanishingly* occurs in contexts like *vanishingly small* and *vanishingly rare* which are well-suited for reanalysis, but for *vanishingly* to be understood as a generic intensifier would also require suppression of its meaning of smallness.

Acknowledgments

We thank Daniel Lassiter, Vivek Kulkarni, and anonymous reviewers for their helpful feedback.

---

[8] For example, the verb *lumber* is an unlikely candidate for undergoing the change from motion verb to tense marker because it explicitly encodes rate and manner of motion, compared to a verb like *go*.

References

Andrea Beltrama and M Ryan Bochnak. 2015. Intensification without degrees cross-linguistically. *Natural Language & Linguistic Theory*, 33(3):843–879.

Andrea Beltrama and Laura Staum Casasanto. 2017. Totally tall sounds totally younger: Intensification at the socio-semantics interface. *Journal of Sociolinguistics*, 21(2):154–182.

Dwight Bolinger. 1972. *Degree Words*. Paris: Mouton.

Michel Bréal. 1964. *Semantics: Studies in the science of meaning*. New York: Dover.

Joan Bybee. 1995. Regular morphology and the lexicon. *Language and Cognitive Processes*, 10(5):425–455.

Joan L Bybee, Revere Dale Perkins, and William Pagliuca. 1994. *The evolution of grammar: Tense, aspect, and modality in the languages of the world*, volume 196. The University of Chicago Press: Chicago.

Mark Davies. 2010-. *The Corpus of Historical American English (COHA): 400 million words, 1810-2009*. Available online at https://corpus.byu.edu/coha/.

Haim Dubossarsky, Daphna Weinshall, and Eitan Grossman. 2017. Outta control: Laws of semantic change and inherent biases in word representation models. In *Proceedings of the 2017 Conference on Empirical Methods in Natural Language Processing*, pages 1136–1145, Copenhagen, Denmark. Association for Computational Linguistics.

Nicholas Evans and David Wilkins. 2000. In the mind's ear: The semantic extensions of perception verbs in Australian languages. *Language*, 76:546–592.

Lea Frermann and Mirella Lapata. 2016. A Bayesian model of diachronic meaning change. *Transactions of the Association for Computational Linguistics*, 4:31–45.

Yoav Goldberg and Jon Orwant. 2013. A dataset of syntactic-ngrams over time from a very large corpus of English books. In **SEM*.

Kristina Gulordava and Marco Baroni. 2011. A distributional similarity approach to the detection of semantic change in the Google books ngram corpus. In *Proceedings of the GEMS 2011 Workshop on GEometrical Models of Natural Language Semantics*, pages 67–71, Edinburgh, UK. Association for Computational Linguistics.

William L. Hamilton, Jure Leskovec, and Dan Jurafsky. 2016a. Cultural shift or linguistic drift? comparing two computational measures of semantic change. In *Proceedings of the 2016 Conference on Empirical Methods in Natural Language Processing*, pages 2116–2121, Austin, Texas. Association for Computational Linguistics.

William L. Hamilton, Jure Leskovec, and Dan Jurafsky. 2016b. Diachronic word embeddings reveal statistical laws of semantic change. In *Proceedings of the 54th Annual Meeting of the Association for Computational Linguistics (Volume 1: Long Papers)*, pages 1489–1501, Berlin, Germany. Association for Computational Linguistics.

Paul J Hopper and Elizabeth Closs Traugott. 2003. *Grammaticalization*. Cambridge: Cambridge University Press.

Vivek Kulkarni, Rami Al-Rfou, Bryan Perozzi, and Steven Skiena. 2015. Statistically significant detection of linguistic change. In *Proceedings of the 24th International Conference on World Wide Web*, pages 625–635. International World Wide Web Conferences Steering Committee.

Yuri Lin, Jean-Baptiste Michel, Erez Aiden Lieberman, Jon Orwant, Will Brockman, and Slav Petrov. 2012. Syntactic annotations for the google books ngram corpus. In *Proceedings of the ACL 2012 System Demonstrations*, pages 169–174, Jeju Island, Korea. Association for Computational Linguistics.

Gunter Lorenz. 2002. Really worthwhile or not really significant? A corpus-based approach to the delexicalization and grammaticalization of intensifiers in Modern English. *New reflections on grammaticalization*, 49:143.

Yiwei Luo and Yang Xu. 2018. Stability in the temporal dynamics of word meanings. In *CogSci*.

Ronald Macaulay. 2006. Pure grammaticalization: The development of a teenage intensifier. *Language Variation and Change*, 18(3):267–283.

George Miller. 1998. *WordNet: An Electronic Lexical Database*. MIT press.

Sunny Mitra, Ritwik Mitra, Martin Riedl, Chris Biemann, Animesh Mukherjee, and Pawan Goyal. 2014. That's sick dude!: Automatic identification of word sense change across different timescales. In *Proceedings of the 52nd Annual Meeting of the Association for Computational Linguistics (Volume 1: Long Papers)*, pages 1020–1029, Baltimore, Maryland. Association for Computational Linguistics.

Marcin Morzycki. 2008. Adverbial modification of adjectives: Evaluatives and a little beyond. *Event structures in linguistic form and interpretation*, 5:103.

Rick Nouwen. 2011. Degree modifiers and monotonicity. In *Vagueness and language use*, pages 146–164. Springer, Palgrave.

Mark Pagel, Quentin D Atkinson, and Andrew Meade. 2007. Frequency of word-use predicts rates of lexical evolution throughout Indo-European history. *Nature*, 449(7163):717.

Carita Paradis. 1997. *Degree modifiers of adjectives in spoken British English*, volume 92. Lund: Lund University Press.

Hans Peters. 1994. *Degree adverbs in Early Modern English*, volume 13. Berlin: Walter de Gruyter.

Christian Ramiro, Mahesh Srinivasan, Barbara C. Malt, and Yang Xu. 2018. Algorithms in the historical emergence of word senses. *Proceedings of the National Academy of Sciences*, 115(10):2323–2328.

Alex Rosenfeld and Katrin Erk. 2018. Deep neural models of semantic shift. In *Proceedings of the 2018 Conference of the North American Chapter of the Association for Computational Linguistics: Human Language Technologies, Volume 1 (Long Papers)*, pages 474–484, New Orleans, Louisiana. Association for Computational Linguistics.

Skipper Seabold and Josef Perktold. 2010. Statsmodels: Econometric and statistical modeling with python. In *9th Python in Science Conference*.

John Simpson, Edmund SC Weiner, et al. Oxford English Dictionary online. *Accessed October 2018*.

Gustaf Stern. 1931. *Meaning and change of meaning*. Bloomington: Indiana University Press.

Eve Sweetser. 1989. *From etymology to pragmatics: Metaphorical and cultural aspects of semantic structure*, volume 54. Cambridge: Cambridge University Press.

Sali A Tagliamonte. 2008. So different and pretty cool! Recycling intensifiers in Toronto, Canada. *English Language & Linguistics*, 12(2):361–394.

Yang Xu and Charles Kemp. 2015. A computational evaluation of two laws of semantic change. In *CogSci*.

A Full set of 250 intensifiers

abnormally	abominably	absolutely
abundantly	abysmally	actually
acutely	adamantly	aggressively
alarmingly	amazingly	amply
annoyingly	astonishingly	astronomically
atrociously	awfully	basically
beautifully	bitterly	blatantly
breathtakingly	brutally	categorically
clearly	cloyingly	colossally
comically	completely	considerably
conspicuously	copiously	crazily
criminally	curiously	dangerously
decadently	decently	decidedly
deeply	defiantly	definitely
delectably	deliciously	delightfully
depressingly	desperately	devastatingly
disastrously	disconcertingly	disgustingly
dismayingly	distinctly	distressingly
disturbingly	dizzyingly	doubly
dramatically	dreadfully	egregiously
embarrassingly	empatically	endlessly
enormously	enthusiastically	entirely
epically	especially	evidently
exceedingly	excellently	exceptionally
excessively	excruciatingly	exorbitantly
extensively	extraordinarily	extravagantly
extremely	exuberantly	fairly
fiercely	firmly	fortunately
frightfully	frustratingly	fully
fundamentally	furiously	genuinely
gorgeously	greatly	grievously
grossly	handsomely	harshly
heavily	hellishly	hilariously
honestly	horribly	horrifically
hugely	hysterically	immensely
immoderately	impossibly	impressively
improperly	inappropriately	inconveniently
indecently	indescribably	inestimably
inexcusably	inexplicably	infinitely
insanely	intensely	intimately
intolerably	justly	laughably
lavishly	legitimately	liberally
literally	ludicrously	luxuriously
madly	magically	magnificently
majorly	marginally	markedly |</pre>

marvellously
mind-blowingly
miserably
needlessly
noticeably
obnoxiously
outrageously
overpoweringly
painfully
pathetically
pleasantly
purely
recklessly
relentlessly
revoltingly
scarily
shamelessly
sickeningly
sincerely
sorely
startlingly
strongly
stupidly
supremely
terribly
thoroughly
tragically
unapologetically
uncommonly
undoubtedly
unfortunately
unnecessarily
unquestionably
unspeakably
utterly
vigorously
visibly
wholly
woefully

massively
mindlessly
monstrously
nicely
notoriously
obscenely
outstandingly
overtly
particularly
perfectly
profusely
radically
regretfully
reliably
richly
seriously
sharply
significantly
sinfully
spectacularly
strangely
stunningly
substantially
surpassingly
terrifically
threateningly
tremendously
unbearably
uncontrollably
unequivocally
unjustly
unnervingly
unreasonably
unusually
vastly
violently
weirdly
wickedly
wonderfully

mightily
miraculously
mysteriously
notably
objectively
offensively
overbearingly
overwhelmingly
passionately
phenomenally
prominently
reasonably
regrettably
remarkably
savagely
severely
shockingly
simply
solidly
splendidly
strikingly
stupendously
superbly
surprisingly
thankfully
totally
truly
uncomfortably
undeniably
unexpectedly
unmistakably
unpleasantly
unsettlingly
unutterably
veritably
virtually
wholeheartedly
wildly
worryingly

B Full set of 178 control adverbs

abruptly
actively
alternatively
apparently
automatically
bitterly
carefully
comparatively
constantly
conversely
daily
directly
easily
efficiently
eventually
explicitly
firstly
frankly
generally
happily
hopefully
importantly
independently
inevitably
invariably
kindly
lightly
mainly
namely
newly
occasionally
originally
permanently
politically
possibly
precisely
presumably
principally
promptly
quickly
readily
reportedly
roughly
secondly
sexually

accordingly
adequately
angrily
appropriately
badly
briefly
comfortably
consequently
continually
correctly
deliberately
duly
economically
equally
exactly
finally
formally
freely
gently
hastily
ideally
incidentally
indirectly
initially
ironically
lately
locally
mentally
neatly
normally
officially
partially
personally
poorly
potentially
predominantly
previously
privately
properly
rapidly
recently
repsectively
sadly
seemingly
shortly

accurately
allegedly
annually
approximately
barely
broadly
commonly
consistently
continuously
currently
differently
easily
effectively
essentially
exclusively
financially
formerly
frequently
gradually
historically
immediately
increasingly
individually
instantly
jointly
legally
loudly
mostly
necessarily
obviously
openly
partly
physically
positively
practically
presently
primarily
probably
publicly
rarely
regularly
rightly
safely
separately
silently

similarly	simultaneously	slowly
smoothly	socially	softly
solely	specifically	steadily
strictly	subsequently	successfully
suddenly	sufficiently	supposedly
swiftly	technically	temporarily
tightly	traditionally	typically
ultimately	urgently	usually
vaguely	weakly	widely

C   Diachronic correlations for W2V embeddings-based rates of bleaching

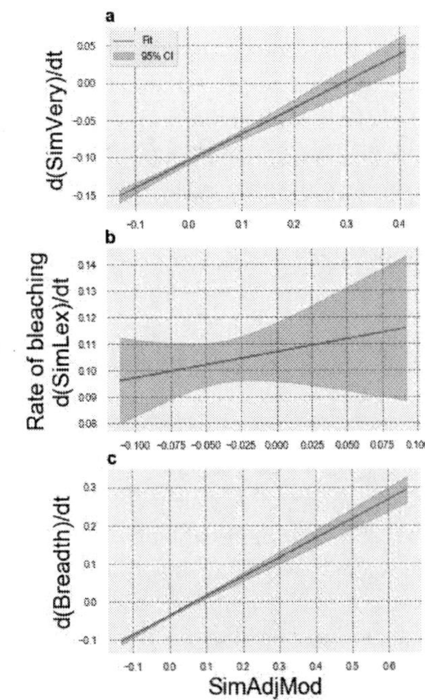

Figure 5. The more semantically similar an adverb is to the adjectives that it premodifies, the greater its rate of bleaching by all three metrics. Rates are computed using HistWords W2V embeddings and data are for all adverbs (intensifiers and control) at all years.

Computational Analysis of the Historical Changes in Poetry and Prose

Amitha Gopidi
IIIT, Hyderabad
amitha.g@research.iiit.ac.in

Aniket Alam
IIIT, Hyderabad
aniket.alam@iiit.ac.in

Abstract

The esoteric definitions of poetry are insufficient in enveloping the changes in poetry that the age of mechanical reproduction has witnessed with the widespread proliferation of the use of digital media and artificial intelligence. They are also insufficient in distinguishing between prose and poetry, as the content of both prose and poetry can be poetic. Using quotes as prose considering their poetic, context-free and celebrated nature, stylistic differences between poetry and prose are delved into. Grammar and meter are justified as distinguishing features. Datasets of popular prose and poetry spanning across 1870-1920 and 1970-2019 have been created, and multiple experiments have been conducted to prove that prose and poetry in the latter period are more alike than they were in the former. The accuracy of classification of poetry and prose of 1970-2019 is significantly lesser than that of 1870-1920, thereby proving the convergence of poetry and prose.

1 Introduction

Language is the mathematics of expression. It is a mathematics because one stitches together an algorithm of concepts in the world, that we identify through words. This world of words is akin to dealing with numbers, because both in their atomic or denotative sense convey very little. But when they combine, they have unlimited potential of justifying profound concepts of time and space.

In this mathematical world of language, however, the origin and definitions of poetry as put forth by philosophers are esoteric in nature with little verifiability. And most of these esoteric definitions, though exotic, can be applied just as well to prose. Plato, in Republic, Book X, writes that poetry has the power to transform its audience, and poets therefore should be held accountable for what they write given this transformative power.

Aristotle (Golden, 1968), differentiates between different artforms but his discussion of poetry as being mainly tragedy or comedy explains that poetry since then has become a much wider artform. Kant (1952) expounded that a "poem may be very neat and elegant, but without spirit" if it lacks imagination, while the same may be said about prose. Shelley (2009) insists that poets are the "unacknowledged legislators of the World" and poetry to him is the "expression of the imagination" which he opines comes naturally to mankind. He also gives a restricted definition of poetry as follows:

> Poetry in a mere restricted sense expresses those arrangements of language, and especially metrical language, which are created by that imperial faculty, whose throne is curtained within the invisible nature of man.

However, as pointed out by Gioia (2003), poetry is a rapidly changing art. He writes that "the general term poetry, for example, now encompasses so many diverse and often irreconcilable artistic enterprises that it often proves insufficient to distinguish the critical issues at stake." Admittedly then, the definition of a poem in the state of the situation is the poem itself. And this causes a problem because anything goes in the name of poetry.

This paper is an attempt to understand what has changed in poetry over the last 150 years within the age of mechanical reproduction of art, named so by Benjamin and Underwood (1998). Comparison, therefore, has been done between the early stages of this age, wherein romantic poetry flourished, namely 1870-1920 and the late stage, 1970-2019, which saw the mechanical reproduction of art occurring through various digital forms. The latter importantly saw the creation of artworks

Proceedings of the 1st International Workshop on Computational Approaches to Historical Language Change, pages 14–22
Florence, Italy, August 2, 2019. ©2019 Association for Computational Linguistics

using artificial intelligence, with many computational poetry generators spewing poetry.

> Whatever one thinks of the artistic quality of the new poetic forms, one must concede that at the very least they reassuringly demonstrate the abiding human need for poetry.
>
> (Dana Gioia)

1.1 Prose and Poetry - Differentiating features

In the attempt to learn how poetry has changed over the last 150 years, the features that are normally attributed to poetry were studied. However, it was noticed that semantic features such as imagery, metaphors, sentiment, choice of words, themes, topics and associations were not strictly ascribed to poetry. All of these features can also be found in prose, and it is for this reason that prose is also called 'poetic', as corroborated by Eagleton (2007). Toni Morrison, for instance, is called a highly 'poetic' writer (Beaulieu, 2003). While we see that many works of prose are poetic, choosing entire novels would cause a lot of noise in the data. It is for this reason that we carefully chose quotes from popular novels as our prose, because quotes are the touchstones of books, are contextually independent of the situation in the book and hence make sense in a stand alone manner.

The visual difference between a quote and a poem are the line breaks.

> A poem is a fictional, verbally inventive moral statement in which it is the author, rather than the printer or word processor, who decides where the lines should end.
>
> (Terry Eagleton)

This, however, is also to say that a quote can be converted to a poem by an individual's decisions as to where to split the sentences into new lines. For this reason, line breaks were avoided as a feature.

Grammar, however, was identified as an important differentiator between poetry and prose by the authors by manual evaluation of the prose and poetry datasets. Within grammar, different types of inversions of word orders in sentences such as verb-subject inversion, along with dependent clauses, questions and conjunctions were chosen as features and are justified under section 2.2.

Meter was also considered as a feature, because as explained by Boulton (2014), meter is only a subsection of rhythm, and meter consists of the most identifiable rhythms. It is also important to note that she makes it abundantly clear that "free verse is not some glorious revolutionary emancipation of poetry, allowing sincerities never before possible." But that it is the kind of poetry with a meter that is neither traditional nor recognizable. And inversions are mentioned to be used in order to enforce a metrical structure in a poem, and therefore, it made all the more sense to consider meter as a feature.

Rhyme, however, was only used in comparing poetry of the two chosen periods and is also aided by inversion.

1.2 Related Work

Classification approaches between poetry and prose have been done by Roxas and Tapang (2010) using word adjacency networks and latent dirichlet allocation. Jamal et al. (2012) have attempted a classification of just poetry using themes. Tanasescu et al. (2016) have done a classification of poetry with respect to only rhyme and meter.

In work related to analysis of prose and poetry, Doumit et al. (2013) have worked on differentiating prose and poetry of two popular poets and authors each, using a semantic neural model. They show that poetry possesses a higher number of associations than prose. However, quotes are as poetic as prose with many metaphors and associations. Therefore, our problem is unique as we differentiate between quotes and poetry.

Kao and Jurafsky (2015) have done a computational analysis of poetic style using amateur and professional poetry. However, they concentrate on parts-of-speech tag occurrences and semantic features such as imagery, emotional language, sound devices and diction. Semantic features in this paper have been avoided with a rationale that quotes and poetry would be very similar with respect to these.

Chen et al. (2014) have worked on converting prose into rhyming verse, which uses substitution choices so as to enforce rhyme and produces sonnets based on an input of source sentences.

Computational poetry generators have used prose in the form of input or as training data, applying constraints on it using meter, rhyme and type of words through deep learning as well as heuristic approaches (Chen et al., 2014; Ghazvininejad et al., 2016; Yi et al., 2017).

Therefore, the use of different sentences styles in poetry as compared to prose contributed by the use of inversion has not been used as a feature so far. While meter was widely used, the dynamics between meter, inversion and rhyme have not been explored. Our high accuracies of classification with just inversion as a feature show the importance of the account of sentences-styling in poetry as compared to prose. The study of change in poetry with respect to prose historically is also unique to this paper, clearly showing the dwindling of the features that were once more prevalent in poetry than they are today. The absence of change in prose over the years with respect to the stylistic features of inversion and meter is also shown.

2 Methodology

2.1 Dataset Overview

The four datasets using which our features for the historical analysis of poetry and prose were derived, belong to two time segments 1870-1920 and 1970-2019. The reasoning behind choosing these particular time segments is explained in Section 1. Each time segment has a dataset of both prose and poetry. Each of the datasets were made computationally by curating content written in the respective time segment by popular poets and books of the time.

For poetry, PoetryFoundation[1] and PoemHunter[2] websites were used. Finding the year of publishing of individual poems was difficult, so lists of popular poets of that time period were manually chosen from the websites mentioned, and their works were collated in the form of pdf files. These pdf files were converted into datasets.

For prose, 30 top liked quotes (or lesser if 30 weren't available) from 500 most popular books of the time segment as listed by Goodreads[3] were computationally collected. The top liked quotes are often quite 'poetic' in their content. The meta structure of our datasets is described in table 1.

2.2 Features

Each line of a poem, and each sentence of a quote was considered as the smallest unit on which the

[1] https://www.poetryfoundation.org/
[2] https://www.poemhunter.com/
[3] https://www.goodreads.com/

Type	Time Period	Count
Prose	1870-1920	7838 quotes
Prose	1970-2019	12623 quotes
Poetry	1870-1920	13635 poems
Poetry	1970-2019	7917 poems

Table 1: Datasets

following features were calculated:

2.2.1 Grammar

While prose is always grammatical, poetry tends to break away from the limitations of grammar. With regard to the celebrated poet Emily Dickinson, Miller (1987) writes that the former often wrote in an ungrammatical manner. The term 'poetic license' (Britannica, 2007) is a testament to the fact that poets often break the rules of grammar. For instance, Kaur (2017) and Cummings (1994) have written without capitalization or punctuation, thus violating grammar.

While the lack of capitalization and punctuation are not universal among poems, by manual evaluation, it was noticed that the styles of the sentences used in poetry greatly differed from those in prose because of the use of inversion. Inversion is defined as, "the syntactic reversal of the normal order of the words and phrases in a sentence, as, in English, the placing of an adjective after the noun it modifies ("the form divine"), a verb before its subject ("Came the dawn"), or a noun preceding its preposition "worlds between")" (Britannica, 2016).

As an example, Wordsworth in his poem, "I Wandered Lonely As A Crowd" (Wordsworth) uses the verb-subject inversion when he writes "Ten thousand saw I at a glance" instead of "I saw ten thousand at a glance".

We use four different kind of inversions that we observed in poetry based on the discussion of styling sentences in Waddell (1993) supplemented by the insights in Literary Devices website (Devices, 2015).

Along with these, features such as dependent clause as a subject, rhetorical questions and lines beginning with conjunctions are used as features. The use of conjunctions at the beginning of a line/sentence is disputed to be ungrammatical (Soanes, 2012), but we noticed that the usage was higher in poetry as compared to prose considering that poetry is a grouping of phrases and clauses.

Waddell (1993) also describes the use of dependent clauses as a pattern of styling sentences and we noted that dependent clause as a subject occurred quite often in poems. The use of rhetorical questions in literature (Devices, 2017) is quite prevalent, and they occurred more in our poetry datasets. The list of features related to grammar with examples are listed in table 2.

In order to implement all of the above features, Stanford CoreNLP (Manning et al., 2014) tools of tokenization, parts of speech tags, dependency parse trees, OpenIE triples were used. Simple heuristics were used to decide which kind of inversions exist in a given sentence using POS tags and OpenIE triple occurrences in the sentence. For instance, if the subject given by OpenIE triple of a line is a noun or pronoun, and it is preceded by a verb, the line would be marked as having subject-verb inversion. The OpenIE tool trained on prose, doesn't always fetch results for lines in poetry and in these cases, we use POS tags as they are accurate for poetry as well. The various inversion counts were normalized by the number of lines in poetry datasets and the number of sentences in prose datasets, so as to remove dependency on the the length of the poem or quote.

2.2.2 Meter

Poets use inversion in order to fit their material into a meter (Britannica, 2016), which is nothing but the arrangement of stressed(s) and unstressed(w) syllables in a certain manner (Boulton, 2014). In order to implement meter, we used Stanford Literary Lab's Poesy (Heuser et al., 2018), which is a python module for poetic processing. The module gives information of a base meter among four types of base meters:

1. Iambic [ws]

2. Trochaic [sw]

3. Anapestic [wws]

4. Dactylic [sww]

It also gives information regarding the number of repetitions of meter in a given line, thus leading to information on whether the poem is a pentameter, hexameter etc.

2.2.3 Rhyme

Inversion is also used often to fit into a rhyme scheme along with meter. Using the Poesy (Heuser et al., 2018) module, we also extract the rhyme scheme of poems. It was only used for comparison between the two poetry datasets. It has not been applied on the prose datasets as the values were null.

2.3 Classification

The feature vectors consisted of 9 features discussed in the previous sections. Seven of them are various inversion types, followed by the base meter and number of feet. The extra feature, 'rhyme type' was only used for classification between the two poetry datasets.

The feature data was trained through a random forest classifier (Breiman, 2001) and KNN classifier with a 70/30 split for the training and testing data. The optimal value of the number of trees for random forest classifier was found to be 100. The value of k is taken be 3 for the KNN classifier. To deal with class imbalance, we adjust weights inversely proportional to class frequencies in the data.

Four experiments of different classifications between poetry and prose were conducted.

3 Results

Random Forest classifier performed better than KNN classifier in all of the below experiments:

3.1 Prose vs Poetry of Each Period

Classification of prose and poetry of each period was done to see if classification accuracy between poetry and prose has reduced for the time segment 1970-2019 as compared to that of 1870-1920. This would indicate that poetry and prose are more similar in 1970-2019 than they were in 1870-1920. Various combinations of features were used with both the classifiers.

The reduction in the classification accuracy of poetry and prose of 1970-2019 as shown in table 4 as compared to 1870-1920 as shown in table 3, indicates convergence in poetry and prose in the period 1970-2019.

3.2 Poetry: 1870-1920 vs 1970-2019

Classification of poetry of 1870-1920 and poetry of 1970-2019 was conducted with rhyme as an additional feature.

The results as shown in table 5 indicate that poetry has undergone a significant change with an accuracy of 77% in classification.

Feature	Example
Adjective Inversion: Adjective occurs right after the noun.	"I sing the body electric"
Subject Verb Inversion: Verb occurs before its subject.	"Ten thousand saw I at a glance."
Prepositional Phrase Inversion: Prepositional phrase occurs before subject and verb, or verb and subject.	"Until we meet again, to be counted as bliss."
The Yoda construction: Modifier followed by subject and verb.	"Whose woods these are I think I know."
Dependent Clause as a subject, followed by verb.	"What man cannot imagine, he cannot create."
Question	"Shall I compare thee to a summers day?"
Beginning with a conjunction	"Two roads diverged in a yellow wood, And sorry I could not travel both And be one traveler, long I stood And looked down one as far as I could To where it bent in the undergrowth;"

Table 2: Grammatical Features

Classifier	Feature	Accuracy	F1 Score	ROC AUC Score
Random Forest	All	98.4	98.4	98.02
Random Forest	Meter	93.7	93.7	93.8
Random Forest	Inversion	91.8	91.8	91.3
kNN	All	97.4	97.4	97.02
kNN	Meter	93.6	93.6	93.8
kNN	Inversion	91.8	91.8	91.2

Table 3: Poetry vs Prose classification results for 1870-1920

Classifier	Feature	Accuracy	F1 Score	ROC AUC Score
Random Forest	All	91.5	91.3	89.7
Random Forest	Meter	83.4	82.8	80.06
Random Forest	Inversion	85.1	84.5	82.06
kNN	All	90.0	89.8	88.2
kNN	Meter	80.6	79.2	75
kNN	Inversion	84.1	83.6	81.07

Table 4: Poetry vs Prose classification results for 1970-2019

Classifier	Accuracy	F1 Score	ROC AUC Score
Random Forest	77.0	76.3	73.11
kNN	72.6	72.5	70

Table 5: Poetry 1870-1920 vs Poetry 1970-2019 classification

Classifier	Accuracy	F1 Score	ROC AUC Score
Random Forest	59.2	50.7	50
kNN	51.4	52.09	51.1

Table 6: Prose 1870-1920 vs Prose 1970-2019 classification

Classifier	Accuracy	F1 Score	ROC AUC Score
Random Forest	94.7	94.7	94.7
kNN	94.04	94.0	94.01

Table 7: Poetry vs Prose classification overall

3.3 Prose: 1870-1920 vs 1970-2019

Classification of prose of 1870-1920 and prose of 1970-2019 was conducted.

The results as shown in table 6 indicate that nothing much has changed in prose as per these features over the two periods because the evaluation scores are close to a random guess (59%).

3.4 Poetry and Prose Both Periods Combined

This classification was done with combined datasets of poetry against combined datasets of prose. As per the results shown in table 7, given an input, this classifier would differentiate between it being a poem or prose with 94.7% accuracy. This is an important result as we do not consider line breaks.

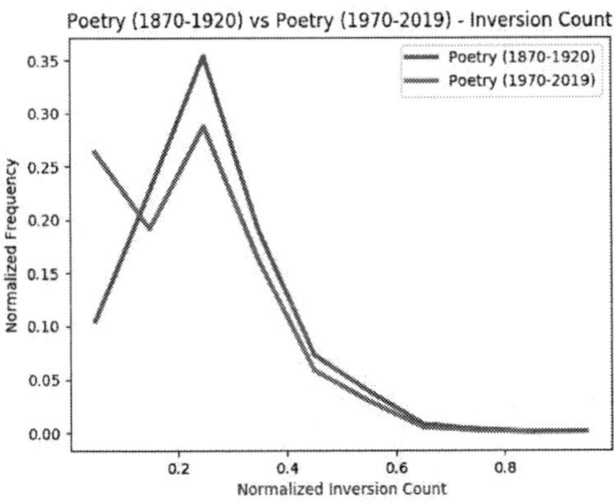

Figure 1: Poetry (1870-1920) vs Poetry (1970-2019) - Inversion Count

4 Analysis

4.1 Inversion

Figures 1 and 2 are plotted between the normalized inversion count(so as to remove any dependency on the length of the poem/prose), and the normalized frequency of the datasets(so as to remove dependency on the number of data points).

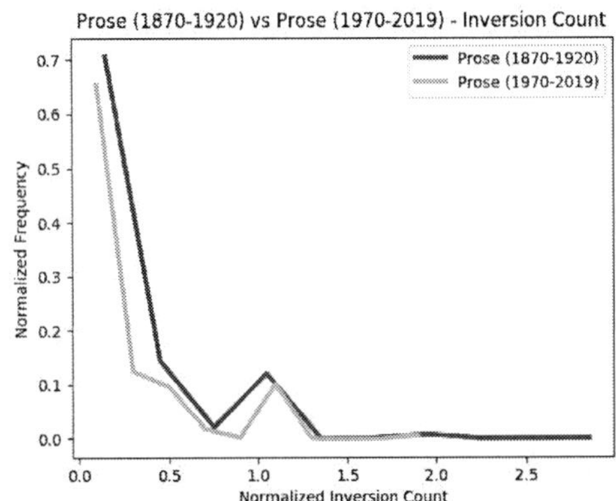

Figure 2: Prose (1870-1920) vs Prose (1970-2019) - Inversion Count

Figure 1 indicates a significant fall in the inversion count in the second time period. And figure 2 shows that the inversion counts of the two periods of prose are more or less the same.

4.2 Meter Base Type

The figures 3 and 4 represent the historical change in meter over the two periods for both prose and poetry. The y axis represents the percentage of dataset, which is a normalized indicator and does not skew the graph towards the period with higher data points.

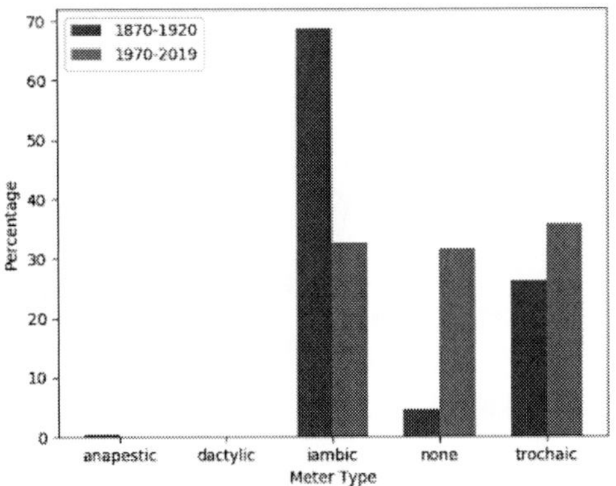

Figure 3: Poetry (1870-1920) vs Poetry (1970-2019) - Meter Type

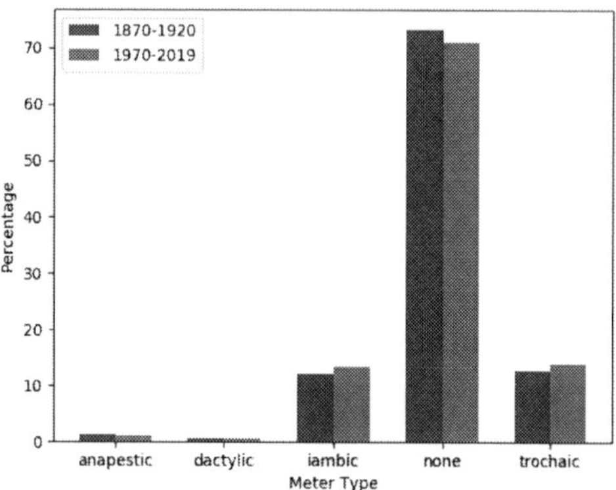

Figure 4: Prose (1870-1920) vs Prose (1970-2019) - Meter Type

Figure 3 clearly shows the dominance of the iambic base meter in poetry datasets, and its fall from 1870-1920 to 1970-2019. It also shows that in 1970-2019, the number of poems with no distinguishable meter has risen considerably with no significant change in anapestic or dactylic base meters.

Figure 4 proves that there is no significant difference in the base meter of prose over the two chosen periods, with none value as the most dominant.

4.3 Popular Meters

Figure 5 and Figure 6 were drawn so as to show the change in meter. Meter plotted is a combination of the base meter and its feet in the poem. The top 7 meters were chosen for the plots.

Figure 5 shows the significant fall of the all the popular meters in the second time period as compared to the first. The increase in the none values also suggests that the second time period consists of poetry with no recognizable meter.

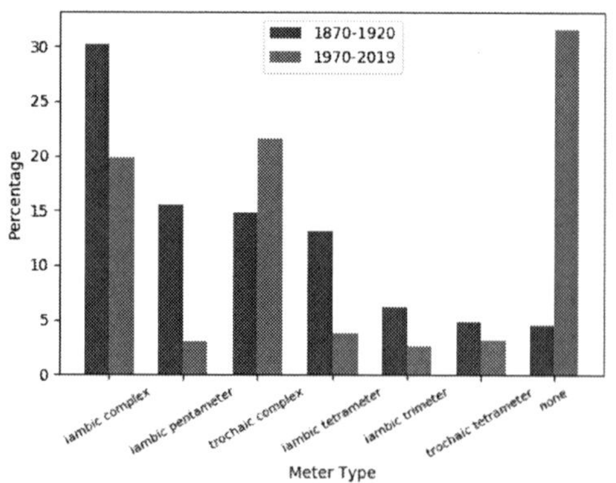

Figure 5: Poetry (1870-1920) vs Poetry (1970-2019)

Figure 6, on the other hand, shows the lack of recognizable meter in prose which is expected.

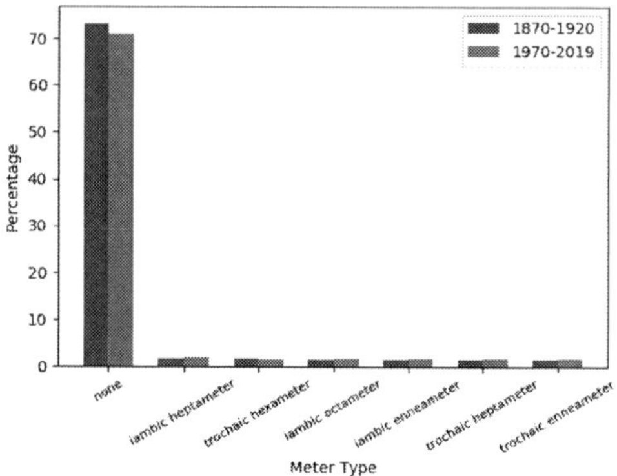

Figure 6: Prose (1870-1920) vs Prose (1970-2019)

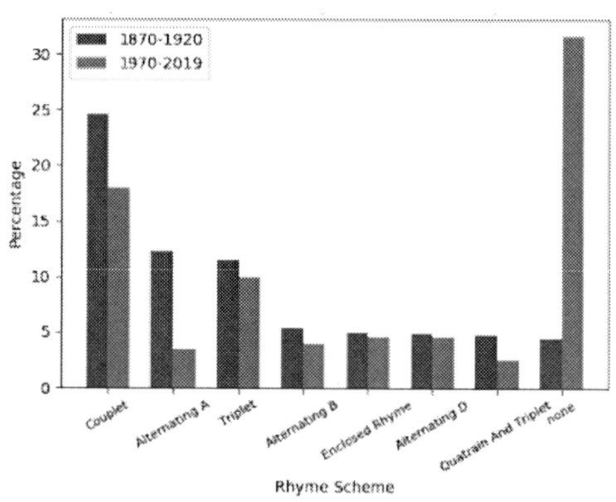

Figure 7: Poetry (1870-1920) vs Poetry (1970-2019) - Rhyme Scheme

4.4 Rhyme

The rhyme feature used in figure 7, shows that a large percentage of 1970-2019 poetry has no rhyme scheme, while also showing that the prevalence of the other rhyme schemes has also come down.

5 Conclusion

From the experiments conducted, it has been proved that the poetry of 1970-2019 is more similar to prose of its period than the poetry of 1870-1920 was to the prose of the same period. The changes in prose of the two periods with respect to stylistic features are minimal, but those in poetry are significant. The convergence of poetry and prose and lack of change in prose, proves that poetry does not possess the liminal boundaries that prose enjoys. The importance of a new age definition of poetry is thus established considering the changes in poetry as an artform.

Apart from justifying the historical changes in poetry and prose, this paper also achieves high accuracy in the classification of poem and prose using no semantic features. This is an important indicator that semantic content of poetry and prose can be very alike and that they can still be differentiated using stylistic features without considering the obvious visual difference of line breaks.

The future work of this paper is to use these features in constructing a personalized poetry assistant that learns the stylistic preferences of the user in inversions and meter, based on user input of creative text. This personalized nature of the assistant would adapt to the user's wishes in becoming a 'modern' or a 'classic' poet.

References

Elizabeth Ann Beaulieu. 2003. *The Toni Morrison Encyclopedia*. Greenwood Publishing Group.

Walter Benjamin and JA Underwood. 1998. *The work of art in the age of mechanical reproduction*. na.

Marjorie Boulton. 2014. *The Anatomy of Poetry (Routledge Revivals)*. Routledge.

Leo Breiman. 2001. Random forests. *Machine learning*, 45(1):5–32.

The Editors of Encyclopaedia Britannica. 2007. Poetic license.

The Editors of Encyclopaedia Britannica. 2016. Inversion.

Quanze Chen, Chenyang Lei, Wei Xu, Ellie Pavlick, and Chris Callison-Burch. 2014. Poetry of the crowd: A human computation algorithm to convert prose into rhyming verse. In *Second AAAI Conference on Human Computation and Crowdsourcing*.

Edward Estlin Cummings and George James Firmage. 1994. *ee cummings: Complete Poems, 1904-1962*. Liveright Publishing Corporation.

Literary Devices. 2015. Inversion Examples and Definition.

Literary Devices. 2017. Rhetorical question.

Sarjoun Doumit, Nagendra Marupaka, and Ali A Minai. 2013. Thinking in prose and poetry: A semantic neural model. In *The 2013 International Joint Conference on Neural Networks (IJCNN)*, pages 1–8. IEEE.

Terry Eagleton. 2007. *How to read a poem*. John Wiley & Sons.

Marjan Ghazvininejad, Xing Shi, Yejin Choi, and Kevin Knight. 2016. Generating topical poetry. In *Proceedings of the 2016 Conference on Empirical Methods in Natural Language Processing*, pages 1183–1191.

Dana Gioia. 2003. Disappearing ink: Poetry at the end of print culture. *The Hudson Review*, 56(1):21–49.

Leon Golden. 1968. *Aristotle's Poetics: a translation and commentary for students of literature*. Prentice-Hall.

Ryan Heuser, Mark Algee-Hewitt, Maria Kraxenberger, J.D. Porter, Jonny Sensenbaugh, and Justin Tackett. 2018. Poesy.

Noraini Jamal, Masnizah Mohd, and Shahrul Azman Noah. 2012. Poetry classification using support vector machines. *Journal of Computer Science*, 8(9):1441.

Immanuel Kant, Immanuel Kant, and Sir James Creed MEREDITH. 1952. *The Critique of Judgement. Translated with Analytical Indexes by James Creed Meredith*. Oxford.

Justine T Kao and Dan Jurafsky. 2015. A computational analysis of poetic style. *LiLT (Linguistic Issues in Language Technology)*, 12.

Rupi Kaur. 2017. *The sun and her flowers*. Simon and Schuster.

Christopher Manning, Mihai Surdeanu, John Bauer, Jenny Finkel, Steven Bethard, and David McClosky. 2014. The stanford corenlp natural language processing toolkit. In *Proceedings of 52nd annual meeting of the association for computational linguistics: system demonstrations*, pages 55–60.

Cristanne Miller. 1987. *Emily Dickinson: A Poet's Grammar*. Harvard University Press.

Ranzivelle Marianne Roxas and Giovanni Tapang. 2010. Prose and poetry classification and boundary detection using word adjacency network analysis. *International Journal of Modern Physics C*, 21(04):503–512.

Percy Bysshe Shelley. 2009. A defence of poetry by percy bysshe shelley.

Catherine Soanes. 2012. Can you start a sentence with a conjunction?

Chris Tanasescu, Bryan Paget, and Diana Inkpen. 2016. Automatic classification of poetry by meter and rhyme. In *The Twenty-Ninth International Flairs Conference*.

Marie L Waddell. 1993. *The art of styling sentences: 20 patterns for success*. Barron's Educational Series.

William Wordsworth. I wandered lonely as a cloud by william wordsworth.

Xiaoyuan Yi, Ruoyu Li, and Maosong Sun. 2017. Generating chinese classical poems with rnn encoder-decoder. In *Chinese Computational Linguistics and Natural Language Processing Based on Naturally Annotated Big Data*, pages 211–223. Springer.

Studying Semantic Chain Shifts with Word2Vec:
FOOD > MEAT > FLESH

Richard Zimmermann
University of Geneva, Switzerland
`richard.zimmermann@unige.ch`

Abstract

Word2Vec models are used to study the semantic chain shift FOOD>MEAT>FLESH in the history of English, c. 1475-1925. The development stretches out over a long time, starting before 1500, and may possibly be continuing to this day. The semantic changes likely proceeded as a push chain.

1 Introduction

A semantic chain shift is a set of directly related semantic changes in one lexical field (Anttila 1989, 146-7). One of the best-known examples, and object of study here, is the semantic chain shift involving MEAT[1] in the history of English. The item used to mean 'food of any kind' in Medieval English, but has acquired the more specific meaning of 'food from animal flesh' in Modern English (e.g., Bejan 2017, 82, and many other textbooks, where the phenomenon is usually discussed as an instance of 'semantic narrowing'). This development is linked to a change in the meaning of FOOD. It meant 'anything required to maintain life and growth' in the Middle Ages, as demonstrated, for instance, by ancient Latin-English glosses, such as Thomas Elyot's 1538 *Dictionary* (Stein 2014), where one reads, *Alimentum, alimonia - sustynaunce, fode, or livinge*. The word has come to denote 'anything to eat' at the present. Likewise, the item FLESH has undergone a related semantic change from 'soft body tissue in any function' in Old and Middle English towards 'soft body tissue, usually not for eating' in Present-Day English (for a discussion of the relation between FLESH and MEAT in terms of analogy, see Bloomfield 1933, 407-8, 440-2). Hence, the innovative meanings of each item must have

encroached on and supplanted their counterpart's conservative semantics, resulting in the chain shift FOOD > MEAT > FLESH.[2]

Table 1 paraphrases the semantics of the three targets of the chain shift, the new meaning being at the top, the old at the bottom. It also presents actual uses of the conservative and innovative variants from the 16th and 19th century, respectively, in the form of KWIC concordances with a search window size of 12 words to the left and the right. The targets are shown in red, and context words likely to signal the intended interpretation in green.

Semantic chain shifts involve confounding factors such as archaism, fixed expressions, domain-dependent technical uses, other genre effects, creative extensions by metaphor and metonymy, noise from polysemy and homonymy, and subtle shifts in connotations. These difficulties impede studying macro-trends in their semantic evolution manually. However, it is possible to trace the developments with word embedding techniques (for an overview, see e.g., Tahmasebi et al. 2018).

The present study employs Word2Vec models (Mikolov et al., 2013) to investigate two questions about the FOOD>MEAT>FLESH chain. (1) What is the general time course of the changes? (2) Does the chain commence at the target FLESH (pull chain) or FOOD (push chain)? Section 2 presents the data used in the study. Section 3 presents the findings. Section 4 concludes.

---

[1]Items in all-caps signify abstract lexemes, both target and context words, which can be realized by a large number of specific spelling variants and inflectional forms.

[2]Several reviewers pointed out that the argument of this paper would be strengthened by the inclusion of additional instances of semantic chain shifts. Time constraints prevented a discussion of further examples. Other well-known cases of semantic chain shifts are the development of tree names in Ancient Greek, ASH > BEECH > OAK (e.g. Gamkrelidze and Ivanov 1995, 537-8; Ancient Greek φᾱγός 'oak,' cognate with English *beech*), or the cycle of facial terms in Latin and early Romance, MOUTH > CHIN > CHEEK > MOUTH (e.g.Mallory and Adams 2006, chapter 11 'Anatomy'; French *menton* 'chin,' cognate with English *mouth*). I leave an investigation of these or similar developments to future research.

Proceedings of the 1st International Workshop on Computational Approaches to Historical Language Change, pages 23–28
Florence, Italy, August 2, 2019. ©2019 Association for Computational Linguistics

Target	Meaning	Example sentence	Text source
FLESH (new)	'soft body tissue, not for eating'	as to marry **girls** of the working class - mere **lumps** of **human flesh**. But most of us know that our **marriage** is a pis aller.	George Gissing, *The Odd Women*, c. 1893
FLESH (old)	'soft body tissue (also for eating)'	**beestes / kyne** ['cows'] **/ & mares**. & lyue of the **mylke** & of the flesshe of these **beestes &** **ete** it & say that it is good	Richard Pynson, *Hayton's Little Chronicle*, c. 1520
MEAT (new)	'soft body tissue for eating'	and the other, a red **breed**, very small and **fat**, excellent for meat, but of no value for **milking** purposes. This last **breed** closely resembles	Rider Haggard, *She: A History of Adventure*, c. 1887
MEAT (old)	'anything for eating'	first **course**, in his daies, one **dish**, or two of good **wholsome** meate was thought sufficient, for a man of great worship to **dine** withalls	Philip Stubbes, *The Anatomy of Abuses*, c. 1583
FOOD (new)	'anything for eating'	coats for pillows. There was a **stove** where they might **cook** their food if they had money to **buy** any. A ha'p'orth of **tea** and	Hall Caine, *The Christians*, c. 1897
FOOD (old)	'anything for sustenance'	Suche suffereth theyr shepe to perysshe for **lacke** of **bodily** and **goostly foode** and **suste-naunce**, for **lacke** of preachynge, for **lacke** of gyuynge good counsell	John Longland, *A Sermonde Made Before the Kynge*, c. 1538

Table 1: Examples of FLESH, MEAT and FOOD in their conservative and innovative uses

2 Data and pre-processing

2.1 Corpora used

The data for this study comes from 4 historical corpora, the *Innsbruck Corpus of Middle English Prose* (Markus, 2010), EEBO[3], ECCO[4] and CL-MET3.0 (Diller et al., 2011). It consists of a total of c. 845 million words or 4,7 GB of uncompressed running text. The material was subdivided into ten 50-year periods covering the time span 1425-1925. Table 2 summarizes the data basis.

2.2 Normalization

The greatest challenge to using the historical data fruitfully lies in the great amount of spelling variation found in earlier English. Word embedding techniques treat different orthographic forms of identical lexemes as distinct items, which might impair the quality of the models and hinder diachronic comparisons (for a study highlighting the importance of consistent pre-processing, see e.g. Camacho-Collados and Pilehvar 2018).

Period	Corpus	Size
1 1425-1475	Innsbruck	2.5m
2 1475-1525	EEBO	9.0m
3 1526-1575	EEBO	35.6m
4 1576-1625	EEBO	149.8m
5 1626-1675	EEBO	330.9m
6 1676-1725	EEBO, ECCO	230.5m
7 1726-1775	ECCO	31.6m
8 1776-1825	ECCO, CLMET	38.7m
9 1826-1875	CLMET	10.9m
10 1876-1925	CLMET	8.1m

Table 2: Periodization of the data, their source corpora, and their size (in million words)

Therefore, a large number of regular expressions were run on the texts, improving spelling coherence (a total of 830 replacements, e.g. regularizing *v-u* variability). Further, several lexemes were lemmatized[5], including FOOD, MEAT,

---

[3]*Early English Books Online* is a collection of c. 25,000 early modern prints, digitized by the Text Creation Partnership (TCP), hosted by the University of Michigan Library. https://quod.lib.umich.edu/e/eebogroup/

[4]*Eighteenth Century Collections Online* is a sister project of EEBO, contributing a sample of c. 2,500 digitized books. https://quod.lib.umich.edu/e/ecco/

[5]There are several attempts at standardizing spelling variation found in Early Modern English texts, including *Virtual Orthographic Standardization and Part Of Speech Tagging* (VosPos) (Mueller, 2006), *VARiant Detector 2* (VARD2) (Baron and Rayson, 2008) and *MorphAdorner v2.0* (Burns, 2013). However, the time investment needed to implement any of these systems would have been incommensurate with the goals of this paper. Therefore, lemmatization targeted only the most important items and not the entire vocabulary.

FLESH and most of their closest neighbors. The Innsbruck and EEBO data was POS-tagged to aid in this task (e.g. to distinguish *wine* vs. *win*, *meat* vs. *meet*). Some word class distinctions could not be maintained as a result (e.g. DRINK now refers to the verb and the noun).

2.3 Training

Word embeddings were created for each of the nine periods by training Word2Vec models on their respective text material with Python's Gensim library (Řehůřek and Sojka, 2010). A continuous bag of words architecture was chosen, the words of interest being of reasonably high frequency, with a vector size of 250, a context window size of 20, and a minimum count of 5.

3 Results

Figure 1 shows the cosine similarities between FOOD-MEAT and MEAT-FLESH across the ten time periods. The former two lexemes have become increasingly more similar from the earliest periods on. Their cosine rose from c. 0.4 in 1450 to c. 0.6 in 1700, where it has remained stable since. In contrast, the latter two items showed some relatedness, but remained quite distinct, throughout the earliest periods. Their cosine then increased from c. 0.3 in 1600, peaking at c. 0.6 between 1700 and 1800, and diverged again to c. 0.4 by 1900.

These findings are compatible with a push chain interpretation: FOOD seems to have initiated the changes by first becoming more similar to MEAT. Only subsequently did MEAT associate more closely with FLESH, which then began to occupy a more distinct semantic niche.

The diachronic trajectories of the targets are visualized in Figure 2. It shows the nearest neighbors of the target words over the time studied from the semantic domains 'sustenance' (green), 'eating' (lime), 'animal food' (orange) and 'human skin' (red). The words are arranged in a two-dimensional principal component plot from the last period. The previous time points were homogenized to it using a procrustes transformation. This method is based on Li et al. (2019), which is in turn inspired by Hamilton et al. (2016).[6]

____

[6]One reviewer remarked that the procrustes transformation must be performed on identical vocabularies for every time period. This is indeed the case. The constant vocabulary consists only of the words shown in Figure 2. Several words

The plot shows that FOOD dissociated from the meaning 'sustenance' early on. This lead to a period of sustained close synonymy between MEAT

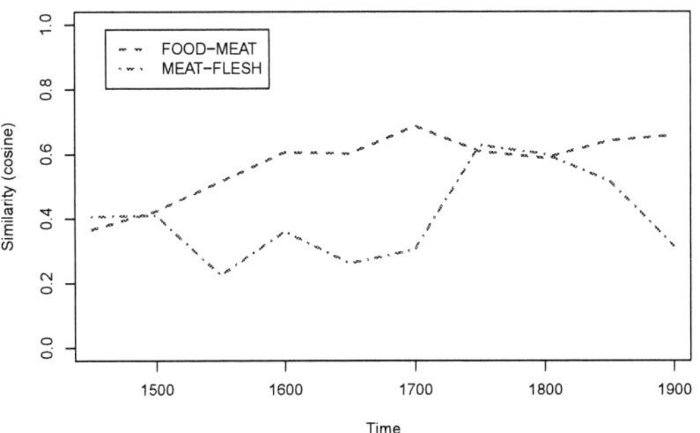

Figure 1: Similarity of target pairs over time

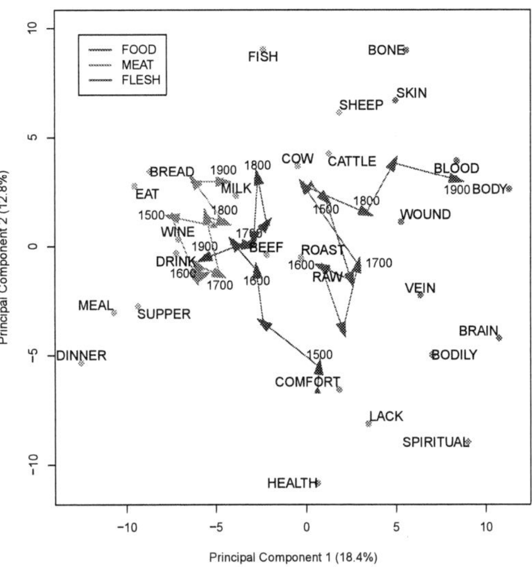

Figure 2: Representation of the semantic chain

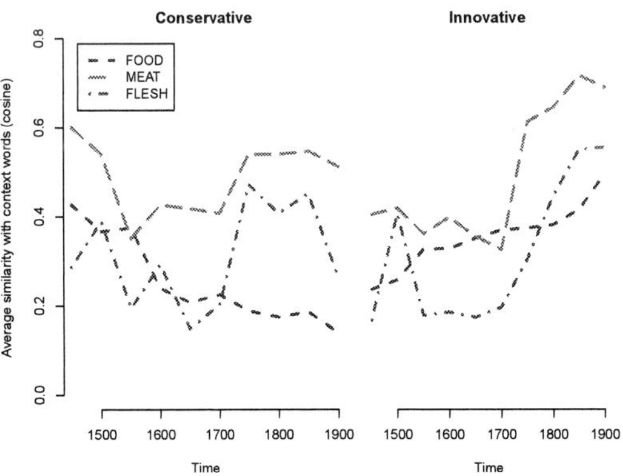

Figure 3: Similarity between a set of conservative / innovative contexts words and each target word

____

had to be left out because they were innovated (e.g. *coffee*, *potato*) or have radically declined in currency (e.g. *concupiscence*, *raiment*) within the time period studied.

and FLESH in the domain 'eating.' In fact, the two lexemes are still strongly connected context words of each other.

While FOOD is now well contained within 'eating' (EAT, MEAL etc.), MEAT is not distinctively associated with 'animal food' (BEEF, ROAST etc.), but rather hovers between the two domains. FLESH was fairly polysemous, cycling around a number of different senses, like 'animal food' (PORK, BROILED etc.) or 'Christian doctrine' (SIN, CHRIST), but has recently become most closely associated with 'human skin' (SKIN, SWEAT etc.).

Figure 3 contains similar information in quantitative, rather than graphical, form. It gives the average closeness of a bag of distinctive context words and the targets as a proxy for their conservative and innovative interpretations.

FOOD consistently moves away from its old towards its new meaning from 1450 on. It thus likely triggered the semantic chain shift. In contrast, the conservative senses of MEAT and FLESH are not entirely lost, but rather fluctuate (witness archaic expressions such as *meat and drink* or *the flesh is weak*). Their modern meanings become frequent from c. 1700 on. This development may happen somewhat earlier and faster for MEAT than for FLESH. If so, this would suggests a secondary push. Here, MEAT may have spread towards semantic space previously held by FLESH, thereby pushing it into a new domain.

4 Summary and outlook

The diachronic developments of the semantic chain shift FOOD > MEAT > FLESH can successfully be investigated with word embedding methods. It was shown that the semantic change of FOOD 'anything for sustenance' > 'anything for eating' can be traced back at least to the middle of the fifteenth century. The acquisition of the new senses 'anything for eating' > 'soft body tissue for eating' for MEAT and 'soft body tissue for eating' > 'soft body tissue not for eating' for FLESH advanced in particular from c. 1700 on. Furthermore, there is evidence to suggest that the semantic change developed as a push chain. FOOD approaches MEAT long before MEAT becomes more closely associated with FLESH. Similarly, MEAT may have encroached upon FLESH somewhat earlier than FLESH became disjoint from the 'animal food' domain.

A number of future research questions are raised by the present study. First, the periodization employed here is not fine-grained enough to establish beyond reasonable doubt that MEAT became specialized before FLESH. The second step of the push chain scenario thus needs to be subject to closer scrutiny. Second, it is possible to follow up the developments during the last century from c. 1900 to 2000. The target items may still be evolving. FLESH might lose its religious connotations; MEAT could move towards a meaning of 'animal body tissue' in general, FOOD is perhaps getting ever more firmly entrenched in the 'eating' domain, etc. Finally, one could investigate a curiously similar chain shift in the history of French, NOURRITURE 'food' > VIANDE 'meat' > CHAIR 'flesh'. It is conceivable that FOOD first changed its meaning under the influence of French loans, such as *nourishment* or *sustenance*. The exact relation between the French and English developments merits closer examination.

It would also be a worthwhile endeavor to compare the results obtained with Word2Vec to other methods suitable for this task. One approach could be to conduct an inter-annotator agreement experiment, in which participants should use the available linguistic context to judge whether FOOD, MEAT and FLESH are used in their innovative or conservative senses in a sample of sentences from every period. The resulting scores could also function as a gold standard for evaluating the goodness of the word embeddings. Another approach could involve collocation measures such as pointwise mutual information or possibly Collostructional Analysis (Stefanowitsch and Griess, 2003).

Several problematic aspects of this research remain. It is very difficult to find a set of context words that remains relatively constant in meaning over as great a time span as considered here. The optimization of the non-modern periods' dimensionality reduction on the modern coordinate space thus becomes increasingly distorted, which may account to some degree for the somewhat erratic movements of the target words in Figure 2. Even worse, some lexemes drop out of use altogether. For example, *potage* 'stew, dish made of a thick liquid' is an important context word of the 'eating' domain at the beginning of the change, but becomes virtually non-existent towards the later periods. Moreover, the corpus sizes of every sub-period vary substantially. This may result in higher-quality embeddings for those periods with more, and poorer embeddings for those with less, textual material. The similarity measurements of the earliest periods of the change, in particular, might be less reliable due to the limited amount of training data. Similarly, the diverse nature of the documents found in the corpora could be problematic. Unbalanced distributions of certain text categories could bias the co-occurrences of target and context words in a considerable way. For example, two corpora might differ by chance in terms of the frequency of religious sermons (associating, say, FLESH with LUST) or culinary recipes (associating FLESH with PORK). Consequently, the embeddings could have been influenced by a random genre effect. Lastly, there are a few minor issues that have not been resolved satisfactorily, such as language mixing in the training texts, in particular with Latin, archaic uses of words in citations, the unprincipled choice of training parameters, and the lack of an appropriate evaluation metric for the task at hand.

Word embedding technologies have advanced to a point where linguists can use them off the shelf to obtain quantitative support for their qualitative assessments (e.g. Traugott and Dasher 2004) without a profound appreciation of the mathematical complexities involved. In particular, they can yield objective measurements and visualizations of the general time course of semantic changes and of the relative sequence of related semantic changes in a chain shift. Yet, the greatest advantage of word embeddings - abstracting over large amounts of text data and their particularities - is also a disadvantage. Linguists are often interested in specific aspects of a semantic change. Is the change more likely to manifest in the writings of a particular social class? Which genres promote or oppose the innovation? What is the role of language contact or dialect? Word embeddings cannot currently output relevant results to help answer such intricate questions. Word embedding methods can supplement but not supplant careful linguistic studies on semantic change.

Acknowledgments

I would like to thank Paola Merlo for her encouragement as well as three anonymous reviewers for helpful feedback. All remaining errors are my own.

References

Raimo Anttila. 1989. *Historical and Comparative Linguistics*. John Benjamins.

Alistair Baron and Paul Rayson. 2008. Vard 2: A tool for dealing with spelling variation in historical corpora. *Proceedings of the Postgraduate Conference in Corpus Linguistics, Aston University, Birmingham*.

Camelia Bejan. 2017. *English Words: Structure, Origin and Meaning*. Addleton Academic Publishers.

Leonard Bloomfield. 1933. *Language*. Henry Holt and Co.

Philip R. Burns. 2013. *MorphAdorner v2: A Java Library for the Morphological Adornment of English Language Texts*. Manuscript, Northwestern University.

José Camacho-Collados and Mohammad T. Pilehvar. 2018. On the role of text preprocessing in neural network architectures: An evaluation study on text categorization and sentiment analysis. *CoRR*, abs/1707.01780.

Hans-Jürgen Diller, Hendrik De Smet, and Jukka Tyrkkö. 2011. A European Database of Descriptors of English Electronic Texts. *The European English Messenger*, 19:21–35.

Thomas V. Gamkrelidze and Vjačeslav V. Ivanov. 1995. *Indo-European and the Indo-Europeans: A Reconstruction and Historical Analysis of a Proto-Language and a Proto-Culture*. de Gruyter.

William L. Hamilton, Jure Leskovec, and Dan Jurafsky. 2016. Diachronic word embeddings reveal statistical laws of semantic change. In *Proceedings of the 54th Annual Meeting of the Association for Computational Linguistics (Volume 1: Long Papers)*, pages 1489–1501, Berlin, Germany. Association for Computational Linguistics.

Ying Li, Tomas Engelthaler, Cynthia S. Q. Siew, and Thomas T. Hills. 2019. The macroscope: A tool for examining the historical structure of language. *Behavior Research Methods*.

James P. Mallory and Douglas Q. Adams. 2006. *The Oxford Introduction to Proto-Indo-European and the Proto-Indo-European World*. Oxford University Press.

Manfred Markus. 2010. *The Innsbruck Corpus of Middle English Prose (Version 2.4)*. University of Innsbruck.

Tomas Mikolov, Kai Chen, Greg Corrado, and Jeffrey Dean. 2013. Efficient Estimation of Word Representations in Vector Space. In *1st International Conference on Learning Representations, ICLR 2013, Scottsdale, Arizona, USA, May 2-4, 2013, Workshop Track Proceedings*.

Martin Mueller. 2006. *VosPos: A project for Virtual Orthographic Standardization and Part of Speech Tagging of Early Modern English texts*. Manuscript, Northwestern University.

Radim Řehůřek and Petr Sojka. 2010. Software Framework for Topic Modelling with Large Corpora. In *Proceedings of the LREC 2010 Workshop on New Challenges for NLP Frameworks*, pages 45–50, Valletta, Malta. ELRA.

Anatol Stefanowitsch and Stefan Th. Griess. 2003. Collostructions: Investigating the interaction of words and constructions. *International Journal of Corpus Linguistics*, 8.2:209–43.

Gabriele Stein. 2014. *Sir Thomas Elyot as Lexicographer*. Oxford University Press.

Nina Tahmasebi, Lars Borin, and Adam Jatowt. 2018. Survey of Computational Approaches to Diachronic Conceptual Change. *CoRR*, abs/1811.06278.

Elizabeth C. Traugott and Richard B. Dasher. 2004. *Regularity in Semantic Change*. Cambridge University Press.

Evaluation of Semantic Change of Harm-Related Concepts in Psychology

Ekaterina Vylomova   Sean Murphy   Nick Haslam

School of Psychological Studies, University of Melbourne, Melbourne, Australia
{vylomovae,nhaslam}@unimelb.edu.au seanchrismurphy@gmail.com

Abstract

The paper focuses on diachronic evaluation of semantic changes of harm-related concepts in psychology. More specifically, we investigate a hypothesis that certain concepts such as "addiction", "bullying", "harassment", "prejudice", and "trauma" became broader during the last four decades. We evaluate semantic changes using two models: an LSA-based model from Sagi et al. (2009) and a diachronic adaptation of word2vec from Hamilton et al. (2016), that are trained on a large corpus of journal abstracts covering the period of 1980–2019. Several concepts showed evidence of broadening. "Addiction" moved from physiological dependency on a substance to include psychological dependency on gaming and the Internet. Similarly, "harassment" and "trauma" shifted towards more psychological meanings. On the other hand, "bullying" has transformed into a more victim-related concept and expanded to new areas such as workplaces.

1 Introduction

During the last decade the area of diachronic language modelling has witnessed substantial progress and development. This technical development enables enhanced understanding of pressing issues in social science disciplines. In this paper, we focus on diachronic change in the semantics of harm-related concepts within psychology. In particular, we test a "concept creep" hypothesis proposed by Haslam (2016). The hypothesis states that during the last half century many concepts related to harm have broadened their meanings. In order to test the hypothesis, we utilize two diachronic models: a count-based approach from Sagi et al. (2009), and a prediction-based approach from Hamilton et al. (2016). In both cases, we estimate the breadth of a concept as its average cosine similarity, i.e. the lower the similarity between concepts vector representations, the broader the concept's meaning. We additionally investigate how exactly the meanings have changed.

2 The Notion of Concept Creep

Haslam (2016) put forward the notion of concept creep to describe an apparent expansion in the meanings of several fundamental psychological concepts. He presented a series of case studies in which psychological researchers and theorists expanded the sense of these concepts by loosening definitions to include milder instances ("vertical creep") or by extending definitions to encompass cognate phenomena ("horizontal creep"). More example, the concept of "mental disorder" has progressively broadened in recent decades by relaxing the diagnostic criteria of some conditions and by expanding the range of problems conceptualized as falling within the psychiatric domain. Haslam documented how similar semantic inflation had occurred for concepts including abuse, addiction, prejudice, and trauma. Haslam proposed that these diverse concepts shared a focus on harm (i.e., the experience or infliction of actual or potential suffering). He therefore speculated that the correlated broadening of the creeping concepts reflected a rising sensitivity to harm within Western cultures.

In the present research we examine the following putatively creeping concepts:

① **Addiction.** This concept originally referred to physiological dependency on an ingested substance, but is increasingly used to identify psychological compulsion to engage in non-ingestive behaviors such as gambling or shopping.

② **Bullying.** This concept, introduced to psychology in the 1970s, initially described peer aggression between children that was repeated, intentional, and perpetrated in the context of power imbalance. More recent definitions extend bullying to adult workplace settings and relax the repetition,

Proceedings of the 1st International Workshop on Computational Approaches to Historical Language Change, pages 29–34
Florence, Italy, August 2, 2019. ©2019 Association for Computational Linguistics

intentionality, and power imbalance criteria.

③ **Harassment.** Early uses of this concept emphasized inappropriate sexual approaches but more recently harassment is also used within psychology to refer to nonsexual forms of unwanted attention.

④ **Prejudice.** The original psychological definitions of prejudice restricted it to overt animosity towards ethnic or racial outgroups. More recent theory and research extend it to many non-racial groups, allow for covert or non-conscious prejudice, and indicate that it may be manifest as anxiety or condescension rather than hostility.

⑤ **Trauma.** Four decades ago only personally encountered life-threatening events that are outside the realm of normal experience were recognized as traumatic by psychologists. More recent definitions include vicarious or indirect experiences of stressful events, including those that are relatively prevalent.

3   Related Work

Existing work on concept creep is primarily theoretical and the idea has been taken up by influential writers. Lukianoff and Haidt (2018) have employed it to understand political conflict on college campuses. Pinker (2018) has argued that concept creep leads people to under-estimate social progress because their definitions of hardship expand to include increasingly minor problems. This phenomenon has been demonstrated by Levari et al. (2018), who showed that concept definitions broaden as concept instances become scarcer. McGrath et al. (2019) has explored the attributes of people who hold relatively broad creeping-related concepts, finding that they tend to be politically liberal and their personal morality is tied to harm and care for others. Wheeler et al. (2019) studied the Google Books English language corpus and showed that words representing harm-based morality has become more culturally salient (i.e., relatively frequent) in the past four decades, consistent with the theory of concept creep. However, to date no research has examined in theory's core claim that the meaning of harm-related concepts have systematically broadened within psychological discourse. The present research aims to remedy this lack using a large new corpus and diachronic language modelling.

Although diachronic studies of language have long history in linguistics, computational approaches to diachronic language modelling were introduced only recently. Jurgens and Stevens (2009), one of the first, proposed an algorithm for tracking temporal semantic changes by learning a sequence of distributional models over time. The work was followed by an LSA-based model from Sagi et al. (2009). Kim et al. (2014) and Hamilton et al. (2016) then proposed the first prediction-based neural models. The latter work also formulated a number of laws of semantic change by exploring correlations between semantic changes and word frequency. Some of the laws were afterwards questioned and reformulated in (Dubossarsky et al., 2017).

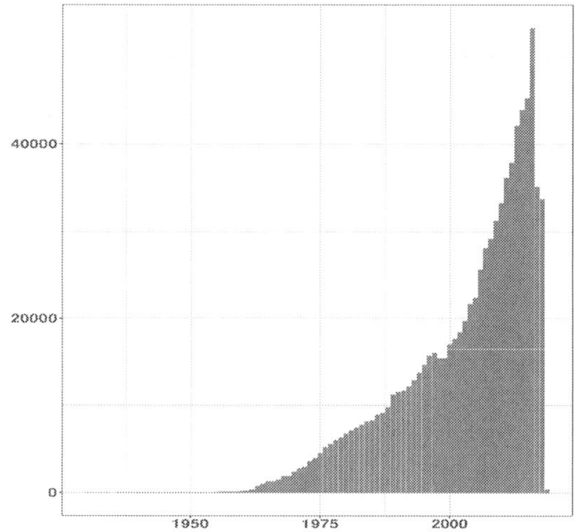

Figure 1: Statistics on the number of abstracts per year.

4   Corpus Description

The corpus comprises abstracts from journals in the field of psychology covering the period of 1930–2019 that were collected from the E-Research and the PubMed databases. In total, there are 871, 340 abstracts from 875 journals resulting in 133, 082, 240 tokens in total. We only focus on abstracts since they distill the core ideas of the paper and provide a compact summary of the main contributions and findings.[1] Fig. 1 presents the number of abstracts for each year . Due to relatively small amount of abstracts during the first half of the 20th century, for the purpose of our experiments we only consider time periods after 1970.

---

[1]Restrictions related to copyright also limited our focus to abstracts.

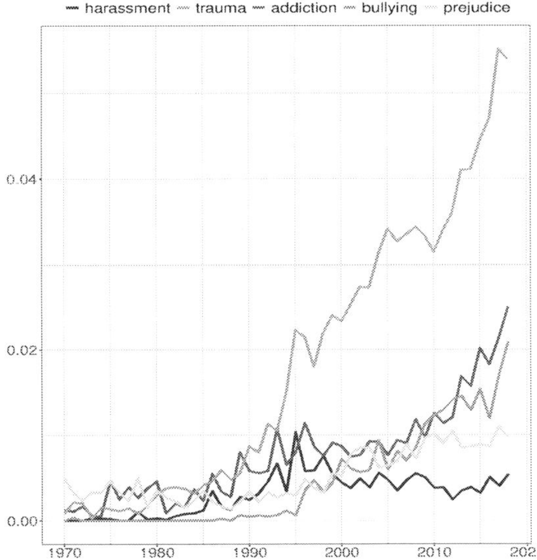

Figure 2: Relative word frequencies based on abstracts from psychology journals.

5 Experiments

5.1 Preprocessing Steps

We tokenized the corpus, removed punctuation, numbers, stop-words and non-English words, did fold-casing and lemmatization using SpaCy.[2]

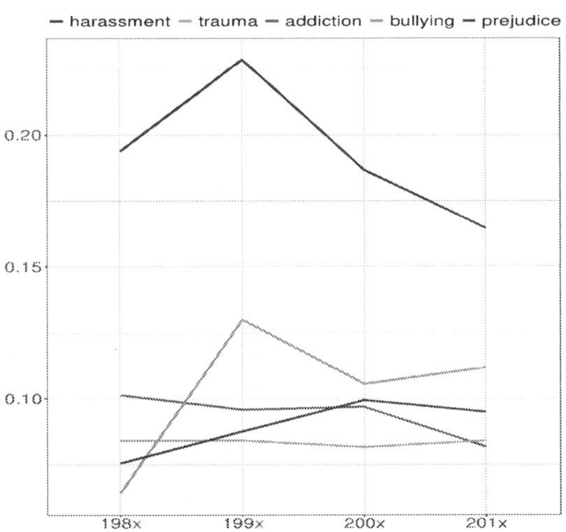

Figure 3: Average cosine similarities over five decades.

5.2 Frequency Analysis

For each of five concepts we first evaluated their (unigram) frequency distribution over time.[3] Al-

though all the concepts demonstrate a certain relative raise of frequency, *Trauma* exhibits the steepest slope, while *Harassment* has its peak in the mid-nineties. Does it mean that *Trauma* became broader over time, i.e. it expanded to a whole range of new contexts? Has *Harassment* expanded to new contexts as well?

In the next section, we adapt two most widely used contemporary models, a count-based model from Sagi et al. (2009) and a prediction-based one from Hamilton et al. (2016). The former provides us with a time-specific measure of semantic breadth for each concept while the latter shows *how exactly* concepts changed. Both models have previously shown their utility at capturing semantic changes over time (Tahmasebi et al., 2018; Kutuzov et al., 2018).

5.3 Sagi et al.'s Model

Our first part of the experiments is based on the LSA-based model proposed by Sagi et al. (2009). We follow their instructions, i.e. we create a term–document co-occurrence matrix on the basis of the whole corpus. The total number of terms is restricted to 40,000 most frequent ones. We follow the vanilla TF-IDF model weights with logarithmic smoothing. The resulting matrix is factorized with SVD and truncated to 200 dimensions.[4] The resulting word embeddings are then contextualized for each decade starting 1980 and finishing 2019.[5] More specifically, in order to obtain a word vector representation for a certain decade, we randomly sample a number of its sentential occurrences[6] from that period, then extract contextual words at the pre-set window size.[7] The final sentence-specific representation is a bag-of-words, i.e. it is an average over corresponding context words representations. To estimate semantic breadth of a word, we evaluate pair-wise cosine similarities across all the sentence-specific representations. To reduce any biases, we repeat the above sampling process 10 times. Fig. 3 shows that concepts behave differently over time. For instance, *Trauma*, although being more frequently used, has not undergone significant changes in its meaning and stayed quite a "broad" concept. The notion of *Harassment*, on

---

[2] https://spacy.io/

[3] We applied a minor "moving average" smoothing with window size of 1, i.e. $f_{1972} = (f_{1971} + f_{1972} + f_{1973})/3$.

[4] Using https://radimrehurek.com/gensim/

[5] We only start with 1980s since certain concepts such as *bullying* were only introduced in 1970s, and the amount of data for them is insufficient for such an analysis.

[6] We set the number to 50

[7] We set the window size to 7

the other hand, was developing until 1990s where it reached the highest similarities in its contextual usages (became more semantically narrow). And during the last three decades the concept became broader again. Similarly, the concept of *Bullying* has been developed before 1990s, and then changed in both ways, becoming broader in 2000s and then narrowing down again in 2010s. Finally, during 2000s *Addiction* has expanded to new contexts such as "internet" and "smartphone". We will further study the changes in the next section.

	1980s-90s	1990s-00s	2000s-10s
addiction	0.35	0.23	0.23
bullying	0.64	0.27	0.19
harassment	0.29	0.21	0.18
prejudice	0.31	0.26	0.16
trauma	0.31	0.18	0.09

Figure 4: Cosine distances between decades.

5.4 Hamilton et al.'s Model

In order to investigate semantic change in a greater detail, we adapt a diachronic model from Hamilton et al. (2016). More specifically, we train a single word2vec model (Mikolov et al., 2013) for each time period, and then align them using the orthogonal Procrustes.[8] Following Hamilton et al. (2016), we consider two metrics to evaluate semantic changes over time:

1. Semantic displacement that shows to what extent an individual word has semantically changed during a certain time period. This is quantified as cosine distance between the aligned word embeddings from the corresponding time periods, i.e. cos-dist$(\mathbf{w}^t, \mathbf{w}^{t+\delta})$. Fig. 4 shows the results of evaluation and confirms our observations made earlier using the model from Sagi et al. (2009).

2. Pair-wise similarity time-series which is quantified as $s^{(t)}(w_i, w_j) = \text{cos-sim}(\mathbf{w}_i^t, \mathbf{w}_j^t)$ and measures how cosine similarity between words w_i and w_j changes over time period $(t; t + \delta)$. For each concept we first constructed a list of words which the concept most often co-occurred with within each time period. Then we calculated cosine similarity between the concept and every word from

---

⁸Due to insufficient amount of data for earlier time periods, we train the models only on the following time frames: 1980-1989, 1990-1999, 2000-2010, 2011-2019.

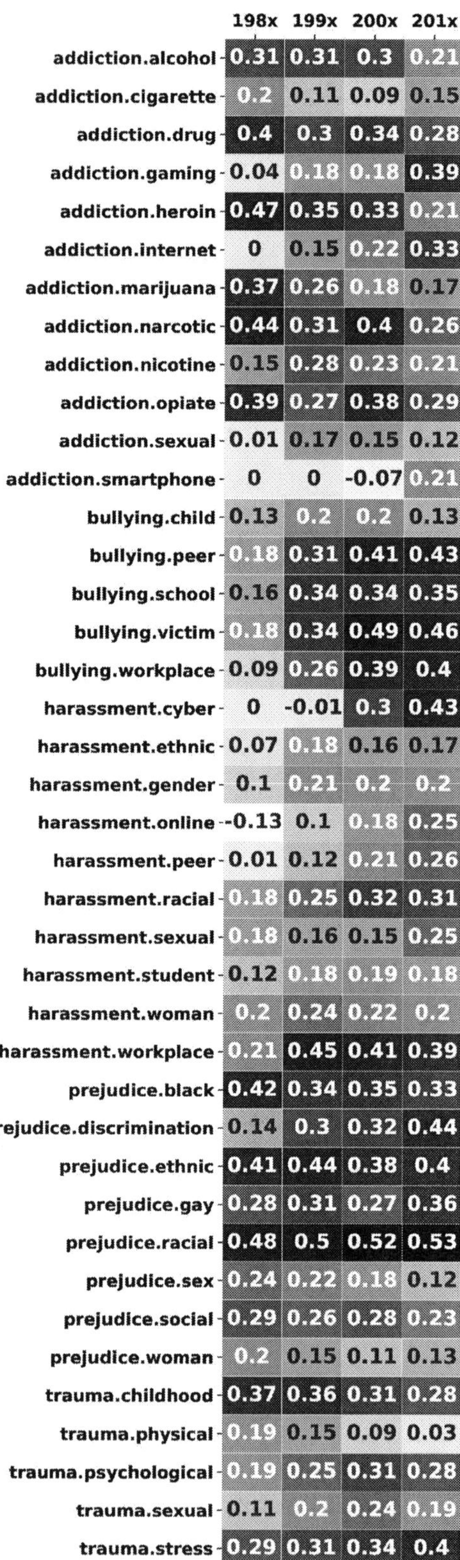

	198x	199x	200x	201x
addiction.alcohol	0.31	0.31	0.3	0.21
addiction.cigarette	0.2	0.11	0.09	0.15
addiction.drug	0.4	0.3	0.34	0.28
addiction.gaming	0.04	0.18	0.18	0.39
addiction.heroin	0.47	0.35	0.33	0.21
addiction.internet	0	0.15	0.22	0.33
addiction.marijuana	0.37	0.26	0.18	0.17
addiction.narcotic	0.44	0.31	0.4	0.26
addiction.nicotine	0.15	0.28	0.23	0.21
addiction.opiate	0.39	0.27	0.38	0.29
addiction.sexual	0.01	0.17	0.15	0.12
addiction.smartphone	0	0	-0.07	0.21
bullying.child	0.13	0.2	0.2	0.13
bullying.peer	0.18	0.31	0.41	0.43
bullying.school	0.16	0.34	0.34	0.35
bullying.victim	0.18	0.34	0.49	0.46
bullying.workplace	0.09	0.26	0.39	0.4
harassment.cyber	0	-0.01	0.3	0.43
harassment.ethnic	0.07	0.18	0.16	0.17
harassment.gender	0.1	0.21	0.2	0.2
harassment.online	-0.13	0.1	0.18	0.25
harassment.peer	0.01	0.12	0.21	0.26
harassment.racial	0.18	0.25	0.32	0.31
harassment.sexual	0.18	0.16	0.15	0.25
harassment.student	0.12	0.18	0.19	0.18
harassment.woman	0.2	0.24	0.22	0.2
harassment.workplace	0.21	0.45	0.41	0.39
prejudice.black	0.42	0.34	0.35	0.33
prejudice.discrimination	0.14	0.3	0.32	0.44
prejudice.ethnic	0.41	0.44	0.38	0.4
prejudice.gay	0.28	0.31	0.27	0.36
prejudice.racial	0.48	0.5	0.52	0.53
prejudice.sex	0.24	0.22	0.18	0.12
prejudice.social	0.29	0.26	0.28	0.23
prejudice.woman	0.2	0.15	0.11	0.13
trauma.childhood	0.37	0.36	0.31	0.28
trauma.physical	0.19	0.15	0.09	0.03
trauma.psychological	0.19	0.25	0.31	0.28
trauma.sexual	0.11	0.2	0.24	0.19
trauma.stress	0.29	0.31	0.34	0.4

Figure 5: Cosine similarities over four decades.

the list for each decade. Fig. 5 presents a sample of nearest neighbors (words with highest cosine similarity) at a certain period of time and reflects changes of semantics of each concept. For instance, for *Addiction* it demonstrates a shift from substance-related concept in 1980s to behaviour-related one in 2010s. More specifically, we observe that it moved from "drug" and "narcotic"-related meaning towards "gaming", "internet", and "smart-phone". *Bullying* has become more "victimized" and associated with workplace while its similarity to "school" and "child" stayed the same. Workplace also started being more related to *Harassment*, although, at the same time, its meaning expanded towards "cyber" and "online". Similarly, for *Trauma* we observe a shift from "physical" to "psychological" as well as an increase of a "stress" meaning. Finally, *Prejudice* has made strong connections to "discrimination" and "racial" while overall reduced for "black" and "woman".

6   Conclusion

The findings of our analyses illuminate and add nuance to our understanding of concept creep within academic psychology. The LSA-based analysis indicated that a sample of harm-related concepts have not undergone a consistent or linear pattern of semantic broadening. Since the 1990s *Addiction*, *Bullying* and *Harassment* have broadened, as the theory of concept creep would suggest, but the breadth of *Trauma* has been relatively static and *Prejudice* has somewhat narrowed. The analysis of semantic displacement points to a more consistent diachronic pattern: all five concepts changed most substantially from the 1980s to the 1990s and changed progressively less thereafter. This finding implies that the final two decades of the 20th century are especially critical for understanding concept creep. Finally, the analysis of pairwise similarities demonstrated changing patterns of co-occurrence for each concept that clarified how its meanings have shifted and expanded over four decades. During this period some concepts have acquired entirely new associations (e.g., cyber-harassment), some have added new semantic domains (e.g., *Addiction* incorporating non-ingestive behaviors such as gaming and smartphone use), and others have shifted emphasis (e.g., *Trauma* becoming associated less with physical injury and more with psychological stress).

The results of the present analyses are in some respects preliminary. From a methodological standpoint, future research will need to optimize the analytic parameters employed in the approaches examined in this research and evaluate whether findings derived from these approaches converge with those using other methods for assessing semantic change. Methods must also be developed to examine horizontal and vertical concept creep separately. The methods used in the present research emphasize "horizontal" changes in the range of semantic contexts in which a concept appears, and do not adequately capture how meanings may shift "vertically" to encompass less severe phenomena.

Substantively, our findings should be replicated with additional hypothetically creeping concepts, such as "mental illness" and "safety". The extent to which expansionary semantic changes are specific to harm-related concepts rather than generalized must also be studied systematically. There is scope for more focused and finely detailed analyses of semantic shifts in single concepts. Ideally, future work will explore concept creep in corpora representing other scholarly disciplines and other languages. A more fundamental challenge is to uncover the cultural factors that contribute to the semantic inflation of harm-related concepts, and to understand its societal implications.

References

Haim Dubossarsky, Daphna Weinshall, and Eitan Grossman. 2017. Outta control: Laws of semantic change and inherent biases in word representation models. In *Proceedings of the 2017 conference on empirical methods in natural language processing*, pages 1136–1145.

William L. Hamilton, Jure Leskovec, and Dan Jurafsky. 2016. Diachronic word embeddings reveal statistical laws of semantic change. In *Proceedings of the 54th Annual Meeting of the Association for Computational Linguistics (Volume 1: Long Papers)*, volume 1, pages 1489–1501.

Nick Haslam. 2016. Concept creep: Psychology's expanding concepts of harm and pathology. *Psychological Inquiry*, 27(1):1–17.

David Jurgens and Keith Stevens. 2009. Event detection in blogs using temporal random indexing. In *Proceedings of the Workshop on Events in Emerging Text Types*, pages 9–16. Association for Computational Linguistics.

Yoon Kim, Yi-I Chiu, Kentaro Hanaki, Darshan Hegde, and Slav Petrov. 2014. Temporal analysis of language through neural language models. *ACL 2014*, page 61.

Andrey Kutuzov, Lilja Øvrelid, Terrence Szymanski, and Erik Velldal. 2018. Diachronic word embeddings and semantic shifts: a survey. In *Proceedings of the 27th International Conference on Computational Linguistics*, pages 1384–1397.

David E. Levari, Daniel T. Gilbert, Timothy D. Wilson, Beau Sievers, David M. Amodio, and Thalia Wheatley. 2018. Prevalence-induced concept change in human judgment. *Science*, 360(6396):1465–1467.

Greg Lukianoff and Jonathan Haidt. 2018. *The Coddling of the American Mind: How Good Intentions and Bad Ideas Are Setting Up a Generation for Failure*. Penguin UK.

Melanie J. McGrath, Kathryn Randall-Dzerdz, Melissa A. Wheeler, Sean C. Murphy, and Nick Haslam. 2019. Concept creepers: Individual differences in harm-related concepts and their correlates. *Personality and Individual Differences*, 147:79–84.

Tomas Mikolov, Ilya Sutskever, Kai Chen, Greg S Corrado, and Jeff Dean. 2013. Distributed representations of words and phrases and their compositionality. In *Advances in neural information processing systems*, pages 3111–3119.

Steven Pinker. 2018. *Enlightenment now: The case for reason, science, humanism, and progress*. Penguin.

Eyal Sagi, Stefan Kaufmann, and Brady Clark. 2009. Semantic density analysis: Comparing word meaning across time and phonetic space. In *Proceedings of the Workshop on Geometrical Models of Natural Language Semantics*, pages 104–111. Association for Computational Linguistics.

Nina Tahmasebi, Lars Borin, and Adam Jatowt. 2018. Survey of computational approaches to diachronic conceptual change. *CoRR*, abs/1811.06278.

Melissa A. Wheeler, Melanie J. McGrath, and Nick Haslam. 2019. Twentieth century morality: The rise and fall of moral concepts from 1900 to 2007. *PLoS one*, 14(2):e0212267.

Contextualized Diachronic Word Representations

Ganesh Jawahar   **Djamé Seddah**
Inria
{firstname.lastname}@inria.fr

Abstract

Diachronic word embeddings play a key role in capturing interesting patterns about how language evolves over time. Most of the existing work focuses on studying corpora spanning across several decades, which is understandably still not a possibility when working on social media-based user-generated content. In this work, we address the problem of studying semantic changes in a large Twitter corpus collected over five years, a much shorter period than what is usually the norm in diachronic studies.

We devise a novel attentional model, based on Bernoulli word embeddings, that are conditioned on contextual extra-linguistic (social) features such as network, spatial and socio-economic variables, which are associated with Twitter users, as well as topic-based features. We posit that these social features provide an inductive bias that helps our model to overcome the narrow time-span regime problem. Our extensive experiments reveal that our proposed model is able to capture subtle semantic shifts without being biased towards frequency cues and also works well when certain contextual features are absent. Our model fits the data better than current state-of-the-art dynamic word embedding models and therefore is a promising tool to study diachronic semantic changes over small time periods.

1 Introduction

Natural language changes over time due to a wide range of linguistic, psychological, sociocultural and encyclopedic causes (Blank and Koch, 1999; Grzega and Schoener, 2007). Studying the semantic change of a word helps us understand more about the human language and build temporally aware models, that are especially complementary to the work done in the digital humanities and his-

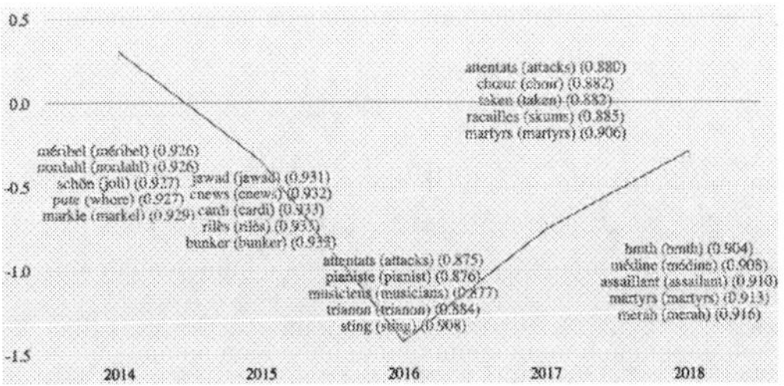

Figure 1: The diachronic embedding computed by our proposed model for the word 'BATACLAN' reveals how the term's usage changed over the years. We list the most similar five words (with English translation in paranthesis) in each year by cosine similarity. The y-axis corresponds to "meaning", a one dimensional PCA projection of the embeddings.

torical linguistics. Recently, diachronic word embeddings based on distributional hypothesis (Harris, 1954) have been used to automatically study semantic changes in a data-driven fashion from large corpora (Kim et al., 2014; Hamilton et al., 2016; Rudolph and Blei, 2018). We refer the reader to Kutuzov et al. (2018) who survey the recent methods in this field and establishes the challenges that lie ahead.

Currently, we find the literature on this problem to be focused on English corpora, spanning across several decades. This has not only created a gap in extending the diachronic word embeddings for a wider scope of languages, but also to datasets spanning across few successive years which are common in digital humanities and social sciences. In this work, we study French text from Twitter collected over just five years, which provides a challenging platform to build models that can capture semantic drifts in a noisy, subtly evolving language corpus.

Figure 1 shows an instance of the evolution of the word 'Bataclan' (a theatre in Paris that was at-

35

Proceedings of the 1st International Workshop on Computational Approaches to Historical Language Change, pages 35–47
Florence, Italy, August 2, 2019. ©2019 Association for Computational Linguistics

tacked by terrorists on November 2015) from the French corpus. It also shows that such embedding representations mostly capture the dominant sense of a word when used in synchrony and can therefore only reflect the evolution of the dominant sense when used diachronically, yet leaving open the question of whether small, subtle changes can be captured (Tahmasebi et al., 2018).

We hypothesize that the current state-of-the-art models lack inductive biases to fit data accurately in this setting. We build on the observation by Jurafsky (2018) that *"it's important to consider who produced the language, in what context, for what purpose, and make sure that the models are fit to the data"*. Hence, we propose a novel model extending on Dynamic Bernoulli word Embeddings (Rudolph and Blei, 2018) (DBE) which exploits the inductive bias by conditioning on a number of contextualized features such as network, spatial and socio-economic variables, which are associated with Twitter users, as well as topic-based features.

We perform qualitative studies and show that our model can: (i) accurately capture the subtle changes caused due to cultural drifts, (ii) learn a smooth trajectory of word evolution despite exploiting various inductive biases. Our quantitative studies illustrate that our model can: (i) capture better semantic properties, (ii) be less sensitive to frequency cues compared to DBE model, (iii) act as better features for 2 out of 4 tweet classification tasks. Through an ablation study, we find in addition that our model can: (iv) work with a reduced set of contextualized features, (v) follow the test of law of prototypicality (Dubossarsky et al., 2015). In sum, we believe our model is a promising tool to study diachronic semantic changes over small time periods. [1]

Our main contributions are as follows:

- Our work is the first to study diachronic word embeddings for tweets from French language to the best of our knowledge. Unlike previous works, we consider dataset from a narrow time horizon (five years).
- We propose a novel, attentional, diachronic word embedding model that derives inductive biases from several contextualized, socio-demographic, features to fit the data accurately.

[1]Code to reproduce our experiments is publicly accessible at https://github.com/ganeshjawahar/social_word_emb

- Our work is also the first to estimate the usefulness of the diachronic word embeddings for downstream task like tweet classification.

2 Related Work

Kim et al. (2014) introduced prediction-based word embedding models to track semantic shifts across time. They extended SkipGram model with Negative Sampling (SGNS) (Mikolov et al., 2013) by training a model on current year after initializing the word embeddings from trained model of previous year. This initialization ensures the word vectors across time slices are grounded in same semantic space. Kulkarni et al. (2015) and Hamilton et al. (2016) utilize ad hoc alignment techniques like orthogonal Procrustes transformations to map successive model pairs together. These approaches have an impractical demand of having enough data in each time slice to learn high quality embeddings.

The work done by Bamler and Mandt (2017), Yao et al. (2018) and Rudolph and Blei (2018) proposed to learn word embeddings across all time periods jointly along with their alignment in a single step. Rudolph and Blei (2018) represent word embeddings as sequential latent variables, naturally accommodating for time slices with sparse data and assuring word embeddings are grounded across time. Our proposed model builds upon this work to condition on several inductive biases, using contextual extra-linguistic (social) and topic-based features, to accurately fit dataset from a narrow time horizon.

3 Contextualized Features

Natural language text is inherently contextual, depending on the author, the period and the intended purpose (Jurafsky, 2018). For instance, features based on authors' demography although incomplete can explain some of the variance in the text (Garten et al., 2019). While diachronic word embeddings' ability to capture semantic shifts is interesting because of its flexibility, we postulate that there is a need to capture contextualized information about tweets such as the characteristics of their authors (including spatial, network, socio-economic, interested topics) and meta-information such as their topic. To extract features, we make use of the largest French Twitter corpus to date proposed in Abitbol et al. (2018). In this section we will describe the set of contextualized feature we propose to inject to our diachronic word embedding model (see Section 4).

3.1 Spatial

Users from similar geographical areas tend to share similar properties in terms of word usage and language idiosyncrasies. Among others, Hovy and Purschke (2018) for German and Abitbol et al. (2018) for French, confirmed regional variations in geolocated users' content in social media. The latter work found the southern part of France to use a more standard language than the northern part. To exploit these geographic variations, we identify geolocated users ($\sim 100K$) and associate each of them to their respective region (out of 22 regions) and department (out of 96 departments) within the French territory. We learn a latent embedding for each region and department which captures the spatial information with different levels of granularity.

3.2 Socioeconomic

Users from similar socioeconomic status tend to share similar online behavior in terms of circadian cycles. Specifically, Abitbol et al. (2018) found that people of higher socioeconomic status are active to a greater degree during the daytime and also use a more standard language. National Institute of Statistics and Economic Studies (INSEE) of France provided the population level salary for each 4 hectare square patch across the whole French territory, estimated from the 2010 tax return in France. We also use IRIS dataset provided by French government which has more coarse grained annotation for socioeconomic status. This information is mapped with the geographical coordinates of users' home location from Twitter so we can roughly ascertain the economic status of every geolocated users. We create 9 socioeconomic classes by binning the income and ensuring that the sum of income is the same for each class. We learn a latent embedding for each such class, which thus captures the variation caused by status homophily.[2]

3.3 Network

Users who are connected to each other in social networks are usually believed to share similar in-

terests. We construct a co-mention network from the set of geolocated users as nodes and edges connecting those users who have mentioned each other at least once. We run the LINE model (Tang et al., 2015) to embed the nodes in the graph using the connectivity information and use the resulting node embedding as fixed features.

3.4 Interest

Interest feature corresponds to the set of important topics a user cares about. We obtain this information by composing a user document capturing all the words used in their posts, ranking the words in the document by the tf-idf score and selecting the top 50 of them. We then construct the user vector by summing the vectors (obtained by running word2vec on the entire corpus or geolocated tweets) corresponding to the top 50 words. We use the user vectors as fixed features.

3.5 Knowledge

Knowledge features keep track of the way the user writes and as such, it is also a summary of their content in Twitter. We learn a latent embedding for each geolocated user.

3.6 Topic

This feature associated with a tweet corresponds to the topic a tweet belongs to. Since the available corpus does not have any annotation about the topic of the tweet, we exploit the distant supervision-based idea proposed by Magdy et al. (2015) to filter geolocated tweets with an accompanying YouTube video link. We then use the YouTube public API to obtain the category of the video, which is then associated to the topic of the tweet. We learn a latent embedding for each YouTube category.

4 Proposed model

In this section we will first briefly discuss the 'Dynamic Bernoulli Embeddings' model (DBE) and then provide the details of our proposal, which uses DBE model as its backbone.

4.1 Dynamic Bernoulli Embeddings (DBE)

The DBE model is an extension of the 'Exponential Family Embeddings' model (EFE, (Rudolph et al., 2016)) for incorporating sequential changes to the data representation. Let the sequence of words from a corpus of text be represented by

---

[2] Some statistical pretreatments were applied to the data by INSEE before its public release to uphold current privacy laws and due to the highly sensitive nature of the disclosed data.

$(x_i, \ldots, x_N)$ from a vocabulary V. Each word $x_i \in {0, 1}^V$ corresponds to a one-hot vector, having 1 in the position corresponding to the vocabulary term and 0 elsewhere. The context c_i represents the set of words surrounding a given word at position i.[3] DBE builds on Bernoulli embeddings, which provides a conditional model for each entry in the indicator vector $x_{iv} \in {0, 1}$, whose conditional distribution is

$$x_{iv} | \mathbf{x}_{c_i} \sim Bern(\rho_{iv}), \qquad (1)$$

where $\rho_{iv} \in (0, 1)$ is the Bernoulli probability and $\mathbf{x}_{c_i}$ is the collection of data points indexed by the context positions. Each index (i, v) in the data represents two parameter vectors, the embedding vector $\rho_v^{(t)} \in \mathbb{R}^K$ and the context vector $\alpha_v \in \mathbb{R}^K$. The natural parameter of the Bernoulli is given by,

$$\eta_{iv} = \rho_v^{\mathsf{T}} \Big(\sum_{j \in c_i} \sum_{v'} \alpha_{v'} x_{jv'} \Big). \qquad (2)$$

Since each observation x_{iv} is associated with a time slice t_i (which is a year, in our case [4]), DBE learns a per-time-slice embedding vector $\rho_v^{(t_i)}$ for every word in the vocabulary. Thus, equation 2 becomes,

$$\eta_{iv} = \rho_v^{(t_i)\mathsf{T}} \Big(\sum_{j \in c_i} \sum_{v'} \alpha_{v'} x_{jv'} \Big). \qquad (3)$$

DBE lets the context vectors shared across the time slices to ground the successive embedding vectors in the same semantic space. DBE assumes a Gaussian random walk as a prior on the embedding vectors to encourage smooth change in the estimates of each term's embedding,

$$\begin{aligned} \alpha_v, \rho_v^{(0)} &\sim \mathcal{N}(0, \lambda_0^{-1} I) \\ \rho_v^{(t)} &\sim \mathcal{N}(\rho_v^{(t-1)}, \lambda^{-1} I). \end{aligned} \qquad (4)$$

4.2 Proposed model

In this work, we argue that the DBE model fails to accurately fit the data spanning across fewer years as it discards other explanatory variables (besides time) about the complicated processes in the language in terms of evolution and construction. These variables, which we defined in Section 3 as contextualized features, carry useful signals to understand subtle changes such as cultural

---

[3] We use 2 words before and after the focal word to determine context for all our experiments.

[4] Our preliminary investigation with different time span units can be found in Appendix A.6.

drifts. Our proposed model extends DBE by utilizing these contextualized features as inductive biases.

In our setting, we represent a tweet as $t_k = (x_i, \ldots, x_N)$ belonging to user u_l. Each tuple (i, c) is associated with a set of contextualized features based on either u_l or t_k, $f_{i,m} \in \mathcal{R}^{d_m}$ ($m = 1, \ldots, |F|$) (where $|F|$ corresponds to the number of contextualized features). Each contextualized feature not only follows a different distribution but also has different degrees of noise (e.g., sparsity of co-mention network, geolocation inaccuracy). Hence, it is harder to unify them in a single model. We propose three ways to introduce inductive bias to the DBE model.

Unweighted sum: The simplest approach is to project all the feature embeddings to a common space and sum them up. This approach is not agnostic to the embedding vector x_i in question and consider all the contextualized features equally. Incorporating this approach, equation 3 now becomes:

$$\eta_{iv} = \Big(\rho_v^{(t_i)} + \sum_{m=1}^{|F|} \mathbf{w}_m f_{i,m} \Big)^{\mathsf{T}} \Big(\sum_{j \in c_i} \sum_{v'} \alpha_{v'} x_{jv'} \Big), \qquad (5)$$

where $\mathbf{w}_m$ corresponds to the learnable weights corresponding to the linear projection of $f_{i,,m}$ with size as $K \times d_m$. Note that K denotes the dimension of both context and target embedding.

Self-attention: Considering all the features equally would be wasteful for certain embedding vector x_i. Henceforth, we propose to let the network decide the important contextualized features based on self attention. This approach gives a provision to our model to handle the effect of spurious contextual signals by paying no attention. Incorporating this approach, equation 5 will now become:

$$\eta_{iv} = \Big(\rho_v^{(t_i)} + \sum_{m=1}^{|F|} \alpha_m \mathbf{w}_m f_{i,m} \Big)^{\mathsf{T}} \Big(\sum_{j \in c_i} \sum_{v'} \alpha_{v'} x_{jv'} \Big), \qquad (6)$$

where α_m are the scalar weights corresponding to the self-attention mechanism:

$$\alpha_m = g(f_{i,m}) = \phi(\mathbf{a} \, \mathbf{w}_m f_{i,m} + b) \qquad (7)$$

where $\mathbf{a} \in \mathcal{R}^K$ and $b \in \mathcal{R}$ are learnable parameters while ϕ is a softmax.

Contextual attention: We can also make the attention mechanism to be context-dependent, that

DBE					Context Attn.				
2014	**2015**	**2016**	**2017**	**2018**	**2014**	**2015**	**2016**	**2017**	**2018**
jdd	*rocard*	*macron*	*macron*	*macron*	jdd	***attali***	*macron*	*macron*	*macron*
brunet	lévy	*matignon*	rugy	*élysée*	*brunet*	lévy	*matignon*	*hollande*	*élysée*
frédéric	*attali*	lejdd.fr	*hollande*	*matignon*	*dupont*	cnrs	fustige	rugy	*elysee*
elysee	*montel*	medef	*élysée*	*pétain*	*frédéric*	monarchie	renoncement	***mélenchon***	**élection**
dupont	monarchie	*élysée*	*bayrou*	interpelle	*révélée*	*rocard*	medef	**présidentielle**	***emmanuelmacron***

Table 1: Embedding neighborhood of 'EMMANUEL' obtained by finding closest word in each time period sorted by decreasing similarity. All named entities are italicized. Interesting words identified by the proposed model are bolded.

DBE					Context Attn.				
2014	**2015**	**2016**	**2017**	**2018**	**2014**	**2015**	**2016**	**2017**	**2018**
genesio	huitiémes	estac	*ogcnice*	*asnl*	*malcuit*	*sampaoli*	*pyeongchang*	*ogcnice*	*asnl*
génésio	*lafont*	*pyeongchang*	amical	tricolore	seri	huitiémes	*estac*	*asnl*	*eswc*
raggi	*génésio*	tgvmax	*slovaquie*	*pariez*	*tousart*	***donnarumma***	çu.e	bleuets	*carrasso*
zambo	*pyeongchang*	u20	*asnl*	affrontera	*raggi*	*lafont*	*ndombele*	*slovaquie*	tricolore
malcuit	*sampaoli*	*lrem*	bleuets	*carrasso*	*asensio*	**sertic**	*auproux*	*mennel*	**euro2016**

Table 2: Embedding neighborhood of EQUIPEDEFRANCE 'French Team' in obtained by finding the closest word in each time period sorted by decreasing similarity. All named entities are italicized. Interesting words identified by the model are bolded.

is, dependent on the embedding vector. Equation 7 then becomes:

$$\alpha_m = g(\rho_i) = \phi(\mathbf{a}_m \rho_i + b) \tag{8}$$

where $\mathbf{a}_m \in \mathcal{R}^K$ corresponds to the learnable attention parameter specific to a contextualized feature f_m.

We fit the diachronic embeddings with the *pseudo log likelihood*, the sum of log conditionals. Particularly, we regularize the pseudo log likelihood with the log priors, followed by maximization to obtain a pseudo MAP estimate. Our objective function can be summarized as,

$$\mathcal{L}(\rho, \alpha) = \mathcal{L}_{pos} + \mathcal{L}_{neg} + \mathcal{L}_{prior} \tag{9}$$

The likelihoods are given by:

$$\mathcal{L}_{pos} = \sum_{k=1}^{|T|} \sum_{i=1}^{N} \sum_{v=1}^{V} x_{iv} log\sigma(\eta_{iv}),$$
$$\mathcal{L}_{neg} = \sum_{k=1}^{|T|} \sum_{i=1}^{N} \sum_{v \in \mathcal{S}_i} log(1 - \sigma(\eta_{iv})), \tag{10}$$

where $\mathcal{S}_i$ correspond to the negative samples drawn at random (Mikolov et al., 2013) and $\sigma(.)$ denote the sigmoid function, which maps natural parameters to probabilities. The prior is given by,

$$\mathcal{L}_{prior} = -\frac{\lambda_0}{2} \sum_v \|\alpha_v\|^2 - \frac{\lambda_0}{2} \sum_v \left\|\rho_v^{(0)}\right\|^2$$
$$- \frac{\lambda}{2} \sum_{v,t} \left\|\rho_v^{(t)} - \rho_v^{(t-1)}\right\|^2. \tag{11}$$

Language evolution is a gradual process and the random walk prior prevents successive embedding vectors $\rho_v^{(t-1)}$ and $\rho_v^{(t)}$ from drifting far apart.

The objective function established in equation 9 is learned using stochastic gradients (Robbins and Monro, 1985) with the help of Adam optimizer (Kingma and Ba, 2014). Negative samples are resampled at each gradient step. Pseudo code for training our model can be found in Appendix A.1.

5 Experiments and Results

In this section we discuss the experimental protocol, qualitative and quantitative evaluation to understand the performance of our model.

5.1 Protocol

Data: We use the French twitter dataset proposed in Abitbol et al. (2018), which is the largest collection of French tweets to date. The original dataset consists of 190M French tweets posted by 2.5M of users between June 2014 and March 2018. To be able to use socio-geographic features and assess the validity of our model, we only considered tweets from users whose home location could be identified to be in Metropolitan France. This filtering step resulted in a data set of 18M tweets from 110K users spread across 5 years. This data set was then enriched using output from the constituency-based Stanford parser in its off-the-shelf French settings (Green et al., 2011) and from the dependency-based parser of Jawahar et al. (2018). We lowercased all the tweets, removed hashtags, mentions, URLs, emoticons and punctuations. We used 80% of the tweets from each year to train our model, split the rest equally to create validation (10%) and test set (10%). Finally, we pick the most frequent 50K words from the train set to create our vocabulary.

Baseline models: We compare our proposed model with three baseline models: **(i) Word2vec (Mikolov et al., 2013)**[5] - We use the SGNS version of Word2vec trained independently for each year with the embedding size as 100, window as 2 and the rest maintained to default; **ii) HistWords (Hamilton et al., 2016)**[6] - We use the SGNS version which is effective for datasets of different sizes and employ similar settings as the previous baseline; **(iii) DBE (Rudolph and Blei, 2018)**[7] - We use the dynamic Bernoulli embedding model (backbone of our model) with the recommended settings. We have three variants of our proposed model: no attention model (unweighted sum), self attention model and contextual attention model. Hyperparameter settings to reproduce our results can be found in Appendix A.2.

5.2 Qualitative Study

Embedding neighborhood: The goal of diachronic word embedding model is to automatically discover the changes in the usage of a word. The current usage at time t of a word w can be obtained by inspecting the nearby words of the word represented by $\rho_w^{(t)}$. From Table 1, we can observe that 'EMMANUEL' (first name of current French president) is associated with his last name ('macron') and office location ('élysée') by both DBE and proposed model. However, proposed model is able to capture interesting neighborhood by bringing words such as 'élection', 'présidentielle' and 'mélenchon' closer to 'EMMANUEL'[8]. Table 2 presents words of interest associated by our proposed model to the French football team like 'euro2016'.

Smoothness of the embedding trajectories:

---

[5]https://radimrehurek.com/gensim/models/word2vec.html

[6]https://nlp.stanford.edu/projects/histwords/

[7]https://github.com/mariru/dynamic_bernoulli_embeddings

[8]Emmanuel Macron became the president of France on May 2017. Jean-Luc Mélenchon stood fourth.

Since language evolution is a gradual process, the trajectory for a word tracked by a model should be changing smoothly. There are exceptions for words undergoing cultural shifts where the changes can be subtle and rapid. We plot the trajectory by computing the cosine similarity between word (e.g., MACRON) and its known, changed usage (e.g., PRESIDENT). Figure 2 shows that models relying on Bernoulli embeddings have smooth trajectories for known relations compared to other models. Despite fusing different, possibly noisy contextualized features, the trajectory tracked by our proposed model and DBE are comparably smooth.

t-SNE: Alternatively, we can overlay the embeddings from all the time slices and visualize them using dimensionality reduction technique like t-SNE (Maaten and Hinton, 2008). From Figure 3, we see a similar result where most of the words modeled by our proposed model has experienced consistent change with time.

5.3 Quantitative Study

Log Likelihood: We can evaluate models by held-out Bernoulli probability (Rudolph and Blei, 2018). Given a held-out position, a better model assigns higher probability to the observed word and lower probability to the rest. We report $\mathcal{L}_{eval} = \mathcal{L}_{pos} + \mathcal{L}_{neg}$ in Table 3. Contextual attention based model which smartly utilizes the contextualized features provides better fits to the data compared to the rest. Interestingly, the other variants of our proposed model performs poorly compared to the DBE model which suggests the importance of utilizing attention appropriately. Since all the competing methods produce Bernoulli conditional likelihoods (Equation 1), where n is the number of negative samples. We keep n to be 20 for all the methods to peform a fair comparison.

Semantic Similarity: Certain tweets are tagged with a 'category' to which it belongs (as discussed in Section 3.6). Similar to Yao et al. (2018), we create the ground truth of word category based on the identification of words in years that are exceptionally numerous in one particular category. In other words, if a word is most frequent in a category, we tag the word with that category and form our ground truth. For each category c and each word w in year t, we find the percentage of occurrences p in each category. We collect such word-time-category $\langle w,t,c \rangle$ triplets, avoid duplication by

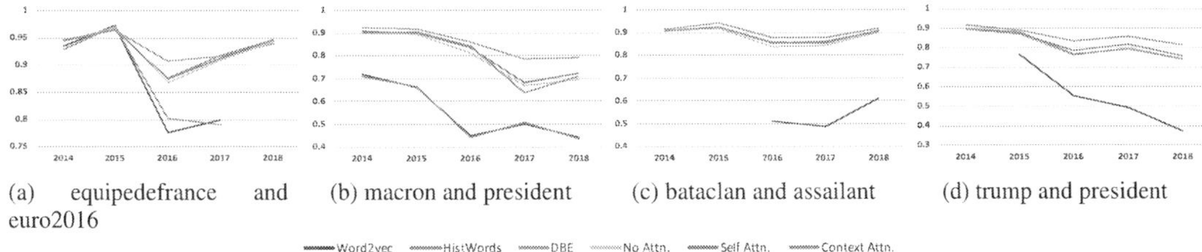

(a) equipedefrance and euro2016   (b) macron and president   (c) bataclan and assailant   (d) trump and president

Figure 2: Smoothness of word embedding trajectories vs. baseline models. High values correspond to similarity. Notice that for Word2vec model, we do not plot the results for time periods where at least one of the word of interest occurs below the minimum frequency threshold.

Model	log lik.	SS	Senti	Htag	Topic	Conv.
Word2vec	Nil	0.034	71.54	37.32	34.98	70.04
HistWords	Nil	0.042	**73.69**	36.75	36.85	70.17
DBE	-7.708	0.065	73.00	41.83	**40.01**	70.98
No Attn.	-8.059	0.058	73.22	42.11*	39.61	71.21*
Self Attn.	-7.840	0.061	73.18	**42.19***	39.67	71.10
Context Attn.	**-7.425**	**0.068**	73.19	41.88	39.65	71.15

Table 3: Quantitative results based on log likelihood, semantic similarity and tweet classification. Higher numbers are better for all the tasks. Statistically significant differences to the best baseline for each task based on bootstrap test are marked with an asterisk. Note that we could not perform statistical significance studies for log likelihood experiment due to the large size of the test set and semantic similarity experiment due to the nature of clustering evaluation.

Figure 3: t-SNE visualization of mid-frequency (between 2000-2500) words for our contextual attention model.

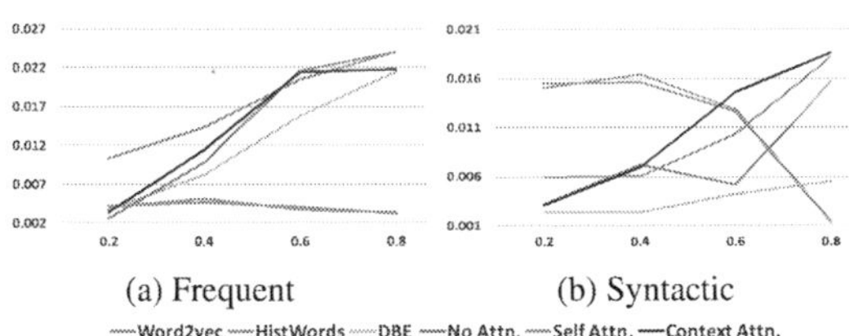

(a) Frequent   (b) Syntactic

Figure 4: Synthetic Evaluation. $p_{replacement}$ vs MRR.

keeping the year of largest strength for each w and s combination, and remove triplets where p is less than 35%. Finally, we pick top 200 words by strength from each category and create a dataset of 3036 triplets across 15 categories, where each word-year pair is essentially strongly linked to its true category. We evaluate the purity of clustering results by using Normalized Mutual Information (NMI) metric. From Table 3, we find a similar trend in the performance of our proposed model.

As we see in Section 6.3, the reason our contextual attention based model excels in this task is due to its superiority in capturing semantic properties of a word.

Synthetic Linguistic Change: We can synthetically introduce the linguistic shift by introducing changes to the corpus and then evaluate if the diachronic word embedding model is able to detect those artificial drifts accurately. We follow the work done by Kulkarni et al. (2015) to duplicate our data belonging to the 2018 year 6 times (along with the extra-linguistic information), perturb the last 3 snapshots and use the diachronic embedding model to rank all the words according to their p-values. We then calculate the Mean Reciprocal Rank (MRR) for the perturbed words and expect it to be higher for models that can identify the words that have changed. To perturb the data, we sample a pair of words from the vocabulary exlcuding stop words, replace one of the word with the other with a replacement probability $p_{replacement}$ and repeat this step 100 times. We employ two types of perturbation - syntactic (where the both the words that are sampled in each step have the same most frequent part of speech tag) and frequent (where there is no restriction for the words being sampled at each step). From Figure 4, we find that DBE model is sensitive to the frequency cues from the data and fails to model subtle se-

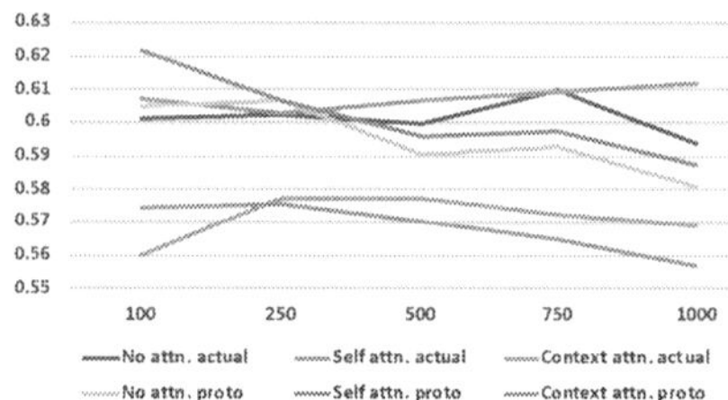

Figure 5: Change in the word's usage correlated with distance for different numbers of clusters between the 2014 and 2018 year.

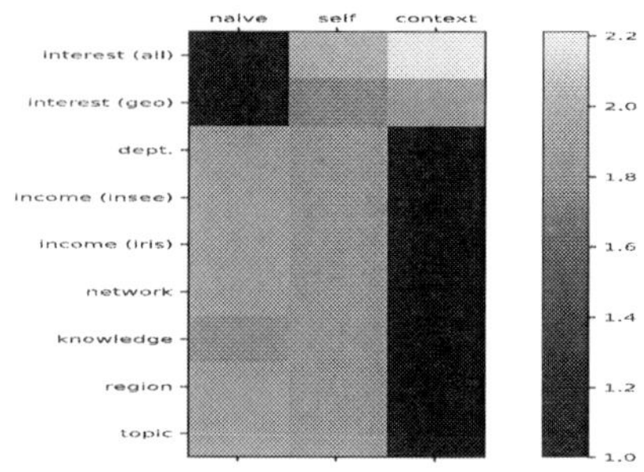

Figure 6: Importance score for each contextualized feature.

mantic shifts (e.g. for words which has evolved in its meaning without substantial change in its syntactic functionality).

Tweet Classification: We find that the existing work skips evaluating the diachronic word embeddings for a downstream NLP task. In this work we propose to test if the diachronic word embeddings can be used as features to build a temporally-aware tweet classifier.[9] We obtain a representation for a tweet by summing the embeddings for the words (belonging to the year in which tweet was posted) present in the tweet. We then train a logistic regression model and compute the F-score on the held-out instances. We establish four tweet classification tasks — Sentiment Analysis, Hashtag Prediction, Topic Categorization and Conversation Prediction (predict if a tweet will receive a reply or not) through distant supervision methods. Details of the task and dataset collection can be found in Appendix A.3. From Table 3, we find that our proposed model provides competitive performance with the baseline models for sentiment analysis and topic categorization while it outperforms them for the hashtag and conversation prediction tasks by a statistically significant margin (computed using bootstrap test (Efron and Tibshirani, 1994)). Note that there is no single best model that works for every tweet classification tasks.

6 Analysis

In this section we perform extended analysis of our proposed model to gain more insights about its functionality.

---

[9]https://scikit-learn.org/stable/
modules/generated/sklearn.linear_model.
LogisticRegression.html

6.1 Ablation Study

We perform ablation studies of the proposed model by considering different set of contextualized features as inductive biases, illustrated in Table 4. It is interesting to find that our model can work with a limited set of contextualized features in practice.

6.2 Law of Prototypicality

Dubossarsky et al. (2015) state that the likelihood of change in a word's meaning correlates with its position within its center. They define the prototypicality measure based on the word's distance from its cluter centroid (e.g., sword is a more prototypical exemplar than spear or dagger) and the prototypicality score reduces when the word undergoes change in its meaning. For all our models, we correlate the distance of word vector corresponding to 2014 and 2018 year with the distance the 2014 (2018) year vector moved from its cluster center. We then check if there is a positive correlation ($r > .3$). From Figure 5, we observe that there exists a positive correlation for all the variants of our model when compared to a prototypical or actual cluster centroid. Interestingly, when the cluster sizes are small (< 250), the word's meaning change is correlated with a prototypical exemplar more than a actual exemplar. On the other hand, this correlation direction gets reversed when the cluster sizes are greater than 250 and there exists more semantic areas.

6.3 Interpretation via Probing Tasks

Our tweet classification experiments (Section 5.3) demonstrated the usefulness of diachronic word embeddings as features in building a diachronic tweet classifier. Understanding the underlying properties of the tweet embeddings that enable it to outperform competing models is hard. This is why, following Conneau et al. (2018), we inves-

Task	log lik.	SS	Senti	Htag	Topic	Conv.
spatial	-7.610	0.059	73.10	42.19	39.61	71.14
income	-7.600	**0.067**	72.98	42.18	39.64	71.10
interest	-7.724	0.061	73.06	**42.21**	39.75	**71.41**
spatial & income	-7.510	0.059	73.21	42.08	39.67	71.22
spatial & interest	**-7.396**	0.059	73.11	42.14	39.77	71.23
income & interest	-7.410	0.059	73.27	42.30	39.75	71.11
spatial & income & network	-7.447	0.062	**73.35**	42.19	39.66	71.06
spatial & interest & network	-7.429	0.064	73.16	42.15	39.64	71.17
interest & income & network	-7.522	0.061	73.11	42.16	**39.82**	71.15
interest & income & network & spatial	-7.489	0.060	73.10	41.95	39.62	71.22
interest & income & network & spatial & knowledge	-7.438	0.059	73.21	41.90	39.70	71.28
interest & income & network & spatial & topic	-7.426	0.064	73.16	41.94	39.65	71.22

Table 4: Ablation Results for contextual attention model based on log likelihood, semantic similarity and tweet classification.

Model/Task (Task type)	SentLen (Surface)	WC (Surface)	TreeDepth (Syntactic)	TopConst (Syntactic)	BShift (Syntactic)	Tense (Semantic)	SubjNum (Semantic)	ObjNum (Semantic)	SOMO (Semantic)	CoordInv (Semantic)
non diachronic										
Word2vec	**84.07**	22.65	**50.34**	37.27	**50.69**	75.99	84.40	82.88	**64.40**	49.79
HistWords	83.40	**34.08**	47.51	**40.43**	49.92	**77**	**84.99**	**83.31**	64.29	**50.46**
diachronic										
DBE	73.48	46.97	43.64	31.41	**50.46**	73.34	**82.57**	82.02	64.85	50.05
No Attn.	**75.51**	46.82	**48.28**	32.78	49.15	**73.45**	82.39	82.07	65.65	49.17
Self Attn.	74.82	**47.37**	47.77	32.49	50.19	73.16	82.38	**82.18**	64.51	**50.18**
Context Attn.	75.47	46.03	47.31	**33.08**	49.98	73.05	82.10	81.81	**65.76**	49.59

Table 5: Probing task accuracies. See Conneau et al. (2018) for the details of probing tasks and classifier used.

tigate that question by setting a diagnostic classifier that probes for important linguistic features on parsed output we mentioned earlier. Those probes are based on various prediction tasks (word content, sentence length, subject or object number detection, etc.) described in (Conneau et al., 2018) and succinctly in our Appendix A.5. In 7 out of 9 tasks the use of contextual features seems to be detrimental, but the relative performance difference between our proposed models and the baseline are negligible for 5 of them. This suggests that the addition of contextualized features does not hurt the syntactic and semantic information captured by our models. Interestingly, all dynamic embeddings models are able to perform twice better in the word prediction task than a Word2vec baseline but it is unclear if those models capture language usage or actual topic prediction within a *degraded* language modeling task.

6.4 Interpretation via Erasure

Alternatively, we can directly compute the importance of a contextualized feature by observing the effects on the model of erasing (setting the weights to 0) the particular feature (Li et al., 2016). By subtracting the erased model performance on the test set from that of the original model performance and post normalization, we can establish the importance score for each feature against each version of our proposed model. Figure 6 empha-

sizes our finding that all contextualized features (except interest) are equally important to the performance of each variant of our proposed model.

7 Conclusion

In this work, we proposed a new family of diachronic word embeddings models that utilize various contextualized features as inductive biases to provide better fits to a social media corpus. Our wide range of quantitative and qualitative studies highlight the competitive performance of our models in detecting semantic changes over a short time range. In the future, we will consider the temporal nature of some of our contextualized features when incorporating them into our models. For example, the static social network we built can be dynamically evolving and more susceptible to accurately model underlying phenomenon.

Acknowledgments

We thank our anonymous reviewers for providing insightful comments and suggestions. This work was funded by the ANR projects ParSiTi (ANR-16-CE33-0021), SoSweet (ANR15-CE38-0011-01) and the Programme Hubert Curien Maimonide project which is part of a French-Israeli Cooperation program.

References

Jacob Levy Abitbol, Márton Karsai, Jean-Philippe Magué, Jean-Pierre Chevrot, and Eric Fleury. 2018. Socioeconomic dependencies of linguistic patterns in twitter: a multivariate analysis. In *Proceedings of the 2018 World Wide Web Conference on World Wide Web, WWW 2018, Lyon, France, April 23-27, 2018*, pages 1125–1134.

Robert Bamler and Stephan Mandt. 2017. Dynamic word embeddings. In *Proceedings of the 34th International Conference on Machine Learning, ICML 2017, Sydney, NSW, Australia, 6-11 August 2017*, pages 380–389.

Andreas Blank and Peter Koch. 1999. *Historical semantics and cognition*. Walter de Gruyter.

Alexis Conneau, Germán Kruszewski, Guillaume Lample, Loïc Barrault, and Marco Baroni. 2018. What you can cram into a single \$&!#* vector: Probing sentence embeddings for linguistic properties. In *Proceedings of the 56th Annual Meeting of the Association for Computational Linguistics, ACL 2018, Melbourne, Australia, July 15-20, 2018, Volume 1: Long Papers*, pages 2126–2136.

Haim Dubossarsky, Yulia Tsvetkov, Chris Dyer, and Eitan Grossman. 2015. A bottom up approach to category mapping and meaning change. In *Proceedings of the NetWordS Final Conference on Word Knowledge and Word Usage: Representations and Processes in the Mental Lexicon, Pisa, Italy, March 30 - April 1, 2015.*, pages 66–70.

Bradley Efron and Robert J Tibshirani. 1994. *An introduction to the bootstrap*. CRC press.

Yanai Elazar and Yoav Goldberg. 2018. Adversarial removal of demographic attributes from text data. In *Proceedings of the 2018 Conference on Empirical Methods in Natural Language Processing*, pages 11–21. Association for Computational Linguistics.

Justin Garten, Brendan Kennedy, Joe Hoover, Kenji Sagae, and Morteza Dehghani. 2019. Incorporating demographic embeddings into language understanding. *Cognitive Science*, 43(1).

Alec Go, Richa Bhayani, and Lei Huang. 2009. Twitter sentiment classification using distant supervision.

Spence Green, Marie-Catherine De Marneffe, John Bauer, and Christopher D Manning. 2011. Multiword expression identification with tree substitution grammars: A parsing tour de force with french. In *Proceedings of the Conference on Empirical Methods in Natural Language Processing*, pages 725–735. Association for Computational Linguistics.

Joachim Grzega and Marion Schoener. 2007. English and general historical lexicology.

William L. Hamilton, Jure Leskovec, and Dan Jurafsky. 2016. Diachronic word embeddings reveal statistical laws of semantic change. In *Proceedings of the 54th Annual Meeting of the Association for Computational Linguistics, ACL 2016, August 7-12, 2016, Berlin, Germany, Volume 1: Long Papers*.

Zellig Harris. 1954. Distributional structure. *Word*, 10(23):146–162.

Dirk Hovy and Christoph Purschke. 2018. Capturing regional variation with distributed place representations and geographic retrofitting. In *Proceedings of the 2018 Conference on Empirical Methods in Natural Language Processing*, pages 4383–4394, Brussels, Belgium. Association for Computational Linguistics.

Ganesh Jawahar, Benjamin Muller, Amal Fethi, Louis Martin, Eric Villemonte de la Clergerie, Benoît Sagot, and Djamé Seddah. 2018. ELMoLex: Connecting ELMo and lexicon features for dependency parsing. In *Proceedings of the CoNLL 2018 Shared Task: Multilingual Parsing from Raw Text to Universal Dependencies*, pages 223–237, Brussels, Belgium. Association for Computational Linguistics.

Dan Jurafsky. 2018. *Speech & language processing*, 3rd edition. Currently in draft.

Yoon Kim, Yi-I Chiu, Kentaro Hanaki, Darshan Hegde, and Slav Petrov. 2014. Temporal analysis of language through neural language models. In *Proceedings of the Workshop on Language Technologies and Computational Social Science@ACL 2014, Baltimore, MD, USA, June 26, 2014*, pages 61–65.

Diederik P. Kingma and Jimmy Ba. 2014. Adam: A method for stochastic optimization. *CoRR*, abs/1412.6980.

Vivek Kulkarni, Rami Al-Rfou, Bryan Perozzi, and Steven Skiena. 2015. Statistically significant detection of linguistic change. In *Proceedings of the 24th International Conference on World Wide Web, WWW 2015, Florence, Italy, May 18-22, 2015*, pages 625–635.

Andrey Kutuzov, Lilja Øvrelid, Terrence Szymanski, and Erik Velldal. 2018. Diachronic word embeddings and semantic shifts: a survey. In *Proceedings of the 27th International Conference on Computational Linguistics, COLING 2018, Santa Fe, New Mexico, USA, August 20-26, 2018*, pages 1384–1397.

Jiwei Li, Will Monroe, and Dan Jurafsky. 2016. Understanding neural networks through representation erasure. *CoRR*, abs/1612.08220.

Laurens van der Maaten and Geoffrey Hinton. 2008. Visualizing data using t-sne. *Journal of machine learning research*, 9(Nov):2579–2605.

Walid Magdy, Hassan Sajjad, Tarek El-Ganainy, and Fabrizio Sebastiani. 2015. Distant supervision for tweet classification using youtube labels. In *Proceedings of the Ninth International Conference on Web and Social Media, ICWSM 2015, University of Oxford, Oxford, UK, May 26-29, 2015*, pages 638–641.

Tomas Mikolov, Ilya Sutskever, Kai Chen, Gregory S. Corrado, and Jeffrey Dean. 2013. Distributed representations of words and phrases and their compositionality. In *Advances in Neural Information Processing Systems 26: 27th Annual Conference on Neural Information Processing Systems 2013. Proceedings of a meeting held December 5-8, 2013, Lake Tahoe, Nevada, United States.*, pages 3111–3119.

Herbert Robbins and Sutton Monro. 1985. A stochastic approximation method. In *Herbert Robbins Selected Papers*, pages 102–109. Springer.

Maja R. Rudolph and David M. Blei. 2018. Dynamic embeddings for language evolution. In *Proceedings of the 2018 World Wide Web Conference on World Wide Web, WWW 2018, Lyon, France, April 23-27, 2018*, pages 1003–1011.

Maja R. Rudolph, Francisco J. R. Ruiz, Stephan Mandt, and David M. Blei. 2016. Exponential family embeddings. In *Advances in Neural Information Processing Systems 29: Annual Conference on Neural Information Processing Systems 2016, December 5-10, 2016, Barcelona, Spain*, pages 478–486.

Nina Tahmasebi, Lars Borin, and Adam Jatowt. 2018. Survey of computational approaches to diachronic conceptual change. *CoRR*, abs/1811.06278.

Jian Tang, Meng Qu, Mingzhe Wang, Ming Zhang, Jun Yan, and Qiaozhu Mei. 2015. LINE: large-scale information network embedding. In *Proceedings of the 24th International Conference on World Wide Web, WWW 2015, Florence, Italy, May 18-22, 2015*, pages 1067–1077.

Jason Weston, Sumit Chopra, and Keith Adams. 2014. #tagspace: Semantic embeddings from hashtags. In *Proceedings of the 2014 Conference on Empirical Methods in Natural Language Processing, EMNLP 2014, October 25-29, 2014, Doha, Qatar, A meeting of SIGDAT, a Special Interest Group of the ACL*, pages 1822–1827.

Zijun Yao, Yifan Sun, Weicong Ding, Nikhil Rao, and Hui Xiong. 2018. Dynamic word embeddings for evolving semantic discovery. In *Proceedings of the Eleventh ACM International Conference on Web Search and Data Mining, WSDM 2018, Marina Del Rey, CA, USA, February 5-9, 2018*, pages 673–681.

A Appendices

A.1 Pseudo code for the training algorithm

Pseudo code for training our proposed model is presented in Algorithm 1.

Algorithm 1 : Training algorithm for the proposed diachronic word embedding model

---

Input: Tweets X^t of size m_t from T time slices, contextual features f_m, context size c, embedding size K, number of negative samples n, number of minibatch fractions m, initial learning rate η, precision λ, vocabulary size V, smoothed unigram distribution $\hat{\rho}$.

for v from 1 **to** V **do**
    Initialize α_v and $\rho_v^{(T)}$ with $\mathcal{N}(0, 0.01)$
end for
for m from 1 **to** $|F|$ **do**
    if f_m is learnable **then**
        Initialize f_m with $\mathcal{U}(0, 1)$
    end if
end for
for number of passes over the data **do**
    for number of minibatch fractions m **do**
        for t from 1 **to** T **do**
            for i from 1 **to** $\frac{m_t}{m}$ **do**
                Sample $c + 1$ consecutive words from a random tweet $X^{(t)}$ and construct: $C_i^{(t)} = \sum_{j \in c_i} \sum_{v'} \alpha_{v'} x_{jv'}$
                Compute contextualized features: $F_i^{(t)} = \sum_{m=1}^{|F|} \alpha_m \mathbf{w}_m f_{i,m}$ Draw a set $S_i^{(t)}$ of n negative samples from $\hat{\rho}$.
            end for
        end for
        Update the parameters $\theta = \alpha, \rho, f_m, w, a, b$ by ascending the stochastic gradient

$$\nabla_\theta \Big\{ \sum_{t=1}^{T} m \sum_{i=1}^{\frac{m_t}{m}} \Big(\sum_{v=1}^{V} x_{iv}^{(t)} log\sigma((\rho_v^{(t)} + F_i^{(t)})^T C_i^{(t)})$$
$$+ \sum_{x_j \in \mathcal{S}_i^{(t)}} \sum_{v=1}^{V} log(1 - \sigma((\rho_v^{(t)} + F_i^{(t)})^T C_i^{(t)})$$
$$- \frac{\lambda_0}{2} \sum_v \|\alpha_v\|^2 - \frac{\lambda_0}{2} \sum_v \left\|\rho_v^{(0)}\right\|^2$$
$$- \frac{\lambda}{2} \sum_{v,t} \left\|\rho_v^{(t)} - \rho_v^{(t-1)}\right\|^2 \Big\}.$$

    end for
end for
We utilize Adam (Kingma and Ba, 2014) to set rate η.

A.2 Hyperparameter settings

We follow the hyperparameter search space provided by Rudolph and Blei (2018) to find the best configuration of our model. Before training our model, we initialize the parameters with one epoch fit of non-diachronic Bernoulli embedding model (as defined in Equation 2 in the paper). We then train our model for 9 more epochs. We fix the embedding dimension to 100, context size to 2 and number of negative samples to 20. We select the initial learning rate $\eta \in [0.01, 0.1, 1, 10]$, minibatch size $m \in [0.001N, 0.0001N, 0.00001N]$ (where N is the number of training records), the precision on context vectors and initial dynamic embeddings $\lambda \in [1, 10]$ ($\lambda_0 = \lambda/1000$). We use the conditional likelihood metric (as discussed in Section 5.3) to sweep over the search space and select the best hyperparameters.

A.3 Tweet Classification Details

We will list down the details of tweet classification tasks where the data comes from our corpus.

- **Sentiment Analysis** - This is a binary task to classify the sentiment of the tweet. Following Go et al. (2009), we create a balanced dataset by tagging a tweet as positive (negative) if it contains only positive (negative) emoticons. We remove the emoticons from the tweets to avoid bias.
- **Hashtag Prediction** - This multiclass classification task is to identify the hashtag present in the tweet. Following Weston et al. (2014), we identify the most frequent 100 hashtags from the corpus, keep the tweets that contain exactly one occurrence of the frequent hashtag, remove the hashtag from the tweet and predict them.
- **Topic Categorization** - This multiclass classification task is to identify the topical category to which a tweet belongs to. Following Magdy et al. (2015), we filter the tweets that has a YouTube video associated with it, query the video category using the public YouTube API and associate that to the topical category of the tweet.
- **Conversation Prediction** - This binary task is to classify if a tweet will receive a reply or not. Following Elazar and Goldberg (2018), we tag the tweet as a conversational tweet if it has at least a mention ('@') in it, otherwise it's a non-conversational tweet. We remove the mentions from the tweets to avoid bias.

A.4 Ablation Results

We perform ablation studies of the no attention and self attention variant of the proposed model by considering different set of contextualized features as inductive biases, illustrated in Table 6.

A.5 Probing Task Description

In this section we will describe briefly the set of probing tasks (proposed in Conneau et al. (2018)) used in our study.

- **SentLen** - The goal for the classification task is to predict the tweet length which has been binned in 6 categories with lengths ranging in the following intervals: $(5-8), (9-12), (13-16), (17-20), (21-25), (26-28)$.
- **WC** - This classification task is about predicting which of the target words appear on the given tweet.
- **TreeDepth** - In this classification task the goal is to predict the maximum depth of the tweet's syntactic tree (with values ranging from 5 to 12).
- **TopConst** - The goal of this classification task is to predict the sequence of top constituents immediately below the sentence (S) node. The classes are given by the 19 most common top-constituent sequences in the corpus, plus a 20th category for all other structures.
- **BShift** - In this binary classification task the goal is to predict whether two consecutive tokens within the tweet have been inverted or not.
- **Tense** - The goal of this task is to identify the tense of the main verb of the tweet.
- **SubjNum** - The goal of this task is to identify the number of the subject of the main clause.
- **ObjNum** - The goal of this task is to identify the number of the subject on the direct object of the main clause.
- **SOMO** - This task classifies whether a tweet occurs as-is in the source corpus, or whether a randomly picked noun or verb was replaced with another form with the same part of speech.
- **CoordInv** - This task distinguishes between original tweet and tweet where the order of two coordinated clausal conjoints has been inverted purposely.

A.6 Selection of time span unit

We performed preliminary experiments with DBE model to identify the time span unit that best fits the data. As shown in Table 7, DBE model fits the data well in terms of log likelihood metric when the time span unit is year.

Time span unit	Yearly	Monthly	Quarterly	Half-yearly
Log lik.	**-5.7323**	-7.1055	-6.4004	-6.0768

Table 7: Log likelihood scores of DBE model with varying time span units.

Task	log lik.	SS	Senti	Htag	Topic	Conv.
No Attention						
spatial	-7.8481	0.0583	73.11	42.1	39.76	71.16
income	-7.8407	0.0616	73.17	41.99	**39.80**	71.22
interest	-7.9704	0.0596	73.24	42.11	39.72	71.17
spatial & income	-7.8407	**0.0718**	73.18	42.07	39.67	71.17
spatial & interest	-7.9774	0.0581	73.27	42.05	39.69	71.14
income & interest	-7.9601	0.0620	**73.3**	42.08	39.68	71.14
spatial & income & network	**-7.7735**	0.0614	73.2	42.13	39.78	71.17
spatial & interest & network	-8.0061	0.0613	73.27	42.17	39.61	71.14
interest & income & network	-8.0170	0.0605	73.22	42.1	39.71	71.17
interest & income & network & spatial	-8.0561	0.0587	73.29	42.18	39.67	71.15
interest & income & network & spatial & knowledge	-8.0734	0.0620	**73.3**	**42.19**	39.7	**71.24**
interest & income & network & spatial & topic	-8.0739	0.0639	73.28	42.13	39.62	71.15
Self Attention						
spatial	-7.8260	0.0624	73.11	41.95	39.75	71.09
income	-7.8248	0.0577	73.13	41.98	39.78	**71.17**
interest	-7.7986	0.0602	73.21	42.14	**39.83**	71.13
spatial & income	-7.8383	**0.0641**	73.08	42.02	**39.83**	71.14
spatial & interest	-7.7874	0.0625	73.2	42.11	39.71	71.12
income & interest	-7.7796	0.0635	73.2	**42.18**	39.75	71.11
spatial & income & network	-7.8613	0.0609	73.09	42.07	39.77	71.19
spatial & interest & network	**-7.7558**	0.0611	73.13	42.1	39.68	71.07
interest & income & network	-7.8432	0.0607	73.11	42.13	39.48	71.09
interest & income & network & spatial	-7.8414	0.0609	73.15	42.16	39.58	71.04
interest & income & network & spatial & knowledge	-7.8554	0.0618	73.2	42.15	39.58	71.06
interest & income & network & spatial & topic	-7.8208	0.0575	**73.22**	42.13	39.58	71.07

Table 6: Ablation results based on log likelihood, semantic similarity and tweet classification.

Semantic Change and Semantic Stability: Variation is Key

Claire L. Bowern
Yale University / 370 Temple St
New Haven, CT 06520
USA
claire.bowern@yale.edu

Abstract

I survey some recent approaches to studying change in the lexicon, particularly change in meaning across phylogenies. I briefly sketch an evolutionary approach to language change and point out some issues in recent approaches to studying semantic change that rely on temporally stratified word embeddings. I draw illustrations from lexical cognate models in Pama-Nyungan to identify meaning classes most appropriate for lexical phylogenetic inference, particularly highlighting the importance of variation in studying change over time.

1 Introduction

All aspects of all languages are changing all the time. And for most of human history, for most of the world's languages, this change is not recorded. Therefore, in order to understand language change adequately, we need methods which allow us to extrapolate back beyond what is identifiable in the written record, which is both shallow and geographically sparse. In this paper, I discuss how evolutionary approaches to language change allow the modeling of cognate evolution. I show how such models can be used to study semantic change at the macro-level, and finally how we can make use of existing data to refine meaning categories for use in inferring language splits. I focus on theoretical models of change.

I begin with a brief outline of contemporary language change, particularly as studied quantitatively (Bowern 2018 provides more context). I then discuss issues of reconstructing meaning and identifying meaning change, before presenting two case studies: one on studying semantic change across a phylogeny, the other about identifying lexical stability.

1.1 What is language change

Much contemporary work on historical linguistics aims to answer one or more of three key questions for the nature of language change:

1. *What* forms have changed?

2. *How* does change work?

3. *Why* does it work the way it does?

The first aspect of diachrony involves establishing the "facts": that is, identifying differences between languages at various stages of their history (or differences between related languages) and establishing which of those differences are due to *change* in the system, and which are artefacts of data gathering or sampling. Research of this type includes how language informs our study of prehistory. Questions of this type include "Where was the homeland of speakers of Proto-Pama-Nyungan?" (Bouckaert et al., 2018) or "What is the origin of the Latin ablative case?"

The second question – how does change work – seeks to establish the general properties of change. These are "mode and tempo" type questions (Greenhill et al., 2010), regarding which items in language change more rapidly than others, what features change into which others, and which features are stable across centuries and millennia. Work in this area include Hamilton et al. (2016b) on semantic change, Wedel et al. (2013) on sound change, Van Gelderen (2018) on change in argument structure, and indeed much work of recent years (Bowern and Evans, 2014).

The third question – the *why* of language change – has received less attention. Until recently, it has been difficult to study changes at the scale necessary, and with the precision necessary, to do more than speculate. Moreover, the focus in historical linguistics on language-internal explanations has made it difficult to grapple with the obvious

Proceedings of the 1st International Workshop on Computational Approaches to Historical Language Change, pages 48–55
Florence, Italy, August 2, 2019. ©2019 Association for Computational Linguistics

fact that languages change in large part because of the way people acquire and use them (see further §1.2). One example of modeling a 'why' of change in meaning comes from Ahern and Clark (2017), which argues that one type of semantic change occurs because of psychological tendencies for interlocutors to assume exaggeration.

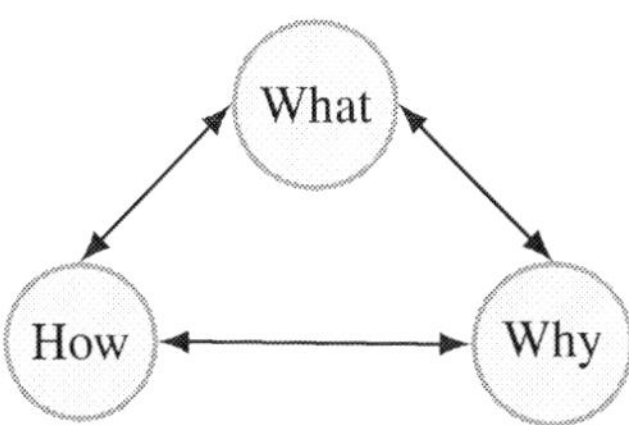

Figure 1: Key questions

All of these questions are related to one another, and the answers to one inform the others. We cannot make plausible inferences about processes without a theory, any more than we can work on a theory of change without data to test it with. The *what* provides us with observations; the *why* provides us with a theory that explains those observations, and the *how* provides us with a framework to structure those observations, and to predict and evaluate implications of the theory.

Language change can be studied at different scales. Phylogenetic approaches typically look across millennia (Bowern, 2018; Greenhill et al., 2010) and concentrate on areas that are assumed to be stable. Other methods look at micro-levels of change; for example, Yao et al. (2018); Hamilton et al. (2016b) and Eisenstein et al. (2014) study change at the range of decades and weeks respectively.

1.2 Traditional explanations of language change

The current 'received view of language change can be summarized as follows (necessarily with much loss of nuance; see further Hock and Joseph 1996). Language change begins with an innovation in a single language user. That innovation catches on and spreads through a community, over time replacing older forms. Because not all members of a language community interact with each other all the time, innovations spread at different rates, and to different extents, across a language area. Thus dialects form, and those dialects eventually become sufficiently different that they come to be regarded as different languages. Innovations may

also be introduced when speakers/signers of a language come into contact with a different language or dialect and adopt some of its features.

Most generative approaches to change assume that the point at which languages change is when children are acquiring language (Lightfoot, 1991; Hale, 2007), a model that goes back ultimately to Paul (1880). Yet we know that language acquisition is not the main driver of all language change. Language change in the historical record happens too fast for children to be solely involved.[1] The evidence is overwhelming that childrens role is minimal (Aitchison, 2003) in the spread of innovations. The errors that children make are not the main types of change we see in the record. Moreover, innovations are spread through social networks, and children acquiring language have peripheral positions in such networks.

The key questions model of change summarized in Figure 1, though fairly common in evolutionary anthropology and in phylogenetic approaches, is not the way historical linguistics has been conceptualized traditionally. Weinreich et al. (1968) or Labov (2001), Lightfoot (1991), and others in the generative tradition have often conceptualized the nature of the task of historical linguistics is being about the *differences* between two stages of a language. That is a simpler problem, since it reduces language change to problem of edit distances. But it does not answer the questions we posed above, except inasmuch as identifying the differences – that is, figuring out that something happened – is just Stage 0 in understanding what happened, how it happened, and why.

1.3 Evolutionary views of change

An alternative approach is a framework which treats language as a complex evolutionary system (e.g. Bowern, 2018; Mesoudi, 2011; Wedel, 2006). This views language as a Darwinian system where changes are modeled through the key properties of variation, selection, and transmission.

In an evolutionary system, change is modeled as follows. The unit of study is the population; for language, our 'population' could be a speech community or members of an ethno-linguistic group (Marlowe, 2005). Such communities are inherently *variable*: we know that not everyone speaks the same way, and that variation has social mean-

---

[1] Compare the arguments in D'Arcy (2017) for the recent spread of 'like' as a discourse particle.

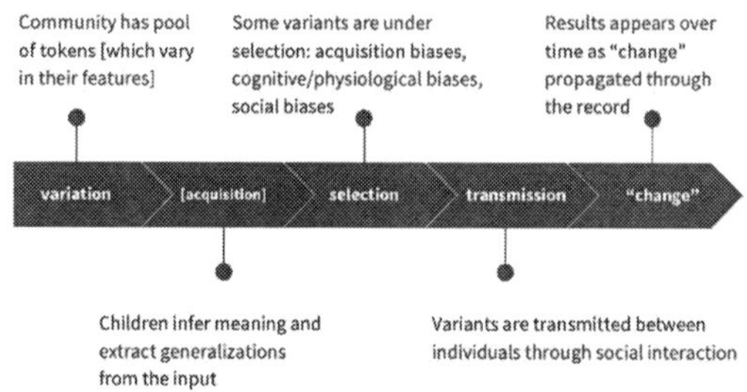

Figure 2: Schematic representation of language change in an evolutionary framework

ing. Systems which contain no variation cannot be modeled in an evolutionary framework.

Much linguistic variation can be described in terms of social variables such as age, gender, socioeconomic class, geography, ethnicity, patri-group, moiety, and the like (though of course, not all of these variables explain linguistic variation). Speakers do not use these variables deterministically, but with them index aspects of social identity (Bucholtz and Hall, 2005). Other inputs to the pool of variation include psychological and physiological aspects of language production and perception. For example, the fundamental frequency (or 'pitch') of speech partly varies physiologically (taller people have deeper voices), partly socially (higher and lower pitch can index femininity and masculinity, respectively), and partly grammatically (for example, the difference between a declarative statement and a question can be signaled solely by an intonational rise at the end of the clause).

Some of these variants are under *selection* (positive or negative). Not all variants have equal chances of spreading within a community. Not all variants are under positive or negative selection; those that are are likely to change faster. Selection can be models as a set of bias biases in language transmission which inhibit or faciliate transmission. Such biases include acquisition, cognitive/physiological biases, and social biases.

Over time, these biases affect the input that children are exposed to, as well as the ways adults use language. We see the results reflected over generations as "change" propagated through the linguistic record.

Conceptualizing language change in this way has consequences for how change is studied. Instead of looking across a system to extract generalizations, we are looking within a system for the points at which features vary. That is, we are not just comparing differences across points in time, but examining variation within a system and how that variation changes over time. Contrast semantic change studied by word embeddings, for example, where words are treated as discrete and uniform entities at each time point. As such, they are unable to distinguish between relative shifts in frequency of use among subsenses, and the spread of genuine innovations. The former may be a precursor to the latter, but the processes are not identical.

Moreover, studying change in this way (correctly) entails that we not conceptualize change as 'facilitating efficient communication'. This is a teleological view. Instead, biases and synchronic features of language make some changes more or less likely (cf. Blevins, 2004).

Finally, the transmission mechanism for language need not be strictly intergenerational. Taking an evolutionary view of language change does *not* entail that it be studied with direct and concrete analogues to biological replication and speciation. A evolutionary view requires that there be a modeled transmission mechanism, not that the transmission mechanism exclusively involves transfer of material from parents to their children.

2 Lexical replacement models

2.1 Types of lexical replacement

With that background, let us now consider 'change' specifically as applied to the lexicon. Like other parts of language, the lexicon is also constantly changing. The lexicon can be viewed as a set of mappings between forms, meanings, and the world. For example, the form we write as *cat* maps to a concept, which relates to language users' knowledge of this animal in the real world.

The following points summarize the types of lexical replacement that are possible in spoken and signed languages. Numerous works on semantic change have typologized the relationships between words and concepts at different stages in time (cf. Traugott and Dasher, 2002). Terms such as subjectification, meronymy, and amelioration all describe different relationships between words across time. Such points are, in this typology, all contained under the concept of "semantic change".

1. Semantic change: that is, change in mappings between a lexical item, concepts, and world

2. Borrowing from other languages

3. Creation of words *de novo*

4. (Loss)

As Bender (2019) has noted, because of the heavy emphasis on English in NLP, the distinction between words and concepts is sometimes obscured. Yet it is vital when considering how concepts change. For example, if I describe a movement as *catlike*, I am evoking aspects of the concept 'cat', not a literal cat. (Someone can walk in a catlike fashion without, for example, being furry or having a tail.)

An emphasis on typologically similar and closely related languages is also problematic for studying tendencies. For example, Hamilton et al. (2016a) argue as an absolute that nouns are more likely to undergo irregular cultural shifts (e.g. expansion due to technological innovations) while verbs are more likely to show regular processes of change, such as drift. Such a view does not take into account that verb numbers differ extensively across languages, and the functional load, levels of polysemy, and lexicalization patterns for events also differ – points that Hamilton et al. (2016b) showed were important in assessing likelihood of change. Technological innovation, while exceptionally salient to those who work in NLP, is unlikely to have been the same driving factor in semantic change across most of human history. And indeed, it plays a small role in the literature on lexical replacement, where euphemism, metaphorical extension, and bleaching play more important roles.

A further type of lexical replacement involves borrowing (Haspelmath and Tadmor, 2009). Both borrowing and creation of words from new resources involve the innovation of mappings between words and concepts within a linguistic system. In the former, lexical material is adapted from another language, while in the latter, it is created from language-internal resources or innovated from scratch. Languages differ in the extent to which novel word formation is utilized, and the strategies, from compounding to acronyms to blends, also vary greatly. Furthermore, there is variation in the extent to which language users borrow words (see further Bowern et al. 2011), but there are regularities in which words are more likely to be borrowed. Word creation has played a role in NLP approaches to semantic change because of the focus on named entity identification, but it is a small part of change overall.

2.2 Evolutionary semantic change

Such changes can be modeled in an evolutionary framework. Some variation is neutral (not under selection). For example, speakers of American English have several distinct systems of contrast in the meanings of the words 'cobweb' and 'spiderweb':[2]

- The two words are synonymous;

- Spiderwebs are spiral or wheel-shaped, cobwebs are collapsed;

- Spiderwebs have spiders in them, other items are cobwebs (including abandoned but intact wheel webs);

- Spiderwebs have spiders, while cobwebs are synonymous with dirt or dust bunnies (detritus that is cleaned when cleaning a house). That is, cobwebs are not necessarily old spiderwebs but could be from other material.

Speakers are unaware of these differences in semantic distinctions, and the variants do not clearly pattern by age, gender, or geography. Such variation is not under selection and is below the level of consciousness. It is, however, very hard to detect (not least because it is usually also invisible to researchers).

Other selectional pressures skew change. Such biases include (but are not limited to) meaning transmission failure and speaker attitudes. For example, there is a bias against using words with novel denotations. Meaning is conventionalized, which is what prevents English speakers from calling a '⋆' a 'sun'. However, language users do make creative and novel associations between objects, which do over time end up as change. For example, several Pama-Nyungan subgroups have words for 'eye' which are etymologically connected to 'seeds' (compare Wati and Pama-Maric languages, which have independently shifted **kuru* 'seed' to 'eye'; the Yolngu language Yan-nhaŋu has a single term *maŋutji*, which means 'eye', 'well', and 'seed'. To study such changes, it is vital to have a good empirical basis for the possibilities for polysemy and shift. List et al. (2013) provides an example using translation equivalents across languages from different families.

---

[2]The source of this observation is 4 years of polling historical linguistics students at Yale.

Finally, words can also fall out of use. They may be tabooed through necronym replacement or protective euphemism, or lost when the knowledge of the concepts they represent is also lost (such as ethnobiological knowledge in many urban English speakers).

In summary, semantic change can be modeled in an evolutionary framework, where meanings vary, have positive or negative selectional biases, and are transmitted through language use. If a word is not used, it is not transmitted. Such a view provides a clue to Hamilton et al.'s findings about polysemy and and frequency. Words are more likely to change if they have low frequency, because speakers have less information about meaning, making them more vulnerable to reinterpretation or replacement (further eroding their frequency). Words are also more likely to change if they exhibit high polysemy, perhaps because they are both more ambiguous and more likely to be further extended.

2.3 Word embeddings

With this theoretical background, let us now turn to an evaluation of methods. Word embeddings (Turney and Pantel, 2010; Kulkarni et al., 2015) are an increasingly common tool for studying change in vocabulary over time. They rely on the intuition that "you can know a word by the company it keeps" (Firth, 1957, 11), and by studying the changes in word use it is possible to quantify and further study language change.

Critiques of the effectiveness of using word embeddings to study change are well known. Dubossarsky et al. (2017) and Tahmasebi et al. (2018) have pointed out issues that limit the utility of embeddings for studying change, such as the necessity for large corpora, the brittleness of results, and the lack of ability to study word senses independently. This latter point is particularly important for theories of meaning change, since as argued above, understanding variation is a prerequisite to an adequate modeling of the evolution of linguistic systems over time.

Embeddings across massive corpora assume that all speakers have the same knowledge of the vocabulary of their language. That is simply not true, as illustrated by the simple example in §2.2 above. Not all speakers/signers know all the words of their languages. Using embeddings across many speakers and documents also con-flates real-world knowledge (e.g. Linnaean classification) with linguistic knowledge. For example, I do not need to know that a koala is a member of the genus Phascolarctos to know what a koala is, any more than the etymology (from Daruk *kula*) is part of the meaning. Yet because word embedding models use encyclopedic corpora such as Wikipedia, they tend to be skewed towards such information.

Finally, embedding changes conflate changes in frequency of a word with conceptual changes, further obscuring mechanisms of change. Yao et al. (2018) identify shifts in frequency and use this as a diagnostic for language change. They use the example of '*apple*'s vectorization changing over time from being more similar to other fruit to being more similar to computer equipment and software. However, just because apple is now more associated in their corpus with software than with fruit, it doesn't entail that the meaning of the word has actually changed over that time period. It is a possible precursor to a change where a word goes through a period of variation and polysemy (an A, A~B, B change), but that is not the only type of change. For a similar problem, see Kulkarni et al. (2015) on word usage time series, and for a more nuanced view, Kutuzov et al. 2018. If we are to study change, we can't just abstract away from variation in the data as "noise". Variation leads to change, and not all differences are changes.

3 Lexical replacement and phylogenetics

3.1 Stability and meaning

So far, I have concentrated discussion on variation and change. However, for studying change at the macro-level, across phylogenetic time, we require items which have high semantic stability. Evolutionary approaches to language split use lexical replacement to model language evolution. That is, they take presumed stable (but nonetheless varying) meaning categories and use the variation in the realization of those meanings to build a model of language split, from which the phylogeny is recovered. Such work is now well established in the literature on language change and the reader is referred to Dunn (2014) and Bowern (2018) for summaries. State of the art methods use Bayesian inference; see Bouckaert et al. (2018) for explanation and details of priors, cognate models, and data treatment.

Such methods can be used to study semantic

change over a phylogeny. They are particularly useful for studying the lexicalization of oppositions within a small semantic space. For example, Haynie and Bowern (2016) used such methods to see how color terms changed across the Australian family Pama-Nyungan. The visible color spectrum is modeled as partitioned by vocabulary (Regier et al., 2005). These partitions obey evolutionary principles. There is variation (people don't have full agreement in the assignment of lexicon to the visible spectrum, and color terms vary across languages); transmission (color terms are acquired and transmitted with other aspects of language) and selection (there are physiological constraints on perception (which are also variable), for example, and visual exemplars which tend to lexicalize as color terms; cf. 'orange'). Keeping the conceptual space constant and varying the partitioning avoids the problem that other types of change are happening simultaneously. That is, we can't study the evolution of particular words in many domains because the words fall out of use or are replaced too many times across the tree.

These models require cognate evolution models. Currently, the main one is Brownian Motion (that is, random change across a tree). Such models fit these types of change well, and allow us to evaluate the effectiveness of such models as well as probabilistically reconstructing ancestral states.

3.2 Lexical replacement in phylogenetics

A final illustration of evolutionary methods for meaning change and lexical replacement concerns a practical issue for phylogenetics: the 'legacy problem' of Swadesh wordlists. Since (Swadesh, 1952, 1955), linguists have been using similar lists of so-called 'basic vocabulary' to construct cognate evolutionary matrices.[3] These wordlists are now a sample of convenience, as lexical resource collection has prioritized vocabulary from Swadesh lists. Other work (McMahon and McMahon, 2006) has reduced the number of comparison items even further. Rama and Wichmann (2018) estimate the number of items needed for small

---

[3]A 'cognate' is a a word which shares an evolutionary history of descent with other words. English 'fish' and German 'Fisch' are cognate, because they continue the same form-meaning correspondence from an ancestor language. English 'much' and Spanish 'mucho' are not cognate, despite their similarity in form, because they continue different lexical roots. 'Much' continues Old English *mickel* (ultimately from an Indo-European root meaning 'big, great', while Spanish *mucho* continues Latin *multus* 'much, many', ultimately from a root meaning 'crumpled'.

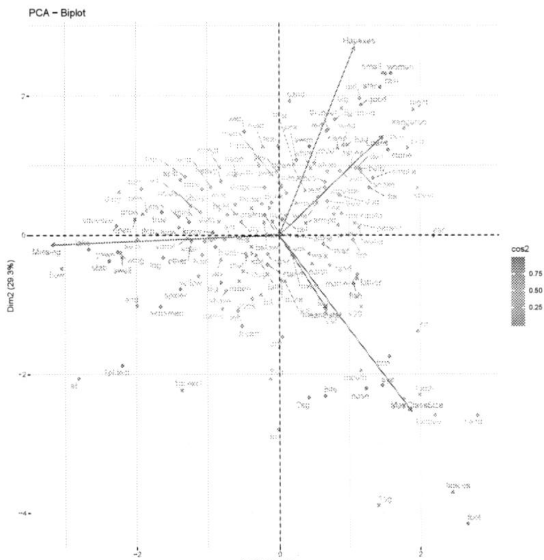

Figure 3: PCA and loadings for meaning classes

phylogenies; however, they do not take stability into account. Their estimate concludes approximately 30 data points per language in the phylogeny. However, the number of such data points varies with both the number of meaning classes and their stability. To illustrate for 300 Pama-Nyungan languages, the number of cognates per meaning class in the Swadesh 200 list ranges from 40 to 199, and the number of languages with a singleton cognate in a meaning class ranges from 20 (for the second person plural pronoun) to 126 (for translations of the concept 'small').

The effect of the choice of vocabulary on phylogeny is not well studied. Bouckaert et al. (2018) point out that the difference between Bowern and Atkinson (2012) and their phylogeny includes additional words; using an additional 20 vocabulary items changed the classification of some languages to be more in line with established subgrouping based on grammatical features. We know that loan rates affect suitability for phylogenetic inference, and that loan rates in basic vocabulary vary. We are left with Swadesh lists being the default instrument for inference, yet they are based on a list whose membership was determined by, to put it bluntly, one person's suggestion of what might be useful to diagnose remote relationships 70 years ago, not on a principled decision of stability in meaning classes.

Many factors contribute to go into making a meaning class a good or poor choice for phylogenetics. If the meaning class is too stable, there is not sufficient variation to recover and date phylogenetic splits. If a word is widely loaned, that will make the evolutionary history harder to uncover and reduce phylogenetic signal. If an item changes too fast, or there are too many singleton reflexes, there is less informative signal higher in the tree. Homoplasy (convergent evolution) is also problematic, as it it difficult to detect and can lead to false language groupings. In order to evaluate the suitability of individual meaning classes, I coded cognate sets in the material used in Bouckaert et al. (2018) and Bowern et al. (2011) for number of loan events, informativeness of phylogenetic signal (D statistic; see Fritz and Purvis 2010), number of singletons, amount of missing data, and mean and maximum meaning class size (that is, how many languages attest a particular cognate in that meaning class). Figure 3 plots the first two PCA and clusters meaning classes based on these variables, using the fviz_cluster() function in the Factoextra package in R (Kassambara and Mundt, 2017). The largest factor contributing to dimension 1 is how much data is missing, while dimension 2's largest contribution is the number of singleton cognates per meaning class. Meaning classes which score relatively highly on dimension 1 and relatively low on dimension 2 are most likely to be optimal for phylogenetic analysis. However, items solely taken from the southeast quadrant are the most stable, and therefore likely to lead to underestimates of splits.

4 Conclusion

In conclusion, evolutionary approaches to language change provide explicit ways of modeling semantic shifts and lexical replacement. They provide researchers with a structure for examining the facts of language differences, the mode and tempo of language change, and a way of framing questions to lead to an understanding of why languages change the way they do. In all this, however, variation is key – it provides the seeds of change, allows the identification of change in progress, and the absence of variation makes it possible to study stability and shift across millennia.

References

Christopher Ahern and Robin Clark. 2017. Conflict, cheap talk, and Jespersen's cycle. *Semantics and Pragmatics*, 10.

Jean Aitchison. 2003. Psycholinguistic perspectives on language change. In *The Handbook of Historical Linguistics*, chapter 25, pages 736–743. Wiley Blackwell.

Emily M. Bender. 2019. English isn't general for language, despite what NLP papers might lead you to believe. Sumposium on Data Science and Statistics, Bellevue, WA.

Juliette Blevins. 2004. *Evolutionary phonology: The emergence of sound patterns*. CUP, Cambridge.

Remco R Bouckaert, Claire Bowern, and Quentin D Atkinson. 2018. The origin and expansion of Pama–Nyungan languages across Australia. *Nature ecology & evolution*, 2:741–749.

Claire Bowern. 2018. Computational phylogenetics. *Annual Review of Linguistics*, 4:281–296.

Claire Bowern and Quentin Atkinson. 2012. Computational phylogenetics and the internal structure of Pama-Nyungan. *Language*, 88(4):817–845.

Claire Bowern, Patience Epps, Russell D. Gray, Jane Hill, Keith Hunley, Patrick McConvell, and Jason Zentz. 2011. Does lateral transmission obscure inheritance in hunter-gatherer languages? *PloS One*, 6(9):e25195.

Claire Bowern and Bethwyn Evans, editors. 2014. *Routledge Handbook of Historical Linguistics*. Routledge, Oxford.

Mary Bucholtz and Kira Hall. 2005. Identity and interaction: A sociocultural linguistic approach. *Discourse studies*, 7(4-5):585–614.

Alexandra D'Arcy. 2017. *Discourse-pragmatic variation in context: Eight hundred years of like*. John Benjamins Publishing Company.

Haim Dubossarsky, Daphna Weinshall, and Eitan Grossman. 2017. Outta control: Laws of semantic change and inherent biases in word representation models. In *Proceedings of the 2017 conference on empirical methods in natural language processing*, pages 1136–1145.

Michael Dunn. 2014. Language phylogenies. In Claire Bowern and Bethwyn Evans, editors, *The Routledge Handbook of Historical Linguistics*, pages 190–211. Routledge, London.

Jacob Eisenstein, Brendan O'Connor, Noah A Smith, and Eric P Xing. 2014. Diffusion of lexical change in social media. *PloS one*, 9(11):e113114.

John R Firth. 1957. *A synopsis of linguistic theory 1930-1955*. Oxford University Press, Oxford.

Susanne A Fritz and Andy Purvis. 2010. Selectivity in mammalian extinction risk and threat types: a new measure of phylogenetic signal strength in binary traits. *Conservation Biology*, 24(4):1042–1051.

Simon J Greenhill, Quentin D Atkinson, Andrew Meade, and Russell D Gray. 2010. The shape and tempo of language evolution. *Proceedings of the Royal Society B: Biological Sciences*, 277(1693):2443–2450.

Mark Hale. 2007. *Historical Linguistics: Theory and Method*. Blackwell Publishing.

William L Hamilton, Jure Leskovec, and Dan Jurafsky. 2016a. Cultural shift or linguistic drift? comparing two computational measures of semantic change. In *Proceedings of the Conference on Empirical Methods in Natural Language Processing*, volume 2016, page 2116. NIH Public Access.

William L Hamilton, Jure Leskovec, and Dan Jurafsky. 2016b. Diachronic word embeddings reveal statistical laws of semantic change. *arXiv preprint arXiv:1605.09096*.

Martin Haspelmath and Uri Tadmor. 2009. *Loanwords in the world's languages: a comparative handbook*. Mouton de Gruyter, Berlin.

Hannah Haynie and Claire Bowern. 2016. A phylogenetic approach to the evolution of color term systems. *PNAS*.

H. H. Hock and B. D. Joseph. 1996. *Language History, Language Change, and Language Relationship: An Introduction to Historical and Comparative Linguistics*. Mouton de Gruyter, Berlin.

Alboukadel Kassambara and Fabian Mundt. 2017. *factoextra: Extract and Visualize the Results of Multivariate Data Analyses*. R package version 1.0.5.

Vivek Kulkarni, Rami Al-Rfou, Bryan Perozzi, and Steven Skiena. 2015. Statistically significant detection of linguistic change. In *Proceedings of the 24th International Conference on World Wide Web*, WWW '15, pages 625–635, Republic and Canton of Geneva, Switzerland. International World Wide Web Conferences Steering Committee.

Andrey Kutuzov, Lilja Øvrelid, Terrence Szymanski, and Erik Velldal. 2018. Diachronic word embeddings and semantic shifts: a survey. *CoRR*, abs/1806.03537.

William Labov. 2001. *Principles of linguistic change: social factors*. Blackwell, Oxford.

David Lightfoot. 1991. *How to set parameters: Arguments from language change*. Cambridge University Press, Cambridge.

Johann-Mattis List, Anselm Terhalle, and Matthias Urban. 2013. Using network approaches to enhance the analysis of cross-linguistic polysemies. In *Proceedings of the 10th International Conference on Computational Semantics (IWCS 2013)–Short Papers*, pages 347–353.

Frank W Marlowe. 2005. Hunter-gatherers and human evolution. *Evolutionary Anthropology: Issues, News, and Reviews: Issues, News, and Reviews*, 14(2):54–67.

April McMahon and Robert McMahon. 2006. *Language classification by numbers*. Oxford University Press, Oxford.

Alex Mesoudi. 2011. *Cultural evolution*. University of Chicago Press, Chicago.

Hermann Paul. 1880. *Prinzipien der Sprachgeschichte*. Aufl. Halle.

Taraka Rama and Søren Wichmann. 2018. Towards identifying the optimal datasize for lexically-based bayesian inference of linguistic phylogenies. In *Proceedings of the 27th International Conference on Computational Linguistics*, pages 1578–1590.

Terry Regier, Paul Kay, and Richard S. Cook. 2005. Focal colors are universal after all. *Proceedings of the National Academy of Sciences*, 102:8386–8391817–845.

M. Swadesh. 1952. Lexicostatistic dating of prehistoric ethnic contacts. *Proceedings of the American Philosophical Society*, 96:452–463.

M. Swadesh. 1955. Towards greater accuracy in lexicostatistic dating. *International Journal of American Linguistics*, 21:121–137.

Nina Tahmasebi, Lars Borin, and Adam Jatowt. 2018. Survey of computational approaches to diachronic conceptual change. *arXiv preprint arXiv:1811.06278*.

E.C. Traugott and R.B. Dasher. 2002. *Regularity in Semantic Change*. CUP, Cambridge.

Peter D Turney and Patrick Pantel. 2010. From frequency to meaning: Vector space models of semantics. *J Artif Intell Res*, 37(1):141–188.

Elly Van Gelderen. 2018. *The diachrony of verb meaning: Aspect and argument structure*. Routledge.

A. Wedel. 2006. Exemplar models, evolution and language change. *The Linguistic Review*, 23(3).

A. Wedel, S. Jackson, and A. Kaplan. 2013. Functional load and the lexicon. *Language and Speech*, 56(3):395–417.

U. Weinreich, W. Labov, and M. Herzog. 1968. Empirical foundations for a theory of language change. In Lehmann & Malkiel, editor, *Directions for historical linguistics: a symposium*, pages 95–195. University of Texas Press, Austin.

Zijun Yao, Yifan Sun, Weicong Ding, Nikhil Rao, and Hui Xiong. 2018. Dynamic word embeddings for evolving semantic discovery. In *Proceedings of the Eleventh ACM International Conference on Web Search and Data Mining*, WSDM '18, pages 673–681, New York, NY, USA. ACM.

GASC: Genre-Aware Semantic Change for Ancient Greek

Valerio Perrone
Amazon, Berlin[*]
vperrone@amazon.com

Marco Palma
University of Warwick
m.palma@warwick.ac.uk

Simon Hengchen
University of Helsinki
simon.hengchen@helsinki.fi

Alessandro Vatri
University of Oxford
The Alan Turing Institute
avatri@turing.ac.uk

Jim Q. Smith
University of Warwick
The Alan Turing Institute
j.q.smith@warwick.ac.uk

Barbara McGillivray
University of Cambridge
The Alan Turing Institute
bmcgillivray@turing.ac.uk

Abstract

Word meaning changes over time, depending on linguistic and extra-linguistic factors. Associating a word's correct meaning in its historical context is a central challenge in diachronic research, and is relevant to a range of NLP tasks, including information retrieval and semantic search in historical texts. Bayesian models for semantic change have emerged as a powerful tool to address this challenge, providing explicit and interpretable representations of semantic change phenomena. However, while corpora typically come with rich metadata, existing models are limited by their inability to exploit contextual information (such as text genre) beyond the document timestamp. This is particularly critical in the case of ancient languages, where lack of data and long diachronic span make it harder to draw a clear distinction between polysemy (the fact that a word has several senses) and semantic change (the process of acquiring, losing, or changing senses), and current systems perform poorly on these languages. We develop GASC, a dynamic semantic change model that leverages categorical metadata about the texts' genre to boost inference and uncover the evolution of meanings in Ancient Greek corpora. In a new evaluation framework, our model achieves improved predictive performance compared to the state of the art.

1 Introduction

Change and its precondition, variation, are inherent in languages. Over time, new words enter the lexicon, others become obsolete, and existing words acquire new senses. These changes are grounded in cognitive, social, and contextual factors, and can be realized in different ways. For example, in Old English *thing* meant 'a public assembly'[1]

and currently it more generally means 'entity'. Semantic change research has a number of practical applications, beyond historical linguistics research, including new sense detection in computational lexicography and information retrieval for historical texts that allows to restrict a search to certain word senses (e.g. the old sense of the English adjective *nice* as 'silly'). To take an example from recent semantic change in English, the verb *tweet* used to be uniquely associated with birds' sounds and has recently acquired a new sense related to the social media platform Twitter. However, in this as in many other cases, the original sense co-exists with the new one, and specific contexts or genres will select one over the other. This is known as synchronic variation, and can be successfully modelled probabilistically, as advocated by several authors (see e.g. Jenset and McGillivray (2017)). The close relationship between innovation and variation is well-known in historical linguistics, and critical to ancient languages. Indeed, the unavailability of balanced corpora due to the limited amount of data at our disposal makes it crucial for models to explicitly account for confounding variables like genre, so as to enable them to use all existing data.

To address these challenges, we introduce GASC (**G**enre-**A**ware **S**emantic **C**hange), a novel dynamic Bayesian mixture model for semantic change. In this model, the evolution of word senses over time is based not only on distributional information of lexical nature, but also on additional features, specifically genre. This allows GASC to decouple sense probabilities and genre prevalence, which is critical with genre-unbalanced data such as ancient languages corpora. The value of incorporating genre information in the model goes beyond literary corpora and historical language data and can be applied to recent data spanning over a period of time where text type information is critical, for example in specialized domains. Explicitly mod-

---

[*]Work done prior to joining Amazon.

[1]In the remainder of this paper, we use *emphasis* to refer to a word and 'single quotes' for any of its senses.

Proceedings of the 1st International Workshop on Computational Approaches to Historical Language Change, pages 56–66
Florence, Italy, August 2, 2019. ©2019 Association for Computational Linguistics

elling genres also makes it possible to address a number of additional questions, revealing the genre most likely associated to a given sense, the most unusual sense for a genre, and which genres have the most similar senses. Naturally, this framework can be applied to different categorical metadata about the text, such as author, geography, or style.

Ancient Greek is an insightful test case for several reasons. First, Ancient Greek words tend to have a particularly high number of senses (Clarke, 2010), and Ancient Greek texts display a large number of literary genres. Second, we can use data spanning several centuries. Third, Ancient Greek scholarship provides high-quality data to validate automatic systems. Top-quality transcribed Ancient Greek texts are available, eliminating the need for OCR correction. Finally, polysemous words are particularly sensitive to register variation and the distribution of senses can vary greatly across registers (Leiwo et al., 2012). As most extant texts are literary and relatively conservative from a linguistic perspective, we expect genre (the type of a text) and register (the fact that different varieties of language are used in particular situations) to play a significant role in the variation of sense distributions in polysemous words. The word *mus*, for instance, can mean 'mouse', 'muscle', or 'mussel'. The effect of genre on the distribution of its meaning can be estimated visually from Figure 1. In this graph, lines represent the percentage of the occurrences of the target word in a literary genre across centuries, while bars represent the percentage of the occurrences of a specific sense of the target word across centuries. If any line shows a similar trend to that of any set of bars, we may estimate that genre might play a more decisive role than diachrony in determining variation in the distribution of senses. Here, the distribution of 'muscle' over time (pink bars) closely follows the distribution of this word in technical genres over time (blue line), suggesting that the effect of genre should be incorporated into semantic change models.

2   Related work

Semantic change in historical languages, especially on a large scale and over a long time period, is an under-explored, but impactful research area. Previous work has mainly been qualitative in nature, due to the complexity of the phenomenon (cf. e.g. Leiwo et al. (2012). In recent years, NLP research has made great advances in the area of semantic change detection and modelling (for an overview of the NLP literature, see Tang (2018) and Tahmasebi et al. (2018)), with methods ranging from topic-based models (Boyd-Graber et al., 2007; Cook et al., 2014; Lau et al., 2014; Wijaya and Yeniterzi, 2011; Frermann and Lapata, 2016), to graph-based models (Mitra et al., 2014, 2015; Tahmasebi and Risse, 2017), and word embeddings (Kim et al., 2014; Basile and McGillivray, 2018; Kulkarni et al., 2015; Hamilton et al., 2016; Dubossarsky et al., 2017; Tahmasebi, 2018; Rudolph and Blei, 2018; Jatowt et al., 2018; Dubossarsky et al., 2019). However, such models are purely based on words' lexical distribution information and do not account for language variation features such as text type because genre-balanced corpora are typically used.

With the exception of Bamman and Crane (2011) and Rodda et al. (2017), no previous work has focussed on ancient languages. Recent work on languages other than English is rare but exists: Falk et al. (2014) use topic models to detect changes in French and Hengchen (2017) uses similar methods to tackle Dutch. Cavallin (2012) and Tahmasebi (2018) focus on Swedish, with the comparison of verb-object pairs and word embeddings, respectively. Zampieri et al. (2016) use SVMs to assign a time period to text snippets in Portuguese, and Tang et al. (2016) work on Chinese newspapers using S-shaped models. Most work in this area focusses on simply detecting the occurrence of semantic change, while Frermann and Lapata (2016)'s system, SCAN, takes into account synchronic polysemy and models how the different word senses evolve across time.

Our work bears important connections with the topic model literature. The idea of enriching topic models with document-specific author meta-data was explored in Rosen-Zvi et al. (2004) for the static case. Several time-dependent extensions of Bayesian topic models have been developed, with a number of parametric and nonparametric approaches (Blei and Lafferty, 2006; Rao and Teh, 2009; Ahmed and Xing, 2012; Dubey et al., 2013; Perrone et al., 2017). In this paper, we transfer such ideas to semantic change, where each datapoint is a bag of words associated to a single sense (rather than a mixture of topics). Excluding cases of intentional ambiguity, which we expect to be rare, we can safely assume that there are generally no ambiguities in a context, and each word instance

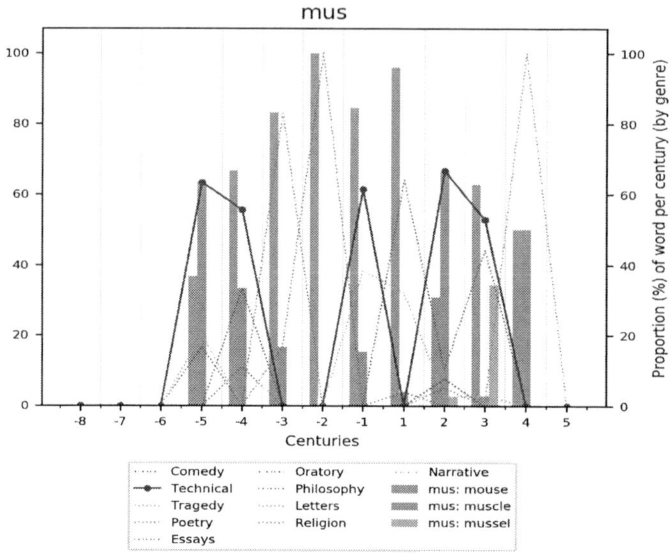

Figure 1: Distribution of *mus* 'mouse'/'muscle'/'mussel' by genre vs its senses over time. Lines track *mus* proportions in each genre and century, while bars show the *mus* occurrence proportions with each sense and century.

maps to a single sense.

3 The model

We start with a lemmatized corpus pre-processed into a set of text snippets, each containing an instance of the word under study (referred to as "target word" in the remainder). Each snippet is a fixed-sized window W of 5 words to the left and right of the target word. The inferential task is to detect the sense associated to the target word in the given context, and describe the evolution of sense proportions over time.

The generative model for GASC is presented in Algorithm 1 and illustrated by the plate diagram in Figure 2. First, suppose that throughout the corpus the target word is used with K different senses, where we define a sense at time t as a distribution ψ_k^t over words from the dictionary. These distributions are used to generate text snippets by drawing each of their words from the dictionary based on a Multinomial distribution (line 13 in Algorithm 1). Based on the intuition that each genre is more or less likely to feature a given sense, we assume that each of G possible text genres determines a different distribution over senses (lines 3-4). Each observed document snippet is then associated with a genre-specific distribution over senses $\phi_{g^d}^t$ at time t, where g^d is the observed genre for document d. Crucially, conditioning on the observed genre we have a specific distribution over senses account-

ing for genre-specific word usage patterns (line 11). On the other hand, to make sure senses can be uniquely identified across genres, we associate each sense to the same probability distribution over words for all genres. We let word (line 7) and sense distributions (line 4) evolve over time with Gaussian changes, ensuring smooth transitions. The coupling between sense probabilities over time is controlled by K^ϕ, the sense probability precision parameter, so that the larger K^ϕ, the stronger the coupling between the sense probabilities over time. We place a Gamma prior over K^ϕ with hyperparameters a and b (line 1), and infer K^ϕ from the data. We fix K^ψ, the word probability precision parameter.

Hyperparameter settings The model can be applied to different inferential goals: we can focus on the evolution of sense probabilities or on the changes within each sense. For each of these aims, we can use several hyperparameter combinations for K^ϕ, which is drawn from the prior distribution as determined by a and b, and K^ψ. Specifically, we consider the following 3 settings. Setting 1: $a = 7, b = 3, K^\psi = 10$, as in Frermann and Lapata (2016). Setting 2: $a = 7, b = 3, K^\psi = 100$. This aims at enforcing less variation within senses over time. Setting 3: $a = b = 1, K^\psi = 100$. This still keeps the bag of words stable for each sense, but also induces less smoothing for sense probabilities over time. Setting 3 allows probabilities to vary widely across centuries. We also expect a large K^ψ to reduce the likelihood of dramatic changes within the same sense across contiguous time periods, and to favour the emergence of new senses. If not otherwise specified, we use setting 3. Other settings (like setting 3 with $K^\psi = 10$) are not recommended since allowing relevant changes over time both in sense probabilities and bag of words might harm interpretability. A final parameter is the window size W, namely the number of words surrounding an instance of the target. While larger windows increase the range of captured dependencies, noise can be introduced in the form of irrelevant contextual words. As in SCAN, we fixed the window size W to 5 for all methods.

Algorithm 1: GASC generative model

---

1   Draw $K^\phi \sim Gamma(a, b)$;

2   **for** *time $t = 1, \ldots, T$* **do**

3   **for** *genre $g = 1, \ldots, G$* **do**

4   Draw sense distribution $\phi_g^t \mid \phi_g^{-t}, K^\phi \sim N(\frac{1}{2}(\phi_g^{t-1} + \phi_g^{t+1}), K^\phi)$

5   **end**

6   **for** *sense $k = 1, \ldots, K$* **do**

7   Draw word distribution $\psi_k^t \mid \psi^{-t}, K^\psi \sim N(\frac{1}{2}(\psi_k^{t-1} + \psi_k^{t+1}), K^\psi)$

8   **end**

9   **for** *document $d = 1, \ldots, D_t$* **do**

10   Let g^d be the observed genre;

11   Draw sense $z^d \mid g^d \sim \text{Mult}(\text{softmax}(\phi_{g^d}^t))$;

12   **for** *context position $i = 1, \ldots, W$* **do**

13   Draw word $w^{d,i} \sim \text{Mult}(\text{softmax}(\psi^{t,z^d}))$;

14   **end**

15   **end**

16 **end**

Posterior inference   For posterior inference, we extend the blocked Gibbs sampler proposed in Frermann and Lapata (2016). The full conditional is available for the snippet-sense assignment, while to sample the sense and word distributions we adopt the auxiliary variable approach from Mimno et al. (2008). The sense precision parameters are drawn from their conjugate Gamma priors. For the distribution over genres we proceed as follows. First, sample the distribution over senses ϕ_g^t for each genre $g = 1, \ldots, G$ following Mimno et al. (2008).

Then, sample the sense assignment conditioned on the observed genre from its full conditional: $p(z^d \mid g^d, \mathbf{w}, t, \phi, \psi) \propto p(z^d \mid g^d, t)p(\mathbf{w} \mid t, z^d) = \phi_g^t \prod_{w \in \mathbf{w}} \psi_w^{t,z^d}$. This setting easily extends to sample genre assignments for tasks where, for example, some genre metadata are missing.

4   Evaluation framework

Evaluating models tackling lexical semantic change is notoriously challenging. Frameworks are either lacking or focus on very specific types of sense change (Schlechtweg et al., 2018; Tahmasebi et al., 2018). Exceptions are Kulkarni et al. (2015), Basile and McGillivray (2018) and Hamilton et al. (2016), who focus on the change points of word senses. However, in the case of Ancient Greek (and other historical languages), corpora typically contain gaps and uneven distribution of text genres, and semantic change is so closely related to polysemy that it is hard to find a specific point in time when a new sense emerged in the language. Therefore, it is more appropriate to take a probabilistic approach to model sense distribution, and devise an evaluation approach that fits this. Although historical dictionaries and traditional philology describe the evolution of word senses over time, they do not necessarily reflect the evidence from corpora on which models can be evaluated, and often only provide insights into the appearance of a new sense, rather than the relative predominance of a word's senses across time. These reasons led us to craft a novel evaluation dataset and framework, which reflects the data on which the model is evaluated, and allows for a finer-grained evaluation of the predominance of word senses across time.

4.1   Ancient Greek corpus

We used the Diorisis Annotated Ancient Greek Corpus (Vatri and McGillivray, 2018), consisting of 10,206,421 lemmatized and part-of-speech-tagged words. The corpus contains 820 texts spanning between the beginnings of the Ancient Greek literary tradition (8th century BC) and the 5th century AD. The corpus covers a number of Ancient Greek literary and technical genres: poetry (narrative, choral, epigrams, didactic), drama (tragedy, comedy), oratory, philosophy, essays, narrative (historiography, biography, mythography, novels), geography, religious texts (hymns, Jewish and Christian Scriptures, theology, homilies), technical literature (medicine, mathematics, natural science,

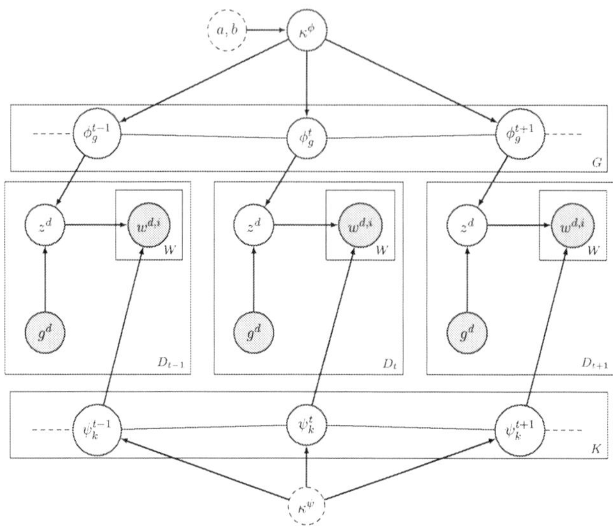

Figure 2: GASC plate diagram with 3 time periods.

tactics, astronomy, horsemanship, hunting, politics, art history, rhetoric, literary criticism, grammar), and letters. In technical texts, we expect polysemous words to have a technical sense. On the other hand, in works more closely representing general language (comedy, oratory, historiography) we expect words to appear in their more concrete and less metaphorical senses; we cannot assume that this distribution holds in a number of other genres such as philosophy and tragedy. Whilst genre-annotated corpora are not especially common in NLP, where most tasks rely on specific genres (e.g. Twitter) or on genre-balanced corpora such as COHA (Davies, 2002), they are more prevailing within humanities, and especially classics. Additionally, research on automated genre identification has been flourishing for decades (e.g. Kessler et al. (1997)), making the need for genre information in a potential corpus not as much of a hindrance as can be thought.

4.2 Log-likelihood evaluation

First, we compared GASC with the state-of-the-art (SCAN) in terms of held-out data log-likelihood. We chose 50 targets that could be identified as polysemous (e.g. the verb *legō*, whose senses are 'gather' and 'tell') based on two criteria: high frequency and a a suitably clear-cut range of meanings. We initially based our selection on the secondary literature and chose 17 words from the well-studied vocabulary of Ancient Greek aesthetics (Pollitt, 1974). We complemented this selection with the inclusion of the 33 most frequent clearly polysemous words identified by an Ancient Greek expert

in a frequency-ranked word list extracted from the Diorisis corpus. The necessity to identify manually suitable words led us to limit their number to 50. For each one of these target words, we randomly divided the corpus into a train (80%) and test set (20%). Results on the 50-word dataset are in Section 5.

4.3 Expert annotation

To evaluate our method against ground truth, we proceeded as follows. We selected three three target words (*mus* 'mouse'/'muscle'/'mussel' and *harmonia* 'fastening'/'agreement'/'musical scale, melody', and *kosmos* 'order'/'world'/'decoration') based on their frequency and clear-cut polysemy, as indicated by the standard scholarly Ancient Greek-English dictionary (Liddell et al., 1996) and traditional philological scholarship on their semantics (Pollitt 1974 on *harmonia* and *kosmos*). These words are especially suitable for an exploratory case study because they exhibit an abstract sense and a concrete counterpart in general, non-technical vocabulary, and are attested in most of the time periods covered by the corpus and across different literary genres. Two Ancient Greek experts manually annotated the whole corpus by tagging the senses of the target words in context. One expert selected the correct sense for each occurrence of *mus* and *harmonia*, and the other expert performed the same task on *kosmos*. The results of each expert's annotation task were not reviewed by the other expert (Vatri et al. 2019 for the dataset). Table 1 shows an example from the annotated dataset for the word *kosmos*. The annotators also marked when the semantic annotation was purely based on the target word context, which is the evidence on which the model can rely (category "collocates"). Only annotations based on collocates were retained in the evaluation. Using this information, the relative frequency of each sense for each target word in any time slice becomes computable, and was used to create ground-truth data on the diachronic predominance of a word's senses as reflected in the corpus.

4.4 Automatic sense labelling

For every time period T, inferred sense k, and genre G, GASC outputs a distribution of words with associated probabilities. For instance, the output for *kosmos* ('order', 'world', or 'decoration') in oratory at time 0 includes:

```
T=0,k=0:
aêr (0.069); mousikos (0.059); gê (0.056); harmonia
    (0.034); ouranos (0.033); logos (0.030);
    gignomai (0.021); sphaira (0.021); pselion
    (0.020); apaiteô (0.019);
T=0,k=1:
polis (0.035); asebeia (0.014); politeia (0.012);
    proteros (0.012); naus (0.012); pentêkonta
    (0.011); aei (0.011); hama (0.011) ; peripeteia
    (0.011); oikia (0.011).
```

These distributions can be interpreted by experts based on the meanings of the words they group and thus associated to the senses of the target word. Here, $K = 0$ includes *aêr* ('air'), *gê* ('earth'), *ouranos* ('sky'), and *sphaira* ('sphere, globe'), which point to the meaning of *kosmos* as 'world'. The list for $K = 1$ includes *polis* ('city'), *asebeia* ('impiety'), *politeia* ('constitution'), and *oikia* ('household'), which point to the meaning of *kosmos* as 'order'. On the other hand, the expert annotation provides lists of corpus occurrences of the target word, each associated to a sense label. In Table 1, the sense label is 'kosmos-world' and we can associate lemmas such as *ouranos* 'sky' and *sphairoeides* 'spherical' to this sense, as these lemmas occur in the corpus context of this target word.

To evaluate against expert annotation, we automatically match the word senses assigned by the annotators (denoted by s) with the senses outputted by the model (denoted by k). To achieve this, we first measured how closely each model sense k matches each expert sense s. We assigned a confidence score to every possible (k, s) pair by comparing the words associated to k in the model output and the words co-occurring with the target word in the annotated corpus sentences labelled with the expert-assigned sense s. For *kosmos* with $k = 0$,

we compare words from the model output, such as *ouranos* 'sky', *gê* 'earth', and *sphaira* 'sphere' with words from the context of the annotated sentences, such as *sphairoeides* 'spherical' and *ouranos* 'sky'. We then considered two elements. For words from the model output, we consider the normalized probability with which these words w_i are associated to the model sense k, i.e. $P(w_i|k)$. For *kosmos*, *aêr* 'air' is associated to probability 0.069, *gê* 'earth' to 0.056, and *ouranos* 'sky' to 0.033. For the context words from the annotated data, we consider the degree to which these words are associated to an expert sense. In the example of *kosmos* from Table 1, this is calculated based on how many different senses a context word like *ouranos* 'sky' or *sphairoeides* 'spherical' is associated to. To measure this degree of association we define the expert score $m(w_i, s)$ of word w_i as 1 divided by the number of senses assigned by the experts to this word. If the word is associated to only one sense s in the annotated data, its expert score $m(w_i, s)$ will be highest (1); if it is associated to two senses, its expert score is 0.5; if it is not assigned to the sense s by the experts, its expert score $m(w_i, s)$ is 0. Formally, we define the confidence score of a pair of model sense k and expert-assigned sense s as $\mathrm{conf}(k, s) = \sum_i P(w_i|k) * m(w_i, s)$. The score is highest when $P(w_i)$ and $m(w_i, s)$ are highest for all words. In extreme cases, $P(w_i)$ will be 1 if the model estimated w_i to be associated to sense k with probability 1 and $m(w_i, s)$ is 1 (i.e. w_i is only found in contexts labelled as s by the experts). This points to k and s being associated to the same words, and thus being the same sense. The confidence is lowest when k and s do not share words, in which case either $P(w_i) = 0$ or $m(w_i, s) = 0$. In contrast with clustering overlap techniques like purity or rand index, we ensure words with a higher inferred probability and uniquely associated to a sense weigh more. The confidence scores were used to find the best matching pair (k, s): for every expert sense s we selected the sense(s) k for which $\mathrm{conf}(k, s)$ was higher than the random baseline (1 over the number of expert senses) and higher than the sum of the 2d and 3rd best confidence scores, when possible, or assigned NA when both conditions were not matched. We consider NA as an additional expert sense whenever the expert assigned a sense based on other factors than lexical context.

After matching inferred and expert-assigned

date	genre	author	work	target word	sense id
-335	Technical	Aristotle	De Mundo	kosmos	kosmos:world

Table 1: Example from annotated dataset displaying *Tou de sumpantos ouranou te kai kosmou sphairoeidous ontos kai kinoumenou kathaper eipon* ("The whole of the heaven, the whole cosmos, is spherical, and moves continuously, as I have said"), containing the target *kosmos* and its expert-assigned sense 'world' (date: 335 B. C.).

senses, we computed precision and recall. For every target word and matched pair (s, k), a word is considered correctly assigned to sense k if it also appeared within a 5-word window of the target word in the expert annotation for s. In the example above for *kosmos*, $k = 0$ and s='kosmos-world', one such word is *ouranos* 'sky' as it appears in the model output for $k = 0$ and in the context window of a sentence labelled as 'kosmos-world' by the annotators. Moreover, we weighted each word by the inferred probability to account for the different degrees of association of words to senses. Specifically, we defined precision as the ratio between the number of words correctly assigned to k, weighted by their respective normalised model-estimated probabilities, and the number of words assigned to k by the model. This metric is based on the distributional hypothesis whereby words occurring in similar contexts tend to exhibit similar meanings. We computed precision after stop word removal, limiting the noise from uninformative contextual words. We defined precision in terms of the words assigned to a sense also appearing within a 5-word window of the target in the expert annotation. Our model, as SCAN, only considers those context words to determine word senses, and for the ground truth evaluation we only retained the cases in which the annotators could disambiguate words based purely on their context. We defined recall as the ratio between the number of all words correctly assigned to k (weighted by their probabilities) and number of words assigned to sense s by the experts (weighted by their expert scores). For each model, precision and recall scores for each (s, k) pair were averaged and used as final scores. Since recall directly depends on the number of expert words, the metric can only be used to compare models for a specific target word. While the proposed assessment focusses on dynamic mixture models, it can be generalised to any probabilistic model by considering the posterior probability of the gold word sense.

5 Experiments

Predictions on held-out words Considering the 50-word dataset described in Section 4, we evaluated the predictive performance in terms of log-likelihood of held-out data for SCAN (not using any genre information), GASC-all (GASC with all the $G = 10$ available genres) and GASC-narr (GASC with 2 genres, Narrative vs. non Narrative). Narrative and Technical are such that all 50 words occurred at least once in the training and test sets, and analogous results are obtained when GASC with Technical vs. non Technical. For each model, we compared the 3 hyperparameter settings previously reported, with higher scores indicating that a model is better at explaining unseen data.

Figure 3 shows predictive log-likelihood scores for a range of K, with the results averaged over 50 leave-one-out folds. Each time, the scores were averaged under the final 10 samples of the latent variables, out of 1000 MCMC iterations. On average, GASC-narr consistently outperforms SCAN across every K and hyperparameter setting. On the other hand, SCAN has a higher held-out log-likelihood than GASC-all. Exploiting some information on the genre yields better predictions, while using all genres attested in the corpus is not effective as some genres are not sufficiently represented by the data. Figure 3 also shows that the best predictions over unseen data are obtained for K between 10 and 15. Higher K values tend to introduce noisy senses with no improvement for the model output. In addition, Setting 3 worked better or on par with other settings. In the next section, we fix the hyperparameters and use a validation set of words that were not part of the 50 targets of this experiment.

Ground truth recovery We explored the ability to recover ground truth when available. For *mus*, experts annotated 205 instances, of which 198 were assigned to one of the 3 senses 'mouse', 'mussel', and 'muscle'; out of these 198 assignments, 114 were based on lexical contextual information only (category 'collocates') and were retained for the evaluation. For *harmonia*, the number of annotated occurrences was 599, of which 411 were of the type

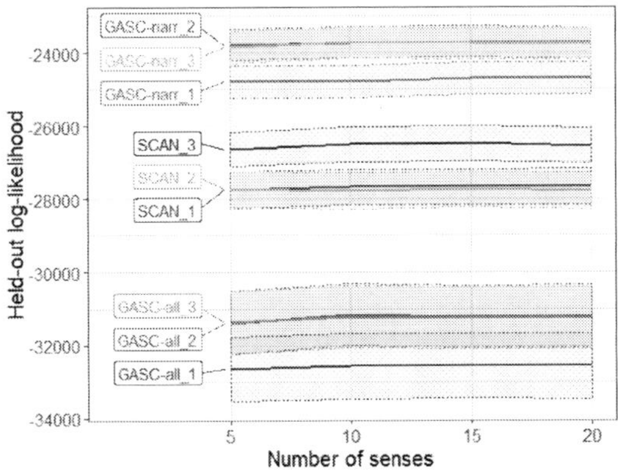

Figure 3: Held-out mean log-likelihood varying K (the larger, the better). Shaded areas are ± 1 standard error.

harmonia	'agreement, harmony'	Technical ($\rho = 0.888$, p < 0.0001) Narrative ($\rho = 0.719$, p $= 0.006$) Essays ($\rho = 0.561$, p $= 0.046$)
	'fastening'	Narrative ($\rho = 0.663$, p $= 0.013$)
	'stringing, music scale'	Technical ($\rho = 0.817$, p $= 0.001$) Philosophy ($\rho = 0.632$, p $= 0.02$) Essays ($\rho = 0.598$, p $= 0.031$)
kosmos	'decoration'	Narrative ($\rho = 0.887$, p $= 0.001$) Technical ($\rho = 0.705$, p $= 0.023$) Oratory ($\rho = 0.664$, p $= 0.036$)
	'order'	Technical ($\rho = 0.875$, p $= 0.001$) Narrative ($\rho = 0.862$, p $= 0.001$
	'world'	Technical ($\rho = 0.792$, p $= 0.006$) Oratory ($\rho = 0.723$, p $= 0.018$)
mus	'mouse'	Narrative ($\rho = 0.813$, p $= 0.001$) Essays ($\rho = 0.743$, p $= 0.004$)
	'muscle'	Technical ($\rho = 0.766$, p $= 0.002$)
	'mussel'	Narrative ($\rho = 0.736$, p $= 0.004$) Essays ($\rho = 0.736$, p $= 0.004$) Poetry ($\rho = 0.613$, p $= 0.026$)

Table 2: Correlations between senses and genres for manually annotated target words.

'collocates'. For *kosmos*, 1,411 occurrences were annotated, of which 1,406 were assigned to a sense, and in 1,102 cases the annotation was of the type 'collocates'. Only the annotations of the type 'collocates' were kept for the expert sense distribution, and thus for the evaluation. We identified genres with the largest effect on the distribution of senses by the Spearman's Rank Correlation Coefficient for each word-sense s between the frequency $f(s)$ of s across centuries and the frequency $f(s, g)$ of s in each genre g across centuries (Table 2). Significant correlation between $f(s)$ and any $f(s, g)$ suggests that variation in the frequency of a word sense across centuries is not due to diachronic change, but to how frequently s is attested in g in each century (and, ultimately, to the amount of texts representing g in each century). Given the amount of available data and the size of the correlations, we considered the genres Technical and non-Technical for *mus* and *harmonia*, and both Technical and

non-Technical and Narrative and non-Narrative for *kosmos*. These words were selected as examples of polysemous words (a) with a range of clearly distinct senses (such as 'mus', whose three senses are strikingly diverse), (b) attested in most, if not all, the time periods covered by the corpus, and (c) attested across a number of genres. As expert annotations of semantic change in Ancient Greek corpora are virtually unavailable, this choice also allowed us to leverage ground truth for validation.

We compared SCAN with GASC and GASC-independent, a simpler version that fits independent models to sets of documents sharing the same genre, so that parameters and senses are inferred independently across genres (while in GASC senses are shared but their probability distributions are independent across genres). First, we compared word senses across time with expert-annotated data. Figure 4 shows the time distribution of the senses of *kosmos* in the expert annotation (top) and as outputted by SCAN and GASC run on Narrative vs. non-Narrative (bottom). For non-narrative texts, the GASC sense distribution successfully captures the 'world' sense arising only after 400 BC, which is less clear for SCAN. Second, we computed precision, recall, and F1 scores (the harmonic mean of precision and recall) to determine how closely the words assigned to a sense match the ones assigned by experts (Table 3). For GASC, the values average precision, recall, and F1-score for {Technical, non-Technical} for *mus* and *harmonia* and {Narrative, Non-Narrative} for *kosmos*. The results show that, for the most represented targets, genre information improves the ability to recover the ground truth.

6   Conclusion

We introduced GASC, a Bayesian model to study the evolution of word senses in ancient texts. We performed this analysis conditional on the text genre, demonstrating that the ability to harness genre metadata addresses a fundamental challenge in disambiguating word senses in ancient Greek. In experiments we showed that GASC provides interpretable representations of the evolution of word senses, and achieves improved predictive performance compared to the state of the art. Further, we established a new framework to assess model accuracy against expert judgement. To our knowledge, no previous work has systematically compared the estimates from a statistical model to manual semantic annotations of ancient texts.

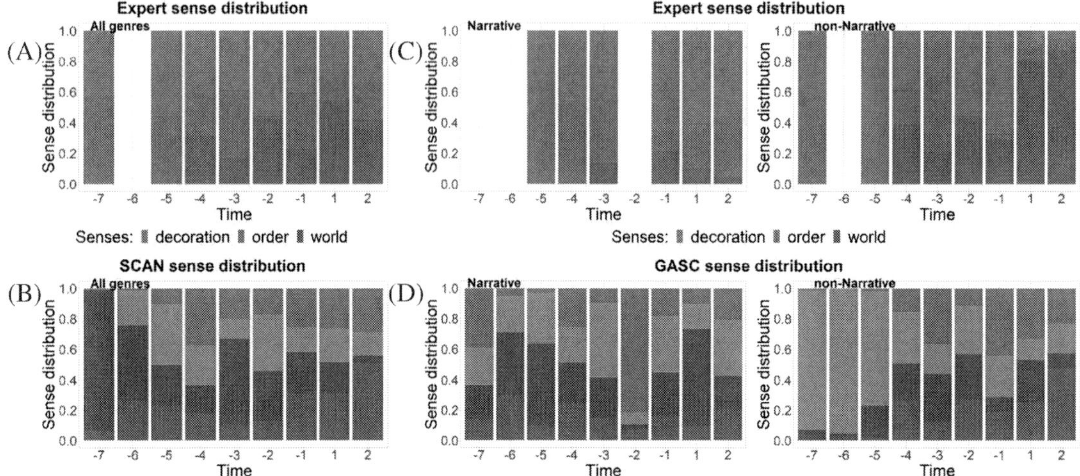

Figure 4: Expert annotation (top) vs SCAN and GASC (bottom). Each stacked bar represents all *kosmos* occurrences in a given time. Colours denoting senses are matched between plots. Both shades of orange map to 'order', but the fourth sense in (B) and (D) is NA (i.e., $\mathrm{conf}(k, s)$ not higher than the random baseline and not higher than the sum of 2nd and 3rd best confidence scores).

Word/Model	SCAN			GASC-independent			GASC		
	P	R	F1	P	R	F1	P	R	F1
mus	**0.430**	**0.477**	**0.452**	0.420	0.442	0.431	0.224	0.298	0.253
harmonia	0.527	0.708	0.603	**0.582**	**0.729**	**0.646**	0.497	0.481	0.484
kosmos	0.405	0.586	0.478	0.362	0.447	0.399	**0.525**	**0.611**	**0.595**

Table 3: SCAN vs GASC on *mus* ('mouse', 'muscle', 'mussel'), *harmonia* ('abstract', 'concrete', 'musical'), and *kosmos* ('order', 'decoration', 'world') in terms of precision ('P'), recall ('R'), and F1-score ('F1').

This work can be seen as a step towards the development of richer evaluation schemes and models that can embed expert judgement. Future work could encode more structured cross-genre dependencies, or allow for change points that occur in the light of exogenous forces by historical events.

Acknowledgements

This work was supported by The Alan Turing Institute under the EPSRC grant EP/N510129/1 and the seed funding grant SF042. We would also like to thank Viivi Lähteenoja for her work on the annotation of the word *kosmos*, Dr Lea Frermann for her advice, Prof Geoff Nicholls for his insights on the model, as well as the anonymous reviewers for their helpful comments.

References

Amr Ahmed and Eric P. Xing. 2012. Timeline: A dynamic hierarchical Dirichlet process model for recovering birth/death and evolution of topics in text stream. *UAI*, abs/1203.3463.

David Bamman and Gregory Crane. 2011. Measuring Historical Word Sense Variation. *Proceedings of the 11th ACM/IEEE-CS Joint Conference on Digital Libraries*, pages 1–10.

Pierpaolo Basile and Barbara McGillivray. 2018. *Discovery Science*, volume 11198 of *Lecture Notes in Computer Science*, chapter Exploiting the Web for Semantic Change Detection. Springer-Verlag.

David M. Blei and John D. Lafferty. 2006. Dynamic topic models. *ICML*, pages 113–120.

Jordan Boyd-Graber, David M. Blei, and Xiaojin Zhu. 2007. A topic model for word sense disambiguation. *EMNLP*.

Karin Cavallin. 2012. Automatic extraction of potential examples of semantic change using lexical sets. In *KONVENS*, pages 370–377.

Michael Clarke. 2010. Register Variation. In Egbert J. Bakker, editor, *A companion to the Ancient Greek language*, pages 120–33. Wiley-Blackwell, Chichester/Malden, Mass.

Paul Cook, Jey Han Lau, Diana McCarthy, and Timothy Baldwin. 2014. Novel word-sense identification. In *Proceedings of COLING 2014, the 25th International Conference on Computational Linguistics: Technical Papers*, pages 1624–1635.

Mark Davies. 2002. *The Corpus of Historical American English (COHA): 400 million words, 1810-2009.* Brigham Young University.

Avinava Dubey, Ahmed Hefny, Sinead Williamson, and Eric P. Xing. 2013. A Nonparametric Mixture Model for Topic Modeling over Time. *SDM*, pages 530–538.

Haim Dubossarsky, Simon Hengchen, Nina. Tahmasebi, and Dominik Schlechtweg. 2019. Time-out: Temporal referencing for robust modeling of lexical semantic change. In *Proceedings of the 57th Annual Meeting of the Association for Computational Linguistics (Volume 1: Long Papers)*, Florence, Italy. Association for Computational Linguistics.

Haim Dubossarsky, Daphna Weinshall, and Eitan Grossman. 2017. Outta control: Laws of semantic change and inherent biases in word representation models. In *Proceedings of the 2017 Conference on Empirical Methods in Natural Language Processing*, pages 1136–1145.

Ingrid Falk, Delphine Bernhard, and Christophe Gérard. 2014. De la quenelle culinaire à la quenelle politique : identification de changements sémantiques à l'aide des Topic Models. In *21ème conférence sur le Traitement Automatique des Langues Naturelles*, page 443.

Lea Frermann and Mirella Lapata. 2016. A Bayesian model of diachronic meaning change. *Transactions of the Association for Computational Linguistics*, 4:31–45.

William L Hamilton, Jure Leskovec, and Dan Jurafsky. 2016. Diachronic word embeddings reveal statistical laws of semantic change. In *Proceedings of the 54th Annual Meeting of the Association for Computational Linguistics*, volume 1, pages 1489–1501.

Simon Hengchen. 2017. *When Does it Mean?: Detecting Semantic Change in Historical Texts*. Ph.D. thesis, Université libre de Bruxelles.

Adam Jatowt, Ricardo Campos, Sourav S Bhowmick, Nina Tahmasebi, and Antoine Doucet. 2018. Every word has its history: Interactive exploration and visualization of word sense evolution. In *Proceedings of the 27th ACM International Conference on Information and Knowledge Management*, pages 1899–1902. ACM.

Gard B. Jenset and Barbara McGillivray. 2017. *Quantitative Historical Linguistics. A Corpus Framework*. Oxford University Press, Oxford.

Brett Kessler, Geoffrey Numberg, and Hinrich Schütze. 1997. Automatic detection of text genre. In *Proceedings of the eighth conference on European chapter of the Association for Computational Linguistics*, pages 32–38. Association for Computational Linguistics.

Yoon Kim, Yi-I Chiu, Kentaro Hanaki, Darshan Hegde, and Slav Petrov. 2014. Temporal analysis of language through neural language models. *ACL 2014*, page 61.

Vivek Kulkarni, Rami Al-Rfou, Bryan Perozzi, and Steven Skiena. 2015. Statistically significant detection of linguistic change. In *Proceedings of the 24th International Conference on World Wide Web*, pages 625–635. International World Wide Web Conferences Steering Committee.

Jey Han Lau, Paul Cook, Diana McCarthy, Spandana Gella, and Timothy Baldwin. 2014. Learning word sense distributions, detecting unattested senses and identifying novel senses using topic models. In *Proceedings of the 52nd Annual Meeting of the Association for Computational Linguistics (Volume 1: Long Papers)*, volume 1, pages 259–270.

Martti Leiwo, Hilla Halla-aho, and Marja Vierros. 2012. *Variation and Change in Greek and Latin. Papers and monographs of the Finnish Institute at Athens*. Foundation of the Finnish Institute at Athens, Helsinki.

Henry George Liddell, Robert Scott, Henry Stuart Jones, and Roderick McKenzie. 1996. *A Greek-English lexicon*, 9th ed. edition. Clarendon PressOxford University Press, Oxford New York.

David Mimno, Hanna Wallach, and Andrew McCallum. 2008. Gibbs sampling for logistic normal topic models with graph-based priors. In *NIPS workshop*.

Sunny Mitra, Ritwik Mitra, Suman Kalyan Maity, Martin Riedl, Chris Biemann, Pawan Goyal, and Animesh Mukherjee. 2015. An automatic approach to identify word sense changes in text media across timescales. *Natural Language Engineering*, 21(5):773–798.

Sunny Mitra, Ritwik Mitra, Martin Riedl, Chris Biemann, Animesh Mukherjee, and Pawan Goyal. 2014. That's sick dude!: Automatic identification of word sense change across different timescales. In *Proceedings of the 52nd Annual Meeting of the Association for Computational Linguistics (Volume 1: Long Papers)*, volume 1, pages 1020–1029.

Valerio Perrone, Paul A. Jenkins, Dario Spanò, and Yee Whye Teh. 2017. Poisson random fields for dynamic feature models. *Journal of Machine Learning Research*, 18(127):1–45.

Jerome Jordan Pollitt. 1974. *The ancient view of Greek art: criticism, history, and terminology*. Number 26 in Yale publications in the history of art. Yale University Press, New Haven. OCLC: 299700455.

Vinayak Rao and Yee Whye Teh. 2009. Spatial normalized gamma processes. In *Advances in neural information processing systems*, pages 1554–1562.

Martina A. Rodda, Marco S.G. Senaldi, and Alessandro Lenci. 2017. Panta Rei: Tracking Semantic Change with Distributional Semantics in Ancient Greek. *Italian Journal of Computational Linguistics*, 3:11–24.

Michal Rosen-Zvi, Thomas Griffiths, Mark Steyvers, and Padhraic Smyth. 2004. The author-topic model for authors and documents. *Proceedings of the 20th Conference on Uncertainty in Artificial Intelligence*, pages 487–494.

Maja Rudolph and David Blei. 2018. Dynamic embeddings for language evolution. In *Proceedings of the 2018 World Wide Web Conference on World Wide Web*, pages 1003–1011.

Dominik Schlechtweg, Sabine Schulte im Walde, and Stefanie Eckmann. 2018. Diachronic usage relatedness (DURel): A framework for the annotation of lexical semantic change. In *Proceedings of the Conference of the North American Chapter of the Association for Computational Linguistics, NAACL 2018*.

Nina Tahmasebi. 2018. A study on word2vec on a historical Swedish newspaper corpus. In *CEUR Workshop Proceedings. Vol. 2084. Proceedings of the Digital Humanities in the Nordic Countries 3rd Conference, Helsinki Finland, March 7-9, 2018*. University of Helsinki, Faculty of Arts.

Nina Tahmasebi, Lars Borin, and Adam Jatowt. 2018. Survey of computational approaches to lexical semantic change detection. *Research Data Journal for the Humanities and Social Sciences*.

Nina Tahmasebi and Thomas Risse. 2017. Finding individual word sense changes and their delay in appearance. In *Proceedings of the International Conference Recent Advances in Natural Language Processing, RANLP 2017*, pages 741–749.

Xuri Tang. 2018. A state-of-the-art of semantic change computation. *arXiv preprint arXiv:1801.09872*.

Xuri Tang, Weiguang Qu, and Xiaohe Chen. 2016. Semantic change computation: A successive approach. *World Wide Web*, 19(3):375–415.

Alessandro Vatri, Viivi Lähteenoja, and Barbara McGillivray. 2019. Ancient Greek Semantic Change - Annotated Datasets and Code [dataset]. doi:10.6084/m9.figshare.c.4445420.

Alessandro Vatri and Barbara McGillivray. 2018. The Diorisis Ancient Greek Corpus. *Research Data Journal for the Humanities and Social Sciences*.

Derry Tanti Wijaya and Reyyan Yeniterzi. 2011. Understanding semantic change of words over centuries. In *Proceedings of the 2011 international workshop on DETecting and Exploiting Cultural diversiTy on the social web*, pages 35–40. ACM.

Marcos Zampieri, Shervin Malmasi, and Mark Dras. 2016. Modeling language change in historical corpora: The case of Portuguese. In *Proceedings of the Tenth International Conference on Language Resources and Evaluation (LREC 2016)*, Paris, France. European Language Resources Association (ELRA).

Modeling markedness with a split-and-merger model of sound change

Andrea Ceolin
University of Pennsylvania
Department of Linguistics
ceolin@sas.upenn.edu

Ollie Sayeed
University of Pennsylvania
Department of Linguistics
sayeedo@sas.upenn.edu

1 Background

The concept of 'markedness' has been influential in phonology for almost a century. Theoretical phonology used it to describe some segments as more 'marked' than others, referring to a cluster of language-internal and language-external properties (Jakobson, 1968; Haspelmath, 2006). We argue, using a simple mathematical model based on Evolutionary Phonology (EP; Blevins, 2004), that markedness is an epiphenomenon of phonetically grounded sound change.

2 Model: random splits and mergers

We propose a simple abstract model of sound change as a discrete-time stochastic process of random splitting and merging of phonemic categories. In the split-and-merger model, sound change belongs to a class of random fragmentation and aggregation processes (Banavar et al., 2004), whose fixed points are power-law frequency distributions over the elements being split and merged. It has been shown that phoneme type and token frequencies in natural languages do indeed follow a power-law distribution, specifically a Yule-Simon distribution (Simon, 1955; Tambovtsev and Martindale, 2007; Martin, 2007).

Say the phoneme inventory of a language is a set of segments $\{x_i\}$, where the ith segment x_i has frequency p_i^t at time step t. At each stage, we apply either a *split* or a *merger* to the language with equal probability:

- To apply a split, pick a random pair of segments x_i, x_j with $i \neq j$. Take away half of x_i's probability mass, and add it to the existing probability mass of x_j.

$$p_i^{t+1} := \frac{p_i^t}{2}$$

$$p_j^{t+1} := \frac{p_i^t}{2} + p_j^t$$

$$p_k^{t+1} := p_k^t$$

- Mergers follow a similar algorithm, except that *all* of x_i's probability mass is transferred to x_j.

$$p_i^{t+1} := 0$$

$$p_j^{t+1} := p_i^t + p_j^t$$

$$p_k^{t+1} := p_k^t$$

- Define a function $P_S(x_j)$ such that $P_S(x_j) \geq 0$ and $\Sigma P_S(x_j) = 1$; this is a probability distribution representing the probability that the jth segment x_j will have its frequency increased when another segment splits. When the splitting algorithm calls for picking a random pair of segments x_i, x_j, pick x_j randomly according to the distribution $P_S(x_j)$.

- Define a second probability distribution $P_M(x_i)$, representing the probability that x_i is lost in a merger. When the merging algorithm calls for picking a random pair of segments x_i, x_j, pick x_i randomly according to $P_M(x_i)$.

Say that segments with *low* $P_S(x_j)$ are 'split-wise marked', and segments with *high* $P_M(x_i)$ are 'mergerwise marked'. In other words, marked segments are segments that either *do not* tend to be created after a split, or *do* tend to be lost in a merger.

3 Predictions: within-language and across-language frequency

Empirically, across-language phoneme frequencies correlate well with within-language frequencies (Gordon, 2016). We show that a split-and-merger model derives this link from stochastic sound change.

Proceedings of the 1st International Workshop on Computational Approaches to Historical Language Change, pages 67–70
Florence, Italy, August 2, 2019. ©2019 Association for Computational Linguistics

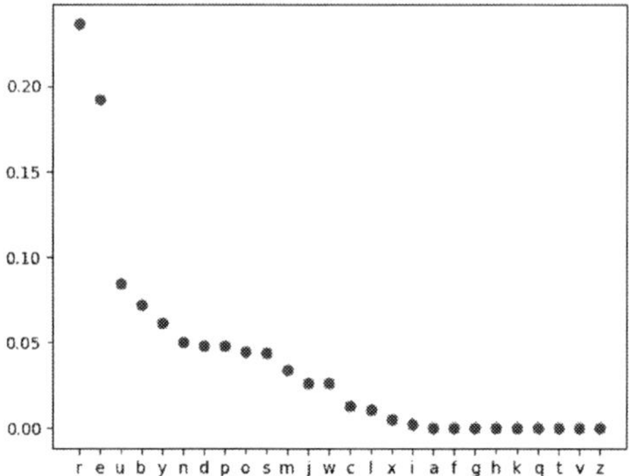

Figure 1: A typical run of our simulation after 500 iterations.

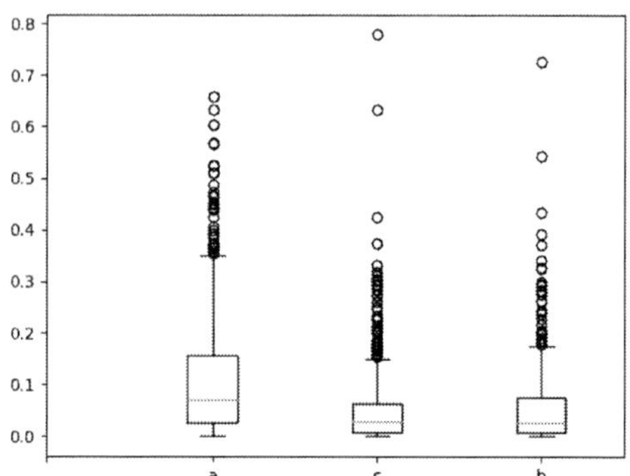

Figure 2: Summary of the final within-language frequencies of 'a', 'c' and 'b, which are modeled in terms of splitwise markedness, after 1000 parallel runs, with r=10.

We run a simulation of the split-and-merger process for 500 iterations with a set of 20 segments arbitrarily labeled $\{a, b, c,....t\}$. We assume that segment frequencies are uniform as a starting point. In addition, six segments $\{u, v,...z\}$ are assigned an initial value of zero. In the sound change simulation, either a split or a merger is applied to the phonemic inventory at each iteration with equal probability. Simulations of the split-and-merger model in action show long-tailed distributions emerging out of an initial flat distribution, qualitatively in line with the results from random fragmentation and aggregation models (Figure 1).

3.1 Splitwise markedness

We re-run the simulation first implementing splitwise markedness. In this simulation, 'a' is 'unmarked' with respect to the other segments by having a probability of increasing its frequency after a split which is higher than that of the other segments, and 'b' is 'marked' by having a probability of increasing its frequency after a split which is lower. The probabilities are determined by a parameter r, which represents the ratio between the probability of the 'unmarked' and the 'marked' segments with respect to the others. This value quantifies how 'unmarked' or 'marked' a segment is with respect to the others.

In a first experiment, we track the average frequencies of 'a' and 'b' across 1000 parallel runs, and we also track the number of runs in which they survive, interpreting each independent run as a separate language. We then compare these numbers with the frequencies exhibited by segments which are neither 'unmarked' nor 'marked', for example 'c'.

Figure 2 shows the average frequencies in the languages in which 'a', 'b' and 'c' survive, and it shows that 'a' has a higher average than 'c' and 'b', while these latter segments do not exhibit a clear difference.

Table 1 shows both within- and across-language frequencies for different values of r. Interestingly, increasing the value for r has the effect of increasing the difference between 'a' and the other symbols, but it does not have any effect on 'b'. On the other hand, across-language frequencies are clearly distinct, and 'a' and 'b' display frequencies different from the neutral segment 'c'. These differences become more salient as r increases.

This experiment shows that when we add a diachronic bias, 'unmarked' segments display higher frequencies both within- and across-languages, while the effect for 'marked' segments appears to be limited to across-language frequencies. This might follow from the fact that while splitwise marked segments tend to appear less in languages, their within-language frequencies are dependent on other factors, for instance the frequency of the segments from which they split or their likelihood of merging with other segments. In the next subsection, we investigate mergerwise markedness.

3.2 Mergerwise markedness

We repeat the simulation modeling mergerwise markedness. This time, 'a' is 'unmarked' with re-

	Markedness	Within-language	Across-language
r=2			
'a'	Unmarked	0.063 ($\pm$0.006)	0.572 ($\pm$0.003)
'c'	Neutral	0.057 ($\pm$0.007)	0.475 ($\pm$0.003)
'b'	Marked	0.056 ($\pm$0.008)	0.410 ($\pm$0.003)
r=5			
'a'	Unmarked	0.081 ($\pm$0.006)	0.702 ($\pm$0.003)
'c'	Neutral	0.058 ($\pm$0.007)	0.452 ($\pm$0.003)
'b'	Marked	0.052 ($\pm$0.008)	0.348 ($\pm$0.003)
r=10			
'a'	Unmarked	0.099 ($\pm$0.008)	0.773 ($\pm$0.002)
'c'	Neutral	0.052 ($\pm$0.007)	0.423 ($\pm$0.003)
'b'	Marked	0.058 ($\pm$0.008)	0.311 ($\pm$0.003)

Table 1: Average within- and across-language frequencies for three segments which differ in terms of splitwise markedness, with different values of r. Confidence intervals at 95% are reported for within-language frequencies. We also report confidence intervals at 95% for across-language frequencies, which we obtained by repeating the whole experiment 100 times.

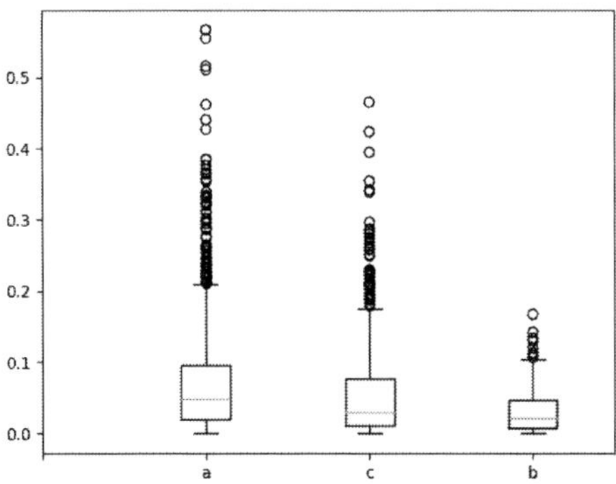

Figure 3: Summary of the final within-language frequencies for 'a', 'c' and 'b', which are modeled in terms of mergerwise markedness, after 1000 parallel runs, with r=10.

spect to the other segments by having a probability of being lost after a merger which is lower than that of the other segments, and 'b' is 'marked' by having a probability of being lost after a merger which is instead higher. The probabilities are determined by the same parameter r.

As previously done, we track the average frequencies of 'a' and 'b' across 1000 parallel runs and the number of runs in which they survive, along with those of a neutral segment 'c'.

Figure 3 shows the average frequencies in the languages in which 'a', 'b' and 'c' survive, and it shows that this time the three segments have different distributions. From Table 2, we see that within- and across-language frequencies line up, exhibiting a correlation. In this case, 'marked' segments exhibit a lower within-language frequency with respect to neutral segments.

4   Conclusions

Both the power-law frequency distribution of phonemes in a language and the cluster of properties associated with 'markedness' can be thought of as epiphenomena of phonetically grounded sound change. A stochastic split-and-merger model predicts the attested language-internal and typological correlations. In particular, mergerwise markedness appears to be responsible for higher within- and across-language frequencies for 'unmarked' segments and lower frequencies for 'marked' segments, while splitwise markedness mainly affects 'unmarked' segments.

	Markedness	Within-language	Across-language
r=2			
'a'	Unmarked	0.065 ($\pm$0.006)	0.652 ($\pm$0.003)
'c'	Neutral	0.056 ($\pm$0.007)	0.485 ($\pm$0.003)
'b'	Marked	0.052 ($\pm$0.008)	0.320 ($\pm$0.003)
r=5			
'a'	Unmarked	0.071 ($\pm$0.006)	0.836 ($\pm$0.002)
'c'	Neutral	0.051 ($\pm$0.005)	0.509 ($\pm$0.003)
'b'	Marked	0.045 ($\pm$0.008)	0.173 ($\pm$0.002)
r=10			
'a'	Unmarked	0.072 ($\pm$0.005)	0.924 ($\pm$0.002)
'c'	Neutral	0.050 ($\pm$0.005)	0.548 ($\pm$0.003)
'b'	Marked	0.032 ($\pm$0.007)	0.109 ($\pm$0.002)

Table 2: Average within- and across-language frequencies for three segments which differ in terms of mergerwise markedness, with different values of r. Confidence intervals at 95% are reported for within-language frequencies. We also report confidence intervals at 95% for across-language frequencies, which we obtained by repeating the whole experiment 100 times.

References

Jayanth R Banavar et al. 2004. Scale-free behavior and universality in random fragmentation and aggregation. *Physical Review E*, 69(3):036123.

Juliette Blevins. 2004. *Evolutionary phonology: The emergence of sound patterns*. Cambridge University Press.

Matthew Kelly Gordon. 2016. *Phonological typology*, volume 1. Oxford University Press.

Martin Haspelmath. 2006. Against markedness (and what to replace it with). *Journal of linguistics*, 42(1):25–70.

Roman Jakobson. 1968. *Child language: aphasia and phonological universals*. 72. Walter de Gruyter.

Andrew Thomas Martin. 2007. *The evolving lexicon*. Ph.D. thesis, University of California, Los Angeles Los Angeles, CA.

Herbert A Simon. 1955. On a class of skew distribution functions. *Biometrika*, 42(3/4):425–440.

Yuri Tambovtsev and Colin Martindale. 2007. Phoneme frequencies follow a Yule distribution. *SKASE Journal of Theoretical Linguistics*, 4(2):1–11.

A method to automatically identify diachronic variation in collocations

Marcos Garcia
Universidade da Coruña, Grupo LyS
Dpto. de Letras, Facultade de Filoloxía
Campus da Zapateira, 15701, Coruña
Universidade da Coruña, CITIC
Campus de Elviña, 15701, Coruña
`marcos.garcia.gonzalez@udc.gal`

Marcos García-Salido
Universidade da Coruña, Grupo LyS
Dpto. de Letras, Facultade de Filoloxía
Campus da Zapateira, 15701, Coruña
`marcos.garcias@udc.gal`

Abstract

This paper introduces a novel method to track collocational variations in diachronic corpora that can identify several changes undergone by these phraseological combinations and to propose alternative solutions found in later periods. The strategy consists of extracting syntactically-related candidates of collocations and ranking them using statistical association measures. Then, starting from the first period of the corpus, the system tracks each combination over time, verifying different types of historical variation such as the loss of one or both lemmas, the disappearance of the collocation, or its diachronic frequency trend. Using a distributional semantics strategy, it also suggests linguistic structures that convey meanings similar to those of extinct collocations. A case study on historical corpora of Portuguese and Spanish shows that the system speeds up and facilitates the finding of some diachronic changes and phraseological shifts that are harder to identify without using automated methods.

1 Introduction

One of the main characteristics of natural language is change, as there is no evidence of any language which does not show different types of variation. Change seems to affect all the strata of natural languages: phonology, morphology, syntax, and semantics. Besides this language-internal perspective, the study of language variation may also take into account the external causes of change: that is, geographical, social, or historical factors, among others (Chambers and Schilling, 2013).

Historical (*diachronic*) studies of language, carried out by philologists and historical linguists, have shown how language evolves over time, finding interesting cross-linguistic generalizations. In those cases where digitalized resources exist, several corpus linguistics and natural language pro-

cessing (NLP) methods have been applied to automate the discovering of language change, thus alleviating the effort of searching for linguistic variation (Curzan, 2008; Dipper, 2008). In this regard, frequency-based strategies are useful to identify increases and decreases in the use of some linguistic phenomena (Hilpert and Gries, 2016). The rise of distributional semantics methods (both count-based and neural network approaches) also allowed researchers to track semantic change in different time periods (Sagi et al., 2009; Gulordava and Baroni, 2011; Kulkarni et al., 2015; Hamilton et al., 2016; Bamler and Mandt, 2017; Gamallo et al., 2018).

A particular case of diachronic variation is the evolution of lexical combinations over time. In this respect, research on the diachrony of complex predicates has provided useful knowledge for theoretical studies on language evolution (Anderson, 2006; Butt and Lahiri, 2013; Elenbaas, 2013). From a different perspective, historical analyses of collocational patterns have shown that some lexical restrictions vary diachronically, while some others seem to be more persistent. Thus, studies such as Alba-Salas (2007) or García-Salido (2017) explore how Spanish causative verbs such as *hacer* ('to make') or *poner* ('to put') were replaced by *dar* (literally, 'to give') to express causation with different nouns such as *miedo* ('fear') or *vergüenza* ('embarrasment'): *hacer vergüenza* ⇒ *dar vergüenza*; *poner miedo* ⇒ *dar miedo*. These examples show the asymmetry of collocations, understood as combinations where one of their lexical units (LUs) (the COLLOCATE: *hacer*, *poner*, or *dar*) is lexically selected by the other (the BASE: *miedo*, *vergüenza*) (Mel'čuk, 1998).

Understanding the properties of collocations and other multiword expressions, both in a specific period of time and diachronically, is crucial not only to understand how a particular lan-

71

Proceedings of the 1st International Workshop on Computational Approaches to Historical Language Change, pages 71–80
Florence, Italy, August 2, 2019. ©2019 Association for Computational Linguistics

guage evolves, but also to develop computational methods for language processing (Sag et al., 2002; Ramisch and Villavicencio, 2018). However, this type of analyses has benefited less from computational approaches, whereby NLP systems could facilitate the automatic identification of variations in lexical combinations. Tools such as *DiaCollo* (Jurish, 2015) or JeSeme (Hellrich and Hahn, 2017) are able to track changes in word associations and lexical semantics, but they are not specifically designed to analyze combinations of syntactically dependent lexical units like the ones exemplified above.

Taking the above into account, we present a new method to analyze, in historical corpora, the diachronic distribution of collocations and their internal components. Besides the period when certain collocations start to be used, the method identifies four variation types: (1) the disappearance of both lexical units of the collocation; the loss of (2) the base or (3) of the collocate, and (4) the loss of certain combinations whose constituent lemmas are still used. In each case, the system searches for other similar combinations and proposes possible replacements. Furthermore, it classifies the increase, decrease, or stability of collocations that continue to be used.

In order to evaluate the usefulness of the proposed method, we carry out a case study on several historical corpora of Spanish and Portuguese. The analyses, both quantitative and qualitative, indicate that the presented approach allows historical linguists to rapidly analyze the diachronic evolution of collocations, showing some interesting changes in lexical combinations of the two languages. The system is freely available and can be applied to any historical corpus parsed in a CoNLL-like format.[1]

The remainder of this paper is organized as follows. Section 2 presents some related work on computational approaches to language change, and Section 3 briefly discusses the theoretical properties of collocations. In Section 4 we describe our method to identify diachronic variation of these expressions. Then, Section 5 shows the results of both quantitative and qualitative evaluations of the system as well as an error analysis, and finally, the conclusions and further work are addressed in Section 6.

---

[1] The annotated corpora and the software used in this paper are released under open-source licences at http://www.grupolys.org/~marcos/pub/diachronic_collocations.zip

2   Related Work

Besides historical linguistic approaches adopted by the philological tradition, the availability of diachronic corpora in digital formats allowed researchers from different areas to implement computational approaches to explore historical language change. In this regard, Lieberman et al. (2007) analyzed the past tense of English verbs over $1,200$ years, showing that the rate of regularization (i.e., the emergence of an *-ed* past form) is directly related to frequency.

Using distributional semantic methods, Sagi et al. (2009) and Cook and Stevenson (2010) found examples of meaning shift by working with historical corpora combining quantitative and qualitative analyses. The former study identified the probability of semantic change by measuring the density of a vector space. The latter concentrated on amelioration and pejoration cases, that is, words that change from negative to positive opinions (e.g., the meaning of *nice* was 'foolish'), or from positive to negative ones (e.g., *vulgar* meant 'common').

More recently, several works have taken advantage of the Google Books Ngrams to train English distributional models of different periods in order to find semantic change over time (Gulordava and Baroni, 2011; Wijaya and Yeniterzi, 2011; Kim et al., 2014; Kulkarni et al., 2015). Similarly, Hamilton et al. (2016) defined a methodology to quantify semantic change using four languages (Chinese, English, German, and French). The results of this article suggest that polysemous words are those with higher rates of semantic change, and that the meaning of frequent words is more stable over time. The Google Books Ngrams were also used to implement dependency-based distributional semantics methods to track the semantic change in Spanish (Gamallo et al., 2017, 2018). To avoid the alignment problem between the vector space of each time period, studies such as Bamler and Mandt (2017) and Rudolph and Blei (2018) learn a joint time-aware semantic space by means of dynamic embeddings.

Designed specifically to explore the diachronic contexts of words, *DiaCollo* allows historical linguists to analyze the typical collocates of a given word over time, providing useful information to identify potential semantic shifts (Jurish, 2015). JeSeme also takes advantage of historical distributional semantics models to create diachronic charts for tracking semantic variation and word emotion over time (Hellrich and Hahn, 2017).[2]

Inspired by several of these works, our method uses natural language processing techniques and distributional semantics methods to support historical linguists to find diachronic changes of collocations in different languages.

3 Collocations

There are at least two main views of the concept of *collocation*. In the Firthian tradition, collocations are arbitrary and recurrent co-occurrences of two or more words within a short space of each other in a text (Benson, 1990; Sinclair, 1991). From this point of view, collocations are word combinations occurring together in a given span with greater frequency than randomly expected (e.g., "night, dark").

Along with this statistical or empirical approach, in the field of phraseology, authors such as Hausmann (1989) or Mel'čuk (1998) conceive collocations as directional combinations of two syntactically related lexical units. According to this approach, one of the LUs that form the collocation (the BASE) is often defined as *autosemantic*, because it is chosen by the speaker due to its meaning. The base, in turn, restricts the selection of the other LU (the COLLOCATE), which conveys a particular meaning depending on a given base (e.g., "take$_{\text{Collocate}}$ (a) picture$_{\text{Base}}$", "black$_C$ coffee$_B$") and is therefore said to be *synsemantic*. This conception of collocations encompasses quite an ample range of compositional lexical combinations (Mel'čuk, 1998), ranging from support verb constructions—in which verbs provide a tenuous lexical meaning (e.g. *Peter took a walk* $\sim$ *Peter's walk*)—to other types of idiosyncratic couplings, where collocates express full meanings, but are not freely interchangeable with theoretical synonyms (see the case of Pt. *arrenegar* with the meaning 'abjure' used in some sections of the corpus almost exclusively in company of *demónio* 'devil' or *diabrura* 'deviltry' in Section 5).

In spite of the differences between the two approaches, there have been recent attempts at using statistical measures to automatically identify phraseological collocations. For instance, Pecina (2010) investigates the performance of a large set of statistical association measures in identifying phraseological combinations. The target collocations of Pecina are only partially coincident with the definition given above, as, along with collocations such as *make a decision*, they also include non-compositional combinations. More recently, Evert et al. (2017) and Uhrig et al. (2018) undertook a research with similar purposes, but, in contrast to Pecina (2010), who started from bigrams, they used dependency parsing to identify collocation candidates and, instead of manual identification of phraseological combinations, they used collocation dictionaries as gold standards.

This paper also combines the statistical and phraseological approaches. Whereas phraseological collocations seem more interesting for diachronic investigations, statistical information can serve as a tool for identifying collocation candidates. The method proposed takes advantage of dependency parsing to identificate syntactically-related base–collocate candidate pairs, and uses statistical analysis in order to identify collocation candidates in each historical period.

4 Identification of diachronic changes on collocations

4.1 Method overview

The strategy for identifying historical variations on collocations consists of analyzing each of these combinations over time, starting from the first epoch when the collocation appears in the corpus. For each collocation, we identify whether it is still used in the following periods, and if it disappears, we verify what type of change it has undergone: loss of one or both LUs, or loss of the combination. As the collocation bases are those elements carrying the bulk of the lexical meaning, we check different candidates with the same base (or a very similar one) in those cases where only the collocate ceased to be used, with a view to finding examples such as the one referred above (*poner$_C$ miedo$_B$* $\Rightarrow$ *dar$_C$ miedo$_B$*). As Section 4.4 will show, other alternatives (e.g., verbs with the same meaning of the collocations) can also be proposed.

4.2 Resources

In order to analyze the diachrony of collocations, our system needs historical corpora divided in different periods p_1, p_2, ..., p_n. Each corpus must have a CoNLL-like format containing lemmas, POS-tags and dependency labels. Also, the system uses word embeddings models to search for

[2] http://jeseme.org/

words with similar distributions. Optionally, it can take advantage of contemporary resources such as a dictionary of lemmas and a reference corpus (e.g., Wikipedia), used to reduce the noise present in historical corpora.

It is worth noting that in diachronic resources the *same word* can be written in different ways, due to variations in spelling, or because of morphological or phonological changes. For instance, the above mentioned Spanish word *vergüenza* can be found written as *berguensa*, *verguensa*, *berguenza*, or *verguença* (among others) in historical corpora (Vaamonde, 2015). As our objective is to find phraseological combinations of words, the system presented in this paper behaves better with normalized texts, where the lemmas have the same spelling across the different resources. Nevertheless, we take advantage of distributional models which encode subword information, so they can effectively tackle rare words present in historical resources (Bojanowski et al., 2017). In this regard, Section 5 includes experiments using normalized corpora (in Portuguese and Spanish) as well as a non-normalized historical corpus of Portuguese.

4.3 Extraction of collocation candidates

Once we have the analyzed corpora, we extract head–dependent pairs of the desired syntactic relations in order to identify candidates of collocations. For example, the *verb-object* dependency will extract instances such as 'eat, sausage' or 'take, shower'. These pairs are then ranked using statistical association measures to identify those candidates that are more likely to be phraseological collocations (Gries, 2013; Carlini et al., 2014; Evert et al., 2017).

4.4 Diachronic track of collocations

The process of tracking the diachronic evolution of collocations consists of the following steps:

- Starting from p_1, we select the n top collocations according the defined association measure and threshold. Optionally, in order to avoid possible noise in historical corpora, we select only those collocations whose internal elements are known (i.e., they appear in a contemporary dictionary), or have a very similar distribution (e.g., 0.9 of cosine similarity) to known present words.

- We calculate the ratio per period of each collocation dividing its frequency by the number

of syntactic dependencies with the same relation (e.g., *subject*) in the same period.

- Then, for each collocation, we verify whether it appears in the next more recent period of the corpus (or ideally, in the reference one). If the collocation is not currently used:

  1. We traverse each period p_{1+i} to identify when the collocation ceased to be used.

  2. Then, we analyze the type of change: (type 1) both the base and the collocate are not used anymore in the corpus; (2) the base, or (3) the collocate do not appear in further periods; (4) both LUs still occur, but the combination ceased to exist. In types 1 and 2 we use the distributional model to search for replacements for the base (for both types) and of the collocate (only for type 1). Using these candidates, we select further collocations whose base and collocate have cosine similarities greater than two given thresholds (*base_simil* and *collocate_simil*). In those cases where the base still appears in phraseological combinations (change 3, and eventually 4), we search for other combinations with the same base to find new collocates with the same lexical function.

     In *verb-object* collocations (e.g., *hacer venganza* or *tomar vingança*, 'take revenge' in Old Spanish and Portuguese) we also search (i) for verbs which convey the same meaning (e.g., *vingar*, 'revenge' in Portuguese), also using the word embeddings model, as well as (ii) for collocations with support verb constructions (*dar venganza*, 'take revenge' in Modern Spanish).

- If the collocation is still used in further historical periods, we obtain its frequency trend using the ratios of each period. This analysis classifies the trend of a collocation as *increase*, *decrease* or *stable* (types 5, 6, and 7, respectively).

Thus, the output of our system contains, for each collocation in the corpus (a) the period when it started to appear, (b) the type of change it undergone (if any), and the time when it happened,

as well as (c) the frequency trend of those collocations which have not suffered lexical variations. Additionally, for some combinations, it
shows other expressions (collocations and eventually verbs) which could be replacements for those
collocations which ceased to be used.

5 Experiments

5.1 Data

To verify the usefulness of the proposed method
for automatically finding changes on collocations,
we carried out a case study on two historical corpora of Portuguese and Spanish (with 648k and
808k tokens of private letters, respectively) from
the *P.S. Post Scriptum* project (CLUL, 2014; Vaamonde, 2015).

Both resources are divided into centuries, from
the 16th to the 19th century, and include versions with normalized spelling. We used the
provided tokens and lemmas, and applied two
NLP pipelines to POS-tag (LinguaKit, Garcia and
Gamallo (2015)) and parse (UDPipe, Straka and
Straková (2017)) the corpora using Universal Dependencies 2.3 (Nivre et al., 2018). As contemporary resources of Portuguese and Spanish, we used
the dictionaries included in LinguaKit, and recent
versions of Portuguese and Spanish Wikipedia
(November, 2018) processed using the same tools
as the corpora.

For computing the distributional similarity we
trained *fastText* embeddings (Bojanowski et al.,
2017) with mixed historical and present corpora,
of about $250M$ for each language. For Spanish, we used *cuentos españoles* and *romances
españoles*;[3] for Portuguese, we combined the
Colonia historical corpus (Zampieri and Becker,
2013) with a collection of novels from XIX century.[4] Apart from that, we randomly selected sentences containing about $200M$ tokens from the
Wikipedia version of each language. These distributional models were also used as pre-trained
word embeddings to train the UDPipe parsers
which analyzed the corpora. Ideally, we could
train different distributional models for each time
period, but we decided to use a single model with
data from different epochs due to the lack of large
resources for historical Portuguese and Spanish.

For both languages we restricted the analyses to *verb-object* collocations, and we used *log-
likelihood* as the association measure (Uhrig et al.,
2018). Moreover, as we deal with historical corpora, we defined a high-coverage approach by selecting candidates with a low *log-likelihood* value
($>=2.5$), and also other very frequent combinations (with a empirically defined ratio per century equal or greater than 0.18). The thresholds
base_simil and *collocate_simil* were defined to 0.9
and 0.7, respectively.

It is worth mentioning that, since, to our knowledge, there is no gold-standard data on collocation
diachronic variation, we cannot carry out a systematic analysis of our approach. Thus, we performed a preliminary evaluation aimed at having
an overview of the precision of the system and
knowing how it could help to automatize the work
of historical linguists.

5.2 Results

First, we present some quantitative results obtained by evaluating a random set of the output in
Portuguese and Spanish. Then, we discuss the outcome from a qualitative perspective, carrying out
a brief analysis using a historical linguistics point
of view. Finally, we also show some results of our
system using a non-normalized diachronic corpus
in Portuguese.

Quantitative analysis: Summing up the data of
the five centuries, the system identified $1,932$ and
$1,980$ changes of types 1 through 4 in Spanish and
Portuguese, respectively. Most of these combinations (about 90%) were of type 4, due to the use of
contemporary resources to restrict the analysis of
unknown words. Besides, it extracted the historical trends (changes 5 to 7) of $3,129$ (Spanish) and
$2,210$ (Portuguese) combinations.

To perform the quantitative evaluation we randomly selected the output of 100 collocations of
types 1 to 4 for each language (we did not evaluated the results of types 5, 6, and 7, since they are
obtained from the observed frequencies of the collocations). From this sample, we removed those
combinations which were not proper collocation
candidates due to parsing errors (e.g., the Spanish *llevar* plus *[el] alférez* –literally 'to take' plus
'the sub-lieutenant'— was incorrectly labeled as
an object relation instead of subject), totaling 32%
in Spanish, and 39% in Portuguese (see Table 1).
Note that these values refer to parsing errors in

---

[3]`https://github.com/cligs/textbox/
tree/master/spanish`

[4]`https://github.com/cligs/
romancesportugueses`

Evaluation	Span.	Port.	Average
Prec_Alt	47.1%	56.8%	52.1%
Prec_Dia	62.5%	73.8%	68.8%
Parsing errors	32.4%	39.0%	36.3%

Table 1: Results of the quantitative evaluations in Spanish and Portuguese. *Prec_Alt* is the precision of the proposed alternatives, while *Prec_Dia* is the overall precision of the system. *Parsing errors* include those source combinations (not the target ones) which were wrongly analyzed by the parser. Average is micro-average.

the source combinations (those which suffered a change), not in the collocations proposed as alternatives for each variation type.

Then, we evaluated the output of each collocation as follows. For those collocations where the system did not give any alternative, we looked for other examples with the same meaning in the lists of collocations (false negatives). In those cases where the system provides alternatives, we checked whether these results have approximately the same meaning (e.g., *dar [um] alegrão* → *alegrar*, 'make happy' in Portuguese). We considered correct (i) the nonexistence of newer collocations with similar meanings (in the first case) as well as (ii) the identification of proper alternatives (in the second). Otherwise, the output was considered incorrect. Then, we carried out an error analysis aimed at knowing into more detail what types of error produced our method (see Section 5.3 below).

We computed two precision values for each language (Table 1). On one hand, *Prec_Alt* evaluates the quality of the proposed alternatives by dividing the number of correct cases by the total number of collocations with alternatives (so this value ignores those cases where the system did not found expressions with similar meanings). On the other hand, *Prec_Dia* performs an overall evaluation of the system by taking into account these cases where it did not provide alternatives (correct cases divided by all the analyzed cases).

The results in Table 1 show that the performance of the system was better in Portuguese, even if this language had a large number of parsing errors. The two evaluation approaches had a similar behaviour in both languages (with differences of 15.4% in Spanish and of 17% in Portuguese).

It is worth mentioning that as our method is not a fully automatic system to identify the changes, but rather a tool for identifying potential variations

to assist historical linguists, a qualitative evaluation is probably more appropriate than a quantitative one. Thus, qualitative analyses in both languages were carried out in order to know the usefulness of the system.

Qualitative analysis: As pointed out, changes of type 4 are the most frequently observed in both Spanish and Portuguese processing of the *P.S. Post Scriptum* corpora. In this regard, a manual revision is in order to evaluate the linguistic interest of these data. Thus, for instance, some of these results point to *bona fide* cases of collocational changes. That is the case of Portuguese *deitar missa* (lit. 'lay, mass', 'say a mass', lost in the 16th century) and *botar [uma] bênção* (lit. 'throw a blessing', 'give a blessing', until 18th c.) and Spanish *prestar paciencia* and *aprestar paciencia* (both meaning 'have patience').

In our setting, changes of type 1 are the less common, since we decided to analyze only those words which are present in further centuries or in present dictionaries. However, the system found some intriguing cases of type 1 (i.e., both words of the collocation do not appear in later periods of the corpus —but they still appear in current dictionaries), such as the Portuguese *obtundir acrimónia* ('lessen the curtness', lost in the 18th c.). Curiously enough, the historical *Corpus do Português* (Davies and Ferreira, 2006)[5] does not have any occurrence of the verb *obtundir*, and only 18 cases of *acrimónia*.

The Portuguese data also offers interesting cases of base loss such as *furtar [o] bisalho* ('steal a bag') and *perdoar [o] enfadamento* ('forgive an annoyance'). Regarding the latter, the system correctly proposes the alternative *perdoar [o] enfado*. Besides, it also identified the loss of the verb *arrenegar* ('to abjure', with a frequency of 3 in the *Corpus do Português*), present until the 18th in combination with bases such as *demónio* ('demon') or *diabrura* ('deviltry'), as examples of type 3 (collocate loss).

In Spanish, instances of change 2 (base loss) correspond to either very infrequent (*réprobo* 'reprobate', *requisitorio* 'requisition') or archaic nouns (*malhecho* 'misdeed'). An interesting case of collocate loss (type 3) is the verb *desenojar* 'to appease', which the system indicates that disappears in the 18th century. In the corpus of the *Nuevo diccionario histórico del español* (hence-

---

[5]https://www.corpusdoportugues.org/

forth CDH), a larger diachronic corpus of Spanish accessible only through a web interface (Instituto de Investigación Rafael Lapesa, 2013), this verb is mostly attested before 1700. Afterwards, in the 18th century its frequency decreases almost by a half (from 2.59 to 1.58 occurrences per million words, *opmw*), and continues to decrease steeply in later periods.

Amongst the changes of type 4, one finds the most relevant cases from a dichronic perspective. In the case of *aprestar|prestar paciencia* the system identifies its loss around the 18th century and correctly predicts its substitution for the nowadays more common light-verb construction *tener paciencia* ('have patience'). In the larger CDH, *prestar paciencia* goes from 0.7 opmw in the 16th and 17th centuries to less than half (0.32) in the 18th c. and keeps decreasing. By the 20th century it seems almost extinct with only one occurrence in 1933.

A similar case is *meter paz* 'to put peace', the last attestations of which are dated by the system in the 16th century in favor of *poner paz*. The loss of this collocation, however, has greater implications, since a broader semantic change affecting the verb *meter* could be at play here. Corominas and Pascual (1996) (s.v. *meter*) point out that that the meanings of *meter* and *poner* ('to put') were more or less interchangeable in medieval Spanish. Nowadays, however, *poner* conveys the meaning 'change of position' and describes non-durative changes (achievements), whereas *meter* has a directional component and a durative interpretation (accomplishment), according to Cifuentes Honrubia (2004).

Results in a non-normalized corpus: Besides the previous experiments, we also carried out a test in a non-normalized and larger historical corpus of Portuguese, Colónia, with 6.2M tokens of essays from 16th to 20th centuries (Zampieri and Becker, 2013).[6] We analyzed combinations with a frequency equal or greater than 2 in the first time period in which it appeared, and used the same association measures and parameters as in the previous experiments.

In this case the system classified $2,622$ changes of types 1 to 4, in which a brief analysis allowed us to identify interesting variations in historical collocational preferences in Portuguese. For instance, examples of type 1 such as *desafivelar gor-*

---

[6]http://corporavm.uni-koeln.de/colonia/

jal ('unfasten, gorjet', lost in the 19th century), of type 2 such as *fazer soído* ('make sound' or 'make noise', where *soído* is currently replaced by *som*) or *corromper [a] pudicícia* (lit. 'to corrupt the shyness') in the 18th and 19th centuries, respectively. Among the observed cases of type 3 there are interesting verb losses (or at least decreases in use) in cases such as *descantar [o] louvor* ('sing praises') or *manear [a] arma* ('handle a weapon'), currently less used than the collocates *cantar* and *manejar*, respectively.

In this analysis, the system also proposed correct alternatives to changes of type 4, including the collocation *tomar aposento* ('to lodge') or the verb *carregar* ('to carry'), from *fazer aposento* and *fazer [a] carregação*, respectively.

In sum, this analysis allowed us to verify the usefulness of the proposed method to rapidly identify the target language changes also in non-normalized corpus such as the *Colónia*. It is worth recalling that, depending on the corpus properties and on the objectives of the research, the parameters of the system can be configured to suit the needs of the analysis.

5.3 Error analysis

In order to know in more detail the type of errors produced by our method we carried out an error analysis of each of the incorrect outputs of the quantitative evaluation. The errors were classified in the following three types, presented by their frequency (see Table 2 for the quantitative results):

1. Different sense of the collocates: the most common error type was the suggestion of a collocate with a different sense in those cases where the base still appears in the corpus, but in other combinations. For instance, the system proposed the combination *dar dilación* (literally 'to give a delay') as a replacement for the Spanish *sentir dilación* ('to regret a delay'). In Portuguese, *fazer recado* ('to do an errand') was suggested as a substitution of *esperar recado* ('to wait for an errand').

2. Different sense of the verbs: another frequent error, similar to the previous one, was the suggestion of single-word verb equivalents for collocations with different meanings. In Portuguese, *encomendar* ('to order') was proposed to replace *tomar encomenda* ('to take an order'), while *desacatar* ('to

Error type	Span.	Port.	Average
Collocate sense	50.0%	75.0%	61.8%
Verb sense	38.9%	18.8%	29.4%
Parsing	11.1%	6.3%	8.8%

Table 2: Quantitative results of the error analysis per language. Average is micro average.

disobey') was the first suggestion for the Spanish *causar desacato* ('to cause disobedience').

3. Parsing: a less frequent error type was produced by incorrect annotations of the dependency parser. As an example, *ver auditor* ('to see an auditor', in Spanish) was analyzed as a *verb-object* relation instead of a *subject-verb* ('the auditor saw [...]').

Error types 1 and 2 were mainly produced due to our distributional semantics approach; as collocates have a particular meaning depending on the base they go with, standard distributional semantics models often fail to capture these specific senses. To avoid these problems, both non-compositional methods (e.g., representing the collocations as multiword units in the distributional models), or contextualized compositional strategies (which combine the vectors of the elements or their most prominent contexts) could be applied.

6 Conclusions and further work

In this paper we presented a system aimed at facilitating the diachronic detection of collocational variation. The method takes advantage of dependency parsing and of statistical association measures, together with a base–collocate approach, to find candidates of phraseological combinations. To the best of our knowledge, this is the first approach focused on the automatic identification of collocational changes in different languages.

For each collocation in the corpus, the system identifies the period it starts to appear and verifies whether it continues to be used. Those combinations which ceased to occur in later historical periods are analyzed in order to infer whether simple lexical substitutions have happened, or if the lexical restrictions of a collocation base have shifted. Also, the strategy takes advantage of distributional semantics methods to propose alternatives for those combinations which ceased to be used.

A case study on Portuguese and Spanish historical corpora shows that the system is useful both to speed up the finding of collocation changes as well as to detect phraseological and semantic variation in diachronic resources. In this regard, some interesting collocational and semantic changes have been pointed out based on a qualitative analysis of the results. It is worth mentioning that, even if the system is better suited for normalized historical corpora, the performed evaluations showed that it works reasonably well also in non-normalized resources. However, further research is needed to reduce the parsing errors in both normalized and non-normalized historical corpora.

Based on an error analysis, in future work we plan to improve the preprocessing with NLP tools adapted for non-normalized corpora as well as with more balanced word embeddings models trained on historical resources. Another future line of research could be the use of contextualized models of distributional semantics able to infer different senses of a word by the contexts where it appears. Finally, it would be interesting to embed the system in a visualization tool to support research in historical linguistics and in digital humanities.

Acknowledgements

This research was supported by a 2017 Leonardo Grant for Researchers and Cultural Creators (BBVA Foundation) and by the Galician Government (Xunta de Galicia grant ED431B-2017/01). Marcos Garcia has been funded by a Juan de la Cierva-incorporación grant (IJCI-2016-29598), and Marcos García-Salido by a post-doctoral grant from Xunta de Galicia (ED481D 2017/009). We gratefully acknowledge the support of NVIDIA Corporation with the donation of the Titan Xp GPU used for this research.

References

Josep Alba-Salas. 2007. On the life and death of a collocation: A corpus-based diachronic study of dar miedo/hacer miedo-type structures in Spanish. *Diachronica*, 24(2):207–252.

Gregory D. S. Anderson. 2006. The Origins of Patterns of Inflection in Auxiliary Verb Constructions. In *Auxiliary Verb Constructions*, Oxford Studies in Typology and Linguistic Theory, chapter 7. Oxford University Press.

Robert Bamler and Stephan Mandt. 2017. Dynamic word embeddings. In *Proceedings of the 34th International Conference on Machine Learning (ICML 2017)*, volume PMLR 70, pages 380–389.

Morton Benson. 1990. Collocations and general-purpose dictionaries. *International Journal of Lexicography*, 3(1):23–34.

Piotr Bojanowski, Edouard Grave, Armand Joulin, and Tomas Mikolov. 2017. Enriching word vectors with subword information. *Transactions of the Association for Computational Linguistics*, 5:135–146.

Miriam Butt and Aditi Lahiri. 2013. Diachronic pertinacity of light verbs. *Lingua*, 135:7–29.

Roberto Carlini, Joan Codina-Filba, and Leo Wanner. 2014. Improving collocation correction by ranking suggestions using linguistic knowledge. In *Proceedings of the third workshop on NLP for computer-assisted language learning*, pages 1–12, Uppsala. LiU Electronic Press.

Jack K. Chambers and Natalie Schilling, editors. 2013. *The Handbook of Language Variation and Change*, 2nd edition. John Wiley & Sons, Inc, New Jersey.

José Luis Cifuentes Honrubia. 2004. Verbos locales estativos en español. *Estudios De Lingüística*, Anexo 2:73–118.

CLUL. 2014. P.S. Post Scriptum. Arquivo Digital de Escrita Quotidiana em Portugal e Espanha na Época Moderna. May 2018. `http://ps.clul.ul.pt`.

Paul Cook and Suzanne Stevenson. 2010. Automatically identifying changes in the semantic orientation of words. In *Proceedings of the 7th International Conference on Language Resources and Evaluation (LREC 2010)*, pages 28–34, Valletta, Malta. European Language Resources Association.

Joan Corominas and José A. Pascual. 1996. *Diccionario crítico etimológico castellano e hispánico*. 5. Gredos, Madrid.

Anne Curzan. 2008. Historical corpus linguistics and evidence of language change. In Anke Lüdeling and Merja Kytö, editors, *Corpus Linguistics. An international handbook*, volume 2, pages 1091–1108. Mouton de Gruyter, Berlin.

Mark Davies and Michael Ferreira. 2006. Corpus do Português (45 milhões de palavras, sécs. XIV-XX). `http://www.corpusdoportugues.org`.

Stefanie Dipper. 2008. Theory-driven and corpus-driven computational linguistics, and the use of corpora. In Anke Lüdeling and Merja Kytö, editors, *Corpus Linguistics. An international handbook*, volume 1, pages 68–96. Mouton de Gruyter, Berlin.

Marion Elenbaas. 2013. The synchronic and diachronic status of English light verbs. *Linguistic Variation*, 13(1):48–80.

Stefan Evert, Peter Uhrig, Sabine Bartsch, and Thomas Proisl. 2017. E-VIEW-alation – a Large-scale Evaluation Study of Association Measures for Collocation Identification. In Iztok Kosem, Carole Tiberius, Milos Jakubíček, Jelena Kallas, Simon Krek, and Vít Baisa, editors, *Electronic lexicography in the 21st century. Proceedings of eLex 2017 conference.*, pages 531–549. Lexical Computing CZ, Brno.

Pablo Gamallo, Iván Rodríguez-Torres, and Marcos Garcia. 2017. A web interface for diachronic semantic search in Spanish. In *Proceedings of the Software Demonstrations of the 15th Conference of the European Chapter of the Association for Computational Linguistics*, pages 45–48, Valencia, Spain. Association for Computational Linguistics.

Pablo Gamallo, Iván Rodríguez-Torres, and Marcos Garcia. 2018. Distributional semantics for diachronic search. *Computers & Electrical Engineering*, 65:438–448.

Marcos Garcia and Pablo Gamallo. 2015. Yet another suite of multilingual NLP tools. In *Languages, applications and technologies. Communications in Computer and Information Science*, International Symposium on Languages, Applications and Technologies (SLATE 2015), pages 65–75. Springer.

Marcos García-Salido. 2017. On causative *dar* and its alternatives in the history of Spanish. *Folia Linguistica*, 51(s38):91–124.

Stefan Th. Gries. 2013. 50-something years of work on collocations. *International Journal of Corpus Linguistics*, 18(1):137–165.

Kristina Gulordava and Marco Baroni. 2011. A Distributional Similarity Approach to the Detection of Semantic Change in the Google Books Ngram Corpus. In *Proceedings of the GEMS 2011 Workshop on GEometrical Models of Natural Language Semantics (GEMS'11)*, pages 67–71, Stroudsburg, PA, USA. Association for Computational Linguistics.

William L. Hamilton, Jure Leskovec, and Dan Jurafsky. 2016. Diachronic word embeddings reveal statistical laws of semantic change. In *Proceedings of the 54th Annual Meeting of the Association for Computational Linguistics (Volume 1: Long Papers)*, pages 1489–1501, Berlin, Germany. Association for Computational Linguistics.

Franz Josef Hausmann. 1989. Le dictionnaire de collocations. *Wörterbücher, Dictionaries, Dictionnaires*, 1:1010–1019.

Johannes Hellrich and Udo Hahn. 2017. Exploring diachronic lexical semantics with JeSemE. In *Proceedings of ACL 2017, System Demonstrations*, pages 31–36, Vancouver, Canada. Association for Computational Linguistics.

Martin Hilpert and Stefan Th. Gries. 2016. Quantitative approaches to diachronic corpus linguistics.

In *The Cambridge Handbook of English Historical Linguistics*, pages 36–53. Cambridge University Press.

Instituto de Investigación Rafael Lapesa. 2013. Corpus del Nuevo diccionario histórico (CDH). http://web.frl.es/CNDHE.

Bryan Jurish. 2015. DiaCollo: On the trail of diachronic collocations. In *Proceedings of the CLARIN Annual Conference*, pages 28–31, Wroclaw.

Yoon Kim, Yi-I Chiu, Kentaro Hanaki, Darshan Hegde, and Slav Petrov. 2014. Temporal analysis of language through neural language models. In *Proceedings of the ACL 2014 Workshop on Language Technologies and Computational Social Science*, pages 61–65, Baltimore, MD, USA. Association for Computational Linguistics.

Vivek Kulkarni, Rami Al-Rfou, Bryan Perozzi, and Steven Skiena. 2015. Statistically Significant Detection of Linguistic Change. In *Proceedings of the 24th International Conference on World Wide Web*, pages 625–635. International World Wide Web Conferences Steering Committee.

Erez Lieberman, Jean-Baptiste Michel, Joe Jackson, Tina Tang, and Martin A Nowak. 2007. Quantifying the evolutionary dynamics of language. *Nature*, 449(7163):713–716.

Igor Mel'čuk. 1998. Collocations and lexical functions. In Anthony Paul Cowie, editor, *Phraseology. Theory, analysis and applications*, pages 23–53. Clarendon Press, Oxford.

Joakim Nivre, Mitchell Abrams, Željko Agić, and Lars Ahrenberg *et al.* 2018. Universal dependencies 2.3. LINDAT/CLARIN digital library at the Institute of Formal and Applied Linguistics (ÚFAL), Faculty of Mathematics and Physics, Charles University.

Pavel Pecina. 2010. Lexical association measures and collocation extraction. *Language Resources and Evaluation*, 44(1-2):137–158.

Carlos Ramisch and Aline Villavicencio. 2018. Computational treatment of multiword expressions. In Ruslan Mitkov, editor, *Oxford Handbook on Computational Linguistics*, 2nd edition. Oxford University Press.

Maja Rudolph and David Blei. 2018. Dynamic Embeddings for Language Evolution. In *Proceedings of the 2018 World Wide Web Conference on World Wide Web (WWW 2018)*, pages 1003–1011. International World Wide Web Conference Committee (IW3C2).

Ivan A. Sag, Timothy Baldwin, Francis Bond, Ann A. Copestake, and Dan Flickinger. 2002. Multiword expressions: A pain in the neck for NLP. In *Proceedings of the 3rd International Conference on Computational Linguistics and Intelligent Text Processing*, volume 2276/2010 of *CICLing '02*, pages 1–15, London, UK. Springer-Verlag.

Eyal Sagi, Stefan Kaufmann, and Brady Clark. 2009. Semantic density analysis: Comparing word meaning across time and phonetic space. In *Proceedings of the Workshop on Geometrical Models of Natural Language Semantics*, pages 104–111, Athens, Greece. Association for Computational Linguistics.

John Sinclair. 1991. *Corpus, concordance, collocation*. Oxford University Press, Oxford.

Milan Straka and Jana Straková. 2017. Tokenizing, POS Tagging, Lemmatizing and Parsing UD 2.0 with UDPipe. In *Proceedings of the CoNLL 2017 Shared Task: Multilingual Parsing from Raw Text to Universal Dependencies*, pages 88–99, Vancouver, Canada. Association for Computational Linguistics.

Peter Uhrig, Stefan Evert, and Thomas Proisl. 2018. Collocation candidate extraction from dependency-annotated corpora: Exploring differences across parsers and dependency annotation schemes. In *Lexical Collocation Analysis*, pages 111–140. Springer.

Gael Vaamonde. 2015. PS Post Scriptum: Dos corpus diacrónicos de escritura cotidiana. *Procesamiento del Lenguaje Natural*, 55:57–64.

Derry Tanti Wijaya and Reyyan Yeniterzi. 2011. Understanding Semantic Change of Words over Centuries. In *Proceedings of the 2011 International Workshop on DETecting and Exploiting Cultural diversiTy on the Social Web (DETECT'11)*, pages 35–40, New York, NY, USA. Association for Computing Machinery.

Marcos Zampieri and Martin Becker. 2013. Colonia: Corpus of Historical Portuguese. In *ZSM Studien, Special Volume on Non-Standard Data Sources in Corpus-Based Research*, volume 5. Shaker.

Written on Leaves or in Stones?: Computational Evidence for the Era of Authorship of Old Thai Prose

Attapol T. Rutherford *
Department of Linguistics
Faculty of Arts
Chulalongkorn University
attapol.t@chula.ac.th

Santhawat Thanyawong
Department of Linguistics
Faculty of Arts
Chulalongkorn University
santhawat.t@gmail.com

Abstract

We aim to provide computational evidence for the era of authorship of two important old Thai texts: *Traiphumikatha* and *Pumratchatham*. The era of authorship of these two books is still an ongoing debate among Thai literature scholars. Analysis of old Thai texts present a challenge for standard natural language processing techniques, due to the lack of corpora necessary for building old Thai word and syllable segmentation. We propose an accurate and interpretable model to classify each segment as one of the three eras of authorship (Sukhothai, Ayuddhya, or Rattanakosin) without sophisticated linguistic preprocessing. Contrary to previous hypotheses, our model suggests that both books were written during the Sukhothai era. Moreover, the second half of the *Pumratchtham* is uncharacteristic of the Sukhothai era, which may have confounded literary scholars in the past. Further, our model reveals that the most indicative linguistic changes stem from unidirectional grammaticalized words and polyfunctional words, which show up as most dominant features in the model.

1 Introduction

The time periods of authorship for many of the old Thai texts are still being disputed and debated, as the identities of the authors are not always well established. Previous approaches often require diachronic close reading of the text to identify the key elements of style or specific linguistic changes that characterize the writing of the era. Such analysis is limited to qualitative accounts drawn from hand-selected textual evidence. In this work, we build a model that infers the time period of authorship for old Thai prose and reveals diachronic linguistic changes while tolerating the natural language processing (NLP) resources and corpora.

Computational approaches analyzing semantic change in old Thai text face many critical challenges due to poverty of NLP resources. The field lacks texts that could serve as representative examples from each era because solid historical evidence can identify the time of writing for only a few texts. Old Thai prose is especially rare. Consequently, we do not have enough texts to re-train syllable and word segmenters or fit classification models. The currently available Thai syllable and word segmentation algorithms do not perform well on old Thai text, owing to dramatically different orthography and vocabulary. Worse still, some representative Thai texts are significantly damaged inscriptions on stones, which impede sentence-level or even word-level analysis. Thus, to analyze old Thai prose, we cannot rely on automatic syllable and word segmentation, nor on models that require large amounts of data from the same era.

In this work, we propose an accurate and interpretable classification model for analyzing the time period of authorship from textual segments of old Thai prose from *Traiphumikatha* (ไตรภูมิกถา) and *Pumratchatham* (ปุมราชธรรม), whose time of authorship is still debated. Unlike most author attribution models, our model scans through and operates at the text segment level; hence the name Maximum Entropy Searchlight model. The model uses varying-length character n-grams as features to classify textual segments into one of the eras. We shrink the model coefficients to reveal the character n-grams that are distinguishing linguistic features of each era. The model spotlights specific text segments that are characteristic of the era where the book was written and provides computational evidence of the era of authorship for the books in question.

The main contribution of this work can be summarized as follows:

*corresponding author

81

Proceedings of the 1st International Workshop on Computational Approaches to Historical Language Change, pages 81–85
Florence, Italy, August 2, 2019. ©2019 Association for Computational Linguistics

- We propose an accurate and interpretable model for identifying the era of authorship of old Thai prose. The model classifies text segments with high accuracy, reveals some of the linguistic changes from the Sukhothai to the Ayuddhya era, and serves as a visualization tool for further linguistic analysis.

- We are the first to provide statistical evidence that *Traiphumikatha* and *Pumratchatham* might be both written in the Sukhothai era, contrary to previous hypotheses.

- As a more general principle, we conclude that grammaticalized words and polyfunctionalized words are the strongest distinguishing indicators of prose from the Sukhothai era.

2 Background and Related Work

In diachronic studies, Thai language eras are roughly divided by historical timeline of state establishment: Sukhothai (1249-1438), Ayuddhya (1350-1767), Thonburi (1767-1782), and Rattanakosin (1767-present). Ayuddhya and Rattanakosin eras are sometimes further divided into 'early,' 'mid,' and 'late,' depending on the individual research purposes. Due to the gradually changing nature of languages, a language change can be observed only when the language samples in comparison are taken from quite distant eras. It is widely believed that *Traiphumikatha* was written in Sukhothai era although the oldest copy was found in Thonburi era and the proof of era of authorship was never rigorously established (Eawsriwong, 1982). *Pumratchatham* is believed to be written during late Ayuddhya (1688-1767) as the orthography and letter types appear on the first page were usually found in late Ayuddhya books.

Our task can be seen as an author attribution problem or style-change detection problem. These models have utilized all levels of features: lexical, character, syntactic, discourse, and structural (Stamatatos, 2009; Ferracane et al., 2017). Various neural network architectures have been explored in the context of this task (Shrestha et al., 2017). Yet, our task differs in that each class has a mixture of authors. We want to use feature-based models for their interpretability, plus want the model to be accurate at the level of small text segments.

3 Data and Model Descriptions

The reference ground truth texts for each era are: stone inscriptions (Sukhothai era), *Histori-*

Text collection	Character count	Segment count
Ground truth		
Sukhothai era	39,700	873
Ayuddhya era	39,872	984
Rattanakosin era	411,134	10,182
Text in question		
Pumratchatham	110,118	2,741
Traiphumikatha	349,162	8,484

Table 1: Data statistics of the five text collections

cal Archive on Kosapan's trip to France (จดหมายเหตุโกษาปานไปฝรั่งเศส) (Ayuddhya era), and *Historical Archive on Luang Udomsombat* (จดหมายเหตุหลวงอุดมสมบัติ) (Rattakosin era). The stone inscriptions vary in their quality, as some are broken stone fragments and not full texts. The identity of the authors of these inscriptions is either unknown or disputed. *Traiphumikatha* and *Pumratchatham* are the two texts whose time of authorship we want to investigate. We use the manually cleaned version of the texts used by literary scholars because different orthography could bias the models. The data sizes and the class distribution are shown in Table 2.

Our goal is to create a three-way (Sukhothai vs Ayuddhya vs Rattanakosin) classification model that is accurate enough to give us statistical evidence for time of authorship, and interpretable enough to reveal linguistic changes that might require further analysis at the small segment level. We propose Maximum Entropy Searchlight model, which is a multi-class logistic regression model (or Maximum Entropy model) with bag of varying-length character n-gram features and an L1 penalty (Tibshirani, 1996). We formulate the task as text segment classification, with each text divided into non-overlapping contiguous character segments. Numerals, indentation, and punctuations serve as segment dividers, but we cap the segment length to be at most 40 characters, which is right around the median segment lengths.

The model scans through each substring of each segment like a searchlight sweeping across the text, hence the name of the model. The L1 penalty acts as a feature selection mechanism to restrain the model to keep only a handful of interpretable features, while shrinking the rest to zero. Since our model is saturated with both redundant and unhelpful features, this penalty is suitable.

Should we use fixed-length n-grams or varying-length n-grams? We run 10-fold cross-validation to compute the accuracy rates of fixed-

Crossvalidated accuracy		n-gram min max		Params	Non-zero params	
0.99	±0.004	2	6	529k	1190	±16
0.98	±0.005	3	6	524k	1278	±24
0.98	±0.008	4	6	487k	2027	±24
0.96	±0.008	5	6	387k	2956	±49
0.98	±0.005	2	2	4k	1079	±14
0.98	±0.006	3	3	37k	1109	±13
0.97	±0.007	4	4	99k	1727	±17
0.96	±0.008	5	5	166k	2477	±33
0.94	±0.012	6	6	221k	3229	±24

Table 2: Varying-length n-gram features perform the best while keeping the number of non-zero parameters relatively low.

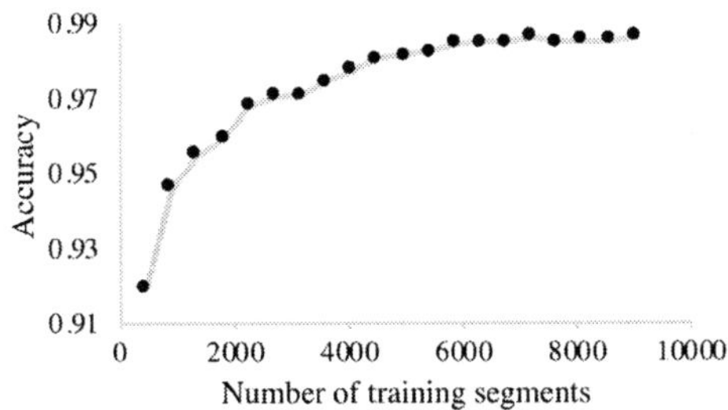

Figure 1: The classifier requires only a small portion of the books to be able to classify the rest at high accuracy.

length n-gram models and varying-length n-gram models ($n \in [2, 6]$). The varying-length n-gram models outperform the best fixed-length models although the L1 penalty shrinks the number of parameters of both types of models to be quite similar (Table 2). The best model only requires (non-zero) 1190 parameters. Our results suggest that varying-length n-gram features are more effective than fixed-length n-gram features even when the number of the parameters are comparable.

Is the model accurate enough to use for unknown texts? We vary the amount of training data from around 4% (454 segments) to 75% (9029 segments) and test the model on the test set, which constitutes the remaining 25% of each book. The final model uses varying-length character n-grams with $n \in [2, 6]$, without fitting the intercepts. The

Era	Precision	Recall	F1
Sukhothai	0.96	0.85	0.90
Ayuddhya	0.98	0.95	0.97
Rattanakosin	0.99	0.99	0.99
Macro average	0.98	0.93	0.95
Micro average	0.98	0.98	0.98

Table 3: Classification results based on the best cross-validated model

accuracy of the model grows logarithmically with the amount of training data, like a typical learning curve of a classifier (Figure 1). Strikingly, the model requires only 40% (4815 segments) of the text from each era to achieve 98% accuracy (Table 3). This low training fraction suggests that the style of writing varies substantially across eras, because the model can capture most of the variation with substantially fewer samples than available. This result also suggests that we can readily apply this model on texts whose era of authorship is unknown.

Does the model present interpretable results? We examine the 30 most salient model coefficients (weights) for linguistic changes. For the Sukhothai era, 15 of those features correspond to known changes studied in Thai historical linguistics. Examples include /lɛ́:w/ and /jù:/ (Sriprasit, 2003), /pen/ (Jaratjarungkiat, 2012), /thǔŋ/ and /thɤ̌ŋ/ (Rodphan, 2012), /mí/ and /bɔ̀mí/ (Jampathip, 2014), and /ʔân/ /nân/ and /nán/ (Suwangphanich, 2017). This correspondence demonstrates how our model can pinpoint specific words for further linguistic analyses.

4 When were *Traiphumikatha* and *Pumratchatham* written?

We classify each 40-character segment of the text and gather the computational evidence for the era of authorship. For each of the two books, we compute the distribution of eras as classified by the model, along with the total log-likelihood of each era given the model. We also compute the distribution of high-confidence classifications for each era, where the score exceeds 0.9. 46% and 41% of the segments from Traiphumikatha and Pumratchatham, respectively, pass this 0.9 threshold (Table 4). The model excludes the intercept terms, to avoid biasing the classification.

Our model supports the hypothesis that *Pumratchatham* was written in the Sukhothai era, contrary to what is popularly believed. 66.8% and 57% of the segments from *Traiphumikatha* and *Pumratchatham* respectively are classified as more similar to the stone inscriptions from the Sukhothai era. Many scholars have hypothesized that *Traiphumikatha* might be written in the Ayuddhya era. Surprisingly, our model gives very little evidence to support this hypothesis, as less than 5% of the segments are classified as Ayuddhya.

The Maximum Entropy Searchlight model vi-

Era	Traiphumikatha					Pumratchatham				
	Classification distribution		>0.9 only distribution		Total likelihood	Classification distribution		>0.9 only distribution		Total likelihood
Sukhothai	5664	67%	2947	75%	-7984	1566	57%	690	58%	-3554
Ayuddhya	286	3%	19	0%	-43511	60	2%	3	0%	-14982
Rattanakosin	2533	30%	956	24%	-24528	1115	41%	498	42%	-5640

Table 4: The distribution of classified segments and the total likelihood suggest that Traiphumikatha and Pumratchatham were likely written in the Sukhothai era, contrary to previous hypotheses.

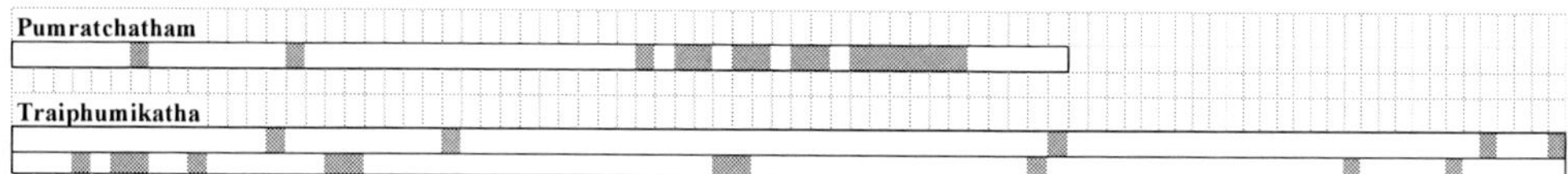

Figure 2: The language of the second half of *Pumratchatham* does not resemble the language from the Sukhothai era. 30-segment blocks are shaded if the majority of its 40-character segments are classified as Rattanakosin era, while the unshaded blocks are Sukhothai.

sualizes potential style changes within the book and spotlights the regions that deserve further investigation. We group 40-character text segments into a blocks and visualize the majority class for each block (Figure 2). It turns out that the non-Sukhothai parts of *Pumratchatham* are clustered towards the end of the book, while non-Sukhothai parts are distributed more uniformly in Traiphumikatha. The era of authorship of this book may be more contested for this reason.

5 Grammaticalization and Polyfunctionalization across Eras

Some of the most common features are words that undergo the process of grammaticalization over time such as /lɛ́ːw/, /jùː/, and /pen/. Grammaticalization refers to the phenomenon where a lexical item becomes a grammatical marker and develops new grammatical functions (Hopper and Traugott, 2003). Grammaticalization is unidirectional in the sense that grammatical forms and markers cannot become lexical again. This implies that the linguistic characteristics of a grammaticalized word are different in each stage of changes. Thus, grammaticalized words can strongly characterize eras.

Polyfunctional words (words that can take multiple part of speech tags) form another group of linguistic changes indicative of eras of authorship. We found 6 words to be polyfunctional observable in synchronic Thai grammar. These are /sǐːa/, as verb and completive aspect marker (Iwasaki et al., 2005), /hɛ̀ŋ/ and /khâːŋ/, as noun and preposition, /thâw/, as noun and adverb, /bâːŋ/, as pronoun and adverb (Royal Institute dictionary B.E. 2554) and /ʔɔ̀ːk/, as verb and adverb (Wongsri, 2004). Poly-

functionality of a word can be seen as a synchronic product of the unidirectional grammaticalization process called `layering', which is the persistence of older forms and meanings alongside newer ones (Hopper and Traugott, 2003) . Our model reveals this synchronic state of grammaticalization and unidirectional linguistic changes that characterize the differences across the eras.

In sum, 15 of 30 extracted words given by the model can be best explained in a single theme of unidirectionality of change, a tendency that forms the backbone of grammaticalization (diachronic change) and layering (synchronic resultant state of the change). Thus, these words, along with grammaticalization perspective, can best validate the Maximum Entropy Searchlight Model as a tool to provide the statistical evidence for the era of authorship.

6 Conclusion

We present the Maximum Entropy Searchlight model, an accurate and interpretable model for identifying the era of authorship of old Thai prose. The model lends reliable computational evidence for the era of authorship because it can classify the era of the ground truth text collections at almost perfect accuracy. In addition, the model can shed light on each individual segment to discover specific linguistic changes that are important indicators for each era. These attributes not only speed up the process of qualitative linguistic analysis, but also reveal an overarching theme of unidirectional grammaticalization, characterizing the differences across the eras.

Acknowledgements

This research is funded by Grants for Development of New Faculty Staff at Chulalongkorn University.

References

Nidhi Eawsriwong. 1982. หลักฐานทางประวัติศาสตร์ใน ประเทศไทย [Historical Evidence in Thailand]. Bhannakij Trading.

Elisa Ferracane, Su Wang, and Raymond Mooney. 2017. Leveraging discourse information effectively for authorship attribution. In *Proceedings of the Eighth International Joint Conference on Natural Language Processing (Volume 1: Long Papers)*, volume 1, pages 584--593.

Paul J Hopper and Elizabeth Closs Traugott. 2003. *Grammaticalization*. Cambridge University Press.

Shoichi Iwasaki, Preeya Ingkaphirom, and Inkapiromu Puriyā Horie. 2005. *A reference grammar of Thai*. Cambridge University Press.

Nida Jampathip. 2014. *The development of the negators "bo" "mi" "pai" "mai" in Thai*. Ph.D. thesis, Chulalongkorn University.

Sureenate Jaratjarungkiat. 2012. *The development of the word /pen/ in Thai*. Ph.D. thesis, Chulalongkorn University.

Krongkan Rodphan. 2012. /thŭŋ/: a historical study. Master's thesis, Chulalongkorn University.

Prasha Shrestha, Sebastian Sierra, Fabio Gonzalez, Manuel Montes, Paolo Rosso, and Thamar Solorio. 2017. Convolutional neural networks for authorship attribution of short texts. In *Proceedings of the 15th Conference of the European Chapter of the Association for Computational Linguistics: Volume 2, Short Papers*, volume 2, pages 669--674.

Mingmit Sriprasit. 2003. A diachronic study of /lææw/, /yuù/ and /yuùlææw/. Master's thesis, Chulalongkorn University.

Efstathios Stamatatos. 2009. A survey of modern authorship attribution methods. *Journal of the American Society for information Science and Technology*, 60(3):538--556.

Wasitthi Suwangphanich. 2017. Development of demonstratives in thai. Master's thesis, Chulalongkorn University.

Robert Tibshirani. 1996. Regression shrinkage and selection via the lasso. *Journal of the Royal Statistical Society: Series B (Methodological)*, 58(1):267--288.

Katbandit Wongsri. 2004. A semantic network of /ʔɔɔk/ in thai: a cognitive semantic study. Master's thesis, Chulalongkorn University.

Identifying Temporal Trends Based on Perplexity and Clustering: Are We Looking at Language Change?

Sidsel Boldsen[1], Manex Agirrezabal[1], Patrizia Paggio[1,2]
(1) Centre for Language Technology
University of Copenhagen
(2) Institute of Linguistics and Language Technology
University of Malta
`{sbol,manex.aguirrezabal,paggio}@hum.ku.dk`

Abstract

In this work we propose a data-driven methodology for identifying temporal trends in a corpus of medieval charters. We have used perplexities derived from RNNs as a distance measure between documents and then, performed clustering on those distances. We argue that perplexities calculated by such language models are representative of temporal trends. The clusters produced using the K-Means algorithm give an insight of the differences in language in different time periods at least partly due to language change. We suggest that the temporal distribution of the individual clusters might provide a more nuanced picture of temporal trends compared to discrete bins, thus providing better results when used in a classification task.

1 Background

Several recent approaches have looked at the task of identifying temporal trends in document collections using NLP methods. An example is the diachronic text evaluation challenge (Popescu and Strapparava, 2015) in SemEval 2015, where newspaper text snippets from 1700-2010 had to be classified into time intervals of different sizes. Models for diachronic text classification are trained based on the way lexical, morphological, syntactic and stylistic features change over time (Abe and Tsumoto, 2010; Garcia-Fernandez et al., 2011; Popescu and Strapparava, 2015; Štajner and Zampieri, 2013; Szymanski and Lynch, 2015; Zampieri et al., 2016; Boldsen and Paggio, 2019).

Diachronic text classification, however, is a simplification. Firstly, no assumption is made about texts from two time spans close to each other being closer than others belonging to time spans further away. Furthermore, how the time spans should be chosen, both in terms of their size and

the exact placing of the boundaries between them, seems often a rather arbitrary decision.

Important insights relevant to the issue may come from research dealing with language distance and language identification. The underlying assumption in this area is that the more difficult it is to identify differences between two languages or language varieties, the shorter is the distance between them. Perplexity has been proposed as a measure of language distance, and recently used to distinguish formal from colloquial tweets (González Bermúdez, 2015), to measure distance between languages (Gamallo et al., 2016, 2017), and, interestingly for our purposes, between historical varieties of the same language (Pichel Campos et al., 2018).

In this paper, we propose a data-driven approach to the identification of temporal trends in a corpus of medieval charters. This is a particularly interesting test-bed in that medieval manuscripts often lack explicit reference to when they were produced, and this knowledge is crucially important for their philological interpretation. We first derive perplexity measures that reflect how similar the documents are to one another, and how this similarity correlates with the time difference between them, and then we cluster the documents based on perplexity. The groups obtained through clustering are evaluated with respect to a manually determined classification into discrete 50-year time periods, a method often used to distinguish historical variants of a language, and which was applied to medieval charters in Boldsen and Paggio (2019).

We believe the idea of clustering documents based on perplexity measures as a method to discover temporal trends in a document collection is a novel and, as we argue below, promising one.

Proceedings of the 1st International Workshop on Computational Approaches to Historical Language Change, pages 86–91
Florence, Italy, August 2, 2019. ©2019 Association for Computational Linguistics

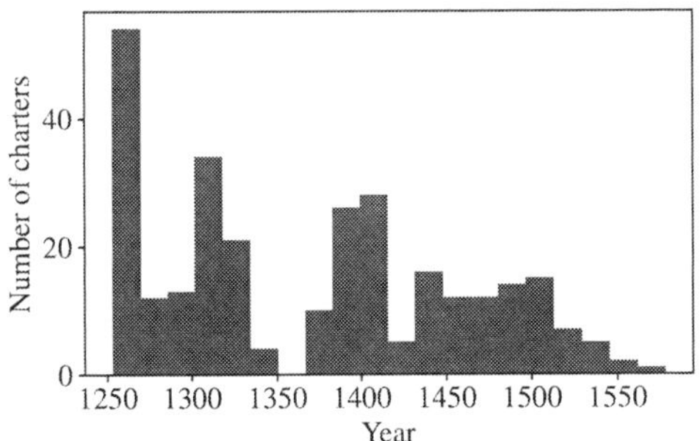

Figure 1: Plot of the distribution of the charters along the temporal line.

2 Methodology

In this section we introduce the dataset and the methods that we have employed in this work.

2.1 Dataset

The dataset in this study consists of 291 charters belonging to a larger collection of charters from St. Clara Convent in Denmark, which is part of the interdisciplinary research project *Script and Text in Time and Space*[1] studying the development of medieval Danish language and script. The charters, which are being prepared for a scholarly edition, document the property and status of the convent from when it was founded in 1256 till it was closed after the Reformation. Two different transcription levels are included in the dataset: (i) the facsimile transcription, where allographic variation is annotated, and (ii) the diplomatic transcription, where this variation is normalised, while spelling variants are kept. Most of the documents are either in Latin or in Danish, with a shift during the 15th century to documents being written in Danish. There are also two texts in Low German from earlier than 1450, and two Swedish ones from 1500-1550. The number of charters available from the various periods varies, as shown in Figure 1.

In addition to the language variation, the charters also vary in length. Therefore, the dataset was resampled by normalising the length of the individual documents. This was done by finding the outliers in the distribution (documents longer than approximately 3000 characters) and

[1]https://humanities.ku.dk/research/
digital-humanities/projects/
writing-and-texts-in-time-and-space

randomly subsampling text from them to get as close as possible to the average length of the rest of the collection. This process produced a more balanced dataset of 291 documents of length between 351 and 3099 characters.

2.2 Perplexity and language modelling

Perplexity is a metric that expresses how well a language model fits a test sample. It is based on the computation of the probability of each sentence in the test set as predicted by the language model. A low perplexity corresponds to a high probability of the sentences in the test sample.

Given a test set consisting of a sequence of characters (CH) and a character-based language model (LM) with n-gram probabilities $P(ch_i|ch_1^{i-1})$, perplexity (PP) is defined by the following equation (Pichel Campos et al., 2018, 148):

$$PP(CH, LM) = \sqrt[n]{\prod_i^n \frac{1}{P(ch_i|ch_1^{i-1})}} \qquad (1)$$

We train document-specific character-based language models and test each model on the remaining documents in the collection. A perplexity measure is then computed for each pair of language model and test document. The measure is used as an estimator of the distance between each document pair. Since the charters represent different stages of language development during a time period of about 350 years, we expect the perplexity related to pairs of language models and test manuscripts to increase with the temporal distance between the text from which a language model is derived and the text to which the same model is applied.

2.3 Language models

As a baseline we used character trigrams to estimate character language models for each of the documents in our corpus, and then calculated the perplexity of each document, given each language model (Stolcke, 2002). We estimated the probabilities by Maximum Likelihood and dealt with zero-counts using Witten-Bell smoothing.

To get more representative language models we then trained Recurrent Neural Network Language Models (Elman, 1990) with LSTM (Hochreiter and Schmidhuber, 1997). The main advantage of RNNs is that the Markov assumption from the trigram language model is relaxed, and thus, the quality of the language model is expected to be better. Our RNN also makes use of an embedding layer that projects each character to a numeric representation. This numeric representation is given as input to the LSTM cell, which, together with the previous layers content, generates a probability distribution of the possible next characters. Then, calculating the perplexity of a language model in a test corpus is relatively simple, if we consider the probability of the whole test sequence.

2.4 Clustering

Having trained a language model, LM, for each of the documents, d, in the collection, D, we let each of the documents in D be represented by a vector, X_i, of size $|D|$, where each value, $X_{i,j}$ corresponds to the perplexity of a language model, LM_i, trained on document d_i, and applied to a document, d_j.

We use k-means clustering to perform cluster analysis of the documents in the collection. In k-means the objective is to find the best k clusters which minimise the distance between cluster centroids and the data points within the clusters (Bishop, 2006). Thus, when applying k-means to the collection of documents, we find clusters of documents which are similar in terms of perplexity. If perplexity is indicative of language change as a measure of (dis)similarity, our hypothesis is that such an analysis will give insights to how a collection of documents changes over time.

3 Results and discussion

In this section first we discuss the usefulness of the perplexity measures as predictors of distance between documents on the temporal line, and then we give an account of the clustering results.

3.1 Perplexity as a predictor of language change

To evaluate whether perplexity was a good basis on which to cluster the charters, in other words whether the perplexity measures modelling similarity between documents are actually related to temporal change, we run a correlation between those measures on the one hand, and differences in years between each document pair on the other. The expectation was that the higher the perplexity between a model and a text is, the greater the temporal distance between them.

The correlation is moderate when using the perplexity calculated by the baseline (Pearson'r = 0.49, p-value < 0.01), and even higher when using the values provided by the RNN model (Pearson'r = 0.65, p-value < 0.01). It thus shows that the neural language model does a better job than the baseline.

However, language change from Latin to Danish during the 15th century might be the main factor behind the correlation strength. To test this, we partitioned the perplexity data from the RNN model into two groups based on the language, and run correlation tests for each partition separately. Although we still found a moderate correlation for the Latin texts (Pearson'r = 0.50, p-value < 0.01), only a weak one was observed for the Danish ones (Pearson'r = 0.20, p-value < 0.01). Nevertheless, for the majority of the charters in the dataset, perplexity still appears potentially useful for the task of modelling temporal change, and was indeed used to drive the clustering.

3.2 Results of clustering

We ran k-means clustering for all values $k \in \{2, ..., 10\}$ and found that $k = 7$ provided a good fit in terms of intra- and inter-cluster distance.

To visualise the results, the document vectors were projected onto two components using t-SNE (Maaten and Hinton, 2008). The resulting projections can be seen in figure 2, in which three groups of documents are clearly distinguished: two groups to the left - one at the top and one at the bottom - and one in the top right corner. The clusters from the k-means clustering are indicated through shapes, revealing that clusters 3, 6 and 7 are gathered in the top left group, whereas the group in the middle mostly consists of instances from cluster 1, and the top right group is mostly made up of texts from clusters 2 and 5. Temporal outliers can be observed in all three groups.

In order to evaluate what the clusters can tell us about the temporal development of documents in the collection, we colour-coded the documents according to their manually assigned temporal bins. Figure 2 shows the distribution of earlier (warmer colours) and later (cooler colours) documents.

First of all, had we coloured the documents to highlight the different languages, we would see that the left groups correspond to the Latin documents and the right one to all the rest, i.e. Danish, Swedish and Low German. This result is highly

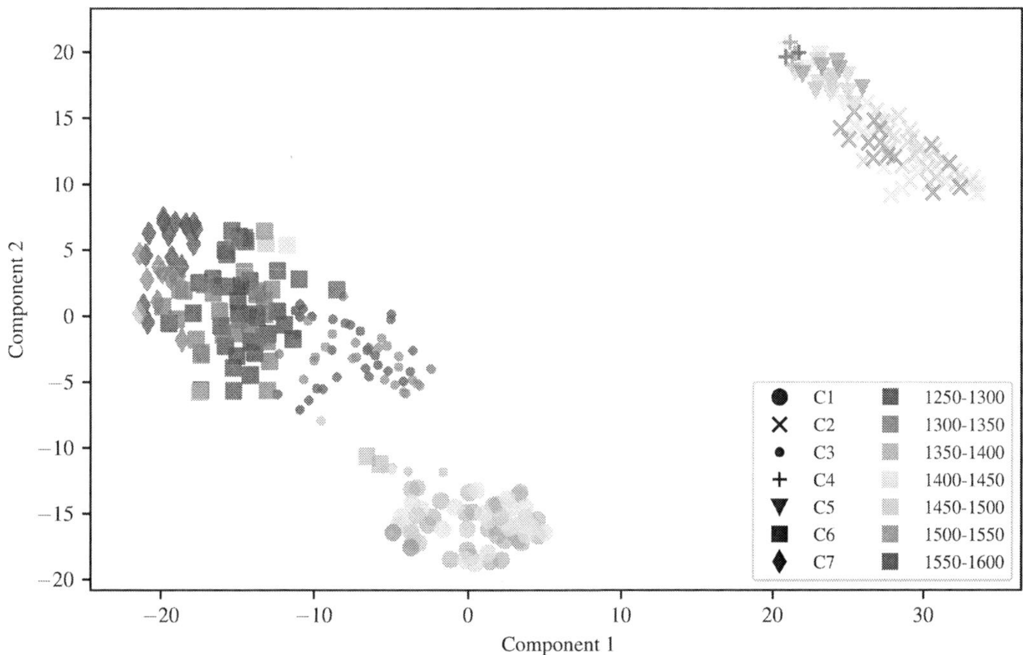

Figure 2: T-SNE projection of the documents in our dataset. Each document is represented as a vector of perplexities. For each document, the shape represents the cluster to which the document belongs based on K-Means. The colour shows the year-span to which the document belongs.

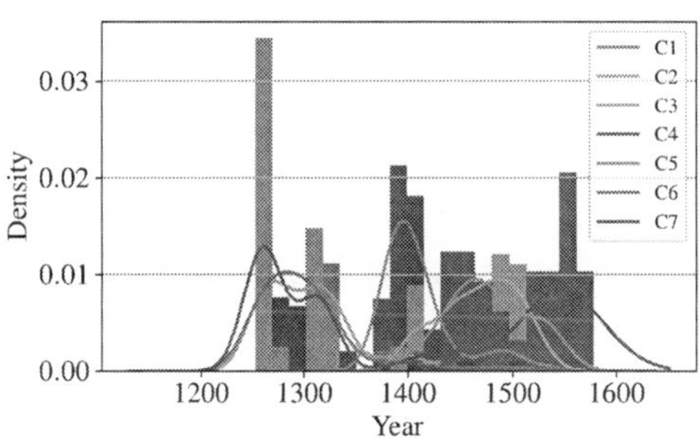

Figure 3: Year distribution for each cluster.

expected given what we know about the language distribution.

Secondly, the top left clusters seem to represent earlier documents (red, dark orange) relative to the internal temporal distribution of the Latin documents, while the lower cluster represents the later ones (light orange, yellow). It remains to be seen if this partition corresponds to time-related language change or some other difference (different scribe, different register, etc.) or whether it is due to a gap in the data just before 1350 (see figure 1).

Looking at the distribution of the temporal bins more closely, however, there is no really clear pattern to how these are distributed between the individual clusters. If we focus on the top left group corresponding to the earliest temporal bins, for instance, it is difficult to interpret the way the three clusters - 3, 6 and 7 - are distributed within the period. This is confirmed in Figure 3 where the clusters are plotted as yearly distributions using Gaussian kernel density estimation (Bishop, 2006). The plot makes it evident that the distributions of the three clusters overlap. This suggests that there may be other factors than language change as such influencing the models. For example, we know that a group of papal letters belong to the early stages of the collection. The special register that these letters use could possibly explain the creation of several clusters within a similar time period. More in-depth analysis is needed, possibly in cooperation with philologists, to understand the exact nature of the differences the clusters are capturing, particularly whether they reflect other textual characteristics than the existence of language variants due to temporal change.

4 Conclusion

In this work we have proposed a methodology for the identification of temporal trends in a document collection. To this end, we relied on perplexities derived from recurrent neural network language models and K-Means clustering.

The perplexities calculated by document-specific language models correlate moderately with time differences. Performing K-Means with $K=7$ based on perplexity measures proved to be a good method for grouping documents based on intrinsic evaluation (inter- and intra-cluster distance). The method allowed us to discover groups that seem at least partially to reflect differences due to language change not only in the sense of radical change in language (from Latin to Danish), but also changes within the same language (Latin).

The remaining question is whether the clusters found can be more deeply characterised. They seem to be somewhat temporally distributed which, however, could partly be explained by the nature of the dataset. Thus, future work involves investigating how other factors could represent temporal trends in the data. This could be done by evaluating how congruent the clusters are with documented trends within the dataset, for example trends that could be caused by the existence of specific types of text such as the group of papal letters.

Another interesting problem is to see how such clusters can be used in relation to the task of temporal document classification (extrinsic evaluation). Using the temporal distribution of the individual clusters might provide a more nuanced picture of temporal trends compared to discrete bins, thus providing better results when used in a classification task.

References

Hidenao Abe and Shusaku Tsumoto. 2010. Text categorization with considering temporal patterns of term usages. In *Proceedings of the 2010 IEEE International Conference on Data Mining Workshops*, ICDMW '10, pages 800–807, Washington, DC, USA. IEEE Computer Society.

Christopher M. Bishop. 2006. *Pattern Recognition and Machine Learning (Information Science and Statistics)*. Springer-Verlag, Berlin, Heidelberg.

Sidsel Boldsen and Patrizia Paggio. 2019. Automatic dating of medieval charters from Denmark. In *Proceedings of the 4th Digital Humanities in the Nordic Countries Conference*.

Jeffrey L Elman. 1990. Finding structure in time. *Cognitive science*, 14(2):179–211.

Pablo Gamallo, Inaki Alegria, José Ramom Pichel, and Manex Agirrezabal. 2016. Comparing two basic methods for discriminating between similar languages and varieties. In *Proceedings of the Third Workshop on NLP for Similar Languages, Varieties and Dialects (VarDial3)*, pages 170–177.

Pablo Gamallo, Jose Ramom Pichel, and Inaki Alegria. 2017. A perplexity-based method for similar languages discrimination. In *Proceedings of the Fourth Workshop on NLP for Similar Languages, Varieties and Dialects (VarDial)*, pages 109–114.

Anne Garcia-Fernandez, Anne-Laure Ligozat, Marco Dinarelli, and Delphine Bernhard. 2011. When was it written? Automatically determining publication dates. In *String Processing and Information Retrieval*, pages 221–236, Berlin, Heidelberg. Springer Berlin Heidelberg.

Meritxell González Bermúdez. 2015. An analysis of twitter corpora and the differences between formal and colloquial tweets. In *Proceedings of the Tweet Translation Workshop 2015*, pages 1–7. CEUR-WS.org.

Sepp Hochreiter and Jürgen Schmidhuber. 1997. Long short-term memory. *Neural computation*, 9(8):1735–1780.

Laurens van der Maaten and Geoffrey Hinton. 2008. Visualizing data using t-SNE. *Journal of machine learning research*, 9(Nov):2579–2605.

José Ramom Pichel Campos, Pablo Gamallo, and Iñaki Alegria. 2018. Measuring language distance among historical varieties using perplexity. Application to European Portuguese. In *Proceedings of the Fifth Workshop on NLP for Similar Languages, Varieties and Dialects (VarDial 2018)*, pages 145–155. Association for Computational Linguistics.

Octavian Popescu and Carlo Strapparava. 2015. Semeval 2015, task 7: Diachronic text evaluation. In *Proceedings of the 9th International Workshop on Semantic Evaluation (SemEval 2015)*, pages 870–878.

Sanja Štajner and Marcos Zampieri. 2013. Stylistic changes for temporal text classification. In *Text, Speech, and Dialogue*, pages 519–526, Berlin, Heidelberg. Springer Berlin Heidelberg.

Andreas Stolcke. 2002. SRILM-an extensible language modeling toolkit. In *Seventh international conference on spoken language processing*.

Terrence Szymanski and Gerard Lynch. 2015. Ucd: Diachronic text classification with character, word, and syntactic n-grams. In *Proceedings of the 9th International Workshop on Semantic Evaluation (SemEval 2015)*, pages 879–883.

Marcos Zampieri, Shervin Malmasi, and Mark Dras. 2016. Modeling language change in historical corpora: The case of Portuguese. In *Proceedings of the Tenth International Conference on Language Resources and Evaluation (LREC 2016)*, pages 4098–4104, Paris, France. European Language Resources Association (ELRA).

Using Word Embeddings to Examine Gender Bias in Dutch Newspapers, 1950-1990

Melvin Wevers

DHLab KNAW Humanities Cluster
Oudezijds Achterburgwal 185
1012DK Amsterdam, the Netherlands
melvin.wevers@dh.huc.knaw.nl

Abstract

Contemporary debates on filter bubbles and polarization in public and social media raise the question to what extent news media of the past exhibited biases. This paper specifically examines bias related to gender in six Dutch national newspapers between 1950 and 1990. We measure bias related to gender by comparing local changes in word embedding models trained on newspapers with divergent ideological backgrounds. We demonstrate clear differences in gender bias and changes within and between newspapers over time. In relation to themes such as sexuality and leisure, we see the bias moving toward women, whereas, generally, the bias shifts in the direction of men, despite growing female employment number and feminist movements. Even though Dutch society became less stratified ideologically (depillarization), we found an increasing divergence in gender bias between religious and social-democratic on the one hand and liberal newspapers on the other. Methodologically, this paper illustrates how word embeddings can be used to examine historical language change. Future work will investigate how fine-tuning deep contextualized embedding models, such as ELMO, might be used for similar tasks with greater contextual information.

1 Introduction

In recent years, public and academic debates about the possible impact of filter bubbles and the role of polarization in public and social media have been widespread (Pariser, 2011; Flaxman et al., 2016). In these debates, news media have been described as belonging to particular political ideologies, producing skewed views on topics, such as climate change or immigration. These contemporary debates raise the question to what extent newspapers in the past operated in filter bubbles driven by their own ideological bias.

This paper examines gender bias in historical newspapers. By looking at differences in the strength of association between male and female dimensions of gender on the one hand, and words that represent occupations, psychological states, or social life, on the other, we examine the gender bias in and between several Dutch newspapers over time. Did certain newspapers exhibit a bias toward men or women in relationship to specific aspects of society, behavior, or culture?

Newspapers are an excellent source to study societal debates. They function as a transceiver; both the producer and the messenger of public discourse (Schudson, 1982). Margaret Marshall (1995) claims that researchers can uncover the "values, assumptions, and concerns, and ways of thinking that were a part of the public discourse of that time" by analyzing "the arguments, language, the discourse practices that inhabit the pages of public magazines, newspapers, and early professional journals."

The period 1950-1990 is of particular interest as Dutch society underwent clear industrialization and modernization as well as ideological shifts (Schot et al., 2010). After the Second World War, Dutch society was stratified according to ideological and religious "pillars", a phenomenon known as pillarization. These pillars can be categorized as Catholic, Protestant, socialist, and liberal (Wintle, 2000). Newspapers were often aligned to one of these pillars (Wijfjes, 2004; Rooij, 1974). The newspaper *Trouw*, for example, has a distinct Protestant origin, while *Volkskrant* and *De Telegraaf* can be characterized as, respectively, Catholic and neutral. In recent years, the latter transformed into a newspaper with clear conservative leanings. Newspaper historians have studied the ideological backgrounds of Dutch newspapers using traditional hermeneutic means to which this study adds a computational analysis of language

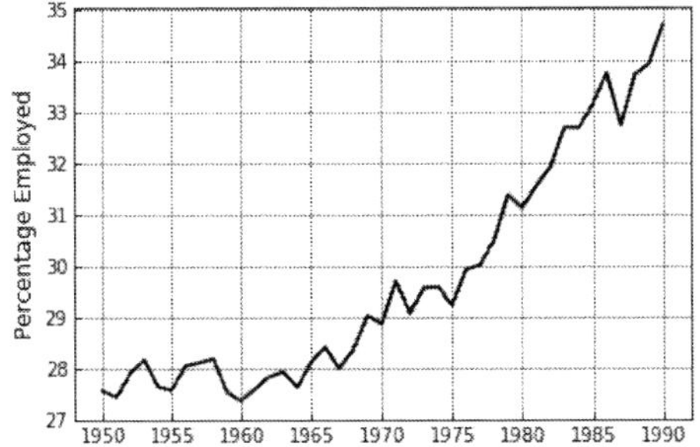

Figure 1: Female Employment Numbers

use related to gender.

The representation of gender in public discourse is related to ideological struggles over gender equality. Several feminist waves materialized in the Netherlands. The origins of the first feminist wave can be traced back to the mid-nineteenth century and lasted until the interwar period. It took until the 1960s for feminism to flare up again in the Netherlands. In between, confessional parties were vocal in their anti-feminist policies. During the 1960s, the second feminist wave, also known as 'new feminism', focused on gender equality in areas such as work, education, sexuality, marriage, and family (Ribberink, 1987).

The increasing equality between men and women is reflected in growing female employment numbers, which increased from 27.5 percent in 1950 to almost 35 percent in 1990 (Figure 1).[1] Apart from Scandinavia, the Netherlands has the highest levels of equality in Europe. Nonetheless, in terms of education and employment, women are still lagging behind and reports of gender discrimination are not uncommon in the Netherlands (Baali et al., 2018; Ministerie van Onderwijs, 2009).

2 Related Work

Word embedding models can be used for a wide range of lexical-semantic tasks (Baroni et al., 2014; Kulkarni et al., 2015). Hamilton et al. (2016) show how word embeddings can also be used to measure semantic shifts by comparing the contexts in which words are used to denote continuity and changes in language use. More recent work focused on the role of bias in word embed-

dings, specifically bias related to politics, gender, and ethnicity (Azarbonyad et al., 2017; Bolukbasi et al., 2016; Garg et al., 2018). Gonen et al. (2019) demonstrate that debiasing methods work, but argue that we should not remove them. Azarbonyad et al. (2017) compare semantic spaces related to political views in the UK parliament, effectively comparing biases between embeddings. Garg et al. (2018) turn to biases in embedding to study shifts related to gender and ethnicity.

This study builds upon the work of Garg et al. (2018), and applies it to the context of the Netherlands—represented by Dutch newspapers. We extend their method further by distinguishing between sources, rather than using a comprehensive gold standard data set. We also incorporate external lexicons, such as the emotion lexicon from Cornetto, the *Nederlandse Voornamenbank* (database of Dutch first names), the Dutch translation of LIWC (Linguistic Inquiry and Word Count) and HISCO (Historical International Classification of Occupations) (Vossen et al., 2007; Tausczik and Pennebaker, 2010; Boot et al., 2017; Zijdeman et al., 2013; Bloothooft, 2010).

3 Data

The data set consists of six Dutch national newspapers: *NRC Handelsblad (NRC)*, *Het Vrije Volk (VV)*, *Parool*, *Telegraaf*, *Trouw*, and *Volkskrant (VK)*.[2] These newspapers can be characterized ideologically as liberal, social-democratic, liberal, neutral/conservative, Protestant, and Catholic.

For the analysis, we rely on the articles and not the advertisements in the newspapers. We preprocess the text by removing stopwords, punctuation, numerical characters, and words shorter than three and longer than fifteen characters. The quality of the digitized text varies throughout the corpus due to imperfections in the original material and limitations of the recognition software. Because of the variations in OCR quality, we only retain words that also appeared in a Dutch dictionary.

We use the Gensim implementation of Word2Vec to train four embedding models per newspaper, each representing one decade between 1950 and 1990.[3] The models were trained using C-BOW with hierarchical softmax, with a dimensionality of 300, a minimal word count

---

[1] https://opendata.cbs.nl/statline/#/CBS/nl/

[2] The digitized newspapers were provided by the National Library of the Netherlands. http://www.delpher.nl

[3] https://radimrehurek.com/gensim/

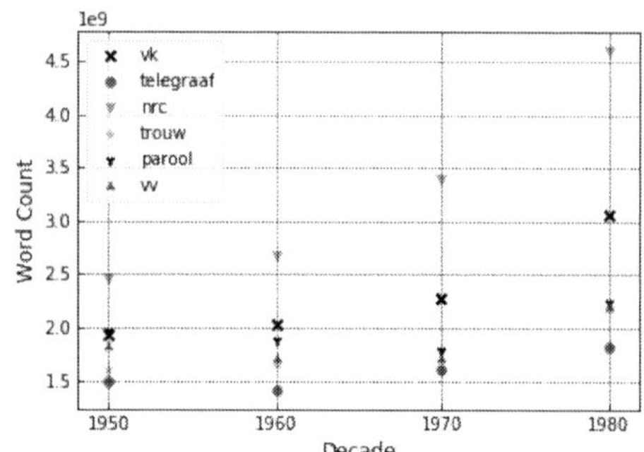

Figure 2: Total number of words per embedding model

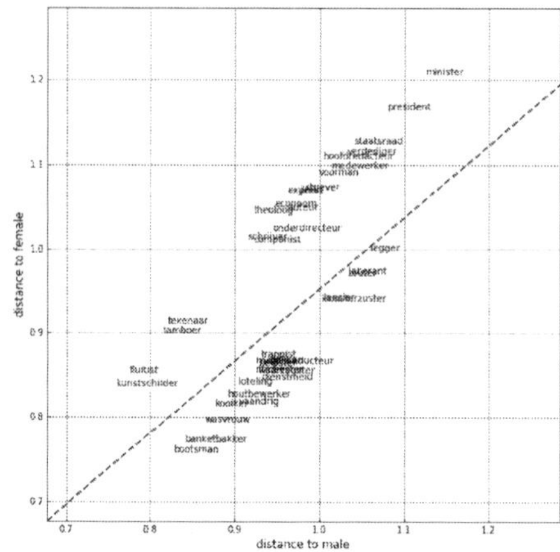

Figure 3: Job titles with strong bias towards men and women in *De Volkskrant*, 1980-1990

and context of 5, and downsampling of 10^{-5}.[4] Figure 2 shows that the size of the vocabulary approximately doubles for some newspapers between 1950 and 1990. The variance of the targets words, however, was small ($\mu \approx 0.003$) and constant ($\sigma[1.3^{-9}, 2.9^{-9}]$), indicating model stability. Since we calculate bias relative to each model, these differences in vocabulary size will have little impact on shifts in bias.

To measure gender bias, we use three sets of targets words. First, we extract a list of approximately 12.5k job titles from the HISCO data set. Second, we select emotion words with a confidence score of 1.0, a positive polarity above 0.5 ($n = 476$) and a negative polarity below -0.5 ($n = 636$) from Cornetto. Third, we rely on the Dutch translation of LIWC2001, which contains lists of words to measure psychological and cognitive states (Pennebaker et al., 2001). We use the following LIWC (sub)categories: Affective and Emotional Processes; Cognitive Processes; Sensory and Perceptual Processes; Social Processes; Occupation; Leisure activity; Money and Financial Issues; Metaphysical Issues; and Physical states.

4 Methodology

For the calculation of gender bias, we construct two vectors representing the gender dimensions (male, female). We do this by creating an average vector that includes words referring to male ('man', 'his', 'father', etc.) or female as well as the most popular first names in the Netherlands

for the period 1950-1990.[5] Next, we calculate the distance between each gender vector and every word in a list of target words, for example, words that denote occupations: a greater distance indicates that a word is less closely associated with that dimension of gender. The difference between the distances for both gender vectors represents the gender bias: positive meaning a bias toward women and negative toward men. Figure 3 shows the biases related to forty job titles. Words above the diagonal are biased towards men, and those underneath the diagonal towards women.

Finally, after standardizing and centering the bias values, we apply Bayesian linear regression to determine whether the bias changed over time. The linear model is formulated as:

$$\mu_i = \alpha + \beta * Y_i + \epsilon,$$

with μ_i the bias for each decade (i) and Y_i the coefficient related to each decade (i). The likelihood function is: $X \sim \mathcal{N}(\mu, \sigma)$ with priors defined: $\alpha \sim \mathcal{N}(0, 2)$, $\beta \sim \mathcal{N}(0, 2)$, and $\epsilon \sim$ HalfCauchy($\beta = 1$). For model training, we use a No-U-Turn-Sampler (NUTS) (5k draws, 1.5k tuning steps, Highest Posterior Density (HPD) of .95).[6] For the target words Job Titles, the proposed model (Model B) outperforms a model that only

---

[4]Code can be found here: `https://github.com/ melvinwevers/historical_concepts` and the models here: `http://doi.org/10.5281/zenodo. 3237380`

[5]The word lists for both vectors can be found in Appendix A. The first names were harvested from `https://www. meertens.knaw.nl/nvb/`

[6]HPD is the Bayesian equivalent of the frequentists confidence interval in Frequentist credible interval. `https: //docs.pymc.io`

	WAIC	pWAIC	dWAIC	weight	SE	dSE
Model B	64624.8	2.9	0	0.99	201.6	0
Model A	64682.1	1.88	57.28	0.01	201.36	15.2

Table 1: Model Comparison

	mean	sd	hpd_2.5	hpd_97.5	n_eff	Rhat
a	-0.164	0.010	-0.185	-0.145	1315.073	1.000
bY	0.046	0.006	0.033	0.055	1261.437	0.999
sigma	1.001	0.005	0.992	1.010	1035.282	1.003

Table 2: Model B Summary

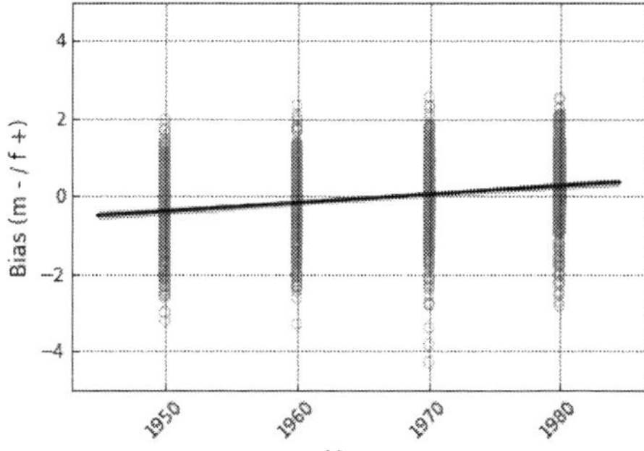

Figure 4: Combined model 'Sexuality'

includes the intercept (Model A), indicating that bias changes as a function of time (Table 1 & Table 2).

We compute a linear model that combines all newspapers for the target words Job Titles, Positive Emotions, Negative Emotions, and the selected LIWC columns. Then, for the same categories, we compute individual linear models for each newspaper. The resulting models are reported in Appendix B.

5 Results

The combined linear models, including all newspapers, generally display minimal shifts in bias. While the effects are weak, they fall within a .95 HPD. Partly, the weak trends are related to opposing shifts in the individual newspapers, cancelling each other out. Nonetheless, the bias associated with the categories 'TV', 'Music', 'Metaphysical issues', 'Sexuality' navigate toward women (0.22, 0.12, 0.15, 0.22), with all of them starting from a position that was clearly oriented toward men (-0.36, -0.20, -0.28, -0.39).[7] Conversely, 'Money', 'Grooming', and Negative Emotion words move toward men (-0.24, -0.17, -0.16), which in the 1950s were all more closely related to women (0.33, 0.20, 0.19). For the Job Titles, we see a slight move toward women (0.05), while words from the LIWC category Occupation move marginally in the direction of men (-0.05). This suggests that job titles might be more closely related to women, while the notion of working gravitates toward men.

The linear models for the individual newspapers demonstrate distinct differences between the newspapers. First, *Volkskrant* is the most stable newspapers with 56% of the categories not changing.[8] When bias changes in this newspaper, it

moves toward women 9 out the 11 categories that change. *Telegraaf*, *NRC*, and *Parool* generally move toward men, respectively (84%, 92%, and 80%). The bias of *Trouw* and *Vrije Volk*, contrarily, move toward women (both 72%).

A noteworthy result is that in all newspapers the bias shifts toward men in the category 'money'. Moreover, they also all exhibit a move toward women for the category 'sexuality', with the clearest shift in *Volkskrant*, *Trouw*, and *Vrije Volk*.

6 Discussion

While the newspaper discourse as a whole is fairly stable, individual newspapers show clear divergences with regard to their bias and changes in this bias. We see that the newspapers with a social-democratic (*Vrije Volk*) and religious background, either Catholic (*Volkskrant*) and Protestant (*Trouw*) demonstrate the clearest shift in bias toward women. The liberal/conservative newspapers *Telegraaf*, *NRC Handelsblad*, and *Parool*, on the contrary, orient themselves more clearly toward men. Despite increasing female employment numbers in the Netherlands, the association with job titles moves only gradually toward women, while words associated with working move toward men. More detailed analysis of the individual trend within each decade is necessary to untangle what exactly is taking place. For example, which words show the biggest shift, and can we identify groups of associated words of which particular words show divergent behavior? Methodologically, this paper shows how word embedding models can be used to trace general shifts in language related to gender. Nevertheless, certain cultural expressions of gender are not captured by distributional semantics represented through word

---

[7]Numbers refer to the slope

[8]Lower confidence interval < 0 and upper > 0

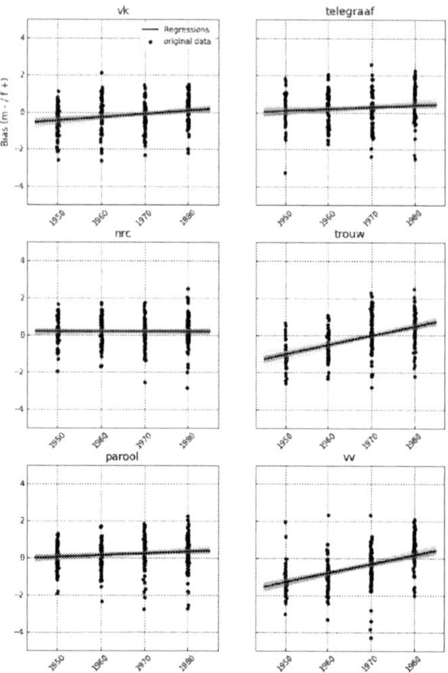

Figure 5: Individual newspaper model 'Sexuality'

embeddings, but rather in syntax, for example, through the use of active of passive sentences. Future work will investigate how fine-tuning state-of-the-art embedding models, such as ELMO and BERT, can be leveraged to gain more contextual knowledge about words and their association with gender (Peters et al., 2018).

Acknowledgments

I would like to thank Folgert Karsdorp for his feedback. This research was part the project "Digital Humanities Approaches to Reference Cultures: The Emergence of the United States in Public Discourse in the Netherlands, 1890-1990", which was funded by the Dutch Research Council (NWO).

References

Hosein Azarbonyad, Mostafa Dehghani, Kaspar Beelen, Alexandra Arkut, Maarten Marx, and Jaap Kamps. 2017. Words are malleable: Computing semantic shifts in political and media discourse. In *Proceedings of the 2017 ACM on Conference on Information and Knowledge Management*, pages 1509–1518. ACM.

Laila Ait Baali, Roos van Os, and Jantien Kingma. 2018. Overheid moet gendergelijkheid centraal stellen. https://www.volkskrant.nl/gs-b6023212.

Marco Baroni, Georgiana Dinu, and Germán Kruszewski. 2014. Don't count, predict! a systematic comparison of context-counting vs. context-predicting semantic vectors. In *Proceedings of the 52nd Annual Meeting of the Association for Computational Linguistics*, volume 1, pages 238–247.

Gerrit Bloothooft. 2010. Nederlandse Voornamenbank. https://www.meertens.knaw.nl/ nvb/veelgesteldevragen.

Tolga Bolukbasi, Kai-Wei Chang, James Zou, Venkatesh Saligrama, and Adam Kalai. 2016. Quantifying and reducing stereotypes in word embeddings. *arXiv preprint arXiv:1606.06121*.

Peter Boot, Hanna Zijlstra, and Rinie Geenen. 2017. The Dutch translation of the Linguistic Inquiry and Word Count (LIWC) 2007 dictionary. *Dutch Journal of Applied Linguistics*, 6(1):65–76.

Seth Flaxman, Sharad Goel, and Justin Rao. 2016. Filter bubbles, echo chambers, and online news consumption. *Public opinion quarterly*, 80(S1):298–320.

Nikhil Garg, Londa Schiebinger, Dan Jurafsky, and James Zou. 2018. Word embeddings quantify 100 years of gender and ethnic stereotypes. *Proceedings of the National Academy of Sciences*, 115(16):3635–44.

Hila Gonen and Yoav Goldberg. 2019. Lipstick on a Pig: Debiasing Methods Cover up Systematic Gender Biases in Word Embeddings But do not Remove Them. *arXiv:1903.03862 [cs]*.

William L. Hamilton, Jure Leskovec, and Dan Jurafsky. 2016. Cultural shift or linguistic drift? comparing two computational measures of semantic change. In *Proceedings of the Conference on Empirical Methods in Natural Language Processing. Conference on Empirical Methods in Natural Language Processing*, volume 2016, page 2116. NIH Public Access.

Vivek Kulkarni, Rami Al-Rfou, Bryan Perozzi, and Steven Skiena. 2015. Statistically significant detection of linguistic change. In *Proceedings of the 24th International Conference on World Wide Web*, pages 625–635. International World Wide Web Conferences Steering Committee.

Margaret Marshall. 1995. *Contesting Cultural Rhetorics: Public Discourse and Education, 1890-1900*. University of Michigan Press, Ann Arbor.

Cultuur en Wetenschap Ministerie van Onderwijs. 2009. Vrouwenemancipatie (gendergelijkheid). https://www.rijksoverheid.nl/onderwerpen/ vrouwenemancipatie.

Eli Pariser. 2011. *The filter bubble: What the Internet is hiding from you*. Penguin, London.

James W. Pennebaker, Martha E. Francis, and Roger J. Booth. 2001. Linguistic inquiry and word count: Liwc 2001. *Mahway: Lawrence Erlbaum Associates*, 71(2001):2001.

Matthew E. Peters, Mark Neumann, Mohit Iyyer, Matt Gardner, Christopher Clark, Kenton Lee, and Luke Zettlemoyer. 2018. Deep contextualized word representations. *arXiv preprint arXiv:1802.05365*.

Anneke Ribberink. 1987. *Feminisme*. Stichting Burgerschapskunde, Leiden.

Maarten Rooij. 1974. *Kranten: dagbladpers en maatschappij*. Wetenschappelijke Uitgeverij, Amsterdam.

Johan Schot, Arie Rip, and Harry Lintsen, editors. 2010. *Technology and the Making of the Netherlands: The Age of Contested Modernization, 1890-1970*. MIT Press, Cambridge.

Michael Schudson. 1982. *The Power of News*. Harvard University Press, Cambridge.

Yla R. Tausczik and James W. Pennebaker. 2010. The psychological meaning of words: Liwc and computerized text analysis methods. *Journal of language and social psychology*, 29(1):24–54.

P. Vossen, Katja Hofmann, M. de Rijke, E. Tjong Kim Sang, and Koen Deschacht. 2007. The Cornetto database: Architecture and user-scenarios.

Huub Wijfjes. 2004. *Journalistiek in Nederland, 1850-2000: beroep, cultuur en organisatie*. Boom, Amsterdam.

Michael Wintle. 2000. *An Economic and Social History of the Netherlands, 1800-1920: Demographic, Economic, and Social Transition*. Cambridge University Press, Cambridge.

Richard Zijdeman, Kees Mandemakers, Sanne Muurling, Ineke Maas, Bart Van de Putte, Paul Lambert, Marco Van Leeuwen, Frans Van Poppel, and Andrew Miles. 2013. HSN standardized, HISCO-coded and classified occupational titles.

Predicting historical phonetic features using deep neural networks: A case study of the phonetic system of Proto-Indo-European

Frederik Hartmann
University of Konstanz
`frederik.hartmann@uni-konstanz.de`

Abstract

Traditional historical linguistics lacks the possibility to empirically assess its assumptions regarding the phonetic systems of past languages and language stages beyond traditional methods such as comparative tools to gain insights into phonetic features of sounds in proto- or ancestor languages. The paper at hand presents a computational method based on deep neural networks to predict phonetic features of historical sounds where the exact quality is unknown and to test the overall coherence of reconstructed historical phonetic features. The method utilizes the principles of coarticulation, local predictability and statistical phonological constraints to predict phonetic features by the features of their immediate phonetic environment. The validity of this method will be assessed using New High German phonetic data and its specific application to diachronic linguistics will be demonstrated in a case study of the phonetic system Proto-Indo-European.

1 Introduction

Since the beginning of historical linguistics, one of the main aims of historical phonology and phonetics has been to reveal phonetic features of now lost sounds and phonological systems of past languages. The study of the phonetic system of earlier stages of languages is a crucial prerequisite to uncover sound change and effects on sound change precisely. The methods, however, are limited for every language whose speakers cannot be invited to a phonetics lab for detailed testing. The temporal scope of inquiries into language change would be fairly limited if we could only examine language change as far back as voice recording and experimental testing methods were present. If we want to study language change over thousands of years, we must rely on robust

techniques to approximate historical phonetic features as well as possible. The most prominent methods in historical linguistics so far to achieve this goal are based on comparative approaches (cf. Campbell, 2013; Beekes and Vaan, 2011; Meier-Brügger et al., 2010). Especially for the reconstruction of proto-languages, historical phonologists use the comparative method to estimate the approximate quality of sounds by investigating their outcomes and effects in the descendant languages. However, approaching historical phonetics by comparative means bears the disadvantage that the more the daughter languages disagree in certain respects, the less precise are the estimates scholars can make for the respective proto-sounds. For some problems for which comparative techniques yield imprecise results, there is a need for alternative methods to tackle these issues. Moreover, there is also no alternative method for cross-checking assumptions obtained through the traditional methods as such an alternative would need to operate on a basis different from diachronic comparison. Thus the method proposed in this paper makes use of synchronic structures and features of a language's phonology and feeds this data into a deep neural network to predict the phonetic features of unknown sounds. The data the network can draw upon is the direct phonetic environment of each sound with the goal to predict its features only by the features of its environment.

The reason for the predictability of sound features in the context of their environment is due to coarticulatory effects, statistical constraints and local predictability. Coarticulation refers to the observation that sounds tend to both influence and be influenced by their environment phonetically (see e.g. Kühnert and Nolan, 1999; Ohala, 1993a; Hardcastle and Hewlett, 2006; Fowler, 1980). This reciprocal influence can be detected synchronically which makes it a possible alterna-

Proceedings of the 1st International Workshop on Computational Approaches to Historical Language Change, pages 98–108
Florence, Italy, August 2, 2019. ©2019 Association for Computational Linguistics

tive to be used for historical phonology if applied to historical language stages or proto-languages: In theory, sounds constantly influence their environment and are affected by it at the same time so that a tight net of interlaced dependencies between sounds and their environment arises. There are indications that sound changes which better fit into this phonetic structure in their initial stage are more likely to become widely adapted (Donegan and Nathan, 2015; Blevins, 2015; Ohala, 1993a,b; Hale, 2003).

Similarly, and partially originating from coarticulatory processes, we find certain types of phonological constraints in languages, be it syllable composition constraints or the prevention of certain consonant clusters which make up a language's phonotactics. These constraints can be both *absolute* and *statistical*, whereby absolute constraints are rules which are never violated, whereas statistical constraints constitute a strong dominance of one phonological shape over others. The network can utilize a language's phonotactics, constraints and coarticulatory effects to predict the phonetic features of a target sound. Feature predictions from environmental properties have already been studied in quantitative phonetics and proven to be possible to some degree due to local predictability effects (see e.g. Priva, 2015; Van Son and Van Santen, 2005; Raymond et al., 2006).

It is important to keep in mind that local predictability on the basis of the phonetic environment is, in fact, *not* contradictory to the observation that different sounds can occur in the same environments which can be demonstrated using minimal pairs. Predictability in this context does not mean that a certain environment of a given sound *always* yields certain phonetic properties, it is rather a probabilistic observation that environments *tend* to occur paired with certain phonetic features and that this tendency of forming patterns is what can be predicted using probabilistic models and machine learning algorithms.

2 The deep neural network approach

Using machine learning algorithms is not new to the field of linguistics, though it is one of the more recent methods.[1] While these approaches are found in an increasing number of studies in lin-

guistics in general, in historical linguistics in particular the method is less used although some studies have been published in this or adjacent fields such as cladistics (Jäger et al., 2017; Jäger and Sofroniev, 2016). Since this approach of predicting sound features by the features in the phonetic environment only works synchronically, the deep neural network used for this needs to be trained on better known phonological features as the basis for predicting unknown features.

The data fed to the network must therefore contain a dataset where the phonetic environment serves as the input that is mapped on the target sound. To achieve this, the lexical corpus data needs to be split into trigrams or pentagrams of phonetic segments which are then categorized with regard to their phonetic features. Afterwards, the middle or target sound is removed and the remaining environment passed through the network with the respective target sound features as labels. Doing this trains the model to detect the correct phonetic features for the target sound given its environment. If the network has successfully trained, the environments of unknown sounds can be passed to the model which will, in turn, predict the features of the sounds on the basis of its weights and biases obtained in the training process. When the network performs well on the training data, we have little reason for it performing worse on the prediction of unknown sounds. Deep neural networks are especially suited for this task since other methods such as random forests or support vector machines have performed worse on this classification in preliminary tests I conducted beforehand. These three approaches, Deep neural networks, random forests and support vector machines, are entirely different approaches to machine learning classification tasks: While random forest classificators aim at finding the best decision tree by partitioning the data in subgroups, support vector machines establish the best splitting function, a hyperplane, to classify new samples according to their position in the multi-dimensional space. Deep neural networks on the other hand aim at optimizing the decision function through means of building abstract representation of the data and 'learning' the occurrence patterns of data features. It is not always possible to determine why some algorithms perform worse on some datasets and better on others. In the task at hand we can merely state that deep neural networks

---

[1]See e.g. Chollet (2018); Nielsen (2015) for a general introduction to deep learning.

seem to find the global minimum, or a better local minimum, of the decision function well while other algorithms do not perform on the same level, presumably due to their characteristics not being ideal for this particular case. In the following section, a case study on Proto-Indo-European shall function as an example study that can be conducted using neural networks.

3 Case study: The phonetic system of Proto-Indo-European

The phonetic system of Proto-Indo-European (PIE) is an ideal field to demonstrate the capabilities of this neural network approach for several reasons: (1) while the phonetic inventory of PIE, along with its phonotactics, has been reasonably well investigated (Clackson, 2007, 64-71; Meier-Brügger et al., 2010, 272-275; Byrd, 2015; Ringe, 2017, 13-17; Fortson IV, 2011, 62-64), there are still unknown aspects that lead to scholarly discussions and diverging theories such as the Glottalic theory.[2] (2) three sounds of PIE, the so-called laryngeals, are still a matter of debate since they are only scarcely attested in PIE's daughter languages and sometimes only through their effects on neighbouring sounds. The case study will therefore aim to propose an attempt to predict the laryngeals and to uncover possible inconsistencies in the phonetic system of PIE. The three laryngeals (h_1, h_2, and h_3) are reconstructed sounds in PIE whose exact phonetic value is unknown. Apart from some direct evidence of laryngeal reflexes in the Anatolian languages, most of our knowledge of those sounds stems from structural and phonetic patterns the laryngeals induced in the daughter languages before they faded altogether. Previous research interprets the laryngeals h_1 : h_2 : h_3 as [ʔ]/[h] : [χ]/[x]/[ɣ]/[ʕ] : [ɣ^w]/[ʕ^w]/[ʁ] .(Rasmussen, 1994; Kümmel, 2007; Meier-Brügger et al., 2010; Beekes, 1994; Bomhard, 2004; Gippert, 1994; Weiss, 2016; Mayrhofer and Cowgill, 1986)

3.1 The data

One of the best resources to obtain reconstructed word data that is already digital is the English version of Wiktionary.[3] Its validity as a repository of data for linguistic research has been as-

sessed by multiple studies and many other studies have already used its database for linguistic inquiry (e.g. Chiarcos et al., 2013; Navarro et al., 2009; de Melo, 2015; Zesch et al., 2008; Meyer and Gurevych, 2012). Especially regarding reconstructed language data, Wiktionary has the decisive advantage that the reconstructions follow certain guidelines (see Wiktionary contributors) unlike data collected from various different traditional dictionaries.

For this study, I extracted all PIE reconstructions found in page headings from the English Wiktionary .xml dump on 20.10.2018. Such a dump file contains all English Wiktionary pages including page and edit histories. The lemmas that were extracted were subsequently split into segments of trigrams: preceding sound, target sound and following sound with a final trigram count of 7782. Where a trigram contained a root ending, '-' was used as following sound to encode the root ending, cases of word-final or word-initial were added as 'zero' in the preceding or following sound slot, respectively. Each sound was ultimately classified according to its place and manner of its articulation according to the reconstructed phonetic inventory of PIE most scholars agree on (e.g. Clackson, 2007, 34; Beekes and Vaan, 2011, 119; Ringe, 2017, 8) without considering the glottalic theory.[4]

3.2 Approaches to verify the method

Before we are able to apply any machine learning techniques to the data, we need to establish whether coarticulatory and statistical constraint effects exist in PIE and that the method is actually feasible for predicting sound features in general. Although there have been studies suggesting the existence of such effects as mentioned above, a preliminary analysis needs to be conducted to *demonstrate* the data shows these effects and that a deep neural network can indeed 'learn' them and make correct predictions on the basis of the observed patterns.

For this reason, I set up a generalized linear logistic regression model as an example to determine the phonetic effects on the occurrence of the feature *aspirated* in PIE. The model was fit for best AIC through both top-down and bottom-up fitting. Before fitting, aliases were removed as

---

[2]See Byrd (2015); Beekes and Vaan (2011); Clackson (2007) for a comprehensive overview of the scientific debate.

[3]https://en.wiktionary.org, accessed: 2019-03-13

[4]For the full list of features used in this study, please refer to the appendix.

well as collinear predictors up to a cutoff-point of Variance Inflation Factor (VIF) greater than 4.

	Estimate	Std. Error	z value	Pr(>|z|)
(Intercept)	-2.302	0.091	-25.312	0.000
labial preceding	-1.504	0.240	-6.269	0.000
sibilant preceding	-2.310	0.587	-3.938	0.000
liquid preceding	-0.843	0.245	-3.446	0.001
syllabic cons. preceding	1.137	0.380	2.994	0.003
back vowel preceding	-1.131	0.267	-4.232	0.000
mid vowel preceding	-1.022	0.178	-5.730	0.000
close vowel preceding	-0.947	0.468	-2.021	0.043
h_1 preceding	-1.519	0.518	-2.933	0.003
h_2 preceding	-2.106	0.513	-4.103	0.000
h_3 preceding	-1.185	0.598	-1.981	0.048
word boundary following	1.439	0.154	9.336	0.000
voiceless cons. following	-2.279	0.390	-5.848	0.000
nasal following	-1.691	0.512	-3.304	0.001
liquid following	0.444	0.175	2.543	0.011
syllabic cons. following	0.381	0.185	2.055	0.040
velar following	1.487	0.509	2.919	0.004
back vowel following	0.526	0.170	3.091	0.002
plosive following	-1.041	0.415	-2.510	0.012
h_2 following	-2.494	1.006	-2.481	0.013

Table 1: Generalized linear logistic regression for the occurrence of the feature *aspirated*

It can be observed in table 1 that several predictors were significant. E.g. preceding sibilant reduces the probability of the target sound being *aspirated* whereas following velar increases this probability. As suggested by this model, the data contains information on coarticulatory and statistical constraint effects the neural network can draw upon.

As a second approach to ensure that the presented method and data is suitable for predicting sound features, I conducted a preliminary study using the same method to predict the features of New High German sounds. For this analysis, I utilized the German phonology lemma data from CELEX2 (Baayen et al., 1995) in the syllabified phonetic lemma transcription with stress in the DISC character set (*PhonStrsDISC*). After extraction from the CELEX2 file, the data were prepared using the same process as for the PIE data with a final sample size of 441236 German trigrams. The method was simultaneously tested with a dataset in which each lemma was oversampled proportional to its frequency of occurrence in the 'Mannheimer Korpus' provided by CELEX2 (*Mann_Freq*) (see Gulikers et al., 1995). While this approach would ideally proportion the dataset more realistically and could, in theory, improve model training, it did not enhance the performance of the network and was therefore discarded.

Each sound of those trigrams was classified according to 38 phonetic features (e.g. *conso-*

nant, nasal, plosive) where 0 and 1 indicate the absence/presence of a particular feature, respectively.[5] Note, that these 38 features contain some redundancies (e.g. *vowels* are entirely contained in the feature *continuant*). This is due to the fact that a deep neural network performs best on as many input features as possible since there might be some relevant signal in a seemingly redundant or unimportant feature vector. Accordingly, specifying two complementary features like e.g. *voiced* and *voiceless* can increase the network's performance since the two categories only apply to consonants. Otherwise, a single binary feature [+voice] would not only encode voiced consonants but also all vowels and therefore decrease the ability of the network to detect voiced consonants specifically. Redundancy itself is also not a problem as redundant or irrelevant information in the data is weighted less important during training while the network focuses on those features that have predictive power.

Also, only basic features (13 features in total for consonants and 10 features for vowels) such as e.g. *consonant, velar* and *labial* were used as target features for the prediction of German sound features. The reason for this decision was that the more fine-grained the distinctions become, the fewer occurrences of the feature there are on which the network can train. Therefore, although the feature *liquid* containing German *r* and *l* was further divided into *rhotic* and *lateral* as features contained in the classification of the phonetic environments, only *liquid* was tested as a target feature. If *rhotic* were tested as target feature on a sound with unknown features, the network would train only on the sound *r* and therefore not necessarily train on the feature *rhotic* but rather learn to discriminate *r* from all other sounds which has in turn little explanatory power when predicting the *rhotic* feature for other sounds.

The method was tested on the German sounds *p, r, ɛː, aː* as an arbitrary preliminary selection that ideally is representative of all other sounds in the New High German phonetic inventory. Therefore, four datasets were prepared, where the respective sound was removed as target sound and its presence in any phonetic environment was indicated by adding a new feature only for this sound. For example when the phonetic environment in a par-

---

[5]For the full list of features used in this study, please refer to the appendix.

ticular trigram contained *r* while *r* was the sound to be later predicted by the network, *r* was classified in a dummy feature category that only encodes presence/absence of this particular sound. This procedure is necessary since removing all instances of the particular sound, *r* in this case, in the phonetic environment would reduce the number of environments and therefore distort the data.

After data preparation, a single network was set up for each feature and trained one feature at a time with a binary output to predict the presence or absence of the feature. I.e. this binary network was trained to detect a particular feature and to predict its presence or absence for unseen sound environment data. After the entire data were shuffled and the test and validation data were separated from the training sets using the Stratified ShuffleSplit cross-validator included in the python package *scikit-learn* (Pedregosa et al., 2011), the training sets were over-sampled before each run to counter class imbalance with the SMOTE algorithm (Chawla et al., 2002) implemented in the 'Imbalanced-learn' (Lemaître et al., 2017) python package. The network was trained for 30 epochs using the optimizer Adam with a learning rate of 0.01 with a batch size of 250 samples with the layer configuration displayed in table 2.

Layer	Layer size	Activation
Dense layer 1	256	ReLU
Dense layer 2	128	ReLU
Dense layer 3	64	ReLU
Dense layer 4	32	ReLU
Output layer	2	softmax

Table 2: Network architecture for the German feature prediction task

For the subsequent evaluation of the model performance, weights and biases were used form the epoch at which the network performed best on the validation data during training using the Keras callback *ModelCheckpoint* (Chollet et al., 2015). This procedure minimizes the risk of the model being stuck at a local minimum in the search space at the time training stops after an arbitrarily chosen number of epochs. It has been established in preliminary tests that the model performance was enhanced when training on an all-consonant or all-vowel subset of the data: First, a model was trained to predict the feature [± consonant] and after the prediction, the main model was trained on consonant or vowel data according to the prediction of the preliminary model. After each training, the network performance was evaluated and

subsequently tasked with predicting the particular feature for the respective test sound. The results are presented in tables 3, 4, 5, and 6 which show which number of samples in the test sets were classified correctly or incorrectly. I.e. 24656 consonant samples in the column *TP* means that 24656 samples of all positive samples in the test set were correctly classified as positive. Similarly, in table 3 in the first row, 7211 samples in *prediction: feature present* denote that 7211 of all tested instances of *p* were classified as [+consonant].

Note that model accuracy metrics such as F1 score, precision, or recall are not given here since these measures only evaluate a classifier's performance on a mixed dataset. Because the method proposed here aims at performing well on determining whether a sound shows a given feature and since this feature is either present in all samples of this sound or absent in all samples, the main goal is that the deep network yields more true positives than false negatives and more true negatives than false positives. Applied to the example in table 3 this means that since German *p* is [+consonant], ideally the majority of classified samples will be classified as such. If after model evaluation the number of false negatives were higher than the number of true positives, the model would likely not be able to classify the majority of samples correctly. More samples would end up being incorrectly labeled as negatives as a result of the poor model training yielding more false negatives than true positives. Therefore, a high false positive or false negative count is not a concern in itself as long as the ratio of true positives to false negatives and true negatives to false positives is always in favor of true positives or true negatives, respectively.

Feature	TP	FN	FP	TN	Pred: feat. present	Pred: feat. absent
consonant	24656	2184	859	15541	7211	1627
nasal	3885	1553	4255	17148	2609	6229
plosive	5417	1984	4341	15099	4860	3978
affricate	732	172	6750	19187	2352	6486
fricative	7156	3627	4272	11786	2394	6444
liquid	4698	1615	5361	15167	1670	7168
sibilant	2148	1072	5676	17945	1634	7204
voiced	11560	3681	3442	8158	3582	5256
labial	3447	864	7656	14874	5507	3331
dental/alveolar	8747	4093	3834	10167	4155	4683
palatal	1019	270	4497	21055	2373	6465
velar/uvular	4896	3035	4200	14710	1972	6866
glottal	428	43	5481	20889	1856	6982

Table 3: Network evaluations and predictions for German *p*

The results show that all 13 tested features of *p* are predicted correctly, *r* is correctly predicted to be a voiced liquid, yet regarding place of articulation, which in German r-allophones is ranging

Feature	TP	FN	FP	TN	Pred: feat. present	Pred: feat. absent
consonant	21986	1739	1311	15089	39071	920
nasal	3722	1716	2702	15585	16238	23753
plosive	5524	2761	3082	12358	6333	33658
affricate	732	172	6339	16482	7972	32019
fricative	4881	1903	4314	12627	11352	28639
liquid	1604	710	5259	16152	22942	17049
sibilant	2172	1048	4683	15822	8997	30994
voiced	8006	3236	3568	8915	30068	9923
labial	3907	1288	6205	12325	12071	27920
dental/alveolar	8974	3865	2844	8042	28021	11970
palatal	1006	283	3138	19298	3895	36096
velar/uvular	2916	1015	4937	14857	11004	28987
glottal	432	39	4728	18526	8695	31296

Table 4: Network evaluations and predictions for German *r*

Feature	TP	FN	FP	TN	Pred: feat. present	Pred: feat. absent
consonant	25884	1840	1111	15105	204	1638
front vowel	3658	1963	2714	7881	589	1253
central vowel	4546	1667	2529	7474	858	984
back vowel	1920	1032	3391	9873	831	1011
round	1395	653	3845	10323	898	944
close	3054	1729	2132	9301	493	1349
mid	5790	1670	2525	6231	585	1257
open	2582	1391	3110	9133	1219	623
diphthong	1097	333	2776	12010	464	1378
long	6595	1544	2365	5712	1248	594

Table 5: Network evaluations and predictions for German *ɛː*

from alveolar to uvular (cf. Meinhold and Stock, 1982, 131-133), only dental/alveolar is predicted which makes a total of 11 out of 13 features. The German vowels were less well detected, with a total of 8 out of 10 for *ɛː* and 6 out of 10 for *aː*. Although the model performs on some sounds and features better than on others, it performs better than expected by chance. Since these results stem from a selected set of sounds in a preliminary study, specific questions as to which features are detected better than others and why some features are incorrectly predicted for certain kinds of sounds need to be established in further research.

3.3 The deep learning method applied to Proto-Indo-European

To prepare the PIE data for training, the data were randomly shuffled and split into training and test set using the Stratified ShuffleSplit cross-validator included in the python package *scikit-learn* (Pedregosa et al., 2011). Afterwards, the training set was first oversampled with the SMOTE algorithm and subsequently under-sampled by removing Tomek links using SMOTETomek (Batista et al., 2003) implemented in the 'Imbalanced-learn' (Lemaître et al., 2017) python package to counter class imbalance in the dataset. Yet the SMOTE over-sampling process performed on the minority group increases the dataset's variation, so to cope with this variation and to make sure that findings were not due to random biases dur-

Feature	TP	FN	FP	TN	Pred: feat. present	Pred: feat. absent
consonant	25694	2030	1102	14445	597	7936
front vowel	3864	1941	2457	7285	4691	3842
central vowel	3996	1364	2302	7885	2760	5773
back vowel	1877	1075	2846	9749	2720	5813
round	1377	671	3550	9949	3848	4685
close	3177	1606	2282	8482	2403	6130
mid	5953	1691	2303	5600	5151	3382
open	2070	1050	2827	9600	3104	5429
diphthong	1164	266	2810	11307	2178	6355
long	5834	1636	2121	5956	4839	3694

Table 6: Network evaluations and predictions for German *aː*

ing oversampling or stratification, I ran each network 100 times to have a representative number of slightly varying model outputs. Each of these runs yields a confusion matrix with the count of true positive, false negative, false positive and true negative predictions of the test samples. To determine whether the model performs significantly better than expected by a random class assignment, all confusion matrices were compared using Wilcoxon signed rank tests with continuity correction. For each model, I performed this test on the output of the 100 runs of true positives vs. false negatives to determine whether the network can clearly find a present feature and a second test on the 100 runs of false positives vs. true negatives to determine whether the network can clearly find the absence of a feature. When the Wilcoxon signed rank test is significant, the tested groups are 'non-identical' populations.

3.4 Example 1: The phonetic quality of the PIE laryngeals

In the following stage, a deep neural network can be set up to learn to detect the feature *aspirated* and to subsequently predict whether the laryngeals had this feature.

The network was trained for 50 epochs using the optimizer Adam with a learning rate of 0.01 and a batch size of 64 samples with the layer configuration displayed in table 7.

Layer	Layer size	Activation
Dense layer 1	128	ReLU
Dropout layer 1	0.25 dropout rate	
Dense layer 2	64	ReLU
Dropout layer 2	0.25 dropout rate	
Dense layer 3	32	ReLU
Output layer	2	softmax

Table 7: Network architecture for the feature *aspirated*

The dropout layers in this network architecture were implemented to reduce the effect of over-fitting due to the limited amount of training samples. Analogous to the training on the modern German dataset above, only weights and biases form the epoch at which the network performed best on the validation data during training were used. As mentioned above, the network was trained and evaluated 100 times in order to further minimize the effect of accidental findings in single runs. The results are listed in table 8 which is a summary of all test set prediction confusion matrices obtained in the 100 runs.[6]

	True positives	False negatives	False positives	True negatives
Mean	58.32	19.68	219.5	602.5
Median	58	20	221	601
Std. dv.	2.044		6.920	

Table 8: Statistics of the confusion matrices from 100 runs for classifying the feature *aspirated*

Subsequently, a Wilcoxon signed rank tests with continuity correction with the alternative hypothesis H_1: True positives greater than false negatives gives $W = 10000.00$ $p < 0.00001$. A second Wilcoxon signed rank tests with continuity correction with the alternative hypothesis H_1: True negatives greater than false positives gives $W = 10000.00$ $p < 0.00001$. These test statistics show that in these 100 runs, the network was able to detect the feature *aspirated* reliably and, most importantly, when presented with an unseen dataset which either contains sounds that have the feature *aspirated* or sounds that do not, the network will correctly identify over 70 percent of the samples. The variance in the prediction accuracy in table 8 can be explained by, as previously addressed, noise in the data and variation in the partitioning and subsequent oversampling of the training set. Having established the functioning network, the model can be used to predict the target feature for sounds with unknown qualities. Since the laryngeals cannot be assigned a phonetic value by means of the comparative method, their properties can be predicted. To achieve this, the phonetic environment was passed through the networks after training at the end of each of the 100 runs. The output of every prediction is a classification matrix for each of the three laryngeals. Table 9 shows the summary of these classification matrices.

To determine the significance of these findings, Wilcoxon signed rank tests with continuity correction were applied to the predictions. Table 10

---

[6]The figures in the tables provided here and below represent the number of classified samples from the test set. E.g. a mean of 58.32 in *true positives* means that from all positive samples in the test set, an average of 58.32 samples were classified correctly as positive.

	h_1		h_2		h_3	
	Positives	Negatives	Positives	Negatives	Positives	Negatives
Mean	113.8	85.2	160.5	187.5	54.06	51.94
Median	115	84	163	187	53	53
Std. dv.	4.141		4.079		1.879	

Table 9: Prediction results by the trained model for the laryngeal feature *aspirated*

shows the test results. The networks trained on de-

	h_1		h_2		h_3	
H_1	W	p-value	W	p-value	W	p-value
P greater N	9991.00	< 0.00001	0	1	7477.00	< 0.00001
N greater P	9.00	1	10000	< 0.00001	2523.00	1

Table 10: Results of Wilcoxon signed rank test with continuity correction applied to the predictions for each laryngeal with H_1: positives greater than negatives and H_1: negatives greater than positives

tecting the feature *aspirated* clearly predict the aspirated feature for h_1. For h_2, the model clearly rejects the feature *aspirated*. In the case of h_3, the statistical tests indicate that the laryngeal possessed the feature *aspirated*, however because of the thin difference in the number of predicted samples, we still need to treat this finding with caution, since the feature is not as clearly predicted for h_3 as it is for h_1. It is likely that the aspiration present in h_3 is weaker than or different from that of h_1.

3.5 Example 2: The internal coherence of PIE nasals

Besides predicting phonetic features of unknown sounds, the deep neural networks can moreover detect inconsistencies or idiosyncrasies in PIE. One such example is the feature *nasal* which is present in both PIE non-syllabic (*m, *n) and syllabic nasals (*m̥, *n̥). While both are regarded to be phonetically identical and only differing in their syllabicity (Clackson, 2007, 35), an investigation using the deep neural network approach gives some insights into their relationship to one another: To analyze this feature, a deep neural network was set up with the architecture displayed in table 11.

Layer	Layer size	Activation
Dense layer 1	128	ReLU
Dropout layer 1	0.25 dropout rate	
Dense layer 2	64	ReLU
Dropout layer 2	0.25 dropout rate	
Dense layer 3	32	ReLU
Output layer	2	softmax

Table 11: Network architecture for the feature *nasal*

The method used in this case is equal to the training and evaluation procedure of the model used in 3.4. The resulting confusion matrices obtained after each evaluation of the 100 training runs are summarized in table 12.

	True positives	False negatives	False positives	True negatives
Mean	49.32	53.68	135.5	661.5
Median	48	55	118.5	678.5
Std. dv.	**6.689**		**38.951**	

Table 12: Statistics of the confusion matrices from 100 runs for classifying the feature *nasal*

As this summary shows, the neural network had more difficulties learning the properties of *nasal* than it had learning the feature *aspirated*. The classifier only detects the feature less than 50 percent of the time it is presented with nasal sounds, which is approximately what could be expected by randomly classifying the rest samples. Moreover, a Wilcoxon signed rank test with continuity correction with the alternative hypothesis H_1: True positives greater than false negatives gives W = 3144 p = 1. As a result, it was not possible to successfully train the network on this feature. Given the large discrepancy in performance between this and the previous network and the fact that both models were optimized using the same methods, the problem must be data inherent. This finding raises the question of why exactly this series differs from the other features. This leaves three possible explanations: (1) The data containing the nasals is noisier compared to the other phonetic features so that the classifier cannot train on a consistent set of properties. Although data can be varying degrees of noisy, it is unlikely that this feature is overly affected by noise. (2) The nasal feature was weakly articulated in PIE and thus it had little effect on its environment. An effect so small that it did not leave stable traces the classifier could detect. (3) The third explanation is that the nasal series does not possess internal coherence. This reason is arguably the most probable given that the nasals consist of two different sets of nasals that contrast in their syllabicity, especially since syllabic and non-syllabic resonants are also allophones and are therefore in complementary distribution (cf. Schindler, 1977). Yet since the model was trained on detecting nasality – not syllabicity – while there were other syllabic consonants in the non-nasal group, it is also possible that the model is not *solely* misled by the difference in syllabicity and their complementary distribution. There might also be a difference in nasality itself which results in the feature not forming a consistent, classifiable group. In other words, the syllabic and non-syllabic nasals might additionally have also differed in their nasality (i.e. nasality being differently articulated in both cases), yet this observation needs to be further investigated before one can make more substantiated claims.

4 Conclusion

As has been demonstrated in this paper, using deep neural networks in historical phonetics is a viable method to predict unknown features and to uncover previously unnoticed inconsistencies within a language's phonetic system. The tool is specifically powerful for historical linguistics since it does not rely on diachronic methods such as the comparative method to analyze and determine phonetic features but can draw upon synchronic phonetic patterns arising from coarticulation and statistical constraints. The results obtained through the machine learning technique presented in this paper are moreover reproducible and empirical, and can therefore be seen as complementary to previous results obtained by other empirical approaches such as the comparative method. However, the specific strengths and weaknesses of this method need to be further investigated in future research.

References

R Baayen, Richard Piepenbrock, and Léon Gulikers. 1995. Celex2 ldc96l14. *Web Download. Philadelphia: Linguistic Data Consortium.*

Gustavo EAPA Batista, Ana LC Bazzan, and Maria Carolina Monard. 2003. Balancing training data for automated annotation of keywords: a case study. In *WOB*, pages 10–18.

R. S. P. Beekes. 1994. Who were the laryngeals. In Jens Elmegård Rasmussen, editor, *In honorem Holger Pedersen*, pages 450–454. Reichert, Wiesbaden.

R. S. P. Beekes and Michiel de Vaan. 2011. *Comparative Indo-European linguistics: An introduction*, 2. ed. edition. Benjamins, Amsterdam.

Juliette Blevins. 2015. Evolutionary phonology: A holistic approach to sound change typology. In Patrick Honeybone and Joseph Curtis Salmons, editors, *The Oxford handbook of historical phonology*, Oxford handbooks in linguistics, pages 485–500. Oxford University Press, Oxford.

Allan R. Bomhard. 2004. The proto-indo-european laryngeals. In Adam Hyllested and Jens Elmegård

Rasmussen, editors, *Per aspera ad asteriscos*, Innsbrucker Beiträge zur Sprachwissenschaft, pages 69–80. Institut für Sprachen und Literaturen der Universität Innsbruck, Innsbruck.

Andrew Byrd. 2015. *The Indo-European Syllable*. Brill, Leiden.

Lyle Campbell. 2013. *Historical linguistics*. Edinburgh University Press, Oxford.

Nitesh V Chawla, Kevin W Bowyer, Lawrence O Hall, and W Philip Kegelmeyer. 2002. Smote: synthetic minority over-sampling technique. *Journal of artificial intelligence research*, 16:321–357.

Christian Chiarcos, John McCrae, Philipp Cimiano, and Christiane Fellbaum. 2013. *Towards Open Data for Linguistics: Linguistic Linked Data*, pages 7–25. Springer Berlin Heidelberg, Berlin, Heidelberg.

François Chollet. 2018. *Deep learning with Python*. Manning Publications Company, Shelter Island.

François Chollet et al. 2015. Keras. `https://keras.io`.

James Clackson. 2007. *Indo-European linguistics: An introduction / James Clackson*. Cambridge textbooks in linguistics. Cambridge University Press, Cambridge.

Patricia J. Donegan and Geoffrey S. Nathan. 2015. Natural phonology and sound change. In Patrick Honeybone and Joseph Curtis Salmons, editors, *The Oxford handbook of historical phonology*, Oxford handbooks in linguistics, pages 431–449. Oxford University Press, Oxford.

Benjamin W Fortson IV. 2011. *Indo-European language and culture: An introduction*, volume 30. John Wiley & Sons, Hoboken.

Carol A Fowler. 1980. Coarticulation and theories of extrinsic timing. *Journal of Phonetics*, 8(1):113–133.

Jost Gippert. 1994. Zur phonetik der laryngale. In Jens Elmegård Rasmussen, editor, *In honorem Holger Pedersen*, pages 455–466. Reichert, Wiesbaden.

Léon Gulikers, Gilbert Rattink, and Richard Piepenbrock. 1995. German linguistic guide. *The CELEX Lexical Database (CD-ROM). Linguistic Data Consortium, Philadelphia, PA*.

Mark Hale. 2003. Neogrammarian sound change. In Brian D. Joseph, editor, *The handbook of historical linguistics*, Blackwell handbooks in linguistics, pages 343–368. Blackwell, Malden, MA.

William J. Hardcastle and Nigel Hewlett. 2006. *Coarticulation: Theory, data and techniques*. Cambridge University Press, Cambridge.

Gerhard Jäger, Johann-Mattis List, and Pavel Sofroniev. 2017. Using support vector machines and state-of-the-art algorithms for phonetic alignment to identify cognates in multi-lingual wordlists. In *Proceedings of Conference: Volume 1: Long Papers,ACL*, pages 1204–1226.

Gerhard Jäger and Pavel Sofroniev. 2016. Automatic cognate classification with a support vector machine. In *Proceedings of the 13th Conference on Natural Language Processing (KONVENS)*, Bochumer Linguistische Arbeitsberichte, pages 128–134.

Barbara Kühnert and Francis Nolan. 1999. The origin of coarticulation. In Nigel Hewlett and William J. Hardcastle, editors, *Coarticulation*, Cambridge studies in speech science and communication, pages 7–30. Cambridge University Press, Cambridge.

Martin Joachim Kümmel. 2007. *Konsonantenwandel: Bausteine zu einer Typologie des Lautwandels und ihre Konsequenzen für die vergleichende Rekonstruktion: Teilw. zugl.: Freiburg, Univ., Habil.-Schr., 2005*. Reichert, Wiesbaden.

Guillaume Lemaître, Fernando Nogueira, and Christos K. Aridas. 2017. Imbalanced-learn: A python toolbox to tackle the curse of imbalanced datasets in machine learning. *Journal of Machine Learning Research*, 18(17):1–5.

Manfred Mayrhofer and Warren Cowgill. 1986. *Indogermanische Grammatik. Bd 1*. Winter, Heidelberg.

Michael Meier-Brügger, Matthias Fritz, and Manfred Mayrhofer. 2010. *Indogermanische Sprachwissenschaft*, 9., durchgesehene und ergänzte auflage 2010 edition. De Gruyter Studium. De Gruyter, Berlin.

Gottfried Meinhold and Eberhard Stock. 1982. *Phonologie der deutschen Gegenwartssprache*, second edition edition. Bibliographisches Institut, Leipzig.

Gerard de Melo. 2015. Wiktionary-based word embeddings. *Proceedings of MT Summit XV*, pages 346–359.

Christian M. Meyer and Iryna Gurevych. 2012. Wiktionary: A new rival for expert-built lexicons? exploring the possibilities of collaborative lexicography. In Magali Gragner, Sylviana;Paquot, editor, *Electronic Lexicography*. Oxford University Press, Oxford.

Emmanuel Navarro, Franck Sajous, Bruno Gaume, Laurent Prévot, Hsieh ShuKai, Kuo Tzu-Yi, Pierre Magistry, and Huang Chu-Ren. 2009. Wiktionary and nlp: Improving synonymy networks. In *Proceedings of the 2009 Workshop on The People's Web Meets NLP: Collaboratively Constructed Semantic*

Resources, People's Web '09, pages 19–27, Strouds-burg, PA, USA. Association for Computational Linguistics.

Michael A. Nielsen. 2015. *Neural Networks and Deep Learning*. Determination Press.

J. J. Ohala. 1993a. Coarticulation and phonology. *Language and speech*, 36 (Pt 2-3):155–170.

J. J. Ohala. 1993b. The phonetics of sound change. In Charles Jones, editor, *Historical linguistics*, Longman linguistics library, pages 237–278. Longman, London.

F. Pedregosa, G. Varoquaux, A. Gramfort, V. Michel, B. Thirion, O. Grisel, M. Blondel, P. Prettenhofer, R. Weiss, V. Dubourg, J. Vanderplas, A. Passos, D. Cournapeau, M. Brucher, M. Perrot, and E. Duchesnay. 2011. Scikit-learn: Machine learning in Python. *Journal of Machine Learning Research*, 12:2825–2830.

Uriel Cohen Priva. 2015. Informativity affects consonant duration and deletion rates. *Laboratory Phonology*, 6(2):243–278.

Jens Elmegård Rasmussen, editor. 1994. *In honorem Holger Pedersen: Kolloquium der Indogermanischen Gesellschaft vom 25. bis 28. März 1993 in Kopenhagen.* Reichert, Wiesbaden.

William Raymond, Robin Dautricourt, and Elizabeth Hume. 2006. Word-medial /t,d/ deletion in spontaneous speech: Modeling the effects of extralinguistic, lexical, and phonological factors. *Language Variation and Change*, 18:55—-97.

Donald A. Ringe. 2017. *From Proto-Indo-European to Proto-Germanic*, second edition edition, volume volume I of *A linguistic history of English*. Oxford University Press, Oxford.

Jochem Schindler. 1977. Notizen zum sieversschen gesetz. *Die Sprache*, 23(1):56–65.

Rob JJH Van Son and Jan PH Van Santen. 2005. Duration and spectral balance of intervocalic consonants: A case for efficient communication. *Speech Communication*, 47(1-2):100–123.

Michael Weiss. 2016. The proto-indo-european laryngeals and the name of cilicia in the iron age. In Andrew Miles Byrd, Jessica DeLisi, and Mark Wenthe, editors, *Tavet tat satyam*, pages 331–340. Beech Stave Press, Ann Arbor and New York.

Wiktionary contributors. Wiktionary:about proto-indo-european — Wiktionary, the free dictionary. Accessed: 2019-03-13.

Torsten Zesch, Christof Müller, and Iryna Gurevych. 2008. Using wiktionary for computing semantic relatedness. In *AAAI*, volume 8, pages 861–866.

A Appendices

word boundary	zero
nasal	m, n, ŋ
plosive	p, t, d, k, g, b
affricate	pf, ts, tʃ
fricative	f, v, s, z, ʃ, ʒ, x/ç, h
liquid	l, r
rhotic	r
lateral	l
sibilant	s, z, ʃ, ʒ
voiced	m, n, ŋ, d, g, ʒ, v, l, r, z, b
voiceless	p, t, k, pf, tʃ, ʃ, s, f, x/ç, h
labial	m, p, pf, f, v, b
bilabial	m, p, b
labiodental	pf, f, v
dental/alveolar	n, t, d, ts, s, z, l, r
palatal	ʃ, ʒ, tʃ, r
velar/uvular	ŋ, k, g, x/ç, r
glottal	h
obstruent	p, b, t, d, k, g, pf, ts, tʃ, f, v, s, z, ʃ, ʒ, x/ç, h, r
sonorant	m, n, ŋ, ɪ, i, ɛ, e, y, ʏ, ø, œ, æ, ə, a, ɑ, u, ʊ, o, ɔ, ai̯, au̯, ɔy̯
occlusive	p, b, t, d, k, g, m, n, ŋ, pf, ts, tʃ
continuant	f, v, s, z, ʃ, ʒ, x/ç, h, r, ɪ, i, ɛ, e, ai̯, ɔy̯, y, ʏ, ø, œ, æ, ə, a, ɑ, u, ʊ, o, ɔ
consonant	m, n, ŋ, d, g, ʒ, v, l, r, b, p, t, k, pf, tʃ, ʃ, s, z, f, x/ç, h
front vowel	ɪ, i, ɛ, e, y, ʏ, ø, œ, æ
central vowel	ə, a, ɑ
back vowel	u, ʊ, o, ɔ
close	i, ɪ, u, ʊ, y, ʏ
mid	ɛ, e, ə, o, ɔ, ø, œ, æ
open	a, ɑ
diphthong	ai̯, au̯, ɔy̯
open diphthong	ai̯, ɔy̯
mid diphthong	au̯
front diphthong	ai̯, au̯
back diphthong	ɔy̯
round	o, ɔ, y, ʏ, ø, œ
unround	ɪ, i, ɛ, e, ə, a, ɑ, u, ʊ, æ
long	i, e, a, u, o, æ, œ, y
short	ɪ, ɛ, ʊ, ɑ, ʏ, ø, ə

Table 13: Phonetic feature assignment of each considered New High German sound

root ending	-
word boundary final/initial	zero
voiced	$*b^h$, $*d^h$, $*\acute{g}^h$, $*g^h$, $*g^w$, $*b$, $*d$, $*\acute{g}$, $*g$, $*g^w$, $*m$, $*\underset{.}{m}$, $*n$, $*r$, $*l$, $*\underset{.}{l}$, $*\underset{.}{r}$, $*y$, $*w$
voiceless	$*p$, $*t$, $*s$, $*\acute{k}$, $*k$, $*k^w$
nasal	$*m$, $*\underset{.}{m}$, $*n$, $*\underset{.}{n}$
aspirated	$*b^h$, $*d^h$, $*\acute{g}^h$, $*g^h$, $*g^{wh}$
labial/labialized	$*m$, $*\underset{.}{m}$, $*p$, $*b$, $*b^h$, $*w$, $*k^w$, $*g^w$, $*g^{wh}$
sibilant	$*s$
liquid	$*r$, $*\underset{.}{r}$, $*\underset{.}{l}$, $*l$
syllabic	$*\underset{.}{r}$, $*\underset{.}{l}$, $*\underset{.}{m}$, $*\underset{.}{n}$, $*i$, $*u$, $*\bar{u}$
coronal	$*n$, $*\underset{.}{n}$, $*t$, $*d$, $*d^h$, $*s$, $*r$, $*l$, $*\underset{.}{l}$, $*\underset{.}{r}$
postvelar	$*k$, $*g$, $*g^h$, $*k^w$, $*g^w$, $*g^{wh}$
velar	$*\acute{k}$, $*\acute{g}$, $*\acute{g}^h$
palatal	$*y$
front vowel	$*e$, $*\bar{e}$, $*i$
back vowel	$*o$, $*\bar{o}$, $*u$, $*\bar{u}$
center vowel	$*a$, $*\bar{a}$
short vowel	$*e$, $*o$, $*u$, $*a$, $*i$
long vowel	$*\bar{e}$, $*\bar{o}$, $*\bar{u}$, $*\bar{a}$
open vowel	$*a$, $*\bar{a}$
close vowel	$*u$, $*\bar{u}$, $*i$
laryngeal 1	$*h_1$
laryngeal 2	$*h_2$
laryngeal 3	$*h_3$
unspecified laryngeal	$*H$
consonant	$*b^h$, $*d^h$, $*\acute{g}^h$, $*g^h$, $*g^w$, $*b$, $*d$, $*\acute{g}$, $*g$, $*g^w$, $*m$, $*\underset{.}{m}$, $*n$, $*r$, $*l$, $*\underset{.}{l}$, $*\underset{.}{r}$, $*y$, $*w$, $*p$, $*t$, $*s$, $*\acute{k}$, $*k$, $*k^w$
back consonant	$*k$, $*g$, $*g^h$, $*k^w$, $*g^w$, $*g^{wh}$, $*\acute{k}$, $*\acute{g}$, $*\acute{g}^h$
front consonant	$*m$, $*\underset{.}{m}$, $*p$, $*b$, $*b^h$, $*w$, $*s$, $*r$, $*\underset{.}{r}$, $*\underset{.}{l}$, $*l$, $*n$, $*\underset{.}{n}$, $*t$, $*d$, $*d^h$
stop	$*\acute{k}$, $*b$, $*b^h$, $*p$, $*\acute{g}$, $*\acute{g}^h$, $*k$, $*g$, $*g^h$, $*k^w$, $*g^w$, $*g^{wh}$, $*t$, $*d$, $*d^h$
obstruent	$*\acute{k}$, $*p$, $*b$, $*b^h$, $*\acute{g}$, $*\acute{g}^h$, $*k$, $*g$, $*g^h$, $*k^w$, $*g^w$, $*g^{wh}$, $*t$, $*d$, $*d^h$, $*s$
sonorant	$*m$, $*\underset{.}{m}$, $*n$, $*\underset{.}{n}$, $*r$, $*\underset{.}{r}$, $*y$, $*w$, $*e$, $*o$, $*u$, $*a$, $*i$, $*\bar{e}$, $*\bar{o}$, $*\bar{u}$, $*\bar{a}$
occlusive	$*\acute{k}$, $*p$, $*b$, $*b^h$, $*\acute{g}$, $*\acute{g}^h$, $*k$, $*g$, $*g^h$, $*k^w$, $*g^w$, $*g^{wh}$, $*t$, $*d$, $*d^h$, $*m$, $*\underset{.}{m}$, $*n$, $*\underset{.}{n}$
continuant	$*s$, $*y$, $*w$, $*e$, $*o$, $*u$, $*a$, $*i$, $*\bar{e}$, $*\bar{o}$, $*\bar{u}$, $*\bar{a}$

Table 14: Phonetic feature assignment of each considered PIE sound

ParHistVis: Visualization of Parallel Multilingual Historical Data

Aikaterini-Lida Kalouli[*] and **Rebecca Kehlbeck**[*] and **Rita Sevastjanova**[*]
and **Katharina Kaiser** and **Georg A. Kaiser** and **Miriam Butt**
University of Konstanz
`firstname.lastname@uni-konstanz.de`

Abstract

The study of language change through parallel corpora can be advantageous for the analysis of complex interactions between time, text domain and language. Often, those advantages cannot be fully exploited due to the sparse but high-dimensional nature of such historical data. To tackle this challenge, we introduce ParHistVis: a novel, free, easy-to-use, interactive visualization tool for parallel, multilingual, diachronic and synchronic linguistic data. We illustrate the suitability of the components of the tool based on a use case of word order change in Romance *wh*-interrogatives.

1 Introduction

Historical linguistics has begun to work with parallel corpora, exploiting the advances in corpus linguistics that facilitate the creation, linkage and analysis of large data sets. For some discussions as to the advantages of using parallel corpora see, e.g., Wälchli (2009); Enrique-Arias (2013). Aspects that stand out are: a) the direct comparability of concrete examples across time periods; b) the ease of analysis due to the known structure of the base text which makes it possible to look selectively at a small number of passages in which relevant structures are likely to occur; c) the facilitation of analysis of languages for which the researcher has no deep knowledge, based on the better known languages. Despite these advantages, it is challenging to use parallel corpora with state-of-the-art statistical/learning methods, because such data is often a) too sparse; b) but too large and too high-dimensional for manual inspection; c) a learning approach necessarily reduces the dimensionality so that important aspects that could in principle be gained from the use of parallel texts are lost. For our study on word order and language change in Romance *wh*-interrogatives, our

goal is to investigate the strict word order observed in Old Romance (Kaiser, 1980; Schulze, 1888; Lapesa, 1992) and the more flexible word order of Modern Romance (Ordóñez, 1997; Rizzi, 2006), based on a parallel corpus of French and Spanish Bible translations of the 12th, 16th and 20th centuries. In particular, it is of interest to determine what factors might interact to determine word order, e.g., particles or the type of interrogative pronoun (Bayer and Obenauer, 2011). However, the relatively small size of our corpus for statistical methods but large size for manual investigation of the interacting factors and the unsuitability of existing visualizations for the inspection of parallel, multilingual, diachronic texts pose a challenge.

To tackle this challenge, but also to assist researchers with similar issues, we designed ParHistVis (Parallel Multilingual Historical Visualization). ParHistVis is a novel, freely-available,[1] easy-to-use, interactive visualization tool for parallel, multilingual, diachronic and synchronic data of a) the same time period across languages; b) of different periods of the same language; c) across languages. The tool employs methods of the field of Visual Analytics (VA) (Keim et al., 2008) and Computational Linguistics. It is suitable for researchers with little or no experience with computational approaches: after defining an input data file, they can directly interact with the visualization. Thus, our contributions are twofold: first, we present an easy-to-use, freely available, interactive tool suitable for the visualization of parallel multilingual data. Concretely, we show what aspects of parallel data can be efficiently explored using streamgraphs and Sankey diagrams. Second, we describe how the tool can be used via a concrete use case: the investigation of word order change in Romance *wh*-interrogatives.

---

[*] The first three authors had an equal contribution.

[1] The tool is available under `https://typo.uni-konstanz.de/parhistvis/`

Proceedings of the 1st International Workshop on Computational Approaches to Historical Language Change, pages 109–114
Florence, Italy, August 2, 2019. ©2019 Association for Computational Linguistics

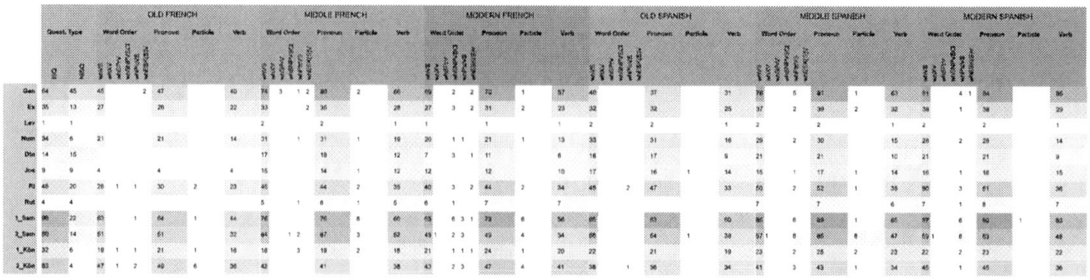

Figure 1: The aggregated matrix view of the books of the Old Testament across time periods and languages.

2 Relevant Work

Visualization as a means of illustration has a long tradition in linguistics, e.g., through spectograms for sound waves, tables for paradigms or graphs and attribute-value matrices for syntactic information. Besides such traditionally established visualizations, recent years have seen the emergence of new visualization ideas coming out of the field of VA (Keim et al., 2008) for the analysis and representation of linguistic data (Sun et al., 2013; Liu et al., 2014; Gan et al., 2014). A considerable amount of research has specifically focused on the visualization of historical linguistic change. One strand of research has focused on the visualization of word meaning across time (Sagi et al., 2009; Rohrdantz et al., 2011; Hilpert, 2011; Tahmasebi and Risse, 2017; Jatowt et al., 2018), while others have approached the same area with state-of-the-art embeddings (see Kutuzov et al. (2018) for a review). Another strand of research has concentrated on visualizing diachronic information in historical dictionaries, e.g., Theron and Fontanillo (2015) and linguistic evolution within the discourse (Lyding et al., 2012). Other work has visualized syntactic historical change (Butt et al., 2014; Schätzle et al., 2017; Schätzle, 2018). This work situates itself in the middle of those approaches, attempting to present a general, easy-to-use tool that can be employed for historical change of any kind (syntactic, semantic, etc.), but particularly targeting parallel, multilingual data.

3 The ParHistVis Tool

The tool works through a web-browser interface and is fully implemented in JavaScript. The only requirement is a tabulated file with the data to be visualized. The file can contain parallel, multilingual text, synchronic or diachronic, with each aligned piece of text (across languages or across time) associated with a row and identified by a unique ID. The rows can contain different columns, each of them encoding linguistic annotations that the researcher has assigned to that specific piece of text/row. In what follows, we call these linguistic annotations *dimensions* and their possible subcategories *features*. These dimensions can be specific to a particular language or time period or be associated with the whole row, i.e. the whole aligned text across languages and periods. The loading of the file in the tool is easy and fast: the researcher creates an online document of her file, e.g., a Google Sheets Document, and feeds its link in the provided field of the interface. This connects the document with the tool and the visualization instantly appears. This method is user-friendly and avoids complex handling of the documents usually found in a server-client environment. An additional merit is that the user can update the input document anytime and the changes will be automatically reflected in the visualization.

3.1 Parallel Analysis of Linguistic Change

One simple but essential requirement for the efficient study of parallel data is that the researcher can indeed observe each data point in a parallel way for each time period and, if multilingual data is available, for each language. Although this is possible with common tools like Excel, such a large document can quickly become overwhelming. To facilitate the direct comparability that parallel corpora enable, our tool builds upon this existing metaphor of a *matrix* visualization, as such a method preserves all dimensions of the data, in contrast to others which use dimensionality reduction techniques and crucial information gets lost. In this initial matrix view, the data follows the format of the input file but is structured in a colorful visualization: the languages and time periods are on the horizontal axis, allowing for interlingual and diachronic analysis of the data, and the course of the corpus is on the vertical axis, allowing for intralingual and synchronic comparisons (see Figure 1). Each time period of each language is assigned a different color. The user can choose to filter a subset of the data, i.e. the features she is interested in, by selecting the corresponding columns. These columns will be automatically highlighted and the rest of the dimensions will be blended out to enable a more focused view on the data. In this detailed view, the user can observe the data in a qualitative way. For example, she can hover over the ID of a row and get the specific text associated with that ID, for each separate time period and language. General trends concerning the whole corpus can also be observed by zooming out on the matrix, e.g., we could observe that the filtered features appear only in the second half of the corpus (on the vertical axis) or only in the later time periods (on the horizontal axis).

3.2 Aggregated View of Linguistic Change

Although the detailed matrix view is suitable for inspecting individual data points, it does not facilitate general quantitative observations for the whole corpus or another natural grouping of the data. But these observations are of interest when comparing the same text across time and languages. We therefore offer an aggregated matrix view. Here, the user can select which data points should be aggregated; the tool offers a standard aggregation option but also makes educated guesses for other natural groupings of the data. The standard option is the aggregation of all data points of the whole corpus. Other aggregation options are offered based on the unique IDs: the tool searches for any reasonable pattern occurring in the IDs and suggests this as a natural aggregation, e.g., IDs with the same prefix will be aggregated to a group. The aggregation function merges all values of each feature of the subgroups contained in the aggregation and calculates their sum (Figure 1). Additionally, a colormap encodes the frequency of the features: the lighter the color of a given feature, the lower its frequency across the aggregated dimension; the darker the color, the higher the frequency.

3.3 Streamgraphs for Pattern Recognition

The aggregated view is suitable for general quantitative observations. Nevertheless, through the aggregation the features of the categorical dimensions are collapsed and thus interesting patterns may disappear. Moreover, the summed aggregated numerical dimensions can be overwhelming

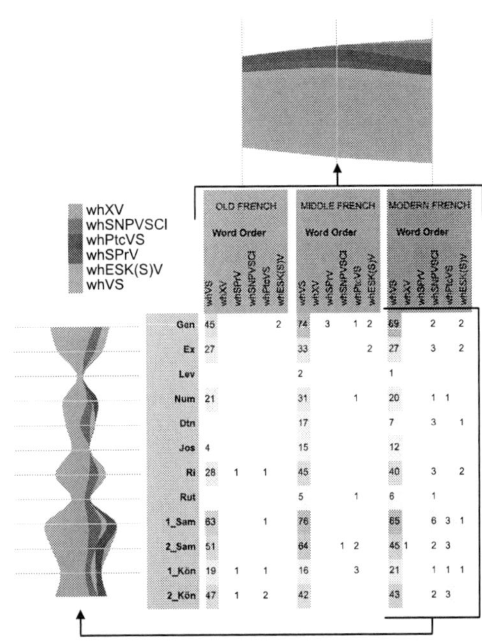

Figure 2: The streamgraphs of word order in French across time (top right) and of word order in Modern French across the aggregated Bible books (bottom left).

when trying to identify patterns. To tackle these drawbacks, the aggregated data is further visualized through *streamgraphs*. A streamgraph (also known as ThemeRiver) is a type of stacked area graph displaced around a central axis, resulting in a flowing, organic shape. Streamgraphs were popularized by Byron and Wattenberg (2008) for movie box office revenues but were already used for topic modelling by Havre et al. (2002) and have been applied to prosody visualization (Martin et al., 2010). Streamgraphs are commonly used to show changes of different categories across a single dimension, e.g., time, where categories might appear or disappear at different times. The height of each individual stream shows how its value has changed over time and the length shows its duration. This allows a comparison of the width of individual features visually, highlighting trends and outliers. Colours are used to differentiate between categories. Such high-dimensional data could also be represented by Parallel Coordinates (Inselberg, 1985), if time and space were considered "simple" quantifiable dimensions. However, as highlighted by Kehrer and Hauser (2013), the independent dimensions of time and space tend to play a central role in spatio-temporal data and should thus be considered independently. The properties of streamgraphs are thus suitable for parallel his-

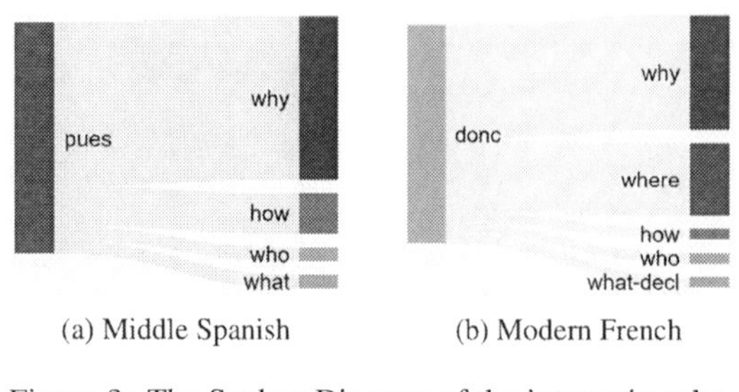

(a) Middle Spanish   (b) Modern French

Figure 3: The Sankey Diagram of the interactions between particles and interrogative pronouns.

torical data. To the best of our knowledge, this is the first work to apply streamgraphs to parallel, multilingual historical data. In ParHistVis, for a selected dimension, two streamgraphs are displayed: a) one for the frequency of the features of this dimension over the aggregated dimension for the specified time period (Figure 2, bottom left) and b) one for the frequency of the features of the dimension over the time periods, if this feature exists in a diachronic scale (Figure 2, top right). By hovering over a stream, the exact frequency of the feature visualized is displayed.

3.4 Sankey Diagrams for Pattern Interaction

Although streamgraphs offer a useful at-a-glance overview of the frequency of the dimensions, they cannot provide any insight into potential interactions between them. However, in the study of language change it is crucial to be able to discover such interactions, as most changes are the outcome of a series of interacting factors. Specifically, in parallel data there is a need for comparing how a concrete interaction has behaved across time or language. We make this kind of visualization available by incorporating *Sankey Diagrams*. These diagrams are traditionally used for visualizing (energy) flows; the entities under investigation are represented as nodes. The links among them are represented with edges with a width proportional to the importance of the flow. The diagrams have already gained attention in the digital humanities, e.g., in the visualization of migration flows and evolution (Abel, 2018), but also in literature (e.g., Campbell et al. (2018)). Here, the user selects the dimensions for which she wants to observe potential interactions. The features of these dimensions are depicted as nodes and the interactions between them as flows connecting them; the thickness of the flow shows the extent of the correlation. Again, a colormap helps the user distinguish between the interacting dimensions. An

example of a Sankey Diagram is shown in Figure 3. The tool does not make predictions about potential interactions to display but lets the user define themselves the dimensions which might show an interesting interaction. This is especially useful for historical data where the data might be too sparse for the tool to be able to find any statistically interesting interactions but the user still wants to observe preliminary patterns and tendencies.

4 Use case

The visualizations above were obtained as part of our study on Romance *wh*-interrogatives. We used a subset of the parallel, multilingual corpus made available by Kalouli et al. (2018). This subcorpus contains three French and three Spanish Bible translations of the 12th, 16th and 20th centuries. We semi-automatically annotated this corpus for a) word order in interrogatives, b) interrogative pronouns and verbs of speaking introducing questions and c) particles used with interrogatives. The ultimate goal was to investigate the differences between the strict word order in Old Romance vs. the greater word order variation in Modern Romance, in correlation with interrogative pronouns, the introducing verbs of the interrogatives and particles. (Old and Modern) Romance languages are characterized by a relatively high stability with respect to word order in *wh*-interrogatives. They generally exhibit the fronting of the *wh*-phrase (*wh*-ex-situ) in combination with subject-verb inversion (*whVS*), so there is a strict adjacency between the *wh*-phrase and the verb. In Modern Romance, however, there is some variation with respect to these word order constraints. Many Modern Romance languages exhibit, mostly under very specific conditions, *wh*-ex-situ interrogatives without subject-verb inversion and allow for non-adjacency of the *wh*-element and the verb with certain elements. With this high-dimensional research question we are interested in a linguistic development within one language, as well as across different languages and time periods, with various interacting factors. ParHistVis can ideally assist us: although a detailed linguistic analysis is beyond the scope of this paper, we can show how the different views facilitate the study of this kind of data. With the color encoding in the matrix view in Figure 1, we can already make at-a-glance observations, e.g., there is a relatively high number of interrogative pronouns in the beginning and the end of the corpus.[2] By using the streamgraph visualization (Figure 2) we can exactly inspect two phenomena attested in the literature: the emergence of complex inversion in Modern French (Roberts, 1993), i.e. the orange stream (*whSNPVSCl*) first appears in Middle French and increases its frequency in Modern French, and the diachronic non-adjacency of the *wh*-element and the verb when a particle is present, i.e. the blue (*whPtcVS*) stream stays stable over time. The visualization with the Sankey Diagram also offers interesting insights: arguably, some interrogative pronouns allow for more variation in the sentence structure, e.g. allow for particles (cf. e.g. Ordóñez (1997)). If we select to view the interaction of the interrogative pronouns and the particles in Middle Spanish and Modern French, Figure 3 shows us that the interrogative pronoun *why* allows for more frequent use of the particle *pues* and *donc* in Spanish and French, respectively, than other pronouns. Through the streamgraphs and Sankey Diagrams, similar observations can be made for other dimensions of the dataset. More importantly, the different available views allow the user to switch between them and inspect patterns that arise from these higher-level graphs. With this, the researcher can recognize and evaluate patterns in an otherwise too multifactorial dataset.

5   Conclusion

We presented ParHistVis, a visualization tool for parallel, multilingual, synchronic and diachronic linguistic data. We showed how the different views of the tool facilitate the inspection of the data, based on our study on word order change in Romance *wh*-interrogatives.

Acknowledgements

We thank the German Research Foundation (DFG) for the financial support within the projects P8 "Questions Visualized" and P2 "Word Order Variation in Wh-questions: Evidence from Romance" of the Research Group FOR 2111 Questions at the Interfaces at the University of Konstanz.

---

[2]For our particular use case this observation is not of great importance. However, for other studies of historical change, e.g. a corpus study on different genres, it is interesting to observe how specific patterns develop across those genres.

References

Guy J. Abel. 2018. Estimates of Global Bilateral Migration Flows by Gender between 1960 and 2015. *International Migration Review*, 52(3):809–852.

Josef Bayer and Hans-Georg Obenauer. 2011. Discourse particles, clause structure, and question types. *The Linguistic Review*, 28(4).

Miriam Butt, Tina Bögel, Kristina Kotcheva, Christin Schätzle, Christian Rohrdantz, Dominik Sacha, Nicole Dehé, and Daniel A. Keim. 2014. V1 in Icelandic: A Multifactorical Visualization of Historical Data. In *Proceedings of the LREC 2014 "Visualization as Added Value in the Development, Use and Evaluation of Language Resources (VisLR)"*, pages 33–40.

Lee Byron and Martin Wattenberg. 2008. Stacked Graphs Geometry Aesthetics. *IEEE Transactions on Visualization and Computer Graphics*, 14(6):1245–1252.

Sarah Campbell, Zheng-Yan Yu, Sarah Connell, and Cody Dunne. 2018. Close and Distant Reading via Named Entity Network Visualization: A Case Study of Women Writers Online. In *Proceedings of the 3rd Workshop on Visualization for the Digital Humanities. VIS4DH*.

Andrés Enrique-Arias. 2013. On the usefulness of using parallel texts in diachronic investigations. Insights from a parallel corpus of Spanish medieval Bible translations. *Corpus Linguistics and Interdisciplinary Perspectives on Language*, 3:105–115.

Qihong Gan, Min Zhu, Mingzhao Li, Ting Liang, Yu Cao, and Baoyao Zhou. 2014. Document visualization: an overview of current research. *Wiley Interdisciplinary Reviews: Computational Statistics*, 6(1):19–36.

S. Havre, E. Hetzler, P. Whitney, and L. Nowell. 2002. ThemeRiver: visualizing thematic changes in large document collections. *IEEE Transactions on Visualization and Computer Graphics*, 8(1):9–20.

Martin Hilpert. 2011. Dynamic visualizations of language change: Motion charts on the basis of bivariate and multivariate data from diachronic corpora. *International Journal of Corpus Linguistics*, 16:435–461.

Alfred Inselberg. 1985. The Plane with Parallel Coordinates. *The Visual Computer*, 1:69–91.

Adam Jatowt, Ricardo Campos, Sourav S. Bhowmick, Nina Tahmasebi, and Antoine Doucet. 2018. Every word has its History: Interactive Exploration and Visualization of Word Sense Evolution. In *Proceedings of the 27th ACM International Conference on Information and Knowledge Management, CIKM 2018, Torino, Italy, October 22-26, 2018*, pages 1899–1902.

Egbert Kaiser. 1980. *Strukturen der Frage im Französischen. Synchronische und diachronische Untersuchungen zur direkten Frage im Französischen des 15. Jahrhunderts (1450-1500).* Tübinger Textbeiträge zur Linguistik, 142. Narr, Tübingen.

Aikaterini-Lida Kalouli, Katharina Kaiser, Annette Hautli-Janisz, Georg A. Kaiser, and Miriam Butt. 2018. A multingual approach to question classification. In *Proceedings of the Eleventh International Conference on Language Resources and Evaluation (LREC 2018)*, pages 2715–2720. ELRA. ISBN: 979-10-95546-00-9.

Johannes Kehrer and Helwig Hauser. 2013. Visualization and visual analysis of multifaceted scientific data: A survey. *IEEE Transactions on Visualization and Computer Graphics*, 19(3):495–513.

Daniel A. Keim, Gennady Andrienko, Jean-Daniel Fekete, Carsten Görg, Jörn Kohlhammer, and Guy Melançon. 2008. Visual Analytics : Definition, Process, and Challenges. In A. Kerren, editor, *Information Visualization*, pages 154–175. Springer, Berlin.

Andrey Kutuzov, Lilja Øvrelid, Terrence Szymanski, and Erik Velldal. 2018. Diachronic word embeddings and semantic shifts: a survey. In *Proceedings of the 27th International Conference on Computational Linguistics*, pages 1384–1397, Santa Fe, New Mexico, USA. Association for Computational Linguistics.

Rafael Lapesa. 1992. La interpolación del sujeto en las oraciones interrogativas. In M. Ariza, editor, *Actas del II Congreso Internacional de Historia de la lengua espaola, Vol. I.*, pages 545–553. Pabellón de Espaa, Madrid.

Shixia Liu, Weiwei Cui, Yingcai Wu, and Mengchen Liu. 2014. A survey on information visualization: recent advances and challenges. *The Visual Computer*, 30(12):1373–1393.

Verena Lyding, Ekaterina Lapshinova-Koltunski, Henrik Dittmann, and Christopher Culy. 2012. Visualising Linguistic Evolution in Academic Discourse. *Proceedings of the European Chapter of the Association of Computational Linguistics (EACL) 2012*, pages 44–48.

JR. Martin, M. Zappavigna, and P. Dwyer. 2010. *Visualising appraisal prosody*, pages 44–75. Continuum, London.

Francisco Ordóñez. 1997. *Word order and clause structure in Spanish and other Romance languages.* Ph.D. thesis, The City University of New York.

Luigi Rizzi. 2006. Selective residual v-2 in Italian interrogatives. In P. Brandt and Eric Fu, editors, *Form, Structure and Grammar. A Festschrift Presented to Gúnther Grewendorf on Occasion of His 60th Birthday.*, Studia Grammatica, 63, pages 229–241. Akademie Verlag, Berlin.

Ian Roberts. 1993. *Verbs and Diachronic Syntax. A Comparative History of English and French.* Kluwer, Dordrecht.

Christian Rohrdantz, Annette Hautli, Thomas Mayer, Miriam Butt, Daniel A. Keim, and Frans Plank. 2011. Towards Tracking Semantic Change by Visual Analytics. In *Proceedings of the 49th Annual Meeting of the Association for Computational Linguistics: Human Language Technologies: Short Papers - Volume 2*, HLT '11, pages 305–310, Stroudsburg, PA, USA. Association for Computational Linguistics.

Eyal Sagi, Stefan Kaufmann, and Brady Clark. 2009. Semantic density analysis: Comparing word meaning across time and phonetic space. *Proceedings of the EACL 2009 Workshop on GEMS: Geometrical Models of Natural Language Semantics*, pages 104–111.

Christin Schätzle. 2018. *Dative Subjects: Historical Change Visualized.* Ph.D. thesis, Universität Konstanz, Konstanz.

Christin Schätzle, Michael Hund, Frederik Dennig, Miriam Butt, and Daniel Keim A. 2017. HistoBankVis: Detecting Language Change via Data Visualization. In *Proceedings of the NoDaLiDa 2017 Workshop on Processing Historical Language*, number 32 in NEALT Proceedings Series, pages 32–39, Linköping. Linköping University Electronic Press.

Alfred Schulze. 1888. *Der altfranzsische direkte Fragesatz. Ein Beitrag zur Syntax des Französischen.* Hirzel, Leipzig.

Guo-Dao Sun, Ying-Cai Wu, Rong-Hua Liang, and Shi-Xia Liu. 2013. A survey of visual analytics techniques and applications: State-of-the-art research and future challenges. *Journal of Computer Science and Technology*, 28(5):852–867.

Nina Tahmasebi and Thomas Risse. 2017. Finding individual word sense changes and their delay in appearance. In *Proceedings of the International Conference Recent Advances in Natural Language Processing, RANLP 2017*, pages 741–749. INCOMA Ltd.

Roberto Theron and Laura Fontanillo. 2015. Diachronic-information visualization in historical dictionaries. *Information Visualization*, 14(2):111–136.

Bernhard Wälchli. 2009. Advantages and disadvantages of using parallel texts in typological investigations. *STUF - Sprachtypologie und Universalienforschung*, 60(2):118–134.

Tracing Antisemitic Language Through Diachronic Embedding Projections: France 1789-1914

Rocco Tripodi   **Massimo Warglien**   **Simon Levis Sullam**   **Deborah Paci**

Ca' Foscari University of Venice

{`rocco.tripodi, warglien, levissmn, deborah.paci`}@unive.it

Abstract

We investigate some aspects of the history of antisemitism in France, one of the cradles of modern antisemitism, using diachronic word embeddings. We constructed a large corpus of French books and periodicals issues that contain a keyword related to Jews and performed a diachronic word embedding over the 1789-1914 period. We studied the changes over time in the semantic spaces of 4 target words and performed embedding projections over 6 streams of antisemitic discourse. This allowed us to track the evolution of antisemitic bias in the religious, economic, socio-politic, racial, ethic and conspiratorial domains. Projections show a trend of growing antisemitism, especially in the years starting in the mid-80s and culminating in the Dreyfus affair. Our analysis also allows us to highlight the peculiar adverse bias towards Judaism in the broader context of other religions.

1 Introduction

Word embeddings are widely used in many Natural Language Processing (NLP) tasks. They provide a machine-interpretable representation of lexical features. Their effectiveness in representing words semantics consists essentially in the ability of learning association patterns in the training dataset. For this reason the learned representations contain human-like biases (Caliskan et al., 2017). These biases can be detected easily and can be related to gender, ethic or racial aspects (Garg et al., 2018; Voigt et al., 2017).

Since the use of word embedding is ubiquitous in many commercial products such as search engines and machine translators, the research community has introduced different techniques to debias them (Bolukbasi et al., 2016; Zhao et al., 2018), especially under the gender dimension. Despite these efforts debiasing word embeddings seems to be harder than expected. In fact, while Bolukbasi et al. (2016) and Zhao et al. (2018) demonstrated that it is possible to debias specific gendered-words, even after the debiasing procedure, the geometry of the embeddings remains almost the same with respect to non gendered-words (Gonen and Goldberg, 2019), preserving their original bias.

In this work, we turn these biases to the historian's advantage and shed light on some aspects of the history of antisemitism in France during the so called *long XIX century*, between the French Revolution and the First Word War, using diachronic word embedding. This technique allows to capture diachronic conceptual changes and to analyse stereotyped historical biases. We tracked how historical events and publications influenced the construction of the collective imaginary related to the Jewish question.

We assume that words do not have a fixed meanings. They can be used in different contexts to evoke a great variety of meanings using different connotational nuances. These multiple meanings are acquired (or lost) over time in correspondence to specific socio-political events. For example, one of the meanings of the word *usurier* (i. e.; *money lender*), as reported by the *French Historical Dictionary*, refers to: *the financial activities of the Jews* [who since the Middle Ages were], *the only ones authorised to lend on pawns* (Rey et al., 2010). This association derives from the fact that especially between the XVI and the XIX century, this word acquired a negative connotation, nurtured by anti-Jewish prejudice and stereotyping developing from the idea of an illegitimate interest attached to this activity. This image, as the above mentioned definition explains, was also fixed in the collective imaginary by Shylock, the Jewish protagonist in Shakespeare's *Merchant of Venice* (1598).

In this work, we trace the conceptual changes of words related to the Jewish question. We collected a large corpus for this purpose, composed of thousands of books and newspapers published in France between 1789 and 1914. We used diachronic word embedding to represent the data, measures of local changes in the semantic space of different words, and embedding projections to quantify biases in different semantic spheres. The measurement of local changes is particularly suited for our study because we do not want to identify new meanings in the words related to the Jewish question, instead we want to trace how the context of their use changed and how these changes affected the representation of Jews at the time of the rise of modern antisemitism. Measuring biases over time is particularly interesting because it allows to connect them with antisemitic streams as identified by historians in the field (Wilson, 1982) and operationalised by us.

2   Related Work

Models for capturing diachronic conceptual changes are associated with the distributional hypothesis (Harris, 1954; Firth, 1957; Weaver, 1955): the semantics of a word is defined by the context in which it is used. Following this assumption, different models have been presented, based on co-occurrence vectors (Sagi et al., 2009; Gulordava and Baroni, 2011; Basile et al., 2016) or word embeddings (Kim et al., 2014; Kulkarni et al., 2015; Hamilton et al., 2016a).

These works are brought together by the idea of analysing the contexts in which a word occurs and have culminated in the measures of *semantic shift* and *cultural drift*, proposed by (Hamilton et al., 2016a) and *the law prototipicality* proposed by Dubossarsky et al. (2015). Semantic shifts are regular linguistic processes such as semantic widening (e.g., *dog*, that in Middle English was used to refer to dogs of a particular breed) (Bloomfield, 1933). This measure was used to derive two laws of semantic change: the *law of conformity*: semantic change scales with a negative power of word frequency; and the *law of innovation*: polysemous words have significantly higher rates of semantic change (Hamilton et al., 2016b). Cultural drifts involve local changes to a lexical form's use (e.g.: the changes in the meaning of the word *cell*: *prison cell → cell phone*) (Hamilton et al., 2016a). The *law of prototipicality* was introduced by Du-

bossarsky et al. (2015): it states that prototypical words, words that are near to the centroid of a cluster in a semantic space, change slower than words that are in a peripheral position. The laws of *conformity, innovation and prototipicality* have been questioned by Dubossarsky et al. (2017), who used controlled conditions to test them.

Different works that tried to measure, directly or indirectly, cultural drifts have been proposed recently. Garg et al. (2018) analysed gender and ethnic stereotypes in the United States during the 20th and 21st centuries, using word embeddings trained on the Google Books and Corpus of Historical American English (COHA) corpora. Kozlowski et al. (2018) used diachronic word embeddings to conduct macro-cultural investigation of social stereotypes. Kutuzov et al. (2017) attempted to model the dynamics of wordwide armed conflicts using word embeddings trained on a news corpus. Zhao et al. (2017) analyzed the amplification effect that learning models present on the gender dimension when trained on biased data.

3   Motivations and historical background

We have looked at linguistics representation of Jews in 19th century France, which was one of the cradles of modern antisemitism in Europe, i.e. of the mostly secularized and racial transformation of the centuries-old Christian prejudice against the Jews (Katz, 1980).

Since the entry and gradual integration of the Jews in French society after the Revolution of 1789, the appearance of anti-Jewish texts, the rise of public controversies, or the burst of cases and scandals in which Jews were supposedly involved marked the emergence and spread of the Jewish question on the French scene, in what have been called *antisemitic moments* or *episodes* (Birnbaum, 2011). Especially during the Third Republic, beginning in 1870, references to Jews entered the French public discourse in relation to a supposed growing influence of the Jews on political and economic affairs, the rise of anticlericalism in the face of Catholic France (for which Jews were considered responsible), the accusation of an alliance between Jews and Freemasonry.

This process reached its climax with the Dreyfus affair (1894), the unfounded accusation against a French army officer to have sold intelligence information to the German enemy (Dreyfus would be exonerated in 1906): the affair caused the heavy spread of antisemitic accusations and anti-Jewish movements of opinion (Wilson, 1982). Different streams of antisemitism ran accross French society throughout this time, together with a pro-Jewish reaction driven by the supporters of Dreyfus' innocence (Kalman, 2010).

The publication in 1845 (republished in 1886) of Alfred Toussenel's *Les Juifs rois de l'epoque* caused especially the rise of the so-called economic antisemitism, which accused the Jews of an increasing economic and financial influence, of which the Rothschilds were considered the protagonists and became a symbol. This accusation was later confirmed by the supposed Jewish role in the crash of the Catholic bank Union Générale (1882) and in the Panama corruption scandal (1892), together with the revival of nationalism tied to the Boulangist crisis (Sternhell, 1998). These events generated a resurgence of antisemitism. In response to the growing secularization and anticlericalism, French Catholics revived an ancient tradition of religious antisemitism, marked in this time by the appearance of works such as Gougenot des Mousseaux's *Le Juif, le judaïsme et la judaïsation des peuples chrétiens* (1869) and by the anti-Jewish campaigns of Catholic periodicals such as *L'Univers* and *La Croix*.

In 1886 the journalist Edouard Drumont published the hugely successful *La France juive. Essai d'histoire contemporaine*, which described a French society under a greedy Jewish influence and control, painting in the style of a novelist (inspired by Balzac and by contemporary feuilletons or serialized novels) the contours of Jewish conspiracies. Although the subtitle of the work suggests an essay of contemporary history, on reading it is as if one is before an enormous cauldron of common place assumptions on Jews which includes Catholic, social, racial, economic, and conspiratorial anti-Semitism. The success of his work depended on the waves it made in the intellectual milieu of the era and its impact on the popular masses attracted by the synthesis of anti-Semitism of the right, of a church worried about laicisation, and anti-Semitism of the left, anti-capitalist and laical. This and other books by Drumont mixed Catholic, socio-political, ethic and conspirationist antisemitism, accusing Jews of all sorts of religious offenses, political machinations, moral perversions and secret plots (Kauffmann, 2008).

The combination of these streams of anti-Jewish accusations, prejudices and stereotypes would christallize - or reach its climax - in the Dreyfus affair. We suggest that the usage in print (books and periodicals) of the term *juif* or other terms related to the Jewish question, all characterised by an adverse bias, was especially connected to antisemitic tendencies. However, we should note that this vocabulary was also present at the time in Biblical and theological scholarship, art and art-historical publications, fictional and theatrical literature, medical treatises and the rising social sciences. References to Jews in the public discourse were therefore not necessarily mobilised in a political context with explicit antisemitics aims. Our investigation asks whether using diachronic word embeddings trained on a large corpus confirms the chronological development of antisemitic language which historians have described on a qualitative level (and if it sheds light on different, previously ignored, *antisemitic moments*). We also examine the relevance of the semantic areas or streams in relation to the *Jew* which we have identified based on (Wilson, 1982), and we show the trends through time of unfavourable biases towards Jews in the period considered.

4   The Corpus and the Embeddings

4.1   The corpus

The corpus[1] was constructed downloading from Gallica, the online library of the *Bibliothèque Nationale de France*[2], the raw text of all the resources that contain a keyword related to Jews (see appendix A for the complete list of keywords) and have been published between 1789-1914. The research was further restricted to those resources that have an OCR quality higher that 98%. The resulting corpus contains 54.403 books and 245.188 periodicals issues. It is important to notice here that we downloaded the full text of a book or newspaper issue even if a keyword appeared only once in it.

Figures 1a and 1b indicate the distribution of resources per year in the periodicals and books subcorpora, respectively, together with the total number of resources in Gallica. The resources distribution per year is not homogenous in neither subcorpora: publications increase significantly year

---

[1]The metadata of the corpus, the embeddings and the code used for the experiments can be downloaded from https://github.com/roccotrip/antisem.

[2]https://gallica.bnf.fr/

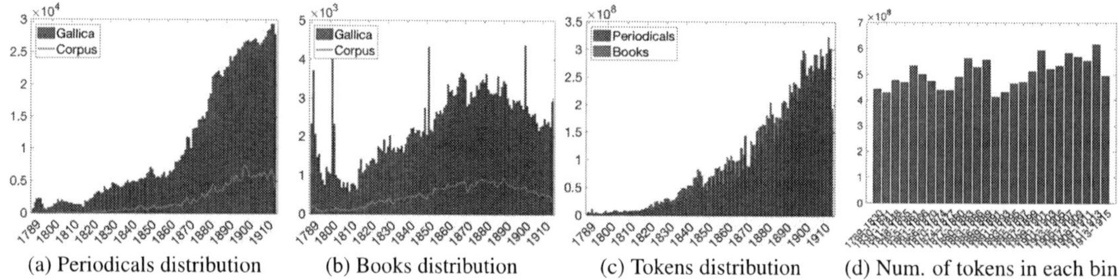

(a) Periodicals distribution   (b) Books distribution   (c) Tokens distribution   (d) Num. of tokens in each bin

Figure 1: Distribuition of resources in the corpus and time bins division.

by year. Several hypotheses can explain this proliferation of documents over time. One straightforward hypothesis can be related to increasing importance of Jews in the French public debate with the proliferation of anti-Semitic movements and newspapers such as *La Croix*, *La libre parole*, *La Lutte antijuive* and *L'Intransigeant*, just to name a few. Yet, a second hypothesis can be related to the fact that the print industry grew over time. In fact, many newspapers and publishers were founded after 1825. For example, *Hachette*, the publisher with the largest number of books in our corpus (1558), was founded in 1826. The newspapers *Le Figaro* was founded in 1826, *L'Univers* in 1833 and *Le Temps* in 1861. Figure 1a and 1b, plotting our corpus compared to the whole Gallica one, seems to suggest that the second hypothesis is the most plausible. In fact, the quantities of resources in our corpora follow a trend similar to those observed in the whole Gallica.

4.2 The embeddings

Figure 1c shows the distribution of tokens per year distinguishing periodicals and books. The greater part of the data is from the periodicals, giving to the corpus a focus on the contemporaneity. Given this distribution it is impossible to train a model using equally sized time bins. For this reason, we decided to group the data into approximately equal bins in terms of tokens. The resulting division comprehend 26 time bins of $\approx$ 450 millions tokens each (see Figure 1d).

For each bin we trained a word2vec skip-gram model (Mikolov et al., 2013) using a window size of 5 words on both sides, a word vector of 300 dimensions and removing the words that occur less than 25 times.

5 Analysis

In this section we analyse the resulting embeddings. First we study the changes in the semantic space of 4 target words. Then we analyse the biases of the same words for 6 different dimensions, each of which corresponds to a predetermined stream.

5.1 Local changes

The first analysis that we conducted is the measurement of the changes in the semantic space of the words used to refer to Jews: *juif* (noun/adjective, masculine, singular), *juifs* (noun/adjective, masculine, plural), *juive* (noun/adjective, feminine, singular) and *juives* (noun/adjective, feminine, plural). For this measurement we used the local neighborhood measure proposed by Hamilton et al. (2016a). To compute this measure it is necessary to create a second order vector, s, according to equation 1,

$$s_i^t = \text{cos-sim}(\mathbf{w}_i^{(t)}, \mathbf{w}_j^{(t)}) \,\forall w_j \in N_k(w_i^{(t)}) \cup \\ N_k(w_i^{(t+1)}), \tag{1}$$

where $N_k(w_i^{(t)})$ represents the k-nearest neighbours $(k - nn)$ at time (t) (according to cosine similarity) of a target word w_i and $\mathbf{w}_*$ is the embedding corresponding to word w_*. Once these vectors are constructed we compute the cosine distance, d, among them to quantify their differences, with equation 2,

$$d(\mathbf{s}_i^{t1}, \mathbf{s}_i^{t2}) = 1 - \text{cos-sim}(\mathbf{s}_i^{t1}, \mathbf{s}_i^{t2}). \tag{2}$$

The results of this experiment are presented in Figure 2 for all the morphological variants of the word *juif*, using $k = 100$[3]. What emerges clearly

---

[3]We noticed that the general trend of the curves in Figure 2 does not change much using different values of k (10, 25,

118

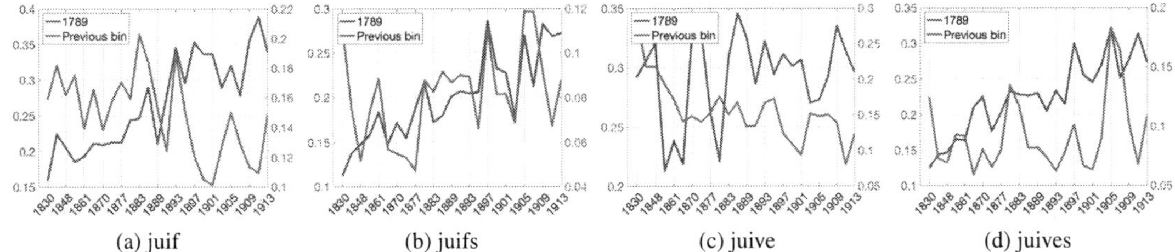

(a) juif   (b) juifs   (c) juive   (d) juives

Figure 2: Local neighborhood measure. The y axes indicates the cosine distance of the second-order vector constructed for each time period compared to the 1789 (blu line) and the preceding time period (red line).

juif		juifs		juive		juives	
⟩ 1841 ⟨		⟩ 1861 ⟨		⟩ 1874 ⟨		⟩ 1870 ⟨	
laquedem	juive	crucifient	juif	huguenots	judaïque	syriennes	négociantes
mécréant	judaïque	schismatiques	israélites	favorite	musulmane	iraniennes	samaritaines
rogatons	rabin	judaïsants	juive	opera	syrienne	musulmanes	réfugiées
blasphémateur	bouddhiste	fétichistes	rabbins	rigoletto	héroine	israélites	ascètes
⟩ 1886 ⟨		⟩ 1870 ⟨		⟩ 1886 ⟨		⟩ 1880 ⟨	
ghetto	judaïque	judaïsants	juif	drumont	iranienne	israélites	épousées
déicides	rabin	hérétiques	synagogues	antisémitisme	apostasié	musulmanes	luthériennes
francmaçon	wanderghen	cabalistes	talmud	circoncis	lithuanienne	femmes	turques
aryen	anabaptiste	lucifériens	sanhédrin	théâtrale	puritaine	célébrations	dissolues
⟩ 1893 ⟨		⟩ 1897 ⟨		⟩ 1893 ⟨		⟩ 1897 ⟨	
déicide	talmud	antisémites	samaritains	juiverie	synagogue	juif	dissolues
youtre	bouddhiste	youtres	talmud	satanisme	héroine	youtres	baptisées
francmaçon	sodomite	youpins	idolâtres	monogamique	lapidée	antijuives	prostituaient
youpins	anabaptiste	enjuivés	pharisiens	opprimée	persécutrice	antisémitiques	ascètes
⟩ 1897 ⟨		⟩ 1905 ⟨		⟩ 1901 ⟨		⟩ 1905 ⟨	
youtre	rabin	judaïsants	synagogues	stigmatisant	dragonnade	massacrées	courtisannes
sémite	usurier	hellénisants	talmud	antijuive	torturée	terrorisées	païennes
judaïsant	shylock	diaspora	pharisiens	antinationale	puritaine	diaspora	prostituaient
antisémite	anabaptiste	massacrant	ismaélites	dreyfusiste	anabaptiste	déportées	émigrées

Table 1: Words that have been introduced (left column ⟩) or eliminated (right column ⟨) for our 4 target words in time periods with a high local neighborhood distance, compared to 1789.

from these figures is that there are certain periods of time in which the relation among a target word and its local neighbourhood changed consistently. What we noticed from them is that besides changes in the relative similarity among two words what changes more is the k-nn itself, with the introduction or elimination of specific words.

Some of the words that were introduced (or eliminated) to (from) the k-nn of relevant time periods (according to local neighbourhood measure) are presented in Table 1. The words in this table are ordered according to the cosine similarity with the target word. We can see an elimination of words related to the religious domain for all the target words that we used, terms like *rabbin* (i.e., rabbi), *talmud* (i.e. the study of the Jewish law),

synagogue and *sanhédrin* (i.e., the Jewish council) are replaced by more negatively connotated words such as *ghetto*, *déicides*, *antisémites* and *antijuives*. From the few words presented in Table 1 one can also notice a possible rise of antisemitic prejudice (or at least of antisemitic language), with the introduction of specific words in the vocabulary specifically tailored to connote Jewish people in a derogatory way. *Youtre* and *youpin* are slang racist insults negatively connoting the *Jew*. They appear increasingly during the period 1880-1900.

Other terms with a negative connotation that entered the semantic area of our target words are *judaïsants* (i.e., judaizers), *enjuivés* (i.e., strongly influenced by the Jewish spirit) and *francmaçon* (i.e., freemason). These terms, as we will see in the next section, are related to the idea of a Jewish conspiracy against the world. This is a clear example of the growth of the antisemitic vocabulary.

50, 100) and that fixing $k = 100$ gives a good representation of the variations over time. Increasing this value gives high fluctuations and introduces many irrelevant words.

119

The analysis of the word *juive* is especially interesting. The word *drumont* entered its space in the time period 1886-1889. It refers to Éduard Drumont, a well known antisemite who published one of the bestsellers of the antisemitism (*La France juive*), in 1886, and was the editor of an antisemitic newspaper (*La libre Parole*), founded in 1892. We can also notice that in the semantic space of the word *juive* there are different words related to theatre. This probably derives from literary and theatre representations of Jewish female characters, as well as references to supposed Jewish inappropriate moral and sexual behaviours. Among the theatre representations we may recall that of *La Juive*, first shown in 1835, one of the most popular French operas of the 19th century, which tells the story of an impossible love affair between a Christian man and a Jewish woman. The fictional Jew, invariably seen as an outsider, provides a mirror for the phobias and obsessions of French society at a time when old Jew hatred becomes politicised, when anti-Semitism begins to permeate French ideology (Weinberg, 1983; Hallman, 2007; Samuels, 2009).

We can also see the introduction of the word *aryen* (i.e.: aryan) in 1886. This word entered the semantic space in a syntagmatic relation with the word *juif* and, as we will see in the next section, the period in which it entered is characterised by a strong antisemitism characterised by an intensification of racial and socio-political stereotypes.

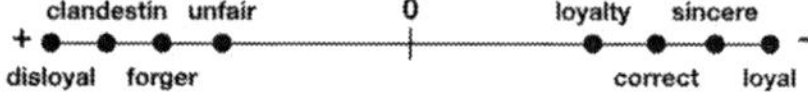

Figure 3: Semantic axis and projections.

5.2 Embedding projections

5.2.1 The streams

To quantify biases in word embeddings semantic spaces it is common to project a specific word vector on a semantic axis (Bolukbasi et al., 2016; Caliskan et al., 2017). The semantic axis can be computed as $\mathbf{g} = \mathbf{w}_i - \mathbf{w}_j$ and its projection as the dot product $\hat{b} = \mathbf{w} \cdot \mathbf{g}$, assuming that the vectors are normalised, the projection is equal to the cosine similarity. The higher the values of the projection, the more biased the word is toward that direction.

In previous literature (Bolukbasi et al., 2016) the gender direction (e.g., $\vec{he} - \vec{she}$) was used to project words related to occupations in order to quantify if these words embed information about gender. In this work we do not want to project words only according to a single direction but we want to analyse different adverse and (or) favourable biases, comparing them over time. For this reason, we defined six different semantic axes, that correspond to six antisemitic streams (S) (Wilson, 1982).

For each stream, $s \in S$, we identified a set of n antonyms pairs, $z_s = \{(a_1^{neg}, a_1^{pos}), ..., (a_n^{neg}, a_n^{pos})\}$ to construct the bias subspace in the embedding. To avoid selection biases we selected the antonyms pairs starting from a positive seed word, that is highly representative for the stream, and used a knowledge base to collect its synonyms and the corresponding antonyms (see appendix B for the complete list of antonyms used). We noticed that computing the PCA of each subspaces the corresponding explained variance is concentrated on the first component and that it is stable over time. For example, the first component of the racial stream has an explained variance of 0.34 (mean) with a standard deviation of 0.012.

The six different semantic areas, which may correspond to related antisemitic discourses are:

1. religious: antisemitism based on theological doctrines or narratives, and on religious prejudices and accusations. The seed word is *believer (unbeliever)*;

2. economic: antisemitism based on a supposed Jewish role in the economy or on stereotypes concerning Jews' economic behaviours. The seed word is *generosity (greed)*;

3. socio-political: antisemitism based on malevolent, e.g. anti-national, political behaviours or on supposedly threatening Jewish actions. The seed word is *honor (shame)*;

4. racial: antisemitism based on the definition of Jews as a race, considered inferior. The seed word is *pure (impure)*;

5. conspiratorial: antisemitism based on conspiracy theories. The seed word is *loyal (disloyal)*;

6. ethic: antisemitism based on Jewish supposed unethical or perverse morals or behaviours. The seed word is *moral (immoral)*;

To quantify the biases for all the time we computed the mean bias, b, for each stream as the

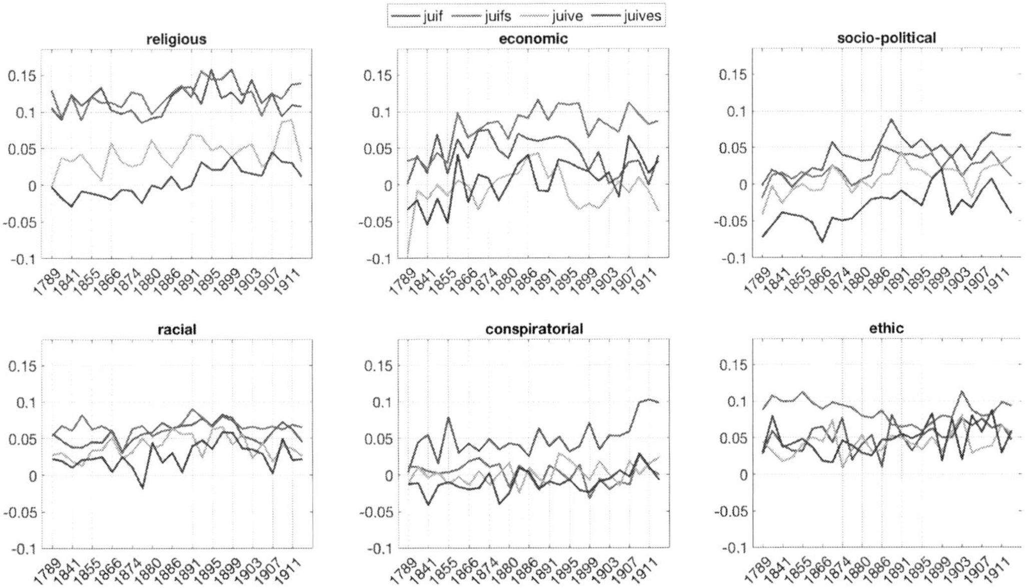

Figure 4: Projections of our 4 target words to the 6 semantic axes. Positive values indicates the adverse bias.

arithmetic mean of the individual biases, $\hat{b}$ on each axis, according to equation 3:

$$b(w_i, s) = \frac{1}{n} \sum_{j=1}^{n} \mathbf{w}_i \cdot (\mathbf{w}_{a_j^{neg}} - \mathbf{w}_{a_j^{pos}}), \quad (3)$$

where n is the number of antonyms pairs in stream s, Given the ordering of the antonyms in the computation of the bias axis ($\mathbf{g} = \mathbf{w}_{a_j^{neg}} - \mathbf{w}_{a_j^{pos}}$) we define an adverse bias when b is positive and a favourable bias when b is negative.

An example of semantic axis constructed with the pair *disloyal* as negative word and *loyal* as positive, is presented in Figure 3 ($\vec{disloyal} - \vec{disloyal}$). From this figure we can see that words that have a high projection value are words very similar to the negative word, on the other hand, words with a low projection are very similar to the word on the other side. The projection tells us if a word is closer to one extreme or the other. Unbiased words should have a projection close to 0.

5.2.2 Biases related to *Jews*

The results of this experiment are presented in Figure 4. The adverse bias is always high for the words *juif*, *juifs* and *juive*. For the word *juives* only on few cases it is negative. Adverse and favourable biases are measured with positive and negative measures respectively.

Our analysis confirms the chronological development of *antisemitic moments* identified by historians, with a steady increase of adverse bias start-

ing in the 1880s, before the Dreyfus affair. We also notice an unexpected peak in adverse bias between 1855 and 1866, in connection with the French Second Empire (1851-1870). The semantic areas or streams in relation to the Jew identified on the basis of (Wilson, 1982) seem relevant for the description of adverse bias in *antisemitic moments*. The highest adverse bias characterises the religious semantic area, followed by the economic and ethic areas. The religious adverse bias shows a peak starting in 1855, after the establishment of Napoleon III's Second Empire, a time of renewed allegiance to the Catholic Church and in 1895 at the beginning of the Dreyfus affair. Also the economic adverse bias shows a peak starting in 1855, perhaps because of the increase of economic discourse on Jews following the publication of Toussenel's *Les Juifs rois de l'époque*, and again coinciding with the establishment of the Second Empire. Another peak comes with the Dreyfus affair. The ethic adverse bias peaks in the period 1830-1855, diminishes afterward and peaks again toward the end of the Dreyfus affair.

Racial, conspiratorial and especially sociopolitical semantic areas show a steady adverse bias and an increase mostly after 1886, i.e. after the publication of Drumont's La France juive (1886). The conspiratorial adverse bias also peaks – like the religious, the economic and the ethic adverse bias – in 1855.

The singular *juif* prevails in the conspiratorial

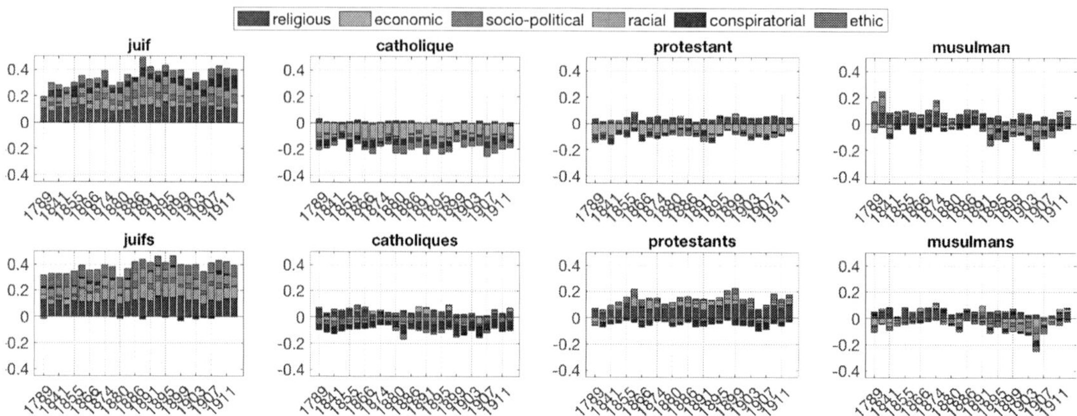

Figure 5: Cumulative bias projections compared to different religious groups.

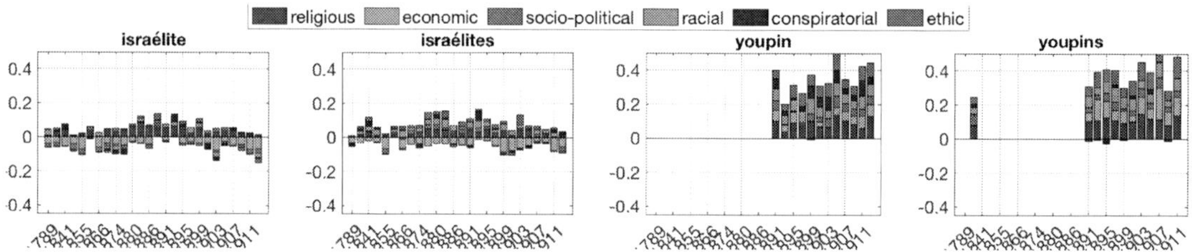

Figure 6: Cumulative bias projections for other words used to refer to Jews.

and socio-political semantic areas, which seem to entail general statements about *the Jew*. This tendency has been noticed by historians as typical of modern antisemitism and has been called *singularisation* (Miccoli, 2003). This underlines that there are features *common to all [Jews], because in all and every one there emerges something which constitutes a common and exclusive feature* of the Jew as *the enemy to be defeated* (Miccoli, 2003). On the other hand, the plural *juifs* prevails in the economic and ethic areas, as implying collective behaviours of Jews.

Racial, sociopolitical and conspiratorial semantic areas show a steady adverse bias and increase especially after 1886. As the racist vision of the Jew increases, it is turned increasingly into a political vision, and it is also nourished by a conspirationist worldview, which will culminate in the Dreyfus affair.

5.2.3 Comparative biases concerning different religious groups

The results of this experiment are presented in Figure 5. They show a comparison with three different religious groups: Catholic, (*catholique*), Protestant (*protestante*) and Muslim (*musulman*). The plots sum positive and negative biases to give a general picture of the biases at each time step.

Juif and *catholic* have a completely opposite bias: exclusively adverse in the first case, entirely favorable in the latter. Confronting *juif* and *protestant* we notice a similar bias, adverse in the first case, favorable in the latter. But the favorable bias of Protestant is much more reduced than that of *catholic*. Confronting *juifs* and *protestantes*, both show an adverse bias (lower in the case of Protestants). The adverse bias concerns *protestantes* especially in relation to the religious domain. *Musulman* and *musulmans* also show an adverse bias concentrated in the religious sphere. If we look at racial stream, this grows for *juif(s)* reference to *protestants* is absent; while there is an occasional emergence of *musulman*, with an adverse bias between 1789 and 1840, when questions of citizenship are being defined (France conquers Egypt in 1798 and in 1834 Algeria is annexed to France; in 1870 the Crémieux Decree granted French citizenship to Algerian Jews but not to Muslims), and a favourable bias in 1891-95 (in 1890 a bill is proposed for the granting of French citizenship to Algerian muslims, see Weill, 2005). The last increase is probably also connected with the availability of a larger quantity of digitised North-African press in the corpus.

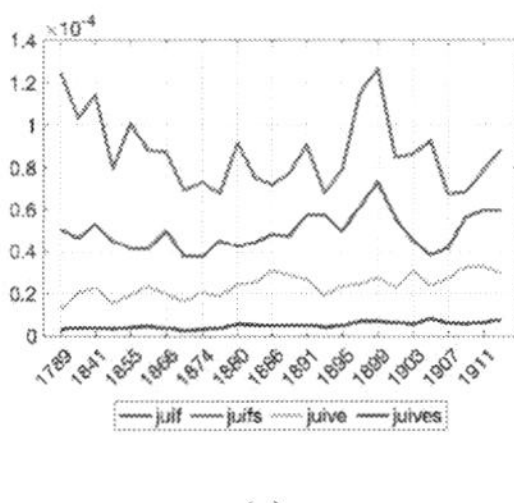 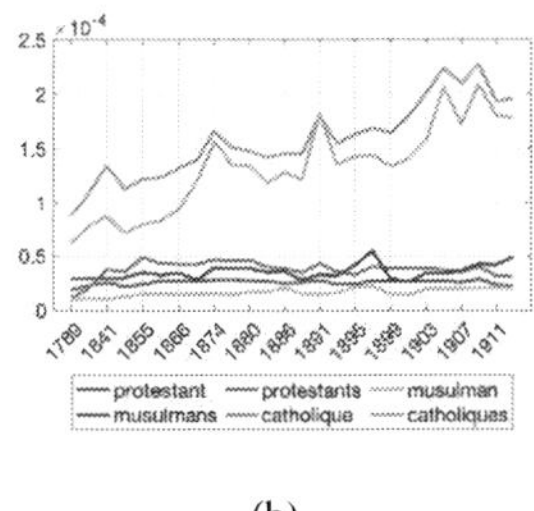 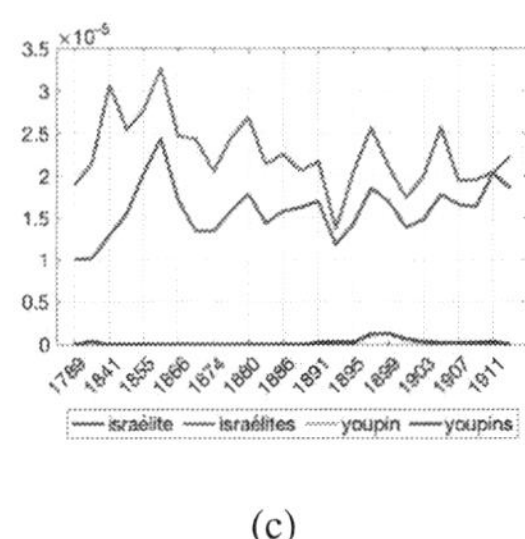

(a)   (b)   (c)

Figure 7: Target words frequency.

5.2.4 Comparative bias concerning different words used to refer to Jews

The results of this experiment are presented in Figure 6. *Israelite* and *israelites* do not show a particular bias as the terms are often used euphemistically (including by Jews themselves), i.e. preferred to the more direct and connotated *juif* and *juifs*. These terms refers to the cultural assimilation and social integration of Jews into French society, as described by Honoré (1981).

The slang and derogatory *youpin* spread starting around 1886; its shows an exclusively adverse bias and a trend similar to *juif*, as if the terms *juif* and *youpin* were interchangeable.

5.3 Target words frequency

Even if the corpus has been constructed selecting documents containing words related to the Jewish question, we noticed that the frequencies of words related to other religious groups is higher for *catholique* and *catholiques* and slightly lower for the words *protestant*, *protestantes*, *musulman* and *musulmanes*. The frequencies of all the target wordsare reported in Figure 7a, 7b and 7c.

6 Conclusions

References to Jews increase throughout the 19th century, as Jews were integrated within French society and these references appear to be mostly associated with an adverse bias in all semantic areas. The adverse bias grows starting in the mid-1880s, i.e. in the second half of the Third Republic, when the rise of anticlericalism and socialism was associated with Jews by the conservative and catholic public opinion. Around this time the publication of Drumont's *La France juive* provokes an adverse bias towards Jews clearly associated to antisemitic discourse in all semantic areas, which prepares the outburst of the Dreyfus affair, and it remains steady during and after the affair.

The highest adverse bias characterises the religious semantic area, followed by the economic and ethic spheres. The conspiratorial and sociopolitical areas show an adverse bias more often associated with the singular *juif*, as if they provoked categorical statements. Adverse bias in the economic and ethic areas is expressed through the plural *juifs* as describing collective behaviours.

The confrontation between *juif* and *catholic* shows an entirely adverse bias in the first case and an entirely favorable bias in the latter case. The adverse bias towards other minorities, i.e. Protestants and Muslims concerns the religious semantic area. No bias concerning protestant emerges in the racial semantic area, while a negative and positive bias emerge in relation to Muslims at times when the question of French citizenship is being defined.

As one evaluates the presence of the word *juif*, and the semantic areas surrounding it, one should also consider that these may emerge in texts which are not antisemitic per se, but still contribute to the spread of images of Jews, with specific biases. We refer here especially to literary texts.

We suggest that the adverse bias in various semantic areas may be associated with antisemitic discourses, but this association should be further explored though an examination of the historical context (for example that of *antisemitic moments*) or an analysis of the textual sources which spread the words associated with *the Jew*.

Acknowledgments

The authors of this work have received funding from the European Union's Horizon 2020 research and innovation programme under grant agreement No 732942. The experiments have been run on the SCSCF cluster of Ca' Foscari University.

References

Pierpaolo Basile, Annalina Caputo, Roberta Luisi, and Giovanni Semeraro. 2016. Diachronic analysis of the italian language exploiting google ngram. *CLiC it*, page 56.

Pierre Birnbaum. 2011. *The anti-semitic moment: A tour of France in 1898*. Chicago University Press.

Leonard Bloomfield. 1933. *Language*. George Allen and Unwin LTD.

Tolga Bolukbasi, Kai-Wei Chang, James Y Zou, Venkatesh Saligrama, and Adam T Kalai. 2016. Man is to computer programmer as woman is to homemaker? debiasing word embeddings. In *Advances in neural information processing systems*, pages 4349–4357.

Aylin Caliskan, Joanna J Bryson, and Arvind Narayanan. 2017. Semantics derived automatically from language corpora contain human-like biases. *Science*, 356(6334):183–186.

Haim Dubossarsky, Yulia Tsvetkov, Chris Dyer, and Eitan Grossman. 2015. A bottom up approach to category mapping and meaning change. In *Net-WordS*, pages 66–70.

Haim Dubossarsky, Daphna Weinshall, and Eitan Grossman. 2017. Outta control: Laws of semantic change and inherent biases in word representation models. In *Proceedings of the 2017 conference on empirical methods in natural language processing*, pages 1136–1145.

John R Firth. 1957. A synopsis of linguistic theory, 1930-1955. *Studies in Linguistic Analysis*.

Nikhil Garg, Londa Schiebinger, Dan Jurafsky, and James Zou. 2018. Word embeddings quantify 100 years of gender and ethnic stereotypes. *Proceedings of the National Academy of Sciences*, 115(16):E3635–E3644.

Hila Gonen and Yoav Goldberg. 2019. Lipstick on a pig: Debiasing methods cover up systematic gender biases in word embeddings but do not remove them. *arXiv preprint arXiv:1903.03862*.

Kristina Gulordava and Marco Baroni. 2011. A distributional similarity approach to the detection of semantic change in the google books ngram corpus. In *Proceedings of the GEMS 2011 workshop on geometrical models of natural language semantics*, pages 67–71.

Diana R Hallman. 2007. *Opera, Liberalism, and Antisemitism in Nineteenth-Century France: The Politics of Halévy's La Juive*. Cambridge University Press.

William L Hamilton, Jure Leskovec, and Dan Jurafsky. 2016a. Cultural shift or linguistic drift? comparing two computational measures of semantic change. In *Proceedings of the Conference on Empirical Methods in Natural Language Processing. Conference on Empirical Methods in Natural Language Processing*, volume 2016, page 2116. NIH Public Access.

William L Hamilton, Jure Leskovec, and Dan Jurafsky. 2016b. Diachronic word embeddings reveal statistical laws of semantic change. *arXiv preprint arXiv:1605.09096*.

Zellig S Harris. 1954. Distributional structure. *Word*, 10(2-3):146–162.

Jean-Paul Honoré. 1981. Le vocabulaire de l'antisémitisme en france pendant l'affaire dreyfus. *Mots. Les langages du politique*, 2(1):73–92.

Julie Kalman. 2010. *Rethinking antisemitism in nineteenth-century France*. Cambridge University Press.

Jacob Katz. 1980. *From prejudice to destruction: anti-Semitism, 1700-1933*. Harvard University Press.

Grégoire Kauffmann. 2008. *Édouard Drumont*. Perrin.

Yoon Kim, Yi-I Chiu, Kentaro Hanaki, Darshan Hegde, and Slav Petrov. 2014. Temporal analysis of language through neural language models. *arXiv preprint arXiv:1405.3515*.

Austin C Kozlowski, Matt Taddy, and James A Evans. 2018. The geometry of culture: Analyzing meaning through word embeddings. *arXiv preprint arXiv:1803.09288*.

Vivek Kulkarni, Rami Al-Rfou, Bryan Perozzi, and Steven Skiena. 2015. Statistically significant detection of linguistic change. In *Proceedings of the 24th International Conference on World Wide Web*, pages 625–635. International World Wide Web Conferences Steering Committee.

Andrey Kutuzov, Erik Velldal, and Lilja Øvrelid. 2017. Temporal dynamics of semantic relations in word embeddings: an application to predicting armed conflict participants. *arXiv preprint arXiv:1707.08660*.

Giovanni Miccoli. 2003. Antiebraismo, antisemitismo: un nesso fluttuante. In *Les racines chrétiennes de l'antisémitisme politique*, pages 1000–1021. École française de Rome.

Tomas Mikolov, Ilya Sutskever, Kai Chen, Greg S Corrado, and Jeff Dean. 2013. Distributed representations of words and phrases and their compositionality. In *Advances in neural information processing systems*, pages 3111–3119.

Alain Rey, Chantal Tanet, and Marianne Tomi. 2010. Dictionnaire historique de la langue française.

Eyal Sagi, Stefan Kaufmann, and Brady Clark. 2009. Semantic density analysis: Comparing word meaning across time and phonetic space. In *Proceedings of the Workshop on Geometrical Models of Natural Language Semantics*, pages 104–111. Association for Computational Linguistics.

Maurice Samuels. 2009. *Inventing the Israelite: Jewish Fiction in Nineteenth-Century France*. Stanford University Press.

Zeev Sternhell. 1998. *La droite révolutionnaire: les origines francaises du fascisme 1885-1914*. Gallimard.

Rob Voigt, Nicholas P Camp, Vinodkumar Prabhakaran, William L Hamilton, Rebecca C Hetey, Camilla M Griffiths, David Jurgens, Dan Jurafsky, and Jennifer L Eberhardt. 2017. Language from police body camera footage shows racial disparities in officer respect. *Proceedings of the National Academy of Sciences*, 114(25):6521–6526.

Warren Weaver. 1955. Translation. *Machine Translation of Languages*, 14:15–23.

Henry H Weinberg. 1983. The image of the jew in late nineteenth-century french literature. *Jewish Social Studies*, 45(3/4):241–250.

Stephen Wilson. 1982. *Ideology and experience: antisemitism in France at the time of the Dreyfus affair*. Fairleigh Dickinson University Press; London: Associated University Presses.

Jieyu Zhao, Tianlu Wang, Mark Yatskar, Vicente Ordonez, and Kai-Wei Chang. 2017. Men also like shopping: Reducing gender bias amplification using corpus-level constraints. In *Proceedings of the 2017 Conference on Empirical Methods in Natural Language Processing*.

Jieyu Zhao, Yichao Zhou, Zeyu Li, Wei Wang, and Kai-Wei Chang. 2018. Learning gender-neutral word embeddings. *arXiv preprint arXiv:1809.01496*.

A Keywords

- Juif (i.e: Jew - masculine, singular)

- Juive (i.e: Jew - feminine, singular)

- Judaisme (i.e: Judaism)

- Israëlite (i.e: Israelite)

- Israël (i.e: Israel)

- Israëlitisme (i.e: Israelitism)

- Mosaïsme (i.e: religions referred to the message of Moses)

- Talmud (i.e: Talmud)

- Judas (i.e: Judass)

- Moloch (i.e: the biblical name of a Canaanite god associated with child sacrifice)

- Ahasverus (i.e: a mythical immortal man whose legend began to spread in Europe in the 13th century. The original legend concerns a Jew who taunted Jesus on the way to the Crucifixion and was then cursed to walk the earth until the Second Coming.)

B Bias axes

The list of antonyms used to compute the bias axes. Note that the translation of the antonyms pairs is provided only for the singular. We used a public resource (http://www.synonyms-fr.com) to collect antonyms relations.

Religious angel, devil; sacred, profane; pious, atheist; pious, pagan; pious, idolater; pious, impious; sacred, cursed; venerable, abject; faithful, unfaithful; believer, unbeliever; religious, irreligious; dedicated, atheist.

Economic give, appropriate; generosity, greed; generous, greedy; generous, miserly; generous, stingy.

Socio-political prodigal, greedy; honest, rabble; honor, shame; friendly, hostile; loyal, deceitful; socialist, capitalist; friend, enemy; ally, antagonist; conservative, progressive.

Racial normal, strange; superiority, inferiority; equality, inequality; pleasant, unpleasant; benign, wicked; worthy, infamous; sympathy, hate; accepted, refused, better, worse; national, foreign; pure, impure; upper, lower; pure, filthy; clean, dirty.

Conspiratorial loyal; spy; honesty, treason; loyal, disloyal; clear, mysterious; obvious, occult; sincere, deceitful; sincere, unfair; benefactor, criminal; clear, secret; friendly, threatening; clear, dark.

Ethic chastity, lust; modest, intriguing; decent, indecent; virtuous, lascivious; faithful, unfaithful; moral, immoral; honest, dishonest; chaste, depraved; chaste, fleshly; pure, degenerate.

DiaHClust: an iterative hierarchical clustering approach for identifying stages in language change

Christin Schätzle
University of Konstanz
christin.schaetzle@uni-konstanz.de

Hannah Booth
Ghent University
hannah.booth@ugent.be

Abstract

Language change is often assessed against a set of pre-determined time periods in order to be able to trace its diachronic trajectory. This is problematic, since a pre-determined periodization might obscure significant developments and lead to false assumptions about the data. Moreover, these time periods can be based on factors which are either arbitrary or non-linguistic, e.g., dividing the corpus data into equidistant stages or taking into account language-external events. Addressing this problem, in this paper we present a data-driven approach to periodization: 'DiaHClust'. DiaHClust is based on iterative hierarchical clustering and offers a multi-layered perspective on change from text-level to broader time periods. We demonstrate the usefulness of DiaHClust via a case study investigating syntactic change in Icelandic, modelling the syntactic system of the language in terms of vectors of syntactic change.

1 Introduction

In historical linguistics, it is now generally acknowledged that language change proceeds gradually rather than abruptly (e.g., Kroch, 2001). Nevertheless, in order to achieve meaningful comparisons and generalizations, it is useful to be able to identify stages in a change's trajectory. In traditional approaches, the progress of a change is typically assessed against a pre-determined and somewhat arbitrary periodization scheme which segments a language's diachrony into discrete periods (e.g., 'Old', 'Middle' and '(Early) Modern'). The problematic nature of this methodology is well known, though rarely made explicit (see, e.g., Curzan, 2012). Such an approach may yield results which conceal the true trajectory of a phenomenon. For instance, relying on a discrete periodization may give misleading findings indicative

of abrupt change, e.g., with a certain year as a turning point. Moreover, transitional stages, which are often of great interest, can be easily obscured. Despite such issues, for a long time this 'periodization problem' was accepted as an unfortunate but unavoidable aspect of historical linguistics.

With the boom in corpus-based and computational studies of language change over recent decades, the periodization problem has been re-addressed, as new data-driven methodologies have emerged, particularly in relation to historical English (see, e.g., Gries and Hilpert, 2008, 2012; Degaetano-Ortlieb and Teich, 2018). Instead of applying a pre-determined periodization to the data at the outset, in such approaches the data is first assessed and periods then suggested based on assessment of this data. The periodization scheme can be arrived at via a range of statistical methods, e.g., hierarchical clustering and relative entropy. This yields objective data-driven periodization schemes which are faithful to the corpus data and can still be used to arrive at meaningful generalizations.

In this paper, we present DiaHClust, a new approach which can be used to identify stages in diachronic change based on quantitative corpus-derived data. As a basis we take the hierarchical clustering approach for historical data from Gries and Hilpert (2008, 2012) and develop this further, specifically for investigating syntactic change. In addition to implementing the methodology from Gries and Hilpert in the software environment R (R Core Team, 2014), we add an extra iterative approach to the hierarchical clustering which results in a multi-layered perspective on change, from text-level to broader periods, while also respecting outliers and genre effects. With DiaHClust, we show that a data-driven periodization methodology can also be applied to a language like Icelandic, where syntactic change is not as extreme as

Proceedings of the 1st International Workshop on Computational Approaches to Historical Language Change, pages 126–135
Florence, Italy, August 2, 2019. ©2019 Association for Computational Linguistics

in other Germanic languages, and where the available annotated corpus data is relatively sparse.

2 Data-driven approaches to periodization

Often, the factors which go into determining a traditional top-down periodization have no direct connection to the linguistic phenomena under investigation. Moreover, the vast majority of traditional periodizations also take into account language-external factors, e.g. historical milestones or migrations. A classic example is the 'Middle English' period, which is often delimited by the onset of the Norman invasions in 1066 and the arrival of printing in the late 15th century. A further issue is that time stages within a periodization scheme are sometimes designed to be equal in length. This results in a periodization scheme whose time stages are not necessarily a best fit with the actual linguistic characteristics. Moreover, since a traditional periodization is a linear sequence of time stages, transitional periods which may overlap with certain time stages cannot readily be identified, despite the fact that understanding these transitions is vital for explaining language change.

In response to such issues, alternative approaches have emerged which are exclusively derived from the data at hand. For example, Degaetano-Ortlieb and Teich (2018) present a data-driven approach which uses relative entropy by calculating the Kullback-Leibler Divergence (KLD) between lexical and grammatical features in texts from temporally adjacent time periods to identify stages in language change. KLD is an information-theoretic measure which is used to compare probability distributions and detect differences between them. Degaetano-Ortlieb and Teich (2018) apply KLD to the detection of periods of change by selecting a starting year and a sliding window of several years to compare the probability distributions of corpus data from the preceding and subsequent years in the sliding window. The KLD models are based on the distributions of lemmas and Part-of-Speech trigrams in historical texts to track changes at the lexical and grammatical level. A change is identified by means of relative peaks or troughs in KLD.

Another methodology is the bottom-up clustering approach to periodization developed by Gries and Hilpert (2008, 2012), 'Variability-based Neighbor Clustering' (VNC) (see also Hilpert and Gries, 2009, 2016; Perek and Hilpert, 2017). In contrast to standard hierarchical clustering, VNC is sensitive to the temporal ordering of data. The basic principle is that parts of the data which exhibit similar linguistic characteristics should form part of the same period, i.e., cluster, and that breaks between periods should be inserted at points where the characteristics of the data show a quantifiable shift.

The VNC algorithm groups together temporally adjacent data points which are most similar to each other in a stepwise fashion. First, the two neighboring data points which exhibit the highest degree of similarity are identified and merged into a single data point. The similarity between data points is measured via the calculation of standard deviations or other distance measurements, e.g. Euclidean distance when the data points represent single values, or correlation measurements such as Pearson's r when the data points represent vectors of values. The data in Gries and Hilpert (2008, 2012) consists of either individual frequency values which represent the occurrence of a given structure over time, e.g., the *get*-passive in historical English, or vectors of values representing the collocations of a linguistic structure with multiple linguistic items, mostly at the lexical level.

The neighboring data points are merged into a single data point according to an amalgamation rule chosen by the researcher. The amalgamation can, for example, be achieved via averaging values or choosing the minimum/maximum of the values. Next, the two neighboring data points with the highest degree of similarity are merged. This process is repeated until all data points have been merged, grouping the data into larger time stages along the way. The result of this process is a hierarchical clustering of all data points which is generally graphically represented as a dendogram. The dendrogram shows the sequence in which the data points were merged into clusters, providing insights into how much the clusters differ from one another. The hierarchical nature of the output is a particular advantage, which – unlike traditional linear periodizations – allows transitional and overlapping stages to be identified and represented. In order to identify the most useful number of clustered time periods, Gries and Hilpert (2012) use a scree plot. Applied to VNC, the scree plot displays how much variability in the data can be explained after each merging step, allowing the researcher to choose the most accurate periods.

Despite the data-driven focus of the VNC methodology, in order to have a suitable number of initial input clusters Gries and Hilpert (2008, 2012) aggregate individual texts into larger temporal episodes, e.g., decades or fifty-year periods. This still involves imposing an abitrary classification on the data at the outset and may bias the clustering, obscuring significant insights about transitional periods – particularly if applied to corpora where data sparsity is an issue. In this paper we present DiaHClust, a method for periodization which implements the VNC algorithm for the analysis of syntactic change, but avoids the a priori aggregation of texts by adding a second level of iteration outside the VNC. One can thus trace the clustering from text-level through several iterations until the final periodization scheme is reached, gaining detailed insights about the progress of change, possible outliers and genre effects.

3 DiaHClust: Methodology

We have developed DiaHClust for a study of syntactic change in Icelandic based on data from the Icelandic Parsed Historical Corpus ('IcePaHC', Wallenberg et al., 2011). The main objective is to provide a better understanding of the progression of previously identified changes in the language in terms of a data-driven periodization. DiaHClust extends Gries and Hilpert's (2008; 2012) vector-based approach to VNC to factor in syntactic changes. Instead of clustering with respect to the distributional features of a single phenomenon, we include multiple known syntactic changes in the vectors to create a model of the syntactic system at different stages. Moreover, we present our implementation of the VNC in R as the DiaHClust package. DiaHClust is readily usable with any kind of diachronic data suitable for hierarchical clustering. In addition to the standard VNC approach, DiaHClust provides an extra iterative approach by calculating silhouette values (Rousseeuw, 1987) to automatically identify the optimal numbers of clusters. This allows us to begin at text-level, tracing the clustering until the final larger time stages are identified, and enables the ad hoc identification of outliers and genre effects. Furthermore, this methodology avoids misleading statistics which may arise when one otherwise aggregates the data into small temporal sequences at the outset.

3.1 Vectors of syntactic change

In the vector-based approach by Gries and Hilpert (2008, 2012) and in the KLD-approach by Degaetano-Ortlieb and Teich (2018), differences in the occurrence of a linguistic feature across various contexts, i.e., its distributional properties, are assessed. These contextual differences often reflect functional, lexical and stylistic factors which are independent of grammar. In generative approaches to syntactic change, a common idea is that multiple 'surface' word order changes which show up in the data often reflect a single 'underlying' change in clause structure (e.g. Kroch, 1989). Syntactic change is thus viewed as deeply interactional, and distributional properties are less relevant in its assessment. Our syntax-specific methodology uses vectors which are packed with information about multiple interrelated syntactic developments.

In our proposal, a vector is created for each text in a given diachronic corpus. Each vector contains relative frequencies of syntactic features which change over time, see (1).

(1)   Text A = {feature$_1$, feature$_2$, ..., feature$_n$}
        Text B = {feature$_1$, feature$_2$, ..., feature$_n$}
        $\vdots$

In this way, existing knowledge about a language's syntactic system across time informs the data-driven periodization. Furthermore, using changing syntactic features to describe the language system at a given point of time is supported by recent work to train a classifier for the dating of early English texts (Zimmermann, 2014; Ecay and Pintzuk, 2016). We provide a more concrete example in Section 4.

3.2 Implementation of VNC

We implemented our DiaHClust methodology using R. The source code and the DiaHClust package, including a detailed documentation, are available on GitHub.[1] DiaHClust implements the VNC approach in the form of the `vnc()` function by manipulating individual steps in the workflow behind R's standard agglomerative hierarchical clustering function `hclust()`.

---

[1] `https://github.com/christinschaetzle/diaHClust`

In the vector-based approach to VNC by Gries and Hilpert (2008, 2012), a correlation statistic is calculated before clustering the data. This is generally done when applying a hierarchical clustering approach to vectorial data (see, e.g., Baayen, 2008). Thus, a correlation matrix is calculated first in the DiaHClust approach, using Pearson's r as correlation coefficient.[2] In DiaHClust, the correlation matrix is calculated based on a data matrix where each column represents a vector containing the changing syntactic features extracted from a text. The vectors are ordered from left to right according to the time stamp of the text. The time stamp is encoded in the vector name, i.e., the name of the corresponding column in the data matrix. For the DiaHClust package to work, the vector name should begin with a four digit year date followed by a dot and the text name, e.g., "1250.STURLUNGA", allowing one to easily identify individual texts in the clustering.[3] Following this, the correlation matrix is transformed into a distance matrix by calculating Euclidean distances between the data points, since hierarchical clustering, including VNC, requires a distance measure to determine the (dis-)similarity between two objects (see, e.g., Gries and Hilpert 2012).

Hierarchical clustering usually begins by clustering together the two most similar objects, i.e., the data points with the smallest distance to one another, merging these two data points. This process continues until all data points have been clustered. This process is illustrated in lines 6–12 in Algorithm 1.[4] Different methods for agglomeration, i.e., the merging or amalgamation of two data points, such as averaging over two data points or taking the minimum value can be applied in hierarchical clustering. When averaging is chosen as the

---

[2]The correlation matrix has to be squared when negative correlation coefficients are produced. Depending on the data distribution, one has to use Spearman correlations instead of Pearson's r (see Baayen, 2008, 150–152 for details on correlation statistics and hierarchical clustering).

[3]This corresponds to token IDs in IcePaHC and other Penn-style treebanks. One could add more information to the vector names, e.g., genre or author, but the longer the vector names, the more difficult it is to read the dendrograms.

[4]Distance matrices in R are designed such that distances between neighboring, in our case temporally-adjacent, data points are depicted on the diagonal of the matrix. Moreover, the cells above the diagonal are empty since they mirror the cells below the diagonal. Line 9 handles the case when the first two data points, i.e., the first two columns, are merged. The first row in a distance matrix in R corresponds to the second data point from the original data matrix. Thus, the first row has to be deleted when it is merged so that the formerly second row can take its place.

Algorithm 1 Implementation of VNC

```
1: function VNC
       ▷ Manipulation of distance matrix (dist):
2:     for i = 1 to numberOfRows(dist) do
3:         for j = 1 to i do
4:             if not i = j then
5:                 dist[i, j] = max(dist)
       ▷ Clustering process:
6:     for k = 1 to numberOfRows(dist) do
7:         find m, n for which dist[m, n] = min(dist)
8:         dist[, n] = (dist[,n]+dist[,n+1]) / 2
9:         if dist[1, 1] = min(dist) then
10:            delete dist[1, ]
11:        else
12:            dist[m, ] = (dist[m−1,]+dist[m,]) / 2
```

agglomeration method, cluster similarity between two clusters is assessed based on the average of the data points in the clusters. Moreover, the two data points with the smallest distance are merged into a new data point by averaging the corresponding values after each iteration, see lines 8 and 12 in Algorithm 1. In general, all agglomeration methods available with `hclust()` are available with our implementation of the VNC. We recommend using averages – following Gries and Hilpert (2008, 2012) – since, in quantitative corpus linguistics, (co-)occurence frequencies are usually assessed by averaging frequencies over texts/time periods.

In order to allow only temporally-adjacent data points (i.e., texts) to be clustered with one another in VNC, we manipulate the distance matrix before clustering the data. This is done by setting all distance values which describe distances between non-temporally adjacent data points to the value which equals the maximum value of the distance matrix, see lines 2-5 in Algorithm 1. As similarity is measured in terms of the minimum distance, it is highly unlikely that two data points which have these maximized distances to one another will be merged in the clustering process. This in turn allows us to use the standard `hclust()` function for clustering according to the ideas of VNC, instead of having to implement a separate clustering algorithm. Moreover, `vnc()` adjusts the permutations of the data points which arise during the merging process in order to guarantee the diachronic ordering of data points for plotting as in the dendrogram in Figure 1.

The most appropriate number of clusters for the data, i.e., the time stages the data points fall into, can now be identified via visual inspection of the dendrogram or by generating a scree plot as proposed by Gries and Hilpert (2008, 2012). In

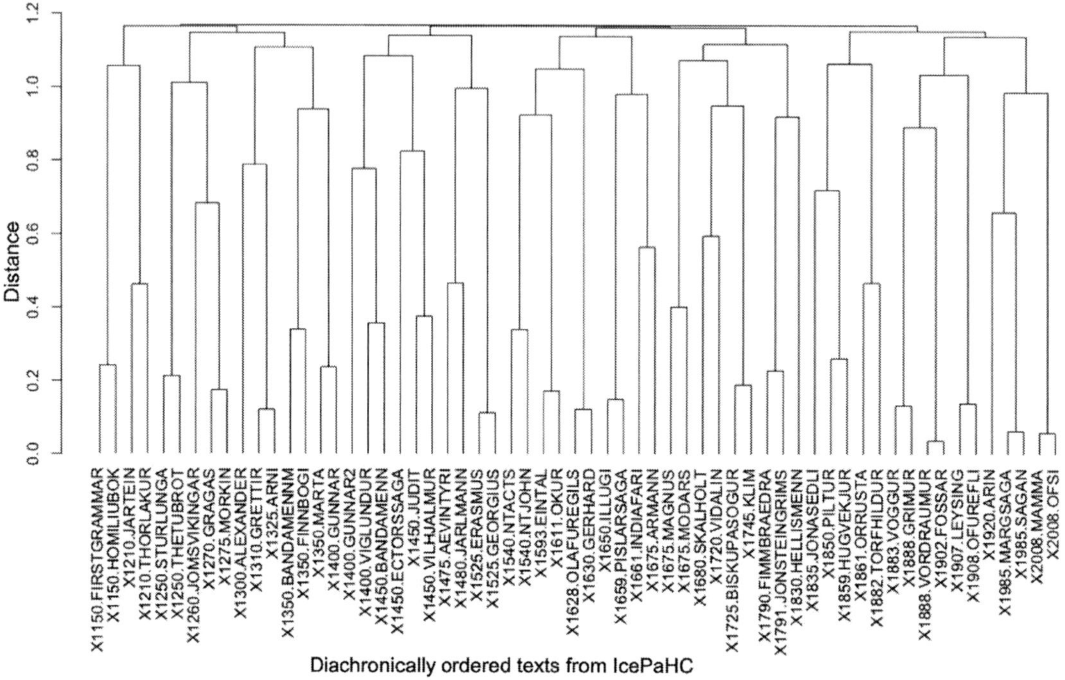

Figure 1: Dendrogram showing the results of the text-based VNC with respect to syntactic change in IcePaHC.

both cases, a decision about the horizontal cut-off point of clusters in the dendrogram has to be made. However, such a visual exploration of the data is often difficult, particularly when the input for the clustering is a large number of individual data points, which is usually the case when clustering individual texts from an entire corpus. Moreover, screeplots rely on the calculation of yet another statistical analysis, i.e., principal components or standard deviations. We therefore decided to calculate silhouettes instead, which provide a quantitative measure of the quality of clusters at different cut-off points. Calculating silhouettes is a standard method for cluster validation. Silhouettes can be used to identify the optimal number of clusters for a given data set, as we explain next.

3.3 Cluster Validation for Cluster Identification

Silhouette values provide information about the consistency of clusters by measuring the dissimilarity of an object to the cluster that it is in, compared to its dissimilarity to other clusters. The silhouette value $s(i)$ of an object i is calculated according to the formula in Equation 1, where $a(i)$ is the average dissimilarity of i to all other objects in the cluster i has been assigned to, and where $b(i)$ corresponds to the average dissimilarity of i to its

next closest cluster (cf. Rousseeuw, 1987, 56). A large silhouette value, i.e., a value close to 1, indicates that the object is clustered well as it is, and a negative $s(i)$ indicates that i has been assigned to the wrong cluster.

$$s(i) = \frac{b(i) - a(i)}{\max\{a(i), b(i)\}} \qquad (1)$$

The silhouette coefficient of a cluster is moreover defined as the average of silhouettes in a cluster. We implement the calculation of silhouette coefficents in the `optimal_clust()` function as part of DiaHClust, in order to be able to find the optimal number of clusters after VNC clustering has been applied.[5] `optimal_clust()` iterates through all clustering possibilities according to the possible number of merges throughout the clustering process, and calculates the average of silhouette coefficients of all clusters in a clustering. Eventually, the clustering with the highest average silhouette coefficient is identified as the best candidate, and returns information about the cluster memberships of data points with respect to the optimal clustering.

When clustering a large number of data points

---

[5]Silhouettes can be easily calculated with R using the `silhouette()` function.

– as is usually the case when the input data represents vectors for texts from an entire corpus – the silhouette coefficient may still imply a large number of optimal clusters. Although this may generate insights about the temporal grouping of the data, such a fine-grained periodization is not suitable for frequency-based investigations of syntactic change. We therefore continue the clustering process iteratively, until the optimal number of clusters is smaller than 10. This is implemented as `diahclust()`, as we now describe.

3.4 Iterative DiaHClust Approach

When the results of the `optimal_clust()` function indicate that the initial VNC clustering yields 10 or more clusters, the clustering process can be continued via the `diahclust()` function. The methodology behind the function is illustrated by the pseudocode in Algorithm 2. Before continuing the clustering process, data points which belong to a single cluster according to the previously assessed optimal clustering are aggregated by averaging the corresponding syntactic vectors in the underlying dataset. To keep track of the texts and time stages which form clusters across the iterations, the names of the new vectors consist of the sequence of the names of the aggregated vectors. The previously applied process of VNC clustering with respect to the new dataset is then repeated, including the recalculation of a correlation statistic and a new distance matrix.[6] Moreover, `diahclust()` automatically plots the clustering as a dendrogram. The labels on the dendrogram are abbreviated for better visibility, representing the range of previously aggregated vectors, with the oldest and the youngest text in the range connected via a hyphen, see Figure 2. The resulting clustering is again evaluated using the `optimal_clust()` function, which returns the cluster memberships listing the full range of texts in the clusters. The application of this process is repeated until the final evaluation arrives at an optimal number of clusters less than 10. In this iterative process, the clusters, i.e., time stages, can be inspected at each step of the iteration, allowing one to track the composition of the clusters with respect to the individual texts from the first iteration onwards. This provides insights

---

⁶When the agglomeration method chosen for VNC clustering is not "average", a different aggregation method, e.g., the minimum with single linkage clustering, should be applied.

Algorithm 2 DiaHClust methodology

```
1: function DIAHCLUST
2:     repeat
3:         aggregate(data)
4:         dist = distanceMatrix(cor(data))
5:         clust = vnc(dist)
6:         plot(clust)
7:         computeOptimalClustering(clust)
8:     until numberOfClusters < 10
```

into how similar the texts in the individual clusters are to one another. We find that this iterative approach very well facilitates the identification of outliers and time stages affected by a genre effect.

In the next section, we illustrate the functionalities of the DiaHClust package by applying the method to a case study which investigates syntactic change in the history of Icelandic.

4 Case study: syntactic change in Icelandic

Icelandic is generally acknowledged to be the most conservative of the present-day Germanic languages with respect to syntactic change. Yet, several recent corpus studies using IcePaHC have brought to light a series of syntactic changes which interact with one another along the diachrony. These changes comprise the increasing use of dative subjects (see, e.g., Schätzle, 2018), an increase in the frequency of the expletive *það* (Booth, 2018), a decrease in the occurrence of declarative V1 (verb-first) structures (Butt et al., 2014), and an increasing preference of subjects to occur in the clause-initial, prefinite position (see Booth et al., 2017). These studies employ a predetermined top-down periodization scheme akin to that suggested by Haugen (1984), which is influenced by language-external factors such as the first Icelandic translation of the New Testament (1540) and separates the corpus data into more or less equidistant time periods. These studies have in common that the frequencies of the individual phenomena seem to change rather abruptly at a similar point in the diachrony, indicating that a series of drastic changes have occurred in Icelandic clause structure during the past two centuries.

The case study presented in this section is intended to shed more light on the trajectories of these changes by applying the DiaHClust method to data extracted from IcePaHC. We create syntactic vectors on the basis of occurrence frequencies with respect to dative subjects, expletives, V1 and subject position in IcePaHC, and also include data which we extracted for two further phenomena of change which have been previously identified in the history of Icelandic: the change from OV (object-verb) to VO (verb-object) order in the verb phrase (see, e.g., Hróarsdóttir, 2000) and a decrease in the Stylistic Fronting phenomenon (Hróarsdóttir, 1998; Rögnvaldsson, 1996).

4.1 IcePaHC

The IcePaHC corpus, from which the data for this case study is drawn, is a Penn-style treebank (Marcus et al., 1993) which is lemmatised, part-of-speech tagged and annotated for constituent structure, with additional tagging for certain grammatical functions (e.g. subject, object). The corpus contains approximately 1,000,000 words, from 61 text extracts spanning 10 centuries (1150-2008), thereby covering all attested stages of Icelandic.

Despite the significant advantages of the IcePaHC annotation scheme for syntactic research, the corpus does have some limitations. Firstly, the texts included represent only a very small sample of attested historical Icelandic. Secondly, these texts are not evenly distributed across time, so that certain centuries are affected by relative data sparsity. Thirdly, although the corpus texts span various genres, there is a strong bias towards narrative texts overall, while in certain centuries other genres (religious, biographical) dominate. These limitations make the application of a top-down periodization extremely difficult. Thus, IcePaHC represents an ideal test case for the application of our DiaHClust method.

4.2 Syntactic factors under investigation

We obtained relative frequencies for the following phenomena to create a syntactic vector for each text from IcePaHC: dative subjects, overt expletives, V1, subjects in the prefinite position, VO order, and Stylistic Fronting. The data was gathered using the CorpusSearch tool (Randall, 2000) and our own programming scripts. In general, we extracted the proportion of matrix declarative sentences in each text in which the respective phenomenon occurred, and calculated average frequencies by means of the total amount of matrix declarative clauses in the corresponding text. For the expletives, we calculated relative frequencies on the basis of the proportion of expletives occurring in presentationals and impersonals, based on the findings of a recent IcePaHC study (Booth,

2018). As an approximation of the frequency of Stylistic Fronting, we counted the matrix declarative clauses with a non-finite verb, verbal particle or negation in the clause-initial position (e.g., Maling, 1990). In order to track the rise of VO in the verb phrase at the expense of OV, we calculated the occurrence frequencies of VO and OV in matrix declaratives with a finite auxiliary and a nonfinite lexical verb, in order to abstract away from the verb-second property (see, e.g. Pintzuk, 2005). For each text, the proportion of VO versus OV was included in our syntactic vectors. The resulting data was loaded into R in the form of a data matrix, where each column represents the syntactic vector of an IcePaHC text.

4.3 Application of DiaHClust

Before applying our implementation of VNC in R via the `vnc()` function, we calculated a correlation and distance matrix for our syntactic vectors. Since we start our clustering process with 61 vectors (IcePaHC texts), the resulting number of clusters is quite large. `optimal_clust()` proposes to cluster the data into 28 clusters via the calculation of silhouette coefficients. Although the silhouettes suggest that the clusters are well structured (average silhouette coefficient > 0.5), analyzing the data quantitatively on the basis of 28 time stages is not sensible. Moreover, the visual exploration of a dendogram with such a high number of vectors is rather difficult, see Figure 1.

Therefore, we iteratively continue the VNC clustering process via the application of the `diahclust()` function until the optimal number of clusters is smaller than 10. In this way, we obtain a clustering which suggests 6 time stages: 1150–1210, 1250–1450, 1475–1630, 1830–1830, and 1835–2008. These groups can also be visually detected in the dendogram in Figure 2. Although the resulting time stages are discontinuous, we do not view this as a problem, as this reflects the distribution of texts over time and how these texts behave with respect to the syntactic phenomena. The time stage '1830–1830' consists of a single text, '1830.HELLISMENN', while the neighboring clusters are quite large. This suggests that '1830.HELLISMENN' is an outlier. This is also captured in the dendogram in Figure 2, where '1830.HELLISMENN' clusters strikingly late. The divergent behaviour of this text is likely explained by the fact that it is a 19th cen-

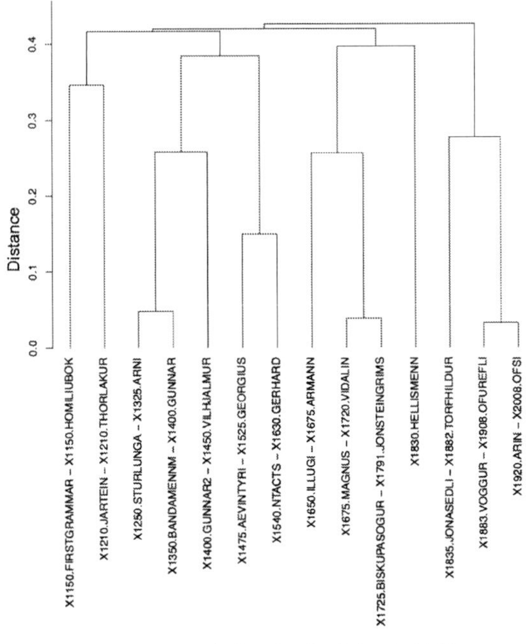

Figure 2: Dendrogram showing the results of the iterative DiaHClust approach with respect to syntactic change in IcePaHC.

tury composition which aims to imitate the older saga style. Moreover, by browsing through the dendrograms generated at each iteration, significant insights about cluster correspondences and genre effects can be obtained. For example, the third time stage (1475–1630) mainly consists of religious texts, which show a close similarity to one another already from the first iteration.

We decided to exclude '1830.HELLISMENN' and repeated the clustering process. This yielded five well-clustered time stages: 1150–1210; 1250–1450; 1475–1630; 1650–1882; 1883–2008. Whereas the first three time stages remain the same, the new clustering sheds more light on the developments occurring in the late 19th century, since '1830.HELLISMENN' no longer blocks the clustering of the surrounding texts. Moreover, the new clustering performs better in terms of average silhouette coefficients in that, with '1830.HELLISMENN' excluded, the coefficient increases from 0.4 to 0.5, indicating a more coherent clustering.

4.4 Investigating syntactic change

Once an appropriate periodization has been identified, the frequencies for the syntactic phenom-

ena can be reassessed against this scheme which respects the corpus design and is faithful to the language-internal developments. Table 1 presents the relative frequencies for the syntactic changes under investigation averaged over the five new time stages obtained via DiaHClust. Compared to previous corpus-based investigations of these changes which made use of a top-down periodization scheme, the changes have a more gradual trajectory, cf. Table 2, which shows comparable findings from Booth et al. (2017) using a pre-determined periodization. Whereas the occurrence frequencies for the syntactic changes in Table 2 remain rather stable until the last time stage, i.e., until 1900 where drastic changes can be observed, investigating the same phenomena via DiaHClust provides a more nuanced picture. Firstly, the most striking developments can be pinned down more precisely to 1650–1882 and 1883–2008. Moreover, some level of change is visible in earlier periods too. In Table 1, the frequencies in the third time stage (1475–1630) deviate from the overall trajectories. This can be attributed to a genre effect, as the DiaHClust method offers easy access to the composition of this time stage, which as mentioned consists almost exclusively of religious texts. Although this genre effect has been noted of IcePaHC by Booth et al. (2017), this effect could not be so clearly isolated using a top-down periodization, leading to a significant loss of information compared to the DiaHClust periodization method.

5 Conclusion

This paper presents a new method for the data-driven periodization of historical corpus data. Our method, DiaHClust, is implemented in R and further develops the VNC approach by Gries and Hilpert (2008, 2012). We use vectors of syntactic change as input to create knowledge-informed models of the syntactic system at different stages of the language. Furthermore, DiaHClust adds an extra iterative layer of clustering, which allows one to start the clustering at text-level, and provides significant insights about the clustering process at different levels of detail.

In order to demonstrate its value, we applied DiaHClust to a corpus-based study of syntactic change in Icelandic. Using DiaHClust reveals that syntactic change follows a more gradual trajectory in Icelandic than has been previously assumed.

Change	1150-1210	1250-1450	1475-1630	1650-1882	1883-2008
Dative subjects	3.4%	4.0%	2.6%	4.1%	5.5%
Expletives	0.1%	0.1%	0.2%	0.5%	1.5%
V1	23.7%	23.2%	6.9%	15.6%	2.3%
Prefinite subjects	44.0%	52.6%	56.2%	55.8%	72.0%
VO	48.1%	56.2%	59.9%	71.2%	83.8%
Stylistic Fronting	1.8%	1.5%	1.2%	1.2%	0.6%

Table 1: Distribution of dative subjects, expletives, V1, prefinite subjects, VO and Stylistic Fronting in IcePaHC according to the periodization scheme obtained via DiaHClust after outlier removal.

Change	1150-1349	1350-1549	1550-1749	1750-1899	1900-2008
Dative subjects	3.9%	3.2%	3.7%	3.8%	5.8%
V1	20.6%	19.9%	14.8%	18.4%	2.7%
Prefinite subjects	51.4%	55.0%	54.2%	57.6%	73.0%

Table 2: Distribution of dative subjects, V1, and prefinite subjects in IcePaHC as per Booth et al. (2017).

Moreover, DiaHClust carves out the effect which genre has on the syntactic phenomena in question and allows the researcher to track changes along the diachrony more easily, without obscuring transitional periods. Finally, we have shown that DiaHClust offers valuable insights into a language like Icelandic, where the available corpus data is relatively sparse and where syntactic change is relatively subtle. As such, applying DiaHClust to a language like English – for which there are several diachronic corpora and where syntactic change is more 'extreme' – should be relatively unproblematic. Testing this, we leave for future work.

Acknowledgments

We thank the Deutsche Forschungsgemeinschaft (DFG, German Research Foundation) – Projektnummer 251654672 – TRR 161 (Project D02) for their financial support. We would also like to thank Aikaterini-Lida Kalouli and Miriam Butt for the valuable feedback that they have provided for this paper.

References

R. Harald Baayen. 2008. *Analyzing Linguistic Data. A Practical Introduction to Statistics Using R*. Cambridge University Press, Cambridge.

Hannah Booth. 2018. *Clause Structure and Expletives: Syntactic Change in Icelandic*. Ph.D thesis, University of Manchester.

Hannah Booth, Christin Schätzle, Kersti Börjars, and Miriam Butt. 2017. Dative subjects and the rise of positional licensing in Icelandic. In Miriam Butt and Tracy Holloway King, editors, *Proceedings of the LFG'17 Conference, University of Konstanz*, pages 104–124. CSLI Publications, Stanford, CA.

Miriam Butt, Tina Bögel, Kristina Kotcheva, Christin Schätzle, Christian Rohrdantz, Dominik Sacha, Nicole Dehe, and Daniel Keim. 2014. V1 in Icelandic: A multifactorial visualization of historical data. In *Proceedings of the LREC 2014 Workshop "VisLR: Visualization as added value in the development, use and evaluation of Language Resources"*, Reykjavik, Iceland.

Anne Curzan. 2012. Periodization in the history of the English language. In Alexander Bergs and Laurel J. Brinton, editors, *The History of English: Vol.1 Historical Outlines from Sound to Text*, pages 8–35. de Gruyter, Berlin.

Stefania Degaetano-Ortlieb and Elke Teich. 2018. Using relative entropy for detection and analysis of periods of diachronic linguistic change. In *Proceedings of the 2nd Joint SIGHUM Workshop on Computational Linguistics for Cultural Heritage, Social Sciences, Humanities and Literature*, pages 22–33, Santa Fe, New Mexico, USA.

Aaron Ecay and Susan Pintzuk. 2016. The syntax of Old English poetry and the dating of Beowulf. In Leonard Neidorf, Rafael J. Pascual, and Tom Shippey, editors, *Old English Philology: Studies in Honour of R.D. Fulk*, pages 219–258. D.S Brewer, Cambridge.

Stefan Th. Gries and Martin Hilpert. 2008. The identification of stages in diachronic data: variability-based neighbour clustering. *Corpora*, 3(1):59–81.

Stefan Th. Gries and Martin Hilpert. 2012. Variability-based neighbor clustering: A bottom-up approach to periodization in historical linguistics. In Nevalainen

Terttu and Elizabeth Closs Traugott, editors, *The Oxford Handbook of the History of English*, pages 134–144. Oxford University Press, Oxford.

Einar Haugen. 1984. *Die skandinavischen Sprachen: Eine Einführung in ihre Geschichte.* Hamburg: Buske.

Martin Hilpert and Stefan Th. Gries. 2009. Assessing frequency changes in multistage diachronic corpora: Applications for historical corpus linguistics and the study of language acquisition. *Literary and Linguistic Computing*, 24(4).

Martin Hilpert and Stefan Th. Gries. 2016. Quantitative approaches to diachronic corpus linguistics. In Merja Kytö and Päivi Pahta, editors, *The Cambridge Handbook of English Historical Linguistics*, Cambridge Handbooks in Language and Linguistics, page 36–53. Cambridge University Press, Cambridge.

Thorbjörg Hróarsdóttir. 1998. *Setningafræðilegar Breytingar á 19. Öld: þróun þriggja málbreytinga.* Málvísindastofnun Háskóla Íslands, Reykjavík.

Thorbjörg Hróarsdóttir. 2000. *Word Order Change in Icelandic. From OV to VO.* John Benjamins, Amsterdam.

Anthony Kroch. 1989. Reflexes of grammar in patterns of language change. *Language Variation and Change*, 1:199–244.

Anthony Kroch. 2001. Syntactic change. In Mark Baltin and Chris Collins, editors, *The Handbook of Contemporary Syntactic Theory*, pages 699–729. Blackwell, Oxford.

Joan Maling. 1990. Inversion in embedded clauses in Modern Icelandic. In Joan Maling and Annie Zaenen, editors, *Syntax and Semantics: Modern Icelandic Syntax*, pages 71–91. Academic Press, San Diego, CA.

Mitchell P. Marcus, Mary Ann Marcinkiewicz, and Beatrice Santorini. 1993. Building a large annotated corpus of English: the Penn Treebank. *Computational Linguistics*, 19(2):313–330.

Florent Perek and Martin Hilpert. 2017. A distributional semantic approach to the periodization of change in the productivity of constructions. *International Journal of Corpus Linguistics*, 22:490–520.

Susan Pintzuk. 2005. Arguments against a universal base: evidence from Old English. *English Language & Linguistics*, 9(1):115–138.

R Core Team. 2014. *R: A Language and Environment for Statistical Computing.* R Foundation for Statistical Computing, Vienna, Austria.

Beth Randall. 2000. CorpusSearch: a Java program for searching syntactically annotated corpora. Dept. of Linguistics, University of Pennsylvania, Philadelphia.

Eiríkur Rögnvaldsson. 1996. Word order variation in the VP in Old Icelandic. *Working Papers in Scandinavian Syntax*, 58:55–86.

Peter J. Rousseeuw. 1987. Silhouettes: A graphical aid to the interpretation and validation of cluster analysis. *Journal of Computational and Applied Mathematics*, (20):53–65.

Christin Schätzle. 2018. *Dative Subjects: Historical Change Visualized.* Ph.D. thesis, University of Konstanz.

Joel C. Wallenberg, Anton Karl Ingason, Einar Freyr Sigurðsson, and Eiríkur Rögnvaldsson. 2011. Icelandic Parsed Historical Corpus (IcePaHC), version 0.9. http://linguist.is/icelandic_treebank.

Richard Zimmermann. 2014. Dating hitherto undated Old English texts based on text-internal criteria. *Ms.*, University of Geneva.

Treat the Word As a Whole or Look Inside?
Subword Embeddings Model Language Change and Typology

Yang Xu
Department of Computer Science
San Diego State University
yxu4@sdsu.edu

Jiasheng Zhang
College of Info Sci and Tech
The Pennsylvania State University
jpz5181@ist.psu.edu

David Reitter
Google AI
reitter@google.com

Abstract

We use a variant of word embedding model that incorporates subword information to characterize the degree of compositionality in lexical semantics. Our models reveal some interesting yet contrastive patterns of long-term change in multiple languages: Indo-European languages put *more* weight on subword units in newer words, while conversely Chinese puts *less* weights on the subwords, but more weight on the word as a whole. Our method provides novel evidence and methodology that enriches existing theories in evolutionary linguistics. The resulting word vectors also has decent performance in NLP-related tasks.

1 Introduction

The roles that subword units play in determining word semantics differ across languages. In typical alphabetic languages, such as English, the smallest grammatical subword unit is *morpheme* (Katamba, 2015). A morpheme can be classified as either free or bound: the former stands by itself as a word (e.g., the *root* of English words), while the latter functions only as part of a word (e.g., *affixes* such as *-ness*, *un-*, etc.). In Eastern-Asian languages, however, the distinction between morphemes and words is not as clear. Particularly in Chinese, the basic subword unit that acts as a morpheme is character (字), but whether a single morpheme or the combination of morphemes constitute a word is open to debate (Hsieh, 2016).

Despite the fact that morphological regularities of words have been extensively applied to improve the dense vector representations of words learned from data, i.e., word embeddings (Chen et al., 2015; Bojanowski et al., 2017; Xu et al., 2018b), the research endeavors so far are less oriented towards linguistic theories about the semantic roles of subword units in word formation. In other words, NLP research has optimized towards

processing languages such as English, but less so Chinese.

This study provides a first attempt (to the best of our knowledge) that uses word embedding models to explore the roles of subword units in the composition of word meanings. The source code is available at https://github.com/innerfirexy/lchange2019. We have shown that a variant based on the current subword-incorporated models can effectively quantify the semantic weights carried by subword units, with the cost of an moderate number of additional parameters, which have clear interpretations. Moreover, we have found that these semantic weights demonstrate temporal patterns that are different between Chinese and Indo-European languages, which implies a fundamental difference in the mechanisms of word formation. More theoretical motivations are discussed in the following section.

1.1 Theoretical Motivation

The direct motivation of this study is based on an empirical conclusion about the evolution of the Chinese language: the relative predominance of the *monosyllabic* words (i.e., single character as a word) in ancient Chinese has shifted to *bisyllabic* words in modern Chinese (Hsieh, 2016), and the long-existing yet unresolved disagreement regarding what a word is in Chinese among lay speakers and linguists (Sproat and Shih, 1996). In other languages, variationist inquiry has turned up regular patterns of shifting from a synthetic (single-word) to analytic (multi-word) constructions. Examples include *des Hauses* (the house's)→*von dem Haus* (of the house), *Edith chanta* (Edith sang)→*Edith a chanté* (Edith has sung) (Haspelmath and Michaelis, 2017). Though these observations are at the phrase level, it is reasonable to check if similar patterns can be found at the word level, because of the self-similarity property in natural language (Shanon, 1993).

The recently developed techniques of learning vector representations of words from data provide a new angle to revisit and contemplate the above theoretical confusions. For example, if we manage to quantify the semantic weight that a Chinese character carries in a word, then we can use it to verify the hypothesis that individual characters play less role in modern Chinese, which is more fine-grained evidence than mere frequency-based statistics.

In this study, we propose an approach that fits additional, theoretically informative parameters to configure a mixture of embeddings. With this, we characterize the relative contributions from words and subword units and capture them with an embedding model.

2 Related Work

2.1 Learning vector representations of words

Among the massive amount of work on learning dense word vectors, one of the most popular method is the word2vec model, which implements two efficient ways of learning word vectors, skipgram and CBOW (continuous bag of words) (Mikolov et al., 2013b,a). Both models learn word embeddings by training a network to predict words that co-occur within a window.

CBOW aims at predicting the target word given context words in a fixed window. For a training dataset of size T from a corpus of vocabulary size V, the learning objective of CBOW is to maximize the log probability: $L_{\text{CBOW}} = \sum_{i=1}^{T} \log p(w_i|C_i)$, where w_i is the target word, and C_i represents the surrounding context words The probability $p(w_i|C_i)$ is formulated by a softmax function:

$$p(w_i|C_i) = \frac{\exp(u_i^\mathsf{T} \cdot v_c)}{\sum_{j \in V} \exp(u_j^\mathsf{T} \cdot v_c)} \quad (1)$$

$$\text{in which } v_c = \frac{1}{|C_i|} \sum_{w_k \in C_i} v_k \quad (2)$$

where v_c is the average vector of all context words, and v_k is the vector of kth context word w_k, and u_i is the vector of the target word.

Skipgram predicts the context word given the target word at the center, by maximizing the log probability objective: $L_{\text{SG}} = \sum_{i=1}^{T} \sum_{w_k \in C_i} \log p(w_k|w_i)$, in which the probability $p(w_k|w_i)$ is also derived from a softmax function:

$$p(w_k|w_i) = \frac{\exp(v_i^\mathsf{T} \cdot u_k)}{\sum_{j \in V} \exp(u_j^\mathsf{T} \cdot v_i)} \quad (3)$$

where u_k is the context word and v_i is the target word. Because the softmax function is impractical to use due to its large amount of computation, hierarchical softmax or negative sampling are used when training the models (Mikolov et al., 2013b,a).

2.2 Word embeddings with subword information

For most languages in the world, the internal structure of words contain information about the semantics of the word. Incorporating parameters associated with those internal structures in the training process can improve word embeddings so that they are more expressive of the meanings of words. We deem that the improvements come from two sources: *semantic compositionality* and *reducing sparsity*.

Improvement from semantic compositionality
Some languages have strong compositionality at the word level. A good example is Chinese, of which a word is usually composed of several characters, and the meaning of the word can be inferred by assembling the meanings of all characters. For instance, the word "教育" (education), can be inferred from the meanings of its first character "教" (teach) and second character "育" (raise). Based on this thought, Chen et al. (2015) propose a character-enhanced word embedding model (CWE) that replaces the context word vector, v_k in eq. (1), with an average vector x_k,

$$x_k = \frac{1}{2}v_k + \frac{1}{2}\left(\frac{1}{N_k}\sum_{t=1}^{N_k} c_t\right) \quad (4)$$

where N_k is the number of characters in word w_k, and c_t is the vector of the tth character. Here the weights on the word and the characters within that word are equal (0.5), which is based on an empirical hypothesis that context words and characters are equally important to determine the semantics of target word. This is an over-simplicity that is reconsidered in our proposal.

Improvement from reducing sparsity
In some morphologically rich languages, one word can have multiple forms that occur rarely, making

it difficult to learn good representations for them. For example, Finnish has 15 cases for nouns[1], while French or Spanish have more than 40 different inflected forms for most verbs. A way to deal with this sparsity issue is to use subword information. Bojanowski et al. (2017) propose to learn representations for character n-grams and represent words as the sum of their n-gram vectors.[2] Their model, *fastText*, alters the training objective of skipgram by replacing the target word vector v_i with the sum of its n-gram vectors. Taking the word *love* for instance, it is represented by the following n-grams ($n = 3$): `<lo, lov, ove, ve>`, in which `<` and `>` are special symbols indicating the beginning and end of words. Each of these trigrams is associated with its own vector. Then the vector of *love*, $\vec{v}_{\texttt{love}}$, is computed as $\vec{v}_{\texttt{love}} + \vec{v}_{\texttt{<lo}} + \vec{v}_{\texttt{lov}} + \vec{v}_{\texttt{ove}} + \vec{v}_{\texttt{ve>}}$, i.e., the summation of all ngram vectors plus the word vector itself. More generally, fastText replaces the target word vector v_i in skipgram (eq. (3)) with an average vector x_i,

$$x_i = v_i + \sum_{t=1}^{N_i} c_t \qquad (5)$$

where N_i is the number of n-grams in word w_i, and c_t is the vector of the tth n-grams. The ideas of fastText and CWE are quite similar, only except that fastText is skipgram-based, while CWE is CBOW-based.

2.3 Word embeddings and language change

Word vectors have been used to study the long-term change of languages from multiple angles. The most straightforward method is to group text data into time bins and then train embeddings separately on these bins (Kim et al., 2014; Kulkarni et al., 2015; Hamilton et al., 2016). Conclusions about language change are reached by observing how the vectors of the same words change over time. The problem with this approach is that the learned word vectors are subject to random noise due to corpus size. Bamler and Mandt (2017) address this with a probabilistic variation of word2vec model, in which words are represented by latent trajectories in the vector space,

and the semantic shift of words is described by a latent diffusion process through time.

Most of the existing approaches describe language change by the trajectories of some representations in a high dimensional space. Even though this provides rich information about every single point in the space (word, character etc.), it is difficult to interpret and summarize these models and discover the general patterns of language change.

3 Method

3.1 Dynamic subword-incorporated embedding model (DSE)

We propose the *Dynamic Subword-incorporated Embedding* (DSE) model, which captures the semantic weights carried by the subword units in words, on top of the architecture of CWE and fastText models. The "dynamic" part is reflected in a design considering that words rely on their internal structures to different degrees in composing a meaning: we associate each word in the vocabulary with a scalar parameter h^w, within the range $[0, 1]$, which is the weight of the word itself in predicting the co-occurred words within a context window. Correspondingly, $1 - h^w$ is the weight of its subword units. Here the subword units refer to characters in a Chinese word, and a subset of n-grams of a word for English and other four languages used in this study. We did not use word roots and affixes as the subword units as did by (Xu et al., 2018b), because of the lack of dictionary data in some languages, and the relative simplicity of n-gram-based models.

In DSE model, we use h^w to compute the weighted average vector for each word, and substitute it for the average context vector x_k in CWE model (eq. (4)), and for the average target vector x_i in fastText model (eq. (5)), as shown below:

$$\begin{cases} x'_k = h_k^w v_k + (1 - h_k^w)\left(\frac{1}{N_k} \sum_{t=1}^{N_k} c_t\right), \\ \quad \text{replacing the } x_k \text{ in eq. (4)} \\ x'_i = h_i^w v_i + (1 - h_i^w) \sum_{t=1}^{N_i} c_t, \\ \quad \text{replacing the } x_i \text{ in eq. (5)} \end{cases}$$

$$(6)$$

in which the subscripts k and i are the indices of words in the vocabulary. We have two versions of model architectures: one is based on CWE (CBOW-like), and the other is based on fastText (skipgram-like). They are referred to as *DSE-*

---

[1]See http://jkorpela.fi/finnish-cases.html

[2]Another approach is to tokenize words into subwords while optimizing a language model acquired over these *word pieces* (Schuster and Nakajima, 2012; Sennrich et al., 2015).

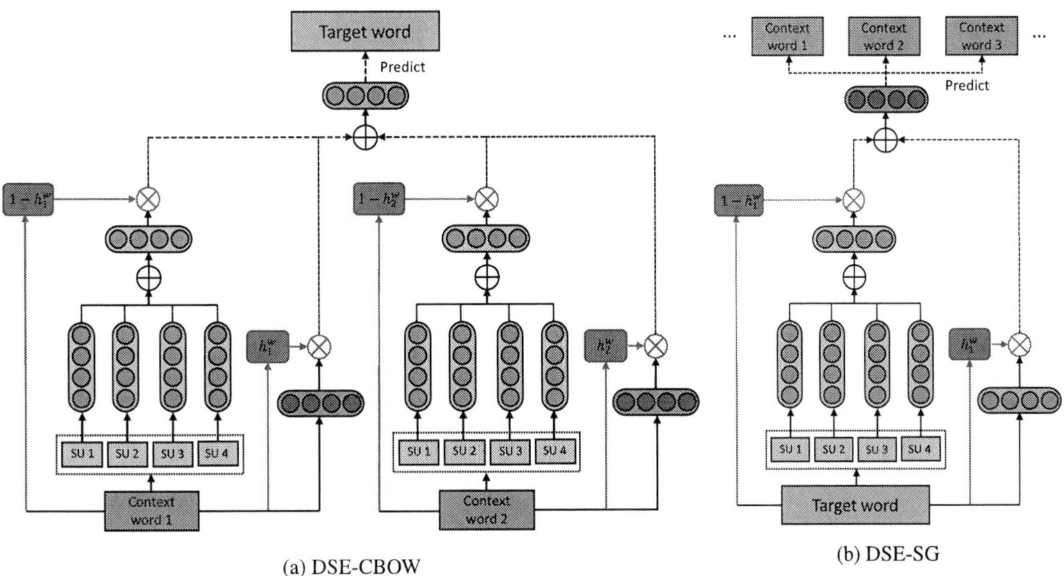

(a) DSE-CBOW   (b) DSE-SG

Figure 1: The architecture of the two version of DSE model. DSE-CBOW associates a semantic weight parameters h^w to each context word, and DSE-SG does this to each target word. The "SU"s in the yellow box stand for "subword units".

CBOW and *DSE-SG* respectively. The architectures of these models are shown in Figure 1.

We call h^w the semantic weight parameter. It describes the proportion of contribution from each word as a solitary semantic unit, while $1 - h^w$ is the total contribution from all the subword units. h^w is a learnable parameter in the model.

3.2 Corpus data and training setup

We use the Wikimedia database dumps[3] (up until July 2017) as our training data. Data in *six* languages are used: Chinese (ZH), English (EN), French (FR), German (DE), Italian (IT) and French (FR). Raw text data are extracted from the dump files using `WikiExtractor`[4]. Further text cleaning are conducted by separating sentences into per line, and converting non-propernouns (proper-nouns are identified using a pretrained NER model provided in the Python package `spacy`[5]) to lower case. For Chinese data particularly, word segmentation is carried out using the `Jieba` segmenter[6]. All traditional Chinese characters are converted to simplified Chinese using OpenCC[7]. All non-Chinese characters are removed, keeping only those within the Uni-

code range U+4E00-9FFF. The training data of all six languages are of similar volumes: 33 to 40 million tokens each after preprocessing.

To accelerate training, we limit the number of *effective* semantic units in each word. For Chinese data, words containing more than 7 characters are ignored. For other languages, if a word contains more than 7 n-grams, we randomly select 7 out of them, and ignore the rest. Here the number 7 is chosen based on the following empirical observation: in a pilot study, we found that numbers larger than 7 will not improve the resulting embeddings, but significantly slow down the training. Other hyper-parameters are kept as close to the previous studies as possible. The detailed hyper-parameter settings and training procedures are described in Appendix A.

As for the size of n-grams, we use a fixed size $n = 4$, i.e., no bigrams or trigrams are considered. This choice is partially based on Bojanowski et al.'s (2017) work showing that $n = 4$ already achieves a satisfactory embedings, and partially due to speed consideration. For words that consist of than 4 letters, we only consider two sources for the mixture embeddings: the word itself and the n-gram ($n < 4$).

The semantic weight parameters h^w are implemented as a $V_w \times 1$ lookup table. Thus, in each training step, the learning algorithm updates three

---

[3] https://dumps.wikimedia.org/
[4] https://github.com/attardi/wikiextractor
[5] https://spacy.io/
[6] https://github.com/fxsjy/jieba
[7] https://github.com/BYVoid/OpenCC

embedding tables: word embeddings E_w, character embeddings E_c, and the semantic weights. Specifically, for DSE-SG model, the average embeddings are first computed from E_w, E_c, h^w, and h^c using eq. (6) and then outputted as the final word vectors. For DSE-CBOW model, just the E_w table is outputted as the learned word vectors[8].

4 Results and Discussion

4.1 Correlation between semantic weights and word ages

We are interested in examining the relationship between the semantic weight h^w of a word and its relative "age". According to the observation that Chinese is shifting from monosyllabic words to bisyllabic words, it is reasonable to expect that newer Chinese words should have larger h^w than those older words, because a higher h^w indicates that the word as a whole rather than the individual subword units is more important in determining its meaning. For other languages, we do not have a clear clue on what the relationship could be, but they should provide an interesting comparison.

First, we need to have a reliable way to measure the "age" of a word. We use the Google Books Ngram (GBN)[9] corpus, which contains word frequency information from about 10 million books published over a period of five centuries (Lin et al., 2012). It is the best resource we can find that provides estimated temporal distributions of words in multiple languages. For each word in GBN we extract the first *year* that it appears in the dataset, and use this first-appearance-year as an approximation of the word's age. Then we check if the word's age is correlated with its h^w from training the DSE model. For example, the word "爱人" (lover) first appears in the year of 1804 (AD) (at least according to the GBN collection). Thus, our examination is focused on the intersection of vocabularies between GBN and the training data. For DE, EN, ES, FR and IT, the intersection covers above 95% of the most common words in the training, and the proportion for ZH is 84%.

In a short summary of the results, we find *opposite* $h^2 \sim$ year relationships in Chinese and the other five languages. h^w *decreases* with the first-appearance-year in the five Indo-European lan-

guages, as shown in Figure 2. Words with subword units count ranging from 2 to 7 are included. Short words that have only 1 n-gram are excluded because the n-grams have the same form as the words. There are some fluctuations but the overall decreasing trends of h^w are salient. As the decrease of h^w is equivalent to the increase of $1-h^w$, it indicates that in these five languages, subword units carry more semantic weights in newer words than older ones. The h^w scores reported in Figure 2 are from DSE-SG, because those from DSE-CBOW are either 0s or 1s, due to the quick saturation of the softmax function, which however does not happen to Chinese data.

As for Chinese, however, h^w *increases* with the first-appearance-year as shown in Figure 3. We choose the subword units (characters) count $= \{2, 3, 4\}$ because they are the majority in the training data, with proportions 57.5%, 31.0%, and 8.6%. Frequency wise, their proportions are more dominant: 82.9%, 11.8%, and 4.6% respectively. Words composed of more than 4 characters are very uncommon in Chinese. From the plot, the increasing trends of the 2-character words are observable, but less so for the 3- and 4-character words. It indicates that our hypothesis in Section 1.1 is supported: characters carry more semantic weight in older Chinese words than in newer Chinese words.

Besides, an interesting finding is that the h^ws from DSE-SG are larger than those from DSE-CBOW in Chinese. It makes sense intuitively: a CBOW-like model is using multiple context words to predict one word, and thus the semantic weight from each individual word is diluted.

4.2 Statistical analysis to verify the results

Considering the fact that word frequency plays a critical role in a broad range of phenomena in language production and comprehension, including word length (Zipf, 1949), syntactic choice (Jaeger, 2010), and alignment (Xu et al., 2018a; Xu and Reitter, 2018), and the fact that during the training of a word embedding model, the more frequent words naturally get more updates on their embedding parameters, it is therefore necessary to rule out the possible confounding effect from word frequencies in the "$h^w \sim$ year" correlation found in previous section.

First, we fit a linear model with h^w as the response variable, and two predictors, the first ap-

---

[8]The discrepancy exists in the original implementations of CWE and fastText, and the reason behind is out of the scope of this study.

[9]http://storage.googleapis.com/books/ngrams/books/datasetsv2.html

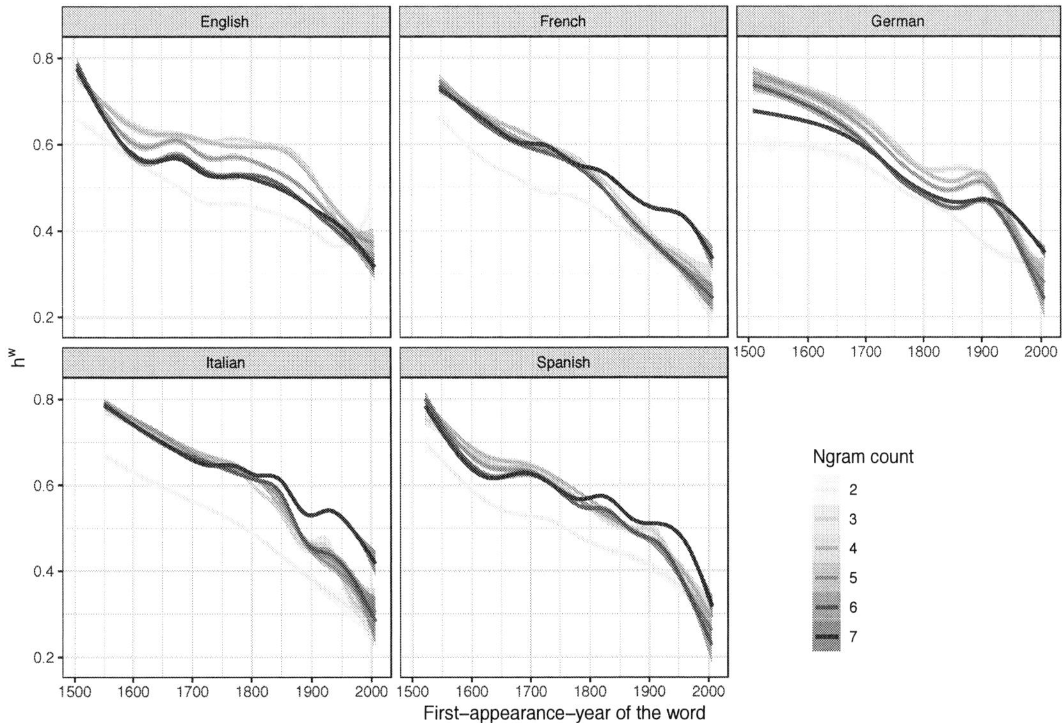

Figure 2: Semantic weight h^w against the first-appearance-year of words in DE, EN, ES, FR, and IT. Words with subword units (n-grams) number ranging from 2 to 7 are plotted separately. Shaded area indicates 95% point-wise confidence intervals of the fitted regression lines. h^w scores are from the DSE-SG model.

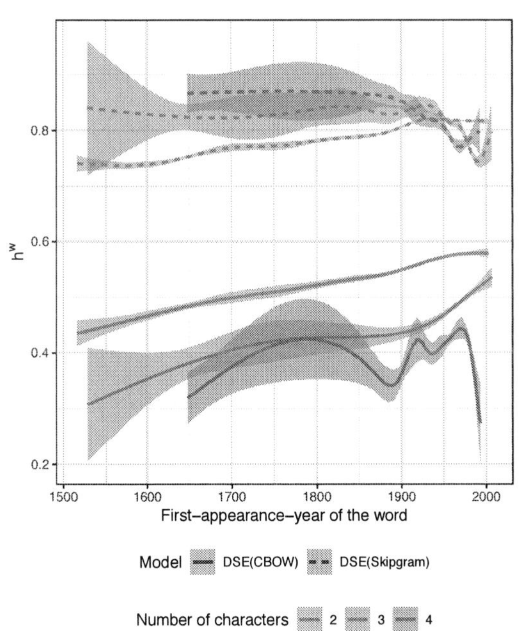

Figure 3: Semantic weight h^w against first-appearance-year for Chinese words with character number = 2, 3, and 4. Shaded area indicates 95% point-wise confidence intervals of the fitted regression lines.

pearance year and the frequency of words in training data, as expressed by the formula: $h^w \sim$ year + frequency. We find that both covariates are significant predictors, as shown in the "Direct model" column of Table 1. The positive and statistically significant ($p < .001$) β_{year} coefficients indicate that the observed decreasing trend of h^w in five Indo-European languages and the increasing trend in Chinese are reliable, after the effect of word frequency is taken into account.

A more conservative method is to fit an auxiliary model m' first, with h^w as the response and word frequency as the sole predictor (regressing it out), and then fit a second model m, using the *residuals* of m' as the new response variable, and the first appearance year as its predictor. If the parameter estimate in m still indicates a significant effect, then that means that the second predictor (year) indeed affects the response (h^w) in a way that is independent on the first predictor (frequency). With this step, we confirm the effect of year on h^w in all languages (see the "Auxiliary model" column in Table 1).

Language	β coefficient of year	
	Direct model	Auxiliary model
DE	$-7.8 \times 10^{-4***}$	$-7.8 \times 10^{-4***}$
EN	$-8.5 \times 10^{-4***}$	$-8.5 \times 10^{-4***}$
ES	$-8.5 \times 10^{-4***}$	$-8.4 \times 10^{-4***}$
FR	$-9.4 \times 10^{-4***}$	$-9.4 \times 10^{-4***}$
IT	$-9.2 \times 10^{-4***}$	$-9.1 \times 10^{-4***}$
ZH (DSE-SG)	$1.2 \times 10^{-4***}$	$1.0 \times 10^{-4***}$
ZH (DSE-CBOW)	$1.5 \times 10^{-4***}$	$1.3 \times 10^{-4***}$

Table 1: Statistical models to verify the decreasing trend of h^w with first-appearance-year in five Indo-European languages and its increasing trend in Chinese. *** indicates a significance level of $p < .001$.

Language	Model	Similarity	Analogy
Chinese	DSE-CBOW	0.597	0.666
	CWE	0.605	0.668
	DSE-SG	0.583	**0.651**
	fastText	0.591	0.588
English	DSE-CBOW	0.659	0.302
	CWE	0.669	0.324
	DSE-SG	0.705	**0.356**
	fastText	0.702	0.338

Table 2: Performance in lexical semantic tasks.

4.3 Evaluation on lexical semantic tasks

Training the DSE model not just results in a lookup table of h^w, but also outputs word embeddings. In theory, these embeddings should be better representations of the semantic space than the CWE and fastText models, because DSE uses more parameters (h^w). Here, we compare the quality of word embeddings resulting from DSE models with those from previous models. Any superiority that DSE could show will indicate that dynamically considering the semantic weight of subword units can be potentially useful in other NLP tasks.

There are several standard lexical semantic tasks commonly used to evaluate the quality of embeddings. We use two of them, word similarity/relatedness and word analogy, and evaluate the embeddings from Chinese and English. For word similarity task, Wordsim-296 Chen et al. (2015) in Chinese and Wordsim-353 (Finkelstein et al., 2002) in English are used. Higher Spearman's correlation score indicates better performance. For word analogy task, the semantic part of the original dataset[10] developed by Mikolov et al. (2013a) and its Chinese translated version are used. The total percentage of correctly answered questions is used to measure the performance on this task.

The performance of DSE are shown in Table 2 compared with CWE and fastText. Here we do not use the original implementations of CWE and fastText (in C and C++), but use our own implementations with the same programming framework as DSE (By disabling the h^w parameters). This is for the consideration of fair comparisons. The models are compared within two groups according to the architecture: DSE-CBOW and CWE are in CBOW group; DSE-SG and fastText are in skip-gram group. We find that DSE-SG achieves *higher* score in word analogy task, and overall speaking, DSE models have comparable or slightly lower performance in word similarity task.

It is surprising that DSE does not show a significant improvement, which could be due to the redundancy in model parameters or the size of training data. That said, what we show here is that the new model performs well enough to be plausible. We do not attempt to improve upon the state-of-the-art in these downstream tasks; rather, the main purpose of the model is for linguistic inquiries.

4.4 Case study

We use several cases of words to intuitively understand what specific aspects in language use causes the finding of this study. First, we find the magnitude of semantic weight h^w is related to the part-of-speech tag of words. For example, some earlier words that contain the character "安" (safe) are mostly used as adjectives, e.g., "安全" (secure, 1581), "安定" (settled, 1632) etc, while some newly appeared words are often nouns of terminology in certain fields, e.g., "安打" (*base hit*, a baseball term) first appears in 1959, "安检" (*security check*, an airport term) first appears in 1987. We find that the h^ws of the domain-specific nouns are higher than the generic adjectives (see Table 3), which indicates that the character "安" plays a lighter semantic role in these nouns. It also indicates that Chinese language users tend to consider the chunk of characters together as standalone semantic unit, and refer less to the original meanings of individual characters within.

We find similar cases in English. For example, the word *acid* first appears in 1517, and its h^w is larger than those words that contain the n-gram "acid" such as *acidosis* and *oxoacid*, both of

---

[10] http://download.tensorflow.org/data/questions-words.txt

Language	Older words	h^w	Newer words	h^w
Chinese	安全(secure), 1581	0.75	安打(base hit), 1959	0.85
	安定(settled), 1632	0.72	安检(security check), 1987	0.87
	组成(consist of), 1568	0.67	课题组 (research group), 1988	0.86
	覆盖 (cover), 1747	0.69	盖帽(block)†, 1972	0.91
	把握(hold), 1591	0.69	拖把 (mop), 1985	0.86
English	**acid**, 1517	0.73	**acid**osis, 1907	0.07
			oxo**acid**s, 1953	0.07
	compare, 1524	0.86	**compar**ison, 1659	0.61
			comparatives, 1810	0.14
	human, 1504	0.87	trans**human**ism, 1955	0.50
	locking, 1600	0.77	un**lock**able, 1854	0.11

†: A basketball term.

Table 3: Case study examples. Earlier words on the left are adjectives and verbs, and have smaller h^w. Later words on the right are nouns, and have larger h^w. Subword units shared across words are highlighted.

which first appear in 1900s. More examples are shown in Table 3. Similarly, some of the newer words (with higher h^w) are domain-specific compounds that consist of several seemingly unrelated n-grams, while some others are inflections of the original verb or adjectives.

We conjecture that a common cause for the changes of h^w in both languages can be the advancement of science and technology, and the need for new vocabulary that comes with it. However, the contrast between the two languages are intriguing: the relatively large h^w of new terms in Chinese seems to indicate that new meanings are assigned to these words without too much inference into the original meanings of the subword units; while the smaller h^w in English indicates the opposite, i.e., the original meanings of the containing subword units are emphasized more.

Through the examples, it indicates that the increasing trend of h^w may reflect the modernization of Chinese as the concepts and terminology in science and technology (and western culture as well) had been introduced since the 19th century, and more so ever after 1900s. Of course, the examples here do not exhaustively cover all possible causes for the change of h^w. We believe that an aggregative analysis over the effect of word types on h^w is necessary in order to get more comprehensive explanations.

5 Conclusions

In this study, we use a subword-incorporated model to characterize the semantic weights of subword units in the composition of word meanings.

We find a major difference in the long-term temporal patterns of semantic weights between Chinese and five Indo-European languages: In Chinese, the weights on subword units (characters) shows a decreasing trend, i.e., individual characters play less semantic roles in newer words than older ones; In Indo-European languages, however, this trend is opposite, i.e., newer words place more weights on the subword units. In a more informal way: Chinese words are treated more as a whole semantic unit "synthetically", while words in Indo-European languages require more attention into the subword units "analytically".

Our findings provide new evidence to linguistic theories about word formation. First, the notion of "word" in Chinese is always changing: compared to its earlier age, modern Chinese tend to have multiple characters as a whole semantic unit. The semantic weight carried by a single character is decreasing. This is strong evidence in favor of the claim in qualitative studies that Chinese has been evolving towards multisyllabic from monosyllabic. Second, the increasing trend of semantic weights on subword units in Indo-European languages is consistent with the "synthetic $\rightarrow$ analytic" pattern shift at the phrase level composition (Hamilton et al., 2016). Moreover, the relative "synthetic" way of composing Chinese word found in this study seems consistent with the holistic encoding hypothesis in the perceptual theories about the Chinese writing system (Dehaene et al., 2005; Mo et al., 2015).

Going forward, we would like to apply the DSE model to other Eastern-Asian languages, such as

Korean and Japanese, which are not included in this study due to the lack of GBN data for them. If we find similar weighting patterns on subword units in these languages as in Chinese (which we anticipate to see), then we can have a bigger picture of the word formation mechanisms of different language families. Second, we would like to use roots and affixes instead of n-grams for Indo-European languages because their semantic meanings are more clearly defined, and thus knowing about their weights change with time can tell a better story of language evolution.

How the semantic meanings are conveyed in subword units is quite different in an Indo-European language such as English (where *word root*, *prefix*, and *postfix* play more important roles than characters) from the case of Chinese. However, it produces meaningful results to quantify and compare the semantic weights of subword units among different languages. At the core of this, there are questions of the universality of semantic subspaces across languages.

Acknowledgments

The authors thank Matthew A. Kelly, Frank E. Ritter, and Saranya Venkatraman for their comments. The authors also thank all the reviewers for their constructive feedbacks. The authors acknowledge support from the National Science Foundation, grant BCS-1734304 to D. Reitter.

References

Robert Bamler and Stephan Mandt. 2017. Dynamic word embeddings. In *Proc. 34th International Conference on Machine Learning*, pages 380–389.

Piotr Bojanowski, Edouard Grave, Armand Joulin, and Tomas Mikolov. 2017. Enriching word vectors with subword information. *Transactions of the Association for Computational Linguistics*, 5:135–146.

Xinxiong Chen, Lei Xu, Zhiyuan Liu, Maosong Sun, and Huan-Bo Luan. 2015. Joint learning of character and word embeddings. In *Proc. 24th International Joint Conference on Artificial Intelligence*, pages 1236–1242.

Stanislas Dehaene, Laurent Cohen, Mariano Sigman, and Fabien Vinckier. 2005. The neural code for written words: a proposal. *Trends in Cognitive Sciences*, 9(7):335–341.

Lev Finkelstein, Evgeniy Gabrilovich, Yossi Matias, Ehud Rivlin, Zach Solan, Gadi Wolfman, and Eytan Ruppin. 2002. Placing search in context: The concept revisited. *ACM Transactions on information systems*, 20(1):116–131.

William L Hamilton, Jure Leskovec, and Dan Jurafsky. 2016. Diachronic word embeddings reveal statistical laws of semantic change. *arXiv preprint arXiv:1605.09096*.

M Haspelmath and SM Michaelis. 2017. Analytic and synthetic: Typological change in varieties of european languages. In *Language Vriation – European Perspectives VI. Selected Papers from the 8th International Conference on Language Variation in Europe*, pages 1–17.

Shu-Kai Hsieh. 2016. Chinese linguistics: Semantics. In Sin-Wai Chan, James W Minett, and Florence Li Wing Yee, editors, *The Routledge Encyclopedia of the Chinese Language*, pages 203–214. Routledge, Abingdon, Oxon.

T Florian Jaeger. 2010. Redundancy and reduction: Speakers manage syntactic information density. *Cognitive Psychology*, 61(1):23–62.

Francis Katamba. 2015. *English Words: Structure, History, Usage*. Routledge.

Yoon Kim, Yi-I Chiu, Kentaro Hanaki, Darshan Hegde, and Slav Petrov. 2014. Temporal analysis of language through neural language models. *arXiv preprint arXiv:1405.3515*.

Vivek Kulkarni, Rami Al-Rfou, Bryan Perozzi, and Steven Skiena. 2015. Statistically significant detection of linguistic change. In *Proceedings of the 24th International Conference on World Wide Web*, pages 625–635.

Yuri Lin, Jean-Baptiste Michel, Erez Lieberman Aiden, Jon Orwant, Will Brockman, and Slav Petrov. 2012. Syntactic annotations for the google books ngram corpus. In *Proceedings of the ACL 2012 system demonstrations*, pages 169–174. Association for Computational Linguistics.

Tomas Mikolov, Kai Chen, Greg Corrado, and Jeffrey Dean. 2013a. Efficient estimation of word representations in vector space. *arXiv preprint arXiv:1301.3781*.

Tomas Mikolov, Ilya Sutskever, Kai Chen, Greg S Corrado, and Jeff Dean. 2013b. Distributed representations of words and phrases and their compositionality. In *Advances in Neural Information Processing Systems*, pages 3111–3119.

Ce Mo, Mengxia Yu, Carol Seger, and Lei Mo. 2015. Holistic neural coding of chinese character forms in bilateral ventral visual system. *Brain and Language*, 141:28–34.

Mike Schuster and Kaisuke Nakajima. 2012. Japanese and korean voice search. In *2012 IEEE International Conference on Acoustics, Speech and Signal Processing (ICASSP)*, pages 5149–5152. IEEE.

Rico Sennrich, Barry Haddow, and Alexandra Birch. 2015. Neural machine translation of rare words with subword units. *arXiv preprint arXiv:1508.07909*.

Benny Shanon. 1993. Fractal patterns in language. *New Ideas in Psychology*, 11(1):105–109.

Richard Sproat and Chilin Shih. 1996. A corpus-based analysis of mandarin nominal root compound. *Journal of East Asian Linguistics*, 5(1):49–71.

Yang Xu, Jeremy Cole, and David Reitter. 2018a. Not that much power: Linguistic alignment is influenced more by low-level linguistic features rather than social power. In *Proc. 56th Annual Meeting of the Association for Computational Linguistics*, volume 1, pages 601–610.

Yang Xu, Jiawei Liu, Wei Yang, and Liusheng Huang. 2018b. Incorporating latent meanings of morphological compositions to enhance word embeddings. In *Proceedings of the 56th Annual Meeting of the Association for Computational Linguistics (Volume 1: Long Papers)*, volume 1, pages 1232–1242.

Yang Xu and David Reitter. 2018. Information density converges in dialogue: Towards an information-theoretic model. *Cognition*, 170:147–163.

George Kingsley Zipf. 1949. *Human Behavior and the Principle of Least Effort*. Addison-Wesley.

A Appendices

The values of the hyper-parameters for training the DSE models are shown in Table 4.

Hyperparameter	Value
Embedding size	300 (Word) 300 (Subword)
Window size	5
Number of negative samples	10
Batch size	128
Minimal word frequency	5
Initial learning rate	0.05 (DSE-CBOW) 0.025 (DSE-SG)

Table 4: Hyperparameter settings.

The training stage consists of three steps:

- Pre-train the word embeddings: set the parameters for word embeddings, i.e., the v_k and v_i in Equation (6) trainable; set all the other parameters not trainable; train the model for 5 epochs.

- Pre-train the subword embeddings: set the parameters for subword units, i.e., c_t in Equation (6) trainable; set all the other parameters not trainable; train the model for 5 epochs.

- Set all the parameters trainable (including embeddings and h^ws); train the model for 5 epochs.

Times Are Changing: Investigating the Pace of Language Change in Diachronic Word Embeddings

Stephanie Brandl, David Lassner
Machine Learning Group, TU Berlin, Berlin, Germany
`{stephanie.brandl, lassner}@tu-berlin.de`

Abstract

We propose Word Embedding Networks (WEN), a novel method that is able to learn word embeddings of individual data slices while simultaneously aligning and ordering them without feeding temporal information a priori to the model. This gives us the opportunity to analyse the dynamics in word embeddings on a large scale in a purely data-driven manner. In experiments on two different newspaper corpora, the New York Times (English) and Die Zeit (German), we were able to show that time actually determines the dynamics of semantic change. However, we find that the evolution does not happen uniformly, but instead we discover times of faster and times of slower change.

1 Introduction

Vectorial representation of natural language, known as word embeddings, have been widely used in e.g. text classification (Joulin et al., 2016) and machine translation (Mikolov et al., 2013). As in Kim et al. (2014); Kulkarni et al. (2015); Hamilton et al. (2016) and Szymanski (2017) aligned sets of embeddings have also been used to detect changes in vectorial representations of words over time. In the past, those changes have mostly been studied at the word-level.

We propose a novel method to investigate the pace of language change based on the entire embedding matrix. Previous approaches have not been able to carry out this type of analysis, as they have taken the continuous change of language for granted and investigated those dynamics in a supervised manner.

Therefore, we present Word Embedding Networks (WEN), a method that has no knowledge about the chronological order of the slices, so we can investigate semantic changes on the whole vocabulary purely data-driven and unsupervised.

Pairwise relations between embeddings and the embeddings themselves are learned simultaneously without feeding the temporal information a priori into the algorithm. In that, it is substantially more flexible than those methods mentioned above. This means that dynamics between any slicing of a text corpus can be learned (especially those where there is no order known) and the result not only contains embeddings for each slice, but an order of slices that corresponds to the dynamics of word meanings.

This method also overcomes the need of a two-step solution for aligned temporal embeddings, as has also been done by Yao et al. (2018) - the two-step solution has, according to Yao et al. (2018), its weaknesses especially in the case of non-uniformly distributed amounts of data across the slices. Closer proximities between embeddings denote time intervals of slower semantic changes, embeddings are farther apart when times are changing faster.

2 Related Work

Rudolph and Blei (2018) analyse dynamical changes in word embeddings based on exponential family embeddings, a probabilistic framework that generalizes the concept of word embeddings to other types data (Rudolph et al., 2016). They focus on word-level changes within and between text corpora spanning from the 19th century until today.

The authors of Yao et al. (2018) proposed a new method to learn individual word embeddings for each year of the New York Times data set (1990-2016) while simultaneously aligning the embeddings to the same vector space. Their neighborhood constraint

$$\frac{\tau}{2}\left(\|U_{t-1} - U_t\|_F^2 + \|U_t - U_{t+1}\|_F^2\right)$$

Proceedings of the 1st International Workshop on Computational Approaches to Historical Language Change, pages 146–150
Florence, Italy, August 2, 2019. ©2019 Association for Computational Linguistics

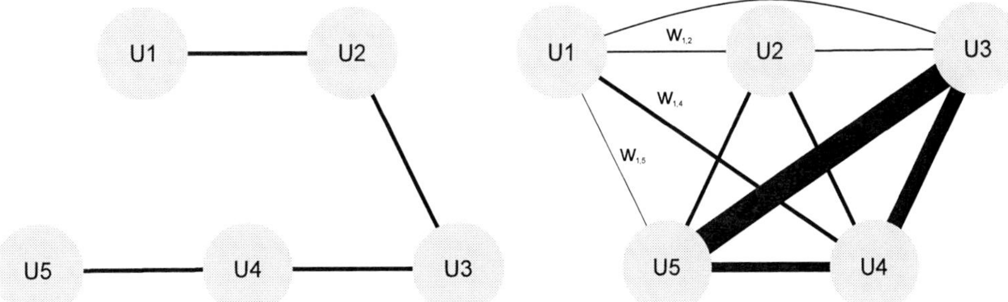

(a) Dynamic Word Embeddings from (Yao et al., 2018) has a predefined ordering of embeddings $U_{\cdot}$.

(b) WEN learns embeddings $U_{\cdot}$ and $\omega_{\cdot,\cdot}$ in turn. Thicker edges denote stronger relation between embeddings.

Figure 1: Comparison of Dynamic Word Embeddings (Yao et al., 2018) and WEN which can be seen as a generalization of the former.

encourages alignment of the word embeddings. The parameter τ controls the dynamic, thus how much neighboring word embeddings are allowed to differ ($\tau = 0$: no alignment and $\tau \to \infty$: static embeddings).

3 Method

To identify the pace of change, we introduce a new method named *Word Embedding Networks* (WEN). WEN learns embeddings for e.g. different time slices while simultaneously aligning and ordering them. WEN starts with assuming an equal distance between all embeddings and then, over time, shapes the relations by moving certain embeddings closer and others farther apart. In Fig. 1 we illustrate an exemplary trained word embedding network and compare it to Dynamic Word Embeddings from Yao et al. (2018).

In order to train the weights of the graph, we include an additional weighting term $\omega_{t,t'}$ into the model and optimize over

$$\min_{U_t} F_t = \min_{U_t} \frac{1}{2} \left\| Y_t - U_t U_t^\top \right\|_F^2 \tag{1}$$

$$+ \frac{\lambda}{2} \|U_t\|_F^2 \tag{2}$$

$$+ \frac{\tau}{2} \sum_{t' \neq t}^{N} \omega_{t,t'} \left(\|U_t - U_{t'}\|_F^2 \right). \tag{3}$$

Here, $U_t \in \mathbb{R}^{V \times D}$ contains the D-dimensional word embeddings in a vocabulary of size V at time point t and $Y_t \in \mathbb{R}^{V \times V}$ represents the PPMI matrix (Yao et al., 2018).

While Term 1 is responsible for training the word embeddings with respect to Y, Term 2 enforces sparse vectorial representations.

By updating $\omega_{t,t'}$ with respect to the distances between word embeddings of different slices it is meant to strengthen connections of word embeddings that lie closer together in the corresponding vector space.

To update $\omega_{t,t'}$ we first introduce a symmetric normalization function

$$\text{norm\_sym}(x_{ij}) = \frac{x_{ij}}{\left(\sum_k x_{ik} + \sum_j x_{kj} \right)}$$

where $x_{ij} \in \mathbb{R}$.

The weighting term $\omega_{t,t'}$ is then updated accordingly:

$$d_{t,t'} = \text{norm\_sym} \left(\frac{1}{\|U_t - U_{t'}\|_F^2} \right)$$

$$\omega_{t,t'}^{\text{new}} = \text{norm\_sym} \left(\omega_{t,t'} + d_{t,t'} \right). \tag{4}$$

We optimize U with gradient descent. We therefore use Adam (Kingma and Ba, 2014) with default values for β and a customized learning rate (see Sec. 4.2).

We did not tune for efficiency and stopped the optimization after 1500 rounds where one round is finished when embeddings of all time slices have been updated once in a random order.

We initialize $\forall t, t'$ $\omega_{t,t'} = 1$ and update every 100 rounds according to Eq. 4.

We have implemented this in PyTorch.

4 Training

4.1 Data Sets

New York Times 1990-2016:
The New York Times data set[1] (NYT) contains

---

[1]https://sites.google.com/site/zijunyaorutgers/

(a) 2-dimensional embedding of the New York Times w matrix. Slices are sorted nicely in a circular structure with only few excepions.

(b) 2-dimensional embedding of the Die Zeit w matrix. The embeddings-embedding still resembles the chronology but there is also a secondary structure of three clusters.

Figure 2: Laplacian eigenmaps of the w matrix to visualize the relationship between embeddings (pace of change). Points are colored with ground truth information.

headlines and lead texts of news articles published online and offline between 1990 and 2016 with a total of 99.872 documents.

Die Zeit 1947-2017:
Die Zeit is a German national weekly newspaper that started publishing in 1946. We obtained titles, teaser titles and teaser texts of 508.698 news articles from the Die Zeit developer API[2] that have been published online and offline between 1947 and 2017.

4.2 Parameters

We perform a grid search to select optimal parameters on the first half (1990-2002) of NYT which results in the same parameter combination as reported by (Yao et al. (2018), $\lambda = 10$, $\tau = 50$, embedding dimension= 32). We start with a learning rate of $\eta = 10^{-3}$, reducing it after 500 rounds to $\eta_{500} = 5 \cdot 10^{-4}$ and after 1000 rounds to $\eta_{1000} = 10^{-4}$.

4.3 Preprocessing

We lemmatize the data with spacy [3].
We only consider the 20.000 most frequent (lemmatized) words of the entire data set that are also under the 20.000 most frequent words in at least

3 yearly slices. This way, we filter out "trend" words that only are of significance within a very short time period. The 100 most frequent words are filtered out as stop words.

4.4 Experiments

New York Times 2003-2016:
We apply WEN with the parameters from Section 4.2 to the second part of NYT (2003-2016) and train embeddings for yearly slices (14 in total). In most of the cases, namely 85%, WEN aligns embeddings closest to each other that in fact also correspond to their chronological neighbor. We define this as the (neighborhood) accuracy of 85%.

Die Zeit 1947-2017:
We further apply WEN on the Die Zeit data set (1947-2017) to evaluate the model on a non-English text corpora which has not been involved in parameter search. We train and sort the word embeddings on the entire data set (71 yearly slices). After 1500 rounds, we achieve an accuracy of 67%.

5 Results

The high neighborhood accuracies, indeed indicate a temporal dynamic in both data sets.
To visualize the network weights as a map, w was used as an affinity matrix to generate Lapla-

---

[2]http://developer.zeit.de
[3]https://spacy.io

cian eigenmaps (Belkin and Niyogi, 2002) of the neighborhoods between yearly slices. In Fig. 2 maps of NYT (second half) and Die Zeit are shown side-by-side.

NYT shows a very nice circular structure of neighborhoods but also how some years lie closer together than others. For instance the years 2008-2010 can be found very close together whereas 2011 having larger gaps to its two closest neighbors 2010 and 2012. By identifying words of largest change within 2011, we found mostly personal names and companies in the high ranks whose media coverage changed during that time. Also, we detected larger gaps in actual neighboring years when there are shifts in how sections are distributed in the data set. As *Sports* remains the section with most articles throughout the entire data set, there are more documents in *Opinion* after 2003 and only half the documents in *New York and Region* after 2005.

Regarding the Die Zeit map, we observe three distinct clusters, one before 1995, one after 2008. The gaps clearly correspond to changes in either publication strategy (starting 2009 with emphasizing the online publication) and archival data storage (there are close to no teaser texts available for 1995). Both events led to a sudden change of the amounts of data available.

6 Conclusion

Word Embedding Networks (WEN) learns word embeddings of individual data slices while simultaneously aligning and ordering them in an unsupervised manner.

After being trained on news articles from the New York Times (1990-2002), the model could successfully be applied to news articles from the same corpus (2003-2016) and to data containing German newspaper articles from 1947-2017 (die Zeit). Results on both data sets show a clear temporal dynamic as 85% and 67% respectively of the closest time slices correspond to the neighboring years. Time can thus be identified as the dominant component that is governing change in word meaning in both data sets.

However, it could be shown for both data sets that change is not introduced at a constant pace hence there are times of slower and times of faster change. We found that distributional changes within the data set can have a huge influence on the perceived pace of semantic change.

Therefore we argue for caution when applying models that assume continuous change, especially concerning the NYT data set, with its widespread use.

For further research, we would like to expand the experiments to corpora where the underlying slices are not ordered. For example given a corpus of works grouped by authors, we could train the model to find proximities between authors based on the similarity of meaning of the words they use.

Acknowledgments

This work was supported by the Federal Ministry of Education and Research (BMBF) for the MALT III project (01IS17058). We thank M. Alber for valuable comments on the manuscript.

References

Mikhail Belkin and Partha Niyogi. 2002. Laplacian eigenmaps and spectral techniques for embedding and clustering. In *Advances in neural information processing systems*, pages 585–591.

William L Hamilton, Jure Leskovec, and Dan Jurafsky. 2016. Diachronic word embeddings reveal statistical laws of semantic change. *arXiv preprint arXiv:1605.09096*.

Armand Joulin, Edouard Grave, Piotr Bojanowski, and Tomas Mikolov. 2016. Bag of tricks for efficient text classification. *arXiv preprint arXiv:1607.01759*.

Yoon Kim, Yi-I Chiu, Kentaro Hanaki, Darshan Hegde, and Slav Petrov. 2014. Temporal analysis of language through neural language models. *arXiv preprint arXiv:1405.3515*.

Diederik P Kingma and Jimmy Ba. 2014. Adam: A method for stochastic optimization. *arXiv preprint arXiv:1412.6980*.

Vivek Kulkarni, Rami Al-Rfou, Bryan Perozzi, and Steven Skiena. 2015. Statistically significant detection of linguistic change. In *Proceedings of the 24th International Conference on World Wide Web*, pages 625–635. International World Wide Web Conferences Steering Committee.

Tomas Mikolov, Quoc V. Le, and Ilya Sutskever. 2013. Exploiting Similarities among Languages for Machine Translation. *CoRR*, abs/1309.4168.

Maja Rudolph and David Blei. 2018. Dynamic embeddings for language evolution. In *Proceedings of the 2018 World Wide Web Conference on World Wide Web*, pages 1003–1011. International World Wide Web Conferences Steering Committee.

Maja Rudolph, Francisco Ruiz, Stephan Mandt, and David Blei. 2016. Exponential family embeddings. In *Advances in Neural Information Processing Systems*, pages 478–486.

Terrence Szymanski. 2017. Temporal Word Analogies: Identifying Lexical Replacement with Diachronic Word Embeddings. In *Proceedings of the 55th Annual Meeting of the Association for Computational Linguistics (Volume 2: Short Papers)*, volume 2, pages 448–453.

Zijun Yao, Yifan Sun, Weicong Ding, Nikhil Rao, and Hui Xiong. 2018. Dynamic Word Embeddings for Evolving Semantic Discovery. In *Proceedings of the Eleventh ACM International Conference on Web Search and Data Mining*, pages 673–681. ACM.

The Rationality of Semantic Change

Omer Korat
Stanford University
omerk@stanford.edu

Abstract

This study investigates the mutual effects over time of semantically related function words on each other's distribution over syntactic environments. Words that can have the same meaning are observed to have opposite trends of change in frequency across different syntactic structures which correspond to the shared meaning. This phenomenon is demonstrated to have a rational basis: it increases communicative efficiency by prioritizing words differently in the environments on which they compete.

1 Introduction

In this paper I propose that as words immigrate to new syntactic environments over time, they tend to push out words that populated these environments prior to immigration. This results from a process of reasoning over the lexicon, in which speakers choose among lexical alternatives in a way that optimizes communicative utility. In particular, I focus on discourse markers (DMs) and prepositions.

Computational modeling of historical change has seen increased popularity in recent years (Xu and Kemp (2015); Kulkarni et al. (2015); Hamilton et al. (2016b,a) (distributional semantics), Basile et al. (2016) (n-gram models), Schaden (2012); Deo (2015); Yanovich; Enke et al. (2016); Ahern and Clark (2017) (evolutionary game theory)). In this paper, parsed historical corpus evidence is used to quantify existing claims about semantic change, some of which have not been empirically assessed (Bréal, 1897; Ullman, 1962; Traugott and Waterhouse, 1969; Clark and Clark, 1979; Sweetser, 1991; Traugott, 1995; Traugott and Dasher, 2002). Data were collected from the Penn Parsed Corpora of Early Modern English (Kroch and Delfs, 2004) and the Parsed Corpora of Early English Correspondence (Taylor and Nevalainen, 2006).

Specifically, I conduct a quantitative investigation of the manifestation of the principle of contrast (Paul, 1898; Bréal, 1897; Clark, 1990; De Saussure, 1916) in semantic change with abstract terms. According to the principle of contrast, difference in form between two lexical items (phonology/orthography) leads to difference in semantics (Section 2.1). The effects of this principle on semantic change have been studied in the literature (Xu and Kemp, 2015; Hamilton et al., 2016a,b), but previous studies have focused on content words using unambiguous bag-of-words based word vectors, while this study focuses on function , employing syntax-based representations which take into account the structural position of the word. These representations allow for a word to have multiple uses, unlike in the bag-of-words approach. Such representations are better suited to study the distribution of function words, because the meaning of these words can vary based on its syntactic position. For example, *so*, when it appears as a complementizer, is a discourse marker, but when it appears inside a verb phrase is a manner adverb. Such distinctions can only be captured with ambiguous representations that take into account structural information beyond the bag-of-word level.

I argue (Section 2.2) that (a version of) this principle leads to the prediction that when some word immigrates to a new environment, it will compete with other words in that environment, leading to older alternatives becoming less frequent in it. This prediction is tested and verified in Section 4.

The environments considered in this paper are defined syntactically, utilizing manually parsed corpora. Semantic change is measured using hand-crafted distributional syntactic features. The advantage of using syntactic features include (i) the ability to distinguish between different uses of lexically ambiguous words and (ii) ability to

151

Proceedings of the 1st International Workshop on Computational Approaches to Historical Language Change, pages 151–160
Florence, Italy, August 2, 2019. ©2019 Association for Computational Linguistics

utilize syntactic information which is absent from unannotated corpora.

This approach can supplement other quantitative approaches, such as distributed semantics, in which all the uses of a word are compressed into one measure (its point in vector space). In previous studies, word vectors were built using pure bags-of-words, and therefore were unable to distinguish different uses of the same word that differ in their syntactic position. Thus, they were not measuring the relative changes in the frequencies of each different use over time. This limitation is addressed in this study by the use of syntactic features taken from parsed corpora.[1]

Hand crafted syntactic features are therefore well suited to analyzing the development of discourse markers. DMs tend to have many different uses, each with its own distributional properties, and capturing them requires tapping into meta-linguistic information which does not exist in unannotated corpora.

2 The Principle of Contrast

2.1 Background

The principle of contrast states that any two forms contrast in meaning (Bréal, 1897; Paul, 1898; Clark, 1990; De Saussure, 1916). The principle is based on the intuition that when speakers choose linguistic expressions, they do so because they mean something they would not mean by some other expression. Part of the meaning of expressions emerges due to the contrast with alternatives. If a given meaning M is already associated with a well-established form F_1, when the speaker uses a different form F_2, the addressee infers that the speaker did not mean M, since it is common knowledge that the speaker assumes that the addressee can readily compute a unique meaning for F_2.

Note that difference in form (phonology or orthography) can motivate difference in distribution but not in meaning. As Wasow (2015) points out, despite the appeal of the idea of contrast (as formulated by Grice (1975)), language is, in fact, ambiguous. This is evident for example by the fact that many sentences have multiple possible parses,

and that speakers sometimes ask for clarification about the sense in which a word was used. Moreover, see the discussion in Section 4.1 for evidence that challenges the principle of contrast.

Contrast should be seen as one motivating force among many in semantic change. Wasow discusses other possible factors which might motivate ambiguity (e.g. such as reliance on speakers' reasoning faculties in order to save time) which lead speakers to leave out information, resulting in ambiguity. Such variables might operate in parallel to the principle of contrast, leading to ambiguity arising in some situations but not others. That is, contrast in the phonology of two words motivates speakers to use those words differently. This can entail difference in semantics, as is claimed by e.g. Clark and Gathercole, but it can also entail distributional difference, that is, difference in likelihood to appear in certain environments, based on social, syntactic or pragmatic conditions.

2.2 Contrast and Function Words

Here, we adopt a relaxed version of the principle of contrast according to which, word pairs that can mean the same thing in some environment will tend to have different distributions in that environment. This version can be thought of as a natural consequence of general logical principles and Bayesian inference, as in (Hobbs, 1985; Frank and Goodman, 2012; Goodman and Stuhlmüller, 2013; De Jaegher and van Rooij, 2014; Ahern and Clark, 2017). Ahern and Clark (2017) demonstrate how rationality principles can account for semantic drift phenomena. This shows that as in the principle of contrast, the distribution of words is modulated at least partially by rational communicative heuristics aimed to save cognitive effort. Speakers exploit these facts to select which words to use when, thus increasing communicative efficiency and saving cognitive effort. In Rational Speech Acts Theory (RSA, Frank and Goodman (2012)) these notions have been generalized to account for pragmatic inference in the general case by assuming that the probability of an utterance is proportional to its information gain over its cost.

This applies directly to the case at hand: by prioritizing function words differently in different environments, speakers can increase the information gain of their utterances, thus reducing the expected cost of communication. Formally, let u_1 and u_2 be identical and synonymous utterances that differ in

---

[1]Note that the same result could be accomplished using syntax-based word vectors (Padó and Lapata, 2007; Weir et al., 2016; Antoniak and Mimno, 2018) or corpus-based semantic models (Baroni and Lenci, 2010; Petrolito and Bond, 2014). However, such corpora typically do not include historical data, unlike the corpora used in this study.

one word. Let this word be w_1 in u_1 and w_2 in u_2. Now, assume u_1 and u_2 compete on some environment E (syntactic, pragmatic, social, etc'). If speakers do not make a distinction between the uses of w_1 and w_2 in E, then there is no reason to store both the E-use of w_1 and the E-use of w_2. Therefore, it is wasteful to use both w_1 and w_2 in the same frequency in E. One efficient way to benefit from the existence of two words that compete on E is by partitioning E into subsets X and Y, and use u_1 more frequently in X, and u_2 more frequently in Y. Thus, when u_1 or u_2 is uttered, it is easier to retrieve the intended sub-environment, since it is more likely to be X or Y, respectively.

For example, the principle of contrast predicts such interaction between *hence* and *therefore*. Originally, *hence* was a locative used to indicate place of origin ("from hence"). An increase in the DM use of *hence* would lead to competition with *therefore* on the sentence-initial DM environment ("hence, John is smart"), so this environment would be partitioned into sentence-initial DM and mid-sentence DM ("John is therefore smart"), such that *hence* is preferred in the former, and *therefore* is preferred in the latter. This way, speakers can save cognitive effort when choosing among DMs which compete on the same meaning - namely, justification. This process is illustrated in Table 1. Refer to Section 4 for the actual distribution of *hence* and *therefore* in this environment.

The relaxed version of the principle of contrast predicts that when a new word immigrates to an environment E, speakers will be motivated to use it with different probabilities than other words that can appear in E without a change in meaning. This entails that when a word is introduced into a new environment, it will lead to words that mean essentially the same in that environment to become increasingly less frequent in that environment over time. This is the prediction tested in this paper.

3 Methodology

3.1 Setup

To test the proposal made in Section 2.2, I computed the co-distributions of groups of words that compete on related uses in the Penn Parsed Corpora of Early Modern English (Kroch and Delfs, 2004) and the Parsed Corpora of Early English Correspondence (Taylor and Nevalainen, 2006). Words chosen for this study were ones that had

two or more distinct annotation schemes in the corpus. Each annotation scheme is treated as a separate use of the word. All distinguishable uses of each highlighted word were identified throughout the corpus. For example, the contrast use of *but* was annotated as a conjunction, while the exception use was annotated as a preposition. For each comparison set of words W which compete on some environment E, the pattern which defines E was chosen to be the weakest possible regular expression over tree structures which captures exactly one of the uses of each $w \in W$.

As was discussed in Section 1, the advantage of this approach is that (i) it enables us to distinguish different uses of one word, and (ii) it yields robust predictions about function words, taking advantage of the information contained in tree structures.

I looked for environments that can be characterized syntactically, in which more than one word can appear without a substantial change in meaning. This enables us to automatically capture groups of words that compete on the same environment. However, the ability to distinguish different uses of function words comes at the cost of limited scope. The only words that can be examined are ones that satisfy the above restrictions. This might introduce some statistical bias, since the examined words are not based on a random sample. However, this bias was traded off in exchange for higher precision and ability to distinguish multiple senses of function words, as explained above. As a point of comparison, bag-of-words based word vectors cannot achieve this level of precision, since (i) they are inherently monosemous and (ii) word vectors for function words are highly uninformative relatively to content words, since function words are frequent nearly everywhere (Section 4.1).[2]

The words selected for this study are *very, thus, but, except, though, therefore, still, yet, from, hence, as* and *when*.

---

[2]There exist vector space models that were trained on syntactically annotated corpora (MacAvaney and Zeldes, 2018; Levy and Goldberg, 2014; Komninos and Manandhar, 2016), which might address point (ii) above, but it would be difficult to apply such models for a historical study since dependency parsers were largely trained on Modern English data, and therefore cannot be used to annotate historical texts. Hence, in this study, manually annotated corpora were used.

	Loc.	Init.	Mid.
Hence	.9	.1	0
Therefore	0	.9	.1

(a) Before increase

	Loc.	Init.	Mid.
Hence	.7	.3	0
Therefore	0	.9	.1

(b) Increase

	Loc.	Init.	Mid.
Hence	.3	.7	0
Therefore	0	.2	.8

(c) After increase

Table 1: Illustration of hypothetical proposed interaction between words. A hypothetical distribution of *therefore* and *hence* over environments (locative, sentence-initial justification DM, mid-sentence justification DM) is taken as an example. The rise in sentence initial uses of *hence* creates competition, and this competition is resolved by *therefore* becoming less frequent in that environment.

3.2 Competing Pairs

Still and *yet* compete on their positive polarity use (denoted by the variables *_adv_pos, demonstrated in (1)). Additionally, they compete on an adverbial use (*_adv) following a raised clause introduced by a complementizer/preposition, as demonstrated in (2).

(1) And consequently, they may still with greater ease begin with it, ...

(2) If I can come again, we are still to have our ball.

Very and *thus* compete on an intensifier degree-adverbial use (*_adv_deg). For *very*, this is the only use, but *thus* has 3 syntactically distinguishable uses, which I term as follows: degree-adverbial (3) (modifying an adjective), manner adverbial (4) (modifying a verb), and discourse particle (5) (modifying a clause). Generally speaking, the degree-use can be paraphrased as 'to that extent'; the manner-use can be paraphrased as 'in that way'; the discourse particle use can be paraphrased as 'for that reason'.

(3) We are, however, thus little acquainted with...

(4) I wished when I heard them say thus, that...

(5) And thus I bid you farewell from my house at foston this ix of november.

But competes with *except* on the exception use (e.g. "all but a few"). This use is marked as a preposition, and therefore it is denoted by the variable *_p. *Though* and *but* are two contrast words that compete on the contrast coordination environment *_conj. The structure corresponding to this use is demonstrated in (6).

Hence competes with *therefore* on the sentence-initial discourse particle environment (*_dp_top). The locative use of *hence*

(6)

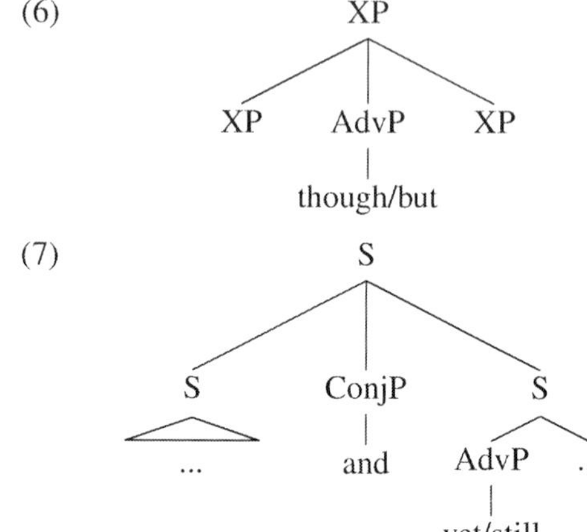

(7)

hence_loc (meaning 'from here'), competes with *from*. *From* is measured by absolute frequency since its only use is the locative one.

As and *when* can both introduce temporal clauses, e.g. 'as/when you arrive'. In the Penn Corpora, temporal complementizers are tagged as prepositions, and therefore I use the pattern *_p to capture these uses.

3.3 Statistical Model

To investigate the hypothesis stated in Section 2.2, relative and absolute frequency counts were collected for each use of each word, and the counts for each competing pair were compared to each other over time. Formally, Each use pattern p of word w was represented as a vector of frequencies over the set T of all 50-year intervals between 1150 CA and 1950 CA (closed to the left and open to the right). For some $\tau \in T$, $\vec{\tau}$ is the vector of intervals that are greater or equal to τ. For example, $\overrightarrow{[1800, 1850)}$ is the vector $([1800, 1850), [1850, 1900), [1900, 1950))$. Each use u is represented as a random variable U, such that $U_{\vec{\tau}}$ is the vector of the count, for each interval $\tau' \geq \tau$ (Read: "following or equal to τ") of matches for the formal pattern that corresponds to

u. For example, the random variable $but_{cont, \vec{\tau}}$ (*cont* for contrast) is the vector of counts of all matches of the formal pattern $[_{conj}\ but]$, that is, all sub-parses that contain a *but* and are directly dominated by a *conj* node, starting from interval τ and onward. $W_{i,\vec{\tau}}$ is the variable corresponding to the vector of counts of the i-th word in τ and the following intervals.

The absolute frequency of a variable $U_{\vec{\tau}}$ is defined as the vector that, for each $s \geq t$, stores in its k-th position the value of $U_{\vec{\tau}}$ at position k divided by the counts of all V words in the vocabulary at position k:

$$\frac{U_{\vec{\tau}}}{\sum_{i=1}^{|V|} W_{i,\vec{\tau}}}$$

If a word has only one relevant use, then its absolute frequency was used as its frequency measure. For example, the word *very* had only one use that was investigated, namely, its adverbial use. The relative frequency of some use of the i-th word, with variable $U_{\vec{\tau}}$, is defined as the proportion of the U values with respect to the W_i values for each interval:

$$\frac{U_{\vec{\tau}}}{W_{i,\vec{\tau}}}$$

If a word had more than one use, its relative frequency was used as its frequency measure. I use $F(U_{\vec{\tau}})$ to denote the frequency measure of $U_{\vec{\tau}}$.

The hypothesis states that for each pair of uses competing on an environment, there exists a point in time t such that one of the uses becomes more frequent following t and the other becomes less frequent following t.[3] That is, for each comparison pair CP, there are $U, V \in CS$ such that there exists some $\tau \in T$ such that $Cov(F(U_{\vec{\tau}}), T_{\vec{\tau}}) <$ o and $Cov(F(V_{\vec{\tau}}), T_{\vec{\tau}}) >$ o. Conceptually, V corresponds to the newer uses which push the older uses, U, out of the environment of competition.

This entails that the trends (i.e. true population regression lines) for U and V in the interval $T_{\vec{\tau}}$ have opposite slopes, which means that they cross at some interval τ' (which may or may not be in T). This means that there is a point in time (τ') starting from which, one use's frequency grows over time, while the other use's frequency decreases over time. Formally, we have that:

$$|F(U_{\tau'}) - F(V_{\tau'})| = O((\tau - \tau')^2)$$

following the definition of O complexity. $\tau - \tau'$ is the difference between the beginning of τ' and the end of τ. In other words, the hypothesis predicts that the difference between the frequencies of the words in each pair grow quadratically as a function of the distance from the point in time in which the trends cross each other.

To model this behavior, a cubic model was fitted to the differences between each pair as a function of T. To account for the fact that the interaction might only take place in a subinterval of T, the model had two splines, one at 1300 and one at 1650.[4] This allows for a coefficient change at those points, which reflects the fact that the effect between the two words might be different for different subintervals of T. The hypothesis predicts that such a model would have a significant fit at $\alpha = .05$.

To verify that the use frequencies indeed change as a linear function of time, for each use U it was tested whether there exists an interval $\tau \in T$ such that the linear model:

$$F(U_{\vec{\tau}}) \sim \vec{\tau}$$

has a significant slope coefficient at $\alpha = .05$. The existence of such a trend shows that U is not constant in time, which entails that if the cubic model is significant, then the two trends have opposite signs (i.e. they are crossing).

4 Results

Coefficients and significance levels for all comparison sets are displayed in Table 2. Each model has 3 coefficients, since the 2 knots partition the intervals into 3 parts. Frequency differences by century are plotted along with model curves. All models were significant, with the exception of the model for *thus* and *very*. All words, with the exception of *still*, were found to change as a linear function of time starting from some year, as described above.

The local extrema of the curves indicate the points at which, according to the hypothesis, the

---

[3]Following the discussion in Section 2.2, the use that becomes less frequent is likely to be the older one, but the hypothesis does not require for this to be the case. The reason is that semantic change can also make words less abstract. For example, *computer* used to denote any computing device, but now typically denotes any computing device which is not tablet-shaped.

[4]As is common practice, the splines were placed at the quantiles of the x axis (rounded).

Env.	Use 1	Use 2	Coef1	Coef2	Coef3	Signif. level
Temporal Adv.	`still_adv`	`yet_adv_pos`	0.83	1.35	0.45	**
Degree/Manner	`very`	`thus_adv_deg`	-0.16	-0.06	-0.0072	.
Justification	`hence_dp`	`therefore_dp_top`	-0.1	-0.73	1.22	***
Locative	`hence_adv`	`from`	1.04	1.56	-0.43	***
Exception	`but_p`	`except`	2.06	0.65	-1e-04	***
Contrast	`though`	`but_contrast`	-3.53	-1.62	-1.42	**
Temporal Comp.	`as_p`	`when_p`	0.1	-1.03	0.12	*

Table 2: Trends by use. Slopes are measured starting from the century the trend started. Signif. codes: 0.001 ** 0.01 * 0.05 '.' .1 ' ' 1

trend lines of the two words cross each other. Due to the X shape formed at those junction points, the absolute difference between the two trends grows cubically around them, which leads to the cubic fit. Curvature change at the splines indicate that the trends have shifted at those points. The chronologically latest trend is indicated by the rightmost parabola, which is the one we are interested in.

For each plot, the order in which the word pair was written reflects the order the subtraction operation applied to the two words' frequencies. Thus, a convex (concave) parabola indicates that the first (second) word's regression line (i.e. its sample trend) has a positive slope while the first (second) word's regression line has a negative slope.

These results suggest that *but*'s contrast use increases at the expense of *though*, and at the same time *except* pushes *but* out of the exception use. *From* pushes *hence* out of the locative use, and *hence* pushes *therefore* out of the justification use. *As* pushes *when* out of the temporal complementizer use. *Yet* seems to interact with *still* in the same way in the positive polarity use, but a definitive linear trend for *still* was failed to be established, so it may be that the difference observed between *stil* and *yet* is only due to a change in *yet* and not a change in *still*. The results also somewhat support the idea that *very* pushes *thus* out of the degree/manner environment, but the model's level of significance warrants further investigation.

4.1 Word Cooccurrence

The proposal made in this paper concerns changes in the structural distribution of semantically similar function words. Function words that share one or more uses are claimed to diverge over time in their syntactic distribution. That is, the syntactic positions they occur in will distribute differently from each other. This claim does not, however, predict that they will occur near different *words*. As Xu and Kemp (2015) report, there is no evidence that semantic similarity leads to difference in word cooccurrence.

Xu and Kemp's hypothesis was formulated in terms of word2vec models (Mikolov et al., 2013), which approximate high-order functions of word cooccurrence. The principle of contrast was translated into the hypothesis that over time, similar words will diverge more than control words in terms of the cosine distance of their vectors. This hypothesis, which was falsified, postulates that two similar words will over time cooccur with different words.

Thus, Xu and Kemp's results suggest that semantically similar words do not tend to diverge in their cooccurrence patterns. They do not, however, exclude the possibility that semantically similar words tend to diverge in the structural positions they assume. This latter possibility is the thesis advocated in this paper.

To verify that the information contained in parsed structures is not fully recoverable from word cooccurrence, I divided the dataset roughly into the Early Modern and Late Modern periods, and for each period, I collected raw cooccurrence matrices for each word that occurred at least twice, with window of size 20. This yields for each word w a vector representation in which the ith position stores the number of times w occurred with the ith vocabulary item in the same sentence. Due to the relatively small size of the dataset, it is not suitable for learning higher order vector representations of words as in word2vec, since such models require larger amounts of data in order to generalize properly. For each pair of words in the vocabulary I computed the change between the early and late periods:

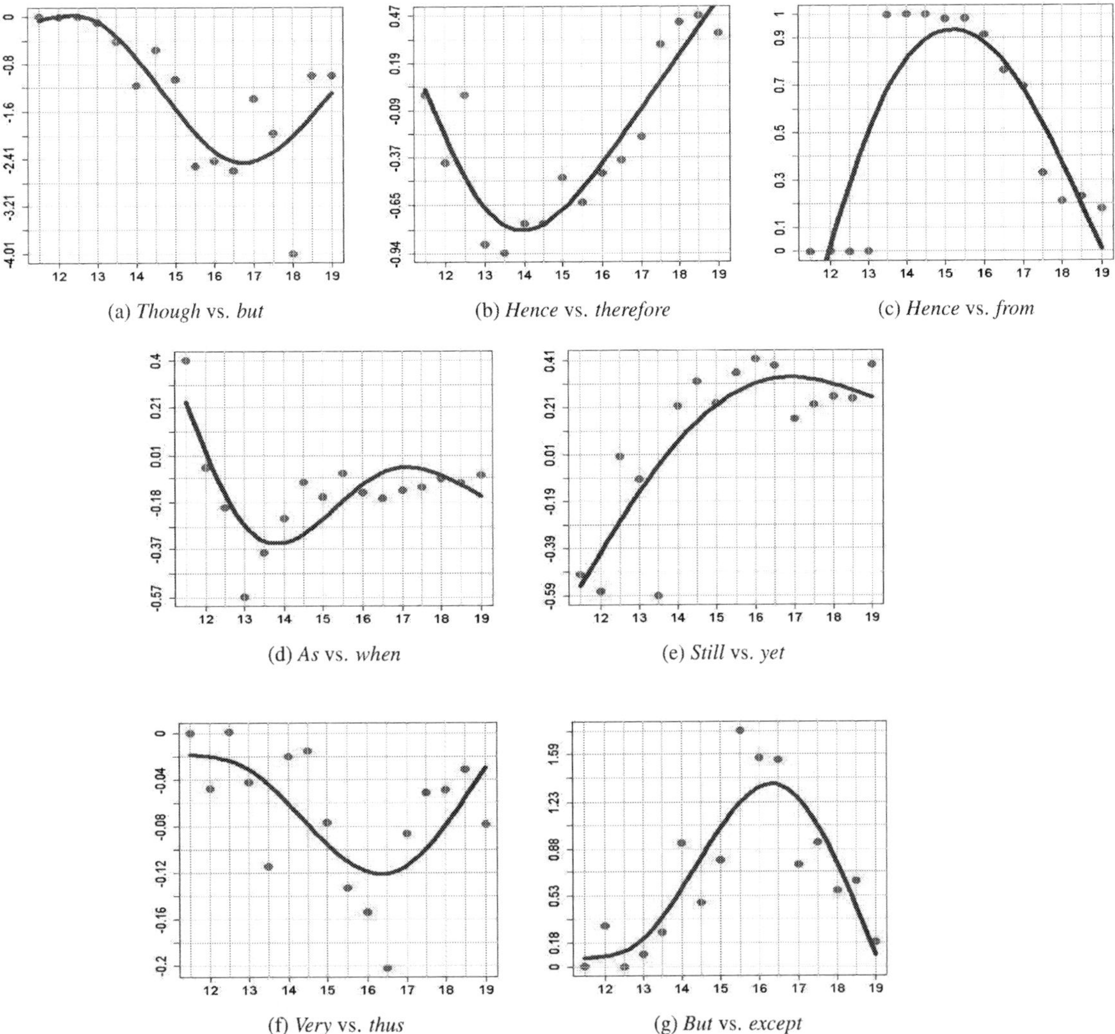

(a) *Though* vs. *but*   (b) *Hence* vs. *therefore*   (c) *Hence* vs. *from*

(d) *As* vs. *when*   (e) *Still* vs. *yet*

(f) *Very* vs. *thus*   (g) *But* vs. *except*

Figure 1: Fitted curves by use pair. The horizontal axis shows centuries and the vertical axis shows the difference between the frequencies of the uses.

$$\delta(w_1, w_2) = |\cos_E(w_1, w_2) - \cos_L(w_1, w_2)|$$

where $\cos_{E/L}$ is the cosine angle between the co-occurrence vectors for w_1 and w_2 for the early and late matrices, respectively. This quantity represents the change in similarities between w_1 w_2 from E to L.

I then considered $\mathbb{E}[\delta(w_1, w_2)]$ for each pair w_1, w_2 of highlighted words as partitioned above (*however-so*, *still-yet*, etc'), and compared it to the $\mathbb{E}[\delta w_1, w_2]$ for every other pair w_1, w_2 of words. This experiment was performed with two cutoff points between the early and late periods: 1700 and 1755 (1755 is the year in which the Dictionary of the English Language, was published which standardized spelling and vocabulary, but 1700 gives a more balanced partition in terms of quantity). For both cutoff points, the two means were different at $\alpha = .01$. The mean for the highlighted pairs was around .1, and the mean for the other pairs was around .33.

This result suggests that no distributional difference is observed between semantically similar word pairs based on word cooccurrence alone. This is in line with (Xu and Kemp, 2015), according to which semantically similar word pairs do not tend to diverge in their cooccurrence patterns over time.

5   Discussion and Conclusions

This paper examined the hypothesis that when a new word immigrates to a new environment, older alternatives tend to decrease in frequency in that environment. Results show that the hypothesis was validated in all cases except `still_adv_pp`. Notice that, in many cases, the r^2 statistic was relatively small. This is unsurprising, since the hypothesis only accounts for a small amount of variation in the data. In other words, time is not the only variable that affects the frequency of different uses of a word.

These results support the proposal detailed in Section 2, namely that as words become more abstract, they compete with old words that share their new environment, leading to the old words being driven to new environments. The results are in alignment with the literature on contrast (Section 2.1). Additionally, it has been shown that these results are not replicated when considering word cooccurrence alone, which suggests that the effects observed are indeed due to structural differences between different uses of the same word. These is fundamentally different from the way content words change, because as has been shown in previous studies (Section 1) content words often move to new distributional environments (in terms of cooccurrence) without any change in syntactic position.

The methodology applied in this study - of using hand-crafted syntactic patterns to distinguish between different uses of the same word - allows for a detailed examination of specific word pairs, which enables us to test highly refined hypotheses. However, this precision is traded off for empirical limitedness, as only a closed set of words satisfies the conditions necessary to be distinguishable in an annotated corpus.

A major limitation of the current study is its narrow empirical coverage, as the study examines a closed set of word pairs. A desirable extension would be testing the same hypothesis across the board for the entire vocabulary. Such an extension would require an innovative method for automatically detecting environments on which word pairs compete.

This phenomenon may be viewed as part of speakers' efforts to maximize utility by conveying the greatest amount of information with the least amount of cognitive effort (as discussed in Section 2). Under this assumption, speakers rely on each other's rational faculties to infer the most likely interpretation of an utterance. lexical meaning is subject to pragmatic considerations of conveying the greatest amount of detail with the least amount of effort. This may explain some of the findings in this study, considering the economic benefit of dividing the labor between different words. These motivations were illustrated in Section 2.

The novelty of the data presented here compared to previous approaches is (i) the application to functional words, specifically prepositions, DMs, and functional adverbs (e.g. *very*, *so*, *really*), and (ii) the ability to compare different uses of the same word. For example, consider the case of *still* vs. *yet*. Figure 1e shows an increase in the positive-polarity and adverbial uses of *still*, followed by a decrease in those same uses of *yet*. This suggests that, following *still*'s immigrating to environments which happen to be shared with *yet*, due to the principle of contrast, those same uses of *yet* are dispreferred, leading to their decrease. This results in the predictions spelled out in Section 2.

Interestingly, note that none of the uses explored in this paper disappear completely. This result is surprising if one considers a naive interpretation of RSA or other game-theoretic approaches to semantic change such as Ahern and Clark (2017). Based on such approaches, one might expect that novel competitors on an environment would eliminate older ones completely, since storing their use in that environment requires unjustified cognitive effort. A possible direction for further research is extending such models to account for the existence of two words that share a use by exploring which distinctions they do mark within that use. A possible explanation is that they are used to mark meta-linguistic information about the utterance, such as the sociology or attitude of the speaker, but this question is left for future experiments.

Acknowledgements

I would like to thank Chris Potts, Paul Kiparsky and Dan Jurafsky for invaluable advise and comments on several drafts of this paper. Their input was essential to the completion of this project. I would also like to thank the Howard B. Kerzner Graduate Fellowship which funds my PhD studies at Stanford University and allowed me access to the resources necessary to complete this project. Additionally, I thank the anonymous reviewers of this workshop who provided detailed comments on the paper.

References

Christopher Ahern and Robin Clark. 2017. Conflict, cheap talk, and Jespersen's cycle. *Semantics and Pragmatics*, 10.

Maria Antoniak and David Mimno. 2018. Evaluating the stability of embedding-based word similarities. *Transactions of the Association for Computational Linguistics*, 6:107–119.

Marco Baroni and Alessandro Lenci. 2010. Distributional memory: A general framework for corpus-based semantics. 36(4):673–721.

Pierpaolo Basile, Annalina Caputo, Roberta Luisi, and Giovanni Semeraro. 2016. Diachronic analysis of the italian language exploiting google ngram. In *Proceedings of Third Italian Conference on Computational Linguistics.*

Michel Bréal. 1897. *Essai de sémantique:(science des significations)*. Paris: Hachette.

Eve V Clark. 1990. On the pragmatics of contrast. *Journal of child language*, 17(02):417–431.

Eve V Clark and Herbert H Clark. 1979. When nouns surface as verbs. *Language*, pages 767–811.

Kris De Jaegher and Robert van Rooij. 2014. Game-theoretic pragmatics under conflicting and common interests. *Erkenntnis*, 79(4):769–820.

Ferdinand De Saussure. 1916. *Cours de linguistique générale: Édition critique*. Lausanne; Paris: Payot.

Ashwini Deo. 2015. The semantic and pragmatic underpinnings of grammaticalization paths: The progressive to imperfective shift. *Semantics and Pragmatics*, 8(14):1–52.

Dankmar Enke, Roland Muhlenbernd, and Igor Yanovich. 2016. The emergence of the progressive to imperfective diachronic cycle in reinforcement-learning agents. In *The Evolution of Language: Proceedings of the 11th International Conference (EVOLANG11). New Orleans.*

Michael C. Frank and Noah D. Goodman. 2012. Predicting pragmatic reasoning in language games. *Science*, 336(3):998–998.

Noah D. Goodman and Andreas Stuhlmüller. 2013. Knowledge and implicature: Modelling language understanding as social cognition. *Topics in cognitive science*, 5(1):173–184.

Herbert P. Grice. 1975. Logic and conversation. In *Syntax and semantics (Vol. 3)*, pages 41–58.

William L Hamilton, Jure Leskovec, and Dan Jurafsky. 2016a. Cultural shift or linguistic drift? comparing two computational measures of semantic change. *Proceedings of EMNLP.*

William L Hamilton, Jure Leskovec, and Dan Jurafsky. 2016b. Diachronic word embeddings reveal statistical laws of semantic change. *Proceedings of ACL.*

Jerry R Hobbs. 1985. *On the coherence and structure of discourse*. Research report, Center for the Study of Language and Information, Stanford University.

Alexandros Komninos and Suresh Manandhar. 2016. Dependency based embeddings for sentence classification tasks. In *Proceedings of the 2016 Conference of the North American Chapter of the Association for Computational Linguistics: Human Language Technologies*, pages 1490–1500.

Beatrice Santorini Kroch, Anthony and Lauren Delfs. 2004. The Penn-Helsinki Parsed Corpus of Early Modern English (PPCEME). CD-ROM, first edition, release 3. Department of Linguistics, University of Pennsylvania.

Vivek Kulkarni, Rami Al-Rfou, Bryan Perozzi, and Steven Skiena. 2015. Statistically significant detection of linguistic change. In *Proceedings of the 24th International Conference on World Wide Web*, pages 625–635. ACM.

Omer Levy and Yoav Goldberg. 2014. Dependency-based word embeddings. In *Proceedings of the 52nd Annual Meeting of the Association for Computational Linguistics (Volume 2: Short Papers)*, volume 2, pages 302–308.

Sean MacAvaney and Amir Zeldes. 2018. A deeper look into dependency-based word embeddings. *arXiv preprint arXiv:1804.05972.*

Tomas Mikolov, Kai Chen, Greg Corrado, and Jeffrey Dean. 2013. Efficient estimation of word representations in vector space. *arXiv preprint arXiv:1301.3781.*

Sebastian Padó and Mirella Lapata. 2007. Dependency-based construction of semantic space models. 33(2):161–199.

Hermann Paul. 1898. *Prinzipien der sprachgeschichte*. Halle: Max Niemeyer Verlag.

Tommaso Petrolito and Francis Bond. 2014. A survey of wordnet annotated corpora. In *Proceedings of the Seventh Global WordNet Conference*, pages 236–245.

Gerhard Schaden. 2012. Modelling the aoristic drift of the present perfect as inflation an essay in historical pragmatics. *International Review of Pragmatics*, 4(2):261–292.

Eve Sweetser. 1991. *From etymology to pragmatics: Metaphorical and cultural aspects of semantic structure*. Cambridge: Cambridge University Press.

Arja Nurmi Anthony Warner Susan Pintzuk Taylor, Ann and Terttu Nevalainen. 2006. The York-Helsinki Parsed Corpus of Early English Correspondence (PCEEC). Oxford Text Archive, first edition. Department of Linguistics, University of York.

Elizabeth C. Traugott and Richard B. Dasher. 2002. *Regularities in semantic change*. Cambridge: Cambridge University Press.

Elizabeth Closs Traugott. 1995. The role of the development of discourse markers in a theory of grammaticalization. *ICHL XII, Manchester*, 123.

Elizabeth Closs Traugott and John Waterhouse. 1969. 'already' and 'yet': a suppletive set of aspect-markers? *Journal of Linguistics*, 5(02):287–304.

Stephan Ullman. 1962. *Semantics: An Introduction to the Science of Meaning*. New York City: Barnes & Noble.

Thomas Wasow. 2015. Ambiguity avoidance is overrated. *Ambiguity: Language and Communication*, page 29.

David Weir, Julie Weeds, Jeremy Reffin, and Thomas Kober. 2016. Aligning packed dependency trees: a theory of composition for distributional semantics. *Computational Linguistics, special issue on Formal Distributional Semantics*, 42(4):727–761.

Yang Xu and Charles Kemp. 2015. A computational evaluation of two laws of semantic change. In *Proc. Annual Conf. of the Cognitive Science Society*.

Igor Yanovich. Analyzing imperfective games. *lingbuzz/002652*.

Studying Laws of Semantic Divergence across Languages using Cognate Sets

Ana Sabina Uban, Alina Maria Ciobanu, and Liviu P. Dinu

Faculty of Mathematics and Computer Science,
Human Language Technologies Research Center,
University of Bucharest

`ana.uban@gmail.com, alina.ciobanu@my.fmi.unibuc.ro,`
`liviu.p.dinu@gmail.com`

Abstract

Semantic divergence in related languages is a key concern of historical linguistics. Intra-lingual semantic shift has been previously studied in computational linguistics, but it can only provide a limited picture of the evolution of word meanings, which often develop in a multilingual environment. In this paper we investigate semantic change across languages by measuring the semantic distance of cognate words in multiple languages. By comparing current meanings of cognates in different languages, we hope to uncover information about their previous meanings, and about how they diverged within their respective languages from their common original etymon. We further study the properties of the semantic divergence of cognates, by analyzing how features of the words, such as frequency and polysemy, are related to their shift in meaning, and thus take the first steps towards formulating laws of cross-lingual semantic change.

1 Introduction and Related Work

Semantic change – that is, change in the meaning of individual words (Campbell, 1998) – is a continuous, inevitable process stemming from numerous reasons and influenced by various factors. Words are continuously changing, with new senses emerging all the time. Campbell (1998) presents no less than 11 types of semantic change, that are generally classified in two wide categories: narrowing and widening.

In recent years, multiple computational linguistic studies have focused on the issue of semantic change, tracking the shift in the meaning of words by looking at their usage across time in corpora dating from different time periods. More than this, computational linguists have also tried to systematically analyze the principles describing semantic change hypothesized by linguists (such as the

law of parallel change and the law of differentiation (Xu and Kemp, 2015)), or even proposed new statistical laws of semantic change, based on empirical observations, such as the law of conformity (stating that polysemy is positively correlated with semantic change), the law of innovation (according to which word frequency is negatively correlated with semantic change) (Hamilton et al., 2016), or the law of prototypicality (according to which prototypicality is negatively correlated with semantic change) (Dubossarsky et al., 2015). More recently, Dubossarsky et al. (2017) revisited some of the semantic change laws proposed in previous literature, claiming that a more rigorous consideration of control conditions when modelling these laws leads to the conclusion that they are weaker or less reliable than reported. More extensive surveys of computational studies relating to semantic change have been conducted by Kutuzov et al. (2018); Tahmasebi et al. (2018).

All previous computational studies on lexical semantic change have, to our knowledge, only looked at the semantic change of the words within one language. However, words do not evolve only in their own language in isolation, but are rather inherited and borrowed between and across languages.

Cognates are words in sister languages (languages descending from a common ancestor) with a common proto-word. For example, the Romanian word *victorie* and the Italian word *vittoria* are cognates, as they both descend from the Latin word *victoria* (meaning *victory*) – see Figure 1. In most cases, cognates have preserved similar meanings across languages, but there are also exceptions. These are called deceptive cognates or, more commonly, false friends. Here we use the definition of cognates that refers to words with similar appearance and some common etymology, and use *true cognates* to refer to cognates

Proceedings of the 1st International Workshop on Computational Approaches to Historical Language Change, pages 161–166
Florence, Italy, August 2, 2019. ©2019 Association for Computational Linguistics

which also have a common meaning, and *deceptive cognates* or *false friends* to refer to cognate pairs which do not have the same meaning (anymore).

Dominguez and Nerlich (2002) distinguish between *chance false friends*, which have similar form but different etymologies as well as different meanings in different languages, and *semantic false friends*, which share the etymological origin, but their meanings differ (to some extent) in different languages. In this study we focus on the latter, which we consider more relevant from the point of view of semantic change since, in principle, they begin with a common meaning then diverge, to a lower or higher degree, while often preserving some common meaning, whereas *chance false friends* usually have entirely distinct meanings.

Most linguists found structural and psychological factors to be the main cause of semantic change, but the evolution of technology and cultural and social changes are not to be omitted. Moreover, when a word enters a new language, features specific to that particular language can affect the way it is used and contribute to shaping its meaning through time: existing words in the same language, as well as socio-cultural and historical factors etc. The evolution of cognate words in different languages can be seen as a collection of different parallel histories of the proto-word from its entering the new languages to its current state. Based on this view, we propose a novel approach for studying semantic change: instead of comparing *monolingual* texts from *different time periods* as ways to track meanings of words at different stages in time - we compare *present meanings* of cognate words across *different languages*, viewing them as snapshots in time of each of the word's different histories of evolution.

Related to our task, there have been a number of previous studies attempting to automatically extract pairs of true cognates and false friends from corpora or from dictionaries. Most methods are based either on orthographic and phonetic similarity, or require large parallel corpora or dictionaries (Inkpen et al., 2005; Nakov et al., 2009; Chen and Skiena, 2016; St Arnaud et al., 2017). There have been few previous studies using word embeddings for the detection of false friends or cognate words, usually using simple methods on only one or two pairs of languages (Torres and Aluísio, 2011; Cas-

tro et al., 2018).

Uban et al. (2019) propose a method for identifying and correcting false friends, as well as define a measure of their "falseness", using cross-lingual word embeddings. We base our study on the method proposed here, and take it further by analyzing the properties of semantic divergence as they relate to different properties of the words, across five Romance languages, as well as English. Similarly to how Hamilton et al. (2016) formulate statistical laws of semantic change within one language, we propose studying the same laws cross-lingually, from the point of view of cognate semantic divergence.

In the following sections, we first present the method for measuring cognate semantic distance in Section 2, then in Section 3 provide details on our experiments for characterizing the properties of semantic change across languages using cognates.

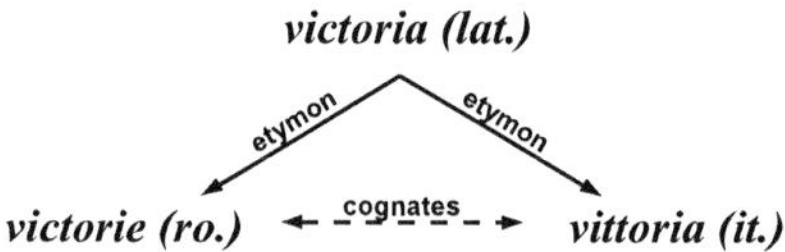

Figure 1: Example of cognates and their common ancestor.

2 Semantic Divergence of Cognates

2.1 Cross-lingual Word Embeddings

Word embeddings are vectorial representations of words in a continuous space, built by training a model to predict the occurrence of a target word in a text corpus given its context, and can be used as representations of word meaning: words that are similar semantically appear close together in the embedding space.

In our study we make use of word embeddings computed using the FastText algorithm, pretrained on Wikipedia for the six languages in question. The vectors have 300 dimensions, and were obtained using the skip-gram model described by Bojanowski et al. (2016) with default parameters. These pre-trained embeddings are suitable for our study since: they are trained on large amounts of text, which minimizes the amount of noise in the vectors, making them good approximators of word meanings; and they are trained on text that is relatively uniform in style and topic - ensuring

Romanian	French	Italian	Spanish	Portuguese	Latin ancestor
arhitect	architecte	architetto	arquitecto	arquiteto	architectus

Table 1: An example of a cognate set: "architect" in Romance languages.

any differences in the structure of the embedding spaces of different languages is dependent on the language, rather than an artifact of topic or genre. Nevertheless, even high quality embeddings can be noisy or biased and this should be kept in mind when interpreting the results of our experiments.

To compute the semantic divergence of cognates across sister languages, we need to obtain a multilingual semantic space, which is shared between the cognates. Having the representations of both cognates in the same semantic space, we can then compute the semantic distance between them using their vectorial representations in this space. For a given pair of languages among the six considered, we can then accomplish this following the steps below:

Step 1. Obtain word embeddings for each of the two languages.

Step 2. Obtain a shared embedding space, common to the two languages. This is accomplished using an alignment algorithm, which consists of finding a linear transformation between the two spaces that on average optimally transforms each vector in one embedding space into a vector in the second embedding space, minimizing the distance between a few seed word pairs (which are assumed to have the same meaning), based on a small bilingual dictionary. The linear nature of the transformation guarantees distances between words in the original spaces (within each language) are preserved. For our purposes, we use the publicly available FastText multilingual word embeddings pre-aligned in a common vector space (Conneau et al., 2017).[1]

Step 3. Compute the semantic distance for the pair of cognates in the two languages, using a vectorial distance (we chose cosine distance) on their corresponding vectors in the shared embedding space.

2.2 Dataset

As our data source, we use the list of cognate sets in Romance languages proposed by Ciobanu and Dinu (2014). It contains 3,218 complete cognate sets in Romanian, French, Italian, Spanish and

Portuguese, along with their Latin common ancestors, extracted from online etymology dictionaries. A subset of 305 of these sets also contains the corresponding cognate (in the broad sense, since these are mostly borrowings) in English.

One complete example of a cognate set for the word "architect" in the Romance languages is illustrated in Table 1.

2.3 Deceptive Cognates and Falseness

The multilingual embedding spaces as defined above can be used to measure the semantic distances between cognates in order to detect pairs of false friends, which are simply defined as pairs of cognates which do not share the same meaning. More specifically, following the false friends detection and correction algorithm of Uban et al. (2019), we consider a pair of cognates to be a false friend pair if in the shared semantic space, there exists a word in the second language which is semantically closer to the original word than its cognate in that language (in other words, the cognate is not the optimal translation). The arithmetic difference between the semantic distance between these words and the semantic distance between the cognates will be used as a measure of the *falseness* of the false friend.

	Accuracy	Precision	Recall
EN-ES	76.58	63.88	88.46
ES-IT	75.80	41.66	54.05
ES-PT	82.10	40.0	42.85
EN-FR	77.09	57.89	94.28
FR-IT	74.16	32.81	65.62
FR-ES	73.03	33.89	69.96
EN-IT	73.07	33.76	83.87
IT-PT	76.14	29.16	43.75
EN-PT	77.25	59.81	86.48

Table 2: Performance for all language pairs using WordNet as gold standard.

Uban et al. (2019) also perform an evaluation of the introduced false friends detection algorithm using multilingual WordNet as a gold standard. In order to provide more context for the method that we employ in our study, we briefly reiterate their results. A pair of words with common etymology are considered true cognates if they belong to the

---

[1] https://github.com/facebookresearch/MUSE

same WordNet synset (are synonyms), and false friends if they are not synonyms. Using this gold standard, the obtained measured accuracy falls between 74% and 82%, depending on the language pair considered. Table 2 presents a breakdown of the obtained performance per language pair considered (limited to languages available in multilingual WordNet).

We select a few results of the algorithm to show in Table 3, containing examples of extracted false friends, along with the suggested correction and the computed degree of falseness. Each row in the table contains a pair of false cognates, among which one is chosen as a reference, and corrected so as to obtain its true translation in the second language using the correction algorithm.

Cognate	False Friend	Correction	False-ness
long (FR)	luengo (ES)	largo	0.50
face (FR)	faz (ES)	cara	0.39
change(FR)	caer (ES)	cambia	0.46
stânga (RO)	stanco (IT)	destra	0.52
tânăr (RO)	tenero (IT)	giovane	0.41
inimă (RO)	anima (IT)	cuore	0.13
amic (RO)	amico (IT)	amichetto	0.04

Table 3: Extracted false friends and falseness.

3 Laws of Cross-lingual Semantic Divergence

We use the measure of falseness of a deceptive cognate pair to quantify the semantic shift between the meanings of a word derived from the same etymon in different languages. We further propose analyzing how the properties of frequency and polysemy of a word relate to semantic shift, and, analogously to what Hamilton et al. (2016) do for monolingual semantic change, we aim to move towards uncovering statistical laws of semantic change across languages.

We first define a measure of the frequency of a word, as well as a measure of its polysemy. Further, we try to correlate these measures of frequency and polysemy with the falseness measure defined in the previous sections. At this step, we

	ES	PT	IT	FR	EN
ES	-	-23.4	-31.5	-39.8	-20.9
PT	-42.0	-	-37.7	-34.2	-31.4
IT	-29.5	-28.5	-	-33.9	-36.2
FR	-25.9	-16.3	-23.3	-	-31.9
EN	-27.7	-39.3	-39.7	-39.2	-

Table 4: Correlations of frequency with falseness.

discard all cognate pairs that, according to the false friend detection algorithm, are true cognates, and focus only on the deceptive cognates. On average across all language pairs, 37% of the cognate pairs in our dataset are found as deceptive cognates. Moreover, we validate these results using multilingual WordNet, and further select only pairs which are confirmed to be deceptive cognates as such: two cognates are considered to be true cognates if they are synonyms according to WordNet, and are considered to be deceptive cognates otherwise. It should be noted that having to use WordNet limits us to languages for which WordNet is available (excluding Romanian).

Although our approach is very similar to the one proposed by Hamilton et al. (2016), an important difference should be noted: while the authors of the monolingual study correlate the magnitude of the shift of meaning in a word to its frequency and polysemy *prior* to the change in meaning, our method looks at the properties of words *after* the meaning shift has already occurred, presumably from the original meaning of the proto-word they derive from to their current meanings in their respective languages.

3.1 Word Frequency and Semantic Divergence

For measuring **frequency**, we use the rankings of words based on their frequency in the corpus used to build the embeddings, which are readily available in the FastText embeddings that we use out of the box. The most frequent words will be associated with the lowest ranks. We normalize the absolute rank of a word dividing by the total number of words in its language, obtaining a relative rank ranging from 0 to 1 (with 0 corresponding to the most frequent words and 1 to the rarest).

For each pair of languages in a cognate set, we compute the Spearman correlation between the frequency rank of the first word in the cognate pair and the falseness of the deceptive cognate. Since frequency and polysemy are correlated, we need to control for polysemy in order to observe the marginal effect of frequency on semantic divergence. To this effect, we compute partial correlations, using polysemy as a covariate variable. Similarly, when computing correlations for polysemy, we set frequency as a covariate.

The results showing the correlations for each language pair are reported in Table 4. The values

	ES	PT	IT	FR	EN
ES	-	56.2	47.3	26.5	12.1
PT	20.2	-	34.5	28.8	4.2
IT	18.6	15.0	-	6.2	2.1
FR	14.2	26.0	16.4	-	-5.4
EN	-9.1	-11.2	-16.5	-14.0	-

Table 5: Correlations of polysemy with falseness.

are considerable for most language pairs, suggesting that the frequency of the word does play a role in the way its meaning shifts.

We also further try to understand the type of relationship between frequency and falseness. Following the results of Hamilton et al. (2016) showing that frequency relates to semantic shift according to a power law, we verify this in our setup by plotting the log of the frequency against the falseness degree, and then the log of polysemy against the falseness degree, confirming a similar type of relationship in our case, as shown for Spanish-Portuguese in Figure 2.

It is interesting to compare our results with those of Hamilton et al. (2016), where the authors observe an inverse correlation between frequency and meaning shift: the more frequent words tend to change their meaning more slowly. Our experiments show the opposite effect: even though the correlation values are negative, here we use frequency ranks rather than raw counts, so a negative correlation indicates a positive relation: more frequent words have diverged more in meaning. This may be related to the fact that we measure frequency *a posteriori*: the cognates we compared had *already* diverged in meaning before we measured their frequency, which may lead to a different effect than the one observed by Hamilton et al. (2016).

3.2 Word Polysemy and Semantic Divergence

For **polysemy**, we make use of WordNet, a semantic network organized in synsets which represent concepts - where each word is part of as many synsets as concepts it designates. In this way, the polysemy of a word can be defined as the number of synsets that it is part of in WordNet.

We perform similar experiments for polysemy, correlating the degree of polysemy of the first word in a cognate pair to the falseness of the pair. The results, shown in Table 5, are noteworthy for most language pairs here as well, though less pronounced than for frequency. Figure 2 shows the relationship between log-polysemy and falseness,

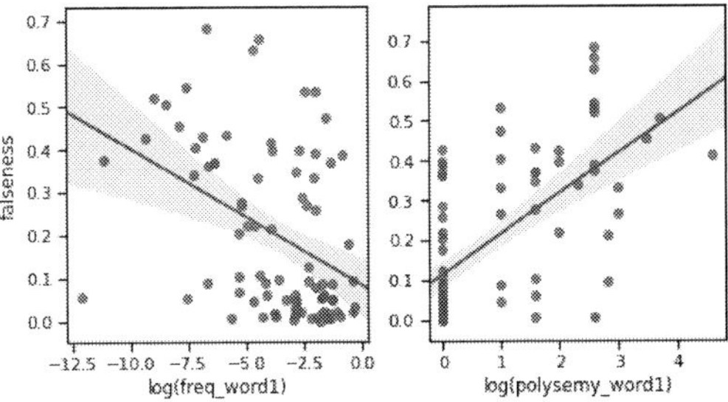

Figure 2: Falseness correlation with log-frequency and log-polysemy for Spanish-Portuguese.

which displays a clear linear trend. More than that, it is interesting to see that the correlations are higher for languages which are known to be more closely related: the strongest effects are observed for Spanish and Portuguese, which are the closest, geographically, of all Romance languages and may have evolved together for parts of their history. English, as the only non-Romance language, also stands out for showing the weakest effects of polysemy on falseness for most language pairs, and for some even shows an inversed effect of negative correlation with falseness with Romance languages.

For Romance languages, polysemy proves to be positively correlated with falseness, confirming the results on monolingual experiments in previous studies: more polysemantic words seem to suffer more semantic shift – or rather, in our case, words which have undergone more semantic shift tend to be more polysemantic.

4 Conclusions

We have proposed in this paper a new perspective for studying semantic change: comparing meaning of cognate words across languages.

We have shown how frequency and polysemy relate to semantic shifts of cognates across languages, demonstrating that both the frequency and polysemy of cognates positively correlate with their cross-lingual semantic shift, taking the first steps towards formulating statistical laws of cross-lingual semantic change. In the future, including the proto-word in the analysis where available (in this case, the Latin etymon) may give further insight into how cognates change their meaning. Additionally, it would be interesting to further explain these correlations, as well as study other hypothesized laws of semantic change in a multilingual setting.

References

Piotr Bojanowski, Edouard Grave, Armand Joulin, and Tomas Mikolov. 2016. Enriching Word Vectors with Subword Information. *arXiv preprint arXiv:1607.04606*.

Lyle Campbell. 1998. *Historical Linguistics. An Introduction.* MIT Press.

Santiago Castro, Jairo Bonanata, and Aiala Rosá. 2018. A high coverage method for automatic false friends detection for spanish and portuguese. In *Proceedings of the Fifth Workshop on NLP for Similar Languages, Varieties and Dialects (VarDial 2018)*, pages 29–36.

Yanqing Chen and Steven Skiena. 2016. False-friend detection and entity matching via unsupervised transliteration. *arXiv preprint arXiv:1611.06722*.

Alina Maria Ciobanu and Liviu P. Dinu. 2014. Building a Dataset of Multilingual Cognates for the Romanian Lexicon. In *Proceedings of the Ninth International Conference on Language Resources and Evaluation, LREC 2014*, pages 1038–1043.

Alexis Conneau, Guillaume Lample, Marc'Aurelio Ranzato, Ludovic Denoyer, and Hervé Jégou. 2017. Word translation without parallel data. *arXiv preprint arXiv:1710.04087*.

Pedro J Chamizo Dominguez and Brigitte Nerlich. 2002. False friends: their origin and semantics in some selected languages. *Journal of pragmatics*, 34(12):1833–1849.

Haim Dubossarsky, Yulia Tsvetkov, Chris Dyer, and Eitan Grossman. 2015. A bottom up approach to category mapping and meaning change. In *NetWordS*, pages 66–70.

Haim Dubossarsky, Daphna Weinshall, and Eitan Grossman. 2017. Outta control: Laws of semantic change and inherent biases in word representation models. In *Proceedings of the 2017 conference on empirical methods in natural language processing*, pages 1136–1145.

William L. Hamilton, Jure Leskovec, and Dan Jurafsky. 2016. Diachronic Word Embeddings Reveal Statistical Laws of Semantic Change. In *Proceedings of the 54th Annual Meeting of the Association for Computational Linguistics, ACL 2016*, pages 1489–1501.

Diana Inkpen, Oana Frunza, and Grzegorz Kondrak. 2005. Automatic identification of cognates and false friends in french and english. In *Proceedings of the International Conference Recent Advances in Natural Language Processing*, volume 9, pages 251–257.

Andrey Kutuzov, Lilja Øvrelid, Terrence Szymanski, and Erik Velldal. 2018. Diachronic word embeddings and semantic shifts: a survey. *arXiv preprint arXiv:1806.03537*.

Svetlin Nakov, Preslav Nakov, and Elena Paskaleva. 2009. Unsupervised extraction of false friends from parallel bi-texts using the web as a corpus. In *Proceedings of the International Conference RANLP-2009*, pages 292–298.

Adam St Arnaud, David Beck, and Grzegorz Kondrak. 2017. Identifying cognate sets across dictionaries of related languages. In *Proceedings of the 2017 Conference on Empirical Methods in Natural Language Processing*, pages 2519–2528.

Nina Tahmasebi, Lars Borin, and Adam Jatowt. 2018. Survey of computational approaches to diachronic conceptual change. *arXiv preprint arXiv:1811.06278*.

Lianet Sepúlveda Torres and Sandra Maria Aluísio. 2011. Using machine learning methods to avoid the pitfall of cognates and false friends in spanish-portuguese word pairs. In *Proceedings of the 8th Brazilian Symposium in Information and Human Language Technology*.

Ana Sabina Uban, Alina Ciobanu, and Liviu Dinu. 2019. A computational approach to measuring the semantic divergence of cognates. In *Proceedings of the 19th International Conference on Computational Linguistics and Intelligent Text Processing*. To be published.

Yang Xu and Charles Kemp. 2015. A computational evaluation of two laws of semantic change. In *CogSci*.

Detecting Syntactic Change Using a Neural Part-of-Speech Tagger

William Merrill,[*†‡] **Gigi Felice Stark,**[*‡] and **Robert Frank**[‡]
[‡]Department of Linguistics, Yale University, New Haven, CT, USA
[†]Allen Institute for Artificial Intelligence, Seattle, WA, USA
`first.last@yale.edu`

Abstract

We train a diachronic long short-term memory (LSTM) part-of-speech tagger on a large corpus of American English from the 19th, 20th, and 21st centuries. We analyze the tagger's ability to implicitly learn temporal structure between years, and the extent to which this knowledge can be transferred to date new sentences. The learned year embeddings show a strong linear correlation between their first principal component and time. We show that temporal information encoded in the model can be used to predict novel sentences' years of composition relatively well. Comparisons to a feedforward baseline suggest that the temporal change learned by the LSTM is syntactic rather than purely lexical. Thus, our results suggest that our tagger is implicitly learning to model syntactic change in American English over the course of the 19th, 20th, and early 21st centuries.

1 Introduction

We define a diachronic language task as a standard computational linguistic task where the input includes not just text, but also information about when the text was written. In particular, diachronic part-of-speech (POS) tagging is the task of assigning POS tags to a sequence of words dated to a specific year. Our goal is to determine the extent to which such a tagger learns a representation of syntactic change in modern American English.

Our method approaches this problem using neural networks, which have seen considerable success in a diverse array of natural language processing tasks over the last few years. Prior work using deep learning methods to analyze language change

has focused more on lexical, rather than syntactic, change (Hamilton et al., 2016; Dubossarsky et al., 2017; Jo et al., 2017). One of these works, Jo et al. (2017), measured linguistic change by evaluating a language model's perplexity on novel documents from different years.

Previous work focusing on syntactic change utilized mathematical simulations rather than empirically trained models. Niyogi and Berwick (1995) attempted to build a mathematical model of syntactic change motivated by theories of language contact and acquisition. They found that their model predicted both gradual and sudden changes in a parameterized grammar depending on the properties of the languages in contact. In particular, they used their simulation to study how verb-second (V2) order was gained and lost throughout the history of the French language. For several toy languages, their model found that contact between languages with and without V2 would lead to gradual adoption of V2 syntax by the entire population.

We use the Corpus of Historical American English (COHA) (Davies, 2010-), an LSTM POS tagger, and dimensionality reduction techniques to investigate syntactic change in American English during the 19th through 21st centuries. Our project takes the POS tagging task as a proxy for diachronic syntax modeling and has three main goals:

1. Assess whether a temporal progression is encoded in the network's learned year embeddings.

2. Verify that the represented temporal change reflects syntax rather than simply word frequency.

3. Determine whether our model can be used to date novel sentences.

---

* Authors (listed in alphabetical order) contributed equally.

† Work completed while the author was at Yale University.

Proceedings of the 1st International Workshop on Computational Approaches to Historical Language Change, pages 167–174
Florence, Italy, August 2, 2019. ©2019 Association for Computational Linguistics

2 Materials and Methods

2.1 Data

2.1.1 Corpus of Historical American English

The COHA corpus is composed of documents dating from 1810 to 2009 and contains over 400 million words. The genre mix of the texts is balanced in each decade, and includes fiction works, academic papers, newspapers, and popular magazines. Because of computational constraints, we randomly selected 50,000 sentences from each decade for a total of 1,000,000 sentences. We selected an equal number of sentences from each decade to ensure a temporally balanced corpus. We put 90% of these into a training set and 10% into a test set. We also cut off all sentences at a maximum length of 50 words. We chose 50 words as our limit to avoid unnecessarily padding a large percentage of sentences. Only 6.95% of sentences in the full COHA corpus exceeded 50 words.

Texts in COHA are annotated with word, lemma, and POS information. The POS labels come in three levels of specificity, with the most specific level containing several thousand POS tags. We used the least specific label for our model, which still had 423 unique POS tags.

2.1.2 Word Embeddings

Our model utilized pre-trained 300-dimensional Google News (Mikolov et al., 2013) word embeddings that were learned using a standard word2vec architecture. When there was no embedding available for a word in the corpus, we assigned the word an embedding vector drawn from a normal distribution, so that different unknown words would have different embeddings. Due to computational constraints, we only included embeddings for the 600,000 most common words in the vocabulary. Other words were replaced by a special symbol *UNK*.

2.2 Methods

2.2.1 Network Architecture

We used a single-layer LSTM model.[1] For a given sentence from a document composed in the year with embedding t, the model's input for the ith word in the sentence is the concatenation of the word's embedding x_i and t. For example, consider a sentence *hello world!* written in 2000. The input

corresponding to *hello* would be the concatenation of the embedding for *hello* and the embedding of the year 2000. A diagram of this architecture can be seen in Figure 1.

An interesting feature of our approach is that a single model can learn information about different time frames. Thus, in principle, learning from sentences in any year can inform predictions about sentences in neighboring years.

The word embeddings were loaded statically. In contrast, year embeddings were Xavier-initialized and learned dynamically by our network. Thus, we did not explicitly enforce that the year embeddings should encode any temporal progression.

We gave both the word embeddings and year embeddings a dimensionality of 300. We picked the size of our LSTM layer to be 512. Due to the size of our training set and our limited computational resources, we ran our network for just one training epoch. Manual tweaking of the learning rate and batch size revealed that the network's performance was not particularly sensitive to their values. Ultimately, we set the learning rate to 0.001 and the batch size to 100. We did not incorporate dropout or regularization into our model since we did not expect overfitting, as we only trained for a single epoch.

In order to calibrate the performance of our LSTM, we trained the following ablation models:

- An LSTM tagger without year input

- A feedforward tagger with year input

- A feedforward tagger without year input

All taggers were trained with identical hyperparameters to the original LSTM. For the feedforward models, the LSTM layer was replaced by a feedforward layer of size 512. The lack of recurrent connections in the feedforward models makes it impossible for these models to consider interactions between words. Thus, these models serve as a baseline that only considers relationships between single words and their POS tags–not syntax.

2.2.2 Analyzing Year Embeddings

We aimed to evaluate the extent to which the learned year embeddings encode a temporal trend. We reduced the year embeddings to one-dimensional space using principal component analysis (PCA). We chose PCA because it is a widely used dimensionality reduction technique

---

[1] `https://github.com/viking-sudo-rm/DiachronicPOSTagger`

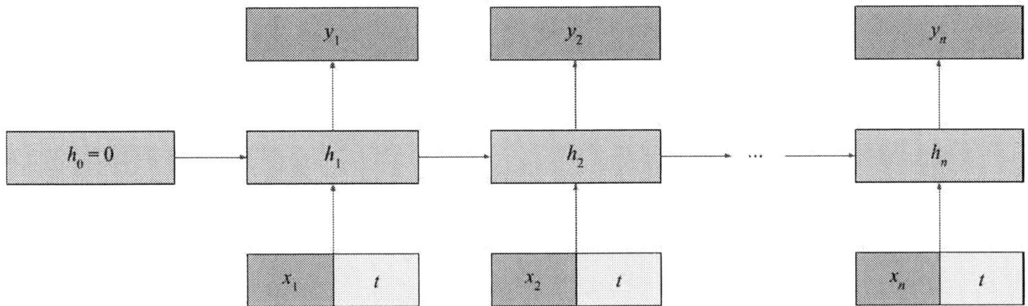

Figure 1: LSTM architecture. The input to the LSTM at each step is the concatenation of the current word's embedding and the corresponding document's year embedding. Each output is the predicted POS tag for the current word.

that requires no hyperparameter tuning. We calculated the correlation between the first principal component of the embeddings and time.

Both the LSTM and feedforward models capture lexical information. However, due to its recurrent connections, the LSTM model is also informed by syntax. To evaluate whether the relationship between years and learned embeddings was due to syntax or simply word choice, we computed the correlation between the first principal component of the embeddings and time for both the LSTM and feedforward models. The difference between the LSTM and feedforward R^2 values reflects the degree to which the LSTM's representation of time is informed by syntactic change.

2.2.3 Temporal Prediction

We evaluated the ability of our model to predict the years of composition of new sentences. Because this task is difficult for a single sentence, we evaluated model performance at the aggregate level, bucketing test sentences by either year or decade. As the year grouping is much more narrow, model performance when these buckets are used should be worse. We report both year and decade metrics to evaluate the extent to which our model is effective at different levels of specificity. We used our model to compute the perplexity of each sentence in a given bucket at every possible

year (1810-2009). We then fit a curve to perplexity as a function of year using locally weighted scatterplot smoothing (LOWESS). These curves provide clear interpretable visualizations that discount extraneous noise. We took the year corresponding to the LOWESS curve's global minimum as the predicted year of composition for the sentences in the bucket.

We compared the effectiveness of the LSTM and the feedforward taggers for temporal prediction. For decade buckets, we quantified the predictive power of each model by calculating the average distance across decades between each decade bucket's middle year and predicted year of composition. Similarly, for year buckets, we measured the average distance between the predicted and actual years of composition. For both metrics, the naive baseline model assigns each bucket a predicted year of 1910 (the middle year in the data set), which results in a metric value of 50.0 for both decade and year buckets.

3 Results

3.1 Tagger Performance

Our LSTM POS tagger with year input achieves 95.5% test accuracy after training for one epoch (see Table 1). While we are not focused on achieving state-of-the-art POS tagging performance, this

	Feedforward	LSTM
Year	82.6	**95.5**
No Year	77.8	95.3

Table 1: Test accuracies for all architectural variants. The networks differed in whether year information was included as input and whether the hidden layer had LSTM or feedforward connections.

	Feedforward	LSTM
Year	82.6	**95.6**
No Year	77.7	95.4

Table 2: Training accuracies for all architectural variants.

relatively high test accuracy suggests that the tagger is legitimate. The LSTM without year input performed marginally worse with a 95.3% test accuracy (see Table 1). These results suggest that temporal information slightly aids tagging.

The feedforward taggers with and without year input had test accuracies of 82.6% and 77.8%, respectively (again, see Table 1). As feedforward networks, unlike LSTMs, do not take into account relations between words, it makes sense that their POS tagging performance is much lower. Additionally, these results bolster the idea that year input improves tagging performance.

To justify not implementing dropout, regularization, or other techniques to combat overfitting, we calculated the training set accuracies of each model. For each type of the model, the training set accuracy was comparable to the test set accuracy (see Table 2). Thus, our models did not overfit.

3.2 Analyzing Year Embeddings

When we plotted the LSTM-learned year embeddings using one-dimensional PCA, a clear linear relationship ($R^2 = 0.89$) between the years and the first principal component emerged (see Figure 2). These results suggest that the most significant information in the year embeddings encodes the relative position of each year within a chronological sequence. As the first principal component seems to encode temporal information well, we did not see a need to investigate additional principal components. This strong linear correlation suggests that, at the aggregate level, change is monotonic and gradual over time. Even if specific changes do not occur monotonically, the aggregation of these changes allows the network to learn a

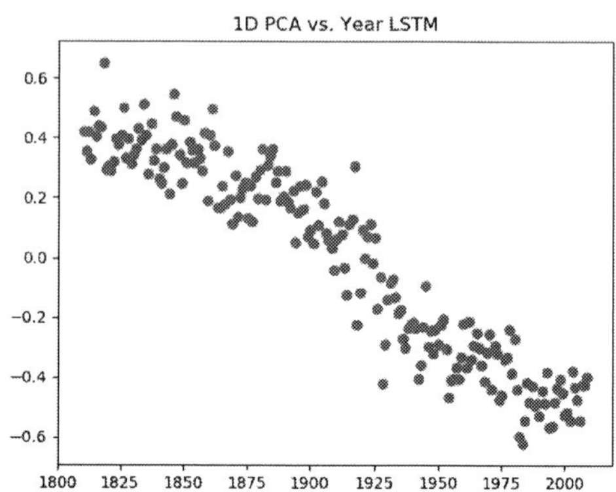

Figure 2: The first principal component of the LSTM year embeddings correlate strongly with time ($R^2 = 0.89$).

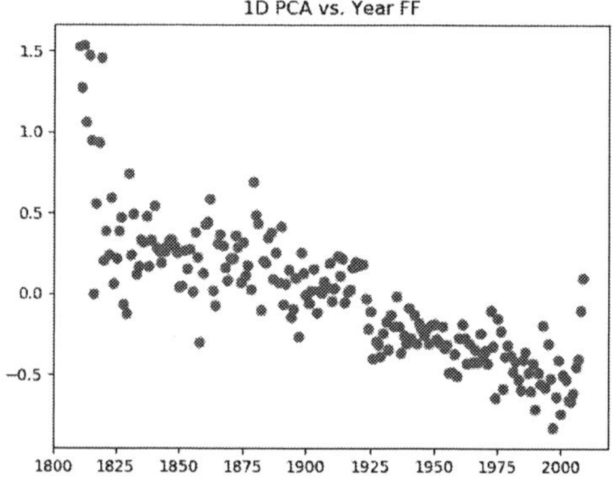

Figure 3: The first principal component of the feedforward year embeddings shows a weaker temporal trend than that of the LSTM ($R^2 = 0.68$).

	Baseline	Feedforward	LSTM
Decade	50.0	26.6	**12.5**
Year	50.0	37.5	**21.9**

Table 3: Average distance between each time period's center and the year that minimizes the perplexity value of the corresponding LOWESS curve. For the decade-level metric, the "center" is the middle year of the decade (1815 for 1810s). For the year-level metric, the "center" is the year itself (1803 for 1803).

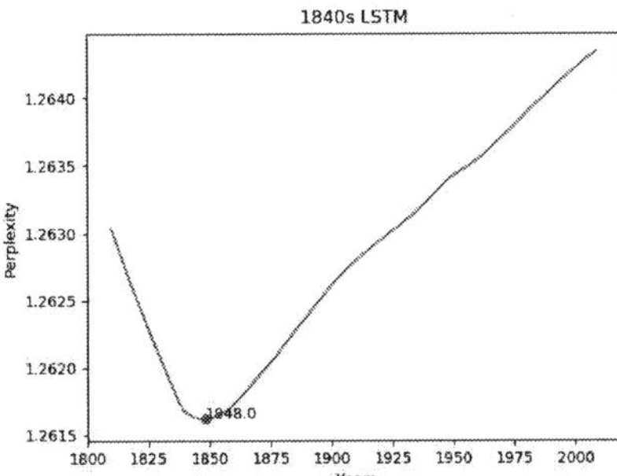

Figure 4: The 1840s LOWESS curve for the LSTM. The year 1848 corresponds to the minimum perplexity.

monotonic representation of change.

The feedforward network's temporal correlation was weaker ($R^2 = 0.68$) (see Figure 3). The discrepancy between the LSTM and feedforward R^2 values indicates that the LSTM does not only identify effects of lexical change, but also syntactic change.

3.3 Temporal Prediction

For both year and decade buckets, the LSTM predicted the years of composition of new sentences much better than the feedforward neural network or the baseline (see Table 3). We also confirmed our hypothesis that for both types of models the prediction error for decade buckets would be lower than for year buckets. Examples of some of the LSTM perplexity curves can be seen in Figures 4, 5, 6, 7, and 8. Examples of some of the feedforward curves can be seen in Figures 9 and 10. For all decades, the feedforward year of composition predictions tended to be skewed towards the middle years of the data set (late 1800s and early 1900s). These findings suggest that the representation of syntactic change learned by the LSTM can be leveraged to date new text.

We examined sample sentences whose years of composition were predicted well. We sam-

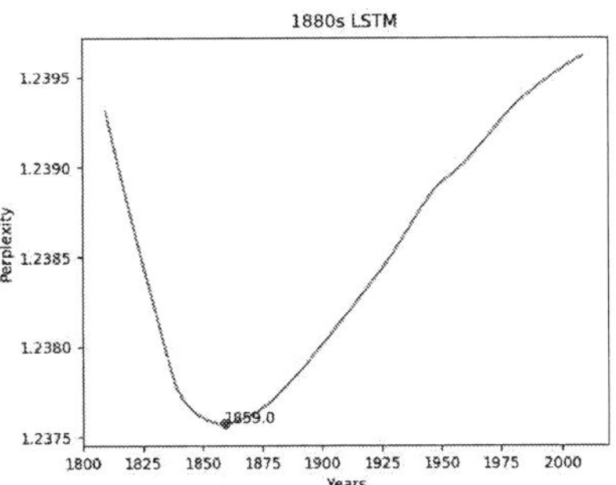

Figure 5: The 1880s LOWESS curve for the LSTM. The LSTM's prediction for this decade is weaker than for the other selected decades. The year corresponding to the minimum perplexity is 1859.

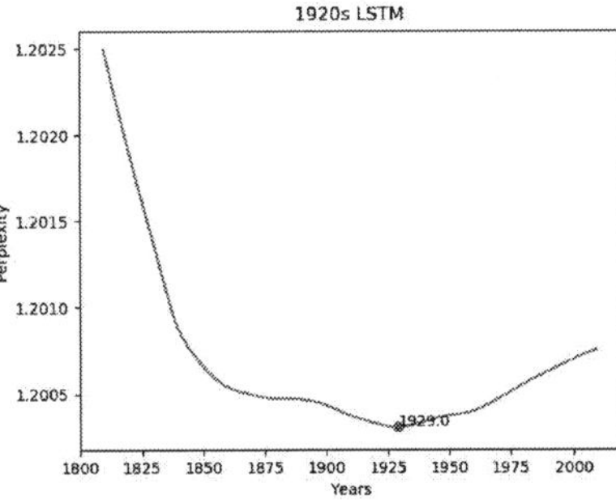

Figure 6: The 1920s LOWESS curve for the LSTM. The year 1929 corresponds to the minimum perplexity.

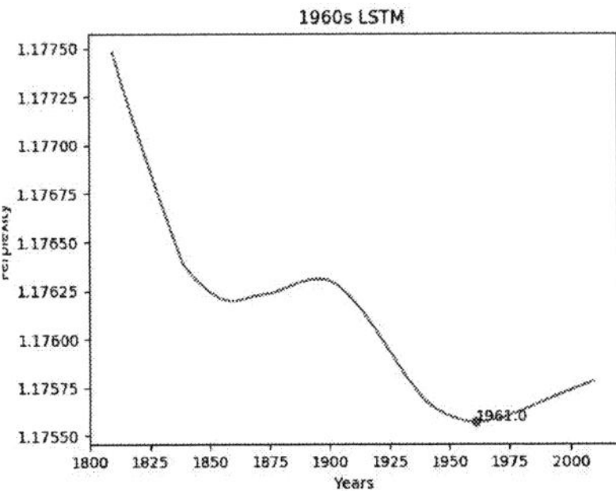

Figure 7: The 1960s LOWESS curve for the LSTM. The year 1961 corresponds to the minimum perplexity.

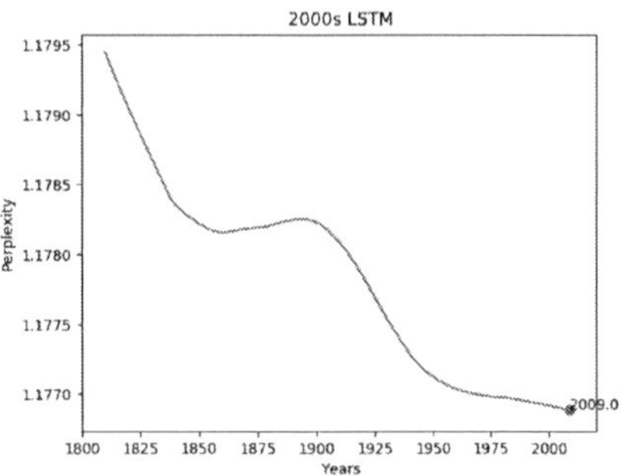

Figure 8: The 2000s LOWESS curve for the LSTM. The year 2009 corresponds to the minimum perplexity.

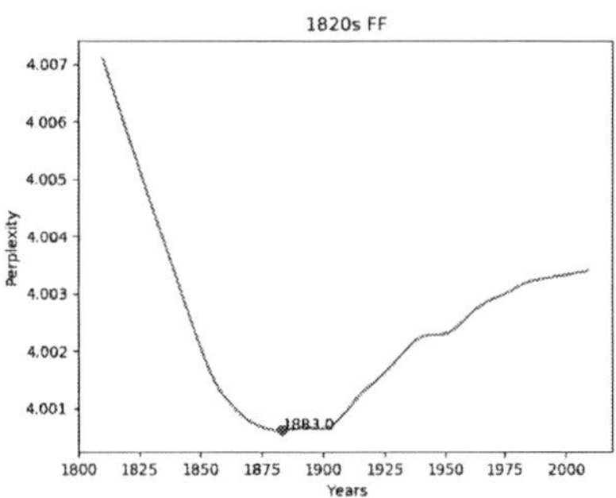

Figure 9: The 1820s LOWESS curve for the feedforward tagger. For this decade, the feedforward network is somewhat off as the year 1883 corresponds to the minimum perplexity. For the feedforward network, there is an evident bias across decades towards the late 1800s and early 1900s, which are the middle years of the data set.

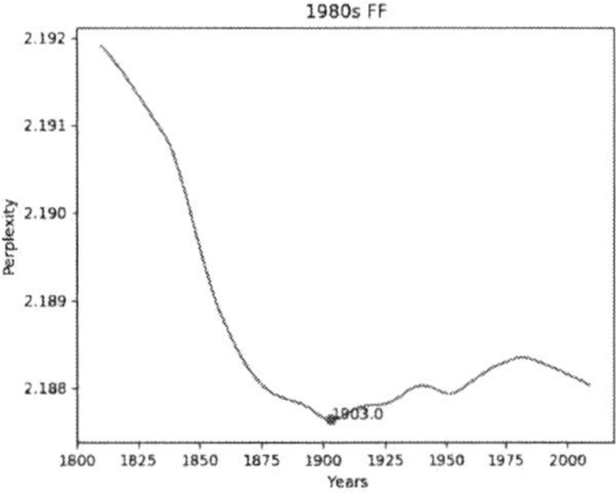

Figure 10: The 1980s LOWESS curve for the feedforward tagger. The feedforward network does not perform well for this decade. The year corresponding to the minimum perplexity, 1903, is somewhat far from the 1980s. Again there is an evident bias in prediction towards the middle years of the data set.

pled 1,000 test data set sentences. Of sentences longer than five words, we examined the ten sentences with the smallest errors (distance between the LSTM-predicted year of composition and the actual year of composition). For each of these sentences, we also calculated the error assigned to the sentence by the feedforward model in order to determine the extent to which syntax aided these predictions. These ten sentences are detailed in Table 4. Generally for these sentences, the feedforward error was comparable to or larger than the LSTM error, which suggests that syntactic information improved prediction for these sentences.

Sentence 1 (again, see Table 4) was one of seven sentences whose year of composition was predicted perfectly. This sentence's predicted year of composition was the same as its actual year of composition (1817). It makes sense that this sentence was predicted well since its syntax is qualitatively archaic. For example, it uses the uninflected subjunctive form *shine* whereas modern American English would prefer *shines*.

4 Conclusion

Through our PCA analysis of the year embeddings, we found that the LSTM learned to represent years in a chronological sequence without any biases imposed by initialization or architecture. The LSTM also effectively predicted the year of composition of novel sentences. Relative performance on these tasks indicates that the LSTM learns a stronger representation of time than the feedforward baseline. Therefore, the diachronic knowledge learned by the LSTM must encompass syntactic–not just lexical–change.

One conceptual puzzle with our results is how to reconcile the continuous notion of change represented by our model with the discreteness of natural language grammar. Some theories explain continuous grammatical change by positing that, at any given time, speakers have multiple grammars, or multiple options for syntactic parameters within a grammar (Aboh, 2015). The relative probabilities of different options can change gradually, permitting continuous grammatical change. Further work could use similar methods to examine how neural networks represent patterns of change in specific grammatical constructions. This analysis could evaluate the degree to which individual syntactic changes–rather than aggregate measures of change–are continuous.

Sentence	Year		Error	
	Pred	**True**	**FF**	**LSTM**
1. it is of great consequence, that we adorn the religion we profess, and that our light shine more and more that we grow in grace as we advance in years, and that we do not resemble the changing wind or the inconstant wave.	1817	1817	86	0
2. what extenuations or omissions had vitiated his former or recent narrative; how far his actual performances were congenial with the deed which was now to be perpetrated, i knew not.	1827	1827	0	0
3. that an unlimited power of making gifts could be narrowed down, by any process of reasoning, to the idea of a grant to an indian, a reward loan informer, and much less to a mere sale for money.	1833	1833	16	0
4. "amiable, generous, kindhearted woman! thou wert anxious to procure for thy poor, afflicted, aged mother, all the repose which her advanced life seemed to require, to wipe away the tear from her dimmed eye and farrowed cheek, and as far as	1817	1817	10	0
5. count when shall we meet again? ther.	1821	1821	11	0
6. in some instances, upon killing them after a full year's deprivation of all nourishment, as much as three gallons of perfectly sweet and fresh water have been found in their bags.	1838	1838	21	0
7. that's a good way to think about me.	1996	1996	12	0
8. the contention between the wife of abraham and her egyptian handmaid, has already been the subject of animadversion; but although their histories are considerably blended, some features in the character of the latter, and some affecting circumstances of her life, have been hitherto omitted,	1816	1817	0	1
9. but what happens when your erotic adventure is stifled by an unwelcome companion, such as a roommate? masturbating in a UNK situation does pose some problems, but where there is a will, there is a way.	2003	2002	22	1
10. it is UNK in truth we are an united people it is true but we are, family united only for external objects; for our common defence, and for the purpose of a common commerce; sharing, in com mop, the UNK and privations of war	1826	1827	3	1

Table 4: Sentences whose years of composition were predicted best by the LSTM model. The table includes the actual and predicted years of composition, and the feedforward and LSTM error measures.

References

Enoch Olad Aboh. 2015. *The Emergence of Hybrid Grammars: Language Contact and Change*. Cambridge Approaches to Language Contact. Cambridge University Press.

Mark Davies. 2010-. The corpus of historical American English: 400 million words, 1810-2009.

Haim Dubossarsky, Daphna Weinshall, and Eitan Grossman. 2017. Outta control: Laws of semantic change and inherent biases in word representation models. In *Proceedings of the 2017 Conference on Empirical Methods in Natural Language Processing*, pages 1136–1145, Copenhagen, Denmark. Association for Computational Linguistics.

William L. Hamilton, Jure Leskovec, and Dan Jurafsky. 2016. Diachronic word embeddings reveal statistical laws of semantic change. In *Proceedings of the 54th Annual Meeting of the Association for Computational Linguistics (Volume 1: Long Papers)*, pages 1489–1501, Berlin, Germany. Association for Computational Linguistics.

Eun Seo Jo, Dai Shen, and Michael Xing. 2017. Backprop to the future: A neural network approach to linguistic change over time. Manuscript, Stanford University.

Tomas Mikolov, Kai Chen, Greg Corrado, and Jeffrey Dean. 2013. Efficient estimation of word representations in vector space. *CoRR*, abs/1301.3781.

Partha Niyogi and Robert C. Berwick. 1995. The logical problem of language change. Technical report. AI Memo 1516, Artificial Intelligence Laboratory, MIT.

Grammar and meaning:
Analysing the topology of diachronic word embeddings

Yuri Bizzoni
Saarland University

yuri.bizzoni@uni-saarland.de

Stefania Degaetano-Ortlieb
Saarland University

s.degaetano@mx.uni-saarland.de

Katrin Menzel
Saarland University

k.menzel@mx.uni-saarland.de

Pauline Krielke
Saarland University

mariepauline.krielke@uni-saarland.de

Elke Teich
Saarland University

e.teich@mx.uni-saarland.de

Abstract

The paper showcases the application of word embeddings to change in language use in the domain of science, focusing on the Late Modern English period (17-19th century). Historically, this is the period in which many registers of English developed, including the language of science. Our overarching interest is the linguistic development of scientific writing to a distinctive (group of) register(s). A register is marked not only by the choice of lexical words (discourse domain) but crucially by grammatical choices which indicate style. The focus of the paper is on the latter, tracing words with primarily grammatical functions (function words and some selected, polyfunctional word forms) diachronically. To this end, we combine diachronic word embeddings with appropriate visualization and exploratory techniques such as clustering and relative entropy for meaningful aggregation of data and diachronic comparison.

1 Introduction

Word embeddings are by now a well established instrument for exploring and comparing corpora in terms of lexical fields and semantic richness (Lenci, 2008). More recently, diachronic word embeddings have been successfully applied to investigate lexical semantic change (e.g. Jatowt and Duh (2014); Hamilton et al. (2016a); Hellrich and Hahn (2016); Fankhauser and Kupietz (2017); Hellrich et al. (2018)). We supplement this line of work using diachronic word embeddings for the analysis of *change in grammatical use*, potentially indicating shifts in style/register. Word embeddings reflect shared usage contexts not only of lexical words but also of grammatical words. By grammatical words we understand function words (determiners, conjunctions, etc.) as well

as some other specific word forms, such as *wh*-pronouns or *ing*-forms of verbs. Typically, the latter are poly-functional (e.g. verbal *ing*-forms can be gerunds, participles or markers of present continuous). Function words are high-frequency words and affected by change only in the long term (e.g. by becoming clitics or bound forms), while lexical words, typically in the lower frequency band, tend to change (meaning) fast. If pressure arises for grammar to change (e.g. for more economical expression), it will likely affect the poly-functional word forms first, which can spread to new syntagmatic environments or attract new lexemes and extend paradigmatically (like lexical words, unlike function words). To capture such developments, we employ diachronic word embeddings with visualization of word clusters on a diachronic axis combined with some other exploratory techniques, such as clustering and relative entropy. For instance, spread of a word/word form will result in the word moving in the overall embedding space, or paradigmatic extension will result in locally higher populate, denser spaces. Comparing lexical words, function words and poly-functional word forms, we inspect the overall topology of the embedding space over time as well as capture the internal composition of (selected) individual sub-spaces.

As a data set we use the Royal Society Corpus (RSC) (Kermes et al., 2016), a diachronic corpus of the Philosophical Transactions and the Proceedings of the Royal Society of London, which includes text material that is linguistically well explored in terms of style, register and diachrony (e.g. Biber and Finegan (1997); Atkinson (1999); Banks (2008); Degaetano-Ortlieb et al. (2018)).

Following related work (Section 2), we present our data and methods (Section 3). In Section 4, we analyze the embedding space in terms of change

175

Proceedings of the 1st International Workshop on Computational Approaches to Historical Language Change, pages 175–185
Florence, Italy, August 2, 2019. ©2019 Association for Computational Linguistics

in overall topology as well as changes in selected clusters. Zooming in on *ing*-forms, we also micro-inspect their (changing) syntagmatic contexts. We conclude with a summary and future work directions (Section 5).

2   Related work

Quantitative corpus-based approaches to language change (e.g. Hilpert (2006); Geeraerts et al. (2011); Sagi et al. (2011); Hilpert and Gries (2016)) share the basic assumption that language use is governed by statistical properties of lexical and grammatical items. In recent years, distributional semantic approaches based on word embeddings, often combined with clustering, capture this assumption in a bottom-up fashion, allowing to model semantic similarity of words from corpora. Approaches such as `word2vec` (Mikolov et al., 2013) and `SVD_PPMI` (Levy and Goldberg, 2014; Levy et al., 2015) trained on corpora covering several time spans allow investigating changes in the semantic usage of lexical items over time (Jatowt and Duh, 2014; Kim et al., 2014; Kulkarni et al., 2015; Hamilton et al., 2016a; Hellrich and Hahn, 2016). To also capture syntactic information, approaches have been developed that account for word order based on structured skip-gram models (Ling et al., 2015) and clustering the model output (Dubossarsky et al., 2015; Fankhauser and Kupietz, 2017).

Particularly targeted at the digital humanities as well as socio-historical corpus-linguistics are approaches which also allow meaningful ways to inspect the data. For instance, Hellrich et al. (2018) provide a visualization website (JeSemE) to inspect change in word meaning over time by means of line and bar plots considering different comparative parameters (word similarity, word emotion, typical context, and relative frequency); Fankhauser and Kupietz (2017) provide a visualization of change in the distributional semantics of words combined with their relative frequency over time.

3   Data and Methods

3.1   Data

As a data set we use v4.0 of the Royal Society Corpus (RSC)[1], containing the publications of the Philosophical Transactions and Proceedings of the

<hr>

[1]Available open source at `http://fedora.clarin-d.uni-saarland.de/rsc_v4/`

Royal Society of London from 1665 to 1869 (ca. 32 million tokens and 10,000 documents). The RSC contains various types of metadata (e.g. author, publication date, text title) and linguistic annotations (e.g. lemma, parts of speech, sentence boundaries). Table 1 gives further statistics on the corpus.

decade	tokens	lemma	sentences
1660-69	455,259	369,718	10,860
1670-79	831,190	687,285	17,957
1680-89	573,018	466,795	13,230
1690-99	723,389	581,821	17,886
1700-09	780,721	615,770	23,338
1710-19	489,857	383,186	17,510
1720-29	538,145	427,016	12,499
1730-39	599,977	473,164	16,444
1740-49	1,006,093	804,523	26,673
1750-59	1,179,112	919,169	34,162
1760-69	972,672	734,938	27,506
1770-79	1,501,388	1,146,489	41,412
1780-89	1,354,124	1,052,006	37,082
1790-99	1,335,484	1,043,913	36,727
1800-09	1,615,564	1,298,978	45,666
1810-19	1,446,900	1,136,581	42,998
1820-29	1,408,473	1,064,613	43,701
1830-39	2,613,486	2,035,107	81,500
1840-49	2,028,140	1,565,654	70,745
1850-59	4,610,380	3,585,299	146,085
1860-69	5,889,353	4,474,432	202,488
total	31,952,725	24,866,457	966,469

Table 1: Corpus statistics of the RSC per decade

3.2   Diachronic word embeddings

For computing word embeddings on a diachronic corpus, we follow the approach of Fankhauser and Kupietz (2017) – based on the structured skip-gram method described in Ling et al. (2015) with a one-hot encoding for words as input layer, a 200-dimensional hidden layer, and a window of [-5,5] as the output layer. Importantly, as this approach takes into account word order, it will capture grammatical patterns in word usage.

Word embeddings are calculated for each decade of the RSC. The embeddings for the first decade are initialized with a first-run training on the whole corpus, and subsequently refined for each decade of the 20 decades taken into consideration (1670–1860). The vocabulary of the models consists of a total of 117.165 100-dimensional points. The vocabulary consists only of "spaced" tokens (i.e. divided by space or punctuation in the original text). Multiword expressions and phrases are not taken into account, to maintain the original modelling as agnostic as possible about the content of the corpus. The models were

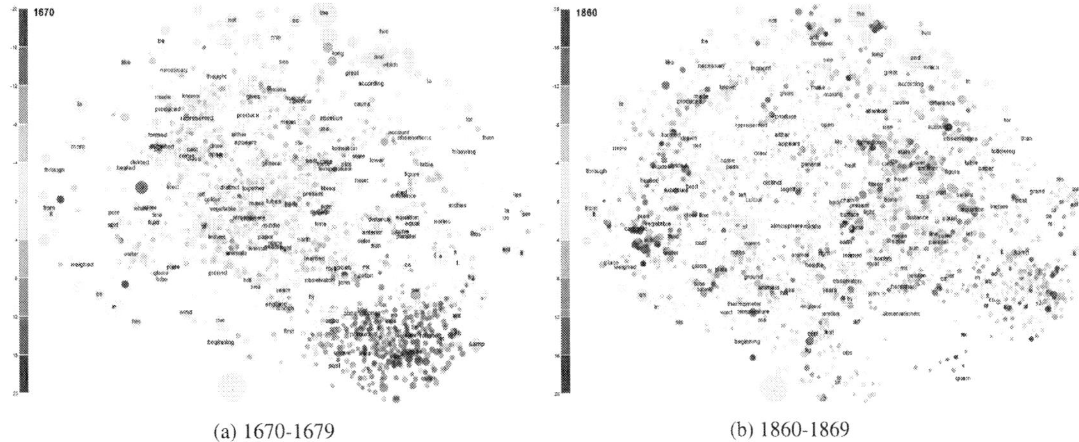

(a) 1670-1679   (b) 1860-1869

Figure 1: Diachronic word embeddings of the 1670s and 1860s decades of RSC. Color denoting increasing (red) and decreasing (green) frequency. Size of the bubbles denoting relative frequency.

trained on non-lemmatized text. For interpretability, Fankhauser and Kupietz apply dimensionality reduction using t-Distributed Stochastic Neighbor Embedding by Maaten and Hinton (2008). Finally, a dynamic, interactive visualization of the resulting embeddings is provided which covers two crucial factors involved in diachronic change: *frequency* (encoded by colour – shades of violet-blue for decreasing frequency, shades of red-orange for increasing frequency) and *similarity in context of use* (encoded by proximity in space). For an example see Figure 1a. This allows us to explore changes in word use as shown in Section 4. As in most studies regarding distributional semantics, we will use cosine distance to compute the similarity between words in the space.

3.3 Investigating change in grammatical use

The large majority of studies performed on diachronic corpora through embedding spaces focuses on lexical semantics: to analyze changes in the distance between specific words over time (Szymanski, 2017), to infer semantic changes between specific categories of words, e.g. words referring to specific objects or concepts (Recchia et al., 2016), or to model the development of new terms with respect to the existing "neighborhoods" to infer their emergent semantic profile (Gangal et al., 2017).

But embedding spaces can be used to go beyond the study of change in lexical meaning (Jenset, 2013; Perek, 2016; Lenci, 2011), as they capture, to varying degrees, both paradigmatic and syntag-

matic properties of words[2]. The same methods used for lexical words can be applied to grammatical words (as defined in Section 1): measuring the distance of individual words from their neighbours, mapping the evolution from their original position in the space, the nearest neighbour similarity, the similarity to other specifically selected words etc. Operating on grammatical words in the same way in which we traditionally operate on lexical words can return interesting observations, exactly as happens studying lexical words. Polyfunctional grammatical words, such as *ing*-forms, are at the boundary between lexis and grammar and are therefore particularly interesting because they can give us insights on the interplay between lexis and grammar. We outline here two main phenomena pertaining to the interplay between lexical semantics and grammatical function in distributional spaces: (1) diachronic expansion of the space; (2) diachronic clustering of poly-functional words with *ing*-forms as an exemplary case.

Considering (1), we measure average distances of lexical and function words as well as polyfunctional word forms. Average distance is the average of the mean distances of each word from the rest of the vocabulary. In addition, we consider the average distance between words within a group (henceforth: inner distance), and the aver-

---

[2]For example, verbs in the past tense have a tendency to cluster with other verbs in the past tense with similar semantic properties, and verbs in the present continuous have a tendency to cluster with other verbs in the present continuous. The "window" size and the type of distribution taken into consideration of course have an important role in magnifying or blurring this aspect of words' distributional profile.

177

age distance of the group from all other words in the space (henceforth: outer distance). Change in inner distance reflects how much the words remain close to each other or drift apart in meaning/usage. Change in outer distance reflects how much semantically similar words become more isolated from all other words, possibly indicating a trend towards more specialized meaning/usage.

Considering (2), we operate in two main steps: (i) We first explore the sub-space of *ing*-forms to see whether meaningful clusters of verbs can be suspected. We do this by simply looking at verbs that have near neighbours, setting a threshold for what we consider *near*[3]. Through this very simple system, we elaborate an idea of what *kinds* of verbs are likely to constitute the clusters we are interested in. (ii) Once we have formed a hypothesis about the structure of the sub-space, we run some fairly popular algorithms of clustering and compare their results with our predictions and interpretations. This double step rises from the conviction that unsupervised clustering algorithms require a hypothesis about the structure of the data to both set their parameters and interpret their results, and that such hypothesis has to be acquired through an exploration of the space.

3.4 Investigating syntagmatic context

For further insights, we inspect the syntagmatic context of selected clusters of *ing*-forms extracting part-of-speech ngrams preceding an *ing*. We then use relative entropy (here: pointwise Kullback-Leibler Divergence (KLD; Kullback and Leibler (1951); Fankhauser et al. (2014); Tomokiyo and Hurst (2003)) to measure how distinctive particular syntagmatic contexts are for particular time periods. This is performed for each inspected feature (in our case a syntagmatic context in terms of a part-of-speech ngram, e.g. preposition-noun-*ing*-verb) comparing two time periods, $T1$ and $T2$ (cf. Equation (1)).

$$D_{feature}(T1||T2) = p(feature|T1)log_2\frac{p(feature|T1)}{p(feature|T2)}$$
$$(1)$$

Basically, the probability of a feature in a time period $T1$ ($p(feature|T1)$) is compared to that feature in time period $T2$ ($p(feature|T2)$), i.e.

the ratio of $T1$ vs. $T2$. To obtain features distinctive of $T1$ the ratio is weighted with the probability of that feature in $T1$. To obtain features distinctive of $T2$, the ratio between $T2$ and $T1$ is calculated and weighted by the feature's probability in $T2$. Divergence is measured in bits of information: the higher the amount of bits, the more the feature is distinctive of a given time period.

4 Analyses

In the analysis, we inspect (1) changes in the overall topology of the embedding space over time, and (2) the development of *ing*-forms of verbs.

4.1 Topology of the overall embedding space over time

Figures 1a and 1b show the embedding spaces for the RSC's first (1670s) and last (1860s) full decades. Most function words (e.g. *the, and, from*) are isolated in both decades indicating their functional status. Lexical words (e.g. verbs, nouns, adjectives), instead, cluster in one large group in the middle. Considering diachronic development, apart from local clusters disappearing altogether (e.g. a cluster of Latin, marked in blue), a visible general trend is the expansion of the overall space to smaller, more spread out and more separated clusters. Thus, the distance between words seems to increase in general, possibly indicating a process of specialization at word level. We test this for three cases: all words, function words and two poly-functional word forms (*ing*- and *-ed* forms of verbs).

All words. Analysing the spaces diachronically, we find that most lexical words[4] tend to drift further from each other over time. This does not mean that they do not form lexico-semantic clusters, but the average distance of each word from both its nearest neighbours (inner distance) and every other word in the space increases (outer distance) (see again Figure 2). Considering different sets of words in the spaces' vocabulary, we observe the same phenomenon: the average distributional distance tends to increase, both within the group (inner distance), and between the group and the rest of the lexicon (outer distance). In Figure 2 we show how this trend is clearly detectable in our spaces, independently of the words' frequencies. It can also be noted that the low frequency

---

[3]We will use a dynamic threshold for this task (see Section 4.2.2)

[4]Here, lexical words are all words that are not conjunctions, prepositions or adpositions.

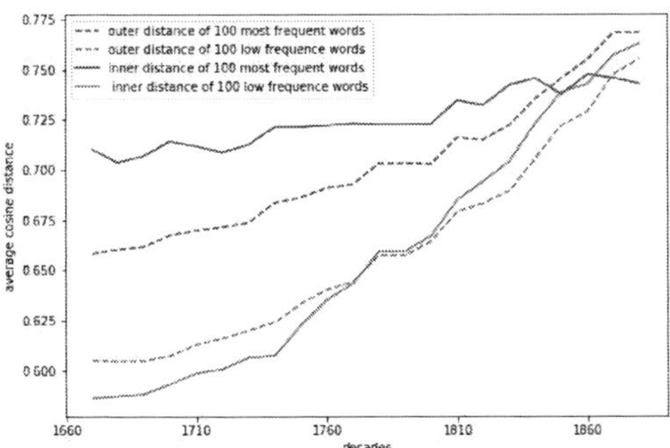

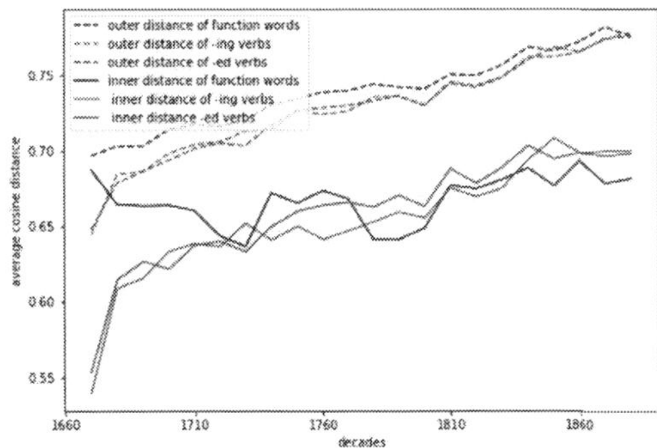

Figure 3: Inner and outer distances for function words, *ed*-verbs, and *ing*-verbs.

Figure 2: Diachronic increase of average distance of words. Average distance: mean of the mean distances of each word from the rest of the vocabulary. Selection of two groups: 100 high and 100 low frequency words in every decade. Inner distance: average distance between words within the group. Outer distance: average distance of the group from all other words in the space.

words maintain most of the time a lower average distance than high frequency words. We consider this a hint that the reason of the expansion of the space is due to *specialization*: the tail of the frequency curve tends to contain many highly technical words, with particularly specialized meanings. These words usually, while being far from the rest of the vocabulary, have a low number of very close neighbours, which represent those few words that happen to share similar specialized contexts. This is often considered an indication of single and specialized meaning (Hamilton et al., 2016b). In fact, words having a frequency lower than three in each decade have, on average, one neighbour which is considerably closer than the closest neighbour of highly frequent words (0.84 vs 0.71 cosine similarity on average). This all leads to the conclusion that the underlying mechanism is lexical specialization.

Function words. If we compare these general distributional behaviours to the behaviour of only function words (here: determiners, conjunctions and adpositions), we observe an interesting difference: function words tend to have an increasingly "reclusive" tendency. While their outer distance increases (see Figure 3), the inner distance stays stable. In other terms, while the average lexical word in our corpus undergoes a process of contextual specialization, function words do not.

Poly-functional word forms. If lexical words undergo expansion in both directions (inner and outer distance), while function words only show an increase in the outer distance, we can assume that the increase in distances is due to the lexico-semantic side of words rather than their functional-grammatical side. This becomes particularly clear when we look at poly-functional word forms which share a common formal feature (e.g., suffix *ed*), but not a common semantic belonging. For example, the average inner distance between *ed*-forms of verbs[5], while increasing over time (see Figure 3), remains lower than their average outer distance: their grammatical side shows its effect on their distributional behaviour, somehow in tension with their semantic change. Among *ing*-forms of verbs, the same tension can be observed: the inner and outer distances both increase, but their inner distance remains smaller. Compare also trends in Figure 3, where the difference between inner and outer distance is immediately evident (outer distance always higher), with those in Figure 2, where such difference does not seem to retain a particular importance. See also Figure 4 for an exemplification of this semantic–grammatical tension.

4.2 Tracing the development of *ing*-forms

We have observed that for poly-functional word forms, which are very much "in between" lexis and grammar, inner distance grows more slowly. To analyze this phenomenon in more detail, we focus on *ing*-forms of verbs.

---

[5]We operate here under the somewhat simplistic assumption that verbs ending in *ed* represent the majority of past tenses.

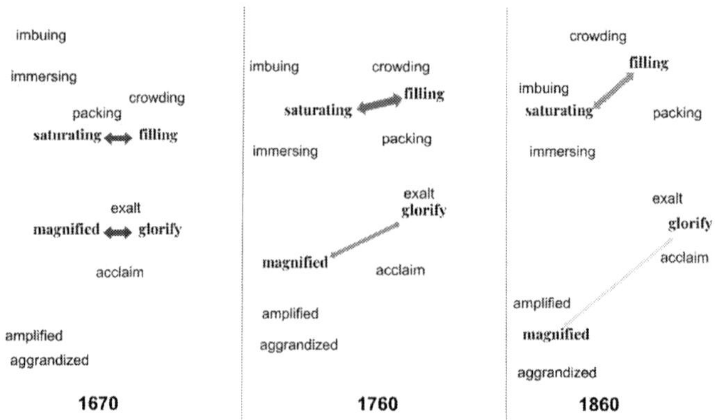

Figure 4: Example of semantic—grammatical tension. Two couples of verbs undergoing a semantic diversification (the left-side verbs become more specialized in meaning). In the lower side of the space, the two verbs have both semantic and grammatical differences. In the upper side of the space, the verbs have a growing semantic distance, but their grammatical profile remains similar; thus their distance grows more slowly.

4.2.1 Diachronic frequency distribution of *ing*-forms

In a first step, to obtain a better understanding of the frequency distribution of *ing*-verb forms in the RSC corpus, we extract all verbs part-of-speech tagged as "gerunds or present participles" (VVG, VBG, VHG). Verbs with this tag include progressives, but exclude other verbs ending in -*ing* (e.g. *sing*, *bring*) or other parts of speech (e.g. *morning*, *spring*). We observe a fairly stable diachronic tendency. In addition, scientific writing is known to use *ing*-verbs most prominently as gerunds and participles rather than progressives (Biber et al., 1999). Indeed, the progressive form (i.e. BE + *ing*-verb) is quite infrequent in the RSC overall and it is declining over time; i.e. 250 occurrences of progressive per million tokens in the 1860s in 13,000 occurrences/million of ing-*forms* altogether.

4.2.2 Inspecting clusters of *ing*-forms

We consider all *ing*-forms per decade and consider as a cluster all neighbours closer than a given threshold distance. In this way, we can analyze (1) how close to other words *ing*-forms are on average, (2) how large their average cluster is (i.e. no. of words in a cluster), and (3) how much they tend to cluster with each other (i.e. whether and which *ing*-forms tend to occur in other *ing*-forms' neighbourhoods).

To build clusters we use a *dynamic* threshold. We set this threshold empirically to the decade's average distance of the nearest neighbours + .05. Thus, for each decade we can see which *ing*-forms have the highest number of "near" neigh-

bours, and how many large clusters are formed, despite the general expansion of the space. From this exploratory analysis we observe that, first, despite our dynamic threshold, the density (i.e. number of words per cluster) of *ing*-clusters diminishes over time. We ascribe this effect, like the more general expansion of the space, mostly to the lexical-semantic component of the verbs involved: their meaning becomes more specific, their context more specialized – and thus less overlap between their contexts is observed. At the same time, the words that are at the *center* of a cluster (i.e. words with relatively large and close neighbourhoods) appear to belong to three increasingly distinct categories.

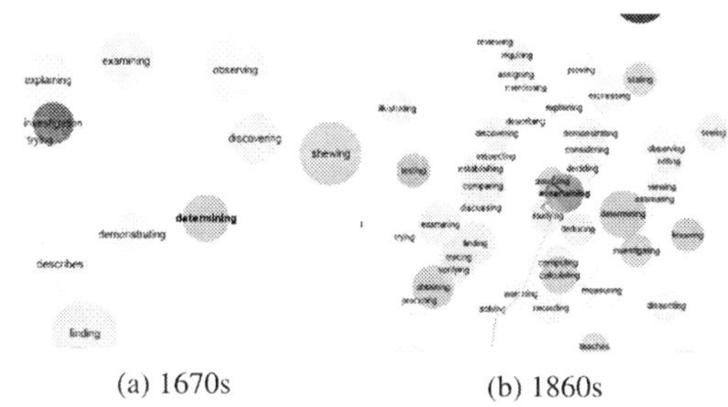

(a) 1670s   (b) 1860s

Figure 5: Academic *ing*-verbs in the RSC

The most prominent category are so-called *academic verbs*, such as *ascertaining, determining, examining* etc. acquiring relatively tight and large neighbourhoods (see Figure 5a and 5b[6]).

---

[6]Figure 5b showing the diachronic trajectory of *ascertaining* moving towards the center of the cluster. Color of the trajectory denoting frequency (green: lower/red: higher)

The complementary analysis of the most frequent neighbours (words that occur most frequently in other words' close neighbourhood) shows the same phenomenon: academic verbs rise in frequency. The two other main categories we observe at the center of large clusters are *change-of-state* verbs (*saturating, diluting*, etc.) and *motion* verbs (*passing, falling*, etc.).

4.2.3 Clustering specialized vs. broader meanings

Based on the above findings, which gave us a general idea of possible clusters, we can now apply some traditional clustering algorithms to our dataset. We will show the results of three algorithms: Affinity Propagation (AP) (Frey and Dueck, 2007), DBSCAN (Ester et al., 1996; Tran et al., 2013), and MiniBatch K Means (Sculley, 2010; Feizollah et al., 2014). Results are presented in Table 2.

Affinity Propagation, much like DBSCAN, does not require a pre-determined number of clusters, i.e. it defines its own number of centroids. While usually seen as an advantage, in our case it could result in a flaw: these algorithms tend towards a micro-clustering (clustering tight relationships), leading to many small clusters of specialized meanings of *ing*-verbs. This would probably shadow the larger and looser clustering resulting from a possible interplay of semantics with more grammatical classes of *ing*-verbs. In fact, Affinity Propagation individuates a large number of *ing*-clusters, and most relevant, an *increasing* number of *ing*-clusters over time. What we see here is lexico-semantic specialization at work: every cluster contains "few" words semantically very close, e.g. *drawing - tracing, preceding - foregoing*.

DBSCAN does not require a pre-determined number of clusters either, but a fixed threshold and a fix minimum of neighbours to consider members of a cluster. While the number of centroids is lower than the number found by Affinity Propagation, it still increases over time.

Unlike the previous two algorithms, MiniBatch K Means requires a heavier pre-interpretation of the data: we need to know how many clusters we are looking for. While usually seen as a disadvantage, once we have more than an educated guess – thanks to our previous exploration of the data – it can turn into a strength: we can force the algorithm to look beyond the most evident micro-clusters and define a larger subdivision of the space. In fact, once we use the K Means algorithm on the *ing*-subspace, setting the number of centroids to 3 (the number of verb classes we have observed through our exploration in Section 4.2.2), we obtain results that are very close to our observations. The verbs falling in the three groups more and more pertain to what we would call academic, change-of-state, and motion verbs (see Table 2, 1860s decade). The centroids determined by the MiniBatch K Means algorithm for these three clusters grow further apart through time, and especially from the beginning of the 19th century we can detect a growing distributional difference between the three centroids of these clusters.

4.2.4 Grammatical classes of *ing*-clusters

To observe whether the use of these main *ing*-clusters differs in terms of grammatical class (gerund vs. participle), we further inspect their syntagmatic context. For this, we generate lists of the top 30 verbs derived from the clusters and extract their preceding part-of-speech ngrams to observe how their use varies in syntactic context. Using Kullback-Leibler Divergence we can inspect which possible grammatical classes (i.e. gerund vs. participle) are distinctive of later time periods in comparison to earlier time periods considering each semantic group of verbs (i.e. academic, change-of-state, motion).

Figure 6 shows the frequency distribution of the three clusters across decades in the RSC. Change-of-state verbs (e.g. *purifying, warming, cooling*) seem to remain relatively stable, showing only a very slight increase. Motion verbs (e.g. *passing, extending, running*) increase especially after 1820. Verbs belonging to the academic semantic sub-space rise until 1810 and decline afterwards. It seems that the beginning of the 19th century (1810-1840) marks a period of change.

Using relative entropy, we compare the part-of-speech ngrams of the three main clusters (academic, motion, and change-of-state verbs in *ing*-form) for the period preceding the 1810s and the period after the 1840s (i.e. 1660-1810 vs. 1850-1869). Table 3 shows the top five ngrams for each cluster, ranked by KLD. By inspecting the grammatical class of each ngram, we see a clear difference between the academic and the motion clusters: while verbs in the academic *ing*-cluster are used as gerunds, those in the motion *ing*-cluster are used as participles. Change-of-state *ing*-verbs are also most distinctively used as gerunds. This

Decade	Affinity Propagation (AP)	DBSCAN	Minibatch KMeans
1660	*Extending, reaching, proceeding. Crying, coughing, sweating. Shading, scattering, tracing.*	*Abounding, according, adding. Whiting, widening, willing.*	*Detaching, wetting, squeezing. Verifying, deciding, transferring. Playing, retiring, accumulating.*
1760	*Pricking, stimulating, snapping. Following, lowing, preceding. Informing, troubling, acquainting.*	*Abating, abounding, abstracting. Lessening. Deducting, subtracting, weighing.*	*Arranging, attaching, immersing. Arranging, studying, illustrating. Interlacing, arranging, transforming.*
1860	*Nourishing, binding, imbibing. Snapping, widening, pricking. Stimulating, promoting, biting.*	*Abounding, absorbing, abstracting. Integrating, introducing, putting. Arching, running, sweeping.*	*Determining, establishing, studying. Passing, extending, running. Purifying, agitating, warming.*

Table 2: Clusters of *ing-* forms with AP, DBSCAN and KMeans.

POS ngram	class	relative entropy (KLD)	example
Academic verbs			
SENT.IN.VVG	Gerund	0.0620	*. **In examining** the laws*
VVN.IN.VVG	Gerund	0.0587	*the formulae **employed in finding** these logarithms*
NN.IN.VVG	Gerund	0.0492	*Potasse for the **purpose of ascertaining** whether*
IN.RB.VVG	Gerund	0.0183	*opportunity **of sufficiently investigating** the errors*
SENT.RB.VVG	Gerund	0.0110	*. **Hence considering** an equation*
Motion verbs			
JJ.NN.VVG	Participle	0.0412	*the **smaller extremity lying** in contact with*
(...VVG	Participle	0.0370	*the tangential force (F), **forming** two equal*
JJ.NNS.VVG	Participle	0.0362	*refracting the **visual rays passing** thorough them*
IN.NNS.VVG	Participle	0.0327	*dark cloud **of ashes falling** from the volcano*
SENT.IN.VVG	Gerund	0.0270	*. **After passing** the central layer*
Change-of-state verbs			
VVN.IN.VVG	Gerund	0.1116	*more strongly **magnetized by placing** them*
SENT.IN.VVG	Gerund	0.0630	*. **By heating** it to above the boiling*
VVZ.IN.VVG	Gerund	0.0590	***crystallizes on cooling***
NN.,.VVG	Participle	0.0254	*a deep oblique **fold , penetrating** from the inner side*
JJ.NN.VVG	Participle	0.0235	*the **chylo-aqueous fluid filling** the ciliated*

IN: preposition, JJ: adjective, NN(S): common noun (pl.), RB: adverb, SENT: full stop, VVG: *ing*-form, VVN: participle, VVZ: present tense

Table 3: Top five part-of-speech ngrams of each verb cluster distinctive for the 1850s period (1850-69 vs. 1660-1800)

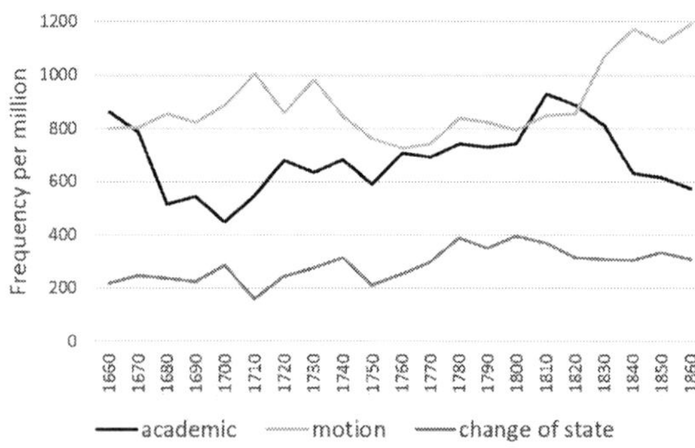

Figure 6: Frequency distribution of main clusters in the RSC

shows that besides capturing semantic relatedness, the diachronic word embeddings also capture grammatical use.

5 Conclusion

We have shown an analysis of diachronic word embeddings based on a diachronic corpus of English scientific writing. The aim of the analysis has been to trace changes in the embeddings of words with grammatical functions (function words, polyfunctional word forms) compared to lexical words. Analyzing the changing topology of the embedding space over time, operating with the notions of inner and outer distance (see Section 3), we were able to show that grammatical words behave differently from lexical words (Section 4). Specifically, we focused on words that have both a lexical meaning and specific grammatical functions, exemplified by *ing-* and *ed*-forms of verbs, because it seemed to us that such forms are common hosts for short to mid-term change in language use in scientific language. Here, we showed that *ing*-forms of verbs form three semantic groups (academic, motion and change-of-state), where change-of-state and academic verbs tend to be gerunds and motion verbs tend to be used as participles.

Methodologically, we showed that diachronic word embeddings are well suited to detect change not only in lexical but also in grammatical use as well as the interplay of lexis and grammar. Diachronic word embeddings combined with informative visualization and appropriate exploratory techniques (here: clustering and relative entropy) presents a powerful tool to investigate changing language use.

In our future work, we plan to inspect other poly-functional words and word forms, such as *wh*-words, because they seem to be involved in the development of scientific style as well. At the level of lexical words, we plan to analyze the embedding space in terms of domain-specific vocabulary. As mentioned in our analyses in various places, the overall trend in scientific vocabulary is specialization. To form distinctive registers (e.g., the language of chemistry, physics, medicine, etc.), vocabulary needs to become diversified. To track diversification related to register formation is therefore a high priority on our research agenda.

Acknowledgments

This work has been supported by *Deutsche Forschungsgemeinschaft* (DFG) under grant 'SFB 1102: Information Density and Linguistic Encoding'. We thank Peter Fankhauser for the initial implementation and visualization of word embeddings for the RSC.

References

Dwight Atkinson. 1999. *Scientific Discourse in Socio-historical Context: The Philosophical Transactions of the Royal Society of London, 1675-1975*. Erlbaum, New York.

David Banks. 2008. *The Development of Scientific Writing: Linguistic Features and Historical Context*. Equinox, London/Oakville.

Douglas Biber and Edward Finegan. 1997. Diachronic Relations among Speech-based and Written Registers in English. In Terttu Nevalainen and Leena Kahlas-Tarkka, editors, *To Explain the Present: Studies in the Changing English Language in Honour of Matti Rissanen*, pages 253–276. Société Néophilologique, Helsinki.

Douglas Biber, Stig Johansson, Geoffrey Leech, Susan Conrad, and Edward Finegan. 1999. *Longman Grammar of Spoken and Written English*. Longman, Harlow, UK.

Stefania Degaetano-Ortlieb, Hannah Kermes, Ashraf Khamis, and Elke Teich. 2018. An Information-Theoretic Approach to Modeling Diachronic Change in Scientific English. In Carla Suhr, Terttu Nevalainen, and Irma Taavitsainen, editors, *From Data to Evidence in English Language Research*, Language and Computers. Brill, Leiden.

Haim Dubossarsky, Yulia Tsvetkov, Chris Dyer, and Eitan Grossman. 2015. A Bottom Up Approach to Category Mapping and Meaning Change. In *Proceedings of the NetWordS Final Conference*, pages 66–70, Pisa, Italy.

Martin Ester, Hans-Peter Kriegel, Jörg Sander, Xiaowei Xu, et al. 1996. A Density-based Algorithm for Discovering Clusters in Large Spatial Databases with Noise. In *Proceedings of 2nd International Conference on Knowledge Discovery and Data Mining*, volume 96, pages 226–231.

Peter Fankhauser, Jörg Knappen, and Elke Teich. 2014. Exploring and Visualizing Variation in Language Resources. In *Proceedings of the 9th LREC*, pages 4125–4128, Reykjavik, Iceland. ELRA.

Peter Fankhauser and Marc Kupietz. 2017. Visualizing Language Change in a Corpus of Contemporary German. In *Proceedings of the Corpus Linguistics International Conference*, Birmingham, UK.

Ali Feizollah, Nor Badrul Anuar, Rosli Salleh, and Fairuz Amalina. 2014. Comparative Study of K-Means and Mini Batch K-Means Clustering Algorithms in Android Malware Detection using Network Traffic Analysis. In *2014 International Symposium on Biometrics and Security Technologies (ISBAST)*, pages 193–197. IEEE.

Brendan J Frey and Delbert Dueck. 2007. Clustering by Passing Messages between Data Points. *Science*, 315(5814):972–976.

Varun Gangal, Harsh Jhamtani, Graham Neubig, Eduard Hovy, and Eric Nyberg. 2017. Charmanteau: Character Embedding Models for Portmanteau Creation. In *Proceedings of the 2017 Conference on Empirical Methods in Natural Language Processing (EMNLP)*, pages 2907–2912, Copenhagen, Denmark. ACL.

Dirk Geeraerts, Caroline Gevaert, and Dirk Speelman. 2011. How Anger Rose: Hypothesis Testing in Diachronic Semantics. *Current Methods in Historical Semantics*, 73:109.

William L. Hamilton, Jure Leskovec, and Dan Jurafsky. 2016a. Cultural Shift or Linguistic Drift? Comparing Two Computational Models of Semantic Change. In *Proceedings of the Conference on Empirical Methods in Natural Language Processing (EMNLP)*, Austin, Texas.

William L Hamilton, Jure Leskovec, and Dan Jurafsky. 2016b. Diachronic Word Embeddings Reveal Statistical Laws of Semantic Change. In *Proceedings of the 54th Annual Meeting of the Association for Computational Linguistics*, pages 1489–1501, Berlin, Germany. ACL.

Johannes Hellrich, Sven Buechel, and Udo Hahn. 2018. JESEME: A Website for Exploring Diachronic Changes in Word Meaning and Emotion. *Proceedings of the 27th International Conference on Computational Linguistics: System Demonstrations (COLING 2018)*, pages 10–14.

Johannes Hellrich and Udo Hahn. 2016. Measuring the Dynamics of Lexico-Semantic Change Since the German Romantic Period. In *Digital Humanities (DH)*, pages 545–547.

Martin Hilpert. 2006. Distinctive Collexeme Analysis and Diachrony. *Corpus Linguistics and Linguistic Theory*, 2(2):243–256.

Martin Hilpert and Stefan Th Gries. 2016. Quantitative Approaches to Diachronic Corpus Linguistics. *The Cambridge Handbook of English Historical Linguistics*, pages 36–53.

Adam Jatowt and Kevin Duh. 2014. A Framework for Analyzing Semantic Change of Words across Time. In *Proceedings of Digital Libraries Conference (JCDL 2014 / TPDL 2014)*, pages 229–238, London, UK. ACM Press.

Gard B Jenset. 2013. Mapping Meaning with Distributional Methods: A Diachronic Corpus-based Study of Existential there. *Journal of Historical Linguistics*, 3(2):272–306.

Hannah Kermes, Stefania Degaetano-Ortlieb, Ashraf Khamis, Jörg Knappen, and Elke Teich. 2016. The Royal Society Corpus: From Uncharted Data to Corpus. In *Proceedings of the 10th LREC*, Portorož, Slovenia. ELRA.

Yoon Kim, Yi-I Chiu, Kentaro Hanaki, Darshan Hegde, and Slav Petrov. 2014. Temporal Analysis of Language through Neural Language Models. In *Proceedings of the ACL 2014 Workshop on Language Technologies and Computational Social Science*, pages 61–5, Baltimore, Maryland, USA.

Vivek Kulkarni, Rami Al-Rfou, Bryan Perozzi, and Steven Skiena. 2015. Statistically Significant Detection of Linguistic Change. In *Proceedings of the 24th International Conference on World Wide Web*, pages 625–635, Florence, Italy.

Solomon Kullback and Richard A. Leibler. 1951. On Information and Sufficiency. *The Annals of Mathematical Statistics*, 22(1):79–86.

Alessandro Lenci. 2008. Distributional Semantics in Linguistic and Cognitive Research. *Italian Journal of Linguistics*, 20(1):1–31.

Alessandro Lenci. 2011. Composing and Updating Verb Argument Expectations: A Distributional Semantic Model. In *Proceedings of the 2nd Workshop on Cognitive Modeling and Computational Linguistics*, pages 58–66, Portland, Oregon, USA. ACL.

Omer Levy and Yoav Goldberg. 2014. Neural Word Embedding as Implicit Matrix Factorization. In *Advances in Neural Information Processing Systems*, pages 2177–2185.

Omer Levy, Yoav Goldberg, and Ido Dagan. 2015. Improving Distributional Similarity with Lessons Learned from Word Embeddings. *Transactions of the Association for Computational Linguistics*, 3:211–225.

Wang Ling, Chris Dyer, Alan W Black, and Isabel Trancoso. 2015. Two/too Simple Adaptations of word2vec for Syntax Problems. In *Proceedings of the 2015 Conference of the North American Chapter of the Association for Computational Linguistics: Human Language Technologies*, pages 1299–1304, Denver, Colorado. ACL.

Laurens van der Maaten and Geoffrey Hinton. 2008. Visualizing Data Using t-SNE. *Journal of Machine Learning Research*, 9(Nov):2579–2605.

Tomas Mikolov, Wen-tau Yih, and Geoffrey Zweig. 2013. Linguistic Regularities in Continuous Space Word Representations. In *Proceedings of the 2013 Conference of the North American Chapter of the Association for Computational Linguistics: Human Language Technologies*, pages 746–751, Atlanta, Georgia, USA. ACL.

Florent Perek. 2016. Using Distributional Semantics to Study Syntactic Productivity in Diachrony: A Case Study. *Linguistics*, 54(1):149–188.

Gabriel Recchia, Ewan Jones, Paul Nulty, John Regan, and Peter de Bolla. 2016. Tracing Shifting Conceptual Vocabularies through Time. In *European Knowledge Acquisition Workshop*, pages 19–28. Springer.

Eyal Sagi, Stefan Kaufmann, and Brady Clark. 2011. Tracing Semantic Change with Latent Semantic Analysis. *Current Methods in Historical Semantics*, 73:161–183.

David Sculley. 2010. Web-scale K-Means Clustering. In *Proceedings of the 19th International Conference on World Wide Web*, pages 1177–1178, Raleigh, North Carolina, USA. ACM.

Terrence Szymanski. 2017. Temporal Word Analogies: Identifying Lexical Replacement with Diachronic Word Embeddings. In *Proceedings of the 55th Annual Meeting of the Association for Computational Linguistics (Volume 2: Short Papers)*, pages 448–453, Vancouver, Canada. ACL.

Takashi Tomokiyo and Matthew Hurst. 2003. A Language Model Approach to Keyphrase Extraction. In *Proceedings of the ACL 2003 Workshop on Multiword Expressions: Analysis, Acquisition and Treatment - Volume 18*, MWE '03, pages 33–40, Stroudsburg, PA, USA. ACL.

Thanh N Tran, Klaudia Drab, and Michal Daszykowski. 2013. Revised DBSCAN Algorithm to Cluster Data with Dense Adjacent Clusters. *Chemometrics and Intelligent Laboratory Systems*, 120:92–96.

Spatio-Temporal Prediction of Dialectal Variant Usage

Péter Jeszenszky
Department of Geography,
Ritsumeikan University
58, Komatsubara Kitamachi, Kita-ku
603-8341 Kyoto
pjeszenszky@gmail.com

Panote Siriaraya
Kyoto Institute of Technology
Matsugasaki, Sakyo-ku
606-8585 Kyoto
spanote@gmail.com

Philipp Stöckle
Austrian Centre for Digital Humanities,
Austrian Academy of Science
Postgasse 7-9
1010 Vienna
philipp.stoeckle@oeaw.ac.at

Adam Jatowt
Department of Social Informatics,
Kyoto University
Yoshida-Honmachi, Sakyo-ku
606-8501 Kyoto
adam@dl.kuis.kyoto-u.ac.jp

Abstract

The distribution of most dialectal variants have not only spatial but also temporal patterns. Based on the 'apparent time hypothesis', much of dialect change is happening through younger speakers accepting innovations[1]. Thus, synchronic diversity can be interpreted diachronically. With the assumption of the 'contact effect', i.e. contact possibility (contact and isolation) between speaker communities being responsible for language change, and the apparent time hypothesis, we aim to predict the usage of dialectal variants. In this paper we model the contact possibility based on two of the most important factors in sociolinguistics to be affecting language change: age and distance. The first steps of the approach involve modeling contact possibility using a logistic predictor, taking the age of respondents into account. We test the *global*, and the *local* role of age for variation where the local level means spatial subsets around each survey site, chosen based on k nearest neighbors. The prediction approach is tested on Swiss German syntactic survey data, featuring multiple respondents from different age cohorts at survey sites. The results show the relative success of the logistic prediction approach and the limitations of the method, therefore further proposals are made to develop the methodology.

1 Motivation

Contact and isolation, in geographic space and in social space, are assumed to be the most impor-

tant factors behind language change. The concept of *apparent time* (Bailey et al., 1991) hypothesizes that mother tongue is mostly acquired until the late teenage, after which one's language is more resistant to change. Throughout an individual's life contact patterns and social network might change (e.g., due to the ease of contact through media and changing migration or commuting patterns – especially from the 20th century). However, based on the apparent time hypothesis, if not uprooted, an individual's linguistic patterns can be assumed to reflect the contact patterns of their early life. With keeping all other variables constant, it can be assumed that for two people that are close in age and spent their youth near each other, the chance for a similar language is higher.

Thus, the quantification of contact possibility allows predicting current language usage and, through the concept of *'apparent time depth'*, future dialect change. If it is possible to predict the usage of variants based on the contact among users, core issues in sociolinguistics and diachronic linguistics such as the diffusion of variants, tracing back and forecasting change in language can be addressed with a better (spatial and temporal) granularity. Besides, through such an approach, linguistic theories long used, such as the apparent time concept (Bailey et al., 1991), language change following gravity-like paths (Trudgill, 1974) or wave-like diffusion (Yokoyama and Sanada, 2009; Blythe and Croft, 2012), can be tested. Further, it can contribute to natural language processing endeavours, such as predicting age from language attributes (Morgan-Lopez et al., 2017).

---

[1] An innovation is, of course, relative. A locally appearing new form with or without attestation elsewhere can be considered an innovation.

Proceedings of the 1st International Workshop on Computational Approaches to Historical Language Change, pages 186–195
Florence, Italy, August 2, 2019. ©2019 Association for Computational Linguistics

This study, tracing language variation back to the patterns of contact between communities, contributes to existing approaches (e.g., Pickl and Rumpf, 2012; Wieling and Nerbonne, 2015; Yamauchi and Murawaki, 2016; Burridge, 2017) in language change and variation studies. So far linguistic geography mostly tested individual phenomena (Willis, 2017), but as obtaining data with better granularity becomes increasingly faster, computational approaches can speed up analysis in language change studies, and highlight variants that can be then more thoroughly investigated with the methods of qualitative and quantitative linguistics.

To account for the diverse roles of contact quantitatively, the relationship of the measured linguistic variation and variables affecting contact patterns – including social, demographic, policy-related or geographic factors – has to be tested. This paper is not the first step in this direction, with sociolinguistics and linguistic geography extensively having researched social status, geographic distances and trade, among others, in these regards (e.g., Labov, 1963; Gooskens, 2004; Nerbonne, 2009; Szmrecsanyi, 2012; Lameli et al., 2015). However, this paper shows one of the first steps towards assembling a model for predicting usage of dialectal variants, and thereby, language change by means of taking as many extralinguistic variables as possible into account. In this paper we start assembling the model by taking two main variable assumed by sociolinguistics to have a crucial impact on language contact and change: age and distance. In a previous paper (Jeszenszky et al., 2018), we provided first steps from the ordination aspect for assessing the spatial predictors of different grammatical domains.

The specific goal of this paper is to analyze the roles that age and distance play in language contact, as explanatory variables for the usage patterns of dialectal variants, tested at the linguistic level of syntax. We build a logistic predictor model at global and local scales for classifying multivariate syntactic data from a Swiss German dialect survey and present first results.

2 Materials and Methods

2.1 Dialect Data

It is often assumed in dialectology that of all linguistic levels, change in syntax is the slowest (Longobardi and Guardiano, 2009). It could mean that the association with age might be lower in syntax than for lexicon (Morgan-Lopez et al., 2017). However, the lower possible number of syntactic variants allows for more robust results with fewer responses in a survey.

The dialectal data used in this paper stems from the database of the *Syntactic Atlas of German-speaking Switzerland* (SADS; (Bucheli and Glaser, 2002; Glaser and Bart, 2015)). The database holds data collected in a series of four dialect surveys, which was conducted between 2000 and 2002, and probed 54 different (morpho)syntactic phenomena. At 383 survey sites, relatively homogeneously distributed throughout the German-speaking area, a total of 3'174 respondents (multiple respondents, 3-26 per survey site, median=7) filled in the questionnaires containing 118 questions. Respondents of several age groups (12-94 years old) were included at most survey sites. However, the age distribution is slightly skewed, with a median of 57 years (Stoeckle, 2018). The multitude of responses shows the local variation in variant usage, and give a higher attribute granularity and thus allows testing the association of variant usage and extralinguistic variables, such as age. Most survey questions involved translation from Standard German to the local dialect and multiple choice (MC) questions. For MC questions however, respondents could accept several answer variants as locally valid, and they were asked to specify their 'preferred' variants. In this work we rely on these preferred variants, as especially younger respondents tended to *accept* more variants (Glaser et al., 2019) – a clue for age as a factor conditioning usage patterns of dialectal variants. It has to be noted that even though dialectological research often refers to survey questions as variables, in this paper we call them *'phenomena'*, as the term 'variable' overlaps with the statistical terms used further on (i.e., explanatory variable, independent variable).

2.2 Predicting Dialectal Variant Usage Based on Age and Spatial Neighborhood

This paper presents the methodology and first results of our proposed approach for analysing the effects of age and regional contact. Regional contact is assumed to be more important in language change, manifesting itself in the variation of dialectal variants by age. We test the following two hypotheses:

- At the global scale, age explains the usage of dialect variants in linguistic phenomena.

- Age is a better predictor for the usage of dialect variants at the local scale.

Firstly, using logistic regression, similarly to Willis (2017), we analyse the predictive power of age at the global level, taking into account all respondents, for the usage of variants that correspond to dialectal phenomena. Secondly, we utilize a regionalisation approach: for every survey site s, taking a set of k nearest survey sites, we predict the usage of each variant in s, based on the age of respondents and the variant preference in the whole set.

Global scale. We test the association between linguistic variation as a categorical (nominal) variable and age as a continuous predictor variable, using logistic regressions. Logistic regression does not provide a good effect size statistic similar to R^2 used for Pearson's product-moment correlation. Nevertheless, its predictive power can be tested by training the logistic regression predictor on a training set in the data and checking whether the predictions of this model correspond to the observed data previously masked. We use a 10-fold cross-validation strategy, with all data used in the training set and all observed data predicted. This tests whether logistic regression based on age provides a significant prediction on the usage of variants at the global level, and if so, with what accuracy. Thus, we report in Figure 1 the significance in a binary way (i.e., whether the prediction of the usage of a certain variant is significant or not). Besides, we present the AUC in Figure 1 as well, as a typical performance measurement for binary classifiers, showing the separability, i.e., to what degree the model is capable of distinguishing between classes. The higher the AUC, better the model is at predicting 0s as 0s and 1s as 1s.

Local scale. The regional approach can be viewed as a classification problem. Our model has to decide for each variant whether respondents at a central survey site s used it or not, based on age as the predictor variable in a set of k nearest neighbor survey sites. We use a logistic regression approach again. Using age as continuous and answer variants of all respondents as boolean variables, we train a logistic model and predict the variant usage for each respondent at s. We do this for all 383 survey sites. In this paper, we choose the k nearest neighbors based on Euclidean distance and we

test models with different k values (5 to 50). Our approach employs distance cut-off, rather than distance decay, however it can also be assumed that the closer survey sites are, the more linguistic influence they have on each other.

3 Results

For this paper, we used 60 phenomena from the SADS survey (approximately half of all), which were already used in Jeszenszky et al. (2017). Appendix A provides some linguistic details on each phenomenon.

Results with regards to the explanatory value of age as a global predictor for variant usage are presented in Figure 1. For more than half of the variants considered, age is not a significant predictor (dark grey squares). The AUC values of separability, reported for the variants where the relationship with age is significant, are relatively low (0.5 means no discriminative capacity of the model). At the same time, variants that reach higher values typically have relatively few users (below 100 out of 3'714), e.g., *II5_3*[2]; 10 users and *II30_7*; 8 users. However, several variants with sparse usage are also found among those not predicted significantly by age. Variants with many users (e.g., *II2_1*; 2'683 users, *I7_3*; 2'880 users, *III2_1*; 2'021 users) typically have an AUC value between 0.5 and 0.6. These values of association between variant usage and age alone are relatively low overall, leading us to investigate the prediction power of age at the regional scale, the patterns of which are possibly concealed by the global patterns.

For each variant in each phenomenon, Figure 2 presents the number of survey sites (out of the total 383) in which age *significantly* predicts the variant's usage, based on $k = 13$ nearest neighbors. It is visible that age proves to be a significant predictor in a large amount or survey sites only for a few variants. These are, however, not always variants with a few users. The first few variants in each phenomenon usually cover the majority of respondents.

The distribution of one such variant (*III7_2*) is mapped in Figure 3 along with the significance and accuracy of the predictor variable age. The patterns in Figure 3 show that the higher number

---

[2] Variant coding includes the survey question number and a variant ID. For example, *II5_3* is Variant #3 in the 5th question of the 2nd survey sheet

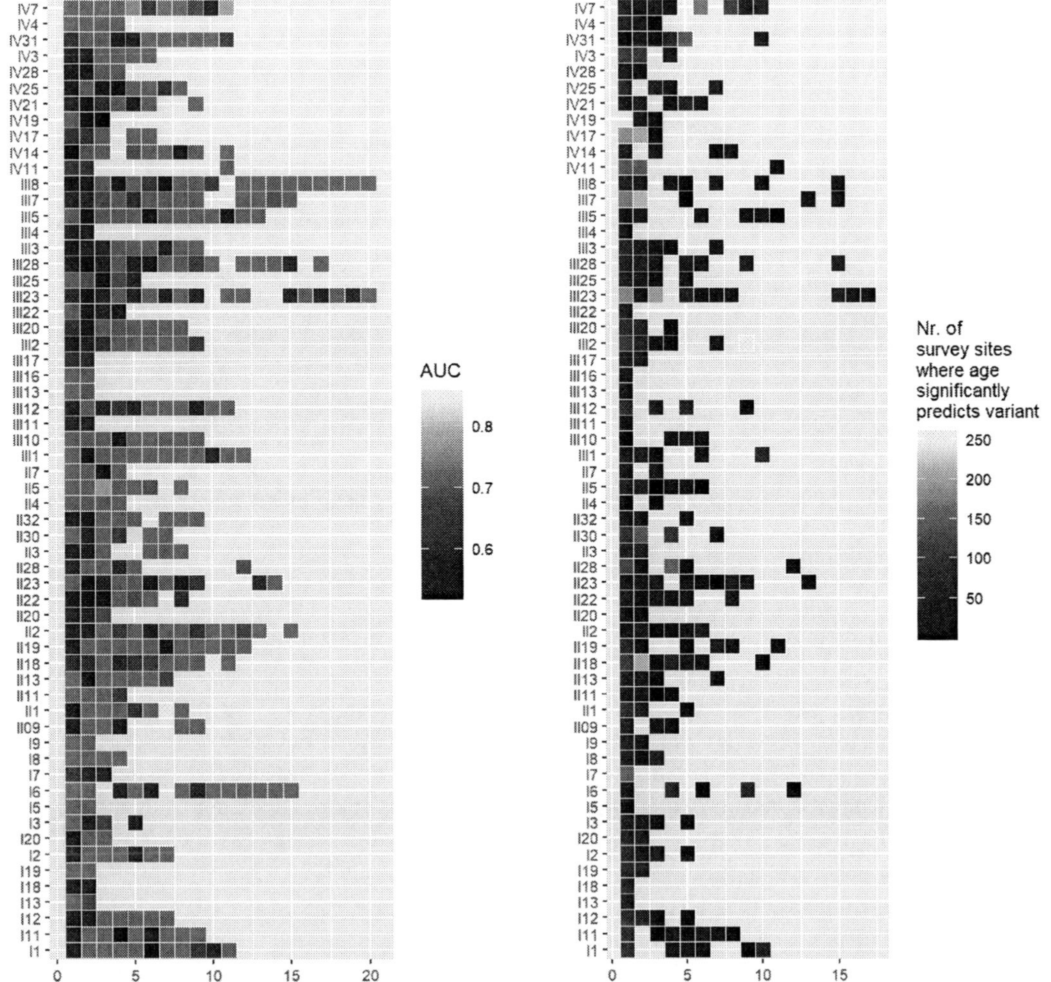

Figure 1: The global prediction power of logistic regression. The AUC values are plotted for each variant (horizontal axis) corresponding to the 60 linguistic phenomenon (vertical axis). Non-significance of the logistic regression is shown by dark grey squares.

Figure 2: The local prediction power of logistic regression. For each phenomenon and variant, the colour corresponds to the number of survey sites for which the logistic regression on age proved significant, based on $k = 13$ nearest neighbors.

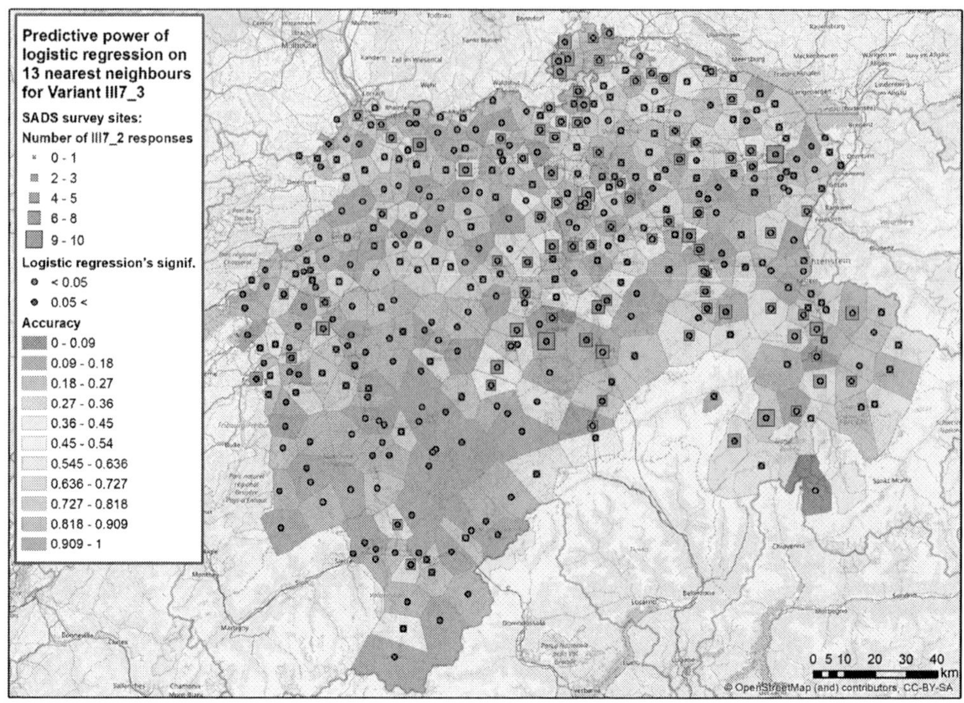

Figure 3: Mapping the significance ($p < 0.05$) and the accuracy of the logistic regression, for an answer variant *'hät s mer erzählt'* of Phenomenon *III7*, investigating the *'position of the personal pronouns'*, based on age and $k = 13$ nearest neighbors. Blue squares show the number of respondents using this variant. Accuracy is calculated by the proportion of correctly predicted usage.

of users does not necessarily make age a significant predictor. Significance of age as a predictor variable is spatially autocorrelated, which can be interpreted as follows. When present, the usage of this variant is characteristic of certain age groups at survey sites with green points, while at red ones it is used by different age groups.

As logistic regression is sensitive to class imbalances, it might not always be the best choice as a predictor when there are a lot of 0s and only a few 1s in the data, as it might result in false accuracy by predicting 0s only and not the 1s.

Interpretations of the first results show that age alone does not prove to be an exceptionally good predictor of syntactic variation. This is partly due to the nature of the data. It has been shown that while lexicon is more prone to have a correlation with age, syntax changes slower. The first results, however, show that already with a relatively simple approach, our research direction seems to be a worthwhile undertaking. Therefore, we have a wide outlook for further developing the methodology. The area and number of respondents involved in each model will be tested through different values of k, a distance decay approach and weights

based on different parameters (including age). The spatial basis of the model will feature estimations of contact potential that have proved more 'informative' than Euclidean distance, such as travel time (Jeszenszky et al., 2017); linguistic gravity (Trudgill, 1974), predicting influence and therefore language change based on settlement populations as weights in a gravity equation; or linguistic distance (Pickl et al., 2014), assuming that the closer dialect varieties should be the outcomes of closer (historical) contact. Furthermore, different algorithms beyond the logistic predictor (e.g., random forests, SVM, XGBoost) will be tested in the prediction model.

Acknowledgments

We are grateful to Elvira Glaser, Gabi Bart and Sandro Bachmann of the Syntactic Atlas of German-speaking Switzerland (SADS) project for the provision and professional help with the linguistic data. Funding by the Swiss National Science Foundation (Project no. P2ZHP2_175019) is gratefully acknowledged. Further, we would like to acknowledge the comments of the anonymous reviewers.

References

Guy Bailey, Tom Wilke, Jan Tillery, and Lori Sand. 1991. The apparent time construct. *Language Variation and Change*, 3(1991):241–264.

Richard A. Blythe and William A. Croft. 2012. S-curves and the mechanisms of propagation in language change. *Language*, 88(Number 2):269–304.

Claudia Bucheli and Elvira Glaser. 2002. The Syntactic Atlas of Swiss German dialects: Empirical and methodological problems. In Sjef Barbiers, Leonie Cornips, and Susanne van der Kleij, editors, *Syntactic Microvariation*, vol. 2. edition, pages 41–73. Meertens Institute Electronic Publications in Linguistics, Amsterdam.

James Burridge. 2017. Spatial evolution of human dialects. *Physical Review X*, 7(031008).

Elvira Glaser and Gabriela Bart. 2015. Dialektsyntax des Schweizerdeutschen. In Roland Kehrein, Alfred Lameli, and Stefan Rabanus, editors, *Regionale Variation des Deutschen. Projekte und Perspektiven.*, chapter 4, pages 79–105. De Gruyter, Berlin.

Elvira Glaser, Philipp Stoeckle, and Sandro Bachmann. 2019. Faktoren und Arten intrapersoneller Variation im Material des syntaktischen Atlas der deutschen Schweiz (SADS). In *Syntax aus Saarbrücker Sicht 3.: Beiträge der SaRDiS-Tagung zur Dialektsyntax 2018*, pages 1–30, Stuttgart. Steiner.

Charlotte Gooskens. 2004. Norwegian dialect distances geographically explained. In *Language Variation in Europe. Papers from the Second International Conference on Language Variation in Europe ICLAVE Vol. 2. 2004.*, pages 195–206, Uppsala.

Péter Jeszenszky, Sandro Bachmann, and Peter Ranacher. 2018. Towards the parameterisation and quantification of dialect contact potential: An extended abstract. In *GIScience 2018 unpublished extended abstract*, pages 1–6.

Péter Jeszenszky, Philipp Stoeckle, Elvira Glaser, and Robert Weibel. 2017. Exploring global and local patterns in the correlation of geographic distances and morphosyntactic variation in Swiss German. *Journal of Linguistic Geography*, 5(2):86–108.

William Labov. 1963. The Social Motivation of a Sound Change. *¡i¿WORD¡/i¿*, 19(3):273–309.

Alfred Lameli, Volker Nitsch, Jens Südekum, and Nikolaus Wolf. 2015. Same same but different: Dialects and trade. *German Economic Review*, 16(3):290–306.

Giuseppe Longobardi and Cristina Guardiano. 2009. Evidence for syntax as a signal of historical relatedness. *Lingua*, 119(11):1679–1706.

Antonio A. Morgan-Lopez, Annice E. Kim, Robert F. Chew, and Paul Ruddle. 2017. Predicting age groups of Twitter users based on language and metadata features. *PLoS ONE*, 12(8):1–12.

John Nerbonne. 2009. Data-Driven Dialectology. *Language and Linguistics Compass*, 3(1):175–198.

Simon Pickl and Jonas Rumpf. 2012. Dialectometric concepts of space: Towards a variant-based dialectometry. In Sandra Hansen, Christian Schwarz, Philipp Stoeckle, and Tobias Streck, editors, *Dialectological and Folk Dialectological Concepts of Space - Current Methods and Perspectives in Sociolinguistic Research on Dialect Change*, linguae & edition, pages 199–214. Walter de Gruyter, Berlin/ New York.

Simon Pickl, Aaron Spettl, Simon Magnus Pröll, Stephan Elspaß, Werner König, and Volker Schmidt. 2014. Linguistic distances in dialectometric intensity estimation. *Journal of Linguistic Geography*, 2(01):25–40.

Philipp Stoeckle. 2018. Zur Syntax von afa (anfangen') im Schweizerdeutschen – Kookkurrenzen, Variation und Wandel. In *Syntax aus Saarbrücker Sicht 2. Beiträge der SaRDiS-Tagung zur Dialektsyntax*, pages 173–203, Stuttgart. Steiner.

Benedikt Szmrecsanyi. 2012. Geography is overrated. In Sandra Hansen, Christian Schwarz, Philipp Stoeckle, and Tobias Streck, editors, *Dialectological and Folk Dialectological Concepts of Space - Current Methods and Perspectives in Sociolinguistic Research on Dialect Change*, pages 215–231. De Gruyter, Berlin, Boston.

Peter Trudgill. 1974. Linguistic change and diffusion: Description and explanation in sociolinguistic dialect geography. *Language in Society*, 2:215–246.

Martijn Wieling and John Nerbonne. 2015. Advances in Dialectometry. *Annual Review of Linguistics*, 1(1):243 – 264.

David Willis. 2017. Investigating geospatial models of the diffusion of morphosyntactic innovations: The Welsh strong second-person singular pronoun chdi. *Journal of Linguistic Geography*, 5:41–66.

Kenji Yamauchi and Yugo Murawaki. 2016. Contrasting Vertical and Horizontal Transmission of Typological Features. *Proceedings of the 26th International Conference on Computational Linguistics (COLING-16)*, pages 836–846.

Shoichi Yokoyama and Haruko Sanada. 2009. Logistic regression model for predicting language change. In Reinhard Köhler, editor, *Studies in Quantitative Linguistics 5, Issues in Quantitative Linguistics*, pages 176–192. RAM-Verlag, Lüdenscheid (D).

A   Appendices

A Appendix contains the 60 dialectal variables from the SADS in Table 1, 2 and 3, based on which the analysis was carried out.

SADS ID	Sentence *(Standard German)*	Sentence in English	Linguistic phenomenon
I.1	Entschuldigung, ich habe zu wenig Kleingeld, *um* ein Billett *zu* lösen.	Excuse me, I don't have enough change *in order to* buy a ticket.	infinitival purposive clause: linkage
I.2	*Wem* will er denn die schönen Blumen bringen?	*To whom* does he want to bring those beautiful flowers?	prepositional dative marking (PDM)
I.3	Oh, ich habe den Fritz *kommen hören*.	Oh, I *heard* Fritz *coming*.	perfect with 'hear': form and position of non-finite verb (IPP)
I.5	Der Korb ist *umgekippt*.	The basket *is toppled over*.	resultative: subject agreement
I.6	Wissen Sie, jetzt brauche ich sogar Tabletten *zum einschlafen*.	You know, now I even need pills *in order to* fall asleep.	infinitival purposive clause: linkage
I.7	Nein, das gehört *meiner* Schwester.	No, it belongs *to my* sister.	prepositional dative marking (PDM)
I.8	Aber ich habe im Fall schon gestern *geholfen abzuwaschen*.	But I already *helped doing the dishes* yesterday.	perfect with 'help': form and position of non-finite verb (IPP)
I.9	Also ich weiss auch nicht, ob er einmal *heiraten will*.	Well, I don't know if he ever *wants to get married*.	modal verb in subordinate clauses: position
I.11	Aber jetzt habe ich mich gerade hingesetzt, *um* ein Buch *zu* lesen.	But I just sat down *in order to* read a book.	infinitival purposive clause: linkage
I.12	Fischstäbchen muss man doch *gefroren anbraten*.	Actually, fish fingers should be fried while still frozen.	copredicative participle
I.13	Da *wird* gearbeitet.	*lit.* Here *will be* worked. (People are working here.)	expletive 'it' (impersonal passive)
I.18	Soll ich *welche* kaufen?	Should I buy some *of that*?	partitive object (pronoun)
I.19	Ich habe keine Ahnung, ob sie das Auto schon *bezahlt hat*.	I have no idea whether she *has* already *paid* for the car.	perfect auxiliary ('have') in subordinate clauses: position
I.20	Aber ich habe doch das Buch *dir* geschenkt.	But I gave the book as a present *to you*.	prepositional dative marking (PDM)
II.1	Hast du die Uhr *flicken lassen*?	Have you *had* the clock *fixed*?	infinitive particle (doubling/position) 'let'
II.2	Das ist doch die Frau, *der* ich schon lange das Buch bringen sollte.	This is the woman *to whom* I should have brought back the book long ago.	relative clause linkage: IO
II.3	Er *lässt* den Schreiner kommen.	*lit.* He *lets* the carpenter come. (He calls the carpenter.)	infinitive particle (doubling/position) 'let'
II.4	Du hast sicher viel *zu erzählen*!	You must have a lot *to tell*!	non-finite form with 'have to' (gerund)
II.5	Ihr dürft alles *liegen lassen*.	*lit.* You can *let* everything *lie*. (You can leave everything.)	infinitive particle (doubling/position) 'let'
II.7	Ich habe erst mit vierzig *fahren gelernt*.	I have only *learnt to drive* at forty.	perfect with 'learn': form and position of non-finite verb (IPP)

Table 1: The linguistic phenomena in SADS used in the experiments (part 1). The grammatical constructs of interest are highlighted in *italics*.

SADS ID	Sentence (*Standard German*)	Sentence in English	Linguistic phenomenon
II.9	Nein, sie ist gerade *verkauft worden.*	No, it *has* just *been sold.*	passive auxiliary and agreement
II.11	Er hat die Hand immer noch *eingebunden.*	He has his arm still *bandaged.*	resultative: object agreement
II.13	Du musst die Milch aber *heiss* trinken!	But you have to drink the milk *hot*!	copredicative adjective
II.18	Das ist der Mann, *dem* ich gestern den Weg gezeigt habe.	That's the man *to whom* I gave directions yesterday.	relative clause linkage: IO
II.19	Und dann ist ein Fuchs *geschlichen gekommen*!	And then a fox *came creeping* around!	verbal construction 'come' + motion verb
II.20	Ich möchte aber ein Auto, *das* ich auch bezahlen kann!	But I want a car *that* I can actually pay for!	relative clause linkage: DO
II.22	Nein, das ist *Peters* [Dreirad].	No, that's *Peter's.* [tricycle]	predicative possessive
II.23	Nein, das ist *Sandras* [Dreirad].	No, that's *Sandra's.* [tricycle]	predicative possessive
II.28	Das ist der Mann, *mit dem* ich immer schwätze.	That's the man *that* I always chat *with.*	relative clause linkage: PP
II.30	Der Hund *des Lehrers*	The *teacher's* dog	adnominal possessive
II.32	Ich habe Fritz *gesehen*	I have *seen* Fritz.	personal name: definite article and case inflection
III.1	Wenn es so warm bleibt, *fängt* das Eis *an* zu schmelzen!	If it stays this warm, the ice will *begin to* melt.	infinitive particle (position/doubling) 'begin'
III.2	*Wen* suchst du?	*Who* are you looking *for*?	interrogative pronoun: case
III.3	Für *wen* sind denn die Blumen?	*Who* are the flowers *for*?	interrogative pronoun: case
III.4	Die sind nicht für *dich*!	They are not *for you*!	personal pronoun (2sg): PP
III.5	Ich habe schon *angefangen* zu kochen.	I have already *started* cooking. (*lit.* have begun to cook)	infinitive particle (position/doubling) 'begin'
III.7	Sie hat *es mir* gestern erzählt.	She told *that* to *me* yesterday [about expecting a baby].	personal pronouns: position
III.8	Sie findet es nicht gut, dass ich *angefangen habe* zu rauchen.	She doesn't find it good that I *have started* smoking. (lit. *have begun* to smoke)	infinitive particle (position/doubling) 'begin'
III.10	Wenn sie dich erwischen, *bekommst* du den Fahrausweis entzogen!	If they catch you, you *get* your driver's license taken away.	'get'-passive
III.11	Also *mich* erwischt keiner!	Well, no one will catch *me*!	personal pronoun (1sg): DO

Table 2: The linguistic phenomena in SADS used in the experiments (part 2).

SADS ID	Sentence *(Standard German)*	Sentence in English	Linguistic phenomenon
III.12	Nimm die Suppe sofort weg, wenn sie zu kochen *anfängt*!	Take the soup off immediately, once it *begins* to boiling.	infinitive particle (position/doubling) 'begin'
III.13	Er gibt *sich* einfach keine Mühe.	He just doesn't put any effort into it. (*lit. for himself*)	reflexive pronoun (3sgm)
III.16	Die Strasse ist schon seit einem Jahr *aufgerissen*.	The street has already been *torn up* for a year.	resultative: subject agreement
III.17	Wir müssen *uns* das überlegen.	We have to think about it. (*lit. for ourselves*)	reflexive pronoun (1pl)
III.20	Er schaut nur für *sich selbst*.	He only thinks about *himself*.	reflexive pronoun (PP)
III.22	Sie ist grösser *als* ich.	She is taller *than* me.	comparative clause linkage
III.23	*Hinkend* ist er gelaufen.	He went home *limping*.	converb
III.25	Sie gehen halt lieber schwimmen *als* laufen.	They would rather go for a swim *than* for a walk.	comparative clause linkage
III.28	Dann ist er ja älter, *als* ich gemeint habe.	So he is older *than* I expected.	comparative clause linkage
IV.3	Ich habe *es ihm* schon geschickt.	I have already sent *it to him*.	personal pronouns: position
IV.4	*Wer* ist das gewesen?	*Who* was it?	interrogative pronoun: case
IV.7	Jetzt kannst du *anfangen*.	Now you can *begin*.	non-finite 'begin' with modal verb
IV.11	Doch, das ist im Fall *er* gewesen.	Yes, that must have been *him*!	personal pronoun (3sgm): subject
IV.14	Du musst das Licht anzünden, *um zu* lesen.	You have to turn the light on *in order to* read.	infinitival purposive clause: linkage
IV.17	Doch, das ist *er* sicher gewesen!	Yes, that was *him* for sure!	personal pronoun (3sgm): subject
IV.19	Ja, ich habe *etwas ganz* Schönes gekauft!	Yes, I have bought *something really* nice!	indefinite pronoun: position/doubling
IV.21	Ich habe nicht gewusst, dass er so spät fahren *gelernt hat*.	I didn't know that he *has learnt* to drive only so late.	perfect with 'learn': form and position of non-finite verb (IPP)
IV.25	Das glaubst du ja selber nicht, dass sie so früh lesen *gelernt hat*.	No way she *has learnt* to read so young!	perfect with 'learn': form and position of non-finite verb (IPP)
IV.28	Ich habe es *(dem)* Fritz gegeben.	I gave it *to* Fritz. (*lit. to the Fritz*)	personal name: definite article and case inflection
IV.31	Das *gefallen* täte mir auch!	approx. That would *do* to my *liking*! (I would like it, too!)	subjunctive auxiliary 'do' (position)

Table 3: The linguistic phenomena in SADS used in the experiments (part 3).

One-to-X analogical reasoning on word embeddings: a case for diachronic armed conflict prediction from news texts

Andrey Kutuzov
University of Oslo
Oslo, Norway
andreku@ifi.uio.no

Erik Velldal
University of Oslo
Oslo, Norway
erikve@ifi.uio.no

Lilja Øvrelid
University of Oslo
Oslo, Norway
liljao@ifi.uio.no

Abstract

We extend the well-known word analogy task to a one-to-X formulation, including one-to-none cases, when no correct answer exists. The task is cast as a relation discovery problem and applied to historical armed conflicts datasets, attempting to predict new relations of type 'location:armed-group' based on data about past events. As the source of semantic information, we use diachronic word embedding models trained on English news texts. A simple technique to improve diachronic performance in such task is demonstrated, using a threshold based on a function of cosine distance to decrease the number of false positives; this approach is shown to be beneficial on two different corpora. Finally, we publish a ready-to-use test set for one-to-X analogy evaluation on historical armed conflicts data.

Performance on the task of analogical inference (or 'word analogies') is one of the most widespread means to evaluate distributional word representation models, with 'KING is to QUEEN as MAN is to ? (WOMAN)' being a famous example. It also has deep connections to the relational similarity task (Jurgens et al., 2012). Most often, analogical inference is formulated as a strict proportion, and the model has to provide exactly one best answer for each question (assuming that it is impossible that, e.g., WOMAN and GIRL are equally correct answers for the question above).

We reformulate the analogical inference task and extend it to include multiple-ended or *one-to-X* relations: one-to-one, one-to-many and one-to-none cases when an entity is not included in this particular relation type, so there is no correct answer for it. This way, the model has to provide as many correct answers as possible, while providing as few incorrect answers as possible. More formally, the task is as follows: for a given vocabulary V, a relation of a type z, and an entity $x \in V$,

identify any pairs $x; i \in V$ such that z holds between x and i. Note that this task has been tackled in NLP using a number of methods, and not necessarily using analogical reasoning; however, in this work we employ a supervised approach implying learning from 'example' or 'prototypical' pairs (similar to analogies). Our method also does not require providing i candidates: they are inferred automatically from an embedding model.

Proper analogy test sets are difficult to compile, especially when the complex structure described above is desired. Thus, we limit ourselves to one particular type of semantic relations, on which objective data can be gathered from extra-linguistic sources: those between a geographical *location* (country) and an *insurgent group* involved in an armed conflict against the government of the country in a given time period. We use the historical armed conflicts data provided publicly by the UCDP project (Gleditsch et al., 2002). These datasets contain the needed relations: several armed groups can operate in one location, one group can operate in several locations, and obviously some locations lack any insurgents to speak of. At the same time, news corpora contain a lot of information about armed conflicts, while being comparatively easy to obtain and train distributional word embedding models on.

Since the UCDP data provides exact dates for all the conflicts, we cast our *one-to-X* analogical reasoning task in a diachronic setup. We attempt to find out whether a distributional vector space retains enough structure to trace the relation after the model was additionally trained with a comparable amount of new in-domain texts created in the subsequent time period.

The **contributions** of this work are: **(1)** We reformulate the well-known word analogy task such that multiple correct answers or no correct answer at all become possible (*one-to-X* relations).

Proceedings of the 1st International Workshop on Computational Approaches to Historical Language Change, pages 196–201
Florence, Italy, August 2, 2019. ©2019 Association for Computational Linguistics

(2) We process historical armed conflicts data and present it as a ready-to-use evaluation set. **(3)** Relying on and partially reproducing the workflow from prior publications, we investigate whether word embedding models are able to solve *one-to-X* analogies diachronically. **(4)** Finally, we show that our learned cosine threshold approach can significantly improve the temporal *one-to-X* analogies performance by filtering out false positives.

1   Related work

The issue of linguistic regularity manifested in relational similarity has been studied for a long time. Due to the long-standing criticism of strictly binary relation structure, *SemEval-2012* offered the task to detect the degree of relational similarity (Jurgens et al., 2012). This means that multiple correct answers exist, but they should be ranked differently. Somewhat similar improvements to the well-known word analogies dataset from (Mikolov et al., 2013b) were presented in the BATS analogy test set (Gladkova et al., 2016), also featuring multiple correct answers.[1] Our *One-to-X* analogy setup extends this by introducing the possibility of the correct answer being 'None'. In the cases when correct answers exist, they are equally ranked, but their number can be different.

Using distributional word representations to trace diachronic semantic shifts (including those reflecting social and cultural events) has received substantial attention in the recent years. Our work shares some of the workflow with Kutuzov et al. (2017). They used a supervised approach to analogical reasoning, applying 'semantic directions' learned on the previous year's armed conflicts data to the subsequent year. We extend their research by significantly reformulating the analogy task, making it more realistic, and finding ways to cope with false positives (insurgent armed groups predicted for locations where no armed conflicts are registered this year). In comparison to their work, we also use newer and larger corpora of news texts and the most recent version of the UCDP dataset. For brevity, we do not describe the emerging field of diachronic word embeddings in details, referring the interested readers to the recent surveys of Kutuzov et al. (2018) and Tang (2018).

2   Learning the armed conflict projection

We rely on the idea that knowing the gold *Location: Insurgent* pairs from a time period n can help us to retrieve the correct pairs bearing the same relation from the next time period $n + 1$, using word embedding models trained incrementally[2] on these time periods. The models are trained using the CBOW algorithm (Mikolov et al., 2013b), and the time periods are yearly subsections of English news corpora (see § 3). A yearly model is saved after the training for a particular year is finished, for later usage.

We deal with pairs of consequent years ('2010–2011', '2011–2012', etc.). Our aim is to predict armed conflicts (or their absence) for a fixed set of locations in the year $n + 1$. Having the gold armed conflict data for all years, we can train a predictor on the 1st year, and then evaluate it on the 2nd one (simulating a real-world scenario where new textual data arrive regularly, but gold annotation is available only for older data). We take the gold *Location: Insurgent* pairs from the year n (as a rule, there are several dozens of them) and their vector representations from the corresponding embedding model M_n. Then, these vector pairs are used to train a linear projection $T \in \mathbb{R}^{p \times d}$, where p is the number of pairs, and d is the vector size of the embedding model used.

Linguistically, T can be seen as defining a 'prototypical armed conflict relation'; geometrically, it can be thought of as the average 'direction' from locations to their active insurgent groups in the M_n vector space [3]. The problem of finding the optimal T boils down to a linear regression which minimizes the error in transforming one set of vectors into another, and we do it by solving d deterministic normal equations (since the number of data points is small, the operation is fast).

After T is at hand, one can find the 'armed conflict projection' vector $\hat{i}$ for any location vector v in M_{n+1} by transforming it with the learned matrix: $\hat{i} = v \cdot T$. In the simplest case, the word with the highest cosine similarity to $\hat{i}$ in M_{n+1} is assumed to be a candidate for an insur-

---

[1]See also the detailed criticism of analogical inference with word embeddings in general in (Rogers et al., 2017).

[2]The model M_{n+1} is initialized with the weights from the model M_n; if there are new words in the $n + 1$ data which exceed the frequency threshold, then at the start of M_{n+1} training they are added to it and assigned random vectors.

[3]A similar approach has been used for naive translation of words from the language L1 to L2 by using monolingual word embeddings for both and a seed bilingual dictionary (set of one-to-one pairs) (Mikolov et al., 2013a).

gent armed group active in this location in the time period $n + 1$; however, a more involved approach is needed to handle cases when the number of insurgents (correct answers) can be different from 1 (including 0), described below. For this workflow to yield meaningful results, it is essential for the paired models to be 'aligned'. This is why we train the models incrementally, thus ensuring that they share common structural properties. Another possible way to cope with this is by using the orthogonal Procrustes alignment (Hamilton et al., 2016).

3 Datasets

Corpora for embeddings We train embeddings on two corpora: **(1)** The *Gigaword* news corpus (Parker et al., 2011), spanning 1995–2010 and containing about 300M words per year, with about 4.8 billion total. This corpus was used in (Kutuzov et al., 2017) and we include it for comparison purposes. **(2)** The *News on Web (NOW)* corpus,[4] spanning 2010–2019. As the UCDP dataset covers conflicts only up to 2017, we use the texts up to that year, yielding on average 730M words per year, with about 5.9 billion total. The time-annotated texts are crawled from online magazines and newspapers in 20 English-speaking countries.

Before training the embedding models, the corpora were lemmatized and PoS-tagged using *UDPipe 2.3 English-LinES* tagger (Straka and Straková, 2017) (during the evaluation, PoS tags were stripped and words lower-cased). Chains of consecutive proper names agreeing in number (`'South_PROPN Sudan_PROPN'`) were merged together with a special character (`'South::Sudan_PROPN'`). This was important to handle multi-word location and insurgent names. Functional words were removed.

Conflict relation data The armed conflict data comes from the UCDP/PRIO Armed Conflict Dataset[5] (ver. 18.1) (Pettersson and Eck, 2018). It is manually annotated with historical information on armed conflicts across the world, starting from 1946, where at least one party is the government of a state, and frequently used in statistical conflict research.

The dataset contains various metadata, but we kept only the years, the names of the locations, and the names of the armed groups (e.g., `'2016: Afghanistan: ["Taliban",`

	Gigaword	NOW
Time span	1995–2010	2010–2017
Locations	52	42
Insurgents	127	78
Conflict pairs	136	102
New pairs share	0.37	0.39
Conflict locations share	0.46	0.56
Insurgents per location	1.65	1.50

Table 1: Comparative statistics of UCDP data subsets

`"Islamic State"]'`). Entities occurring less than 25 times in the corresponding yearly corpora were filtered out, since it is difficult for distributional models to learn meaningful embeddings for such rare words.

We create one such conflict relation dataset for each news corpus; one corresponding to the time span of NOW and another for Gigaword. Table 1 shows various statistics across these UCDP subsets, including the important 'new pairs share' parameter, showing what part of the conflict pairs in the years $n + 1$ was not seen in the years n (how much new data to guess).

The *NoW* dataset features 102 unique *Location: Insurgent* pairs, with 42 unique locations and 78 unique armed groups. On average, each year 56% of these 42 locations were involved in armed conflicts, based on the UCDP data. The remaining (different each year) serve as 'negative examples' to test the ability of our approach to detect cases when no predictions have to be made. For the areas involved in conflicts, the average number of active insurgents per location is about 1.5, with the maximum number being 5[6].

A replication experiment In Table 2 we replicate the experiments from (Kutuzov et al., 2017) on both sets. It follows their evaluation scheme, where only the presence of the correct armed group name in the k nearest neighbours of the $\hat{i}$ mattered, and only conflict areas were present in the yearly test sets. Essentially, it measures the recall @k, without penalizing the models for yielding incorrect answers along with the correct ones, and never asking questions having no correct answer at all (e.g., peaceful locations). The performance is very similar on both sets, ensuring that the *NOW* set conveys the same signal as the *Gigaword* set; however, in the next section we make

---

[4] https://corpus.byu.edu/now/
[5] https://www.ucdp.uu.se/

[6] Congo (2017) features 5 active armed groups: `'Kamuina Nsapu'`, `'M23'`, `'CMC'`, `'MNR'`, `'BDK'`.

Dataset	@1	@5	@10
Gigaword	0.356	0.555	0.610
NOW	0.442	0.557	0.578

Table 2: Average recall of diachronic analogy inference

the task more realistic by extending the evaluation schema to the *one-to-X* scenario described above.

4 Evaluation setup

In our workflow, each yearly test set contains all locations, but whether a particular location is associated with any armed groups, can vary from year to year. Conceptually, the task of the model is to predict correct sets of active armed groups for conflict locations and to predict the empty set for peaceful locations. For a test year, an 'armed conflict projection' $\hat{i}$ is produced for each location using the learned transformation T_n. The k nearest neighbors of $\hat{i}$ in M_{n+1} become armed group candidates (k is a hyperparameter). We calculate the number of true positives (correctly predicted armed groups), false positives (incorrectly predicted armed groups), and false negatives (armed groups present in the gold data, but not predicted by the system). These counts are accumulated and for each year standard precision, recall and F1 score are calculated. These metrics are then averaged across all years in the test set. Using false negatives ensures that we penalize the systems for yielding predictions for peaceful locations.

4.1 Cosine threshold

It is clear that such a system (dubbed 'baseline') will always yield k incorrect candidates for peaceful areas. Inspired partially by the ideas from Orlikowski et al. (2018), we implemented a simple approach based on the assumption that the correct armed groups vectors will tend to be closer to the $\hat{i}$ point than other nearest neighbours. Thus, the system should pick only the candidates located within a hypersphere of a pre-defined radius r centered around $\hat{i}$. r_n can be different for different years, and we infer it from the p training conflict pairs from the previous year by calculating the average cosine distance between the 'armed conflict projections' $\hat{i}$ and armed groups:

$$r = \frac{1}{p} \sum_{p=0}^{p} \cos\left(\hat{i}_p, g_p\right) + \sigma \qquad (1)$$

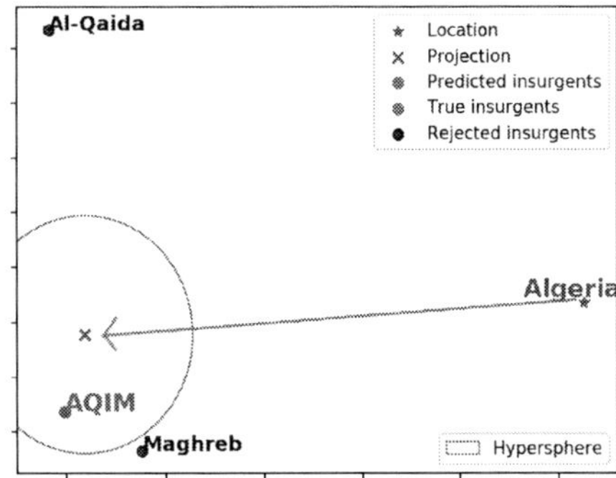

Figure 1: Prediction of armed groups in Algeria, 2014 (2-dimensional PCA projection).

	Algorithm	Precision	Recall	F1
Giga	Baseline	0.19	0.51	0.28
	Threshold	0.46	0.41	**0.41**
NOW	Baseline	0.26	0.53	0.34
	Threshold	0.42	0.41	**0.41**

Table 3: Average diachronic performance

where g_p is the armed group in the pth pair, and σ is one standard deviation of the cosine distances in p. The hypersphere serves as a cosine threshold.

This allows us to keep only the candidates which are not farther from $\hat{i}$ than the armed groups in the previous year tended to be. Figure 1 shows a PCA projection of predicting armed groups for Algeria in 2014. With $k = 3$, the system initially yielded 3 candidates ('AQIM', 'Al-Qaida' and 'Maghreb'), with only the first being correct. The red circle is a part of the hypersphere inferred from the 2013 training data. It filters out the wrong candidates (in black), since the cosine distance from the conflict projection (in blue) to their embeddings is higher than the inferred threshold.

5 Experiments

For the experiments, we chose $k = 2$, to be closer to the average number of armed groups per location in our sets. Table 3 shows the *diachronic* performance of our system in the setup when the matrix T_n and the threshold r_n are applied to the year $n + 1$.

For both *Gigaword* and *NOW* datasets (and the corresponding embeddings), using the cosine-based threshold decreases recall and increases precision (differences are statistically significant with *t-test*, $p < 0.05$). At the same time, the integral

	Algorithm	Precision	Recall	F1
Giga	Baseline	0.28	0.74	0.41
	Threshold	0.60	0.69	**0.63**
NOW	Baseline	0.39	0.88	0.53
	Threshold	0.50	0.77	**0.60**

Table 4: Average synchronic performance

metrics of F1 consistently improves ($p < 0.01$). Thus, the thresholding reduces prediction noise in the *one-to-X* analogy task without sacrificing too many correct answers. In our particular case, this helps to more precisely detect events of armed conflicts termination (where no insurgents should be predicted for a location), not only their start.

As a sanity check, we also evaluated it *synchronically*, that is when T_n and r_n are tested on the locations from the same year (including peaceful ones). In this easier setup, we observed exactly the same trends (Table 4).

6 Conclusion

We presented a new *one-to-X* word analogy task formulation, applying it to the problem of temporal armed conflicts detection based on word embedding models trained on English news texts. A historical armed conflicts test set was prepared for evaluation of diachronic word embedding models. We also showed that a simple thresholding technique based on a function of cosine distance allows us to significantly improve the relation detection performance, especially for reducing the number of false positives. This approach outperformed the baseline both with the corpora used in the prior work (*Gigaword*) and with the *NOW* corpus which to the best of our knowledge was not used for diachronic semantic shifts research before.

Our future plans include using negative sampling when calculating optimal projections, along with testing recent diachronic modeling algorithms representing time as a continuous variable (Rosenfeld and Erk, 2018). Another interesting issue is how to avoid catastrophic forgetting when training embeddings incrementally (semantic relation structures tend to completely change after significant updates).

Our code, test sets and best-performing embeddings are available at `https://github.com/ltgoslo/diachronic_armed_conflicts`.

References

Anna Gladkova, Aleksandr Drozd, and Satoshi Matsuoka. 2016. Analogy-based detection of morphological and semantic relations with word embeddings: What works and what doesn't. In *Proceedings of the NAACL-HLT SRW*, pages 47–54, San Diego, California, June 12-17, 2016. ACL.

Nils Petter Gleditsch, Peter Wallensteen, Mikael Eriksson, Margareta Sollenberg, and Håvard Strand. 2002. Armed conflict 1946-2001: A new dataset. *Journal of peace research*, 39(5):615–637.

William Hamilton, Jure Leskovec, and Dan Jurafsky. 2016. Cultural shift or linguistic drift? Comparing two computational measures of semantic change. In *Proceedings of the Conference on Empirical Methods in Natural Language Processing*, pages 2116–2121, Austin, Texas.

David Jurgens, Saif Mohammad, Peter Turney, and Keith Holyoak. 2012. Semeval-2012 task 2: Measuring degrees of relational similarity. In **SEM 2012: The First Joint Conference on Lexical and Computational Semantics – Volume 1: Proceedings of the main conference and the shared task, and Volume 2: Proceedings of the Sixth International Workshop on Semantic Evaluation (SemEval 2012)*, pages 356–364. Association for Computational Linguistics.

Andrey Kutuzov, Lilja Øvrelid, Terrence Szymanski, and Erik Velldal. 2018. Diachronic word embeddings and semantic shifts: a survey. In *Proceedings of the 27th International Conference on Computational Linguistics*, pages 1384–1397. Association for Computational Linguistics.

Andrey Kutuzov, Erik Velldal, and Lilja Øvrelid. 2017. Temporal dynamics of semantic relations in word embeddings: an application to predicting armed conflict participants. In *Proceedings of the Conference on Empirical Methods in Natural Language Processing*, pages 1824–1829, Copenhagen, Denmark.

Tomas Mikolov, Quoc Le, and Ilya Sutskever. 2013a. Exploiting similarities among languages for machine translation. ArXiv preprint arXiv:1309.4168.

Tomas Mikolov, Ilya Sutskever, Kai Chen, Greg S Corrado, and Jeff Dean. 2013b. Distributed representations of words and phrases and their compositionality. *Advances in Neural Information Processing Systems*, 26:3111–3119.

Matthias Orlikowski, Matthias Hartung, and Philipp Cimiano. 2018. Learning diachronic analogies to analyze concept change. In *Proceedings of the Second Joint SIGHUM Workshop on Computational Linguistics for Cultural Heritage, Social Sciences, Humanities and Literature*, pages 1–11. Association for Computational Linguistics.

Robert Parker, David Graff, Junbo Kong, Ke Chen, and Kazuaki Maeda. 2011. English Gigaword Fifth Edition LDC2011T07. Technical report, Linguistic Data Consortium, Philadelphia.

Therése Pettersson and Kristine Eck. 2018. Organized violence, 1989–2017. *Journal of Peace Research*, 55(4):535–547.

Anna Rogers, Aleksandr Drozd, and Bofang Li. 2017. The (too many) problems of analogical reasoning with word vectors. In *Proceedings of the 6th Joint Conference on Lexical and Computational Semantics (*SEM 2017)*, pages 135–148. Association for Computational Linguistics.

Alex Rosenfeld and Katrin Erk. 2018. Deep neural models of semantic shift. In *Proceedings of the 2018 Conference of the North American Chapter of the Association for Computational Linguistics: Human Language Technologies*, pages 474–484, New Orleans, Louisiana, USA.

Milan Straka and Jana Straková. 2017. Tokenizing, pos tagging, lemmatizing and parsing UD 2.0 with UD-Pipe. In *Proceedings of the CoNLL 2017 Shared Task: Multilingual Parsing from Raw Text to Universal Dependencies*, pages 88–99. Association for Computational Linguistics.

Xuri Tang. 2018. A state-of-the-art of semantic change computation. *Natural Language Engineering*, 24(5):649–676.

Measuring diachronic evolution of evaluative adjectives with word embeddings: the case for English, Norwegian, and Russian

Julia Rodina[1], Daria Bakshandaeva[1], Vadim Fomin[1],
Andrey Kutuzov[2], Samia Touileb[2], and Erik Velldal[2]

[1]National Research University Higher School of Economics, Moscow, Russia
[2]Language Technology Group, University of Oslo, Oslo, Norway
{julia.rodina97,dbakshandaeva,wadimiusz}@gmail.com
{andreku,samiat,erikve}@ifi.uio.no

Abstract

We measure the intensity of diachronic semantic shifts in adjectives in English, Norwegian and Russian across 5 decades. This is done in order to test the hypothesis that evaluative adjectives are more prone to temporal semantic change. To this end, 6 different methods of quantifying semantic change are used.

Frequency-controlled experimental results show that, depending on the particular method, evaluative adjectives either do not differ from other types of adjectives in terms of semantic change or appear to actually be less prone to shifting (particularly, to 'jitter'-type shifting). Thus, in spite of many well-known examples of semantically changing evaluative adjectives (like 'terrific' or 'incredible'), it seems that such cases are not specific to this particular type of words.

1 Introduction

Words change their meaning over time. It has become widespread recently to trace such shifts using word embedding models (that is, using contextual cues from raw corpora). However, most of this research is centred on the English language, and focuses on *nouns* specifically. In this paper, we work with 3 different languages (English, Norwegian and Russian), and focus our attention on *adjectives*.

Particularly, we aim to test empirically whether *evaluative adjectives* are more susceptible to diachronic semantic shifts than other types of adjectives. Evaluative adjectives are defined as those which describe object qualities from the subjective point of view of the speakers, expressing their opinions about the object being described. Typical English examples are '*good*', '*bad*' or '*brilliant*'.

Sometimes, adjectives can become evaluative in the course of semantic shifts happening across time: consider the history of the English word

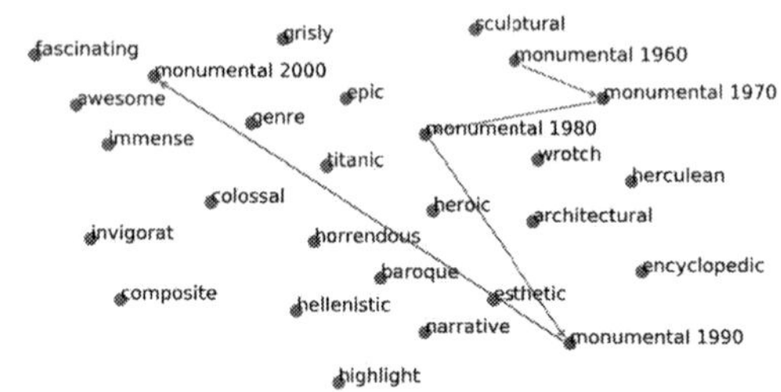

Figure 1: Alterations in meaning of the English adjective '*monumental*': from *sculptures* in the sixties to *awesome* in the 2000s

monumental from the 60s to the 2000s (Figure 1)[1] or how the word *sick* slowly acquires a (colloquial) evaluative sense ('*That's sick, dude!*') as described in Mitra et al. (2014). On the other hand, intuitively, evaluative adjectives are naturally prone to amelioration and pejoration as major types of diachronic semantic shifts. One can immediately recall, for example, the English words *incredible* and *terrific* which underwent amelioration and started to denote positive instead of negative qualities.

But are these words only isolated hand-picked examples, or is there a general trend in human languages which makes evaluative adjectives change more intensely over time? In this paper, we try to answer this question. Section 2 puts this work in the context of previous research. In section 3, we describe the corpora and word lists we relied upon. Our experiments are described in 4. In sections 5 and 6 we outline the limitations of the presented research, our plans for the future, and conclude.

---

[1]See Appendix A for details on visualisation

Proceedings of the 1st International Workshop on Computational Approaches to Historical Language Change, pages 202–209
Florence, Italy, August 2, 2019. ©2019 Association for Computational Linguistics

2 Related work

The nature of semantic change processes has always been of special interest to linguistics. This interest started at least as early as in Bréal (1883) who asserted the intellectual (cognitive) laws of semantic change as opposed to 'natural' ones. Later, Bloomfield (1933) proposed a popular categorisation of semantic shifts into classes. Further on, the academic community tried to develop a theoretical understanding of reasons behind semantic shifts, and to refine their classification (Meillet, 1974).

Moving on to specific types of semantic shifts, amelioration (acquiring more positive sentiment) and pejoration (acquiring more negative sentiment) were studied in Borkowska and Kleparski (2007), who mentioned these types to be one of the strongest and most wide-spread.

As the amount of language data available to computational linguistics increased,[2] the focus of research interest moved from theoretical reasoning about the nature of semantic shifts to more empirical approaches, mainly based on corpus-based analysis (see Michel et al. (2011) and Jatowt and Duh (2014), among many others).

Recently, the usage of pre-trained word embeddings (Bengio et al., 2003; Mikolov et al., 2013a) has become widespread in the publications related to diachronic semantic shifts (Kim et al., 2014; Hamilton et al., 2016c; Liao and Cheng, 2016; Kutuzov et al., 2017b,a; Rosenfeld and Erk, 2018). The main reason for this is the powerful abilities of such approaches to model word meaning based solely on non-annotated corpora. Additionally, vector representations of words allow for easy calculation of their similarities and changes. The baseline method here consists of simply training embedding models on the texts created in different time periods, and then comparing the vector representations for the same words. For further information on the current state of the field, see Kutuzov et al. (2018) and Tang (2018).

One of the difficulties brought by these approaches is the necessity to somehow 'align' the vector spaces trained on different time bins (time periods). A variety of methods have been proposed to overcome this. They include initialising the models for each time bin with the weights from models trained on the previous time bin ('incremental training') (Kim et al., 2014); Procrustes alignment of independent embedding models (Hamilton et al., 2016c); dynamic models trained across all time bins at once (Bamler and Mandt, 2017; Yao et al., 2018; Rosenfeld and Erk, 2018); Global Anchors (measuring the vectors of words' similarities to other words) (Yin et al., 2018), etc. In this paper, we employ Procrustes alignment and the Global Anchors methods, applying them to the task of measuring the speed of semantic shifts of evaluative adjectives across time.

An important publication related to our work is Hamilton et al. (2016a). In it, the authors induce historical sentiment lexicons from English corpora (using word embeddings, among other methods). They further show that amelioration and pejoration do occur on a massive scale: many evaluative adjectives in English have completely switched their sentiment during the last 150 years. We extend this work by studying not only sentiment changes, but semantic shifts in evaluative adjectives in general. Additionally, we analyse data from 3 languages (English, Norwegian and Russian). However, we focus on a more narrow time span: only the decades from 1960s to 2000s.

3 Data

In this section, we describe our data: the corpora employed to train word embedding models, and the sentiment lexicons serving as the source of evaluative adjectives.

3.1 Corpora

For the purposes of our research, we employed corpora in three languages, selecting texts which were created during the five decades from 1960s to 2000s. We lemmatized (it was especially important for Russian with its rich morphology) and POS-tagged all the corpora ourselves, using the corresponding UDPipe models (Straka and Straková, 2017).

For *English* data, we used The Corpus of Historical American English (COHA).[3] This is a corpus of English texts annotated with creation dates and balanced by genres. It is composed of fiction, magazine and newspaper articles, as well as non-fiction texts.

Decade	**English**	**Norwegian**	**Russian**
1960s	12	6	10
1970s	12	21	10
1980s	13	25.5	9
1990s	14.5	40.5	20
2000s	15	21	39.5

Table 1: Corpora sizes (in millions of words)

For *Norwegian* data, we used the NBdigital corpus.[4] It contains texts in Norwegian Bokmål from the National Library of Norway's collection of free texts, obtained by OCR processing (only texts with the OCR confidence higher than 0.9). These texts were mainly produced by various public institutions.

For *Russian* data, we used the Russian National Corpus (RNC).[5] It includes a wide variety of genres of written and spoken language, such as non-translated works of fiction, memoirs, essays, journalistic works, scientific and popular scientific literature, public speeches, letters, diaries, documents, etc. It is important that the RNC is also rigorously balanced across genres and types of texts.

Table 1 lists the corpora sizes for each decade under consideration.

3.2 Word embeddings

Continuous bag-of-words (CBOW) embedding models (Mikolov et al., 2013b) were trained on each decade for each of the three languages. All the models share the same set of hyperparameters: vector size 300, symmetric context window size 3, and 10 iterations over the corpus. We discarded all the words which occurred less than 5 times in the training corpus, and additionally limited the maximum vocabulary size to be 100 000, more or less following the hyperparameters from Kutuzov et al. (2017a). The models are made available via the NLPL word vector repository[6] (Fares et al., 2017).

3.3 Evaluative adjectives lists

In order to find out whether evaluative adjective are more prone to diachronic semantic shifts, we need an authoritative source providing us with a list of such adjectives, more than only several words in size. Unfortunately, even for English

such a list is hard to find in the published works, and the same is true for Norwegian and Russian. For this reason, we turned to sentiment lexicons: lists of positive and negative words widely used for the purposes of automatic sentiment analysis. The ratio is that such words are almost always evaluative by definition. Below we describe these lexicons for each of the three languages under analysis.

The lists for *English* and *Norwegian* come from the same source. The English lexicon is a general sentiment lexicon composed of a positive and a negative lexicon. These were created by assigning the positive and negative labels using a WordNet-based bootstrapping approach (Hu and Liu, 2004)[7]. We thereafter automatically translated (from English to Norwegian) these positive and negative sentiment lexicons. The translations were manually checked, and corrected when necessary. Furthermore, if an English word had several senses that could be translated into different Norwegian words, these were added to the translations. We have omitted all multi-word expressions, and only kept single word translations. This resulted in a collection of 3961 negative and 1646 positive Norwegian words. The original English lexicons contained 4783 negative and 2006 positive words. We did not investigate rigorously to what extent the translated lexicon is representative of the Norwegian language, but we believe that it is representative enough, since it is a general lexicon equivalent to its original English counterpart, and because the Norwegian list was checked manually to filter out non-evaluative adjectives.

The Norwegian lexical resource SCARRIE[8], a full-form lexicon, was used to identify which of the Norwegian translations were adjectives. Once these Norwegian adjectives were identified, we selected only the English words that had a Norwegian adjective as translation. Subsequently, we used the WordNet (Miller, 1995) to identify which of the selected English words were actually adjectives. If an English word was not identified as an adjective, we used WordNet to find its adjective form by analysing the derivationally related forms of its lemma. If no such form could be found, then the English word was removed from our list. Both lists were thereafter lemmatized and manu-

---

[4] https://www.nb.no/sprakbanken/show?serial=oai:nb.no:sbr-43&lang=en

[5] http://ruscorpora.ru/en/

[6] http://vectors.nlpl.eu/repository/

[7] Available at https://www.cs.uic.edu/~liub/FBS/sentiment-analysis.html

[8] https://www.nb.no/sprakbanken/show?serial=sbr-9&lang=nb

ally filtered to remove non-evaluative adjectives. This resulted in 2250 English adjectives and 1939 Norwegian adjectives.

We borrowed *Russian* evaluative adjectives from *RuSentiLex* (Loukachevitch and Levchik, 2016): a list of sentiment-related words and expressions. There are three types of entries in *RuSentiLex*, depending on their source: 'opinion', 'feeling' and 'fact' (words or expressions that do not express an opinion of the author, but have a positive or negative connotation). Also, each entry is labelled with its part of speech, lemmatized form and polarity, which can be positive, negative, neutral or positive/negative for strong context-dependent semantic orientation. Polysemous words have separate entries for different senses. The current version of the lexicon contains more than 12 thousand words and expressions, which were semi-automatically obtained from existing domain-oriented sentiment vocabularies (initial list), news articles (words with connotations) and Twitter (slang and curse words). For this research we used only one-word adjectives labelled with the 'opinion' source. Since differences in the sentiment and polarity of polysemous words are not taken into account in this paper, repeated entries have been removed. In total, there are 2435 Russian evaluative adjectives.

After acquiring the lists of evaluative adjectives and training word embedding models on the texts created for each decade under analysis, we were able to move on to the experiments.

4 Experiments

Our general aim is to measure the speed of temporal semantic shifts in evaluative adjectives compared to all other adjective types. This is necessary to confirm or reject the hypothesis that evaluative adjectives are less stable than other words of the same part of speech. We want to find evidence across all three languages under analysis. We also would like to control for frequency and to exclude its influence on the results, since it is known that word frequency often correlates with the speed of semantic change (Hamilton et al., 2016c) [9].

We measure the speed of semantic changes using a variety of methods:

1. *Jaccard distance* (Jaccard, 1901) between sets of 10 nearest neighbours of one word (by cosine distance) in two embedding models;

2. *Procrustes alignment* (Hamilton et al., 2016c): the models' vector spaces are first aligned using an SVD-based orthogonal transformation, and then cosine distance is calculated between one word's vectors in two transformed models;

3. *Global Anchors* (Yin et al., 2018): here, the degree of semantic change is defined as the cosine distance between the vectors of a word's cosine similarities to all other words in the intersection of two models' vocabularies ('anchors').

The aforementioned methods measure the distance between the meanings of one word in two different embedding models. However, our data includes five models (trained on five consequent decades from 1960s to 2000s). In order to quantify the speed of semantic change across the whole time span, two techniques were used:

1. *Mean distances*: simple mean between the 4 pairwise distances ('60s to 70s', '70s to 80s', '80s to 90s', and '90s to 2000s'). It measures the degree of 'semantic jitter' that the word undergoes: it is not necessarily a steady movement into one direction, but can instead be fluctuations around one centre point (points).

2. *Mean deltas from the 60s*: here, at each decade we calculate the distance of the current word representation to its representation in the 60s (the initial point of our time span). If the distance increased, one point is added to the word's score, if the distance decreased, one point is subtracted. Then, the average score is calculated for each word. The rationale behind this is to measure how steady the shift in meaning is from the initial point for a given word. The score here will be low for the words which fluctuate but do not really substantially change their semantics. At the same time, it will be high for consistent cases (like, for example, the English adjective *'solid'* steadily moving toward denoting not only qualities of materials, but also generally being of good quality). See, e.g., Figure 2 for an example of how a word can first move away from the original meaning, but then start to slowly return back.

---

[9]Note, however, that this was disputed in Dubossarsky et al. (2017).

Figure 2: Alterations in meaning of the Russian adjective 'бескомпромиссный' (*uncompromising*): from *ruthless* over *fanatical*, *passion*, later *conviction*, *heroic* to *intransigence*, *confrontation*

Method	English	Norwegian	Russian
# fillers	8994	3989	7535
Freq diff	0.00001	0.00003	0.00001
Mean pairwise distances			
Jaccard	-11.08	-4	-15.05
Procrustes	-15.52	-5.04	-12.01
GlobAnchors	11.91	-4.40	12.62
Mean deltas from 1960s			
Jaccard	3.28	0	0
Procrustes	2.98	0	3.92
GlobAnchors	3.57	3.24	3.11

Table 2: Difference in the intensity of semantic shifts between evaluative adjectives and fillers. Positive values correspond to evaluatives changing significantly faster, and vice versa.

Both *mean distances* and *mean deltas from the 60s* can be used with any method of measuring semantic change of the 3 described above, thus overall we have 6 scores to assign to each word in our word lists.

Note that we have *two* word lists for each language: the one with *evaluative* adjectives (extracted from sentiment lexicons) and another with what we will refer to as *fillers*: that is, simply all other adjectives present in the vocabularies of all five models for the current language. We compare the semantic change speed scores of the first list to those in the second one. If the average values differ with the Welch's T-test p-value not exceeding 0.1[10], we conclude that one type of adjectives is more subject to diachronic semantic change than the other, and report the t-statistics of the difference between the averages. If the p-value exceeds the 0.1 threshold, we conclude there is no difference between two lists, and report it as 0 (full anabridged tables available at `https://github.com/ltgoslo/diachronic_multiling_adjectives/tree/master/full_tables`).

Table 2 presents the results calculated this way. Positive t-statistic values mean that evaluative adjectives change faster than other types of adjectives, according to particular metrics; negative values mean they change slower. We also report the number of filler adjectives ('# fillers') for each language.

As can be seen, across all languages, evaluative adjectives seem to fluctuate less (*mean pairwise distances*), as measured by all methods, except for Global Anchors applied to English and Russian. At the same time, the majority of methods agree that evaluative adjectives are more likely to steady shift in one direction, farther and farther away from the original meaning (as measured by *mean deltas from the 60s*). This is less expressed for Norwegian (with Jaccard and Global Anchors methods, the difference between two types of adjectives was not significant).

However, these values are potentially problematic. As already mentioned, the speed of semantic change can correlate with word frequencies. The 'Freq diff' line in the table 2 shows the difference between average word frequencies in both word lists (expressed as word probabilities relative to corpora sizes). All these values are statistically significant and positive: this means that evaluative adjectives are on average more frequent than other adjectives.

Table 3 proves that there are indeed statistically significant correlations between word frequencies and all our methods for measuring the intensity of temporal semantic shifts, across all languages. More frequent words consistently get *lower* scores from *mean distances*.[11] Vice versa, they get *higher* scores from the *mean deltas* technique, suggesting that frequent words are more prone to steady semantic shifting.

---

[10] The p-value threshold of 0.1 was used intentionally, instead of the more standard 0.05. We could as well use 0.05, and it wouldn't change the final results of the research (the original hypothesis would still be rejected). The reason behind choosing 0.1 was to be able to show that some differences in the speed of semantic change between evaluative adjectives and fillers can be found, but they are rare and fragile even with a very permissive p-value threshold.

[11] It seems to support the law of conformity from Hamilton et al. (2016c)

Method	English	Norwegian	Russian
Mean distances			
Jaccard	-0.37	-0.33	-0.32
Procrustes	-0.19	-0.21	-0.17
GlobAnchors	0.29	-0.08	0.11
Mean deltas from 1960s			
Jaccard	0.05	0.10	0.08
Procrustes	0.07	0.12	0.08
GlobAnchors	0.07	0.12	0.05

Table 3: Correlation of semantic change speed and normalised word frequency across all adjectives (evaluative and fillers). Positive values correspond to frequent words changing significantly faster, and vice versa.

Method	English	Norwegian	Russian
# fillers	1133	571	929
Freq diff	0	0	-0.00002
Mean distances			
Jaccard	0	-1.68	-2.54
Procrustes	-4.77	-3.24	-5.03
GlobAnchors	-3.70	-4.07	0
Mean deltas from the 1960s			
Jaccard	0	0	-2.44
Procrustes	0	2.94	0
GlobAnchors	0	0	-1.79

Table 4: Difference in the intensity of semantic shifts between evaluative adjectives and fillers (frequency > 100). Positive values correspond to evaluatives changing significantly faster, and vice versa.

To get rid of the influence of the frequency factor in comparing evaluative and non-evaluative adjectives, we have to make the average frequencies of both lists more like each other. Since we observed that evaluative adjectives are more frequent, we decided to use the *frequency threshold*. All adjectives with corpus frequency in at least one decade lesser than the threshold (which is a hyperparameter) were removed from the word lists (both evaluative adjectives and fillers) [12]. This allowed us to get rid of low-frequency long-tail and make both lists to better fit each other in terms of frequency. In the table 4, we report the results using the threshold of 100.

The number of fillers has naturally declined.

[12]We did not down-sample the evaluative adjectives instead, since they are the main focus of our research, and we did not want to reduce their number (not huge to begin with).

Also, the 'Freq diff' line shows that this way we managed to eliminate any statistically significant difference between evaluative and non-evaluative word lists for English and Norwegian. For Russian data, the situation has reversed: now evaluative adjectives are on average *less* frequent. Interestingly, the overall results for the 'mean distances' methods did not change or even became more expressed. Even when controlled for frequency, evaluative adjectives seem to be less prone to 'fluctuating' semantic shifts. Thus, to some extent they are more semantically stable than other adjectives. This makes us reject the initial hypothesis about them being less stable.

Note that for the *mean deltas* technique, filtering out the low-frequency words led to the differences between evaluative and non-evaluative adjectives losing their statistical significance in almost all combinations of languages and methods. Thus, we cannot prove any specificity of evaluative adjectives with respect to the 'steadiness' of diachronic semantic changes.

5 Limitations and future work

First of all, sentiment lexicons as sources of 'evaluative adjectives' are by all means only proxies. It is quite probable that there are evaluative adjectives beyond sentiment lexicons, and vice versa. In the future, we plan to refine our datasets and probably come up with more linguistically justified word lists.

Although we used the well-known methods of measuring semantic shifts across word embedding models, there is still a need to evaluate the methods themselves. One option here it to use the *SentProp* historical sentiment datasets from Hamilton et al. (2016b). These datasets are created automatically, but still this sanity check could allow us to find out which of the algorithms produces results better correlated with the output of other systems. At the same time, it is known that distributional models can have a hard time handling the differences between antonyms, and those constitute a significant part of diachronic changes in *SentProp* (cf. *'incredible'* changing it sentiment from negative to positive in the last 40 years). There is an ample room for further research here.

Note also that the interplay between semantic shift detection methods and word frequencies is quite complex, and there is still a room to investigation. We didn't analyse it deeply, so we cannot exclude the possibility that the results could change if controlling for other related factors.

6   Conclusion

We measured the intensity of diachronic semantic shifts in adjectives across 3 languages (English, Norwegian and Russian) and 5 decades (60s, 70s, 80s, 90s, 2000s), to test whether evaluative adjectives change faster (or more intensely) than other adjectives.

Our results show that, contradictory to the initial hypothesis, evaluative adjectives change over time *less* intensely (statistically significant at $p < 0.1$), if we measure change as the mean of pairwise differences between successive decades, and not as a steady 'movement' in one particular direction. This is not an artefact of frequency, since we observe the same behaviour when controlling for word frequencies.

At the same time, when measuring the probability of steady 'moving away' from an original meaning across time, evaluative adjectives *do not differ from other adjectives at all* (at least on any statistically significant level).

To sum up, it seems that evaluative words (in our case, adjectives) are not more prone to semantic shifts than other word types. Vice versa, under some circumstances, they can be even more stable than their counterparts, with this observation holding across languages and methods of semantic shifts tracing.

Our diachronic embedding models, word lists and code can be found at `https://github.com/ltgoslo/ diachronic_multiling_adjectives`.

Acknowledgements

Parts of this work has been carried out in context of the SANT project, as funded by the Research Council of Norway (project number 270908).

References

Robert Bamler and Stephan Mandt. 2017. Dynamic word embeddings. In *Proceedings of the International Conference on Machine Learning*, pages 380–389, Sydney, Australia.

Yoshua Bengio, Rejean Ducharme, and Pascal Vincent. 2003. A neural probabilistic language model. *Journal of Machine Learning Research*, 3:1137–1155.

Leonard Bloomfield. 1933. *Language*. Allen & Unwin.

Paulina Borkowska and Grzegorz Kleparski. 2007. It befalls words to fall down: pejoration as a type of semantic change. In *Studia Anglica Resoviensia*, volume 47(4), pages 33–50.

Michel Bréal. 1883. Les lois intellectuelles du langage: fragment de sémantique. *Annuaire de l'Assocaition pour l'encouragement des études grecques en France*, 17:132–142.

Haim Dubossarsky, Daphna Weinshall, and Eitan Grossman. 2017. Outta control: Laws of semantic change and inherent biases in word representation models. In *Proceedings of the 2017 Conference on Empirical Methods in Natural Language Processing*, pages 1147–1156, Copenhagen, Denmark.

Murhaf Fares, Andrey Kutuzov, Stephan Oepen, and Erik Velldal. 2017. Word vectors, reuse, and replicability: Towards a community repository of large-text resources. In *Proceedings of the 21st Nordic Conference on Computational Linguistics*, pages 271–276. Association for Computational Linguistics.

William Hamilton, Kevin Clark, Jure Leskovec, and Dan Jurafsky. 2016a. Inducing domain-specific sentiment lexicons from unlabeled corpora. In *Proceedings of the Conference on Empirical Methods in Natural Language Processing*, pages 595–605, Austin, Texas.

William Hamilton, Kevin Clark, Jure Leskovec, and Dan Jurafsky. 2016b. Inducing domain-specific sentiment lexicons from unlabeled corpora. In *Proceedings of the 2016 Conference on Empirical Methods in Natural Language Processing*, pages 595–605, Austin, Texas. Association for Computational Linguistics.

William Hamilton, Jure Leskovec, and Dan Jurafsky. 2016c. Diachronic word embeddings reveal statistical laws of semantic change. In *Proceedings of the 54th Annual Meeting of the Association for Computational Linguistics*, pages 1489–1501, Berlin, Germany.

Minqing Hu and Bing Liu. 2004. Mining and summarizing customer reviews. In *Proceedings of the tenth ACM SIGKDD international conference on Knowledge discovery and data mining*, pages 168–177. ACM.

Paul Jaccard. 1901. *Distribution de la Flore Alpine: dans le Bassin des dranses et dans quelques régions voisines*. Rouge.

Adam Jatowt and Kevin Duh. 2014. A framework for analyzing semantic change of words across time. In *Proceedings of the 14th ACM/IEEE-CS Joint Conference on Digital Libraries*, JCDL '14, pages 229–238, Piscataway, NJ, USA. IEEE Press.

Yoon Kim, Yi-I Chiu, Kentaro Hanaki, Darshan Hegde, and Slav Petrov. 2014. Temporal analysis of language through neural language models. In *Proceedings of the 52nd Annual Meeting of the Association for Computational Linguistics*, pages 61–65, Baltimore, USA.

Andrey Kutuzov, Lilja Øvrelid, Terrence Szymanski, and Erik Velldal. 2018. Diachronic word embeddings and semantic shifts: a survey. In *Proceedings of the 27th International Conference on Computational Linguistics*, pages 1384–1397. Association for Computational Linguistics.

Andrey Kutuzov, Erik Velldal, and Lilja Øvrelid. 2017a. Temporal dynamics of semantic relations in word embeddings: an application to predicting armed conflict participants. In *Proceedings of the Conference on Empirical Methods in Natural Language Processing*, pages 1824–1829, Copenhagen, Denmark.

Andrey Kutuzov, Erik Velldal, and Lilja Øvrelid. 2017b. Tracing armed conflicts with diachronic word embedding models. In *Proceedings of the Events and Stories in the News Workshop at ACL 2017*, pages 31–36, Vancouver, Canada.

Xuanyi Liao and Guang Cheng. 2016. Analysing the semantic change based on word embedding. In *Natural Language Understanding and Intelligent Applications*, pages 213–223. Springer International Publishing.

Natalia Loukachevitch and Anatolii Levchik. 2016. Creating a general Russian sentiment lexicon. In *Proceedings of Language Resources and Evaluation Conference (LREC-2016)*, pages 1171–1176.

Laurens Van der Maaten and Geoffrey Hinton. 2008. Visualizing data using t-SNE. *Journal of Machine Learning Research*, 9(2579-2605):85.

Antoine Meillet. 1974. Wie die wörter ihre bedeutung ändern. *G. Disner (ed.) Zur Theorie der Sprachveränderung*, pages 19–67.

Jean-Baptiste Michel, Yuan Kui Shen, Aviva Presser Aiden, Adrian Veres, Matthew K Gray, Joseph P Pickett, Dale Hoiberg, Dan Clancy, Peter Norvig, Jon Orwant, et al. 2011. Quantitative analysis of culture using millions of digitized books. *science*, 331(6014):176–182.

Tomas Mikolov, Kai Chen, Greg Corrado, and Jeffrey Dean. 2013a. Efficient estimation of word representations in vector space. *arXiv preprint arXiv:1301.3781*.

Tomas Mikolov, Ilya Sutskever, Kai Chen, Greg S Corrado, and Jeff Dean. 2013b. Distributed representations of words and phrases and their compositionality. *Advances in Neural Information Processing Systems*, 26:3111–3119.

George Miller. 1995. Wordnet: a lexical database for English. *Communications of the ACM*, 38(11):39–41.

Sunny Mitra, Ritwik Mitra, Martin Riedl, Chris Biemann, Animesh Mukherjee, and Pawan Goyal. 2014. That's sick dude!: Automatic identification of word sense change across different timescales. In *Proceedings of the 52nd Annual Meeting of the Association for Computational Linguistics*, pages 1020–1029, Baltimore, Maryland.

Alex Rosenfeld and Katrin Erk. 2018. Deep neural models of semantic shift. In *Proceedings of the 2018 Conference of the North American Chapter of the Association for Computational Linguistics: Human Language Technologies*, pages 474–484, New Orleans, Louisiana, USA.

Milan Straka and Jana Straková. 2017. Tokenizing, pos tagging, lemmatizing and parsing ud 2.0 with udpipe. In *Proceedings of the CoNLL 2017 Shared Task: Multilingual Parsing from Raw Text to Universal Dependencies*, pages 88–99. Association for Computational Linguistics.

Xuri Tang. 2018. A state-of-the-art of semantic change computation. *Natural Language Engineering*, 24(5):649–676.

Zijun Yao, Yifan Sun, Weicong Ding, Nikhil Rao, and Hui Xiong. 2018. Dynamic word embeddings for evolving semantic discovery. In *Proceedings of the Eleventh ACM International Conference on Web Search and Data Mining*, pages 673–681, Marina Del Rey, CA, USA.

Zi Yin, Vin Sachidananda, and Balaji Prabhakar. 2018. The global anchor method for quantifying linguistic shifts and domain adaptation. In *Advances in Neural Information Processing Systems*, pages 9433–9444.

A Visualization

Visualisation algorithm is based on the method described in (Hamilton et al., 2016c). To trace visually the movement of a given word in the semantic space we take a union of m most similar words for all periods that are of interest for us. Then t-SNE (Van der Maaten and Hinton, 2008), a technique for dimensionality reduction, is used to fit embeddings into two dimensional space: for m nearest neighbours, t-SNE embedding is found only on the most recent period (which represents the most recent meanings of these words), whereas for the word under consideration, embeddings from all time periods are taken into account. Procrustes alignment is preliminarily applied so that embeddings of the target word from all time bins are placed in common embedding space.

Semantic Change in the Language of UK Parliamentary Debates

Gavin Abercrombie and **Riza Batista-Navarro**
School of Computer Science
University of Manchester
Kilburn Building, Manchester M13 9PL
`gavin.abercrombie@postgrad.manchester.ac.uk`
`riza.batista@manchester.ac.uk`

Abstract

We investigate changes in the meanings of words used in the UK Parliament across two different decade-long epochs. We use word embeddings to explore changes in the distribution of words of interest and uncover words that appear to have undergone semantic transformation in the intervening period. We explore different ways of obtaining target words for this purpose. We find that semantic changes are generally in line with those found in other corpora, and little evidence that parliamentary language is more static than general English. It also seems that words with senses that have been recorded in the dictionary as having fallen into disuse do not undergo semantic changes in this domain.

1 Introduction

Commonly known as *Hansard*, transcripts of debates held in the United Kingdom (UK) Parliament from 1802 to the present day are publicly and freely available in digitized format. These transcipts are important sources of historical and current information for many people including scholars in the political and social sciences, the media, politicians, and members of the public who wish to scrutinize the activities of elected representatives.

Natural languages (such as English) are known to be dynamic, with the meaning of many lexical items drifting over time (for example., *gay: cheerful* → *homosexual* (Wijaya and Yeniterzi, 2011)).

Knowledge of the level of such semantic change existing in a particular domain can assist in the design of systems for downstream natural language processing tasks such as sentiment analysis. For example, training and testing on in-domain data from different periods of time has been shown to negatively affect perfomance in named entity recognition (Fromreide et al., 2014) and sentiment analysis (Kapovciute-Dzikiene and Krupavicius,

2014). Successful analysis of such changes in Hansard could therefore be an important element in the development of civic technology applications for parliamentary analysis.

In this paper, we investigate to what extent diachronic semantic change occurs in the Hansard record by examining the contexts in which words appear during two different periods in the corpus.

2 Analysis

2.1 Data: The Hansard record

We collected the transcripts of debates in the House of Commons chamber from the parliamentary Hansard website[1] in `html` format and extracted the text elements that correspond to speaker utterances. These 'substantially verbatim'[2] transcripts are recorded by parliamentary reporters present at the debates.

Comparison across epochs Following Dubossarsky et al. (2017), we organised the transcripts into two decade-long epochs for comparison. We selected the periods 1909-18 and 2009-18 due to (a) the latter being the most recent period to comprise data from 10 complete years, and (b) the former consisting of transcripts from a full century prior, with the intervening period having seen a variety of significant changes, both in Parliament (for example, women's suffrage, the rise of the Labour party) and in wider society (two World Wars, the growth of technology). We considered the data for periods prior to the twentieth century to possibly be insufficiently complete for comparison with recent transcripts.[3]

Examination of the data available in the two

---

[1] `https://hansard.parliament.uk`
[2] `https://hansard.parliament.uk/about?`
`historic=false`
[3] The Hansard record of debates from the 19th century includes only 92 days per year on average.

Proceedings of the 1st International Workshop on Computational Approaches to Historical Language Change, pages 210–215
Florence, Italy, August 2, 2019. ©2019 Association for Computational Linguistics

periods (see Table 1) shows that, due to changes in Hansard transcription practice, the more recent epoch consists of a larger amount of data. Additionally, the large quantity of unique tokens (around 46 thousand items) that appear in only one of the epochs (the disjunctive union of the two sets) indicates that the vocabulary of the corpus changes considerably in this period.

	1909-18	2009-18	Total
Debate days	975	1455	2430
Utterances	448k	2.1M	2.5M
Tokens	33.7M	105.8M	124.9M
Unique tokens	95.6k	174.2k	222.8k

Table 1: Comparison of Hansard over two epochs. Each day's transcript typically includes several debates, which can be broken down into individual utterances (unbroken passages of text) and tokens (words).

2.2 Representation of the distributional space

In preproceesing, we stripped all utterances of punctuation, lowercased and tokenized them.

We extracted embedding vectors using `gensim`[4]'s `word2vec`[5] (Mikolov et al., 2013), with a context window of four tokens and vector dimensionality of size 300 (following settings used in previous work (Hamilton et al., 2016)).

As in Dubossarsky et al. (2017) and Hamilton et al. (2016), we trained word embeddings on each epoch, and aligned these using orthogonal procrustes transformation (Schönemann, 1966). We then compared word embedding vectors for each word of interest across the different time windows by calculating the cosine similarity of its embedding vectors in the two different periods. Assuming that lower similarity between these vectors indicates a higher degree of difference in the meaning and usage of a term, we use these calculations to identify which of these words has undergone semantic change in Hansard over time.

We calculate the cosine similarity between the word embedding vector of each word that appears in both epochs. The mean similarity across the entire vocabulary is only 0.154, indicating that the distributions of words in these two periods is quite different overall. We use this figure for comparison with our target words.

2.3 Target words of interest

We investigate instances of semantic change in the Hansard record from the two chosen epochs in four groups of lexical items: (1) words known from previous work to have undergone semantic change in the twentieth century; (2) words with senses that are no longer in use according to the Oxford English Dictionary (OED); (3) words from the parliamentary website's glossary;[6] and (4) words not appearing in the first three categories that demonstrate the greatest degree of distributional change across epochs. We consider words in the latter category to represent 'discovered' changes from this domain.

Known words from prior work Overall, it seems that words known to have undergone semantic change in English, have also done so in the Hansard record. Of the 21 known items (see Table 2), 18 have lower cosine similarity than the mean, suggesting that these semantic shifts also take place in Hansard. Observing the words with most similar embedding vectors in each epoch, we consider that 14 of these exhibit clear shifts in usage. The word with most dissimilar embedding vectors for the two periods is *checking*, which appears to undergo a similar shift in meaning as that described by Kulkarni et al. (2015) (see Figure 1).

Figure 1: T-SNE visualisation (Maaten and Hinton, 2008) of the embedding space for 'checking' across both epochs, where it's sense appears to shift from *stopping* towards *verifying*.

While some items do appear to have undergone change in this data, this is not always of the form reported in the original literature. For example, while Hamilton et al. (2016) observe *broadcast* moving from being an agricultural term to the media and technology domain, in Hansard, it's earlier

---

[4]Řehůřek and Sojka (2010).

[5]`https://radimrehurek.com/gensim/models/word2vec.html`

[6]`https://www.parliament.uk/site-information/glossary/`

Word of interest	Earlier sense	Later sense	Source
actually	—	—	Hamilton et al. (2016)
broadcast∗	cast out seeds	transmit signal	Hamilton et al. (2016)
calls	—	—	Hamilton et al. (2016)
check	—	—	Hamilton et al. (2016)
checking	stop doing	look at	Kulkarni et al. (2015)
diet	foods	weight-loss regime	Kulkarni et al. (2015)
gay∗	happy	homosexual	Hamilton et al. (2016)
headed	top of body/entity	direction	Hamilton et al. (2016)
honey∗	foodstuff	form of address	Kulkarni et al. (2015)
major	—	—	Hamilton et al. (2016)
monitor∗	—	screen	Hamilton et al. (2016)
mouse∗	rodent	device	Jatowt and Duh (2014)
plastic	flexible	synthetic polymer	Kulkarni et al. (2015)
propaganda	Papal committee	political information	Jatowt and Duh (2014)
record	—	album	Hamilton et al. (2016)
recording	set down in writing	stored copy	Kulkarni et al. (2015)
sex	biological gender	have intercourse	Kulkarni et al. (2015)
started	—	—	Hamilton et al. (2016)
starting	—	—	Hamilton et al. (2016)
transmitted∗	pass	broadcast	Kulkarni et al. (2015)
wanting	lacking	wishing for	Hamilton et al. (2016)

Table 2: List of words of interest known to have undergone semantic change during the twentieth century, their sense shifts (if stated in the literature), and sources. Words we deem to have also undergone semantic change in Hansard are in bold. Those which appear to have shifted, but between different senses than those reported in the prior work, are marked with an asterisk (∗). Note: Hamilton et al. (2016) compiled their original word list from Jatowt and Duh (2014); Jeffers and Lehiste (1979); Kulkarni et al. (2015); Simpson and Weiner (1989).

sense seems to be related to the *distribututon* of printed material.

A number of observations seem to be artifacts of this particular dataset. A feature of the earlier epoch is that many of the MPs were ex-military officers, so in this period the most similar words to *major* are other rank titles such as *colonel* and *captain*, while this term later adopts the sense of *important* or *significant*. The word that appears to have changed the least according to vector similarity is *honey*. This is perhaps unsurprising, as the later sense recorded by Kulkarni et al. (2015) is both an informal term of address and associated with American English—and therefore unlikely to feature in UK parliamentary language. Given this, the fact that this item still has fairly low cosine similarity may be attributible to its frequent appearance as a surname in debates in the earlier epoch.

Disused words We obtained a list of words which have a least one sense that has fallen out of use and was last recorded by the OED between 1900 and the present day.[7] Of these, 39 appear in both epochs of Hansard. While we determine that most of these have not undergone semantic change in the corpus, even the three items that do seem to have shifted appear not to have been used in the disused sense listed in the dictionary (see Table 3).

Word of interest	Disused sense (OED)	1910s sense	2010s sense
slag	chain	coal bi-product	criticize
screen	banknote	barrier	electronic display
sky	enemy	? (unclear)	media organisation

Table 3: Words with a disused sense in the OED together with the senses in which thay are apparently used in the two epochs of the Hansard record.

---

[7]Downloaded from the API `https://developer.oxforddictionaries.com/our-data#!/word/get_words`.

| ↑ | *racket*, *levers*, *balances*, *abet*, *leans*, *tailor*, *consensual*, *implements*, *riddle*, *teen*, *invalidates*, *delivering*, *honouring*, *relay*, *technological*, *traverse*, *directs*, *capitalise*, *plurality*, *disguised* |
| ↓ | *porcelain*, *whales*, *lesions*, *moat*, *professors*, *turnip*, *exceptionally*, *decreased*, *employ*, *suicides*, *insist*, *scaffold*, *assertions*, *daughters*, *murders*, *lasted*, *unfurnished*, *seeking*, *dams*, *fishes* |

Table 4: Top 20 words that have undergone the most (↑) and least (↓) semantic change. Words the authors verify as clearly having undergone semantic change are in bold.

Parliamentary vocabulary Examination of the 51 single-word items in the parliamentary glossary reveals that only 56.9% of these have cross-epoch cosine similarity above the mean for the whole corpus, indicating that, as might perhaps be expected, these words have been semantically stable in Hansard through the last century. Among the most stable items are aristocratic titles such as *earl*, *bishop*, and *baron* that are used to refer to particular MPs and members of the House of Lords.

Discovered changes We examined the top 20 words from the whole vocabulary that are most and least similar according to cosine measurement across the two epochs of interest, excluding proper nouns, foreign words and numerals (see Table 4). Examining the words with most similar embedding vectors, we were able to confirm that most of the top changed words have indeed undergone semantic shifts, while none of those with the most similar embeddings across epochs appear to have done so. Examples, which may reflect societal changes between the epochs are *tailor* (*profession* → *adapt*) and *riddle* (*sieve* → *puzzle*).

3 Discussion

Words that have been shown to experience semantic change in English, in general seem to exhibit similar behaviour in parliamentary speeches. When compared to nearest neighbours from the distributional spaces in each epoch, it seems that the words that are least similar over time do indeed undergo semantic change in Hansard during this period. While it might be expected that words with senses specific to Parliament should not exhibit semantic change over time, they do not in fact seem to be much more stable than other items. This fact, combined with the overall low similarity across epochs for all words, may suggest that the differences in quantity and recording of the data in the two observed periods makes alignment of the word vectors problematic.

Additionally, words acknowledged to be in dis-

use in the OED tend to remain constant in this domain, and even those that do undergo change do not always seem to be used in the previously observed senses in this dataset. It would seem that, while these words had their last ever recorded uses in the period in question, they had already fallen out of use in Parliament.

In making the above observations, we acknowledge that it remains to be seen to what extent the observed changes are actually representative of diachronic change and how many of these are simply artifacts of the changing topics of dicussion in Parliament and the extent and manner of their recording in the Hansard record over the two epochs. We leave exploration of these questions for future work.

4 Related work

The phenomenon of language change has long been recognised (Sapir, 1921), and various social, cultural and cognitive factors have been proposed to explain it (Labov, 2011).

In recent years, efforts have been made to perform computational analyses of semantic change in dichronic corpora, and a number of methods have been proposed.[8] For example, (Wijaya and Yeniterzi, 2011) used topic modelling and clustering to investigate changes in the meanings of words in the Google Books corpus, while Frermann and Lapata (2016) proposed a Bayesian sense modelling approach to uncover gradual changes in meaning.

Much work in this area has focused on the use of vector space models such as Latent Semantic Analysis (LSA). Sagi et al. (2011) use this approach to track differences in the use of target words in historical texts, and Jatowt and Duh (2014) compare LSA with other distributional measurements.

A popular approach, which we adopt for this paper, is to use word embeddings. Kulkarni et al. (2015) compare distributional with

---

[8]For a recent overview, see Tang (2018).

frequency-based and syntactic analyses for diachronic change investigation, while Hamilton et al. (2016) and Dubossarsky et al. (2017) use embeddings to test hypotheses about the causes of such changes.

While Bamler and Mandt (2017) and Rudolph and Blei (2018) explore semantic change in the political domain on US State of the Union and Senate speeches repectively, we are unaware of any similar work on UK parliamentary debate transcripts.

5 Conclusion

We have explored four ways of obtaining target words of interest for diachronic semantic change analysis and conducted an initial study of this task in the domain of parliamentary debate transcripts. We found that using similarity measurement of word embedding vectors trained on two different epochs of the data, we are able to verify shifts in meaning in words that are known to have undergone this process in general English, and that we are also able to identify previously unknown changes in this data. We also observe that words with senses specific to parliamentary language do not appear to be particularly stable across time.

Future work will focus on conducting more comprehensive and systematic analyses of semantic change throughout the whole Hansard corpus in an effort to track senses and identify changes. We would also like to explore the possibility of using dynamic embeddings (e.g., Bamler and Mandt, 2017; Rudolph and Blei, 2018; Yao et al., 2018) to jointly train on different subsets of the data.

Acknowledgments

The authors would like to thank the anonymous reviewers for their helpful and insightful comments.

References

Robert Bamler and Stephan Mandt. 2017. Dynamic word embeddings. In *Proceedings of the 34th International Conference on Machine Learning - Volume 70*, ICML'17, pages 380–389. JMLR.org.

Haim Dubossarsky, Daphna Weinshall, and Eitan Grossman. 2017. Outta control: Laws of semantic change and inherent biases in word representation models. In *Proceedings of the 2017 Conference on Empirical Methods in Natural Language Processing*, pages 1136–1145, Copenhagen, Denmark. Association for Computational Linguistics.

Lea Frermann and Mirella Lapata. 2016. A Bayesian model of diachronic meaning change. *Transactions of the Association for Computational Linguistics*, 4:31–45.

Hege Fromreide, Dirk Hovy, and Anders Søgaard. 2014. Crowdsourcing and annotating NER for Twitter #drift. In *Proceedings of the Ninth International Conference on Language Resources and Evaluation (LREC'14)*, Reykjavik, Iceland. European Language Resources Association (ELRA).

William L. Hamilton, Jure Leskovec, and Dan Jurafsky. 2016. Diachronic word embeddings reveal statistical laws of semantic change. In *Proceedings of the 54th Annual Meeting of the Association for Computational Linguistics (Volume 1: Long Papers)*, pages 1489–1501, Berlin, Germany. Association for Computational Linguistics.

Adam Jatowt and Kevin Duh. 2014. A framework for analyzing semantic change of words across time. In *Proceedings of the 14th ACM/IEEE-CS Joint Conference on Digital Libraries*, JCDL '14, pages 229–238, Piscataway, NJ, USA. IEEE Press.

Robert Jeffers and Ilse Lehiste. 1979. *Principles and Methods for Historical Linguistics*. MIT Press.

Jurgita Kapovciute-Dzikiene and Algis Krupavicius. 2014. Predicting party group from the Lithuanian parliamentary speeches. *Information Technology And Control*, 43(3):321–332.

Vivek Kulkarni, Rami Al-Rfou, Bryan Perozzi, and Steven Skiena. 2015. Statistically significant detection of linguistic change. In *Proceedings of the 24th International Conference on World Wide Web*, WWW '15, pages 625–635, Republic and Canton of Geneva, Switzerland. International World Wide Web Conferences Steering Committee.

William Labov. 2011. *Principles of linguistic change, volume 3: Cognitive and cultural factors*, volume 36. John Wiley & Sons.

Laurens van der Maaten and Geoffrey Hinton. 2008. Visualizing data using t-sne. *Journal of machine learning research*, 9(Nov):2579–2605.

Tomas Mikolov, Kai Chen, Greg Corrado, and Jeffrey Dean. 2013. Efficient estimation of word representations in vector space. In *1st International Conference on Learning Representations, ICLR 2013, Scottsdale, Arizona, USA, May 2-4, 2013, Workshop Track Proceedings*.

Radim Řehůřek and Petr Sojka. 2010. Software framework for topic modelling with large corpora. In *Proceedings of the LREC 2010 Workshop on New Challenges for NLP Frameworks*, pages 45–50, Valletta, Malta. ELRA. http://is.muni.cz/publication/884893/en.

Maja Rudolph and David Blei. 2018. Dynamic embeddings for language evolution. In *Proceedings of the 2018 World Wide Web Conference*, WWW '18, pages 1003–1011, Republic and Canton of Geneva, Switzerland. International World Wide Web Conferences Steering Committee.

Eyal Sagi, Stefan Kaufmann, and Brady Clark. 2011. Tracing semantic change with latent semantic analysis. In Kathryn Allan and Justyna A. Robinson, editors, *Current methods in historical semantics*, pages 161–183. De Gruyter Mouton Berlin.

Edward Sapir. 1921. *Language: An Introduction to the study of speech*. NY: Harcourt, Brace & Co.

Peter H Schönemann. 1966. A generalized solution of the orthogonal procrustes problem. *Psychometrika*, 31(1):1–10.

John Simpson and Edmund Weiner. 1989. *The Oxford English Dictionary (20 Volume Set)*. Oxford University Press, USA.

Xuri Tang. 2018. A state-of-the-art of semantic change computation. *Natural Language Engineering*, 24(5):649–676.

Derry Tanti Wijaya and Reyyan Yeniterzi. 2011. Understanding semantic change of words over centuries. In *Proceedings of the 2011 international workshop on DETecting and Exploiting Cultural diversiTy on the social web*, DETECT '11, pages 35–40, New York, NY, USA. ACM.

Zijun Yao, Yifan Sun, Weicong Ding, Nikhil Rao, and Hui Xiong. 2018. Dynamic word embeddings for evolving semantic discovery. In *Proceedings of the Eleventh ACM International Conference on Web Search and Data Mining*, WSDM '18, pages 673–681, New York, NY, USA. ACM.

Semantic Change and Emerging Tropes
In a Large Corpus of New High German Poetry

Thomas Nikolaus Haider
MPI for Empirical Aesthetics, Frankfurt
IMS, University of Stuttgart
`thomas.haider@ae.mpg.de`

Steffen Eger
Natural Language Learning Group
Technical University of Darmstadt
`eger@aiphes.tu-darmstadt.de`

Abstract

Due to its semantic succinctness and novelty of expression, poetry is a great test bed for semantic change analysis. However, so far there is a scarcity of large diachronic corpora. Here, we provide a large corpus of German poetry which consists of about 75k poems with more than 11 million tokens, with poems ranging from the 16th to early 20th century. We then track semantic change in this corpus by investigating the rise of tropes ('love is magic') over time and detecting change points of meaning, which we find to occur particularly within the German Romantic period. Additionally, through self-similarity, we reconstruct literary periods and find evidence that the law of linear semantic change also applies to poetry.

1 Introduction

Following in the footsteps of traditional poetry analysis, Natural Language Understanding (NLU) research has largely explored *stylistic variation* (Kaplan and Blei, 2007; Kao and Jurafsky, 2015), (over time) (Voigt and Jurafsky, 2013), with a focus on *sound devices* (McCurdy et al., 2015; Hench, 2017) and broadly canonised form features such as *meter* (Greene et al., 2010; Agirrezabal et al., 2016; Estes and Hench, 2016) and *rhyme* (Reddy and Knight, 2011; Haider and Kuhn, 2018), as well as *enjambement* (Ruiz et al., 2017) and *noun+noun metaphor* (Kesarwani et al., 2017).

However, poetry also lends itself well to semantic change analysis, as linguistic invention (Underwood and Sellers, 2012; Herbelot, 2014) and succinctness (Roberts, 2000) are at the core of poetic production. Poetic language is generally very dense, where concepts / ideas cannot be easily paraphrased. With a distributional semantics model, Herbelot (2014) finds that the coherence of poetry significantly differs from Wikipedia and random text, allowing the conclusion that poetry is – compared to ordinary language – unusual in its word choice, but still generally regarded comprehensible language. Recently, there has been research with topic models on poetry with Latent Dirichlet Allocation. Navarro-Colorado (2018) explores the overarching topical motifs in a corpus of Spanish sonnetts, while Haider (2019) sketches the evolution of topics over time in a German poetry corpus, identifying salient topics for certain literature periods and applying these for downstream learning how to date a poem.

Following in this vein, we offer a method to explore poetic tropes, i.e. word pairs such as 'love (is) magic' that gain association strength (cosine similarity) over time, finding that most are gaining traction in the Romantic period. Further, we track the self-similarity of words, both with a change point analysis and by evaluating 'total self-similarity' of words over time. The former helps us to reconstruct literary periods, while the latter provides us with further evidence for the law of linearity of semantic change (Eger and Mehler, 2016) using our new method.

We do this with a model that learns diachronic word2vec embeddings jointly over all our time slots (Bamman et al., 2014), avoiding the need to compute the cosine similarity of two word vector representations on second order to align the embeddings.

Our contributions are: we (1) provide a large corpus of German poetry which consists of about 75k poems, ranging from the 16th to early 20th century with more than 11 million tokens.[1] We then track semantic change in this corpus with (2) two self-similarity experiments and finally (3) by investigating the rise of tropes (e.g. 'love is magic') over time.

---

[1] `http://github.com/`
`thomasnikolaushaider`

Proceedings of the 1st International Workshop on Computational Approaches to Historical Language Change, pages 216–222
Florence, Italy, August 2, 2019. ©2019 Association for Computational Linguistics

2 Related Work

Semantic change has been explored in various works in recent years. One focus has been on studying laws of semantic change. Xu and Kemp (2015) explore two earlier proposed laws quantitatively: the law of differentiation (near-synonyms tend to differentiate over time) and the law of parallel change (related words have analogous meaning changes), finding that the latter applies more broadly. Hamilton et al. (2016) find that frequent words have a lower chance of undergoing semantic change and more polysemous words are more likely to change semantically. Eger and Mehler (2016) find that semantic change is linear in two senses: semantic self-similarity of words tends to decrease linearly in time and word vectors at time t can be written as linear combinations of words vectors at time $t - 1$, which allows to forecast meaning change. Regarding methods, Xu and Kemp (2015) work with simple distributional count vectors, while Hamilton et al. (2016) and Eger and Mehler (2016) use low-dimensional dense vector representations. Both works use different approaches to map independently induced word vectors (across time) in a common space: Hamilton et al. (2016) learn to align word vectors using a projection matrix while Eger and Mehler (2016) induce second-order embeddings by computing the similarity of words, in each time slot, to a reference vocabulary. Kutuzov et al. (2018) survey and compare models of semantic change based on diachronic word embeddings. Dubossarsky et al. (2017) caution against confounds in semantic change models.

An interesting approach besides computing independent word embeddings in each time period has been outlined by Bamman et al. (2014) who *jointly* compute embeddings across different linguistic variables: each word w has an embedding

$$\mathbf{w} = \mathbf{e}_w \mathbf{W}_{\mathrm{main}} + \mathbf{e}_w \mathbf{W}_C,$$

where $\mathbf{W}_{\mathrm{main}} \in \mathbb{R}^{|V| \times d}$ is a main embedding matrix and $\mathbf{W}_C \in \mathbb{R}^{|V| \times d}$ is an embedding matrix for linguistic variable C, and $\mathbf{e}_w$ is a 1-hot vector (index) of word w. In their original work, C ranges over geographic locations (US states). A joint model has several advantages: it better addresses data sparsity (for specific variables) and it directly learns to map words in a joint vector space without necessity of ex-post projection. In our work, we use this latter model for temporal embeddings in that each linguistic variable C corresponds to a time epoch t:

$$\mathbf{w}(t) = \mathbf{e}_w \mathbf{W}_{\mathrm{main}} + \mathbf{e}_w \mathbf{W}_t$$

This dispenses the need to align independently trained embeddings for every time slot. Instead, a joint (MAIN) model is learned that is then re-weighted for every time epoch. While this is convenient, it does not necessarily mean that embeddings of a certain low-frequency word in a given time slot are stable. If there is not enough context for a given word in a certain time period t, the model just learns the MAIN embedding with little to no re-weighting, i.e., the matrix $\mathbf{W}_t$ may not be well estimated (at certain rows).

Corpus

We compile the largest corpus of poetry to date, the **German Poetry Corpus v1**, or Deutsches Lyrik Korpus version 1, **DLK** for short. See table 1 for a size overview. We know of no larger poetry collections in any language. Only the collection from the English Project Gutenberg offers a similar size, but due to a lawsuit, as of 2018 it is not available in Germany anymore.[2]

Tokens	11,849,112
Lines	1,784,613
Stanzas	280,234
Poems	74,155
Authors	269

Table 1: Corpus Size, Deutsches Lyrik Korpus v1

DLK covers the full range of the New High German language (of public domain literature), ranging from 1575 AD (Barock period) up to 1936 AD (Modern period). It is collected from three resources: (1) Textgrid[3] (TGRID), (2) The German Text Archive[4] (DTA), and (3) Antikoerperchen (ANTI-K). The latter two were first described by Haider and Kuhn (2018). All three corpora are set in TEI P5 XML.

TGRID offers around 51k poems with the label 'verse' (TGRID-V). Many of these texts have a unique timestamp. Where this is not the case, we take the average year between the author's birth and death.

---

[2]http://block.pglaf.org/germany.shtml
[3]textgrid.de
[4]textarchiv.de

DTA offers around 28k poems with the label 'lyrik' (DTA-L). The poetry in DTA is organized by editions (whole books), rather than by single poems. The timestamps are therefore guided by these few books, but give very accurate stamps.

ANTI-K is a collection of only 156 poems of school canon that was mined from `antikoerperchen.de/lyrik`. It has very accurate annotation, including literary periods, that allow us to gauge the distribution of poems according to canonic periods.

For training our model, we organize the corpus by stanzas, where every stanza represents a document. The reasoning behind this is that for poetic tropes, words are likely to stand in local context. We merge our collections and remove duplicate stanzas that match on their first line. This removes 9600 duplicates. Filtering Dutch and French material further eliminates 3200 stanzas. Since the earliest time slot 1575–1625 is too small, we merge it with the adjacent slot.

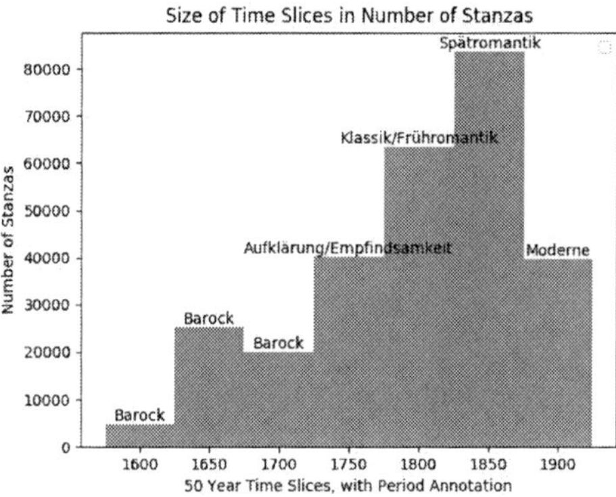

Figure 1: Distribution of stanzas in 50 year slots, 1575–1925 AD. Period labels: Barock (baroque), Aufklärung (enlightenment), Empfindsamkeit (sentimentalism), Klassik (Weimar classicism), Frühromantik (early romantic), Spätromantik (late romantic), Moderne (modernity). First slot (1600) is merged into the adjacent slot.

See figure 1 for the distribution of stanzas in 50 year time slots. The slots are labelled with approximate literature period information based on the clustered annotation in ANTI-K. We can see that the Romantic period (approx. 1750–1875) is overly heavy, while the Barock period is somewhat underrepresented.

We lemmatize based on a gold token:lemma mapping that was extracted from DTA-L in tcf format. Where this does not cover a token, we pos-tag the line with *pattern.de* to feed into germalemma.[5] We publish our corpus in json format.[6]

Experiments

Self-similarity

We investigate semantic self-similarity of words over time in two ways: (1) How does poetic diction change over successive time steps (change point detection), and (2) how does contextual word meaning change in total over the whole time frame with respect to the word's frequency (laws of conformity and linearity)? We use a model with a 25+50 sliding window, where time steps increase by 25 years, with a window size of 50 years. This doubles the data and allows a more fine grained analysis.

Pairwise Self-Similarity

We compute how the contextual use of words changes over successive time steps. We do this by determining the self-similarity of a word w over time by calculating the cosine similarity of the embedding vectors $\mathbf{w}(t)$ for w at time periods $t = t_i$ and $t = t_{i+1}$ as in equation (1):

$$\mathrm{cossim}(\mathbf{w}(t_i), \mathbf{w}(t_{i+1})) \qquad (1)$$

where $\mathrm{cossim}(\mathbf{a}, \mathbf{b})$ is defined as $\mathbf{a}^\mathsf{T}\mathbf{b}$ for two normalized vectors $\mathbf{a}$ and $\mathbf{b}$.

Thus, we can aggregate the self-similarity for the most frequent words at every time step and plot the change for all these words combined. See figure 2 for a boxplot of this pairwise self-similarity for the 3000 most frequent words.

Results

Our interpretation is that rising similarity signifies a homogenization of overall word use (diction), while a falling similarity signifies semantic diversification. In particular, we see a steady falling trajectory in the period between 1600 and 1675, with a dip at 1700. This period is generally regarded as the 'Barock' period. Then, word use slowly homogenizes, until we see a sharp dip around 1750, the onset of the Romantic period. Then it homogenizes during the Romantic period, until a dip at 1850, the end of the Romantic period, and then a homogenization into the the the onset of modernity.

<hr>

[5] `https://github.com/`
`WZBSocialScienceCenter/germalemma`
[6] `http://github.com/`
`thomasnikolaushaider`

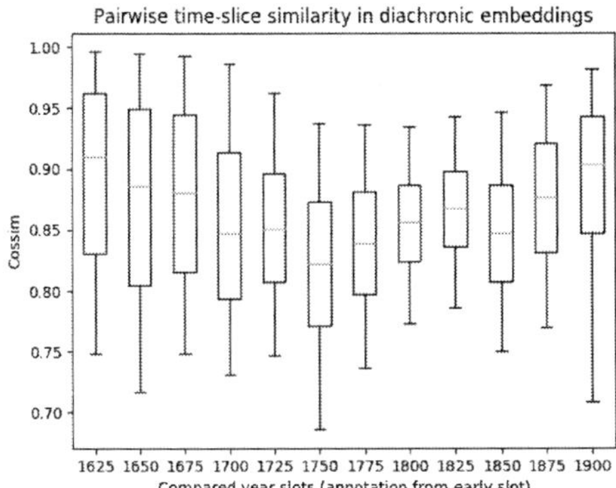

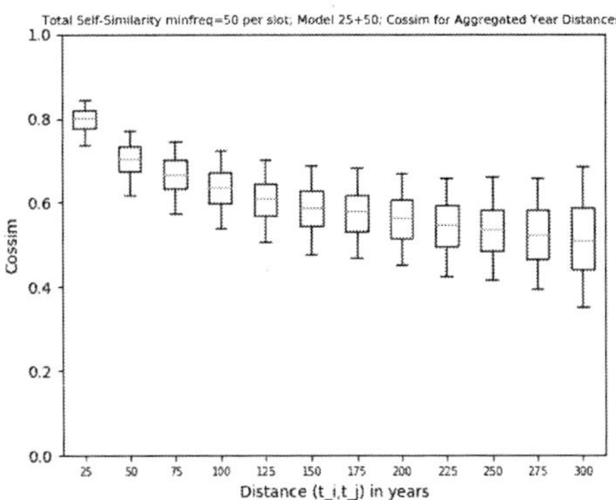

Figure 2: **Pairwise Self-Similarity. Top-3000 most frequent words. Cossine similarities of word w with itself in adjacent time slots** $cossim(w(t_i), w(t_{i+1}))$

Figure 3: **Total Self-Similarity of words that occur at least 50 times in every time slot. Cossine similarities aggregated by the distance of compared time slots** (t_i, t_j) **averaged for every time slot given a word. Removed stopwords. Whiskers: [5,95] percentiles.**

Total Self-Similarity

We determine change of word meaning across any possible time distances as a probing for the linearity of semantic change in our corpus.

For this, we calculate the semantic self-similarity of a word across all time periods t_i and t_j with $t_i < t_j$. We then aggregate all pairwise distances in years

$$\text{dist}(t_i, t_j) = |t_i - t_j|$$

for all words w.[7] To obtain robust estimates of embeddings, we only allow words that occur at least 50 times in every time slot and remove stopwords, leaving us with 472 words.

The x-axis in Figure 3 gives the distances $\text{dist}(t_i, t_j)$ while the y-axis shows the distribution of cossims over all words w within each distance.

We find that there is approximately a linear relation between the distance of timeslots for an average word, where close slots are more similar, and far apart slots are increasingly dissimilar. However, the variance also increases with distance.

Additionally, we equally divide our words into a low-frequency and a high-frequency band. We find that the low-frequency band shows a generally higher self-similarity than the high-frequency band over all distances. This would mean that, overall, high frequency words tend to be more semantically diverse over time, i.e. stand in more diverse contexts. In contrast, low-frequency words stand in fewer contexts, therefore undergo less

change. However, this could also come from the tendency of the model to revert to MAIN.

Emerging Tropes: Collocations & Metaphors

Method

To detect emerging tropes, we calculate the cosine similarity of word pairs over time. For the sake of visualization we use a 50+50 model with 6 time slots. We then perform Principal Component Analysis (PCA) over the resulting trajectories (Eger, 2010). The resulting principal components show that similar trajectories are co-variant. Component 1 aggregates stable high/low trajectories, while component 2 aggregates rising/falling trajectories. We illustrate our finding with the tropes for the concept 'love' ('Liebe' in German) and determine the most salient word pairs over the whole dataset. 'Love' is a very frequent word in poetry. Nevertheless, this approach works equally well for any word, except very low frequency words that show idiosyncratic behavior as they are not well distributed.

Results

We calculate the distance of 'love' against every other word w, where w has to occur at least 30 times in the corpus, and it needs to be represented in every time slot at least twice. We allow one slot to be empty.

The first 4 components of PCA explain >.95 variance, where component 1 explains 73%, component 2 13%, and component 3 5%. We retrieve the top-25 word pairs at every component extreme.

---

[7]For all 25,50,…,300 year distances, cossims per word in these distances are averaged, so we are left with one value per distance and word.

rising traj.	falling traj.	high traj.	low traj.
frische	aufrechen	liebe	brummen
veilchen	alsbald	freundschaft	krähen
niedersinken	billigkeit	lust	rasseln
duftig	erzeigen	treue	rum
jenseits	unterstehen	trieb	bock
zauber	betragen	seligkeit	dum
entgleiten	stracks	hoffnung	prasseln
künden	zuerkennen	glaube	trommel
hoffend	hierin	keusch	säbel
efeu	schmeissen	treu	traben
enthüllen	anlaß	erkalten	bellen
erfüllung	jederzeit	wahr	block
heimat	muhen	immerdar	bügel
trübe	schimpfen	regung	gaul
gloria	stecken	gegenliebe	grasen

Table 2: Top 15 words per dimension for 'love' tropes from PCA extremes, plotted in figures 4, 5, 6 and 7.

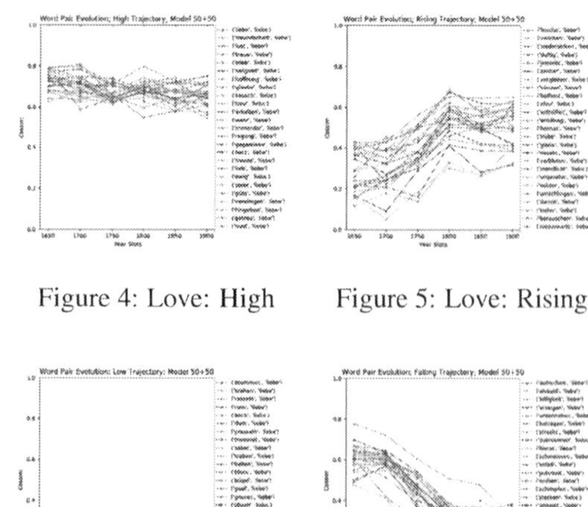

Figure 4: Love: High   Figure 5: Love: Rising

Figure 6: Love: Low   Figure 7: Love: Falling

We find that component 1 orders trajectories based on high/low semantic similarity, while component 2 orders based on rising/falling trajectories. See figures 4 (high trajectory), 5 (rising trajectory), 6 (low trajectory) and 7 (falling trajectory). See table 2 for the respective word pairs (collocations) with 'love' as they are plotted.

Stable High Trajectories Trajectories in figure 4 (table 2 column 3) have a consistently high cosine, meaning that these collocations have remained unchanged since the Baroque period: 'love is fidelity',[8] 'love is friendship',[9] or 'love is lust'. These are conventional near-synonyms, just as ('apple', 'tree')[10] or idioms ('apples', 'pears').[11] A k-nearest neighbor (KNN) analysis retrieves these collocations. Performing this analysis for multiple words, we find that the idiom ('apple', 'pear') is a special case, as it strongly loads into both rising and stable high PCA dimensions (both top 20).

Rising Trajectories Figure 5 (table 2 column 1) shows rising collocations that emerge during the Romantic period, i.e. 'fresh love',[12] 'love is magic / enchantment'[13] and 'love is violets'.[14] A metaphorical (trope) interpretation is most likely here.

Falling Trajectories As illustrated in figure 7 (column 2), these collocations fall into obscurity.

We find 'cheap love'[15] or things like 'raking'[16] or 'manners / accounting'.[17]

Stable Low Trajectories The lines in figure 6 (column 4) signify word pairs that are always far apart. We find things that make noise, like drums.[18] The 'drums of love' seems to be an oxymoron.

Conclusion

We constructed the largest poetry corpus to date and investigated distributional semantic change with different methods. With self-similarity, we can reconstruct literature period transitions and find that the the law of linear semantic change also applies to poetry. However, for confident analysis of other laws more data and a more robust model is still called for. Finally, we extract emerging and vanishing poetic tropes based on the co-variance of time trajectories of word pairs. This method is applicable more broadly to cluster similar trajectories for any given word pairs. We found trajectories of word similarities that are beyond simple nearest-neighbor analysis, and illustrated findings for reasonable tropes with 'love'. While large, our dataset is still somewhat sparse in the distribution of words over all time slots, partially because many word forms simply emerge / vanish at a certain point ('excitement' is not in Baroque).

---

[8]('Treue', 'Liebe')

[9]('Freundschaft', 'Liebe')

[10]('Apfel', 'Baum')

[11]('Äpfel', 'Birnen'), 'compare apples and oranges'.

[12]('Frische', 'Liebe')

[13]('Zauber', 'Liebe')

[14]('Veilchen', 'Liebe')

[15]billigkeit

[16]aufrechen

[17]betragen

[18]trommel

References

Manex Agirrezabal, Iñaki Alegria, and Mans Hulden. 2016. Machine learning for metrical analysis of English poetry. In *Proceedings of COLING 2016, the 26th International Conference on Computational Linguistics: Technical Papers*, pages 772–781, Osaka, Japan. The COLING 2016 Organizing Committee.

David Bamman, Chris Dyer, and Noah A Smith. 2014. Distributed representations of geographically situated language. In *Proceedings of the 52nd Annual Meeting of the Association for Computational Linguistics (Volume 2: Short Papers)*, volume 2, pages 828–834.

Haim Dubossarsky, Daphna Weinshall, and Eitan Grossman. 2017. Outta control: Laws of semantic change and inherent biases in word representation models. In *Proceedings of the 2017 Conference on Empirical Methods in Natural Language Processing*, pages 1147–1156, Copenhagen, Denmark.

Steffen Eger. 2010. Investigating lexical competition - an empirical case study of the german spelling reform of 1996/2004/2006. *JLCL*, 25(1):3–21.

Steffen Eger and Alexander Mehler. 2016. On the linearity of semantic change: Investigating meaning variation via dynamic graph models. In *Proceedings of the 54th Annual Meeting of the Association for Computational Linguistics (Volume 2: Short Papers)*, pages 52–58, Berlin, Germany. Association for Computational Linguistics.

Alex Estes and Christopher Hench. 2016. Supervised machine learning for hybrid meter. In *Proceedings of the Fifth Workshop on Computational Linguistics for Literature*, pages 1–8.

Erica Greene, Tugba Bodrumlu, and Kevin Knight. 2010. Automatic analysis of rhythmic poetry with applications to generation and translation. In *Proceedings of the 2010 conference on empirical methods in natural language processing*, pages 524–533.

Thomas Haider and Jonas Kuhn. 2018. Supervised rhyme detection with siamese recurrent networks. In *Proceedings of the Second Joint SIGHUM Workshop on Computational Linguistics for Cultural Heritage, Social Sciences, Humanities and Literature. At COLING 2018, Santa Fe, New Mexico*, pages 81–86.

Thomas Nikolaus Haider. 2019. Diachronic topics in new high german poetry. In *In Proceedings of the International Digital Humanities Conference DH2019, Utrecht*.

William L. Hamilton, Jure Leskovec, and Dan Jurafsky. 2016. Diachronic word embeddings reveal statistical laws of semantic change. In *Proceedings of the 54th Annual Meeting of the Association for Computational Linguistics (Volume 1: Long Papers)*, pages 1489–1501, Berlin, Germany. Association for Computational Linguistics.

Christopher Hench. 2017. Phonological soundscapes in medieval poetry. In *Proceedings of the Joint SIGHUM Workshop on Computational Linguistics for Cultural Heritage, Social Sciences, Humanities and Literature*, pages 46–56.

Aurélie Herbelot. 2014. The semantics of poetry: a distributional reading. *Digital Scholarship in the Humanities*, 30(4):516–531.

Justine T Kao and Dan Jurafsky. 2015. A computational analysis of poetic style. *LiLT (Linguistic Issues in Language Technology)*, 12.

David M Kaplan and David M Blei. 2007. A computational approach to style in american poetry. In *Seventh IEEE International Conference on Data Mining (ICDM 2007)*, pages 553–558. IEEE.

Vaibhav Kesarwani, Diana Inkpen, Stan Szpakowicz, and Chris Tanasescu. 2017. Metaphor detection in a poetry corpus. In *Proceedings of the Joint SIGHUM Workshop on Computational Linguistics for Cultural Heritage, Social Sciences, Humanities and Literature*, pages 1–9.

Andrey Kutuzov, Lilja Øvrelid, Terrence Szymanski, and Erik Velldal. 2018. Diachronic word embeddings and semantic shifts: a survey. In *Proceedings of the 27th International Conference on Computational Linguistics*, pages 1384–1397, Santa Fe, New Mexico, USA. Association for Computational Linguistics.

Nina McCurdy, Julie Lein, Katharine Coles, and Miriah Meyer. 2015. Poemage: Visualizing the sonic topology of a poem. *IEEE transactions on visualization and computer graphics*, 22(1):439–448.

Borja Navarro-Colorado. 2018. On poetic topic modeling: extracting themes and motifs from a corpus of spanish poetry. *Frontiers in Digital Humanities*, 5:15.

Sravana Reddy and Kevin Knight. 2011. Unsupervised discovery of rhyme schemes. In *Proceedings of the 49th Annual Meeting of the Association for Computational Linguistics: Human Language Technologies*, pages 77–82.

Phil Roberts. 2000. *How Poetry Works*. Penguin UK.

Pablo Ruiz, Clara Martínez Cantón, Thierry Poibeau, and Elena González-Blanco. 2017. Enjambment detection in a large diachronic corpus of spanish sonnets. In *Proceedings of the Joint SIGHUM Workshop on Computational Linguistics for Cultural Heritage, Social Sciences, Humanities and Literature*, pages 27–32.

Ted Underwood and Jordan Sellers. 2012. The emergence of literary diction. *The Journal of Digital Humanities, 1(2)*, pages http://journalofdigitalhumanities.org/1–2/theemergence–of–literary–diction–by–ted–underwoodand–jordan–sellers/.

Rob Voigt and Dan Jurafsky. 2013. Tradition and modernity in 20th century chinese poetry. In *Proceedings of the Workshop on Computational Linguistics for Literature*, pages 17–22.

Yang Xu and Charles Kemp. 2015. A computational evaluation of two laws of semantic change. In *CogSci*. cognitivesciencesociety.org.

Conceptual Change and Distributional Semantic Models: an Exploratory Study on Pitfalls and Possibilities

Pia Sommerauer and Antske Fokkens
Computational Lexicology and Terminology Lab
Vrije Universiteit Amsterdam
De Boelelaan 1105 Amsterdam, The Netherlands
`pia.sommerauer@vu.nl, antske.fokkens@vu.nl`

Abstract

Studying conceptual change using embedding models has become increasingly popular in the Digital Humanities community, while critical observations about them have received less attention. This paper investigates what the impact of known pitfalls can be on the conclusions drawn in a digital humanities study through the use case of "Racism" in the 20th century. In addition, we suggest an approach for modeling a complex concept in terms of words and relations representative of the conceptual system. Our results show that different models created from the same data yield different results, but also indicate that (i) using different model architectures, (ii) comparing different corpora and (iii) comparing to control words and relations can help to identify which results are solid and which may be due to artefacts. We propose guidelines to conduct similar studies, but also note that more work is needed to fully understand how we can distinguish artefacts from actual conceptual changes.

1 Introduction

Distributional models have been used to detect shifts in meaning with various degrees of success (Hamilton et al., 2016; Kim et al., 2014; Kulkarni et al., 2015; Gulordava and Baroni, 2011, e.g.). Based on promising examples such as the shift of the word *gay* from meaning 'carefree' to 'homosexual', researchers in digital humanities have been inspired to explore the use of distributional semantic models for studying the more complex phenomenon of concept drift (Wohlgenannt et al., 2019; Orlikowski et al., 2018; Kenter et al., 2015; Kutuzov et al., 2016; Martinez-Ortiz et al., 2016, e.g.). In most cases, standard methods with high results on identifying known examples of semantic shift are adopted and applied to specific data and use-cases.

Literature that raises critical questions concerning the reliability of these methods (e.g. (Hellrich and Hahn, 2016a; Dubossarsky et al., 2017)), however, seems to have received less attention in the digital humanities community. It is, in fact, far from trivial to apply distributional semantic models to study a complex phenomenon such as concept drift in a methodologically sound manner. We distinguish three main challenges: First, distributional semantic models reflect the way words are used and not directly how concepts are perceived. This leads to the question of which words should be studied and how shifts in their meaning relate to the underlying concept. Second, the relation between data, frequency and information emphasized by different model types is not fully understood (Dubossarsky et al., 2017). Third, the semantic models resulting from neural network-inspired architectures as provided by (e.g.) word2vec (Mikolov et al., 2013) depend on random factors such as initialization and the order in which data is presented (Hellrich and Hahn, 2016a).

If these challenges are not taken into account, researchers may end up publishing insights and results that are the result of artefacts in the data or models rather than valid observations on change. Existing research has shown that these variations exist, but we are not aware of previous work that explored their consequences in a typical digital humanities set-up, which does not just consider the most extreme changes or words in commonly used evaluation sets, but considers words of a specific topic under consideration. In order to enable digital humanities research that makes use of distributional semantic models, it is essential to establish how these models can be used in a methodologically sound manner and to communicate this to potential users.

In this paper, we illustrate this importance and

Proceedings of the 1st International Workshop on Computational Approaches to Historical Language Change, pages 223–233
Florence, Italy, August 2, 2019. ©2019 Association for Computational Linguistics

propose methods that take these risks into account when investigating conceptual change using word embeddings. We illustrate this through a use case of a concept known to have changed radically during the 20th century, namely "Racism". We define a set of words that represent this complex conceptual system and test various hypotheses concerning how relations between these words changed. We investigate the impact of artefacts by (1) using two datasets, (2) testing the impact on control words and (3) creating different models. In particular, we compare predict models both to count models and to other predict models created with different random initializations.

The results show that not all conclusions drawn in a naive methodological set-up can withstand a more critical investigation. The main contributions of this work are the following:

- We propsose ways of critically investigating apparent changes with respect to artefacts of the data and/or model.
- We formulate recommendations for Digital Humanities studies that aim to use diachronic embeddings to study conceptual change.

In addition, this paper provides a first illustration of how a generic hypothesis around a changing concept may be translated into concrete hypotheses concerning changes of language use.

We present this work in a somewhat unusual way to highlight the danger of uninformed use of distributional semantic models for studying concept drift. After an overview of related work (Section 2) and introducing our hypotheses (Section 3), we first take a naive approach using existing embeddings created according to the state-of-the-art and test our hypotheses in Section 4. We then report additional experiments that verify the robustness of the naively obtained insights in Section 5. Section 6 provides a set of recommendations on how to increase the reliability of research using distributional models to study language change based on the outcome and previous work. We then conclude and discuss open challenges.

2 Background and Related Work

Based on the distributional hypothesis (Firth, 1957), studying meaning change using distributional representations of words seems natural: Since words with similar meanings appear in similar contexts, it follows that changes in the contexts of words are a good indication of meaning change. This notion has been taken up in the Computational Linguistics community and implemented using distributional semantic models. The idea underlying diachronic distributional models is to create a series of semantic spaces representative of specific time periods that can be compared. While earlier approaches relied on count-based semantic space models (Gulordava and Baroni, 2011), more recent approaches made use of prediction-based models and suggested different methods to make embedding representations comparable across time periods (Kim et al., 2014; Kulkarni et al., 2015; Hamilton et al., 2016). Nowadays, prediction-based models (the skip-gram and CBOW architectures in the word2vec toolkit (Mikolov et al., 2013) and Glove (Pennington et al., 2014) seem to be the dominant choices (Kutuzov et al., 2018).

A number of studies warn about the reliability of distributional semantic models for detecting change. Dubossarsky et al. (2017) illustrate that it is not known what properties in the underlying corpora are emphasized by various models and that count-based models in particular are sensitive to frequency effects. Hellrich and Hahn (2016a) point out that predictive models trained on the same data return different nearest neighbors, because they are influenced by random factors such as their initialization and the order in which examples are processed. Antoniak and Mimno (2018) present an investigation of the extent to which only small changes in the underlying corpus impact the resulting representations. They show that the impact of the processing order increases when smaller corpora are used.

Researchers in other domains (mainly Digital Humanities, but also biomedical text minig (Yan and Zhu, 2018)) have embraced the promising initial results from studies such as Mitra et al. (2014) and Hamilton et al. (2016) without being aware of the pitfalls of these methods. This is particularly concerning, as these fields typically work with comparatively small datasets restricted to a specific domain (Wohlgenannt et al., 2019). For instance, Kenter et al. (2015) and Martinez-Ortiz et al. (2016) study conceptual change in a corpus of Dutch Newspapers collected by the Royal Dutch Libary. The same corpus is taken up by Orlikowski et al. (2018), who proposes a model of conceptual change using analogical relations between words. Kutuzov et al. (2016) extend the idea of diachronic changes to genre differences and explore subgenres of the BNC. Wohlgenannt et al. (2019) recognize problem of small specialized datasets and propose a new evaluation set constricted of data from the Game of Thrones and Harry Potter novels, but they do not address the problems related to robustness and frequency effects in their experimental set-up.

Even diachronic general purpose corpora, such as the Corpus of Historical American English (Davies, 2002, COHA) introduced to the Computational Linguistics community by Eger and Mehler (2016), are rather limited in size. The much larger Google n-grams data set (used by Mitra et al. (2014); Gulordava and Baroni (2011), e.g.) does not have this limitation, but full texts cannot be accessed and it suffers from a bias towards scientific publications from 1950 onwards (Pechenick et al., 2015). The Google n-grams fiction component, used by e.g. Michel et al. (2011); Dubossarsky et al. (2015), is smaller and limited in genre but avoids unbalanced differences in genre across time periods.

In addition to these model-specific caveats, the translation from (potentially complex) concepts to words which can be observed by a distributional model is not straight forward. Betti and van den Berg (2014) propose the use of conceptual models to study concept change in a clearly defined and somewhat formalized way. This notion is rarely treated explicitly in applications of diachronic embedding models. Studies such as Bjerva and Praet (2015) provide a start, but we are not aware of previous work that investigates a conceptual system consisting of several subconcepts and of a similar complexity to the use-case of "Racism" presented in this paper.

To the best of our knowledge, this work is furthermore the first to investigate how arteficial components influence a digital humanities research question. The scope of this research is still limited to investigating the impact of different methods and random artefacts leaving questions concerning the underlying data to future work.

3   Use Case: The Concept of Racism

The first step for studying concept drift by means of linguistic corpora is to identify words that refer to (components of) the concept and related concepts. Following Betti and van den Berg (2014)'s observation that change applies to conceptual net-

works, this can not be simplified by looking at words referring to the concept and their near synonyms alone. We distinguish four classes of words that can be relevant for studying conceptual change: (i) words referring to the core of the concept, (ii) relevant subconcepts, (iii) instances of a core or subconcepts and (iv) words referring to related concepts. In this paper we investigate how the concept of "Racism" changed during the 20th century. We use literature from various disciplines within Social Science and Humanities to select relevant words and formulate hypotheses. A brief overview is provided in this section.

Barker (1981) identifies a shift from 'old' to 'new' racism. Race used to be understood in biological terms related to visual attributes, particularly, skin color. Due to social changes (triggered by the Nazi regimes cruelties and the Civil Rights Movement), biological interpretations were relinquished as explanations for prejudice and increasingly replaced by cultural interpretations of differences between groups (Augoustinos and Every, 2007; Lentin, 2005; Morning, 2009; Omi, 2001; Wikan, 1999; Winant, 1998). We therefore identify "Culture" and "Race" as the core concepts of "Racism" investigated through the words *race* and *culture* as well as *racial* and *cultural* which are less polysemous. This shifting interpretation led to different ways of defining and comparing social groups (subconcepts and instances) and different justifications for racist ideologies (related concepts) summarized in Tables 1 and 2.

We hypothesize that words representing subconcepts, instances and related concepts associated with old racism will have moved further away (i.e. the similarity of their vectors has decreased) from the core concepts as this vision is no longer supported whereas words related to new racism have moved closer to the core concepts (i.e. the similarity between the vectors has increased) during the 20th century. Furthermore, we expect that within the core concepts, the word *cultural* is increasingly used to describe social groups, while the biologically connotated word *racial* is avoided. A detailed overview of all word pairs and their expected change can be found in the appendix to the paper (Appendix A).[1]

---

[1]Conceptual change in different corpora and models: `https://github.com/cltl/semantic_space_navigation/tree/master/projects/conceptual_change`, comparing models of the same corpus with different initializations: `https://github`.

Conceptual system of old racism		target words
Subconcepts	'Race defined in terms of visual attributes, first and foremost skin color	*skin color* (not investigated as compound nouns are not in the model vocabularies)
instances	Groups defined in terms of skin color	*whites, blacks*
Related concepts	Emphasis on a racial hierarchy	*superior, inferior*
	Biological justification of hierarchical structures	*genetics*
	Fear of intimacy between people of different racial groups	*marriage, relationship*

Table 1: Conceptual system and representative words of old racism.

Conceptual system of new racism		target words
Subconcepts	'Race' defined in terms of cultural background consisting of nationality, language and religion	*linguistic, national, religious*
instances	Group labels of immigrants	*immigrants, foreigners*
	Ethnic group labels	*Jews, Turks, Arabs*
Related concepts	Emphasis on differences	*different*
	Defense of seemingly liberal values	*values, attitudes, beliefs*
	The reason for differences lies in history (rather than genetics)	*historic*

Table 2: Conceptual system and representative words of new racism.

4 Basic Experimental Results

In this section, we outline the outcome of a 'naive' approach to testing our hypotheses, using the methods with best results in Hamilton et al. (2016). We use two corpora: COHA with the advantage of being well-balanced and disadvantage of being relatively small (on average 24,5 million words per decade) and the larger but unbalanced English Google Ngram corpus (hencforth ngram).

change direction	ngrams	both	coha
$\leftarrow\longrightarrow$	*inferior - cultural superior- cultural*	*whites - races marriage - cultural*	
$\rightarrow\leftarrow$	*linguistic - cultural*	*values - cultures*	*religious - racial religious - racial different- cultural national - cultural*

Table 3: Hypotheses about changes in relations between words confirmed in the n-grams corpus, the COHA or both. The changes significantly correlate with time (either over the entire century or over the second half only).

Embeddings are created by Hamilton et al. (2016) with the skip-gram with negative sampling model (SGNS) of the Word2vec toolkit.[2] We first explore whether cosine distances between vectors changed according to our hypotheses. Because we are ultimately interested in the reliability of positive results, we limit our presentation to the statistically significant confirmations presented in Table 3. We observe three hypotheses confirmed in both corpora, four only in the COHA corpus and three just in the Google Ngram corpus.[3]

We furthermore explore changes in nearest neighbors of *cultural* and *racial* illustrated in Figures 1 and 2. The shifts observed in nearest neighbors indicate that biologically connoted term *racial* is increasingly avoided in contexts in which racially constructed groups are described or compared. The results indicate that it is used to name social problems partly rooted in racist ideologies.

This naive approach seems to confirm that the shift in "Racism" established by scholars is indeed reflected in language use to a certain extent. We observed stastically significant shifts between ten word pairs in the direction that was expected.

com/cltl/semantic_space_navigation/tree/
master/projects/neighbor_stability

---

[2] The embeddings can be donloaded from the HistWords project webiste: https://nlp.stanford.edu/projects/histwords/

[3] Out of 47 hypotheses in total (see Appendix). A complete overview of the negative results is not included here due space limitations, but can be found in the Appendix.

(a) Nearest neighbors of *racial* in 1900 (small darker), 1950 (small lighter) and both decades (big).

(b) Nearest neighbors of *racial* in the 1950s (small darker), 1990 (small lighter) and both decades (big).

Figure 1: Changes in the nearest neighbors of *racial*.

(a) Nearest neighbors of *cultural* in 1900 (small darker), 1950 (small lighter), and both decades (big).

(b) Nearest neighbors of *cultural* in the 1950s (small darker), 1990 (small lighter) and in both decades (big).

Figure 2: Changes in the nearest neighbors of *cultural*.

We furthermore found changes in the environment of the nearest neigbors of *racial* and *cultural* that confirm the change of discourse from a biological racial vision of difference between people to a more cultural one. In the next section, we test whether the conclusions hold when being tested through alternative means.

5 Diving Deeper

At first sight, the approach and outcome outlined in the previous section may seem solid: we have taken the models evaluated best by Hamilton et al. (2016), who reported 100% accuracy on 18 evaluation pairs for the SGNS models created on the Google corpus. However, these results do not take into account that (1) predictive models are influenced by random components as pointed out by Hellrich and Hahn (2016a) and (2) significant change can also be spotted for words that did not exhibit change as (a) observed in the top-10 changing words reported in Hamilton et al. (2016) and (b) by the Dubossarsky et al.'s 2017 experiments showing that change is difficult to distinguish from frequency effects.

In this section, we present the results of additional experiments to test whether our initial findings hold when tested with alternative models. In addition, we use control words to verify whether changes between words referring to instances of racial groups and core concepts reflect indeed a change between these instances and the concept or whether similar changes are observed between the concepts and unrelated words or pairs of words whose distance should have remained stable.

5.1 Variations between Models

We first test whether a subset of our conclusions hold as well when we use Hamilton et al.'s 2016 count-based distributional semantic models, which are provided with their paper: a PPMI (Positive Pointwise Mutual Information) model and its high-density derivative SVD (Singular Value Decomposition). Though these models were less successful in detecting change in Hamilton et al.'s 2016 paper, they reflect the data directly without being influenced by their initialization or the or-

word pair	SGNS	PPMI-SVD	PPMI
culture-values	→←	→←	→←
races-immigrants	←→	←→	–
cultural-different	–	–	←→
racial-different	–	←→	←→
cultural-inferior	←→	←→	→←

Table 4: Comparison across different models using the ngrams corpus.

der in which examples are processed (Hellrich and Hahn, 2016b). Table 4 presents an overview of the conclusions drawn from different model types when analyzing changes in the relations between word pairs. Some changes are only significant in one model (e.g. *cultural-different*), others reveal contradictory results with significant changes in opposite directions (e.g. *cultural-inferior*). A conclusion that remains stable and is thus supported by all models is the increasing similarity of *cultures* and *values*.[4]

Next, we test variation between nearest neighbors confirming Hellrich and Hahn's 2016a observation about the instability of nearest neighbors. Out of 25 nearest neighbors, only 2-5 are shared across all model types (an example is shown in Figure 3). However, these shared neighbors do confirm the initial observation about the changing meaning of *racial* and *cultural* (as presented in Tables 5 and 6).

In addition to differences between model algorithms, we also expect differences between SGNS models trained on the same corpus but with different initializations. We trained three SGNS models[5] for the COHA slices representative of the 1900s, 1950s and 1990s and compared the 25 nearest neighbors of *racial*. When considering the differences in the top 25 nearest neighbors of *racial* in the SGNS model trained on this comparatively small corpus, it can be seen that the number of shared neighbors between all three models ranges between 11 and 18 (Table 7). This means that as much as 14 out of 25 nearest neighbors vary depending on the three initializations, showing that drawing conclusions based on artefacts is

---

[4]In the experiments, equivalent part of speech (e.g. noun - noun) and number (e.g. plural - plural) have been chosen for investigating changes in word pairs.

[5]To train these models, we used a modified version of the code used by Levy et al. (2015) allowing us to fix the initialization vectors. We preprocessed the corpus with our own scripts, which may be slightly different from the preprocessing used by Hamilton et al. (2016).

indeed a risk. The number of shared neighbors increases with the size of the underlying subcorpus.

In order to gain deeper insight into the variation displayed by nearest neighbors, we examine the difference in rank of a specific word across various models. For instance, if *language* were ranked 5th closest in the model initialized with init1 and 15th closest in the model initialized with init2, the rank difference would be 10. Table 8 presents the average rank differences for the top 25 nearest neighbors of *racial* for each model pair. The average differences range from as high as 49 ranks difference in the smallest corpus to 6.24 in the largest corpus, again indicating higher stability with an increasing corpus size.

These results confirm Hellrich and Hahn's 2016a observation that even models trained on the same data created with the same method can lead to different conclusions depending on their initialization. As the initialization vectors are chosen randomly, there is a high risk of drawing conclusions due to artefacts rather than actual changes in the data when relying on a single, prediction-based model, in particular when trained on a small corpus. These risks can be reduced by creating multiple models and measuring the degree of difference between them. Based on the differences in rank of nearest neighbors, a larger environment can be studied to verify which changes are stable across models and larger than variations caused by artefacts.

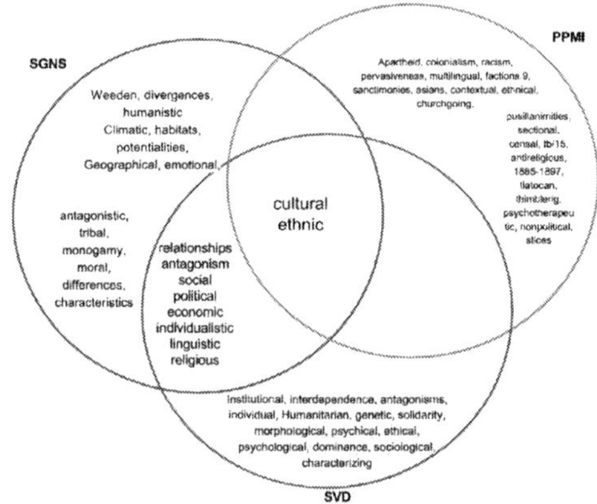

Figure 3: Nearest neighbors of *racial* in 1900 in different models created with the ngrams-corpus.

5.2 Control Words

Observations that hold across different models can still be a result of a bias or artefact in the

1900	1950	1990
cultural ethnic	stereotypes ethnic backgrounds discrimination	discrimination segregation

Table 5: Nearest neighbors of *racial* shared across all three models in the n-gram corpus.

1900	1950	1990
racial morphological economic	socio racial social backgrounds ethnic	socio ethno

Table 6: Nearest neighbors of *cultural* shared across all three models in the n-gram corpus.

decades million tokens	1900 25.7	1950 29.0	1990 33.2
init1-init2	15 (0.60)	15 (0.60)	20 (0.80)
init1-init3	16 (0.64)	18 (0.72)	20 (0.80)
init2-init3	16 (0.60)	16 (0.64)	19 (0.76)
init1-init2-init3	11 (0.44)	14 (0.56)	18 (0.72)

Table 7: Number of shared top 25 nearest neighbors of *racial* in the models created with three different initializations on the same decades of COHA.

decades million tokens	1900 25.7	1950 29.0	1990 33.2
init1-init2	47.08	31.92	6.24
init1-init3	27.04	31.00	7.20
init2-init1	22.60	13.32	7.68
init2-init3	22.32	33.48	8.96
init3-init1	35.16	13.28	14.12
init3-init2	49.00	26.52	12.72

Table 8: Average differences in rank between the top 25 nearest neighbors of *racial* in the models created with three different initializations on the same decades of COHA.

data. Control words can potentially reveal such an underlying cause. If observations are indicative of changes in the relation between these specific words, control words should not reveal similar changes. To illustrate the insights that can result from such a test, we show the outcome of comparing *immigrants* and *races* in the COHA corpus in Figure 4. In this case, the control words may yield insights in addition to calling into question an apparent change in the usage of the word *immigrant*. It may have led to a new insight, namely that the actual change might lie in how the general concept of "People" relates to *races*, as the neutral control

'naive'	data	models	control
nn of *racial* indi- cate shift towards meta-discourse	yes	yes	n.a
cultures ←→ *values*	yes	yes	yes
races ←→ *immi- grants*	no	partly	no
cultural ←→ *su- perior*	no	yes (SVD), data sparsity (PPMI)	yes in n- grams, no in COHA
cultural ←→ *in- ferior*	no	yes (SVD), no (PPMI)	yes

Table 9: Summary of results in line with the hypotheses in the 'naive' set-up.

word *nurse* shows a highly similar pattern to the other social group labels. This outcome calls for further investigations to try and establish whether this is a pattern related to biological race, to *race* in the sense of speeding contest or to a difference in which one of these meanings occurs more frequently.

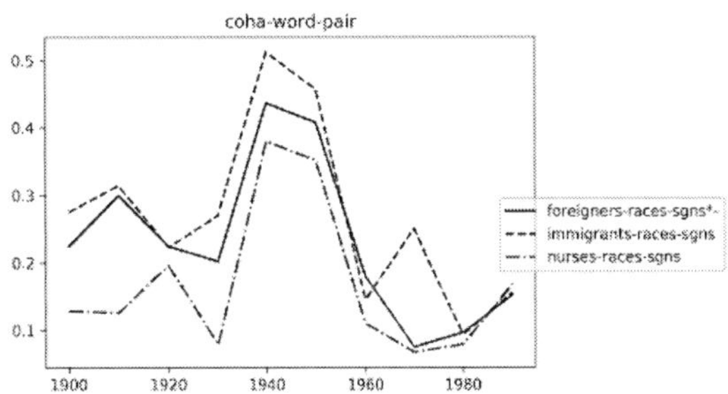

Figure 4: Changes in the cosine similarities between races and words representing social groups.

Overall, the results from the control experiments show that only a handful of the hypotheses were confirmed by all methods. Tables 9 and 10 provide an overview of the final outcome of our experiments in the different settings used to control for instability.

6 General Guidelines

Our experiments have shown that different models created from the same data do not always provide the same answers to our hypotheses. This outcome confirms the risk of naively applying distri-

'naive'	data	models	control
nn of *racial - different*	no	no	no
racial - different $\longleftrightarrow$ *values*	yes	no	yes

Table 10: Summary of results contradicting the hypotheses in the 'naive' set-up.

butional semantic technologies to explore conceptual change. In particular when they seem plausible, there is a risk that results based on artefacts are presented as valid observations. Based on the outcome of this study, we propose the following guidelines for studying conceptual change using distributional semantics:

1. Define a wide range of verifiable hypotheses to study the overall question before diving into actual changes.
2. Compare the outcome of multiple models. Count-based models directly reflect the distribution in the data, but can be influenced by word frequency. When using predictive models, test variations with different initializations and different ordering of examples.
3. Adapt the range of nearest-neighbors based on the variation in rank across models to ensure that changes are indeed changes in distribution and not due to random artefacts of a predictive model.
4. Use control words that should not exhibit the same change to further verify your hypotheses. Ideal control words are close to those from the hypotheses, but lack the property that is supposed to have triggered the change (e.g. descriptions of racial groups vs. other descriptions of groups of people).

In addition, properties of the data (balance and size) should be taken into consideration. Control words can capture some of the problems that may be introduced by the data, but not all. Additional insights may be obtained by running verification experiments with shuffled and synchronic corpora as done in Dubossarsky et al. (2017).

7 Discussion and conclusion

Computational linguistics research has shown that distributional semantic models can be used to detect linguistic shifts (Hamilton et al., 2016), but has also shown that (a) not all observed changes are actual shifts (Hamilton et al., 2016; Dubossarsky et al., 2017) and that (b) predictive models can yield unstable results (Hellrich and Hahn, 2016a). We investigated the implications of this for a digital humanities use case: the concept "Racism". Though the main insights from social science were confirmed by our study, most results turned out to be unstable.

A possible explanation is that our selection of words and relations is not representative of the actual conceptual system. As non-experts in the field of race studies, we selected the words and relations we investigated to the best of our abilities using existing literature. An interdisciplinary team might have proposed sounder hypotheses that would have been consistently confirmed. However, this does not undermine the, in our opinion, most important finding of this work. A standard, seemingly sound, experimental setup originally confirmed five hypotheses and showed clear patterns in nearest neighbors. Only two results could be reproduced by alternative methods and just 2-5 out of 25 nearest neighbors overlapped across all models. Furthermore, considerable variation was observed in the nearest neighbors of *racial* of models resulting from the same architecture and corpus with fixed different random initializations. Moreover, it should be noted that the impact of the order in which word-context pairs are considered by a prediction-based model has an impact on the results as well (Hellrich and Hahn, 2016b; Antoniak and Mimno, 2018). This variation has not been explored in this paper.

At this point, it is not possible to determine whether differences between models are due to random factors in prediction-based models, frequency effects in count-based models or a combination of both. However, the proposed checks and, in particular, investigations of the impact of random factors and patterns observed by control words provide a first step towards determining which results are artefacts and which are not. Identifying methods for answering this question is an important task for future work. We propose combining the guidelines resulting from this paper with the kind of experiments carried out by Dubossarsky et al. (2017) as a first next step.

This main contribution of this study is that it shows the risks of applying methods that work for specific examples and data to new use cases. It is tempting to assume that the method works when it provides an expected outcome or, otherwise, an outcome that can easily be explained. At this point, the relation between linguistic data and resulting semantic models is not understood well enough to draw conclusions from diachronic comparisons. Until we have more profound knowledge about the interpretation of shifts, conclusions about conceptual change should be drawn with care and verified through multiple means.

Acknowledgments

This research is funded by the PhD in the Humanities Grant provided by the Netherlands Organization of Scientific Research (Nederlandse Organisatie voor Wetenschappelijk Onderzoek, NWO) PGW.17.041 awarded to Pia Sommerauer and NWO VENI grant 275-89-029 awarded to Antske Fokkens. We would like to Minh Le for providing the adapted version of word2vec that allows us to select a specific initialization model and we thank anonymous reviewers for their comments. All remaining errors are our own.

References

Maria Antoniak and David Mimno. 2018. Evaluating the stability of embedding-based word similarities. *Transactions of the Association of Computational Linguistics*, 6:107–119.

Martha Augoustinos and Danielle Every. 2007. The language of race and prejudice a discourse of denial, reason, and liberal-practical politics. *Journal of Language and Social Psychology*, 26(2):123–141.

Martin Barker. 1981. *The new racism: conservatives and the ideology of the tribe*. Junction Books.

Arianna Betti and Hein van den Berg. 2014. Modelling the history of ideas. *British Journal for the History of Philosophy*, 22(4):812–835.

Johannes Bjerva and Raf Praet. 2015. Word embeddings pointing the way for late antiquity. In *LaTeCH@ ACL*, pages 53–57.

Mark Davies. 2002. *The Corpus of Historical American English (COHA): 400 million words, 1810-2009*.

Haim Dubossarsky, Yulia Tsvetkov, Chris Dyer, and Eitan Grossman. 2015. A bottom up approach to category mapping and meaning change. In *NetWordS*, pages 66–70.

Haim Dubossarsky, Daphna Weinshall, and Eitan Grossman. 2017. Outta control: Laws of semantic change and inherent biases in word representation models. In *Proceedings of the 2017 conference on empirical methods in natural language processing*, pages 1136–1145.

Steffen Eger and Alexander Mehler. 2016. On the linearity of semantic change: Investigating meaning variation via dynamic graph models. In *Proceedings of the 54th Annual Meeting of the Association for Computational Linguistics (Volume 2: Short Papers)*, volume 2, pages 52–58.

John Rupert Firth. 1957. A synopsis of linguistic theory, 1930-1955. *Studies in linguistic analysis*.

Kristina Gulordava and Marco Baroni. 2011. A distributional similarity approach to the detection of semantic change in the google books ngram corpus. In *Proceedings of the GEMS 2011 Workshop on GEometrical Models of Natural Language Semantics*, pages 67–71. Association for Computational Linguistics.

William L Hamilton, Jure Leskovec, and Dan Jurafsky. 2016. Diachronic word embeddings reveal statistical laws of semantic change. In *Proceedings of the 54th Annual Meeting of the Association for Computational Linguistics (Volume 1: Long Papers)*, volume 1, pages 1489–1501.

Johannes Hellrich and Udo Hahn. 2016a. Bad companyneighborhoods in neural embedding spaces considered harmful. In *COLING (16)*, page 27852796.

Johannes Hellrich and Udo Hahn. 2016b. An assessment of experimental protocols for tracing changes in word semantics relative to accuracy and reliability. In *LaTeCH 2016Proceedings of the 10th SIGHUM Workshop on Language Technology for Cultural Heritage, Social Sciences, and Humanities@ ACL*, pages 111–117.

Tom Kenter, Melvin Wevers, Pim Huijnen, and Maarten de Rijke. 2015. Ad hoc monitoring of vocabulary shifts over time. In *Proceedings of the 24th ACM International on Conference on Information and Knowledge Management*, pages 1191–1200. ACM.

Yoon Kim, Yi-I Chiu, Kentaro Hanaki, Darshan Hegde, and Slav Petrov. 2014. Temporal analysis of language through neural language models. *ACL 2014*, page 61.

Vivek Kulkarni, Rami Al-Rfou, Bryan Perozzi, and Steven Skiena. 2015. Statistically significant detection of linguistic change. In *Proceedings of the 24th International Conference on World Wide Web*, pages 625–635. ACM.

Andrey Kutuzov, Lilja Øvrelid, Terrence Szymanski, and Erik Velldal. 2018. Diachronic word embeddings and semantic shifts: a survey. In *Proceedings of the 27th International Conference on Computational Linguistics*, pages 1384–1397.

Andrey Borisovich Kutuzov, Elizaveta Kuzmenko, and Anna Marakasova. 2016. Exploration of register-dependent lexical semantics using word embeddings. In *Proceedings of the Workshop on Language Technology Resources and Tools for Digital Humanities (LT4DH)*, pages 26–34.

Alana Lentin. 2005. Replacing race, historicizing culturein multiculturalism. *Patterns of prejudice*, 39(4):379–396.

Omer Levy, Yoav Goldberg, and Ido Dagan. 2015. Improving distributional similarity with lessons learned from word embeddings. *Transactions of the Association for Computational Linguistics*, 3:211–225.

Carlos Martinez-Ortiz, Tom Kenter, Melvin Wevers, Pim Huijnen, Jaap Verheul, and Joris Van Eijnatten. 2016. Design and implementation of shico: Visualising shifting concepts over time. In *HistoInformatics 2016*, volume 1632, pages 11–19.

Jean-Baptiste Michel, Yuan Kui Shen, Aviva Presser Aiden, Adrian Veres, Matthew K Gray, Joseph P Pickett, Dale Hoiberg, Dan Clancy, Peter Norvig, Jon Orwant, et al. 2011. Quantitative analysis of culture using millions of digitized books. *science*, 331(6014):176–182.

Tomas Mikolov, Wen-tau Yih, and Geoffrey Zweig. 2013. Linguistic regularities in continuous space word representations. In *HLT-NAACL*, volume 13, pages 746–751.

Sunny Mitra, Ritwik Mitra, Martin Riedl, Chris Biemann, Animesh Mukherjee, and Pawan Goyal. 2014. That's sick dude!: Automatic identification of word sense change across different timescales. *arXiv preprint arXiv:1405.4392*.

Ann Morning. 2009. Toward a sociology of racial conceptualization for the 21 st century. *Social Forces*, 87(3):1167–1192.

Michael A Omi. 2001. The changing meaning of race. *America becoming: Racial trends and their consequences*, 1:243–263.

Matthias Orlikowski, Matthias Hartung, and Philipp Cimiano. 2018. Learning diachronic analogies to analyze concept change. In *Proceedings of the Second Joint SIGHUM Workshop on Computational Linguistics for Cultural Heritage, Social Sciences, Humanities and Literature*, pages 1–11.

Eitan Adam Pechenick, Christopher M Danforth, and Peter Sheridan Dodds. 2015. Characterizing the google books corpus: Strong limits to inferences of socio-cultural and linguistic evolution. *PloS one*, 10(10):e0137041.

Jeffrey Pennington, Richard Socher, and Christopher D. Manning. 2014. Glove: Global vectors for word representation. In *Empirical Methods in Natural Language Processing (EMNLP)*, pages 1532–1543.

Unni Wikan. 1999. Culture: A new concept of race. *Social Anthropology*, 7(01):57–64.

Howard Winant. 1998. Racism today: Continuity and change in the post-civil rights era. *Ethnic and Racial Studies*, 21(4):755–766.

Gerhard Wohlgenannt, Ariadna Barinova, Dmitry Ilvovsky, and Ekaterina Chernyak. 2019. Creation and evaluation of datasets for distributional semantics tasks in the digital humanities domain. *arXiv preprint arXiv:1903.02671*.

Erjia Yan and Yongjun Zhu. 2018. Tracking word semantic change in biomedical literature. *International journal of medical informatics*, 109:76–86.

A Detailed overview of hypotheses and outcomes

word1	word2	Hypothesis	Coha-sgns	Ngrams-sgns
racial	cultural	closer	-	-
racial	superior	apart	-	-
racial	inferior	apart	apart	-
racial	blacks	apart	-	-
racial	whites	apart	apart	closer
racial	marriage	apart	-	closer
racial	relationships	apart	-	-
racial	genetics	apart	OOV	OOV
racial	nigger	apart	closer	closer
racial	yankee	apart	-	-
racial	gypsy	apart	-	-
cultural	superior	apart	closer	apart
cultural	inferior	apart	-	apart
cultural	blacks	apart	-	closer
cultural	whites	apart	-	closer
cultural	marriage	apart	-	apart
cultural	relationships	apart	-	-
cultural	genetics	apart	OOV	OOV
cultural	nigger	apart	closer	-
cultural	yankee	apart	-	-
cultural	gypsy	apart	-	-
racial	immigrant	closer	-	apart
racial	foreigner	closer	apart	-
racial	national	closer	-	apart
racial	Turks	closer	OOV	OOV
racial	Arabs	closer	-	-
racial	Jews	closer	apart	-
racial	religious	closer	closer	-
racial	linguistic	closer	-	-
racial	values	closer	apart	closer
racial	attitudes	closer	-	apart
racial	beliefs	closer	-	apart
racial	historic	closer	apart	-
racial	different	closer	-	-
cultural	immigrant	closer	-	-
cultural	foreigner	closer	-	-
cultural	national	closer	closer	-
cultural	Turks	closer	-	-
cultural	Arabs	closer	-	-
cultural	Jews	closer	-	-
cultural	religious	closer	closer	-
cultural	linguistic	closer	-	closer
cultural	values	closer	closer	closer
cultural	attitudes	closer	-	-
cultural	beliefs	closer	-	-
cultural	historic	closer	-	-
cultural	different	closer	closer	-

Table 11: Overview of hypothesized changes and results in of the SGNS model in COHA and the google n-grams. The forms of *racial* and *cultural* have been adapted to match word2 in part of speech and number. *closer* indicates a significant change towards each other and *apart* a significant increase in distance, - means no significant change

Measuring the compositionality of noun-noun compounds over time

Prajit Dhar
Leiden University
dharp@liacs.leidenuniv.nl

Janis Pagel
University of Stuttgart
pageljs@ims.uni-stuttgart.de

Lonneke van der Plas
University of Malta
lonneke.vanderplas@um.edu.mt

Abstract

We present work in progress on the temporal progression of compositionality in noun-noun compounds. Previous work has proposed computational methods for determining the compositionality of compounds. These methods try to automatically determine how transparent the meaning of the compound as a whole is with respect to the meaning of its parts. We hypothesize that such a property might change over time. We use the time-stamped Google Books corpus for our diachronic investigations, and first examine whether the vector-based semantic spaces extracted from this corpus are able to predict compositionality ratings, despite their inherent limitations. We find that using temporal information helps predicting the ratings, although correlation with the ratings is lower than reported for other corpora. Finally, we show changes in compositionality over time for a selection of compounds.

1 Introduction

Compositionality is a long debated issue in theoretical linguistics. The principle of compositionality (Partee, 1984) states that the meaning of an expression is a function of the meanings of its parts and of the way they are syntactically combined. It is often used to describe how the meaning of a sentence can be derived from the meaning of single words and phrases, but the principle might also be postulated for *compounding*, i.e. the process of combining two or more lexemes to form a new concept (Bauer, 2017, p. 1 and 4). Compounds can often be directly derived from the meanings of the involved compound constituents (e.g. *graduate student*, *speed limit*), however, we also find compounds whose meanings can only be derived partially from their components (*night owl*, *hot dog*).

Surprisingly, diachronic perspectives on compositionality[1] are virtually absent from previous work. To the best of our knowledge, we present the first study on the compositionality of compounds over time. We bring two strands of research together. On the one hand we are inspired by the synchronic work on predicting the degree of compositionality of compounds by comparing the vector-based representations of the parts to the vector-based representations of the compound as a whole. On the other hand, we rely on methods designed for detecting semantic change, such as presented in Hamilton et al. (2018), to study compositionality in compounds from a diachronic viewpoint.

2 Related Work

From a synchronic perspective, Reddy et al. (2011), Schulte im Walde et al. (2013) and Schulte im Walde et al. (2016a) are closest to our approach, since they predict the compositionality of compounds using vector space representations. However, Schulte im Walde et al. (2013) use German data and do not investigate diachronic changes. They report a Spearman's ρ of 0.65 for predicting the compositionality of compounds based on the features of their semantic space and find that the modifiers mainly influence the compositionality of the whole compound, contrary to their expectation that the head should be the main source of influence. This is true for both the human annotation and their vector space model.

---

[1] A notable exception is Vincent (2014), although he mainly focuses on syntactic processes in Romance languages and only briefly covers numeral words.

Proceedings of the 1st International Workshop on Computational Approaches to Historical Language Change, pages 234–239
Florence, Italy, August 2, 2019. ©2019 Association for Computational Linguistics

Schulte im Walde et al. (2016a) further investigate the role of heads and modifiers on the prediction of compositionality and report ρ values between 0.35 and 0.61 for their models on German and English data. Reddy et al. (2011) also report Spearman's ρ between their surveyed compositionality values and word vectors. They achieve ρ values of around 0.68, depending on the model.

From a diachronic perspective, we follow the general methodological approach of Hamilton et al. (2018), who use PPMI, SVD and word2vec based vector spaces to investigate a shift in meaning for chosen words with a known semantic change (*gay*, *broadcast*, etc.). They use time series to detect a significant change-point for two words, using cosine similarity and Spearman's ρ. They also compute the displacement for a single word embedding by calculating the cosine similarity between a point in time t and a later point in time $t + \Delta$. We adapt this methodology and make use of the same corpus (Google Books Ngram).

3 Methods and Data

Several studies have been conducted in order to measure compositionality for compounds in different languages (von der Heide and Borgwaldt, 2009; Reddy et al., 2011; Schulte im Walde et al., 2016b). Some of these works have used large corpora to extract vector-based representations of compounds and their parts to automatically determine the compositionality of a given compound. The models were validated on the basis of their correlation with human compositionality ratings for a set of compounds.

Because we are interested in the diachronic perspective on compounds, we use a time-stamped corpus: the Google Books Ngram corpus[2] (Michel et al., 2011) It contains books from the 1500s to the 2000s, from which we retrieve the contextual information of compounds and their constituents per year. We operate on 5-grams, which is the largest unit provided by Google Ngrams and use the words appearing in the 5-grams as both target words and context. We use the Part-of-Speech information already included in the Google Ngram corpus to extract noun-noun patterns. We then regard all other tokens in the 5-gram as context words and from this build up a semantic space representation of noun compounds for each year. We use a sliding window approach, wherein we capture the context of a compound based on its position in the 5-gram. That means that a bigram (say the compound *gold mine*) could occur in four different positions in the 5-grams (1-2, 2-3, 3-4 and finally 4-5). We then capture the contexts for each of these positions, in order to enrich the representation of a compound and its constituents (which similarly have five such positions, as they are unigrams).

Ideally, we would validate our diachronic model on diachronic test data. However, as it is not possible to survey compositionality rating for diachronic data, we instead use the synchronic data provided by Reddy et al. (2011) (henceforth referred to as REDDY) for evaluating the quality of the Google Books Ngram data as a source for investigating the compositionality of compounds in general. Reddy et al. (2011) compiled a list of 90 English compounds and asked annotators to rate the compositionality of these compounds on a scale from 0 to 5. They provide three mean values of their ratings for the compounds (*compound-mean*), heads (*head-mean*) and modifiers (*modifier-mean*). We make use of REDDY in order to verify that our methods are capable of capturing compositionality (synchronically) and use the diachronic data of Google Books Ngram to investigate the temporal change of compositionality.

A common challenge in building semantic spaces on a diachronic scale is that when building the spaces for individual spans of time, the spaces need to be aligned later on in order to compare models (see e.g. Kutuzov et al., 2018, Section 3.3). We circumvent this problem by jointly learning the spaces for the target words. To do this, we take the sparse representations of the compounds and their constituents and jointly learn their dense representations using SVD. Similar to Hamilton et al. (2018) we also choose the dimensions of our embeddings to be 300. We carry out row normalization on the embeddings, in order to remove the bias of the frequency of the compounds and their constituents.

We make use of six different semantic features that have been proposed in the literature to capture compositionality (Schulte im Walde et al., 2016a) and plausibility of noun-noun compounds (Günther and Marelli, 2016; Dhar and van der

---

Plas, 2019). Three features are based on the cosine similarity between the embeddings of different compound parts (see Günther and Marelli, 2016):

1. Similarity between compound constituents (*sim-bw-constituents*)

2. Similarity of the compound with its head (*sim-with-head*)

3. Similarity of the compound with its modifier (*sim-with-mod*)

The three information theory based features given below were proposed by Dhar and van der Plas (2019):

4. Log likelihood-ratio (*LLR*)

5. Positive Pointwise Mutual Information (*PPMI*)

6. Local Mutual Information (*LMI*)

Such formulas have been used prior to calculate collocations and associations between words (compare Manning and Schütze, 1999). Each feature will be tested individually for its ability to capture compositionality.

4 Experiments

We ran a total of two experiments[3] (Section 4.2 and 4.3) with different goals.

4.1 Experimental Setup

Hyper-parameters We experiment with certain hyper-parameters, in particular we varied the *time span length*, e.g. single years, decades or a span of 20 years etc. and *frequency cut-off* of compounds and their constituents in a specific time span, i.e. compounds and constituents have to occur above a certain frequency threshold. Choosing a greater time span will increase the observable data per compound and might improve the vector representations. We only consider compounds which retain representations in all time spans starting from the year 1800, which reduces the number of total compounds depending on the specific setup.

---

[3]The code is available at https://github.com/prajitdhar/Compounding

Compound-centric setting Dhar and van der Plas (2019) found the compound-centric set up, where the distributional representations of words are based on their usage as constituents in a compound to outperform compound-agnostic setups, for predicting novel compounds in English. They were inspired by research on N-N compounds in Dutch that suggests that constituents such as -molen '-mill' in pepermolen 'peppermill' are separately stored as abstract combinatorial structures rather than understood on the basis of their independent constituents (De Jong et al., 2002). We hence adopt the compound-centric setting.

4.2 Correlation

We first carry out a quantitative experiment, to see if our features bolster the prediction of compositionality in noun-noun compounds. To do so, we calculate correlation scores between our proposed metrics and the annotated compositionality ratings of REDDY. Like Reddy et al. (2011) and Schulte im Walde et al. (2013), we opt for Spearman's ρ.

To find the best configuration of a time span and cut-off for the regression models, we use the R^2 metric. Table 1 presents our findings; we will discuss them in the following Section 5.

4.3 Progression of Compositionality over Time

Based on the results of our correlation experiment, we proceed to analyze the temporal progression of compositionality. Our goals are two-fold: First, investigate if temporal information helps in predicting the contemporary REDDY data and second, use the best feature and setup in order to model the progression of compositionality over time.

5 Results

We find the best predictors for the compositionality ratings of REDDY to be *LMI* and *LLR* (compare Table 2). The overall highest correlation occurs between *compound-mean* and *LMI* with ρ of 0.54. We also see that *sim-bw-constituents* and *sim-with-heads* are generally good predictors as well. Contrary to Schulte im Walde et al. (2013) we do not find a strong correlation between modifiers and the REDDY ratings. Interestingly, *PPMI* is always weakly negatively correlated with the ratings. This could be due to *PPMI*'s property of inflating scores for rare events. As can also be seen

Time span	Cut-off	$R^2 \pm$ sd
	20	0.343 ± 0.028
NA (Non-temporal)	50	0.344 ± 0.026
	100	0.337 ± 0.035
	20	0.350 ± 0.029
1 (Year)	50	0.171 ± 0.039
	100	0.326 ± 0.030
	20	0.332 ± 0.024
10 (Decade)	50	0.328 ± 0.034
	100	0.360 ± 0.062
	20	0.341 ± 0.039
20 (Score)	50	0.331 ± 0.031
	100	$\mathbf{0.370 \pm 0.012}$
	20	0.352 ± 0.038
50 (Half-century)	50	0.360 ± 0.029
	100	0.364 ± 0.034
	20	0.351 ± 0.037
100 (Century)	50	0.343 ± 0.033
	100	0.344 ± 0.034

Table 1: R^2 values and standard deviation for the different configurations.

from Table 2, our correlation values are considerably lower than that of Reddy et al. (2011), but on par with a replication study by Schulte im Walde et al. (2016a) for *compound-mean*. We speculate that these differences are potentially due to the use of different data sets, the fact that we use a considerably smaller context window for constructing the word vectors (5 due to the restrictions of Google Ngram corpus vs. 100 in Reddy et al. (2011) and 40 in Schulte im Walde et al. (2016b)) and the use of a compound-centric setting (as described in 4.1).

From Table 1 we see that our best reported R^2 value occurs when observing time in stretches of 20 years (scores) and compounds having a frequency cut-off of at least 100. A few other observations could be made: In general the cut-off seems to improve the R^2 metric and the time spans of 10 and 20 years appear to be the most informative and stable for the cut-off values. Also, using temporal information almost always outperforms the setup that ignores all temporal information.

For our following experiment, we choose to use the configuration with the highest R^2 value: a time span of 20 years and a cut-off of 100. Since LMI

achieved the highest ρ values, we also choose LMI over the other features. We group the compounds of REDDY into three groups based on the human ratings they obtained: *low* (0-1), *med* (2-3) and *high* (4-5). Each group contains around 30 compounds. We then plot the LMI values of these three groups with their confidence interval across the time step of 20 years, shown in Figure 1. We can observe that there is a separation between the groups towards the later years, and that the period between 1940s and 1960s caused a noticeable change in the compositionality of the REDDY compounds. We find the same trends for all three information theory based features. Although care should be taken given the small data sets (especially for the earlier decades) on which the models were build and tested, the slope of the lines for the three groups of compounds seems to suggest that less compositional compounds go through a more pronounced change in compositionality than compositional compounds, as expected.

We also show the graphs for *sim-with-head* and *sim-with-mod* (Figures 2 and 3) for the different groups of compounds across time, as these underperformed in our previous experiment. Both figures based on cosine based features largely confound the three groups of compounds across time, reinforcing our previous findings.

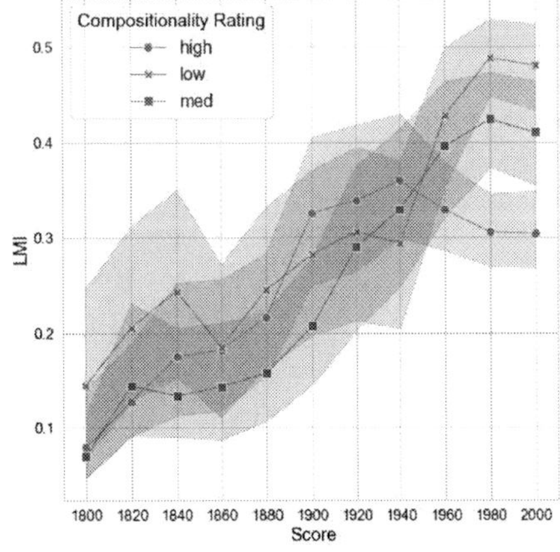

Figure 1: LMI of a compound in time point t and $t+1$, with a time span of 20 years and a frequency cut-off of 100. Compounds are grouped according to their rating in REDDY.

	modifier-mean	head-mean	compound-mean
sim-bw-constituents	0.35	0.41	0.48
sim-with-head	0.26	0.43	0.43
sim-with-mod	0.1	0.18	0.2
LLR	0.36	0.44	0.52
PPMI	-0.12	-0.1	-0.14
LMI	**0.38**	**0.45**	**0.54**

Table 2: Spearman's ρ of our measures and the compositionality ratings of REDDY.

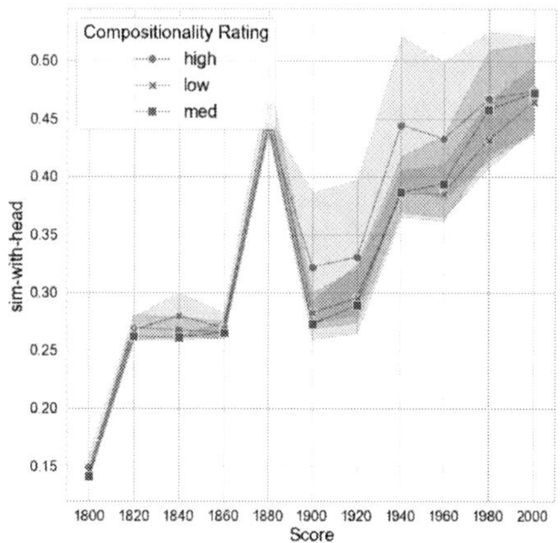

Figure 2: *sim-with-head* of a compound in time point t and $t + 1$, with a time span of 20 years and a frequency cut-off of 100. Compounds are grouped according to their rating in REDDY.

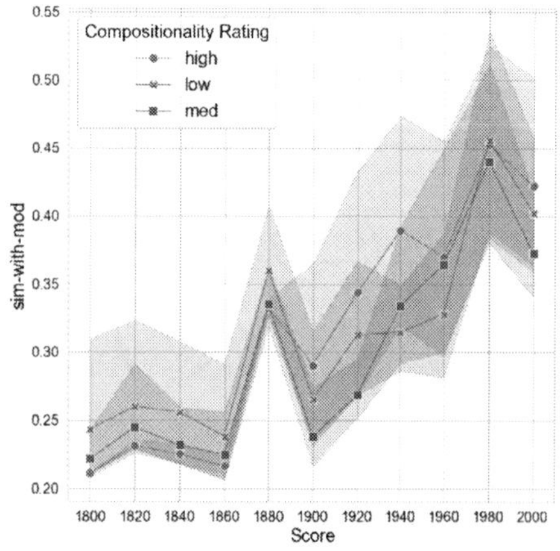

Figure 3: *sim-with-mod* of a compound in time point t and $t + 1$, with a time span of 20 years and a frequency cut-off of 100. Compounds are grouped according to their rating in REDDY.

6 Future Work

Our current work was limited to English compounds from Reddy et al. (2011). We plan to expand our models to other languages for which compositionality ratings are available, such as German. We would also like to further investigate the fact that the information theory based measures outperform the ones based on cosine similarity. We intend to do so by incorporating more compounds and their compositionality ratings, as well as by using larger corpora.

Lastly, we will seek to find ways to harvest proxies for compositionality ratings of compounds over time. A possible avenue could be to use the information available in dictionaries.

7 Conclusion

We have shown work in progress on determining the compositionality of compounds over time. We showed that for our current setup, information theory based measures seem to capture compositionality better. Furthermore, we showed that adding temporal information increases the predictive power of these features to prognosticate synchronic compositionality. Finally, we showed how our best performing models trace the compositionality of compounds over time, delineating the behavior of compounds of varying levels of compositionality.

Acknowledgements

We would like to thank the anonymous reviewers for their valuable comments. The second author has been funded by the Volkswagen Foundation in the scope of the QuaDramA project.

References

Laurie Bauer. 2017. *Compounds and Compounding*, volume 155 of *Cambridge Studies in Linguistics*. Cambridge University Press, Cambridge.

Nivja H. De Jong, Laurie B. Feldman, Robert Schreuder, Matthew Pastizzo, and R. Harald Baayen. 2002. The processing and representation of dutch and english compounds: peripheral morphological and central orthographic effects. *Brain and Language*, 81:555–67.

Prajit Dhar and Lonneke van der Plas. 2019. Learning to predict novel noun-noun compounds. In *Joint Workshop on Multiword Expressions and WordNet (MWE-WN 2019)*.

Fritz Günther and Marco Marelli. 2016. Understanding Karma Police: The Perceived Plausibility of Noun Compounds as Predicted by Distributional Models of Semantic Representation. *PLoS ONE*, 11(10):1–36.

William L. Hamilton, Jure Leskovec, and Dan Jurafsky. 2018. Diachronic word embeddings reveal statistical laws of semantic change. *CoRR*, abs/1605.09096.

Andrey Kutuzov, Lilja Øvrelid, Terrence Szymanski, and Erik Velldal. 2018. Diachronic word embeddings and semantic shifts: a survey. In *Proceedings of the 27th International Conference on Computational Linguistics*, pages 1384–1397, Santa Fe, New Mexico, USA.

Christopher D. Manning and Hinrich Schütze. 1999. *Foundations of Statistical Natural Language Processing*. MIT Press, Cambridge, MA, USA.

Jean-Baptiste Michel, Yuan Kui Shen, Aviva Presser Aiden, Adrian Veres, Matthew K. Gray, The Google Books Team, Joseph P. Pickett, Dale Hoiberg, Dan Clancy, Peter Norvig, Jon Orwant, Steven Pinker, Martin A. Nowak, and Erez Lieberman Aiden. 2011. Quantitative analysis of culture using millions of digitized books. *Science*, 331(6014):176–182.

Barbara H. Partee. 1984. Compositionality. In *Varieties of Formal Semantics: Proceedings of the 4th Amsterdam Colloquium, Sept. 1982*, pages 281–311. Foris Publications.

Siva Reddy, Diana McCarthy, and Suresh Manandhar. 2011. An empirical study on compositionality in compound nouns. In *Proceedings of the 5th International Joint Conference on Natural Language Processing*, pages 210–218, Chiang Mai, Thailand. AFNLP.

Sabine Schulte im Walde, Anna Hätty, and Stefan Bott. 2016a. The role of modifier and head properties in predicting the compositionality of English and German noun-noun compounds: A vector-space perspective. In *Proceedings of the Fifth Joint Conference on Lexical and Computational Semantics (*SEM 2016)*, pages 148–158.

Sabine Schulte im Walde, Anna Hätty, Stefan Bott, and Nana Khvtisavrishvili. 2016b. $G_h$ost-NN: A Representative Gold Standard of German Noun-Noun Compounds. In *Proceedings of the 10th International Conference on Language Resources and Evaluation*, pages 2285–2292, Portoroz, Slovenia.

Sabine Schulte im Walde, Stefan Müller, and Stephen Roller. 2013. Exploring Vector Space Models to Predict the Compositionality of German Noun-Noun Compounds. In *Proceedings of the 2nd Joint Conference on Lexical and Computational Semantics*, pages 255–265, Atlanta, GA, USA.

Nigel Vincent. 2014. Compositionality and change. In Claire Bowern and Bethwyn Evans, editors, *The Routledge Handbook of Historical Linguistics*, pages 103–123. Routledge, United Kingdom.

Claudia von der Heide and Susanne Borgwaldt. 2009. Assoziationen zu Ober-, Basis- und Unterbegriffen. Eine explorative Studie. In *Proceedings of the 9th Norddeutsches Linguistisches Kolloquium*, pages 51–74, Bielefeld, Germany.

Towards Automatic Variant Analysis of Ancient Devotional Texts

Amir Hazem[1] **Béatrice Daille**[1] **Dominique Stutzmann**[2] **Jacob Currie**[2] **Christine Jacquin**[1]

(1) Université de Nantes, LS2N, France
(2) IRHT-CNRS, France

{amir.hazem, beatrice.daille, christine.jacquin}@ls2n.fr
{dominique.stutzmann, jacob.currie}@irht.cnrs.fr

Abstract

We address in this paper the issue of text reuse in liturgical manuscripts of the middle ages. More specifically, we study variant readings of the *Obsecro Te* prayer, part of the devotional Books of Hours often used by Christians as guidance for their daily prayers. We aim at automatically extracting and categorising pairs of words and expressions that exhibit variant relations. For this purpose, we introduce a linguistic classification that allows to better characterize the variants than edit operations. Then, we study the evolution of *Obsecro Te* texts from a temporal and geographical axis. Finally, we contrast several unsupervised state-of-the-art approaches for the automatic extraction of *Obsecro Te* variants. Based on the manual observation of 772 *Obsecro Te* copies which show more than 21,000 variants, we show that the proposed methodology is helpful for an automatic study of variants and may serve as basis to analyse and to depict useful information from devotional texts.

1 Introduction

Among the most popular texts of the late middle ages were Books of Hours, used by Christians as a guidance book for their daily prayers. Appearing in the thirteenth century, in France, the Netherlands, and England and, later on, in Italy, Spain, and many other European countries, Books of Hours constitute one of the bestsellers of the late medieval period. Books of Hours evolved over the years and additional texts were included. Mostly written in Latin, they often include parts in Vernacular languages (esp. French). The whole was arranged in a particular repetitive structure that varied in its details depending on times of the day, seasons, liturgical use, patrons, origin (Wieck, 1988; Hindman and Marrow, 2013), etc.

Despite their success, the content of Books of Hours has been rarely studied on a large-scale in NLP, mainly due to the lack of available transcriptions. few of them are available. One textual element of Books of Hours which offers an opportunity for study is *Obsecro Te*. This devotional prayer to the Virgin Mary was manually transcribed and annotated based on 772 Books of Hours (Plummer and Clark, 2015). More than 21,000 textual variants were recorded. Plummer and Clark (2015) observed and reported three types of variants present in the *Obsecro Te* dataset, that is: (i) addition (marked "+", e.g. "peccatis + vel mortalibus" for *criminalibus peccatis / criminalibus peccatis vel mortalibus*), (ii) substitution (marked ":", e.g. "opera misericordia: misericordia opera" for *opera misericordia / misericordia opera*), and (iii) omission (marked "-", e.g. "-gloriosam" for *ostendem michi gloriosam / ostende michi*). This classification is roughly based on a surface assessment and does not allow a more fine-grained analysis of variants characteristic while no linguistic information is included. In order to study in a more precise way *Obsecro Te* variant readings, we adopt a linguistic classification based on both synformic and conceptual (similar words form) concepts (Laufer, 1988; Daille, 2017). Clark's variants consist in addition, suppression or omission operations at the word level. The same operation groups diverse linguistic operations. Substitution operation for instance, may refer to flexional variants (*crucem / cruce*), paradigmatic variants obtained by synonymic substitution (*gratie / indulgencie*), etc. Also, two consecutive substitution operations may characterise variant permutation (*opera misericordia / misericordia opera*). We conduct an automatic empirical study of the main unsupervised state-of-the-art approaches dealing with variant extraction and discuss our findings according to the proposed linguistic variant classification. Finally, we study variant-relation phenomena and the evolu-

Proceedings of the 1st International Workshop on Computational Approaches to Historical Language Change, pages 240–249
Florence, Italy, August 2, 2019. ©2019 Association for Computational Linguistics

Num	Obsecro Te 1	Obsecro Te 2
1	Obsecro Te domina sancta maria mater dei pietate plenissima summi	Obsecro Te domina sancta maria mater dei pietate plenissima summi
2	regis filia mater gloriosissima mater orphanorum consolatio	regis filia mater gloriosissima mater orphanorum consolatio
3	desolatorum via errantium salus in te sperantium virgo ante	desolatorum via errantium salus et spes in te sperantium virgo ante
4	partum virgo in partu et virgo post partum Fons misericordie	partum virgo in partu virgo post partum
5	fons salutis et gratie fons pietatis et leticie fons consolationis	fons salutis et gratie fons pietatis et leticie fons consolationis
6	et indulgencie Per illam sanctam ineffabilem leticiam	et indulgencie Et per illam sanctam inestimabilem leticiam
7	qua exultavit spiritus tuus in illa hora quando tibi per gabrielem	qua exultavit spiritus tuus in illa hora quando tibi per gabrielem
8	annunciatus filius dei fuit	archangelum annunciatus et conceptus filius dei fuit
9	Et per illud divinum mysterium quod tunc operatus est spiritus sanctus	Et per illud divinum mysterium quod tunc operatus est spiritus sanctus in te

Table 1: Comparison of the first lines of two *Obsecro Te* variants. Text in red indicates *Obsecro Te* variants.

tion of *Obsecro Te* readings from a temporal and geographical axis and discuss several aspects of Books of Hours.

This work constitutes a first step in the automatic study of Book of Hours content in order to discover the similarities and differences in practices of the middle age. The similarities can for instance serve to detect structural, geographical or terminological correlations between Books of Hours. Whether issued from different regions of the same country or from different countries of medieval Europe.

2 Books of Hours and *Obsecro Te*

Books of Hours contain a set of prayers to be used at eight hours of the day. The structure and content of Books of Hours vary from one book to another and this particularity is certainly due to the nature of textual transmission in a world before the printing press. Books of Hours did not appear as such until the thirteenth century. Before, other types of books were used. For their daily prayers, Christians adopted the Psalter previously used by the Jews for their devotions. Over the years, a number of additional texts came to enrich the Psalter, such as, antiphons, canticles, hymns, readings from the Bible, etc. The whole was arranged in a repetitive structure that varied in its details depending on times of the day and seasons. Also, a calendar was used to record local saints, days and feast's seasons. Finally, rubrics were employed as guidance on what to say and when to say it. This resulted in a complex book known as breviary. The breviary was used by clerks and was not intended to be used by lay people for whom it was too complex. However, the desire of lay people to imitate monastic practices resulted in the creation of a simpler book, that was easier to use: the Book of Hours. Amongst the prayers in Books of Hours is

the *Obsecro Te*, a supplication to the Virgin Mary. As the content of a Book of Hours may vary due to writing choice, local liturgical practices, etc., we aim in this paper to study the amount and nature of variants of *Obsecro Te*.

Table 1 shows an example of the first lines of two copies of *Obsecro Te*. Red are the variants according to an arbitrary lines alignment of the two texts (Plummer and Clark, 2015). As highlighted by the passages in red, several variants can be observed. In line 3, for instance, the words "*et spes*" in *Obsecro Te* 1 are added between the words "*salus*" et "*in*" ((Plummer and Clark, 2015) notes that "*salus + et spes*", while in line 4, the words "*et*" and "*Fons misericordie*" are omitted in *Obsecro Te* 2. Also, at lines 7-8, the Annunciation is addressed with the expression *per Gabrielem annunciatus* (*Obsecro Te* 1), while *Obsecro Te* 2 expands upon the passage by specifying the announcer, the *archangelum*, and the effect *et conceptus*. If the reasons of such variants are a matter of interpretation, we aim at depicting the most common ones. For that purpose, we define in the next section our proposed classification of the observed variants before presenting an empirical study for variant extraction and categorisation.

3 Obsecro Te Variant Categorization

We introduce in this section a new variant classification inspired by similar lexical forms (Synforms) introduced in (Laufer, 1988) and the terminological variant typology proposed in (Daille, 2017) applying to nominals.

3.1 Similar Lexical Forms (Synforms)

The concept of synforms was first introduced to deal with lexical confusions of English learners (Laufer, 1988). Synforms are defined at the word level and can be classified on the basis of their

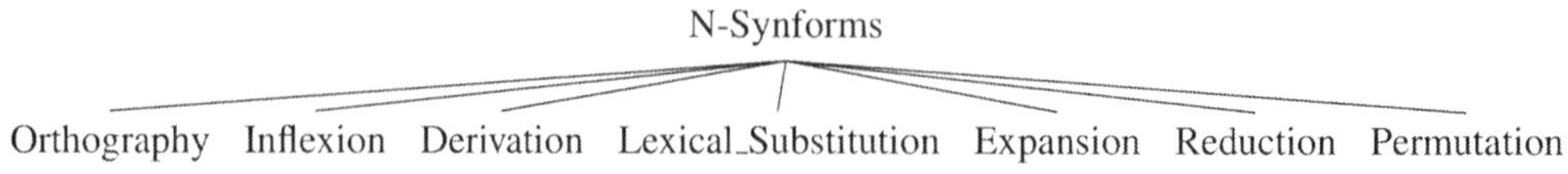

N-Synforms

Orthography   Inflexion   Derivation   Lexical_Substitution   Expansion   Reduction   Permutation

Figure 1: N-Synforms variant representation

similarity features. Words can be different in their affix and similar in their root, different in one phoneme, consonant or vowel. Usually, ten categories including letter addition, substitution and omission, are reported (Laufer, 1988; Kocic, 2008). These categories include: productive synforms with the same root and different suffixes (*considerable / considerate, successful / successive*); non-productive synforms with the same root and different suffixes (*credible / credulous, capable / capacious*); synforms which, although identical in consonants, have different vowels (*base / bias, manual / menial*); synforms with identical phonemes except for one consonant (*price / prize, extend / extent*), etc.

3.2 Lexical Similarity at the Word Ngram Level (N-Synforms)

We extend the similar lexical forms concept (Laufer, 1988; Kocic, 2008) to the word ngram level. Nonetheless, we do not exploit the ten categories presented in (Laufer, 1988), as it deals with confusions of English learners. Therefore, we keep the word level categorization of unigrams as defined in Daille (2017) and extend it using linguistic operations often applied to complex terms and to ngrams. Base on the copies of the *Obsecro Te* prayer and the variant annotations in (Plummer and Clark, 2015), we propose a linguistic representation of variant's typology that can be applied to word ngrams of any length. Our typology includes basic linguistic variants at the word level (orthography, inflexion, derivation), lexical substitution, as well as operations specific to sequence of words (reduction, expansion and permutation). Figure 1 illustrates our typology. We describe the proposed categorization as follows:

Orthography letter substitution (consonant or vowel) like *dilecto / delecto*;

Inflexion latin inflexions like *crucem / cruce*;

Derivation is defined as an operation which creates a new lexical unit from one existing word through modification processes such as affixation or convertion *dilecto (Adj)/ dilectissimo (Adj superlative)*;

Lexical substitution refers to any operation of substitution of a lexical unit by another. Lexical substitution allows variants in semantic relation, such as synonymy (*tribuas / concedas*), near-synonymy (*gratie / indulgencie*) and other variants with no clear semantic relation such as (*tribuas / obtineas*);

Expansion refers to several linguistic operations such as modification which specifies the nominal phrase, predication which inserts the nominal phrase into a nominal argument structure, coordination that emphasize an aspect (*criminalibus peccatis / criminalibus peccatis vel mortalibus*);

Reduction removes one of the lexical constituents of ngrams such as *ostendem michi gloriosam / ostendem michi*;

Permutation of the n-gram elements such as *criminalibus peccatis / peccatis criminalibus*.

Of course, like any typology, ours does not claim to be exhaustive. Nonetheless, it can be extended, if necessary, to other linguistic operations like composition. Also, variants that combine multiple operations like lexical substitution and expansion or substitution exist but they are marginal.

4 Variant Extraction Approaches

We introduce in this section four unsupervised state-of-the-art approaches to the task of variant extraction: Edit distance (Levenshtein, 1966), Jaccard Index (Jaccard, 1901), distributional bag of words (Harris, 1971) and its adaptation to variable length variants extraction and finally, distributed word embeddings (Mikolov et al., 2013; Arora et al., 2017).

4.1 Edit Distance (Levenshtein)

Edit distance, also known as the distance of Levenshtein (Levenshtein, 1966), aligns local similarities and differences between strings and calculates string-alignment. Distance is calculated from the number of necessary operations (insertions, deletions and substitutions) for transforming the string x into the string y. Among the edit distance applications, we find plagiarism detection and orthographic corrections. Edit distance formula is represented as follows:

$$D(i,j) = min \begin{cases} D[i-1,j] + SuppCost(i) \\ D[i,j-1] + InsCost(i) \\ D[i-1,j-1] + SubCost(i,j) \end{cases} \quad (1)$$

where D(i,j) represents the distance between two ngrams i et j and $Suppcost(i)$, $InsCost(i)$ represent respectively the deletion, insertion costs of i. Finally, $SubCost(i,j)$ represents the substitution cost of i by j. When the three cost functions are put to 1, Edit distance is equivalent to Levensthein distance. The use of Edit Distance is based on the observation that several *Obsecro Te* variants may be synformic (graphically similar). For instance, *salvatione* is very close to *salvationis* or *salvationem*. In this case, Edit distance score is 2 between *salvatione* and *salvationis* (the letter *e* is substituted by *i* and the addition of *s*) and a score of 1 between *salvatione* and *salvationem* (addition of the letter *m*).

4.2 Jaccard Index

Jaccard Index (JI) (Jaccard, 1901) measures the degree of similarity between two sets. This is represented by the number of elements in common normalized by the elements of the two sets. One advantage of Jaccard Index is that it is insensitive to element's position and for this reason is not affected by element's permutation. This particularity makes the JI well suited to semantic variants of permutation type, such as *crucifixum vulneratum* and *vulneratum crucifixum*. In this case, JI score is 0 which means that the pair of variants is similar according to permutation property. JI formula is as follows:

$$Jaccard(\mathbf{A}, \mathbf{B}) = \frac{A \cap B}{A \cup B} \quad (2)$$

where the two sets A and B correspond to two word ngrams, with B a variant candidate. The intersection and union are both considered at the character level.

4.3 Distributional Bag of Words

In the distributional Bag of Words (BoW) approach each word w is represented by its context vector (Harris, 1971). The context vector of w gathers all the words with which it appears in the corpus within a size n context window. The context window represents a set of surrounding words often close to the sentence level size. To measure the similarity between words, the cosine (Salton and Lesk, 1968) is applied between the context vector of w and all the word context vectors of the corpus. The closest word to w is a potential variant. We adapt BoW approach and extend it to the ngram level. The procedure remains the same, the main change lying in the context representation of each variant. Let us consider the following example: *Levitae autem in tribu **familiarum suarum** non sunt numerati cum eis*. The context vector of ***familiarum suarum*** is represented by the following ngrams: Unigrams: *Levitae, autem, in, tribu, non, sunt, numerati, cum, eis*; Bigrams: *Levitae autem, autem in, in tribu, non sunt, sunt numerati, numerati cum, cum eis*; 3grams: *Levitae autem in, autem in tribu, non sunt numerati, sunt numerati cum, numerati cum eis*; 4grams: *Levitae autem in tribu, non sunt numerati cum, sunt numerati cum eis*; and 5grams: *non sunt numerati cum eis*. Once the context vectors have been computed, an association measure is used as a way to better characterize the contextual relation between the head of the vector (**familiarum suarum**) and its constituents. We consider three different association measures: mutual information (Fano, 1961), discounted odds ratio (Evert, 2005) and log-likelihood (Dunning, 1993). Finally, to extract the candidates, we compute cosine similarity (Salton and Lesk, 1968) between all ngrams of the corpus. Our adaptation takes into account broken ngrams. Hence, in addition to the above cited ngrams, based on *non sunt numerati cum eis*, we add the following bigrams: *non numerati, non cum, non eis, sunt cum, sunt eis, numerati eis*. Therefore, we assume that the unigrams *sunt, numerati*, and *cum* may not appear or were omitted.

4.4 Word Embeddings

In the word embedding approach, each variant is represented by an embedding vector which is a linear combination of the word embeddings composing the variant (Arora et al., 2017). For instance,

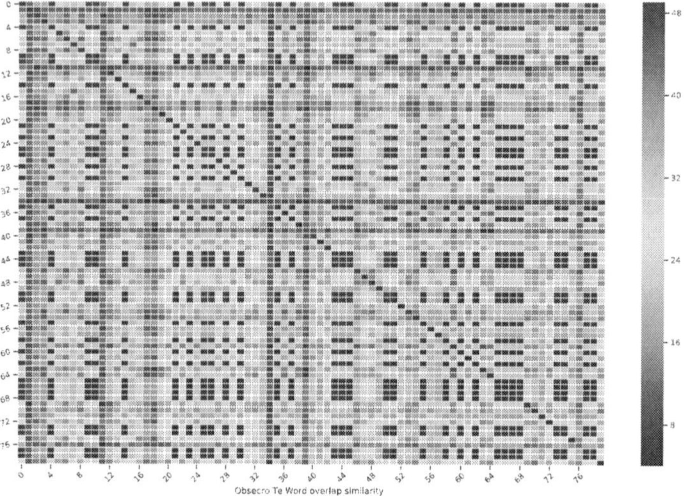

Figure 2: Word overlap similarity of 80 randomly selected *Obsecro Te* texts.

the embedding vector of *familiarum suarum*, is the sum of the word embedding vector of *familiarum* plus the word embedding vector of *suarum*. Finally, after computing the embedding vectors of all the ngrams which compose the corpus, cosine similarity is used to extract the variant candidates. The computation of the embedding vector of a given variant is represented as follows:

$$Embedding(A) = \sum_{j=1}^{n} Embedding(w_j) \quad (3)$$

where A is a variant and n the number of words composing A. $Embedding(w_j)$ corresponds to the chosen embedding model of w_j. We use two pre-trained models: Word2Vec[1] and FastText[2].

5   Experimental Data

To evaluate the automatic extraction of *Obsecro Te* variants, we exploit the *Beyond Use* [3] database which contains variants extracted manually from 772 manuscripts (Plummer and Clark, 2015). The given prayer contains 49 segments (passages) defined arbitrarily. This segmentation allowed Clark to compare each line of the *Obsecro Te*, manuscript by manuscript, and to extract

21,329 variants, of which 3,298 distinct variants. In order to study the impact of variant length, we build four distinct evaluation lists. Each one corresponds to an ngram size. Hence, we obtain a list of unigrams that contains only unigrams as variants; a list of bigrams that contains only bigrams as variants and so on. We do not go beyond four-grams because very few ngrams are characterized by a length longer than four in the corpus. We finally build a fifth list that contains all the ngrams of the four previous lists as well as ngram variants of any length (20% of the variants have a variant of a different size).

6   Results

Our experimental procedure targets three points: (i) an empirical evaluation of *Obsecro Te* reading similarity; (ii) an empirical evaluation of automatic variant extraction; (iii) a qualitative variant analysis with regard to linguistics, geographic and diachronic changes.

6.1   Similarity of Obsecro Te Texts

There is substantial variation in the text of the prayer *Obsecro Te*. As has been shown in (Wieck, 1988; Plummer and Clark, 2015), the manual analysis of 772 *Obsecro Te* prayers revealed several dissimilarities as well as the existence of more than 21,000 variants. Figure 2 illustrates the simi-

---

[1] www.cs.cmu.edu/~dbamman/latin.html
[2] github.com/facebookresearch/fastText/blob/master/pretrained-vectors.md
[3] http://www6.sewanee.edu/BeyondUse/

| | Ngram size (size of the evaluation list) | | | | | | | | | | | | | | | | | | | |
| | 1 (208) | | | | 2 (82) | | | | 3 (53) | | | | 4 (28) | | | | ALL (482) | | | |
Method	P	R	F	MAP	P	R	F	MAP	P	R	F	MAP	P	R	F	MAP	P	R	F	MAP
EditDist	**14.0**	**59.1**	**22.6**	48.3	1.82	10.4	3.11	4.65	2.83	8.49	4.24	6.04	2.85	8.06	4.21	5.43	7.01	28.1	11.2	23.1
Jaccard	11.4	50.8	18.7	37.9	7.80	**66.0**	13.9	48.7	**11.3**	**66.0**	**19.3**	38.2	7.85	43.0	13.2	22.8	7.12	35.7	11.8	25.3
BOW (IM)	10.2	46.2	16.8	17.3	5.24	45.3	9.40	12.5	9.24	51.9	15.6	14.8	3.21	15.6	5.33	10.5	2.54	10.8	4.11	8.36
BOW (OR)	10.1	46.2	16.7	17.1	4.87	41.6	8.73	12.3	9.05	50.1	15.3	14.5	3.21	15.6	5.33	10.5	2.54	10.9	4.12	8.39
BOW (LL)	12.6	52.6	20.3	**48.5**	**8.04**	60.9	**14.2**	28.6	10.7	60.0	18.2	25.7	2.85	17.7	4.78	12.1	**9.70**	**41.7**	**15.7**	**31.9**
W2V	7.74	33.7	12.5	23.3	6.95	63.3	12.4	**62.3**	9.43	65.0	16.4	**49.1**	**12.5**	**64.0**	**20.9**	**40.9**	3.89	21.6	6.60	17.2
FastText	6.39	30.2	10.5	28.7	6.95	60.9	12.4	59.7	9.43	63.9	16.4	41.1	12.1	57.3	20.0	29.0	3.25	19.5	5.57	11.6

Table 2: Evaluation of EditDist, Jaccard, BoW and Embedding approaches (W2V and FastText). The results are presented in terms of precision (P), Recall (R) and Fmeasure (F) at top 10 as well as the mean average precision (MAP). Between parentheses we display, for each ngram size, the size of the evaluation list. For instance: 1(208) corresponds to 208 ngrams (variants) of length 1.

larities between 80 randomly[4] selected *Obsecro Te* texts. The similarity is measured in terms of word overlap. Strong similarities are shown by the dark red colour, while weak similarities by dark blue. Figure 2 shows that none of the 80 sampled *Obsecro Te* texts are identical. This empirical finding confirms the observations of Clark and supports the idea that different copies of the prayer *Obsecro Te* differ substantially from one another.

6.2 Automatic Variant Extraction

In this section, we aim at evaluating unsupervised approaches to variant extraction. Hence, no clue, such as verse or segment alignment, is considered in variant modelling. This leads to the assumption that any ngram extracted from the corpus is a variant candidate. The side effect of this assumption is its error productivity while many ngrams are not variants.

Table 2 illustrates the results of the implemented approaches. Edit distance shows the best results for unigram variants. Nonetheless, its performance significantly drops when variants are of length greater than 1. This can be explained by the large number of permutations that are not identified by Edit distance.

Jaccard Index obtains better results than Edit distance for ngrams greater than 1, which means that conversely to Edit distance, it better handles the permutation phenomenon. Our adaptation of the bag of words approach (BOW (LL)) using log-likelihood shows the best results on the entire evaluation list (*ALL*). This indicates that BOW (LL) better handles variants of variable length. The lower results of BOW (MI) and BOW (OR)

---

[4]The number of texts was limited to 80 to enable a clear visualisation of the results. The same behaviour was observed over the entire *Obsecro Te* dataset.

Rare Variants	Category
salvationem / salvatione	inflectional
victoria / victoriam	inflectional
viscerum / viscerum	orthographic
dolose / dolore	lexical substitution
gaudii / gaudio	inflectional
ancilla tua / famulo tuo	lexical substitution + inflectional (f./ m.)
michi annuncies / annuncies michi	permutation
sensum erigat mores imponat	reduction
/ mores componat	+ lexical substitution
Frequent Variants	**Category**
gaudia / gaudio	inflectional (f./ m.)
misericordie / gratie	lexical substitution (Adjective)
domina / virgo	lexical substitution (Noun)
cordis dolorem / dolorem cordis	permutation
a dilecto filio / de filio	lexical substitution + reduction
regat / custodiat	lexical substitution (Verb)
super / per	lexical substitution (Preposition)

Table 3: Examples of extracted *Obsecro Te* variants.

lead to the assumption that these two association measures fail to capture strong ngram association relations. The lack of training data can also explain this behaviour. The word embedding approach (w2v) shows the best Map scores for ngrams greater than 1. This suggests that w2v is the most appropriate when variants are not unigrams. The lower results for unigrams can be explained by the nature of the embedding models. Indeed, w2v and fastText are pre-trained models and many *Obsecro Te* words are not present in these models. Finally, a linear combination of the approaches has been carried out without significant improvements.

If some phenomena can be detected such as synforms at the word level (with Edit distance for unigrams), permutations using Jaccard index, or lexical substitution using bag of words and embedding vector approaches, other phenomena are more difficult to handle, such as expansion and reduction variants where the two segments are of variable length. We also report that some words and expressions are often substituted by connectors (*et, a, que, de, in...*), such as *sanctam / et, de filio tuo / a, vulneratum / et, in omnibus / et in*. Very frequent connectors represent one of the most difficult variants to extract as they show a big discrepancy of distribution between the two elements.

6.3 Qualitative Variant Analysis

Variant categories can be analysed based on Edit distance, Jaccard Index, BoW and Embedding scores as follow: (i) if Edit distance score is lower than few characters (generally 3), we can effectively pinpoint, thanks to a regular expression, one of the three synformic categories (orthographic, inflectional or derivational); (ii) if Jaccard index score is equal to 0, we face a permutation; (iii) if we combine two criteria, i.e., high Edit distance score and low Jaccard index score, we extract variants that exhibit both expansion and permutation; (iv) lexical substitution variants can be extracted using BoW or Word embedding approaches. A high cosine similarity score has also been used to give more confidence about lexical substitution variants.

Based on the observation that a large number of variants (406) appears in less than five copies of *Obsecro Te*, we divide our analysis into two parts: rare variants and frequent variants. Table 3 reports some examples of variants identified by our automatic extraction. For rare variant pairs (*salvationem / salvatione*, for instance), each reported left side variant appears only in one copy, while its right side counterpart variant appears in hundreds of copies. Rare variants may indicate either a rare usage or a misspelling error. On the other hand, frequent variants may offer a high confidence in their usage.

We observe inflectional variants as rare or frequent variants: *salvationem* (singular accusative) and *victoria* (singular) appear only once in the corpus, while *salvatione* (singular ablative) and *victoriam* (singular accusative) appear respectively 961 and 966 times. In one case the accusative mode is used, while in the other, the ablative is used. Misspellings as rare variants: *viserum* and *vicerum* are both misspellings of *viscerum*. Lexical substitution applies mostly to frequent variants and leads to semantic variants. Synonym lexical substitu-

Rare (freq=1)	Frequent (freq >500)
in me instruat (Savoy)	instituat
ancilla tua n (Netherlands)	famulo tuo
sensum sursum dirigat (Paris)	cursum dirigat
famule tue leonarde (Provence)	famulo tuo
aliis rebus quas (Val d'Oise)	illis rebus in quibus
in cruce denudatum (Netherlands)	ante crucem nudatum
siscientem ac hely (Paris)	sicientem fel apponi
mea et desideria (Paris)	et desideria mea
venias et festine (Netherlands)	veni et festina
bene per me (Amiens)	me bene per
omni auxilio consilio (Netherlands)	omni consilio
cursum meum regat (Besançon)	cursum dirigat
scicientem fel aponi (Bourges)	sicientem fel apponi
venias et sustines (Valenciennes)	veni et festina
pace omni salvatione (Besançon)	omni salvatione pace
petitionibus et requestis (Western Fr)	orationibus et requestis
et etiam abundantiam (Val d'Oise)	etiam habundantiam
in omnibus etiam (Central France)	et in omnibus
deus filius tuus (Netherlands)	filius dei
mentem sensum et (Netherlands)	mentem erigat
gratie et salutis (Paris)	salutis et gratie
in ea elevatum (Netherlands)	in ipsa levatum
regat et mentem (Paris)	regat mentem
veni et festinam (Rouen)	veni et festina
probet et vota (Mons)	probet vota
cursum sensum erigat (Paris)	cursum dirigat
honnestam et honnourabilem (Mons)	honestam et honorabilem
venies et festinas (Netherlands)	veni et festina
meum in consilium (Rouen)	et consilium
horam et diem (Netherlands)	diem et horam

Table 4: Examples of 3 gram variants. First column shows variants that appear only once. Column 2 shows the corresponding frequent variants.

tion, such as *domina /virgo*, is encountered in every grammatical category (noun, verb, adjective, preposition). One exception is the rare variant *ancilla tua / famulo tuo*, the result of two linguistic operations, lexical substitution and inflection, that may refer to a customisation of Books of Hours according to its owner, either a woman or a man. We expect that looking to the whole text of Books of Hours and increasing the number of Books of Hours, this variant will be more frequent. Indeed, Books of Hours are personal objects, and are not intended to be shared. Finally, the last example of rare variants shows the application of two lexical operations, reduction and lexical substitution.

Figure 3 illustrates the number of *Obsecro Te* (and therefore, Books of Hours) produced between 1375 and 1530 and used in this experiment[5]. This

---

[5]Given that the Books of Hours are not dated by their scribes, a date range is generally devised by scholars. The

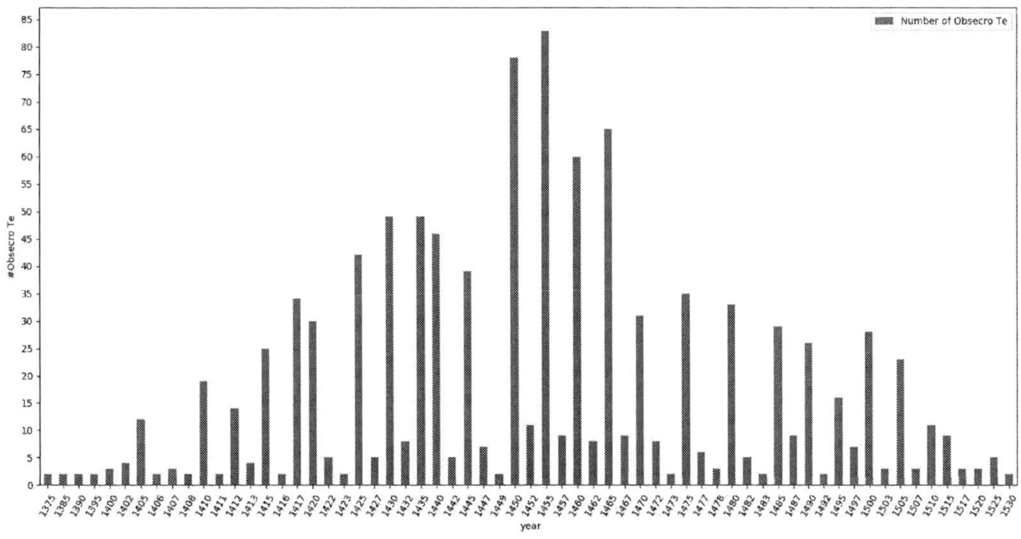

Figure 3: Number of Obsecro Te prayers per year

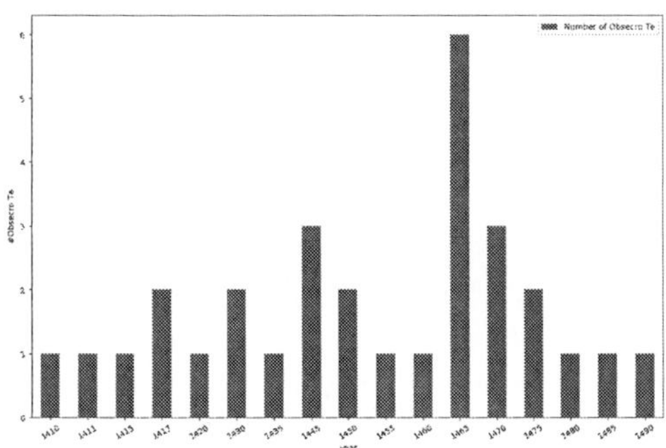

Figure 4: Obsecro Te per Year: 3gram variants over temporal axis

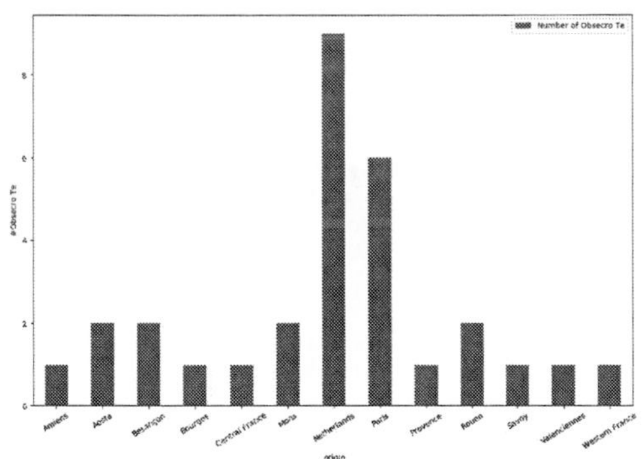

Figure 5: Obsecro Te Origin: 3gram variants over geographical axis

corpus illustrates how the production of Books of Hours increased until the second half of the fifteenth century and decreased afterwards. A larger corpus suggests that production reached it highest level during the last third of the fifteenth century (Stutzmann, 2019). An empirical overview through approximately a century and half of Book of Hours production, does not allow to draw a direct relation in the diachronic change of *Obsecro Te* prayer copies. Nonetheless, our method allows to target a variant category and to observe its years of use and origins. Table 4 provides some examples of rare 3gram variants of which it is not always obvious to assign a linguistic category. We can notice that rare 3gram variants are often expansion of frequent bigrams *omni auxilio consilio / omni consilio*. Figures 4 and 5 illustrate the use of rare orthographic 3gram variants that have less than ten character substitutions (respectively per year and per origin). This is performed by fixing the edit distance score to 10 (which means a maximum of ten substitutions) and choosing only the variants that appear only once in the corpus. We obtain for instance, the variant pair obtained by lexical substitution *petitionibus et requestis / orationibus et requestis*, where the former appears only once and the latter appears 983 times. From a geographic perspective, Netherlands is the country that produces this synformic category followed by Paris. Both places are the ones producing the

corpus in (Plummer and Clark, 2015) has a strong focus on the mid-fifteenth century, with a maximum of 80 copies ascribed to the year 1455. Figure 3 illustrates the number of witnesses by year using the arithmetic mean between the extreme dates, which explains the peaks on round numbers, particularly those ending in 0 and 5, and the important variation from one year to another

largest number of copies, so that it comes as no surprise that scribes generates more variants, including the rare ones that we have isolated here. From a temporal perspective, however, we see that 3gram variants mostly appeared in 1465 and 1470. This is unexpected, since the maximum number of manuscripts in the corpus is for the years 1450 and 1455. This increase is perhaps correlated with the higher production levels of Books of Hours in the last third of the century (not strictly represented in Clark's corpus) whose variety would be reflected in Clark's corpus, but this would not explain why the 1460s and 1470s are more variant than the end of the century. We may now formulate an original hypothesis, that we observe here a loosening of the copying discipline for the *Obsecro Te* as a very common text, perhaps due to the multiplication of workshops or to other causes such as text memorisation, resulting in the emergence of many new, isolated variants. Even though our analysis cannot draw factual conclusions for now, it can nonetheless guide experts to analyse such phenomena.

7 Conclusion

We conducted for the first time a large-scale study of medieval devotional texts for the purpose of variant analysis. We used linguistic operations rather than edition operations to characterise variants in order to facilitate the interpretation of variants. We also design a suitable methodology for their detection that we hope will help medievalists in their research. If the automatic variant extraction is encouraging, further investigations are certainly needed to distinguish between orthographic in one hand, and inflectional and derivative variants in the other hand. Some computational methods well designed to deal with a particular variant detection fail when they face problematic cases: word embedding approach does not succeed to detect lexical substitutions showing a difference of distributions between the two elements, typically those substitutions that imply connectors. None of the methods is adapted to discover expansion and reduction at the n-gram level. This work constitutes a first step in the automatic study the content of Book of Hours in order to discover temporal and geographical correlations between Books of Hours, whether issued from different regions of the same country or from different countries of medieval Europe.

Acknowledgments

This work is part of the HORAE project (Hours - Recognition, Analysis, Editions) and is supported by the French National Research Agency under grant ANR-17-CE38-0008. We would like to thank professor Gregory Clark for making available *Obsecro Te* dataset and the annotations of variants.

References

Sanjeev Arora, Liang Yingyu, and Ma Tengyu. 2017. A simple but tough to beat baseline for sentence embeddings. In *Proceedings of the 17th International Conference on Learning Representations (ICLR'17)*, pages 1–11.

Batrice Daille. 2017. *Term Variation in Specialised Corpora: Characterisation, automatic discovery and applications*, volume 19 of *Terminology and Lexicography Research and Practice*. John Benjamins.

Ted Dunning. 1993. Accurate methods for the statistics of surprise and coincidence. *Computational Linguistics*, 19(1):61–74.

Stefan Evert. 2005. *The statistics of word cooccurrences : word pairs and collocations*. Ph.D. thesis, University of Stuttgart.

Robert M. Fano. 1961. *Transmission of Information: A Statistical Theory of Communications*. MIT Press, Cambridge, MA, USA.

Z. S. Harris. 1971. *Structures mathématiques du langage*. Dunod. Traduit de l'Américain par C. Fuchs.

Sandra Hindman and James H. Marrow. 2013. *Books of hours reconsidered*. Harvey Miller Publishers, London.

Paul Jaccard. 1901. tude comparative de la distribution florale dans une portion des alpes et des jura. *Bulletin de la Socit Vaudoise des Sciences Naturelles*, 37:547–579.

Ana Kocic. 2008. The problem of synforms. *Facta Universitatis*, 6(1):51–59.

Batia Laufer. 1988. The concept of synforms (similar lexical forms) in vocabulary acquisition. *Language and Education*, 2(2):113–132.

V. I Levenshtein. 1966. Binary codes capable of correcting deletions, insertions, and reversals. *Cybernetics and Control Theory*, 10(8):707–710.

Tomas Mikolov, Ilya Sutskever, Kai Chen, Greg S Corrado, and Jeff Dean. 2013. Distributed representations of words and phrases and their compositionality. In C. J. C. Burges, L. Bottou, M. Welling,

Z. Ghahramani, and K. Q. Weinberger, editors, *Advances in Neural Information Processing Systems 26*, pages 3111–3119. Curran Associates, Inc.

John Plummer and Gregory T. Clark. 2015. Obsecro te. *Beyond Use: A Digital Database of Variant Readings In Late Medieval Books of Hours.* `http://www6.sewanee.edu/BeyondUse/` `texts_list.phptexts=ObsecroTe`.

Gerard Salton and Michael E. Lesk. 1968. Computer evaluation of indexing and text processing. *Journal of the Association for Computational Machinery*, 15(1):8–36.

Dominique. Stutzmann. 2019. Résistance au changement ? les écritures des livres d'heures dans l'espace français (1200-1600). In *'Change' in Medieval and Renaissance Scripts and Manuscripts. Proceedings of the 19th Colloquium of the Comit international de palographie latine (Berlin, 16-18 September, 2015).*, pages 101–120, Turnhout. Brepols.

Roger. Wieck. 1988. *Time sanctified : the Book of Hours in medieval art and life.* G. Braziller, New York.

Understanding the Evolution of Circular Economy
through Language Change

Sampriti Mahanty[1], Frank Boons[2], Julia Handl[3], Riza Theresa Batista-Navarro[4]
Alliance Manchester Business School, The University of Manchester[1, 2,3]
School of Computer Science, The University of Manchester[4]
sampriti.mahanty@postgrad.manchester.ac.uk[1]
{frank.boons, julia.handl, riza.batista}@manchester.ac.uk[2,3,4]

1 Introduction

Drawing on the work of Thomas Kuhn, philosophers of science have developed understandings of the process of scientific development (Campbell, 1974b; Popper, 1972; Toulmin, 1967, 1972; Hull, 1988) using metaphors relating to Darwin's theory of natural selection. The consequence of this is the conceptualization of scientific development as constituting an "evolutionary process". The defining feature of adopting an evolutionary orientation in understanding scientific development is suggesting an analogy between the process of biological evolutionary process and that of gain in knowledge (Bradie, 1986). According to this perspective, in the course of evolution, species become more adaptive to their natural environment by undergoing natural selection. Likewise, scientific progress is a result of selection mechanisms on an individual level and in the scientific community.

Scientists are the "central subjects" in the process of scientific development since they are the entities who read the literature, perform experiments, publish the results and pass on knowledge. Textbooks, journal articles are "vehicles" in this process of scientific and conceptual development. Scientists then go on to form communities based on common cognitive, social and philosophical grounds (Hull, 1988).

While the production of scientific knowledge is an outcome of selectionist mechanisms, it is closely related to evolution of human language

(Popper, 1984; Bradie, 1986). Scientific communities tend to use the same umbrella terms ("lexicon kind-terms") at the least, having meanings that are shared and understood by members of such communities. Language thus becomes a crucial indicator to assess the shift or development in ideas (Kuhn, 1990).

For our study, we propose to focus on a specific concept—that of *Circular Economy (CE)*. The evolutionary perspective of understanding scientific development is the framework that we implement to understand this concept. While this forms a part of our larger ongoing work to determine the process of emergence, diffusion and evolution of the concept of 'circular economy' in academic discourse, the focus of this study is to understand the evolution of CE from the lens of language change, as language can be a crucial indicator of the shift in ideas in a particular scientific field.

There are two aspects of language change that can be investigated. The first one is *lexical change*, i.e., the generational shift in the representation of words over time, and the second is *semantic change*, i.e., the evolution of word usage, sometimes to the point that the modern meaning is radically different. In some cases, the semantic change that words undergo happens by means of acquiring additional meanings, rather than original meanings becoming outdated or being replaced. In this study we will be analysing how the language used in academic discussions pertaining to CE has changed semantically. It is worth noting that

Proceedings of the 1st International Workshop on Computational Approaches to Historical Language Change, pages 250–253
Florence, Italy, August 2, 2019. ©2019 Association for Computational Linguistics

the meaning and central theme of this concept has remained the same; however, we hypothesise that it has undergone semantic change by way of additional layers being added to the concept.

2 Circular Economy

Circular Economy (CE) refers to a system of provision in which resources are circulated between production and consumption rather than linearly transformed from production to consumption to waste. It has gained immense traction amongst academics, practitioners and policy-makers for its perceived capacity to operationalise Sustainable Development[1]: (Geissdoerfer et al., 2017). It is only in the last 15 years that it has emerged as a field in its own right, being referred to directly and independently in the academic literature, distancing itself from the antecedent fields (e.g., industrial ecology) (Prendeville et al., 2018).

The diffusion of CE has become prominent since 2015 as indicated by the steep increase in the number of academic articles published (Appendix Figure 1). This can be attributed to the fact that more recently, CE has gained dominance in literature discussing issues related to sustainability. While CE has its roots in Industrial Ecology focused on industrial processes, pollution etc., nowadays CE is actively being referred to in the context of micro-level interventions for sustainable development, e.g., circular product design, circular business models (Bocken et al., 2016). The contemporary understanding of CE and its practical applications to industrial processes and economic systems has evolved to incorporate different features and contributions from concepts beyond CE which share the theme of closed loops (Geissdoerfer et al., 2017). This kind of change in context makes CE suitable as the focus of our study in scientific concept evolution.

3 Methodology and Findings

The first step towards the analysis of language for detecting semantic change w.r.t CE is the collection of academic literature on CE from the Scopus database[2]. Using the query "circular economy", we retrieved a total of 3,300 scientific papers. For the pre-processing of the corpora, we performed word stemming and the removal of stop-words, extraneous white spaces and punctuations. We conducted topic modelling using the Latent Dirichlet Allocation algorithm (Blei et al., 2003) on the academic abstracts by using the topic models3 package available in R. The number of topics (K) was fixed at 20, based on the examination of coherence scores4 of the topic model coupled with manual analysis. The results from the topic model were plotted to visualize the topics over time. Based on the results from the topic model we noticed a structural change in academic discussions pertaining to CE in the year 2015 (Appendix Figure 2). There was a significant change in the proportion of topic distribution before and after 2015. Based on this finding, two datasets were formed: an early set consisting of papers published from 2006 to 2014, and a contemporary CE set composed of papers published from 2015 to March 2019.

We investigated and compared the CE literature across the early and contemporary data sets using two approaches to analyse semantic change in language over time. First is the development of co-occurrence networks based on keywords associated with the documents. Nodes of the network correspond to the keywords (with a node for CE as the centroid), and edges indicate the co-occurrences. A co-occurrence network using the bibliometrix package[5] in R was generated based on each of the early (Figure 1) and contemporary (Figure 2) data sets. We observed that there is a significant difference between the two co-occurrence networks. Contemporary CE literature was found to be more strongly linked to "business models", "supply chain", "product design". Meanwhile the focus of early CE literature was more on "ecology", "industrial economics" and

---

[1] Development that meets the needs of the present without compromising on the ability of future generations to meet their own needs

[2] https://www.scopus.com/search/form.uri?display=basic

[3] https://cran.r-project.org/web/packages/topicmodels/topicmodels.pdf

[4] The coherence score is for assessing the quality of the learned topics. For one topic, the words i, j being scored in $\Sigma i<j$Score (wi, wj) have the highest probability of occurring for that topic.

[5] http://bibliometrix.org

"environmental management". These observations confirm that the concept of CE has undergone some change over the years that are reflected by a shift in focus in the context of its application (as discussed in Section 2). We note that despite this expansion, the core meaning of the concept has not changed over time (as evidenced by the nodes that are common between the two networks, e.g., "sustainable development, "waste management", "recycling".

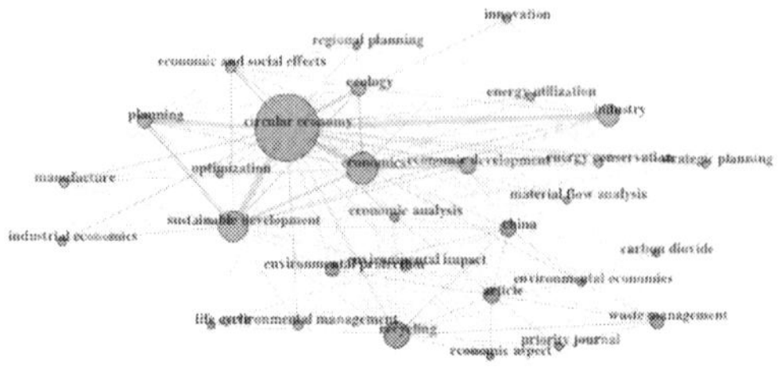

Figure 1: Co-occurrence network drawn from the early dataset (2006-2014)

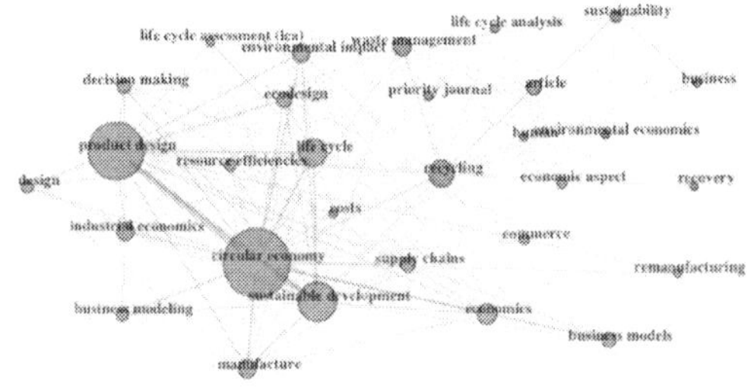

Figure 2: Co-occurrence network drawn from the contemporary dataset (2015-2019)

Our second method is underpinned by the development of word embedding vectors (Bojanowski et al., 2017). We obtained word embeddings using gensim's word2vec[6] implementation on the full text of academic articles. The word embeddings were trained on each of the two data sets i.e., early and contemporary CE literature. We then compared the word embeddings based on the target word of interest "circular economy" across the two time periods. The cosine similarity between word embedding vectors across the two time frames is only 0.195. To better understand the similarity measure between the word embeddings we conduct a random sampling on each of the early and contemporary datasets to create two subsets out of each, then trained embeddings on each of the subsets. The cosine similarity between each of the subsets came across to be quite high i.e., 0.62 and 0.743 in the early and contemporary dataset respectively. This provides us with the basis of comparing the cosine similarities and we can conclude that the cosine similarity of word vectors between the late and early dataset is considerably low at 0.195.

If we examine the nearest neighbours of CE (i.e., words with highest similarity to CE) from the two time periods in Table 1, we see a shift from the environmental and industrial focus to a perspective, which integrates an approach, which is innovation, business focused and incorporates the social dimension of CE as well. The results from the word embeddings conform to the results from the co-occurrence networks. The early literature primarily address macro-level themes in the context of environmental management and industries while the contemporary literature focuses on more micro- level interventions like business models, product design and supply chain.

Early dataset	Contemporary dataset
Resource	Innovation
Materials	Business Models
Recycling	Social
China	Strategies
Environmental	Companies
Economic	Supply Chain
Industrial	Sustainable development

Table 1: Closely associated word vectors to CE for each of the early and contemporary datasets, ordered by decreasing similarity.

3. Conclusion

We have discussed that semantic change in language is a reflection of shifts in scientific ideas, which in turn help explain the evolution of a concept. This helps us to build an understanding of conceptual evolution. This forms a part of our ongoing work to understand the concept of CE starting from the emergence of the concept, to its adaption, diffusion and evolution.

---

[6]https://radimrehurek.com/gensim/models/word2vec.html

References

Bocken Nancy, Pauw Ingrid de, Bakker Conny & Grinten Bram van der. (2016). Product design and business model strategies for a circular economy, *Journal of Industrial and Production Engineering*, 33:5, 308-320, DOI: 10.1080/21681015.2016.1172124

Bojanowski, Piotr, Grave Edouard, Joulin Armand, and Mikolov Tomas (2017). Enriching word vectors with subword information. *Transactions of the Association for Computational Linguistics*: 135-146.

Blei, D.M.; Jordan, M.I.; Ng, A.Y. (2003) Latent dirichlet allocation. *Journal of Machine Learning*. Res. 2003, 3, 993–1022.

Bradie, Michael. "Assessing evolutionary epistemology. (1986)" *Biology and Philosophy* 1.4: 401-459.

Campbell, Donald. T. (1974b). *"Evolutionary Epistemology". In: Schlipp, P. A. (Ed.), The philosophy of Karl Popper.* LaSalle, IL: Open Court, 413–63.

Geissdoerfer, Martin & Savaget, Paulo & Bocken, Nancy & Hultink, Erik. (2017). The Circular Economy – A new sustainability paradigm? *Journal of Cleaner Production.* 143. 757–768. 10.1016/j.jclepro.2016.12.048.

Hull, David L. (1988). *Science as a Process an Evolutionary Account of the Social and Conceptual Development of Science.* University Of Chicago Press.

Kuhn, Thomas S. (1990). The Road since Structure. _PSA: *Proceedings of the Biennial Meeting of the Philosophy of Science Association_ 1990*:3-13.

Popper, Karl. R. (1972) (1979). *Objective Knowledge: An Evolutionary Approach*, Oxford: The Clarendon Press

Popper, Karl R, and William Warren Bartley. (1984) *"Postscript to the logic of scientific discovery."*

Prendeville, Sharon, Emma Cherim, and Nancy Bocken. (2018). Circular cities: mapping six cities in transition. *Environmental innovation and societal transitions.* 26 171-194.

Toulmin, Stephen. (1967). "The Evolutionary Development of Natural Science", *American Scientist* 55, 456–471

Toulmin, Stephen. (1972). *Human Understanding: The Evolution of Collective Understanding*, Volume 1. Princeton, NJ: Princeton University Press.

Appendices

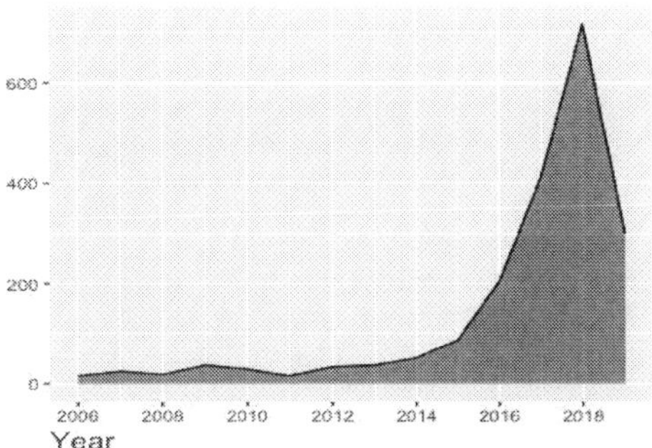

Figure 1: Production of academic articles on CE

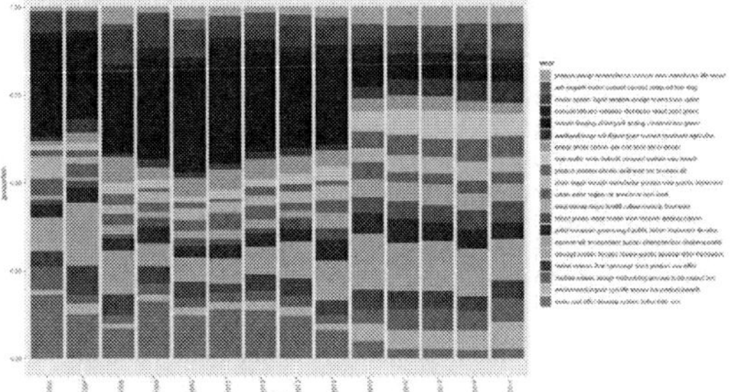

Figure 2: Proportion of topic distribution over time

Gaussian Process Models of Sound Change in Indo-Aryan Dialectology

Chundra A. Cathcart
Department of Comparative Linguistics
University of Zurich
Plattenstrasse 54
CH-8032 Zürich
chundra.cathcart@uzh.ch

Abstract

This paper proposes a Gaussian Process model of sound change targeted toward questions in Indo-Aryan dialectology. Gaussian Processes (GPs) provide a flexible means of expressing covariance between outcomes, and can be extended to a wide variety of probability distributions. We find that GP models fare better in terms of some key posterior predictive checks than models that do not express covariance between sound changes, and outline directions for future work.

1 Introduction and Background

There exists today a wealth of digitized etymological resources from which etymological headwords (e.g., words in Latin, Sanskrit, etc.) and their reflexes in modern language can be extracted, and by proxy, information regarding sound changes operating between ancestral and descendant languages. This information can be used to address hypotheses regarding dialectal relationships between these descendant languages, and the accumulation of large data sets allows such hypotheses to be addressed probabilistically.

This paper builds upon Cathcart to appear, which seeks to address the issue of Indo-Aryan dialect groupings using data extracted from Turner (1962–1966). It has generally been held that sound change holds a great deal of power in determining dialectal relationships in Indo-Aryan (Masica, 1991), and a number of sound changes thought to be probative with respect to Indo-Aryan dialectology have been put forth (Hock, 2016). A problem, however, is that Indo-Aryan languages have developed in close contact with each other, and intimate lexical borrowing between closely related languages has been widespread. Forms showing irregular outcomes of sound change are so great in number that it is difficult to characterize the expected outcomes of sound changes in many languages, much less identify the so-called "residual forms" deviating from what is expected (cf. Bloomfield, 1933).

For this reason, we seek to represent Indo-Aryan languages using a shared-admixture model whereby a given Indo-Aryan language (e.g., Hindi) inherits its vocabulary from multiple LATENT DIALECTAL COMPONENTS in which different SOUND CHANGES have operated; we believe that this approach explicitly models intimate borrowing between Indo-Aryan dialects, a sociolinguistic process that many scholars have argued for (Turner, 1975 [1967]). We restrict the dossier of sound changes we work with to include relatively transparent changes thought to be highly diagnostic for purposes of Indo-Aryan dialectology, with the additional hope of excluding those where multiple intermediate developments have been telescoped into a single change.

The main objective of this paper is to determine the most appropriate way to represent dialect component-level distributions over sound changes. Cathcart to appear compared a shared-admixture model where a Dirichlet prior was placed over sound change probabilities with a model that used a Partitioned Logistic Normal prior, the latter distribution generating Multinomial/Categorical probabilities (like the Dirichlet distribution) but capable of expressing covariance between outcomes within and across distributions (unlike the Dirichlet distribution), and found no major differences in behavior between these two models. At the same time, this procedure relied on a fixed covariance matrix for the Logistic Normal distribution based on the similarity of segments across the sound changes in which they are involved. Working within a similar modeling framework, this paper seeks to model this covariance via a Gaussian Process. Gaussian Processes (GPs) are a flexible family of prior distributions over covari-

Proceedings of the 1st International Workshop on Computational Approaches to Historical Language Change, pages 254–264
Florence, Italy, August 2, 2019. ©2019 Association for Computational Linguistics

ance kernel functions. For our purposes, GPs allow us to assess the extent to which sound changes in an evolving linguistic system are correlated, and which features of sound changes influence this correlation. Our results are somewhat open ended at this stage, but we find that GP models fare better in terms of certain critical posterior predictive checks than models that do not express covariance between sound changes.

2   Sound Change

The sound changes that operate within a language's history tend to be subject to certain constraints. In general, most sound changes are thought to stem from low-level phonetic variation, though this view has been challenged (Blust, 2005). Additionally, it is often the case that similar sounds behave similarly in similar environments; hence, if earlier p undergoes voicing to b between two vowels, it is reasonable expect the changes $t > d$ and $k > g$ in the same environment. However, this systematicity and symmetry cannot always be relied upon. Different sounds, regardless of their similarity along a large number of phonetic dimensions, are subject to different articulatory and perceptual constraints. For instance, it is less likely for velar plosives such as k to undergo voicing, because considerable articulatory effort is required to pronounce g relative to d and b (Maddieson, 2013). The voiceless labial plosive p lacks perceptual salience, and often is debuccalized, losing its oral constriction, to h (as in Japanese and Kannada, among other languages) or perceptually enhanced (e.g., to f), though other voiceless stops may not undergo the same type of behavior. In other examples, the phonetic grounding is less clear: in most High German dialects, the Old High German consonant shift involved the changes *p > (p)f and *t > (t)s; in southern dialects, the shift also involves the change *k > k(x); see Schrijver 2014, 97–121 for a sociolinguistic explanation of this asymmetry. In short, while sound change has the tendency to be highly systematic, with similar sounds moving in lockstep, it is clear that this is not always the case; an ideal architecture for modeling sound change will allow for, but not enforce, the possibility of correlation between changes involving similar sounds.

3   Quantitative models of sound change

Under the Neogrammarian view, sound change is a tightly constrained process with discrete binary outcomes; a sound in a given environment has one and only one regular reflex. If irregularity is seen, it is due to analogy or language contact; if neither analogy nor language contact (or, according to some, a small number of additional minor processes that are poorly understood) can be convincingly invoked, then we do not understand the conditioning environment properly. In probabilistic treatments of language change, however, this assumption is infeasible to implement; generally some probability mass, however small, must be allocated to unobserved events (cf. Laplace's law of succession). For this reason, it is standard to relax the Neogrammarian hypothesis by assuming a multinomial/categorical distribution over possible reflexes of a given sound in a language's history (cf. Bouchard-Côté et al., 2007, 2008, 2013); all of the sound changes that operate in the history of a given language can be represented as a collection of multinomial probability distributions, with each distribution in collection corresponding to the possible outcomes of an Old Indo-Aryan (OIA) input in the relevant conditioning environment.

3.1   Prior distributions

In the Bayesian context, an obvious prior for each Multinomial distribution in a collection is the DIRICHLET DISTRIBUTION, which generates probability simplices. The concentration parameter of a SYMMETRIC DIRICHLET DISTRIBUTION can determine the smoothness/sparsity of the resulting multinomial distribution; this is a desirable property, since many phenomena in natural language, sound change being no exception, are best represented using sparse distributions (cf. Ranganath et al., 2015). The Dirichlet distribution has been used to model sound change in previous work (Bouchard-Côté et al., 2007).

However, the Dirichlet lacks an explicit means of expressing correlations between the probabilities of events, such as similar outcomes of sound change, or of modeling dependence between events across multinomial distributions in a collection (like the one we use to represent sound change). An alternative is the LOGISTIC NORMAL DISTRIBUTION (Aitchison, 1986). Under the logistic normal distribution, unbounded values representing unnormalized log probabilities are generated from a multivariate normal distribution; these are subsequently transformed to probability simplices summing to one via the softmax function. Since the underlying distribution is multivariate normal, the logistic normal distribution is capable of modeling covariance between different outcomes. At the same time, it is not possible to control the sparsity of a logistic normal distribution unless there is high variance and no covariance between different outcomes (this makes it possible to control sparsity in Laplace's approximation to the Dirichlet distribution). Despite this tradeoff, we believe that the logistic normal distribution has promise for modeling sound change, particularly when distributions are noisy. Crucially, the partitioned logistic normal distribution (Cohen and Smith, 2009) allows us to capture dependencies across distributions in a collection as well as within them (i.e., with an eye to modeling low-level variation within dialect groups), allowing us to treat our collection as a large, interdependent distribution.

3.2 Gaussian Processes

Use of the logistic normal distribution in Natural Language Processing usually estimates the covariance between outcomes empirically (cf. Blei and Lafferty, 2007). At the outset, we are unsure of how covariance between two sound changes drawn from a logistic normal prior should be modeled. In principle, covariance should be based on the phonetic similarity of the segments involved, but it is not clear whether all features of all participating segments should have equal influence on the covariance between two changes.

For this reason, we adopt a Gaussian Process approach (Rasmussen and Williams, 2006) to generate our unnormalized sound change probabilities. GPs define a flexible prior over continuous covariance functions. A zero-mean GP assumes that for a given observable response variable, the values of N data points are generated from a multivariate normal distribution with a mean of zero and some covariance. The distribution's covariance is modeled via a kernel function, which takes as its input a measure of distance or dissimilarity between two covarying data points. A popular function is the squared exponential kernel (K_{SE}), which we employ in this paper. A basic squared exponential kernel models the covariance between two data points with values x_i and x_j for some

variable in the following manner:

$$K_{\mathrm{SE}}(x_i, x_j) = \alpha^2 \exp\left(\frac{(x_i - x_j)^2}{2\rho^2}\right) \quad (1)$$

The function is parametrized by a parameter α^2, determining the dispersion of the variance-covariance matrix, and a parameter ρ, often referred to as the CHARACTERISTIC LENGTH SCALE, since it controls the distance threshold at which two data points can influence one another, with high values permitting greater influence between distant data points. A third dispersion parameter σ^2 is generally added to diagonal values of the variance-covariance matrix to ensure that it is positive definite. Given a set of data points differing according to a predictor value for which response values are recorded, the parameters α^2, ρ and σ^2 can be fitted conditioned on the data.

We wish to exploit the flexibility of GPs in order to determine how much influence features of segments participating in sound changes should have on other coextensive sound changes. Take the changes $p > b$ and $t > d$, setting aside the conditioning environment. Both straightforwardly involve voicing of a voiceless plosive. Care must be taken in representing these changes in a way that the relevant dimensions of similarity can be detected by a probabilistic model. If we compute similarity between them on the basis of whether the segments involved are identical, we will not be able to take into account processes such as voicing — i.e., $p > b$ and $t > d$ (which both involve voicing) will be treated as being as dissimilar as $p > b$ and $d > t$ (which involve voicing and devoicing, respectively). Such a model may not be completely useless, as it will still capture correlations between identical changes across different environments, a generalization that the Dirichlet distribution is not explicitly capable of capturing.

In contrast to a binary approach concerned with segmental identity, we can make use of distinctive phonological features to capture granular relationships between similar sound changes. If we assume a simple featural representation for each change, these changes will differ along the dimension of PLACE OF ARTICULATION (labial > labial ≠ dental > dental) but not VOICING (voiceless > voiced = voiceless > voiced).

We are faced with similar questions when deciding how to represent the conditioning environment. While it makes sense that the featural representations of the input and output of each individual change should be considered jointly, it is not clear that the environment should be treated in such a manner. If we look only at the joint dissimilarity of the lefthand and righthand contexts of each pair of changes, there is the potential that the dissimilarity between changes where only one side of the environment is a relevant conditioning factor will be inflated if the other side differs. Therefore it may be more instructive to model similarity between conditioning environments as a composition of the similarities of the left- and righthand contexts, though this model may have the potential to overgeneralize. We opt to treat the environment as a whole as a feature of interest, based on a survey of conditioning environments (Kümmel, 2007), setting this question aside for future work.

There are several ways to deal with multiple variables or featural dimensions in a GP framework. The simplest approach is to assume a single length scale for all features, which can potentially induce behavior similar to an interaction in a linear model — if the length scale is low, covariance between two data points will be high only if their similarity across all dimensions is high as well. An alternative is to assume a kernel function for each dimension $d \in \{1, ..., D\}$, and add these together. A third approach is to model an additive combination of the dimensions within the kernel function, as follows:

$$K_{\text{SE}}(\boldsymbol{x}_i, \boldsymbol{x}_j) = \alpha^2 \exp\left(\sum_{d=1}^{D} \frac{(x_{i,d} - x_{j,d})^2}{2\rho_d^2}\right) \tag{2}$$

A consequence of the structure of this kernel, known as an Automatic Relevance Determination (ARD) kernel, is that covariance will not be sensitive to or vary according to differences along dimensions for which ρ_d is large, allowing us to gauge which featural dimensions have greater "relevance" (Neal, 1996). While interpreting relevance is challenging for featural dimensions which have different scales (Piironen and Vehtari, 2016), this is not a concern for our data, since distances between sound changes across featural dimensions are binary (i.e., 0 or 1).

We employ an ARD kernel for two types of GP prior over covariance between sound changes. The first kernel, the binary GP (BGP) takes into account two dimensions concerning (1) segmental identity between inputs and outputs and (2) seg-mental identity between environments across each pair of changes. The granular GP (GGP) generalizes this approach to a larger number of dimensions corresponding to phonological features of interest, described below.

3.3 Feature representation and kernel structure

We assume an n-ary featural representation for the sound types in our data set, similar to that found in models such as that of Futrell et al. (2017). In theory, it would be possible to employ binary distinctive features à la *The Sound Pattern of English* (Chomsky and Halle, 1968) and related works, which would potentially allow a richer representation (Duvenaud, 2014), but with considerable computational cost. Embedding representations for continuous phonetic values present a promising avenue (cf. Cotterell and Eisner, 2017). The feature space looks as follows:

- A feature indicating whether a segment is a CONSONANT or VOWEL

- A set of consonant-specific features:

  - Place of articulation: labial, dental, palatal, retroflex, velar, glottal
  - Manner of articulation: plosive, affricate, fricative, approximant, nasal
  - Voicing: $\pm$
  - Aspiration: $\pm$

- A set of vowel-specific features:

  - Height: low, mid, high
  - Frontness: front, back
  - Rounding: $\pm$
  - Orality: oral, nasal

This yields 9 featural dimensions. Each segment takes an n-ary or binary value for each relevant attribute; for irrelevant attributes (i.e., consonant-specific features, if the segment is a vowel, or vice versa), the segment is assigned a null value.

4 Data

We extracted all modern Indo-Aryan (NIA) forms from Turner (1962–1966) along with the OIA headwords from which these reflexes descend (Middle Indo-Aryan languages such as Prakrit and Pali were excluded). Transcriptions of the data were normalized and converted to the International Phonetic Alphabet (IPA). Systematic morphological mismatches between OIA etyma and reflexes were accounted for, including stripping the endings from all verbs, since citation forms for OIA verbs are in the 3sg present, while most NIA reflexes give the infinitive. We matched each dialect with corresponding languoids in Glottolog (Hammarström et al., 2017) containing geographic metadata, resulting in the merger of several dialects. Languages with fewer than 100 forms in the data set were excluded, yielding 50 remaining languages; the best represented language is Hindi, with 4012 forms, followed by Sinhala, Marathi, Panjabi and Gujarati. We excluded sound changes appearing fewer than 7 times in our data set, ultimately yielding 38479 modern Indo-Aryan words. We preprocessed the data, first converting each segment into its respective sound class, as described by List (2012), and subsequently aligning each converted OIA/NIA string pair via the Needleman-Wunsch algorithm, using the Expectation-Maximization method described by Jäger (2014), building off of work by Wieling et al. (2012). This yields alignments of the following type: e.g., OIA /aːntra/ 'entrails' > Nepali /aːn∅ro/, where ∅ indicates a gap where the "cursor" advances for the OIA string but not the Nepali string. Gaps on the OIA side are ignored, yielding a one-to-many OIA-to-NIA alignment; this ensures that all aligned cognate sets are of the same length. We restrict our analysis to changes affecting OIA ʃ, ʋ, ɲ, ɳ, ʂ, ɽ, h, i, iː, j, kʂ, l, n, r, s, u, uː, which are thought to play a meaningful role in Indo-Aryan dialectology (Southworth, 2005; Hock, 2016).

5 Model

Complete information regarding this paper's model specification and inference can be found in the Appendix. Our data set contains W OIA etyma, each of which is continued by some of the L languages in our sample. The data set contains R OIA inputs (e.g., sounds in a conditioning environment), each of which have S_r reflexes. We assume $K = 10$ dialect groups. At a high-level, our model is a mixed membership model which assumes that EACH WORD in EACH LANGUAGE is generated by one of K latent dialect components, according to the relevant sound changes whose operation the word displays. Key parameters are θ (language-level distributions over dialect components) and ϕ (component-level collections of distributions over sound changes). The stochastic generative process we assume to underlie the data looks as follows (for information regarding priors over θ and ϕ, refer to the Appendix):

For $\boldsymbol{w}_i : i \in \{1, ..., W\}$, the vector of relevant inputs in each OIA etymon

> For each language $l \in \{1, ..., L\}$ continuing $\boldsymbol{w}_i$
> $z_{i,l} \sim$ Categorical($\boldsymbol{\theta}_l$) [Draw a dialect component label]
> For each OIA input $w_{i,t}$ in etymon $\boldsymbol{w}_i$ at index $t : \{1, ..., |\boldsymbol{w}_i|\}$
> $y_{i,l,t} \sim$ Categorical($\boldsymbol{\phi}_{z_{w,l},w_{i,t},\cdot}$) [Generate each output]

The likelihood of a given NIA word's reflexes (i.e., outcomes of relevant sound changes) $\boldsymbol{y}_{i,l}$ and its OIA predecessor $\boldsymbol{w}_i$ under the generative process described above is the following, with the discrete variable $z_{i,l}$ marginalized out:

$$P(\boldsymbol{y}_{i,l}, \boldsymbol{w}_i | \boldsymbol{\theta}, \boldsymbol{\phi}) = \sum_{k=1}^{K} \theta_{l,k} \prod_{t=1}^{|\boldsymbol{w}_i|} \phi_{k,w_{i,t},y_{i,l,t}} \quad (3)$$

We carry out inference for three flavors of this model involving different versions of ϕ. In the Diagonal model, there is no covariance across outcomes of ϕ. In the Binary GP (BGP) and Granular GP (GGP) models, ϕ is generated by GPs with the ARD kernels described in 3.2; these models differ in that the former takes a 2-dimensional featural input, while the latter takes a 18-dimensional one (2 times the number of features given in 3.3). We fit a variational posterior to the data for multiple separate initializations (as described in the Appendix) from which we can draw samples.

6 Results

6.1 Geographic distribution

Averaged language-level component distributions can be visualized geographically in Figure 1. A number of redundant components are shared across all languages in each model; this is likely an artifact of the prior placed over $\boldsymbol{\theta}$; changes to this prior (see discussion in the Appendix) would likely assign less probability mass to redundant components. In general, for all models, certain linguistic groups show a similar component makeup: these groups include Romani dialects and their close relatives Domari and Lomavren; Dardic languages of northern Pakistan; languages of Eastern South Asia and the Eastern Indo-Gangetic Plain; the insular languages Sinhala and Dhivehi; and western languages such as Marathi and Gujarati.

We measure correlation coefficients to assess how well the language-level dialect component makeup inferred in each of our models reflects the geography of Indo-Aryan dialects. For each of our three models, we compute the Jensen-Shannon divergence between θ_l and $\theta_{l'}$ for each pair of languages l, l', averaging across samples of $\hat{\theta}$, the language-level posterior over components. We measure the correlation between (1) average inter-language JS divergence between dialect component makeup and (2) pairwise great circle geographic distance, using Spearman's ρ (although pairwise distances violate the independence assumption). These values are .28 for the Diagonal model, .34 for the BGP model, and .26 for the GGP model. We see that the BGP model shows the strongest geographic signal. We note that this metric serves as a basis for comparison, but not evaluation; if the language contact we are detecting is chronologically deep, it is less likely to show a strong geographic signal (cf. Haynie, 2012).

6.2 Relevance

We inspect posterior values of ρ^{-2}, the squared inverse characteristic length scales for each featural dimension of interest, for both the BGP and GGP models. Since we work with inverse scales, high values indicate relevance, while values close to zero indicate irrelevance.

Figure 2 shows the squared inverse length scales for the BGP model. The squared inverse length scale for change is higher than that of environment, though the multimodality seen may be due to a lack of convergence across initializations for the BGP model. This is perhaps not particularly surprising, though perhaps something of a sanity check: given a large number of sound changes involving a large number of conditioning environments, some of them redundant, it is likely that changes with different environments and identical input-output pairs will show similar behavior.

Figure 3 shows the squared inverse length scales for the GGP model. The results seem to suggest that when input-output pairs and conditioning environments are decomposed into featural representations, very few featural dimensions have a strong

influence on the co-occurrence of sound changes that show featural identity in terms of input-output pair or conditioning environment — essentially, these features are the most meaningful when they are bundled together into individual segments. An exception is the feature VOWEL HEIGHT for environment, indicating that changes are likely to co-occur if their conditioning environments have the same values for vowel height. Further work is needed to determine which combination of feature values for the left- and righthand context in the conditioning environments actually serves as a meaningful determinant of correlation.

6.3 Posterior Predictive Checks

6.3.1 Entropy

We carry out model criticism using a posterior predictive check proposed by Mimno et al. (2015) for mixed-membership models, inspecting the uncertainty with which each model assigns dialect component labels to each word. Recall that during inference, we marginalized out the discrete variables $z_{i,l}$, which indicate the dialect component label selected for the reflex of OIA word w_i in language l. Given our fitted parameters $\hat{\theta}$ and $\hat{\phi}$, it is straightforward to reconstruct the probability of a label for a given NIA word:

$$P(z_{i,l} = k | \boldsymbol{y}_{i,l}, \boldsymbol{w}_i, \boldsymbol{\theta}, \boldsymbol{\phi}) \propto \theta_{l,k} \prod_{t=1}^{|\boldsymbol{w}_i|} \phi_{k, w_{i,t}, y_{i,l,t}}$$

$$(4)$$

If $P(z_{i,l} | \boldsymbol{y}_{i,l}, \boldsymbol{w}_i, \boldsymbol{\theta}, \boldsymbol{\phi})$ shows high entropy, then our fitted parameters do not allow us to assign a label with certainty. We average the entropy of $P(z_{i,l} | \boldsymbol{y}_{i,l}, \boldsymbol{w}_i, \boldsymbol{\theta}, \boldsymbol{\phi})$ across each word for 100 samples of $\hat{\theta}, \hat{\phi}$ in each model. Histograms of these entropy measures can be seen in Figure 4. The averages of these averaged values are 1.058 for the Diagonal model, 1.255 for the BGP model, and 1.259 for the GGP model, with the Diagonal model outperforming the GP models; these values show a decrease rather than an increase in posterior predictive checks with greater granularity in the underlying GP.

6.3.2 Accuracy

We assess the extent to which each model's posterior parameters can accurately regenerate the observed data. For each word, we sample $z_{i,l} \sim$ Categorical$(\hat{\theta}_l)$, and then draw outcomes of sound change $\hat{y}_{i,l,t} \sim$ Categorical$(\phi_{z_{i,l}, w_{i,t}, \cdot}) : t \in$

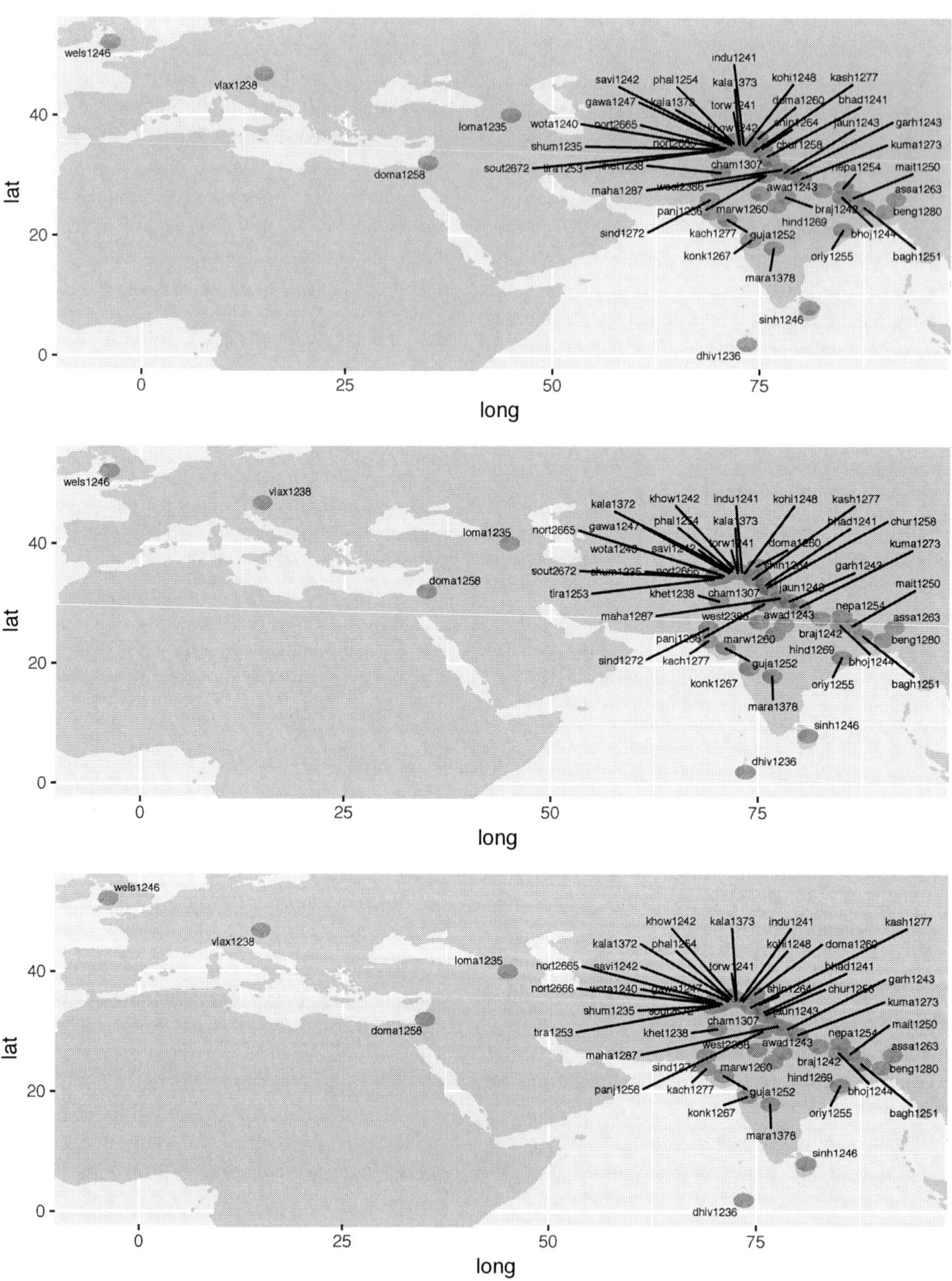

Figure 1: Averaged language-level component distributions for Diagonal (top), BGP (middle), and GGP (bottom) models.

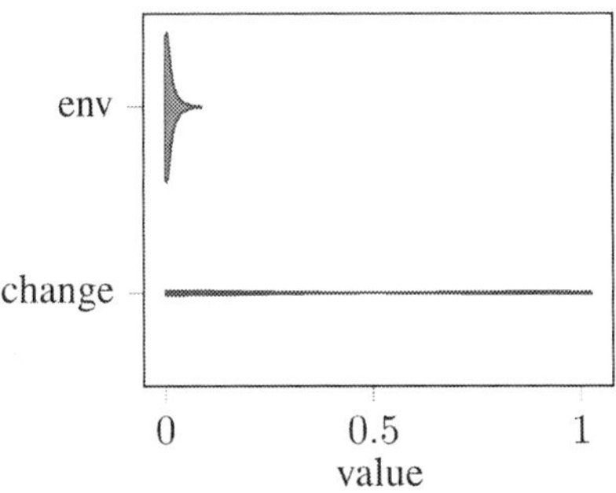

Figure 2: Squared inverse scales for the BGP model by featural dimension.

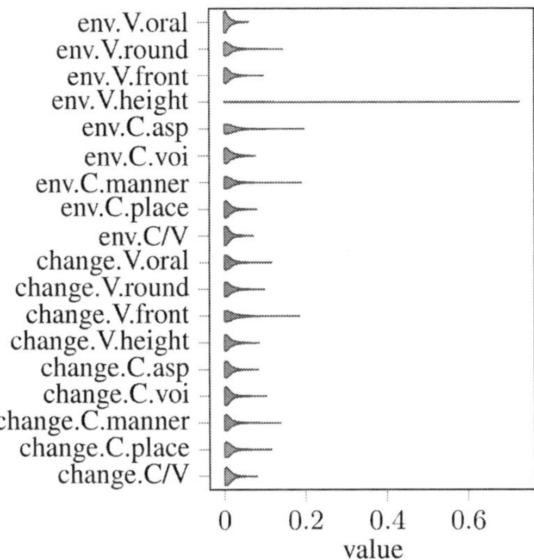

Figure 3: Squared inverse scales for the GGP model by featural dimension.

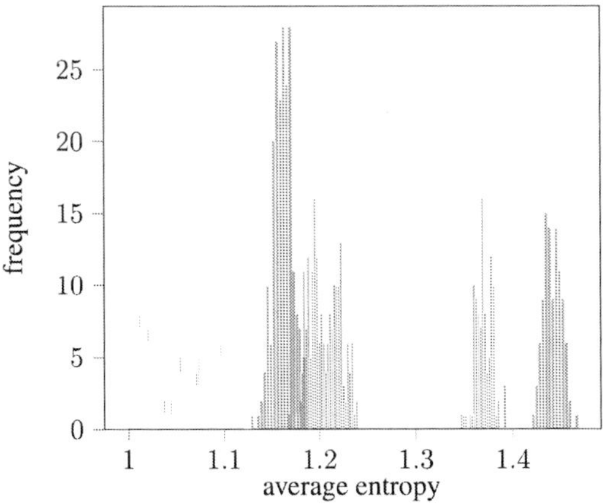

Figure 4: Average word-level component assignment entropies from posterior samples for each model (Diagonal = blue, BGP = red, GGP = green).

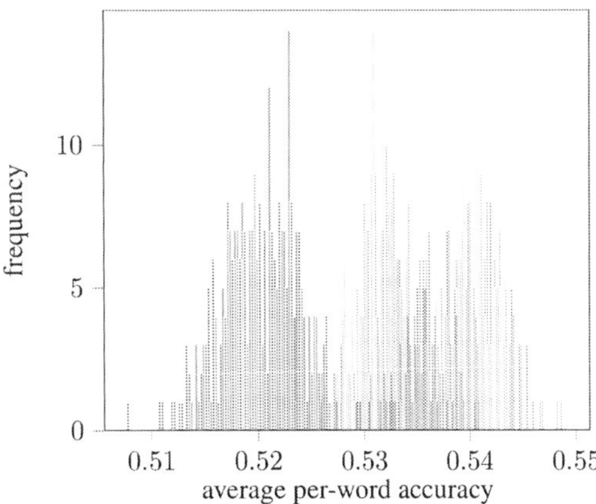

Figure 5: Average per-word accuracies from posterior samples for each model (Diagonal = blue, BGP = red, GGP = green).

$\{1, ..., |\boldsymbol{w}_i|\}$. We measure per-word accuracy by dividing the number of instances of $\hat{y}$ that were correctly simulated by the number of relevant sound changes in the word, $|\boldsymbol{w}_i|$. We take the mean of per-word averages across the data set for 100 samples of $\hat{\boldsymbol{\theta}}, \hat{\phi}$ in each model. Histograms of these accuracy measures can be seen in Figure 5. We find that the GP models re-generate the data with greater accuracy than the Diagonal model, but the BGP model outperforms the GGP model. This suggests that the sound change posterior distributions $\hat{\phi}$ of the GP models are more informative than those of the Diagonal model, and better capture the structure of the data. It is possible that the Diagonal model fared better in terms of entropy due to a trade-off in sparsity between $\hat{\theta}$ and $\hat{\phi}$, where more informative $\hat{\theta}$ and flatter $\hat{\phi}$ allowed for component labels to be assigned with greater certainty.

7 Outlook

This paper proposed a probabilistic formalization of sound change according to the logistic normal distribution, a distribution that has been underused for such a modeling purpose. We attempted to use GPs in order to induce more realistic sound change distributions for application to dialectological questions. We described a generative Bayesian model in which unnormalized logistic normal weights are generated by a Gaussian Process, a powerful and flexible prior distribution over functions that can be used to model covariance for multivariate normal data. GPs have been put forth as a means of modeling continuous phonetic changes (Aston et al., 2012), but this paper is the first to use them as a prior for multinomial sound change distributions.

While some aspects of our results were difficult to interpret and remain inconclusive, we did demonstrate a marginal increase in terms of key posterior predictive checks with the use of Gaussian Process models. It is clear that much work is required in order to bring the automated methodology described here into line with gold standards in linguistics as well as the intuitions of historical linguistics; however, we believe that this research program is promising and has high potential impact. Specifically, received wisdom can be used in the process of prior selection for Bayesian models. In this paper, we used a standard and simple covariance kernel function for our Gaussian process, the squared exponential kernel. We placed relatively uninformative priors over the parameters of the kernel function in the hopes that well-informed, highly identifiable parameters would fall out of the data. Further empirical work is required to determine which priors over kernel parameters are suitable, if a squared-exponential kernel is to be used in future work. Additionally, it is worth noting that there are many kernel functions to choose from, and that the squared-exponential kernel has its limitations. It (along with many other popular functions used for GPs) cannot model negative covariance, for example, whereas highly sophisticated alternatives can (Wilson and Adams, 2013).

If the methodology described here can be refined, the potential for quantitative historical linguistics is significant. Sound change and morphological change are the cornerstones of traditional historical linguistics (Meillet, 1922). High-definition data sets like the one used in this paper are largely unexploited. If the issues outlined above can be tackled, models like the one employed in this paper will undoubtedly serve as a powerful means of inferring key aspects of linguistic prehistory.

References

John Aitchison. 1986. *The statistical analysis of compositional data*. Chapman & Hall, London/New York.

JAD Aston, D Buck, J Coleman, CJ Cotter, NS Jones, V Macaulay, N MacLeod, JM Moriarty, and A Nevins. 2012. Phylogenetic inference for function-valued traits: speech sound evolution. *Trends in Ecology & Evolution*, 27(3):160–166.

David M Blei and John D Lafferty. 2007. A correlated topic model of Science. *The Annals of Applied Statistics*, 1(1):17–35.

Leonard Bloomfield. 1933. *Language*. Holt, Rinehart and Winston, New York.

Robert A Blust. 2005. Must sound change be linguistically motivated? *Diachronica*, 22(2):219–269.

Alexandre Bouchard-Côté, David Hall, Thomas L. Griffiths, and Dan Klein. 2013. Automated reconstruction of ancient languages using probabilistic models of sound change. *Proceedings of the National Academy of Sciences*, 110:4224–4229.

Alexandre Bouchard-Côté, Percy Liang, Thomas Griffiths, and Dan Klein. 2007. A probabilistic approach to diachronic phonology. In *Proceedings of the 2007 Joint Conference on Empirical Methods in Natural Language Processing and Computational Natural Language Learning (EMNLP-CoNLL)*, pages 887–896, Prague. Association for Computational Linguistics.

Alexandre Bouchard-Côté, Percy S Liang, Dan Klein, and Thomas L Griffiths. 2008. A probabilistic approach to language change. In *Advances in Neural Information Processing Systems*, pages 169–176.

Chundra Cathcart. to appear. A probabilistic assessment of the Indo-Aryan Inner-Outer Hypothesis. *Journal of Historical Linguistics*.

Noam Chomsky and Morris Halle. 1968. *The Sound Pattern of English*. Haper & Row, Publishers, New York.

Shay B. Cohen and Noah A. Smith. 2009. Shared logistic normal distributions for soft parameter tying in unsupervised grammar induction. In *Proceedings of Human Language Technologies: The 2009 Annual Conference of the North American Chapter of the Association for Computational Linguistics*, pages 74–82. Association for Computational Linguistics.

Ryan Cotterell and Jason Eisner. 2017. Probabilistic typology: Deep generative models of vowel inventories. In *Proceedings of the 55th Annual Meeting of the Association for Computational Linguistics (Volume 1: Long Papers)*, pages 1182–1192.

David Duvenaud. 2014. *Automatic Model Construction with Gaussian Processes*. Ph.D. thesis, University of Cambridge.

Richard Futrell, Adam Albright, Peter Graff, and Timothy J. O'Donnell. 2017. A generative model of phonotactics. *Transactions of the Association for Computational Linguistics*, 5:73–86.

Harald Hammarström, Robert Forkel, and Martin Haspelmath. 2017. Glottolog 3.3. Max Planck Institute for the Science of Human History.

Hannah Haynie. 2012. *Studies in the History and Geography of California Languages*. Ph.D. thesis, University of California, Berkeley.

Philipp Hennig, David Stern, Ralf Herbrich, and Thore Graepel. 2012. Kernel topic models. In *Proceedings of the 15th International Conference on Artificial Intelligence and Statistics (AISTATS)*, volume 22 of *JMLR*, La Palma, Canary Islands.

Hans Henrich Hock. 2016. The languages, their histories, and their genetic classification. In Hans Henrich Hock and Elena Bashir, editors, *The Languages and Linguistics of South Asia: A Comprehensive Guide*, pages 9–240. De Gruyter, Berlin, Boston.

Gerhard Jäger. 2014. Phylogenetic inference from word lists using weighted alignment with empirically determined weights. In *Quantifying Language Dynamics*, pages 155–204. Brill.

Mohammad Khan, Shakir Mohamed, Benjamin Marlin, and Kevin Murphy. 2012. A stick-breaking likelihood for categorical data analysis with latent gaussian models. In *Artificial Intelligence and Statistics*, pages 610–618.

Diederik P. Kingma and Jimmy Ba. 2015. Adam: A method for stochastic optimization. In *International Conference on Learning Representations (ICLR)*.

Diederik P. Kingma and Adam Welling. 2014. Auto-Encoding Variational Bayes. In *International Conference on Learning Representations (ICLR)*.

Martin Kümmel. 2007. *Konsonantenwandel*. Dr. Ludwig Reichert Verlag, Wiesbaden.

Johann-Mattis List. 2012. SCA. Phonetic alignment based on sound classes. In M. Slavkovik and D. Lassiter, editors, *New directions in logic, language, and computation*, pages 32–51. Springer, Berlin, Heidelberg.

Ian Maddieson. 2013. Voicing and gaps in plosive systems. In Matthew S. Dryer and Martin Haspelmath, editors, *The World Atlas of Language Structures Online*. Max Planck Institute for Evolutionary Anthropology, Leipzig.

Colin P. Masica. 1991. *The Indo-Aryan languages*. Cambridge University Press, Cambridge.

Antoine Meillet. 1922. *Les dialectes indo-européens*. E. Champion, Paris.

Yishu Miao, Edward Grefenstette, and Phil Blunsom. 2017. Discovering discrete latent topics with neural variational inference. In *Proceedings of the 34th International Conference on Machine Learning-Volume 70*, pages 2410–2419. JMLR. org.

David Mimno, David M. Blei, and Barbara E. Engelhardt. 2015. Posterior predictive checks to quantify lack-of-fit in admixture models of latent population structure. *Proceedings of the National Academy of Sciences*, page 201412301.

Radford Neal. 1996. *Bayesian Learning for Neural Networks*. Springer, Berlin and Heidelberg.

J. Piironen and A. Vehtari. 2016. Projection predictive model selection for Gaussian processes. In *Machine Learning for Signal Processing (MLSP), 2016 IEEE*.

Rajesh Ranganath, Linpeng Tang, Laurent Charlin, and David Blei. 2015. Deep exponential families. In *Artificial Intelligence and Statistics*, pages 762–771.

C. E. Rasmussen and C. K. I. Williams. 2006. *Gaussian Processes for Machine Learning*. MIT Press, Cambridge, MA.

Danilo Jimenez Rezende, Shakir Mohamed, and Daan Wierstra. 2014. Stochastic backpropagation and variational inference in deep latent gaussian models. *arXiv preprint arXiv:1401.4082*.

Peter Schrijver. 2014. *Language contact and the origin of Germanic languages*. Routledge, New York.

Franklin C. Southworth. 2005. *Linguistic Archaeology of South Asia*. Routledge, London.

Akash Srivastava and Charles Sutton. 2017. Autoencoding variational inference for topic models. In *International Conference on Learning Representations (ICLR)*.

Ralph L. Turner. 1962–1966. *A comparative dictionary of Indo-Aryan languages*. Oxford University Press, London.

Ralph L. Turner. 1975 [1967]. Geminates after long vowel in Indo-aryan. In *R.L. Turner: Collected Papers 1912–1973*, pages 405–415. Oxford University Press, London.

Martijn Wieling, Eliza Margaretha, and John Nerbonne. 2012. Inducing a measure of phonetic similarity from pronunciation variation. *Journal of Phonetics*, 40(2):307–314.

Andrew Wilson and Ryan Adams. 2013. Gaussian process kernels for pattern discovery and extrapolation. In *Proceedings of the 30th International Conference on Machine Learning*, Atlanta. `https://arxiv.org/pdf/1302.4245.pdf`.

8 Appendix

Here, we describe our model specification as well as the inference procedure used to fit our model's parameters.[1] We parameterize our model such that

---

[1] All relevant code can be found at `https://github.com/chundrac/IA_dial/tree/master/LChange2019`.

no random variables are dependent on other random variables, treating such variables as deterministic variables dependent on an auxiliary noise variable and one or more random variables. This allows us to construct a straightforward variational approximation to our model.

8.1 Language-component prior

The parameter θ, representing language-level distributions over latent dialect components, is generated as follows:

$$\eta_{l,k} \sim \mathcal{N}(0, 10) : l \in \{1, ..., L\}, k \in \{1, ..., K\}$$

$$\theta_l = \text{softmax}(\eta_l)$$

Placing a large standard deviation on the Gaussian prior passed to the softmax function allows for sparser multinomial distributions to be generated, but unlike symmetric Dirichlet priors with a concentration parameter below 1, does not penalize smoother distributions relative to sparse ones.

In theory, the Gaussian Stick-Breaking construction of (Khan et al., 2012; Miao et al., 2017) can be used to allow the language-level prior over dialect components to favor a large or small number of groups, conditional on the data. We do not use the GSB prior in this paper, but are exploring it in ongoing work.

8.2 Component-sound change prior

8.2.1 Diagonal Prior

The diagonal prior (i.e., the prior over sound changes that is insensitive to correlation) is a softmax-transformed diagonal multivariate Gaussian distribution with high variance:

$$\psi_{k,r,s} \sim \mathcal{N}(0, 10) : k \in \{1, ..., K\},$$
$$r \in \{1, ..., R\}, s \in \{1, ..., S_r\}$$

$$\phi_{k,r,\cdot} = \text{softmax}(\psi_{k,r,\cdot})$$

8.2.2 GP Prior

The following process holds for both the Binary GP (BGP) and Granular GP (GGP), the only difference being that the dimensionality D of the $D \times S \times S$ matrix δ containing pairwise featural distances between sound changes is larger for the GGP model. We use the Cholesky decomposition of the variance-covariance matrix Σ generated by the SEK function, coupled with an auxiliary noise

variable, in order to treat ψ as a deterministic random variable.

$$\alpha \sim \mathcal{N}(0, 1), \sigma \sim \mathcal{N}(0, 10)$$
$$\rho_d^{-1} \sim \mathcal{N}(0, .1) : d \in \{1, ..., D\}$$

[2]

$$\Sigma = \alpha^2 \exp\left(-\sum_{d=1}^{D} \frac{\delta^d}{2\rho^2}\right) + I\sigma^2 = LL^\top$$

$$z_{k,r,s}^{\Sigma} \sim \mathcal{N}(0, 1) : k \in \{1, ..., K\},$$
$$r \in \{1, ..., R\}, s \in \{1, ..., S_r\}$$

$$\psi_{k,\cdot,\cdot} = Lz_k^{\Sigma}$$

$$\phi_{k,r,\cdot} = \text{softmax}(\psi_{k,r,\cdot})$$

8.3 Inference

We use Stochastic Gradient Variational Bayes (Kingma and Welling, 2014) to learn each model's parameters. Since all of our priors are Gaussian, it is straightforward to construct a Gaussian variational approximation for each parameter with its own trainable mean and standard deviation. The objective of Variational Inference is to maximize the evidence lower bound (ELBO), given below:

$$\text{ELBO} = \mathbb{E}_{z \sim q(z|x)}[P(x|z)] - D_{KL}(q(z|x)||p(z))$$

where the first term denotes the expectation of the model log likelihood (see eq. 3) under samples z from the variational posterior $q(z|x)$, and the second denotes the sum of Kullback-Leibler (KL) divergences between the variational posterior parameters and their corresponding priors in $p(z)$, all of which are Gaussian. We use the Adam optimizer (Kingma and Ba, 2015) with a learning rate of .1 to optimize the variational parameters for 5000 iterations over 3 separate initializations via batch inference (i.e., fitting the parameters on the entire dataset at each iteration), using 10 Monte Carlo samples per iteration to estimate $\mathbb{E}_{z \sim q(z|x)}[P(x|z)]$ according to the reparameterization trick (Rezende et al., 2014; Kingma and Welling, 2014). To deal with label switching across initializations, we choose the permutation of labels $\{1,...,K\}$ of the posterior parameters of initializations 2 and 3 such that the KL divergence to the posterior parameters of the first initialization is minimized.

---

[2]In theory, a more informative prior over σ such as $\mathcal{N}(10, 1)$ may be a good choice in order to encourage sparser distributions.

Modeling a historical variety of a low-resource language: Language contact effects in the verbal cluster of Early-Modern Frisian

Jelke Bloem
ILLC
University of Amsterdam
`j.bloem@uva.nl`

Arjen Versloot
ACLC
University of Amsterdam
`a.p.versloot@uva.nl`

Fred Weerman
ACLC
University of Amsterdam
`f.p.weerman@uva.nl`

Abstract

Certain phenomena of interest to linguists mainly occur in low-resource languages, such as contact-induced language change. We show that it is possible to study contact-induced language change computationally in a historical variety of a low-resource language, Early-Modern Frisian, by creating a model using features that were established to be relevant in a closely related language, modern Dutch. This allows us to test two hypotheses on two types of language contact that may have taken place between Frisian and Dutch during this time. Our model shows that Frisian verb cluster word orders are associated with different context features than Dutch verb orders, supporting the 'learned borrowing' hypothesis.

1 Introduction

If we want to use computational methods to answer linguistic research questions, a major restriction is that the data-driven methods that are popular in natural language processing today are only applicable to a tiny part of the world's language varieties. Last decade, it was estimated that significant computational resources were available for "perhaps 20 or 30 languages" (Maxwell and Hughes, 2006). Efforts to address this have been proposed, such as the Human Language Project (Abney and Bird, 2010), and to a limited degree executed (i.e. the Universal Dependencies project, Nivre et al., 2016 or SeedLing, Emerson et al., 2014). However, the reality is still that relatively few languages are being studied using quantitative methods. Many phenomena that are of interest to linguists do not occur in these 20 or 30 languages, of which the larger available corpora mainly contain modern standard varieties in common registers and within easily recorded domains of language.

Specifically, certain phenomena of interest to linguists are characteristic of minority languages, which are by definition used less, and are less likely to have computational resources available. For example, in cases of language contact where there is a majority language and a lesser used language, contact-induced language change is more likely to occur in the lesser used language (Weinreich, 1979). Furthermore, certain phenomena are better studied in historical varieties of languages. Taking the example of language change, it is more interesting to study a specific language change once it has already been completed, such that one can study the change itself in historical texts as well as the subsequent outcome of the change.

For these reasons, contact-induced language change is difficult to study computationally, and we consider it a great test case for applying some insights from the recent wave of articles discussing computational linguistics for low-resource languages. In this work, we apply computational methods, to the extent that it is possible, to gain insight into the nature of language change that occurred in historical West-Frisian, a lesser-used language spoken in the Dutch province of Fryslân.

2 Case study

Our case study of language change focuses on word order changes in the verbal cluster. This phenomenon has been studied thoroughly in the larger West-Germanic languages such as Dutch (Coussé, 2008; Coupé, 2015), but not the smaller Frisian language[1], which has been in extensive contact with Dutch for most of its history, continuing up to the present (Breuker, 1993; Ytsma, 1995). This gives us a good basis for comparison. While Frisian is a lesser-used language, its historical data is exceptionally well-accessible: all known West-Frisian

---

[1]In this article, we will use the term *Frisian* to refer to the West-Frisian language (*Westerlauwers Fries*), as opposed to Saterland Frisian or North Frisian, or the West-Frisian dialect of Dutch.

Proceedings of the 1st International Workshop on Computational Approaches to Historical Language Change, pages 265–271
Florence, Italy, August 2, 2019. ©2019 Association for Computational Linguistics

texts written until 1800 are digitally available.

In Frisian, when there are two verbs in a cluster (an auxiliary verb and a main verb), the normative word order is the one in example 1 below, as prescribed in the reference grammar of Popkema (2006). However, both logically possible orders are being used in present-day Frisian:

(1)   Anne sei dat er my **sjoen hie**.
        Anne said that he me seen   had

        'Anne said that he had seen me'

(2)   Anne sei dat er my **hie sjoen**.
        Anne said that he me had seen

        'Anne said that he had seen me'

Example 1 shows the 2-1 order, so called because the syntactically higher head verb (referred to as 1) comes after the lower lexical verb (2). Example 2 shows the opposite 1-2 order. The present-day use of the 1-2 order appears to be recent, and influenced by language contact with Dutch (de Haan, 1996). It has even been found that Frisian bilingual children have similar word order preferences in their Frisian as in their Dutch (Meyer et al., 2015). However, the non-normative 1-2 order also appears in older sources: in Early-Modern texts, Hoekstra (2012) found 10% 1-2 orders, and noted that the 1-2 ordered clusters exhibit some Dutch-like properties that do not occur in 2-1 ordered clusters, suggesting a contact effect during this time period.

A particularly interesting Middle Frisian set of texts with regards to language contact are the *Basle Wedding Speeches*, notable for mixing in Middle Low German and Middle Dutch forms (Buma, 1957): a clear case of 'contact' Middle Frisian. Two conflicting hypotheses have been proposed in the literature regarding the nature of this language contact. (Bremmer, 1997, p. 383) argues that the writer was a bilingual with "a full command neither of Frisian nor Low German, certainly not in his writing, nor in all likelihood in his spoken usage". This type of contact may have resulted in this mixed-language text. Blom (2008, p. 21) instead proposes the existence of a shared written register in which using borrowed forms was normal: authors of the time show familiarity with texts written in Middle Dutch and Middle Low German, which may have influenced their written Frisian. These two proposals correspond to two kinds of language change that have been distinguished in the literature: change from below and change from above (Labov, 1965, 1994). Furthermore, they correspond

to two types of language acquisition: early acquisition and late acquisition (Weerman, 2011). These theories make different usage predictions that allow us to identify which of the two hypotheses is more plausible:

1. Variation in Early-Modern Frisian texts is due to contact through bilingualism, with early acquisition of the optionality, based on Bremmer (1997) and like the present-day situation (de Haan, 1996).

2. Variation in Early-Modern Frisian texts is due to learned borrowing, with late acquisition of the optionality, based on Blom (2008).

To test these hypotheses, we compare features of verb clusters in Early-Modern Frisian texts to those in modern Dutch, as those have been studied thoroughly (De Sutter, 2009; Meyer and Weerman, 2016; Bloem et al., 2014; Augustinus, 2015; Hendriks, 2018). We are particularly interested in the contexts in which the 'Dutch' 1-2 cluster order is used in the Frisian corpus. Specifically, we test whether the Frisian 1-2 orders occur in the same contexts as modern Dutch 1-2 orders to see what type of contact is responsible for them. It has been argued that verb cluster order variation in Dutch has the function of facilitating sentence processing: the verb cluster order that is 'easier' or more economical in a particular context is used (De Sutter, 2009; Bloem et al., 2017). By studying whether the variation in the Frisian texts is predicted by the same features as the variation in modern Dutch, we can infer whether Early-Modern Frisian verb cluster order variation has the same functions as modern Dutch verb cluster order variation.

If Early-Modern Frisian 1-2 order clusters occur in similar contexts as modern Dutch clusters in the 1-2 order this would indicate that this order has the same function in both varieties, and is part of the grammar of the writer of the Early-Modern Frisian text. This can mean two things: Firstly, it could be the case that the order is used in the same way as its modern Dutch counterpart. This supports the idea that 'contact through bilingualism' is the source of the variation: hypothesis 1. If the contexts of use are not similar between Early-Modern Frisian and modern Dutch, this means it is likely that the 1-2 order has been borrowed in some way, but with a different function than the function it has in modern Dutch. In this case, learned borrowing would be the source of the variation: this would support hypothesis 2. There is a third option, which is that these 1-2 orders are not due to contact, but for Early-Modern Frisian we will skip over this possibility with reference to the contact evidence found by Hoekstra (2012). In future work, a study of older Frisian texts is needed to investigate whether this non-contact hypothesis is plausible for older stages of Frisian.

3 Task description

Our task is to test the aforementioned two hypotheses by taking a model that shows what features are associated with the Dutch 1-2 order, and then creating a model from Frisian data based on those features. We first identify a suitable data source containing sufficiently annotated Early-Modern Frisian text. We then operationalize the relevant verb cluster features (as modelled for Dutch, Bloem et al., 2014) in terms of the annotation. Next, we automatically identify and extract verb clusters and their relevant features from the data. Lastly, we identify the features that are associated with the Dutch-like 1-2 order in the Frisian data, and compare them to those that are associated with the 1-2 order in Dutch. For reasons of comparability, we use logistic regression to identify the features, a method commonly used in quantitative linguistics (Speelman, 2014) and in the studies on Dutch verb clusters that we use as a basis for comparison (De Sutter, 2009; Bloem et al., 2014).

Our approach of taking a case study that is well-studied in a related language is inspired by cross-lingual learning in NLP: in studies involving low-resource languages, closely related languages that are more rich in resources are used as a source of additional data. Examples of this are cross-language parse tree projection (Xia and Lewis, 2007), where structural information about a sentence in one language is transferred to parallel data in another language, and data point selection (Søgaard, 2011), where a tool for a low-resource language is trained on data from a high-resource language, while selecting the data that is most similar to the low-resource language. In both of these cases, general knowledge about a language family is also transferred to a low-resource language.

Frisian language resources When working with a low-resource language, a brief overview of the available resources for that language can be helpful. Most Frisian resources are of the traditional kind. The *Wurdboek fan de Fryske Taal*, a dictionary that has been in development since 1984, currently contains about 115.000 lemmas (Sijens and Depuydt, 2010), and has an online version[2]. Frisian grammar has been studied since at least the start of the 20th century (Collitz, 1915), leading to collections of linguistic studies such as Hoekstra et al. (2010). Its minority language status has been researched as well (Ytsma, 1995; Breuker, 2001; de Graaf et al., 2015).

As for digital resources, the Fryske Akademy is working on the Frisian Integrated Language Database[3] (Taaldatabank, TDB). This corpus contains all of the attested Frisian texts from the years 1550-1800 and is planned to include modern material. The Early-Modern Frisian texts have been tokenized, lemmatized and part-of-speech tagged manually. The Fryske Akademy is also compiling a Corpus of Spoken Frisian[4] for the purpose of developing speech technology. The aforementioned dictionary is also included in a digitalization effort of Dutch historical dictionaries (Duijff and Kuip, 2018), forming a bilingual lexical-semantic database. A parallel corpus with aligned sentences from the Fryske Akademy exists[5].

Besides spell-checking, the only available NLP tools appear to be the statistical machine translation system by van Gompel et al. (2014) and two text-to-speech systems: one using an existing Dutch text-to-speech system (Dijkstra et al., 2004) and one using a bilingual system capable of handling code-switching between Dutch and Frisian (Yılmaz et al., 2016). While there is a part-of-speech tagger for historical (Middle) Low German (Koleva et al., 2017), a related low-resource language, none are available for historical or modern Frisian, and neither are syntactic parsers.

The TDB corpus is the most relevant resource for the present study, as it contains annotated Early-Modern Frisian texts. The size of this section of the corpus is around 480,000 tokens and 20,000 types, though this includes repeated text and non-contemporaneous front/back matter. After selecting representative texts without duplicate material or non-Frisian material, we obtain a subcorpus con-

---

[2]`http://gtb.inl.nl//?owner=WFT`
[3]`https://argyf.fryske-akademy.eu/en/undersyk/taalkunde/yntegrearre-taaldatabank/`
[4]`https://www.narcis.nl/research/RecordID/OND1287823`
[5]`https://www.sketchengine.eu/fryske-akademy-parallel-corpus/`

taining 125,842 tokens and 10,405 types. Unfortunately, no tools are available for further annotation that would be relevant for word order phenomena.

4 Experiments

We automatically annotate verb clusters and extract their features from the corpus using a Python script that detects verb clusters based on the information already available in the annotation. In previous work on Dutch, verb clusters were defined using dependency structure or phrase structure, with one verb being the syntactic head of the other (Bloem et al., 2014; Augustinus, 2015). However, as no syntactic annotation is available, we must rely on part-of-speech tags. As there is no gold standard data for this task, and little data in general, a statistical modeling approach is infeasible. Therefore, the script is rule-based, and we define a verb cluster based on the occurrence of bigrams of verbs (according to the existing annotation), or trigrams containing grammatical verb cluster interruptions, as well as the verb classes in the annotation. The word order of the verb cluster is then determined based on the relative positions of its constituent verbs (a main verb and an auxiliary verb) in the linear order of the sentence. This procedure is not 100% reliable, especially in clusters with infinitival auxiliary verbs, where auxiliary verbs and main verbs may have the same form.

We checked the classification of a random sample of 50 1-2 order clusters and 50 2-1 order clusters, using only prose text for this evaluation because the script appears to make more mistakes there. We evaluate only for precision, not for recall, as we have no gold standard data for evaluating recall. Of the 50 automatically extracted candidate 1-2 clusters, 34 were found to be actual two-verb clusters from subordinate clauses: a precision of 68%. Of the 50 2-1 clusters, all 50 met this requirement (100% precision). Most of the erroneous candidate 1-2 order clusters were cases of a finite auxiliary verb in V2 position in a main clause, immediately followed by the main verb in final position, with no intervening objects. This looks exactly like a 1-2 order cluster consisting of a finite auxiliary verb and a main verb at the end of a subordinate clause. Main clause clusters cannot look like 2-1 order clusters, which explains the 100% precision for the 2-1 order. This evaluation shows that a statistical model based on this annotation is likely to overestimate the probability of 1-2 orders.

Due to annotation limitations, several features from Bloem et al.'s (2014) Dutch model could not be extracted from our corpus: the tree depth of the verb cluster, the definiteness of the preceding noun, extraposition of the prepositional object, multiword units and the length of the clause. Verb frequency was estimated by counting over the entire Early-Modern Frisian part of the TDB. Another factor is that Dutch 1-2 orders have a more uniform information density (Bloem, 2016). This was found by training a n-gram language model on Dutch corpus data, and then measuring its perplexity over sentences containing verb clusters that were not in its training data. A 145 million word corpus was used for this, but for Early-Modern Frisian we have less than 0.5 million words available. A model trained on such diverse texts spanning hundreds of years would require more training data to achieve reasonable perplexity rates than a model trained on newspaper text from a small range of years, thus we cannot reliably operationalize this factor. However, the Dutch result is likely to apply to Frisian as well, as the reasons for the perplexity values that were found for Dutch can equally apply to Frisian: in both languages, there are few clustering auxiliary verbs and many possible main verbs, and in both languages, the first verb of a cluster helps to predict its second verb and is highly unlikely to be followed by something that is not a verb, as verb cluster interruption rarely occurs in present-day Frisian (Barbiers et al., 2008, p. 25–41). The main difference between the languages in this regard is that present-day Frisian shows more noun incorporation into the verb cluster's main verb (Dyk, 1997), which may increase informativity of the main verb compared to Dutch in 1-2 orders, but seems rare. Therefore, we can transfer the knowledge gained with a Dutch language model to Frisian and assume that there is not much difference between the languages regarding verb cluster information density.

Next, we have created a multifactorial logistic regression model using the remaining features. We model verb cluster order as a binary variable predicted by these features, in which the order can be 1-2 or 2-1. The advantage of this method over neural networks or other methods involving dimension reduction is that the contribution of each feature is transparent. The goal is after all not to make an optimal classifier for 1-2 and 2-1 order contexts, but to find out more about why language users produced a 1-2 or 2-1 order given a context. Table 1 shows the contribution of each feature to the model. The effect size of each variable is given as an odds ratio, and in line with previous work, we are reporting associations with the 1-2 order. The model has acceptable multicollinearity (VIF < 1.3)[6]. The text type and year features were not used in previous work, but are necessary control factors when working with historical text. Much of the text is rhyme, which affects word order: 1-2 orders are estimated to be 18.69 times more likely in rhyming text.

Feature	Odds ratio
Text type +Rhyme	*** 18.69
Text year	0.99
Auxiliary verb +Modal	1.19
Auxiliary verb +Future	0.98
Auxiliary verb +Aspectual	** 7.15
Auxiliary verb +Copula	** 7.88
Auxiliary verb +Past	*** 2.50
To-infinitival verb	*** 8.33
Priming +1-2	0.95
Separable verb	0.64
Information value +High	0.91
Information value +Medium	*** 0.24
Verb log frequency	0.96

Table 1: Effect of different features on the likelihood of 1-2 verbal cluster orders. ** $p < 0.01$, *** $p < 0.001$.

Of the auxiliary verb features, *modal* is the most important feature in Dutch, with an odds ratio of 148 (Bloem et al., 2014), while our model shows no evidence for an effect. We find an association between copular verbs and the 2-1 order, while Dutch shows the reverse — a difference that supports Hypothesis 2, the learned borrowing hypothesis. The *aspectual* and *to-infinitival* effects we found are consistent with Hoekstra's (2012) observations, who shows that no equivalent construction existed in Frisian, making these easy candidates for borrowing, along with the Dutch word order.

Other factors from the Dutch model are not significant in this model (*priming, separable, frequency*) and are all related to complexity (Bloem, 2016). The *information value* feature has opposite associations compared to the Dutch model. Thus, the model shows evidence for only some of the features from the Dutch model. Under Hypothe-

sis 1, we would expect significant effects here — use of 1-2 orders in contexts that are more difficult to process, as in Dutch (Bloem et al., 2017). Instead, the only significant features are associated with borrowed constructions, or are significant in the opposite direction as in Dutch and therefore associated with the other word order. These clear usage differences support hypothesis 2: the 1-2 orders appeared due to learned borrowing, and unlike in Dutch, did not have a clear function besides stylistic marking (i.e. in rhymed text). Unfortunately a direct, number by number comparison to the Dutch model is not possible due to different categories (i.e. for the types of auxiliary verbs), stemming from different corpus annotation schemes used for the Dutch and Frisian data. Furthermore, the numbers cannot be compared directly because both models include different features.

5   Conclusion

Our study has shown that it is possible to apply computational methods to a historical variety of a lesser used language. We investigated a case of contact-induced change, a phenomenon that is mainly found in low-resource languages, and were able to test hypotheses regarding the nature of this change. In doing so, we made use of what is known about the construction in a closely related but higher-resourced language, Dutch. This allowed us to limit the hypothesis space, reducing the problem to a comparison with Dutch and testing whether features that model the observed variation in Dutch, are also relevant in Frisian, although the limited availability of data and annotation did not allow us to test all features. There was also not enough data to train a language model for estimating complexity through model perplexity. Nevertheless, by combining findings from our Frisian data and from previous studies on Dutch, we are able to get a good impression of the origin of the 1-2 order construction in Early-Modern Frisian.

As verb cluster order variation is a probabilistic phenomenon that is affected by multiple factors, we could not have found the verb cluster usage patterns described here without making use of computational models. Even when little data is available, computational methods can help supplement other types of evidence in historical linguistics, particularly on research questions involving variation, complexity and other matters that go beyond grammaticality versus ungrammaticality.

---

[6]Variable Inflation Factor (VIF) quantifies linear dependence of a feature on other features. With VIF $= 1.3$, the variance of a feature is inflated by 30% due to collinearity.

References

Steven Abney and Steven Bird. 2010. The human language project: building a universal corpus of the world's languages. In *Proceedings of the 48th annual meeting of the association for computational linguistics*, pages 88–97. Association for Computational Linguistics.

Liesbeth Augustinus. 2015. *Complement Raising and Cluster Formation in Dutch. A Treebank-supported Investigation.* Ph.D. thesis, KU Leuven.

Sjef Barbiers, Johan van der Auwera, Hans Bennis, Eefje Boef, Gunther De Vogelaer, and Margreet van der Ham. 2008. *Syntactische Atlas van de Nederlandse Dialecten Deel II / Syntactic Atlas of the Dutch Dialects Volume II.* Amsterdam University Press.

Jelke Bloem. 2016. Testing the processing hypothesis of word order variation using a probabilistic language model. In *Proceedings of the Workshop on Computational Linguistics for Linguistic Complexity (CL4LC)*, pages 174–185.

Jelke Bloem, Arjen Versloot, and Fred Weerman. 2014. Applying automatically parsed corpora to the study of language variation. In *Proceedings of COLING 2014, the 25th International Conference on Computational Linguistics: Technical Papers*, pages 1974–1984, Dublin. Dublin City University and Association for Computational Linguistics.

Jelke Bloem, Arjen Versloot, and Fred Weerman. 2017. Verbal cluster order and processing complexity. In Enoch Aboh, editor, *Complexity in human languages: A multifaceted approach*, volume 60, pages 94–119. Elsevier.

Alderik H Blom. 2008. Language admixture in the Old West Frisian Basle Wedding Speeches? *Amsterdamer Beiträge zur älteren Germanistik*, 64(1):1–27.

Rolf H Bremmer. 1997. Bad Frisian and bad Low German: Interference in the writings of a medieval West Frisian. *Multilingua*, 16:375–388.

Pieter Breuker. 1993. *Noarmaspekten fan it hjoeddeiske Frysk*, volume 70. Stifting FFYRUG.

Pieter Breuker. 2001. West Frisian in language contact. *Handbuch des Friesischen*, pages 121–129.

Wybren Jan Buma. 1957. *Aldfryske houlikstaspraken.* van Gorcum.

Hermann Collitz. 1915. Phonology and grammar of Modern West Frisian. *Modern Language Notes*, 30(7):215–217.

Griet Coupé. 2015. *Syntactic extension. The historical development of Dutch verb clusters.* Ph.D. thesis, Radboud University Nijmegen.

Evie Coussé. 2008. *Motivaties voor volgordevariatie. Een diachrone studie van werkwoordvolgorde in het Nederlands.* Ph.D. thesis, Ghent University.

Ger de Haan. 1996. Recent changes in the verbal complex of Frisian. In A Petersen and H F Nielsen, editors, *A Frisian and Germanic miscellany published in honour of Nils Århammar on his sixty-fifth birthday, 7 August 1996*, pages 171–184. Odense University Press.

Gert De Sutter. 2009. Towards a multivariate model of grammar: The case of word order variation in Dutch clause final verb clusters. In A Dufter, J Fleischer, and G Seiler, editors, *Describing and Modeling Variation in Grammar*, pages 225–255. Walter De Gruyter.

Jeltske Dijkstra, Louis C W Pols, and Rob J J H van Son. 2004. FRYSS: A first step towards Frisian TTS. Institute of Phonetic Sciences, University of Amsterdam.

Pieter Duijff and Frits van der Kuip. 2018. Lexicography in a minority language: A multifunctional online Dutch-Frisian dictionary. *International Journal of Lexicography*, 31(2):196–213.

Siebren Dyk. 1997. *Noun incorporation in Frisian.* Ph.D. thesis.

Guy Emerson, Liling Tan, Susanne Fertmann, Alexis Palmer, and Michaela Regneri. 2014. Seedling: Building and using a seed corpus for the human language project. In *Proceedings of the 2014 Workshop on the Use of Computational Methods in the Study of Endangered Languages*, pages 77–85.

Maarten van Gompel, Antal van den Bosch, and Anne Dijkstra. 2014. Oersetter: Frisian-dutch statistical machine translation. *Boersma, P.; Brand, H.; Spoelstra, J.(ed.), Philologia Frisica anno 2012*, pages 287–296.

Tjeerd de Graaf, Cor van der Meer, and Lysbeth Jongbloed-Faber. 2015. The use of new technologies in the preservation of an endangered language: The case of Frisian. *Endangered languages and new technologies*, pages 141–149.

Lotte Hendriks. 2018. *Not another book on verb raising.* Ph.D. thesis, Utrecht University.

Eric Hoekstra. 2012. Reade wurdfolchoarders en dêrmei gearhingjende aspekten yn 17e-ieusk Frysk. In ûndersyk nei de tiidwurdkloft yn Gysbert Japicx syn "Yen suwnerlinge forhânlinge Fen it Libben In fenne Deade". *It Beaken*, 72 (2010)(3-4):223–239.

Jarich. Hoekstra, Willem. Visser, and Goffe. Jensma. 2010. *Studies in West Frisian Grammar: Selected Papers by Germen J. de Haan.* John Benjamins Publishing Company.

Mariya Koleva, Melissa Farasyn, Bart Desmet, Anne Breitbarth, and Véronique Hoste. 2017. An automatic part-of-speech tagger for Middle Low German. *International Journal of Corpus Linguistics*, 22(1):107–140.

William Labov. 1965. On the mechanism of linguistic change. *Georgetown University Monographs on Language and Linguistics*, 18:91–114.

William Labov. 1994. *Principles of Linguistic Change, Volume 1: Internal Factors*. Oxford: Blackwell.

Mike Maxwell and Baden Hughes. 2006. Frontiers in linguistic annotation for lower-density languages. In *Proceedings of the workshop on frontiers in linguistically annotated corpora 2006*, pages 29–37. Association for Computational Linguistics.

Caitlin Meyer, Doatske de Haan, Martina Faber, and Fred Weerman. 2015. Language acquisition and language change: the case of verb clusters. Presented at A Germanic Sandwich 2015, University of Nottingham.

Caitlin Meyer and Fred Weerman. 2016. Cracking the cluster: The acquisition of verb raising in Dutch. *Nederlandse Taalkunde*, 21(2):181–212.

Joakim Nivre, Marie-Catherine De Marneffe, Filip Ginter, Yoav Goldberg, Jan Hajic, Christopher D Manning, Ryan T McDonald, Slav Petrov, Sampo Pyysalo, Natalia Silveira, et al. 2016. Universal dependencies v1: A multilingual treebank collection. In *LREC*.

Jan Popkema. 2006. *Grammatica Fries*. Prisma Woordenboeken en Taaluitgaven.

Hindrik Sijens and Katrien Depuydt. 2010. Clarin-NL project WFT-GTB.

Anders Søgaard. 2011. Data point selection for cross-language adaptation of dependency parsers. In *Proceedings of the 49th Annual Meeting of the Association for Computational Linguistics: Human Language Technologies: short papers-Volume 2*, pages 682–686. Association for Computational Linguistics.

Dirk Speelman. 2014. Logistic regression. *Corpus Methods for Semantics: Quantitative studies in polysemy and synonymy*, 43:487–533.

Fred Weerman. 2011. Diachronic change: Early versus late acquisition. *Bilingualism: Language and Cognition*, 14(2):149–151.

Uriel Weinreich. 1979. *Languages in contact: Findings and problems*. 1. Walter de Gruyter.

Fei Xia and William Lewis. 2007. Multilingual structural projection across interlinear text. In *Proc. of the Conference on Human Language Technologies (HLT/NAACL 2007)*, pages 452–459.

Emre Yılmaz, Henk van den Heuvel, and David van Leeuwen. 2016. Investigating bilingual deep neural networks for automatic recognition of code-switching Frisian speech. In *Procedia Computer Science*, volume 81, pages 159–166. Elsevier.

Jehannes Ytsma. 1995. *Frisian as first and second language: sociolinguistic and socio-psychological aspects of the acquisition of Frisian among Frisian and Dutch primary school children*. Fryske Akademy.

Visualizing Linguistic Change as Dimension Interactions

Christin Schätzle, Frederik L. Dennig, Michael Blumenschein,
Daniel A. Keim and **Miriam Butt**
University of Konstanz
`firstname.lastname@uni-konstanz.de`

Abstract

Historical change typically is the result of complex interactions between several linguistic factors. Identifying the relevant factors and understanding how they interact across the temporal dimension is the core remit of historical linguistics. With respect to corpus work, this entails a separate annotation, extraction and painstaking pair-wise comparison of the relevant bits of information. This paper presents a significant extension of HistoBankVis, a multi-layer visualization system which allows a fast and interactive exploration of complex linguistic data. Linguistic factors can be understood as data dimensions which show complex interrelationships. We model these relationships with the Parallel Sets technique. We demonstrate the powerful potential of this technique by applying the system to understanding the interaction of case, grammatical relations and word order in the history of Icelandic.

1 Introduction

Historical linguistic research is corpus-based by nature. In recent years, a large amount of digitized and linguistically well-annotated corpora have been made available and the historical linguistic research community is increasingly employing quantitative and statistical methods for their analysis. This includes the calculation of co-occurrence frequencies, correlations, dispersion statistics, and more sophisticated methods such as clustering (see, e.g., Hilpert and Gries, 2016). Statistical measurements are well-established for the analysis of linguistic change with respect to the quantification of individual structures. However, these methods are not per se suitable for the uncovering and understanding of the complex interactions between various linguistic structures typically involved in a change.

This paper extends our HistoBankVis system (Schätzle et al. 2017) by a powerful visualization to analyze and explore the interrelationship between multidimensional linguistic factors. HistoBankVis was specifically developed for the analysis of historical linguistic data. The system allows for an interactive exploratory access to a complex data set by using several interlinked visualization and filtering techniques. The extension presented in this paper integrates a *Dimension Interaction* visualization, based on the Parallel Sets technique (Bendix et al., 2005; Kosara et al., 2006), into the HistoBankVis system. Parallel Sets support the flexible analysis, visual presentation, and exploration of correlations between a large number of features from different *data dimensions*, i.e., linguistic factors, which immensely facilitates the analysis of interactions between features from changing dimensions.

We demonstrate the efficacy of the Dimension Interaction technique for historical linguistic research using a concrete case study which investigates interrelations between word order changes and subject case in Icelandic. The visualization not only proved to be an extremely valuable tool for the analysis of complex interactions across different data dimensions, but also facilitated the uncovering of previously unknown interdependencies in the data.

2 Challenges for Diachronic Linguistics

More and more digitized text corpora have been made available for historical linguistic research in recent years. These comprise large linguistically unannotated collections of historical texts, e.g., the Bibliotheca Augustana,[1] TITUS[2] and GRETIL,[3] but also increasingly include annotated corpora.

Annotated corpora are usually smaller in size and have undergone a manual annotation process in addition to an automatic preprocessing. The

---

[1] https://www.hs-augsburg.de/~harsch/augustana.html
[2] http://titus.uni-frankfurt.de/indexd.htm
[3] http://gretil.sub.uni-goettingen.de/

272

Proceedings of the 1st International Workshop on Computational Approaches to Historical Language Change, pages 272–278
Florence, Italy, August 2, 2019. ©2019 Association for Computational Linguistics

Texts	Indefinite NPs			Definite NPs			NPs as proper names		
	OV	VO	% OV	OV	VO	% OV	OV	VO	% OV
14th century	28	33	45.9%	11	57	16.2%	3	8	27.3%
15th century	23	30	43.4%	10	25	28.6%	1	3	25.0%
16th century	15	28	34.9%	17	26	39.5%	1	5	16.7%
17th century	28	59	32.2%	18	50	26.5%	0	20	0.0%
18th century	6	28	17.6%	7	31	18.4%	1	7	12.5%
19th century	34	425	7.4%	14	351	3.8%	4	68	5.6%
	134	603	18.2%	77	540	12.5%	10	111	8.3%

Table 1: Definiteness distribution of NPs across different word orders in Icelandic (Hróarsdóttir, 2000, 136).

manual annotation procedure allows for a linguistically sophisticated annotation which often includes a deep syntactic analysis of hierarchies and dependencies between phrase structure constituents. Prototypically, such structural information is annotated in the Penn Treebank-style (Marcus et al., 1993). Examples are the Penn Parsed Corpora of Historical English (Kroch and Taylor, 2000; Kroch et al., 2004, 2010), the Icelandic Parsed Historical Corpus (IcePaHC, Wallenberg et al., 2011), the Heliand Parsed Database (Walkden, 2015), the Latin Dependency Treebank (Bamman and Cane, 2006), the Prague Dependency Treebank (Hajič, 1998), and PROIEL (Haug and Jøhndal, 2008).

The standard procedure within diachronic corpus linguistics incorporates the use of programming languages for text processing and statistical analysis, e.g., Python, Perl, and R (Baayen, 2008; Bird et al., 2009; Christiansen et al., 2012), to extract the relevant patterns on the basis of the annotation and to calculate co-occurrence frequencies and statistical significances across different time stages. A multitude of high-dimensional data tables containing different features and data characteristics are generated. For example, Table 1 represents a prototypical historical linguistic data set.

Finding significant patterns and feature interactions across such tables is by no means a trivial task, as a temporal component not only has to be factored in, but numbers computed for several features belonging to different data dimensions need to be compared across many data tables of varying size. Moreover, statistical significances are difficult to interpret and often calculated on the basis of only very few occurrences of the actual observation, derogating the significance measures and statistical conclusions. Thus, meaningful patterns may not be identified, whereas irrelevant patterns are likely to surface as significant. Interesting patterns may furthermore stay hidden when an analyst chooses temporal episodes that are either too coarse or too fine grained for the statistical analysis. The factors causing a language to change are often unknown or at least highly debated among researchers. Therefore, a researcher may have to conduct several different analyses, experimenting with different combinations of data dimensions. This is time-consuming and the resulting data is difficult to navigate.

HistoBankVis addresses these challenges by providing an exploratory access to a high-dimensional data set by means of different visualization layers combined with a structured statistical analysis. The system is part of on-going work which investigates visualization possibilities and the needs of historical linguistic data stored in treebanks.

3   HistoBankVis: a multilayer visualization system

As part of our on-going work, we developed HistoBankVis, a visualization system originally designed for the investigation of syntactic change in Icelandic based on IcePaHC (see Schätzle et al. 2017 for details). The tool is an online browser app and publicly available.[4] HistoBankVis requires well-structured, tabular datasets in the csv-format as input. Thus, corpus data needs to be processed by extracting linguistic factors relevant for the research task, usually identified by consulting the theoretical literature. HistoBankVis stores these factors as data dimensions in an SQL database, with the corresponding values referred to as features.

The user can filter for a subset of the data, specifically for dimensions and features from particular time periods. Before visualizing the historical developments of the selected data dimensions, the researcher has to define time periods for the temporal comparison, either by specifying them manually or by selecting predefined periods.

---

[4]http://histobankvis.dbvis.de

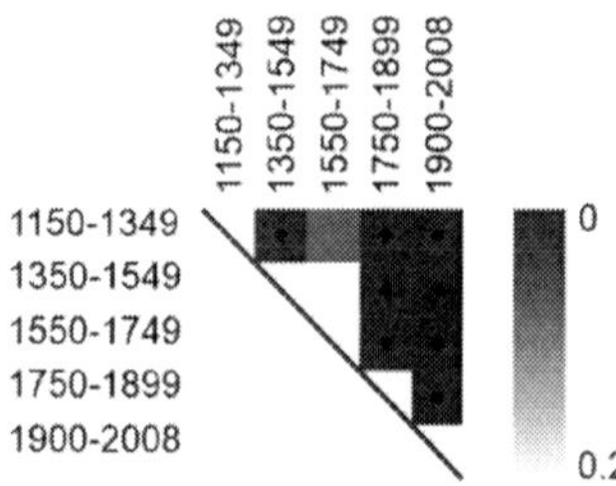

Figure 1: Compact matrix visualization showing statistically significant differences between data distributions from different time periods.

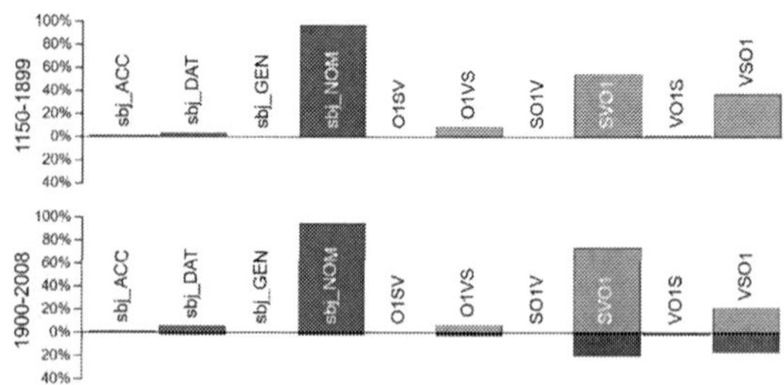

Figure 2: Difference histograms for the distribution of subject case and word order pre- and post-1900.

The original HistoBankVis version (Schätzle et al., 2017) has two main visualization components, the *Compact Matrix* and the *Difference Histograms Visualization*. Both visualizations allow researchers to interactively compare the distributions of selected features and dimensions of the filtered sentences across time periods on different granularity levels. The compact matrix visualizes differences between the selected data dimensions across time stages. Each row and column represents one period as shown in Figure 1. The differences are measured by χ^2-tests or Euclidean distances and represented by color. The matrix is a useful means to show differences among all time period combinations.

Difference histograms provide a more nuanced view on the diachrony of individual features and dimensions. The difference histograms visualize each time period as one composed bar chart, see Figure 2. For each time period, the dimensions are encoded via different colors and can be inspected in parallel. The bar height corresponds to the percentage of sentences containing a given feature in the respective time period. To facilitate the comparison of periods, we show the difference between the distributions of two neighbouring time periods with a separate bar chart below each feature bar. A green bar indicates that a feature increased compared to the previous period and red indicates that the feature decreased. For example, in Figure 2, SVO1 (Subject-Verb-Direct Object) word order increases, while VSO1 (Verb-Subject-Direct Object) decreases.

While the matrix and the histograms allow for the exploration of differences between linguistic factors across different time periods, the representations lack a perpendicular comparison of interactions between different factors to correlate, e.g., the occurrence of a particular type of subject case with the observed word order variation. That is, while it

is clear that most of the subjects have nominative case (sbj_NOM) in Figure 2, one cannot correlate this information directly with word order: the question of which attested word order possibilities the subjects appear in must be tackled in a different way. To this end, we extended HistoBankVis with a visualization of dimension interactions.

4 Dimension Interaction Visualization

To provide insights into the interrelation between multiple features of different dimensions, we extended the HistoBankVis system by a *Dimension Interaction* visualization, based on the Parallel Sets technique (Bendix et al., 2005; Kosara et al., 2006). Parallel Sets extend the idea of Parallel Coordinates (PC; Inselberg 1985, 2009) to a frequency-based representation of categorical data dimensions.

PC represent relations between individual data points from a multidimensional data set on a 2D plane by visualizing each dimension along a vertical axis with the related features of the dimensions being connected by a polyline. This allows to identify both relationships between data points and neighboring dimensions. Structured Parallel Coordinates (Culy et al., 2011), a specialized version of PC for the analysis of linguistic data, have been used to analyze word co-occurrences (Culy et al., 2011) and to investigate meanings of modal verbs within historical academic discourse (Lyding et al., 2012). Moreover, the diachronlex diagrams by Theron and Fontanillo (2015) which track the evolution of meanings as represented in historical dictionaries make use of PC.

Parallel Sets visualize the frequency of each feature as proportions of equally spaced vertical lines (data dimensions). In this way, Parallel Sets allow for the sophisticated investigation of interactions between features from different data dimensions, whereas PC only allow for the analysis of co-occurrence frequencies of specific features. For ex-

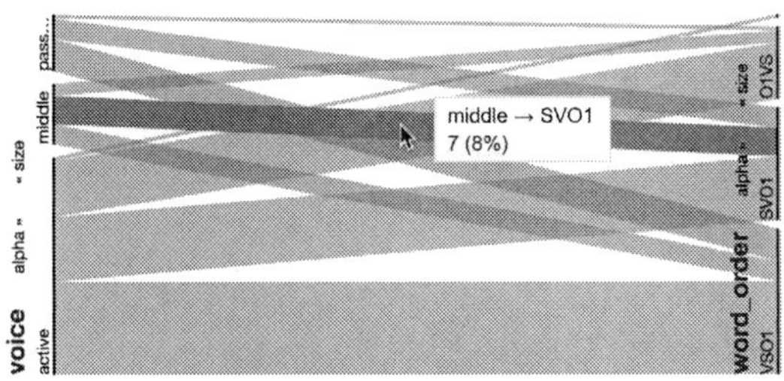

Figure 3: Dimension interaction for voice and word order in dative subject sentences from 1750–1899.

ample in Figure 3, the interactions between the dimensions voice and word order are visualized. The dimensions are connected by colored ribbons. The size of a ribbon indicates the share which a feature holds of a feature from another dimension from left to right, allowing for the investigation of interactions between the features. In Figure 3, active constructions occur most often with VSO1, while middles are mostly SVO1.

In our Parallel Sets implementation, dimensions can be reordered via drag&drop, allowing for a flexible investigation of different types of interactions.[5] To provide a better overview, the features on each dimension axis can be sorted according to their size or alphabetically. Additionally, details of a feature correspondence can be accessed via mouse interaction techniques, see Figure 3.

To our knowledge, Parallel Sets have not yet been used in the context of linguistic research. In this paper, we show that our implementation of Parallel Sets, i.e., the dimension interaction visualization, is an extremely effective and powerful device for historical linguistic research as it fosters the identification and understanding of interactions between a variety of features contained in a multi-dimensional data set.

5 Tracking Syntactic Change

In the visualization community, the general practice is to use case studies to evaluate the usefulness of a visualization with regard to whether significant and novel insights about the data could be yielded (Carpendale, 2008; Isenberg et al., 2013). This section presents a case study which shows how HistoBankVis can be employed for the flexible investigation of syntactic change in Icelandic, focusing on the interaction between subject case and word order. Previous studies (e.g., Rögnvaldsson, 1996;

---

[5]This is based on Jason Davies' work: `https://www.jasondavies.com/parallel-sets/`.

Barðdal, 2011) that investigate changes with respect to these phenomena do not factor in potential interactions between the changes. By visualizing the data, we found that the two phenomena are closely interlinked.

Overview and Differences. We first looked at the diachronic development of word order in transitive sentences, i.e., sentences containing a subject (S), a finite verb (V), and a direct object (O1), vis-á-vis subject case (nominative, accusative, dative, or genitive) via the difference histograms. The compact matrix visualization showed at-a-glance that the distribution of word order and subject case changes significantly as of 1900, see Figure 1. Figure 2 provides the difference histogram distributions for subject case and word order in the periods before and after 1900. The most striking change with respect to word order is that SVO1 is increasing in the period from 1900–2008 (green bar), whereas VSO1 is decreasing concomitantly (red bar). At the same time, dative subjects increase slightly. The question is whether these two developments are linked to one another.

Dimension Interactions. The dimension interaction visualization allows for a detailed view of correlations between the features of each selected data dimension in order to investigate potential interactions. Figure 4 shows the dimension interaction for subject case and word order in the period 1900–2008 in the upper right corner. Both dimensions have been sorted according to the size of their features, with the largest feature displayed at the bottom. The shares of the subject cases on the left are mapped onto the shares they hold of the word orders on the right. The dimension interaction shows that SVO1 is the most prominent word order overall. The large majority of nominatives occur together with SVO1, while the share of SVO1 of the dative subjects is considerably smaller.

The patterns observed in the period from 1900 to 2008 differ from the interactions in an earlier time period (1150–1350), compare the top right with the top left of Figure 4. In contrast to the period post-1900, the shares of SVO1 and VSO1 are about equal for nominative subjects. Additionally, dative subjects occur most frequently with VSO1. Thus, word order develops differently with respect to subject case over time. The difference histograms in Figure 2 indicated that subjects are increasingly realized preverbally, the dimension interaction shows

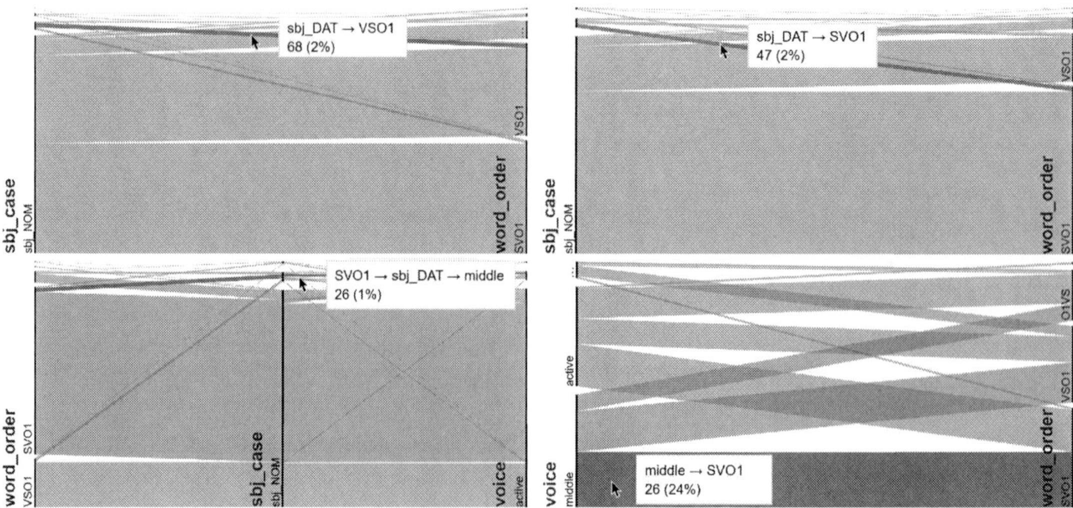

Figure 4: Top: Dimension interactions for subject case and word order from 1150–1350 (left) and 1900–2008 (right). Bottom: Dimension interactions from 1900–2008 for word order, subject case and voice (left) and voice and word order in dative subject sentences (right).

that dative subjects lag behind this development.

It is well-known that voice influences the occurrence of dative subjects in Icelandic (e.g., Zaenen et al., 1985; Sigurðsson, 1989). However, whether there is an actual correlation between voice, subject case and word order has not yet been investigated. This can be accomplished easily with the help of HistoBankVis since we can simply integrate the dimension voice for an analysis of the dimension interactions between subject case, word order and voice, cf. Figure 4-bottom-left for the period 1900–2008. The dimension interactions show that SVO1 occurs most often with nominative subjects in active constructions. With dative subjects though, SVO1 order mainly occurs in middle constructions. A separate analysis of the interaction between voice and word order for dative subjects allows for a more nuanced look at interactions, see Figure 4-bottom-right (1900–2008). Dative subjects occur most frequently with middle voice and SVO1 is the most prominent word order for both, active and middle constructions. However, in earlier stages of the language, word order and voice pattern differently, see Figure 3 for the dimension interaction from 1750 to 1899. First, dative subjects occurred most often in active clauses and not with middles. Moreover, SVO1 is already the dominant word order for middle forms, but not for the active constructions in which VSO1 prevails.

Concluding, these findings indicate that the increasing realization of dative subjects in before the verb correlates with an increasing use of dative sub-jects together with middle voice. With the aid of HistoBankVis, in particular the dimension interactions, we were able to easily identify a previously unknown link between word order, dative subjects and voice in a matter of minutes.

6 Conclusion

HistoBankVis serves as an efficient and powerful tool for historical linguistic investigations as it provides multiple perspectives of the data at different levels of detail on demand, fostering an iterative process of hypothesis testing and generation. In particular, we introduced the use of Parallel Sets to provide an interactive visualization of complex interactions across different dimensions of data. To our knowledge, this is the first use of Parallel Sets in a linguistic visualization.

We illustrated the flexibility and strength of HistoBankVis on the basis of a concrete case study which investigated changing linguistic features in Icelandic. We demonstrated that our system can yield new insights and we have shown that the analysis of dimension interactions as provided by the extended system represents an effective new means for historical linguistic research.

Acknowledgements

We thank the Deutsche Forschungsgemeinschaft (DFG, German Research Foundation) – Projektnummer 251654672 – TRR 161 (Projects A03 and D02) for their financial support.

References

R. Harald Baayen. 2008. *Analyzing Linguistic Data. A Practical Introduction to Statistics Using R*. Cambridge University Press, Cambridge.

David Bamman and Gregory Cane. 2006. The design and use of a Latin dependency treebank. In Jan Hajič and Joakim Nivre, editors, *Proceedings of the Fifth International Treebanks and Linguistic Theories*. pages 67–78.

Jóhanna Barðdal. 2011. The rise of dative substitution in the history of Icelandic: A diachronic construction grammar account. *Lingua* 121(1):60–79.

Fabian Bendix, Robert Kosara, and Helwig Hauser. 2005. Parallel sets: Visual analysis of categorical data. In *Information Visualization, 2005. INFOVIS 2005. IEEE Symposium on*. IEEE, pages 133–140.

S. Bird, E. Klein, and E. Loper. 2009. *Natural Language Processing with Python*. O'Reilly.

Sheelagh Carpendale. 2008. Evaluating information visualizations. In *Information Visualization - Human-Centered Issues and Perspectives*, pages 19–45. https://doi.org/10.1007/978-3-540-70956-5_2.

Tom Christiansen, Jon Orwant, Larry Wall, and Brian Foy. 2012. *Programming Perl*. O'Reilly, 4 edition.

Chris Culy, Verena Lyding, and Henrik Dittmann. 2011. Structured Parallel Coordinates: a visualization for analyzing structured language data. In *Proceedings of the 3rd International Conference on Corpus Linguistics, CILC-11*. April 6-9, Valencia, Spain, pages 485–493.

Jan Hajič. 1998. Building a Syntactically Annotated Corpus: The Prague Dependency Treebank. In E. Hajičová, editor, *Issues of Valency and Meaning. Studies in Honour of Jarmila Panevová*, Karolinum, Charles University Press, Prague, Czech Republic, pages 106–132.

Dag T. T. Haug and Marius L. Jøhndal. 2008. Creating a Parallel Treebank of the Old Indo-European Bible Translations. In Caroline Sporleder and Kiril Ribarov, editors, *Proceedings of the Second Workshop on Language Technology for Cultural Heritage Data (LaTeCH 2008)*. pages 27–34.

Martin Hilpert and Stefan Th. Gries. 2016. Quantitative approaches to diachronic corpus linguistics. In Merja Kytö and Päivi Pahta, editors, *The Cambridge Handbook of English Historical Linguistics*, Cambridge University Press, Cambridge, pages 36–53.

Thorbjörg Hróarsdóttir. 2000. *Word Order Change in Icelandic. From OV to VO*. John Benjamins, Amsterdam.

Alfred Inselberg. 1985. The plane with parallel coordinates. *The Visual Computer* 1:69–91.

Alfred Inselberg. 2009. *Parallel Coordinates: VISUAL Multidimensional Geometry and its Applications*. Springer, New York.

Tobias Isenberg, Petra Isenberg, Jian Chen, Michael Sedlmair, and Torsten Möller. 2013. A systematic review on the practice of evaluating visualization. *IEEE Trans. Vis. Comput. Graph.* 19(12):2818–2827. https://doi.org/10.1109/TVCG.2013.126.

R. Kosara, F. Bendix, and H. Hauser. 2006. Parallel Sets: interactive exploration and visual analysis of categorical data. *IEEE Transactions on Visualization and Computer Graphics* 12(4):558–568. https://doi.org/10.1109/TVCG.2006.76.

Anthony Kroch, Beatrice Santorini, and Lauren Delfs. 2004. The Penn-Helsinki Parsed Corpus of Early Modern English (PPCEME). First edition.

Anthony Kroch, Beatrice Santorini, and Ariel Diertani. 2010. The Penn-Helsinki Corpus of Modern British English (PPCMBE). First edition.

Anthony Kroch and Ann Taylor. 2000. Penn-Helsinki Parsed Corpus of Middle English (PPCME2). Second edition.

Verena Lyding, Stefania Degaetano-Ortlieb, Ekaterina Lapshinova-Koltunski, Henrik Dittmann, and Christopher Culy. 2012. Visualising linguistic evolution in academic discourse. In *Proceedings of the EACL 2012 Joint Workshop of LINGVIS & UNCLH*. Association for Computational Linguistics, pages 44–48.

Mitchell P. Marcus, Mary Ann Marcinkiewicz, and Beatrice Santorini. 1993. Building a large annotated corpus of English: the Penn Treebank. *Computational Linguistics* 19(2):313–330.

Eiríkur Rögnvaldsson. 1996. Word order variation in the VP in Old Icelandic. *Working Papers in Scandinavian Syntax* 58:55–86.

Christin Schätzle, Michael Hund, Frederik L. Dennig, Miriam Butt, and Daniel A. Keim. 2017. HistoBankVis: Detecting language change via data visualization. In Gerlof Bouma and Yvonne Asedam, editors, *Proceedings of the NoDaLiDa 2017 Workshop on Processing Historical Language*. Linköping University Electronic Press, Linköping, pages 32–39.

Halldór Á. Sigurðsson. 1989. *Verbal Syntax and Case in Icelandic. In a Comparative GB Approach*. Institute of Linguistics.

Roberto Theron and Laura Fontanillo. 2015. Diachronic-information visualization in historical dictionaries. *Information Visualization* 14(2):111–136. https://doi.org/10.1177/1473871613495844.

George Walkden. 2015. HeliPaD: the Heliand Parsed Database. Version 0.9. http://www.chlg.ac.uk/helipad/.

Joel C. Wallenberg, Anton Karl Ingason, Einar Freyr
Sigurðsson, and Eiríkur Rögnvaldsson. 2011. Icelandic Parced Historical Corpus (IcePaHC). Version
0.9. http://www.linguist.is/icelandic_treebank.

Annie Zaenen, Joan Maling, and Höskuldur Thráins-
son. 1985. Case and grammatical functions: the
Icelandic passive. *Natural Language and Linguistic
Theory* 3(4):441–483.

Author Index